POLA

Patrice M. Dabrowski

Poland

THE FIRST THOUSAND YEARS

NIU PRESS / DEKALB, IL

Published by the Northern Illinois University Press, DeKalb, Illinois   60115
Manufactured in the United States using acid-free paper.
first printing in paperback, 2016
ISBN 978-0-87580-756-0
Design by Shaun Allshouse

Several photographers and collectors have granted permission to use their work. Gratitude
goes to Janusz Juda (Figures 1.2, 3.1, 10.1), Nancy Wingfield (Figure 6.1), Jagiellonian Library, Kraków (Figure 11.2), Jerzy Polak [bwsolidarnosc.com] (Figure 13.2). Other photo-
graphs were taken by the author.

Library of Congress Cataloging-in-Publication Data
Dabrowski, Patrice M., 1960
Poland : the first thousand years / Patrice M. Dabrowski.
    pages cm
Includes index.
ISBN 978-0-87580-487-3 (cloth : alkaline paper) —ISBN 978-1-60909-166-8 (e-book)
1. Poland—History. I. Title.
DK4140.D33 2014
943.8—dc23   2014007233

NAJ
(zawsze)

Contents

List of Illustrations

List of Maps

List of Figures

Preface

What Poland? What Poles?

The action of an 1896 play, *Ubu Roi,* reportedly took place "Nowhere, that is, Poland." Readers of this book will find out that "nowhere" could indeed be Poland's location. But not only—and far from only. The thousand-plus-year-old country we call Poland has been a moving target, geographically as well as demographically. Not only—amazingly—is there no single piece of territory that has been part of a Polish state throughout the country's entire history. The very definition of who is a Pole has not been constant either. Thus, Polish history is not your "average" national history.

Poland has had more than its share of highs and lows. In the late medieval and early modern periods, it grew to be the largest country in continental Europe. Then it was wiped off the map for over a century. The phoenix that was Poland rose out of the ashes of World War I, only to be obliterated by the joint Nazi-Soviet occupation that began World War II. The postwar entity known as Poland was both shaped and controlled by the country's Big Brother, the Soviet Union. Yet even under those constraints, Poles proved persistent in their desire to wrest from the communists a modicum of national dignity, and they ultimately achieved much more than that.

This is in part because Poles have long marched to their own drummer. They have straddled East and West, not always comfortably but often creatively. At various times, political or cultural considerations have inclined them and their polity to focus attention on various specific directions of the compass. This is seen in the opening chapters of the book, where Poles are considered "connecting with the West," or "embracing the East," with their influence "spreading southward." Nonetheless, it would be impossible to relegate Poles to any one particular direction—despite the insistence of most contemporary Poles on being fully "Western" and having their country referred to as part of "Central Europe."

And Poles have often been caught in the middle. Poland's central location, which one historian termed the "heart of Europe," has been both a blessing and a curse. Indeed, Poles have often been victims of their own unenviable geography (see chapters 5–7), which placed them in between rising states to the east (Muscovy/Russia/Soviet Union) and west (Prussia/Germany). They and their state also perched, at times precariously, along a religious fault line dividing western and eastern Christianity.

Yet being in the middle meant that the country has had more opportunity than most to profit from exposure to ideas emanating from many directions. This made Poland perhaps less the heart of Europe than its crossroads. Poles took inspiration from this wealth of interactions emanating from all directions. At one point in the late medieval/early modern period (see chapter 4), they even created their own sui generis state (the Commonwealth of Both Nations, Polish and Lithuanian) and nation (noble, or Sarmatian). At that time, the people we call Poles were trailblazers of tolerance and defenders of diversity.

But who were these people, and what made them Poles? This question is hardly moot. Who was considered a Pole varied over the course of Polish history. Given the multiethnic and multidenominational composition of Poland's most creative, early modern incarnation as a state, the Polish-Lithuanian Commonwealth, readers would be wrong to assume that the "Poles" under consideration were always ethnic Poles, Roman Catholics, or native speakers of Polish (the way we tend to define the nation in modern times). The "noble (Sarmatian) nation" of the early modern period extended the full rights of citizenship to nobles across the breadth and length of this state and of different ethnic backgrounds. The country's inhabitants included people whom today we would call Lithuanians, Belarusians, Ukrainians, Germans, Jews, Armenians, Tatars, among others. The legacy of this broader, more inclusive conception of Polishness would continue to color the evolution of Polish national thought, sometimes even inclining the nation to fight "for our freedom and for yours," despite the fact that, ultimately, the nation would come to be defined in modern ethnic terms.

The Paradoxical Persistence of Poland

In most tellings of European history, one is lucky to hear Poland mentioned at all. It figures only sporadically, coming in and out of the picture (seemingly more out than in), and quite often history textbooks get the facts wrong. The picture of Poland has often been unflattering. The country has been mentioned in conjunction with the late eighteenth century "partitions of Poland," that is, precisely at the moment when it disappeared from the map of Europe for over a century. This disappearance was generally presented as something almost inevitable—certainly natural. There were good reasons, so the argument goes, for the Poles to be denied independent statehood. But the reasons for partitioning a large and long-established state, which is what Poland was at the time, were questionable.

In accounts of twentieth-century history, Poland's trajectory has long been seen as depressing. The country generally is mentioned as one of the new states created after World War I. It disappears from the map again during World War II. After that painful caesura, it becomes subsumed within an area called variously "Eastern Europe" or the East or Soviet Bloc—suggesting (correctly) that many general works of history assumed that any references to the Soviet Union (which did become an obsession during the Cold War) would by extension apply to the countries of Eastern Europe. Indeed, one history textbook saw fit to write in its index, "See Soviet Union," under the entry for "Eastern Europe."

Polish Pertinence and Impertinence

Thus, the picture of Poland (insofar as the country has been depicted at all) has tended to be depressing. The only hope during periods of oppression lay in something called "The Polish Question." This phenomenon referred to the Poles' seemingly impertinent or even provocative demand for independent statehood—something they considered their right. The question was a feature of what is often called the "long nineteenth century," a period when there was no Polish state, and no truly independent Polish state (see chapters 8–10). This period established the idea of "Poland," featured in courses on or readings in European or world history. It was a paradoxical, even problematic, country that, according to some interpretations, "did not deserve" to exist, as during World War II (see chapter 12), or else was fated by its unfavorable geopolitical position to exist only as part of the Soviet bloc (see chapter 13).

History tends to be written by the victors. Given that the modern history profession dates from a period when there was no Polish state, we should not be surprised that Poland has so often been presented in such a sporadic, unflattering, even disheartening way. It has often been in the interest of the victors to underestimate, downplay, or even obscure the history of the "losers."

But times have changed. Polish history is no longer a totally depressing story. Some still seem to tell it that way and to emphasize periods of trials and tribulations, the nation's faults and weaknesses. And there is a tendency to which many Poles subscribe to treat Poles as a long-suffering people, as a nation of victims. But it would be wrong to read Polish history as a tale of helpless Polish victims incapable of doing anything to help themselves. Poles were not powerless pawns in big-power politics. Indeed, readers will see that they were in fact able to influence outcomes—even some outcomes that affected not only the history of their own nation but that of their neighbors as well. More than that: some outcomes involving Polish actors were of world-historical significance.

The Poles have as interesting a historical profile as any of the peoples of this part of the world—arguably, the most interesting. Among other things, they have boldly forged their own unique type of government and embraced diversity within their state borders. Poles have also been the quintessential "freedom fighters"—fighters for the freedom of other nations as well as for their own.

Poland's pertinence to European and world history, thus, is varied. With the country's accession to the European Union in 2004, its history has become an integral part of European history. It is seen, for better or worse, as part of the "New Europe." Yet such an approach suggests that Poland, despite its being the largest country of this new cohort, is but an appendage, a country on the outskirts of Europe, rather than a major player in its own right.

Such an interpretation does not do justice to the roles played by the country and its people. If one reads history backward, one should not underestimate the role the Poles have played in bringing down the prevalent European or world systems. In the most recent past, Poles contributed to the collapse of communism in the East. Even prior to that, Poles and their desire for independent statehood likewise helped to undermine the great Central and East European empires of the long nineteenth century.

These accomplishments stemmed—again, taking a step backward—from the unique experience of Poles in the early modern period. Poland was long a big player in Central and Eastern Europe. While Poland was not itself an empire, in a certain incarnation it was the largest political entity in this part of Europe, one that had a multiethnic population. Think of it as Europe writ small. This premodern Polish permutation represented the pinnacle of Polish creativity, a road not taken by other countries within Europe during that period. Its citizens valued democratic, consensual, constitutional approaches long before such ideas were embraced by the rest of Europe. The country also was strong enough to become a federative state, allowing a patchwork of peoples and territories to join of their own accord in the Polish experiment. Some might consider this particular Polish permutation a precursor of sorts to the European Union. That Poland has recently concluded its successful turn at the helm of the council of the European Union while also weathering the global economic crisis significantly better than much of the continent suggests that, even today, there may be lessons to be learned from both Poles and Poland.

The writers of big books incur big debts. I would like to thank the Polish Ministry of Culture and National Heritage as well as Professor Jacek Purchla, director of the International Cultural Centre in Kraków, Poland, for the opportunity to spend the fall of 2011 in Kraków with a very generous Thesaurus Poloniae Fellowship. My lectures there and elsewhere in Poland convinced me of the need for this kind of popular history of the country. All the same, this book would never have been written without the repeated urging of J. Alex Schwartz, former director of Northern Illinois University Press. I am indebted to him for pushing me in this direction, and to my editor Amy Farranto and the team at NIUP for their very professional assistance. The maps are the work of cartographer Daniel Huffman. They are based on maps in a Polish historical atlas given to me by Professor Krzysztof Zamorski of the Jagiellonian University. Both men deserve my utmost gratitude, as do the anonymous readers of the manuscript. I also had the privilege of taking part in the conference "Recovering Forgotten History: The Image of East-Central Europe in English-Language Textbooks," in the course of which a number of distinguished scholars, mostly Polish, generously reviewed my manuscript. I am extremely grateful to Professors Dobrochna Kałwa, Igor Kąkolewski, Robert Kostro, Adam Kożuchowski, John Merriman, Andrzej Nowak, Endre Sashalmi, and Marek Wierzbicki for their invaluable comments and suggestions. Of course, all errors of interpretation are mine alone.

If the text of the book is any good, it is thanks not only to these reviewers and the stellar examples of historians who have served me as mentors over the years. It is also due in no small part to the students who took my classes at the University of Massachusetts Amherst, where I have happily taught under the aegis of the Amesbury Professorship of Polish Language, Literature, and Culture, in the person of Professor Robert A. Rothstein. In teaching them, I learned more than they could ever guess.

While I have my husband, Janusz, to thank for his endless support and love, which can never be repaid, this book is dedicated to my daughter, Natalie. While she is not a historian, her connection to Poland is deeper than mine (in that it dates from birth). While I hope this book might be read by history buffs in the United States, Poland, and beyond, during the process of conceptualizing and writing I have had in mind Natalie and all our relatives around the globe who might wish to learn more about their Polish heritage.

Note on Names

A somewhat simplified version of the Library of Congress system of transliteration has been used to render names from the East Slavic (Cyrillic alphabet) realm, that is, from Russian, Belarusian, and Ukrainian. An attempt has been made for many Christian names and surnames from a number of languages—these include Polish, Ukrainian, Russian, Belarusian, Czech, Hungarian, and German—to retain their native flavor (for example, the Polish Bolesław instead of the Latinized Boleslaus, or the German Friedrich instead of English Frederick or Polish Fryderyk). The only cases where this approach has not been followed concern the Russian, Hungarian, or Austrian royalty or the occasional world-renowned individual—for example, we have Catherine the Great, not Ekaterina the Great, and Genghis Khan, not the less familiar Chinghis Khan. A Polish pronunciation guide follows for those who wish to decipher the original Polish names or the occasional word.

The names of countries and many major cities have been left in their Anglicized form—therefore, Poland, not Polska. With several exceptions, the less familiar place names used are the current ones, with an alternate form given in parentheses at first mention: for example, Gdańsk (German: Danzig). Current toponyms are also found on the book's maps. While this modern usage may at times ring false to the historian, it enables the general reader to locate the places on a general map of the world, while it is also suggestive of the reach of the Poles and of Polish history.

Pronunciation Guide

This guide is for those who wish to pronounce Polish words correctly—an admirable goal! In Polish, every letter is pronounced distinctly. Consonants are crisp and vowels are full. There are very few exceptions to the rules of pronunciation presented below. In addition, note that the *penultimate* syllable is always stressed: Mic-KIE-wicz, Czar-to-RYS-ki, POL-ska, etc.

Written Pronunciation
Regular vowels:

a	ah
e	eh
i	ee
o	oh
u	oo
y	like the i in "hit"
j	like the y in "boy"

Nasal vowels:

ą	nasal a ("own")
ę	nasal e ("ehwn")

The bane of spelling bees (pronounced just like the letter u):

ó	oo

Gratis:

b	b
f	f
g	g as in "good"
h	h
k	k

m	m
p	p
t	t

Near Wictory:

w	v

Just when you think it's safe . . . (beware these letters with diacritical marks or in combinations, as given below)

c	ts
d	d
l	l as in "let"
n	n
r	r-rrolled!
s	s
z	z

Struck by ŁIghtnIng . . .

ć (ci)	c as in "cello"
dź (dzi)	like j in "jeans"
ł	w
ń (ni)	n as in "canyon"
ś (si)	s as in "sure"
ź (zi)	like g in "Gigi"

Dot your . . . ?

ż	like s in "pleasure"

It's all in the company one keeps . . .

ch	h
cz	ch as in "church"
dz	like ds in "woods"
dż	like dg in "bridge"
rz	ż
sz	sh
szcz	shch as in "fresh cheese"

POLAND

Part I

POLAND IN EUROPE

CHAPTER 1

Connecting with the West

The Piast Dynasty

Windows onto a Distant Past

Many generations have looked deep into the past for the origins of the Poles and a Polish state—the earlier the better being the working premise. (In this, Poles are no different from the peoples of other nations who as a rule tend to seek an ancient lineage for themselves.) Using the available archaeological and linguistic sources, among others, some scholars have pieced together a neat trajectory—from the prehistoric cave dwellers in the limestone caves of Ojców, through the wooden settlement of Biskupin, existing from circa 750 BC to 550 AD, and in the process moving from hypothetical Proto-Indo-European beginnings to the emergence of Slavic languages and distinct Slavic peoples. They claim that this represents the rise of Poland. For the historian, however, such an approach raises more questions than it answers, especially as quite a parade of peoples had crisscrossed this part of Europe by the end of the first millennium, including Scythians, Celts, Germanic tribes, not to mention Goths, Huns, and Avars. The evidence of life in such ancient times cannot, thus, convincingly be put into "national" boxes.

Not that making sense of traditional historical sources is easy. The historian interested in early medieval Poland must make do with a sparse and fragmented historical record. That Romans never conquered these lands (a good thing) meant that there was no early record of them (a bad thing). Commercial links of some kind clearly connected this part of Central and Eastern Europe with the Roman world—with Roman coins exchanged, perhaps, for precious Baltic amber. Legible signs of the beginnings of what can be called "Poland" are available to us only in tantalizing snippets, however.

While the occasional source makes reference to tribes, settlements, or leaders in this part of the world, even these are frustratingly hard to locate on the map in any precise way. So, how are we to deal with the origins of the Poles, and the origin of Poland?

Three Foundational Legends

A different window onto the past is provided by legends. While some may disdain such tales as ahistorical and thus not worthy of our attention, there is much to be learned from these primitive yet enduring attempts to explain the world of the past. As received wisdom, legends also shape the views of new generations. Some of the more interesting legends tell us something about perceptions of relations between peoples—here, between the Poles and their neighbors. The following selection of three foundational legends will provide a working framework for an understanding of Polish history and Polish perceptions.

Consider the legend of three brothers: Lech, Czech, and Rus. Lech was the forerunner of the Poles; Czech, of course, the forerunner of the Czechs; and Rus of the broader Slavic family further east, today's Belarusians, Ukrainians, and Russians. Each brother decided to set off in a different direction in search of a place to call home. Whereas Czech headed south and Rus traveled east, Lech was led north by a white eagle until he arrived at a tree. From its top branches, Lech took in the view. To the north he spied a mighty ocean, to the east he could see vast fertile plains. Mountains dominated the southern horizon, and dense forests spread out to the west. Was this land not ideal? Enthralled with what he saw, Lech decided to settle right there—indeed, to build a nest of his own. In thanks, he made his emblem the white eagle with outstretched wings.

This legend addresses the larger Slavic family of Central and Eastern Europe and explains how various peoples ended up in their present location. Slavic tribes came to populate much of Central and Eastern Europe around the fifth century. Over time, they became more differentiated, eventually giving rise to more recognizable national groups. The Polish legend speaks of only three brothers, clearly reflecting the local Polish neighborhood. The Poles and Czechs were both members of the western branch of the Slav family, while Rus represented the entirety of the eastern Slav family. Given Lech's particular location, the southern Slavs (the peoples we associate with the former Yugoslavia) were out of view; they were located to the south of the Czech homeland. The legend likewise hints that the descendants of Czech and Rus were not only the Poles' closest brothers; we might expect them to figure more prominently within the Polish purview.

The legend also provides some geographical cues regarding Lech's territory, which was depicted in glowing terms. As we will see, the Polish "nest" founded by Lech was a place called Gniezno, a toponym related to the modern Polish for "nest" (*gniazdo*). Gniezno, incidentally, is located in the heart of modern Poland. The lands of the Poles are in part described by natural boundaries: the Baltic Sea in the north and the Carpathian Mountains in the south. The western and eastern borders of Lech's land—those forests and plains—are not as easily delineated, suggesting that such determinations may be more open to adjustment. (It is worth noting that the other Slavic peoples who figured in the legend, the descendants of Czech and Rus, lay to the southwest and east, respectively.) In a nice touch, the legend also provides an ancient justification for a historical detail: the white eagle remains Poland's emblem to this day.

Another legend tells us about the founder of the city of Kraków, a man called Krak. He was a wise villager who, through a clever ruse, managed to kill the dragon that terrorized his people. Krak smeared a sheep with sulfur and cast it into the dragon's cave; after ingesting this free but unusually spicy meal, the dragon drank from the Vistula (Polish: Wisła) River until he burst. The dragon had lived in the cave beneath Wawel Hill, the future site of the city that long would be Poland's capital. The legend thus explains both the city's subsequent rise in importance and the existence of the so-called Krak Mound, a hill on the outskirts of Kraków that was erected in honor of Krak by his thankful subjects. Such mounds, incidentally, were an ancient Slavic way of honoring the dead.

And who can deny the grain of truth in the legend of Wanda, Krak's daughter, who drowned herself in the Vistula River rather than marry a German who threatened to invade the country if she refused him. Does her tale not suggest the fact, borne out by subsequent history, of a certain long-standing tension in the interactions between Poles and Germans? (For lovers of music, Dvořák's 1875 opera *Vanda* is based on this tale, reflecting the Czechs' own sometimes rocky relations with their German neighbors.) The persistence of the legend of Wanda suggests that Slavic peoples such as Poles and Czechs felt their German neighbor to be a distinct "Other." Corroboration can be found in the name given by such Slavs to the Germans. The latter were from early days referred to as *Niemcy*—the mute ones. These Germans were probably not tongue-tied but, rather, spoke an unintelligible (Germanic) language, whereas the Slavic languages were more or less mutually intelligible. Could this be enough reason for a pagan princess to have preferred

Figure 1.1: The Wawel dragon, crawling out of his cave beneath the Wawel Castle, as depicted in a sixteenth-century woodcut. From Sebastian Münster, *Cosmografia universalis*, Basel, 1544.

a different husband? Some versions of the legend interestingly depict the Germans as rather uncouth—let us say barbaric—warriors, in contrast to the more cultured Cracovians. Regardless of the reason for her embracing a watery death, Wanda, like her father Krak, was honored with a mound.

These three legends set the stage for our foray into Polish history. Coming to us out of the mists of time, they hint at the deep prehistoric and pagan beginnings, including the emergence of distinct peoples within the larger Central and East European space. They also provide clues to certain central places and prominent features of the country we will call Poland, as well as evidence that from the very outset Poles have functioned within a world peopled by "brothers" (Slavs) and "others" (Germanic peoples).

From Legends to History

Polish history, as opposed to prehistory, dates only from the late tenth century. Prior to this period, various tribes in this general vicinity of Central and Eastern Europe get only the briefest of mention in written sources. A Bavarian geographer in the mid-ninth century enumerated a series of tribes, which appear to have lived in the region. These included the Vuislane-Wiślanie (people of the Vistula River region) and Lendizi-Lędzianie (also in Małopolska, or Lesser Poland, somewhat further to the east); the Glopeani-Goplanie (near Lake Gopło, fed by the Noteć River); the Sleenzane-Ślężanie, Dadosesani-Dziadoszanie, Opolini-Opolanie, and Golensizi-Goleszycy, all in the area of present-day Silesia; and the Prissani-Pyrzyczanie and Velunzani-Wolinianie in the region of Pomerania, on the coast of the Baltic Sea.

An early mention of an emerging threat in the region came from one of the first Slavic states, Greater Moravia, which formed in the vicinity of today's Czech Republic and Slovakia. Baptized by the missionaries Cyril and Methodius circa 863 AD, Moravians noted the presence of a powerful pagan prince in the region of the Vistula. The reference was likely to a tribe in the region of Kraków, the site not only of the historic mounds already mentioned but also of an enormous cache of ancient metal blades, which suggests that it was a seat of some power, even in this early period. The Vuislane tribe at some point probably came under Czech rule or influence before becoming part of a dynamic state emerging to the north.

Polish Beginnings: The Gniezno "Nest"

The beginnings of Polish statehood emanated from the region of today's city of Gniezno, part of the region later termed Greater Poland (Wielkopolska). As mentioned earlier, the name "Gniezno" is related to the present-day Polish word for "nest" (*gniazdo*). The avian metaphor suggests there might be some truth in the legend of Lech. The archaeological record also allows us to see the region's rise. Given that Lake Gopło is not far from Gniezno, there may well be a relation between the Glopeani mentioned by the Bavarian geographer and the tribe that started a rapid ascendance in the region.

Gniezno had become a stronghold of note, a town where craftsmen settled and trading took place. This nameless people settled along the surrounding rivers and lakes, where they constructed settlements. Around the year 920 AD, the apparent military expansion and buildup of fortified settlements near Gniezno (including Poznań) speak of a significant and speedy expansion; the next half-century would witness further expansion and consolidation in the region as well as beyond. The Gniezno state expanded its influence northward to the seacoast region of Pomerania, although the link was likely loose, and perhaps based on paying tribute. It incorporated territories in the east (Mazovia and Sandomierz) and made inroads into the southeast circa 970; the Lendizi of that last region, however, soon fell under the control of the Rus' princes to the east.

The dynamic tribe with its seat in Gniezno was only later (around the year 1000) labeled the Polanie—Poles. Etymologically, these are the people of the fields or plains (*pole*). The sixteenth-century Polish historian Marcin Kromer provided two more hypotheses as to the origins of the name. It could be a contraction of "*po Lech*" (after Lech), the reference being to the legendary first Pole, or the term could be related to the Poles' love of hunting (*polowanie*). Given that Lech's legendary territory also was rich in forests (and thus probably also in game), any of these explanations could have merit.

The earlier, still prehistorical, period is associated with figures such as the famous Popiel (an evil ruler who, according to legend, was devoured by rats and the ancestors, whether apparent or legendary, of the first Polish ruler of whose name and historical existence we can truly be certain, Mieszko (?–992). Before we turn to him, however, we must decipher the chapter title's reference to the Piasts. Who were the Piasts, and why were they important?

The Piasts

The first written account of their origins was penned in the early twelfth century by an anonymous monk. He is traditionally called the Anonymous Gaul, as the assumption is that he hailed from France. Scholars more recently have surmised that he spent time at the monastery of Saint-Gilles and was educated somewhere in France or Flanders. The peripatetic monk may also have come to Poland via Hungary, perhaps with a stay in the monastery in Somogyvár, and perhaps expressly to write about the Polish lands. The Anonymous—a sojourner in Poland—was the first to write of "the deeds of the princes of the Poles." This was the title of his work, in Latin, *Gesta principum Polonorum*. Indebted to his hosts, the Anonymous wrote so as "not to eat Poland's bread in vain." He began, as did so many authors of his time, by praising the land to which he had come:

> Although this land is thickly forested, yet it has ample resources of gold and silver, bread and meat, fish and honey; but in one respect it is especially to be preferred to all others, for in spite of being surrounded by all the many aforementioned peoples, Christian and pagan alike, and frequently attacked by all and sundry, it has never been completely subjugated by anyone. A land where the

air is healthy, the fields fertile, the woods full of honey, the water abounding in fish, the warriors warlike, the peasants hardworking, the horses hardy, the oxen strong at plowing, the cows give abundant milk and the sheep abundant wool.[*]

In a way, it seems to reflect the legend of Lech, who saw similar goodness in the land, while amplifying something that doubtless would cheer every Polish heart: that the land had never been subjugated by foreigners, despite their many attempts. To be sure, prior to its swift rise and expansion, the Gniezno state had been shielded on all sides from direct interference on the part of the growing powers in Central and Eastern Europe. A series of small Slavic tribes to the west, inhabiting the region between the Oder and Elbe Rivers, kept the Germans at bay; the Vuislane of what would be called Lesser Poland to the south themselves dealt with the neighboring Czechs; and the Lendizi tribe served as a buffer between the nascent Polish state and the Ruthenes to the east.

The Anonymous related the tale of an ancient ritual, that of cutting the hair of young boys once they reached a certain age, as a sign of their maturity, and bestowing a new name on them. According to legend, on a certain day, the son of Duke Popiel and the son of a poor plowman Piast were both undergoing this ceremonial cutting. Two mysterious strangers came upon the ducal ceremony but were chased away. Setting out once again, the two mysterious strangers came upon the plowman Piast, who received them hospitably. Although he had only one barrel of homebrewed ale and a piglet to celebrate his son, he treated the strangers to them. What happened next was a miracle: the barrel amazingly replenished itself, so that all those present could drink their fill—while the cups ran dry at the ducal feast. Furthermore, there was so much leftover pork that ten buckets (*cebri* in Polish, added the Anonymous) full of leftovers were collected. On the advice of the guests, Piast extended his hospitality to Duke Popiel, who was amazed at the sight. The guests cut the boy's hair and bestowed upon him the name Siemowit—which meant "welcome here." Siemowit ultimately succeeded Popiel, who later would meet an ignominious fate, being beset by a horde of rats.

According to the Anonymous's chronology, Mieszko figured as the great-grandson of Siemowit and, thus, the great-great-grandson of the hospitable Piast. Regardless of his prehistoric lineage either real or legendary, it is Mieszko who brings us into the historical era as the first historically verifiable, authentic Polish ruler. All that is known of Siemowit and the next two generations of Piasts—Leszek and Siemomysł—comes from this twelfth-century

---

[*]   *Gesta principum Polonorum: The Deeds of the Princes of the Poles*, trans. and annotation, Paul W. Knoll and Frank Schaer (Budapest: Central European University Press, 2003), 15.

account. In other words, the Anonymous's tale is of the origins of a dynasty: the first dynasty to rule over the nascent Polish state, the Piasts.

The anonymous French monk had a tale to relate about Mieszko. The future Polish ruler reportedly was born blind, but in his seventh year, at a feast given by his father Siemomysł, he gained his sight. How to explain this? The wise folk of that period reportedly explained that Mieszko had been blind, as Poland had been, until this time; only in the future would Poland "be illuminated by Mieszko and exalted over all the neighboring nations."* In this way, they presaged what Mieszko would be most known for. Not only was he the first ruler of Poland to make the historical record, but he would bring enlightenment of a certain sort to the Poles—something that would forever change their outlook on the world.

Medieval Poland: Becoming Part of the Christian World

Mieszko seems to have led the Polanie as of about the year 960. The reason we know of him and his state is that, like the Moravians to the south, the Germans (that is, the Christian population to the west, which was part of post-Carolingian Europe, the eastern part of which was ruled by the German emperor) were beginning to pay attention to this emerging state centered around Gniezno. Early recorded mention of Mieszko's doings has come down to us from a Jewish trader, Ibrahim Ibn Jakub, who, while on business in Magdeburg in 966, learned of the existence of a well-organized state that was conquering some of the Slavic tribes to its west. A Saxon monk noted the existence of the dynamically expanding state, which likewise caught the attention of Otto I. Titled Emperor of the Romans by the pope only in 962, the German Otto had pretentions to the same region. Before long, Mieszko's realm came to be referred to as Poland, or the land of the Poles.

It is customary to date the beginnings of the history of Poland to 966. This choice of date reflects a momentous decision made that year. Until this point, the Polanie and the neighboring tribes in the vicinity of Central and Eastern Europe were for the most part pagans. This was not true of the Germans further west, who had already converted to Christianity in late antiquity or the early medieval period; nor was it true for the Moravians, who had witnessed the ninth-century ministry of Cyril and Methodius, the missionaries to the Slavs, although by this time—a century later—they were under German influence. (Note that Kyivan Rus', lying further to the east, was baptized only as of 988, but its baptism came from Greek sources, that is, Constantinople.) In

---

*   Ibid., 27.

this part of the world, of world-historical significance was what religion these pagan rulers chose, and at whose hands they were baptized.

It is in 966 that the baptism of Mieszko—head of the Gniezno state, this nascent Polish polity—took place. It is both interesting and important that this was facilitated not by the Germans but by a Bohemian (Czech) connection. A Czech state had emerged around the turn of the eighth and ninth centuries; first baptized by Saint Methodius, the Czechs relatively quickly came under Bavarian influence, their church under the bishop of Regensburg. In 965 Mieszko strengthened the connection with this Slavic neighbor by marrying a Bohemian princess, the daughter of Boleslav I. This Dubravka, known variously also as Dąbrówka or Dobrava, was a Christian, and she likely brought some Christian clergy with her to Gniezno. The next year, Mieszko accepted baptism at their hands.

What is important for the future history of Poland is that this was Western, and not Eastern, Christianity—that is, Mieszko was baptized into the Church of Rome, as it was then known. No less important is that baptism came from Bohemia, not from the imperial power to the west.* Mieszko furthermore took care to ensure that his state was placed under the care of missionaries. As missionary priests were directly subordinated to the papacy and not to a bishop within any given territory, this gave the nascent Polish church more flexibility because it was not placed under another sovereign state.

Thus began the Poles' connection with Roman Catholicism, one that dates back a millennium. It is a connection that has stuck. Until very recently, many people around the world associated Poland above all with the man who, until not so long ago, was head of the Universal Church—Karol Wojtyła, better known as Pope John Paul II. During his first trip to Poland after he became pontiff, John Paul II famously declared to his countrymen that "it was impossible, without reference to Christ, to understand the history of the Polish nation, this great thousand-year-old community that so profoundly shapes my existence and that of each of us."† While clearly there is much to this statement, one cannot say that the Christianization of Poland or the Poles' historic identification with Roman Catholicism were inevitable. Nor (as we shall see) is the belief that all "real" Poles have always been, or must be, Roman Catholics borne out by the country's history, certainly not if one examines that history in its entirety. (Such Polish paradoxes await the patient reader.)

---

* The baptism of the Poles clearly came long before the Great Schism of 1054, which henceforth separated Western from Eastern Christianity; however, even in Mieszko's time one could speak of the Roman Church and the Greek Church.

† "Pope John Paul II Speaks in Victory Square, Warsaw, June 2, 1979," in *From Stalinism to Pluralism: A Documentary History of Eastern Europe since 1945*, ed. Gale Stokes, 2d ed. (Oxford: Oxford University Press, 1996), 202.

So what motivated Mieszko's conversion? The baptism of "Poland" into the larger Roman Catholic family appears to have been, above all, a political decision and not simply (if such matters are ever simple!) a matter of spiritual conversion. It likely extended originally only to Mieszko's court and entourage, who through the person of his wife and her entourage were pulled into the Christian orbit. Surely Mieszko realized that, by accepting Christianity, he would no longer be subject to incursions from the west—at least, the types of incursions from the eastern marches that doubtless had long been intended to turn these Slavic peoples from paganism to Christianity. By converting, he would deny the Holy Roman Empire the pretext to interfere with his state. The fact that the baptism came at the hands of a missionary who was under papal jurisdiction proved important. The Polish church thus would not be subordinated to the Holy Roman Empire or any other lay power. Moreover, as denizens of a Christian power the Poles could now seek to spread Christianity to other pagan tribes in the region (for example, the Pomeranians or the tribes further east), thus expanding their own influence.

So much for Mieszko and his entourage, who, as was common elsewhere in medieval Europe, constantly made the rounds of his lands. Perhaps you wonder, what did the common folk think of their ruler's conversion? Sources on this—as with all of Polish early medieval history—are thin. By this time, nonetheless, the population of Mieszko's state was already differentiated: Mieszko had a strong army of three thousand men (some of them likely Vikings), advisers, as well as a number of vassals, who all helped him to "rule" over a series of fortified settlements, outside of which lay the farms and forests that provided their inhabitants with much of what they needed. The diet of these early Poles consisted primarily of meat and fish (the latter gaining ground after the introduction of Christianity), barley and millet, peas and lentils, cucumbers and cabbage, cheeses, breads made with a beer leaven, as well as beer and other fermented drinks. Among these settlements and royal residences for the peripatetic king and his entourage were the capital of Gniezno, as well as Poznań and Kruszwica in Greater Poland; Płock in Mazovia; Kraków and Sandomierz in Lesser Poland; and Wrocław, Opole, and Głogów in Silesia. On their outskirts were places where trading took place. Certain settlements on the major overland trade routes were peopled by traders, merchants, and artisans; these locales facilitated the making of connections between Byzantium and Scandinavia along the north–south line as well as between the important east–west destinations of Kyiv and Regensburg. On the Polish market, foreign traders sought furs and hides, honey and wax, even slaves.

The idea of replacing pagan gods such as Perun, the god of thunder, with a Christian God received a varied reception in the Polish lands. While many people rebelled, others came around relatively quickly to support this new world-view. The conversion of Mieszko to Christianity may also have helped to raise the ruler's profile among the disparate tribes bordering on his state, certainly as more and more conversions took place and the church gained a foothold in the region. The Christian church—which established itself in the Polish lands through the introduction of hermitages and monastic orders, with the Benedictines the most important—surely would support the ruler who shared its beliefs.

Mieszko's baptism brought with it other benefits. He and his state came into the orbit of the West. The nascent Polish state gained international status and recognition of its existence within the Western fold. Witness the fact that Mieszko's second wife would be the daughter of a Saxon margrave, indicating that the Germans further west considered an alliance with the new convert to be advantageous. Elites within the new country were introduced to high Latin culture and "Western" civilization. Foreign priests and monks (at the outset primarily Czechs, Bavarians, and southern Germans) who came to Poland to help with the conversion process also helped to increase the ranks of the faithful. They brought "Western" ways with them, such as new tools and agricultural methods, not to mention the ways of the church. Establishing churches in Romanesque style (an early and still extant example is the Church of Saint Andrew in Kraków), they maintained relations with their home bases in the West, thus enabling further contacts with places as distant as Italy and France as well as cultural transmission.

Yet all such inroads were not made right away. Nor was paganism vanquished overnight. Indeed, we know it was not, as the imposition of the tithe circa 1030 brought about something of a pagan backlash. Time and again the infant Catholic Church faced challenges within this new Polish state, with church authority undermined more than once. Yet, seen in the perspective of the millennium of Polish history, these were but growing pains. The final defeat of paganism in the Polish lands allowed for Roman Catholi-.cism to gain what turns out to be an extraordinarily strong foothold. The Polish people—here, most certainly the common folk, if not always the nobility—would remain loyal to the church throughout the centuries to come.

So 966 was a crucial date for the Poles, and for Poland.

The Brave Exploits of Poland's First Crowned King

This is not the sole date worth remembering from the medieval period, however. Let us now turn to the events of the reign of Mieszko's son and successor, Bolesław I Chrobry (r. 992–1025). The sobriquet of Chrobry (Gloriosus or

Chrabri in some early sources) means "the Brave." Bolesław's reign straddled the end of the first millennium AD, which brought a new distinction to the land of the princes of the Poles.

Mieszko's son had come to rule over Lesser Poland as a result of the Czech connection. It is Bolesław who would integrate both the Silesian and Lesser Polish lands into the Gniezno state built by the Piasts who preceded him. Bolesław's father had continued the country's expansion in the west; this had led to conflicts with the Czechs over control of Silesia as well as attempts to gain territories at the expense of the Slavs beyond the Oder, so as to gain control over that river's mouth.

As would be the case in ensuing years, decades, and centuries, there were conflicts between the Poles and the Holy Roman Empire (or parts thereof). Yet for a miraculous moment during the reign of Bolesław, the relationship between the two polities was entirely positive. To understand the reasons for this, we must backtrack for a minute and focus on the church in the Polish lands, which was strengthened in the wake of the murder, by pagan Prussians, of the former bishop of Prague in the year 997. Known variously as Vojtěch (in Czech), Wojciech (Polish), or Adalbert (English), the peripatetic former-bishop-turned-missionary had made his way to Poland, where he was received with great veneration; with the significant support of Bolesław, he set off to convert the pagans to the north. Despite some early successes along the Baltic Sea coast, he met an untimely death there when some Prussians came to suspect he was a Polish spy.

Learning of the fate of the revered missionary, Bolesław sought permission to ransom the body of the martyr and bring it back to Gniezno. The price the pagans extracted from the Polish ruler was the weight of Vojtěch's body in gold—no small sum. But it was a valuable relic for the young Polish church. Before two years had passed, the Church of Rome had canonized Vojtěch, bishop, missionary, and martyr.

This new development did not elude the other major power in the West: the Holy Roman Emperor. In the year 1000, Emperor Otto III traveled to Gniezno to pay his respects to the remains of Saint Vojtěch. In this context of demonstrable Polish piety, the emperor reaffirmed the independence of the Polish church and established further bishoprics. Thus, in addition to Gniezno (now an archbishopric), three new bishoprics were installed in Kraków (in Lesser Poland), Wrocław (in Silesia), and Kołobrzeg (in Pomerania, along the Baltic). That their jurisdiction coincided with the borders of the state was a positive sign, and one that boded well for the strengthening of a Polish church that sought to retain its independence despite its proximity to the Holy Roman Empire.

If we are to believe the anonymous monk who first wrote of the "deeds of the princes of the Poles" (*Gesta principum Polonorum*) in the early twelfth century, there was an important political dimension to this meeting between Otto III and Bolesław as well. The Anonymous took pains to illustrate the wealth of the Polish state. In his words, the Polish ruler received the Holy Roman Emperor

> with the honor and ceremony with which such a distinguished guest, a king and Roman emperor, should fittingly be received. Marvelous and wonderful sights Boleslaw set before the emperor when he arrived: the ranks first of the knights in all their variety, and then of the princes, lined up on a spacious plain like choirs, each separate unit set apart by the distinct and varied colors of its apparel, and no garment there was of inferior quality, but of the most precious stuff that might anywhere be found. For in Boleslaw's time every knight and every lady of the court wore robes instead of garments of linen or wool, nor did they wear in his court any precious furs, however new, without robes and orphrey. For gold in his days was held by all to be as common as silver, and silver deemed as little worth as straw. So when the Roman emperor beheld his glory and power and richness, he exclaimed in admiration, "By the crown of my empire, the things I behold are greater than I had been led to believe," and after taking counsel with his magnates he added before the whole company, "Such a great man does not deserve to be styled duke or count like any of the princes, but to be raised to a royal throne and adorned with a diadem in glory."*

As the story goes, Otto then placed his crown atop Bolesław's head, indicating his wish that the Polish ruler be crowned. The two men also exchanged gifts. Otto bestowed upon his Polish counterpart the spear of Saint Maurice; this insignia representing the power of the German kings and emperors is still today in Polish possession. Bolesław reciprocated with no less royal gifts: the shoulder of Saint Vojtěch as well as three hundred armored warriors. Aptly symbolic, the very dead holy relic and still very much alive military assistance were doubtless both appreciated by the Holy Roman Emperor.

This "coronation" at the hands of Otto III presaged the official coronation of Bolesław the Brave. For the Polish ruler was eventually to receive a crown, with the permission of Pope John XIX. Crowned on April 18, 1025, Bolesław died later that same year. The victory was more symbolic than anything else, but it demonstrated how the young Polish state was truly entering into the European scene. Bolesław the Brave was crowned by both temporal and spiritual

---

* *Gesta principum Polonorum*, 35, 37.

authorities, and this dual blessing helped to strengthen his claims—and those of his descendents—to the right to rule.

This was not the reason that Bolesław was called the Brave, however. He faced up to many various forces—including Otto III's relative and successor, Henry II, who unlike his cousin sought to undermine the Polish ruler. Polish-German wars ensued, and they continued throughout Bolesław's reign. In 1002 an attempt was even made on the Polish ruler's life. Perhaps this only served to galvanize the brave Pole. Availing himself of substantial military forces—thousands of knights in armor as well as foot soldiers—Bolesław expanded Poland's frontiers in all directions. He gained access to the Baltic Sea, in the north. He acquired territories in the vicinity of Kraków, stretching all the way to the Carpathian Mountains. Further south, he came to occupy Prague for a time. He was even raised to the Bohemian throne, though he was then expelled when he refused to render homage to the Holy Roman Emperor (for whom the independent-minded Polish ruler was becoming an increasing threat). He even held some Upper Lusatian lands, peopled by other Slavic tribes to his west, first as imperial fiefs and later independently.

This first Polish king likewise turned his attention eastward, to the Kyivan state. As early as 1012, Bolesław got involved in Kyivan Rus' on account of his Ruthenian son-in-law, Sviatopluk, the eldest son of Volodimer I. The four sons of Volodimer—Sviatopluk, Boris, Gleb, and Yaroslav—vied for the throne of Kyiv. Bolesław's intervention was not successful, although in the course of this succession conflict two of Sviatopluk's half-brothers, Boris and Gleb, were murdered. This pair of warrior-princes (by some accounts rather militarily inept or even pacifistic) would become the first Orthodox saints of Kyivan Rus'.

Bolesław nonetheless intervened once more in the affairs of Kyivan Rus' in 1018. The story of the encounter is told rather entertainingly (if improbably) by the Anonymous. The invading Bolesław found the ruler of Kyivan Rus', Yaroslav the Wise, out fishing—in other words, completely unprepared to defend his state. If one is to believe the Anonymous, Polish cooks on one bank of the River Bug pelted the Ruthenes with offal, while the Ruthenes hurled abuse and showered them with arrows from the other bank.

This time, the Poles triumphed. Bolesław occupied the capital Kyiv, and ultimately made off with much booty and many prisoners of war; some say he wished to rule instead of his son-in-law Sviatopluk. While Sviatopluk eventually got rid of his father-in-law, he was not able to hold onto the throne; it was his younger brother Yaroslav who eventually triumphed.

Legend has it that while in Rus' Bolesław put a notch in his sword by striking the Golden Gate of Kyiv—a powerful image, though rather unlikely

Map 1.1: Piast Poland under Bolesław the Brave, ca. 1025

because the Golden Gate is believed to have been built only in 1037. The legend may in fact refer to Bolesław II, who captured Kyiv in 1069 and who may have struck the gate in this way. Yet the story persists and is reinforced by a potent symbol of material culture. For from the fourteenth century onward a copy of this jagged sword, henceforth known as Szczerbiec, was the coronation sword of the kings of Poland.

The Polish state underwent upheaval in the wake of Bolesław's death in 1025. The king's sons fought over the throne, their Latin education clearly not making them any more civil in their relations with each other. The ensuing period included a popular revolt and foreign interventions. An example of the latter: in 1038 Bohemians sacked the capital of Gniezno, including its churches, and absconded with the remains of Saint Vojtěch. This caused one of Bolesław's grandsons—the peripatetic Kazimierz the Restorer (Odnowiciel) (r. 1034–1058)—to move his capital south to Kraków.

Bolstered by good relations with both the Germans and Kyivan Rus', Kazimierz managed to reunite much of the country he had inherited from his father, Mieszko II (r. 1025–1034), which consisted of the central Polish lands of Greater and Lesser Poland, Silesia, Mazovia, and Cuiavia. He began the process of reestablishing the foundations for church and state development, one of the reasons he is remembered in history as the Restorer.

Kazimierz was as much an innovator as a restorer, however, and he changed the way the country functioned. How? By bestowing land on both his knights and the church. No longer would the knights be supported directly by the ruler, to whom the entirety of the state personally belonged. In exchange for becoming self-supporting landowners the knights would be obliged to render military service to their ruler, under the regional leadership of a palatine, as needed. As to the church, it would no longer have to depend on the tithe (perhaps a good thing, given the popular revolt) but would become a powerful landowner in its own right. While freeing the monarch from direct responsibility for the well-being of his subjects, Kazimierz's innovation nonetheless meant that, with time, both knights-turned-nobles and clergy would have the wherewithal to challenge the monarch for power and influence within the Polish lands.

Church versus State?

The rising power of both would be felt by Kazimierz's eldest son. The Anonymous called this son Bolesław the Bountiful (Latin: Largus; Polish: Szczodry). He has gone down in history, however, as Bolesław the Bold (Polish: Śmiały). He reigned from 1058 to 1079.

Bolesław was crowned king of Poland in 1076, the third ruler to achieve this honor. His coronation took place one year before his counterpart in the Holy Roman Empire, Henry IV, made his famous trip to Canossa. Henry had been excommunicated in 1076, the previous year, by Pope Gregory VII and needed to make penance to be reunited with the church. Bolesław II sided with the pope, not the emperor, in this famous dispute, known as the Investiture Conflict.

Yet soon the Polish king also found himself in hot water. Back home in Poland, there was still support for his younger brother Władysław Herman. And not all the noble knights in the different parts of the country were happy about the increasing centralization of the country, which meant that more power was concentrated in the hands of the monarch. While Bolesław the Bold was engaged in the east, helping to place the eldest son of Yaroslav the Wise upon the throne in Kyivan Rus', rebellion broke out back home in 1079—a rebellion that apparently was supported by the bishop of Kraków, Stanisław. The king had Stanisław executed in 1079 for treason.

Some maintain that the king killed the bishop himself. The contemporary sources on the Kraków conflict are all silent, which has allowed many different parties to interpret the events as they each saw fit—whether in favor of the church (Stanisław) or the state (Bolesław). What is clearly evident is that Stanisław's death provided the impetus for the opposition to the king to coalesce.

This somewhat enigmatic event of 1079 became the most famous instance in Polish history of the struggle between church and state. In it one can see parallels to the more famous but much later clash between Thomas à Becket and King Henry II of England—with one major difference. Henry II did not have to escape into exile afterward as Bolesław did. Ultimately, Stanisław's murder proved more injurious for the Polish state—especially as Bolesław's successor, Władysław Herman, proved a weak ruler. Nonetheless, the tragedy did provide Poland with its first native martyr, for Stanisław, bishop of Kraków, was canonized in 1253.

The fact that Bolesław had to go into exile following the murder suggests a degree of influence of the church and church hierarchy within the medieval state. Yet the church had only recently begun to rise again, after a surge of popular protests circa 1030 that threatened to undermine both religion and state. Paradoxically, it was Bolesław the Bold who, following in the footsteps of his father, strengthened the church in Poland—in part as a result of his strong relationship with Pope Gregory. Church historians contend that it was only during Bolesław's rule that the church in Poland, like the Polish kingdom, was truly on a strong footing once again.

And indeed, the Polish king had sought to strengthen the church at all levels. Bolesław saw to it that a series of bishoprics (including a new one in the Mazovian town of Płock) came under the metropolitan of Gniezno. He strengthened the church on a diocesan level and founded a Benedictine monastery in the environs of each cathedral, each to be supported by landholdings and other sources of permanent income. Still standing today, for example, is the beautifully situated monastery of Tyniec, perched aside the Vistula River not far from Kraków. And it was from Tyniec as well as from other Polish monasteries that there emanated some major achievements of Western Christian culture—not only the religious rites of Western Christianity but also the use of the Latin language.

In many ways Bolesław the Bold was one of the early kingdom's better monarchs. Legend has it that he commanded iron piles to be pounded into the riverbeds of the Dnieper, Saale, and Elbe Rivers to signify where the borders of the Polish state should reach. This suggests Bolesław the Bold had ambitions to extend the country significantly westward in the direction of the Elbe and the Saale as well eastward toward the Dnieper. If it had not been for his ill-fated clash with Bishop Stanisław, perhaps the kingdom of Poland might have been strong enough to withstand the forces that would wrack the medieval state before another series of kings literally pieced it back together again.

The new Polish state, emerging into the light of history, established itself on the eastern fringes of the West. In the shadow of the Holy Roman Empire, it nonetheless managed to retain its independence. A key factor in its development was Mieszko's acceptance of Western Christianity and later the acquisition of a royal crown from the West and the respect that came with this honor. Yet the trajectory of the young Polish polity was not the proverbial upward one. The new state alternated between moments of triumph and moments of tragedy. Its relationship with the church had its rocky moments, for example, as attested by the murder of Bishop Stanisław at the hands of King Bolesław the Bold. Nonetheless, the acceptance of Christianity by the Polish masses would shape the rest of Poland's history—to the extent that Poles are now generally considered to be among the world's most devout Catholics and most devoted servants of the Holy See. This doubtless was the greatest legacy of Mieszko, the first of the Piast rulers.

The Fall and Rise of the Piasts

The saga of the Piasts began with the story of the poor but hospitable peasant plowman Piast, who with his wife entertained two mysterious guests. The guests not only worked miracles. They helped turn a spotlight on the coming of age of Piast's son, Siemowit. Aptly so. For it was Siemowit who reportedly ousted Popiel, the ruler who according to legend was devoured by rats. Several generations later (if the Anonymous's account is to be believed), it was the turn of Piast's great-great-grandson Mieszko to rule. He and his descendants would be the princes of the Poles.

It was only later, however, that this native ruling clan was labeled the Piast dynasty. Odd as it may seem, this is the only dynasty to rule Poland that can be thought of in ethnic Polish terms. This is one of the paradoxes of Polish history: only in medieval times was there truly a "Polish" dynasty. This later led the term "Piast" to become synonymous with a native Pole. The use of the word to describe native sons—as we shall see—was especially true when it came time to elect kings . . . but that is a story for a later chapter.

Despite a strong beginning, the Piast dynasty eventually fell upon challenging times. The murder of Bishop Stanisław at the hands of Bolesław the Bold in 1079 played a pivotal role in this development. The revolt of the

Polish knights, appalled by the murder of the bishop (or at least using it as a pretext to continue the conflict), forced Bolesław the Bold into exile.

The fact that Bolesław had to give up his throne caused huge repercussions for the still relatively young Polish kingdom. The situation remained shaky under his brother, Władysław Herman (1079–1102), who never was crowned king. Before long, the Polish state went through a period that used to be termed "feudal disintegration." Perhaps it is best considered an experiment in sharing the burdens and responsibilities of ruling, an experiment that went horribly wrong.

The problems began in 1138, with the death of another Polish ruler named Bolesław—Władysław Herman's son Bolesław III Krzywousty, known as the Wrymouth (1102–1138). Although he was a much better ruler than his father, the Wrymouth encountered numerous serious difficulties during his reign: first involving his elder brother, Zbigniew, then involving the Germans. To be sure, he did manage to gain control over the Baltic Sea region of Pomerania, which means that his Poland had borders in many ways close to those of present-day Poland. Nonetheless, in order to maintain control over these territories he was forced to swallow a bitter pill: Bolesław was compelled to pay homage to the Holy Roman Emperor.

Clearly something had to be done to beef up Poland's position. Taking example from the Kyivan grand dukes to the east, who also faced the daunting challenge of how to control a large and lightly populated territory, Bolesław the Wrymouth decided to parcel out control over the country among his numerous sons, and he wrote that stipulation into his will. His eldest son, Władysław—the so-called "senior prince"—would control the choicest lands, including the capital of Kraków, and his remaining sons would be awarded the lesser territories. Each would be responsible for keeping in line his own region, and the sometimes troublesome land-owning magnates within it. The younger Piasts would learn how to rule, and thus be ready to take over after the death of the senior prince. More a system of rotation than primogeniture, despite its complexities this plan seemed to make sense while promising to keep the dynasty in control of the entirety of the Polish lands.

Yet this experiment in dynastic power sharing backfired. Before too long, the princely Piast brothers ceased to work together. The new system simply provided each brother with a provincial base from which he could entertain pretentions to the lands of his siblings. Nor did the country's leading churchmen and powerful magnates cooperate. This led to civil war—and to the involvement of Emperor Frederick Barbarossa. The latter tried to bolster the position of Władysław—without success. Wrymouth's oldest son and onetime senior prince is remembered as Władysław the Exiled (1138–1146), for such was his fate.

Over the next decades the Wrymouth's experiment disintegrated, and its results were not at all what the king had imagined. The country was torn apart, not strengthened. Ultimately, the Piast dynasty split along regional lines. Five main branches were established: Lesser Poland, Greater Poland, Silesia, Mazovia, and Pomerania, each controlling a different part of the formerly unitary Polish state. And these were subject to further division and fragmentation: the Wrymouth's sons also managed to sire numerous sons and naturally wanted to provide for them. The most egregious (and lasting) example of fragmentation, the Silesian branch of the Piast dynasty, eventually disintegrated into some nine separate lines. The latter increasingly came under the influence of their neighbors to the west—as did the Piasts to the north, who had to contend with the new and rising March of Brandenburg. It would take another two hundred years before the crown was regained and monarchy reestablished in the Polish lands.

The Menace from the East

The Polish lands, subdivided into provinces and more, were in no position to fend off enemies who would prove frequent callers over the next centuries. These were the Mongols, also known (particularly later, when they were based in the region of the Black Sea) as Tatars. Who has not heard of Genghis Khan? This brilliant Mongol leader was one of the most famous military commanders of all time. He assembled an enormous army of fighters on horseback, mobile, swift, and well trained. And they attacked: first in northern China, Siberia, and Central Asia, and then they proceeded west toward the Caspian Sea, through the Caucasus and the Crimea, to engage the Europeans for the first time in battle in 1223, in the vicinity of the Sea of Azov.

This Asian people proved to be a true terror for the Europeans, who lacked light cavalry, and thus could easily be outmaneuvered. Although Genghis Khan died in 1227, leadership of the Mongol forces in the West was assumed by his grandson, Batu Khan. The latter, with his Golden Horde, made light work of the Ruthenes: Riazan, Moscow, Suzdal, and Vladimir all fell. In 1240 the Mongols made their way across the Dnieper River and sacked Kyiv.

In 1241 the Mongol forces made their way into Poland and Hungary. The latter was their ultimate goal: the Hungarian king Bela IV had refused to agree to Mongol demands and had even killed their emissaries. The Mongols attacked the Poles in order to keep them from coming to the aid of the

Hungarians. In this, the Mongols were successful. Poles proved no match for the Mongol hordes. City after city fell. First Sandomierz was sacked, then Kraków; various localities in Silesia—for the Mongols pressed on further west—witnessed the escape of populations into more distant fortresses or even the forests.

By April, the Mongols had made their way to Legnica (German: Liegnitz). The Polish duke Henryk the Pious (Pobożny), ruler of Lesser Poland, was there, waiting for Czech allies, who never arrived. However, he had the support of two religious crusading orders, the Knights of the Cross and the Knights Templars. What took place was nothing any of these central European forces had ever experienced before. The Mongols not only had their advantage of speed and mobility over the heavily armored western troops; they also used irritating gasses and smoke to disorient the Poles and their allies.

The result was out-and-out slaughter. Henryk perished, as did most of his men. Even his dead body met a gruesome fate: Mongols paraded his head on a stick outside the fortress of Legnica, which they were not able to penetrate. The Asian horde continued on its way to Hungary, which subsequently fell to them. Only news of the death of the great khan Ögödei brought about their return home, which saved the lands further west from devastation. This defeat at Legnica would have further repercussions for the Poles. Henryk had been in the process of uniting the Polish lands, and his death left them divided and weak.

Even today Poles have not forgotten the Mongol invasion. Evidence of this is seen by practically every visitor to the city of Kraków. The southern Polish town was sacked in 1241, its population annihilated, and the city burned in its entirety—with one exception: the only Cracovians to survive were those who hid in the Romanesque church of Saint Andrew, solidly built of durable stone. In commemoration of the invasion, every hour, on the hour, a trumpeter plays a tune from one of the towers of Saint Mary's Church, on the corner of the main market square. The tune comes to a sudden end—as if the trumpeter were felled by an arrow as he played, summoning Cracovians to come to the defense of the city. This melody is known as the Hejnał. Thus, the legend of the trumpeter of Kraków is kept alive. The Hejnał is even played by Polish radio at noon every day (a tradition that began in the early part of the twentieth century), thus reminding the entire Polish community of this historic conflict between West and East. At this time, of course, it was the East that proved victorious.*

---

* Kraków has yet another tradition connected to the Mongol invasion. That is the Lajkonik—a person wearing Mongol dress, atop a hobbyhorse, who makes his appearance in the city every summer, on the eighth day following Corpus Christi.

While the Poles clearly smarted from the Mongol invasions (they were invaded several more times that same century), the lands further east of them were hit harder. Kyiv (today's capital of Ukraine) was sacked. Repeated incursions led to a period known as the Tatar Yoke, when the Ruthenian principalities were subjugated to the Mongols. They had to pay tribute to the khanate for several centuries—and this period influenced later developments in what would come to be called Muscovy or Muscovite Russia.

Why is this worthy of our attention? Because the weakness of the Ruthenian principalities had repercussions for another neighbor of the Poles as well. The power vacuum in the east meant that the Lithuanians, located to the northeast of the Polish state, were able to expand in a southerly direction, into territories that in better times had belonged to Rus', which was now in no position to defend itself. With time, the Lithuanians would come to occupy a territory that reached far beyond their northeastern lands: from the basin of the Rivers Neman (Polish: Niemen) and Dnieper all the way to the Black Sea. They would also gain sovereignty over the East Slavic population of that vast region. (While the East Slavs dominated numerically, other peoples came to settle in Lithuania, including a Kipchak Turkic–speaking Jewish sect known as the Karaites.) Not a Slavic people themselves, the Lithuanians speak an ancient Baltic language that is related to that of the pagan Prussians and the Latvians. Yet their fate was much different from these peoples' fate. Their star was only beginning to rise . . .

The Menace from the North

The menace from the east was not the only threat posed to the Polish lands at this time. Witness the rise of a new and somewhat unusual power in the north: the Teutonic Knights. The real name of this curious entity was the Order of the Hospital of the Blessed Virgin Mary of the German House of Jerusalem. A religious order of crusading knights, it originated in the Holy Land in the twelfth century, just in time to be expelled by the Moslems. The order then, after reconstituting itself, eventually—and significantly for us—made its way to Hungary and Transylvania, ready to fight the infidel on any front (as long as payment were forthcoming).

In 1226 Konrad of Mazovia extended an invitation to the Teutonic Knights to settle along the border of Mazovia and Prussia, as he needed help in fighting the pagan Prussians and Yazwingians of the northern seacoast. It seemed a good idea at the time—Konrad thought he would gain support in the fight against the pagans, which would allow him to focus his

Figure 1.2: The thirteenth-century Gothic Church of the Blessed Virgin Mary, where a trumpeter now plays the Hejnał every hour, on the hour. In 1240, the year the city was destroyed by the Tatar invasion, a trumpeter might have been on the lookout from the tower of the already extant Romanesque Church of St. Andrew the Apostle.

ambitions elsewhere; for, in addition to his landholdings in the north, he had hopes of gaining control over Lesser Poland. The Polish prince did not realize the Pandora's box he opened in this fashion. The Teutonic Knights were not content to fight the Prussians for Konrad. They asked for further land grants—the Mazovian prince had given them the district of Chełmno (German: Kulm) as well as the right to control the territories they subdued. In this, they sought both papal and imperial support, both of which proved forthcoming. In the process they painted a rather false picture of their agreement with Konrad, demonstrating a lack of scruples that would continue to characterize their work in the region.

Given this highly placed support, the Polish princes were soon powerless to regain control over the north. Furthermore, the Teutonic Knights worked together with the support of the so-called Knights of the Sword, who sought conquests further north along the Baltic, in the region of the River Dvina. The Teutonic Knights became an efficient, impersonal machine of an organization, able to hold the lands they had conquered with the sword. These lands were soon populated, at the Order's behest, by German settlers—naturally, under the rule of the Knights. They founded hundreds of villages as well as many towns, including Königsberg (today's Kaliningrad, in Russia) and Marienburg (Polish: Malbork). The Knights encouraged and facilitated trade, in general appearing to further development of the region. This earned them the admiration and the support of the papacy, the Holy Roman Empire, the international trading organization known as the Hanseatic League, and others.

The work of this religious order was regarded by some to be very unChristian. The Knights energetically set about converting the pagan peoples of the north (at the point of a sword) and plagued neighboring Catholics long after their evangelizing services were no longer necessary. The crusading order made great strides within a very short space of time, and toward the end of the thirteenth century the hold of the Teutonic Knights on the Prussian lands was complete. They now ruled what we have come to call Prussia, with the support of both the pope and the German emperor. In their crusading zeal, they well nigh annihilated the pagans whom they were supposed to convert. This has led one historian to call them "the incarnation of the most un-Christian elements of the Christian world."* They were a formidable foe.

These were trying times for the already weakened Poles, weakened by fragmentation and infighting. During this period, Poland—insofar as it ex-

---

* Norman Davies, *God's Playground: A History of Poland* (New York: Columbia University Press, 1982), 1:91.

isted in anyone's mind—lost its power and influence in the region. These various menaces only exacerbated the problem, leaving anyone wishing to reunite the country with a major challenge.

The German Presence

In the thirteenth and fourteenth centuries, another development worth noting was the influx of some 250,000 German settlers into the Polish lands. The German label we understand broadly as those speaking unintelligible languages: they could be of Dutch or Flemish as well as German origin. By the thirteenth century, new ideas from the West were not only making their way to the rulers and their courts, the church, and the wealthier barons and magnates, they were also penetrating Polish society in general as well. Many settlers were recruited from various parts of the Holy Roman Empire. They brought in medieval technological innovations, introducing mills (that is, the harnessing of water power), better ploughs, and the like. These Germans were settled on lands not subject to the whims of the prince but, rather, under terms referred to as German Law, *ius teutonicum.*

In the Polish towns, a new form of governance commonly referred to as Magdeburg Law was established. Magdeburg Law established municipal autonomy and would eventually lead to municipal self-rule, providing for aldermen and a mayor (*wójt*). Magdeburg had been the closest significant German town, and it served as the pattern for many a Polish town by the end of the thirteenth century. Towns founded on this principle inherited a set pattern of spatial development: an urban grid opening onto a central market square, with a church at its corner—a pattern still found all over Poland. At the market square, knights also could acquire various goods, as could peasants, who monetized their grain to buy salt, metal tools, and clothing. Magdeburg Law was first introduced into the Silesian town of Złotoryja, known for its gold mines, in 1211. The same municipal rights were conferred upon Kraków at its reestablishment, following the Mongol invasion, in 1257. The spread of Magdeburg Law continued to radiate throughout the Polish lands, although the German presence itself was felt most in the western part of the country.

The new influx of foreigners led to a mosaic of peoples. The towns in the Polish lands were increasingly German and German-speaking, especially in the Silesian territories adjacent to the Holy Roman Empire. Polish was the language of the peasants in the surrounding territories, though clergymen throughout the country tended to favor the maintenance of the local language in their schools to keep Germans from becoming too influential within the ranks of the church, as seen in the 1285 synod at Łęczyca. That Polish was indeed being used by clergy can be seen from the earliest extant Polish-language document, the Holy Cross Sermons; these texts, containing a mixture of Latin and Polish, were written at the end of the thirteenth or beginning of the fourteenth century.

All told, these new developments led to an economic and cultural boom. Villages began to specialize in the cultivation of grain and the breeding of livestock, which later were traded in or near the towns. In addition to trade, the rapidly multiplying towns could become centers for a full complement of urban handicrafts, the work of guilds. Schools run by the cathedrals, monasteries, and others paid attention to both Latin and the vernacular in their teaching. The Polish lands were looking more and more like the lands to their west.

So all was not lost. Even if Poland was in pieces, the lands were developing and its people were thriving. Nor had the broader population lost its identity and connection to the Polish past. Indeed: despite a series of hurdles, an entity to be called Poland once more would come together, as a monarchy, in the early fourteenth century.

Poland: From Lows to Highs—or the Triumph of the Vertically Challenged . . .

This coming together was the work of one of the Piast princes, Władysław Łokietek. A grandson of Duke Konrad of Mazovia, Łokietek hailed from neighboring Cuiavia, in the central-northern reaches of the Polish lands. His sobriquet was "Elbow-High," which suggests the prince was short of stature. What Łokietek lacked in height, he surely made up for in chutzpah. This plucky—and lucky—Piast prince would begin what can be seen as an upward trajectory for the Poles.

The vertically challenged Łokietek was chosen prince of Greater Poland after the death of a different Piast ruler, Przemysł II (1257–1296), who was assassinated on Ash Wednesday on orders of the margraves of Brandenburg. The German margraves were unhappy with Przemysł's attempts to unify the Polish lands: Przemysł had brought together Greater Poland and the seacoast region known as Gdańsk-Pomerania, and in 1295 was even crowned king in Gniezno, albeit of those two regions alone. Łokietek hoped to build on these achievements.

In his race to consolidate his hold over these lands, however, the young

Piast made several missteps and, in the process, alienated some of his subjects. This led to Łokietek being outmaneuvered by his powerful neighbor, the king of Bohemia, Václav (Wenceslas) II. Václav was son of the ambitious Přemysl Otakar I, who had made an unsuccessful bid for the imperial crown that went instead to Rudolf Habsburg. Ambitious like his father, Václav nonetheless sought to expand eastward (into the Polish lands), and not westward (into the Austrian lands). The Bohemian king seized control over Gdańsk-Pomerania from the short Piast prince and subsequently conquered further Polish territories. More significantly, Václav managed to get himself crowned king of Poland in Gniezno in 1300. The long-standing tradition of crowning only members of the Piast dynasty as king of Poland was broken.

The coronation of his Bohemian rival might have put an end to Łokietek's ambitions—or worse. He was forced to flee the country. Legend tells us how the plucky Polish Piast hid from Václav's troops in one of the limestone caves at Ojców. A spider wove a large web over the entrance to Łokietek's cave before the troops arrived, which convinced them their quarry was not to be found inside.

The Piast was aided in other, more prosaic ways as well. One was the problem faced by many a medieval dynasty: life was brutish and short. The reign of King Václav II came to an end with his sudden death in 1305. His son and successor, also named Václav (who had become king of Hungary before inheriting Bohemia and Poland from his father), was assassinated in Bohemia the following year. The extinction of the Czech Přemyslid dynasty left the throne open (in fact, it left several thrones open), which was then contested from all sides. Habsburgs, Luxemburgs, as well as a number of Piast princes (if not Łokietek) all sought to claim the throne. Married to a Bohemian Přemyslid princess, John of Luxemburg ultimately proved victorious—thus initiating a new Bohemian dynasty. He would consider himself also heir to the Polish throne.

Tiny but tenacious, Łokietek was not one to abandon the cause of conquest and unification so lightly. Whereas Václav II and subsequent Bohemian monarchs had found support in the Germanized towns, the Piast prince managed to rally the knights (if not the towns) to his side. And he was willing to fight. With Hungarian help, Łokietek reconquered Lesser Poland, Cuiavia, and other territories, thus establishing himself as a legitimate ruler of the Polish lands circa 1306. Holding onto them proved a challenge: for example, at one point burghers rebelled in Kraków and other towns of Lesser Poland, and they had to be subdued. The Polish unifier sought to rid Kraków of the miscreants by use of a shibboleth. Those burghers who could pronounce the four words "soczewica, koło, miele, młyn" (lentil, wheel, grinds, mill) were allowed to stay. Native German speakers stumbled over the pronunciation of the Polish letters "ł" and "s," which allowed the authorities to shuffle and rearrange the city's population. Henceforth, the Kraków burghers would find it politic to Polonize. The process of unification was anything but smooth.

Nonetheless, the Piast was persistent—and his persistence paid off. The sixty-year-old Łokietek was crowned King Władysław Łokietek in 1320. His coronation on January 20 of that year took place not in Gniezno but in Kraków, which had been gaining in political significance since Kazimierz the Restorer moved there in the eleventh century. Still, the Elbow-High succeeded in unifying only two provinces: Lesser Poland and Greater Poland. His Poland had no Mazovia, no Prussia (despite Łokietek's best efforts, the Teutonic Knights had seized control there), no Gdańsk-Pomerania (treacherously taken by the Teutonic Knights), and no Silesia (the Silesian Piasts did not feel compelled to subordinate themselves to the upstart Łokietek, and they remained firmly in the Bohemian orbit). Once again coronation was an important symbolic act, if still just a beginning.

The return of the Piasts to the crown and the dynasty's subsequent strengthening were made possible by several developments. Initially, a series of succession pacts among the Piast princes resulted in some consolidation, leaving certain territories in Łokietek's hands. This was no guarantee of success, though: the efforts of earlier unifiers—Przemysł as well as Henryk Probus, who had sought to unite Silesia and Lesser Poland—were cut short by assassination. Yet Łokietek importantly secured the support of Pope John XXII. The pope actually preferred Poland to be an independent entity. Why was that? Because as a papal fief Poland paid the so-called Peter's Pence. When the Czech Václav II sat on the throne, the money went into the coffers of the Holy Roman Empire, as the Czech king was the vassal of the emperor. Furthermore, any strengthening of Bohemia would then result in a strengthening of the Holy Roman Empire, which was frequently at odds with the church in Rome. The same would have held true for the rule of the Luxemburg or Habsburg candidates.

Łokietek also entered into dynastic alliances. He gained an ally in the impressive and ambitious king of Hungary, Charles Robert of Anjou (son of Charles Martel of Naples). With papal support, the Angevin had succeeded the last of the native Hungarian Árpád dynasty at the beginning of the fourteenth century. Poles and Hungarians both were concerned about the rise of neighboring Bohemia under the Luxemburgs. This Polish-Hungarian alliance—as with so many in the medieval and later periods—was cemented by a marriage. In 1320, Łokietek's daughter Elżbieta (Elizabeth) became the third wife of the recently widowed Charles Robert.

This was not the only strategic marriage arranged by Łokietek. The Polish king also married his sole surviving son to Aldona (baptized as Anna), the daughter of the Lithuanian prince Gediminas. As luck would have it, this alliance with their aggressive pagan neighbor Lithuania to the east left the Mazovians peeved. However, as we will see, these marriage alliances set the tone for later developments.

That Łokietek lived to be seventy-three—he died in 1333—added to the stability of the Polish kingdom, as it reemerged from its fractious and fragmented recent past. And, as only one son survived him, the question of succession was, thankfully, an easy one. This son was named Kazimierz.

The Greatest Piast

King Kazimierz III—Łokietek's sole surviving son as well as his heir—was the only Polish king ever to be called Great. His father laid the groundwork for a genuinely hereditary monarchy. It was now up to Kazimierz to consolidate his holdings and lend some stability to the country. That Kazimierz—who would turn out to be the last of the Piast dynasts—was able to do this and more doubtless earned him the sobriquet.

Kazimierz proved an able diplomat and an effective nation-builder. As historian Paul Knoll has written, Kazimierz demonstrated, still at an early age, that he was "master of the art of the possible."[*] The new king knew how to cut his losses and turn enemies into—well, if not friends, at least then foes not actively seeking his demise. This is seen through a series of negotiations he undertook with his neighbors.

As mentioned earlier, the princes of Silesia had long flirted with the Bohemians, preferring to be vassals of the Bohemian king than to return to Polish control. Their continued alienation from the unified Polish state was ultimately confirmed by the Treaty of Namysłów (Namslau) of November 22, 1348. In exchange for this concession, the Luxemburgs of Bohemia renounced their claim to the Polish crown and their claim to control over Mazovia, which then became a fief of the Polish crown. Thus, one potential enemy was neutralized. All the same, this decision to relinquish Polish claims to the territory—which Kazimierz did not relish—was fateful. After this time, the lands and people of Silesia were not to return to a Polish state for another six centuries. (They would become

---

[*] Paul W. Knoll, *The Rise of the Polish Monarchy: Piast Poland in East Central Europe, 1320–1370* (Chicago: University of Chicago Press, [1972]), 82.

part of the Habsburg landholdings in 1526 and were taken over by the Prussians in 1740.)

Kazimierz also sought to pacify the North. His father had defeated the Teutonic Knights at Płowce in 1331, but the victory had not resulted in any return of territory. Kazimierz the Great tried a different, more diplomatic tack. A peace with the Teutonic Knights (negotiated first in 1335 in Visegrád and then in 1343 in Kalisz) gave the Poles some breathing room. The new Polish king was even able to regain strategically located Cuiavia and neighboring Dobrzyń in the north, although he had to relinquish hold over Chełmno to their north.

The stabilizing of the long contested borders in the west and the north inclined Kazimierz, determined to strengthen his country's position in Europe, to set his sights eastward. The objective was the nearby Ruthenian kingdom of Halych and Volodymyr (*regnum Galiciae et Lodomeriae*). In 1323, the kingdom had come under the control of a Mazovian Piast prince, Bolesław Trojdenowic. His mother, Maria, daughter of Yuri I, was the last of the Rurikids in Halych; her son came to rule after her two brothers had perished in battle with the Tatars.

The reign of Yuri II (this was Bolesław's name, after his conversion to Orthodox Christianity) was nonetheless fraught with tension. In 1340 Yuri was poisoned by his boyars; according to some accounts, they objected to inroads being made within the kingdom by Catholicism, thus destabilizing the region. At the news of the murder of Yuri (who, incidentally, had been put on the throne in part due to Łokietek's efforts), Kazimierz invaded. The country was still ostensibly under Tatar rule, thus the Polish king's military campaign could be presented as a crusade of sorts. It is also possible that Yuri himself had earlier offered the Polish king the succession to the Ruthenian throne.

Regardless of how motivated, Kazimierz's efforts at seizing control over the region were successful. The kingdom of Halych and Volodymyr would eventually become known, in Polish history, as Red Ruthenia and Volhynia. However, the Polish takeover of the Ruthenian kingdom led to conflict with Lithuania, which also took a lively interest in the Ruthenian lands. Ultimately the territory was divided between the two countries. Poland gained the southernmost part, Red Ruthenia.

Kazimierz's addition of Heir of Ruthenia to his royal title did not go unnoticed. Poland's neighbors to the west and north began to take greater notice of the great king and his doings in the east. The German emperor arranged a marriage alliance for Kazimierz, ultimately setting him up with Adelheid of Hesse; and relations between Bohemia and Poland took a turn for the better. This in turn unnerved the Teutonic Knights; they were unhappy about

Map 1.2: Piast Poland under Kazimierz the Great, ca. 1370

the Poles' improved relations with Lithuania, which incidentally marked a return to Łokietek's earlier policy.

Kazimierz also renegotiated relations to the south. In the process of securing his claim to Red Ruthenia, ties to Hungary were further strengthened. The king's sister was the third wife of Charles Robert and mother of his son and heir Louis (Hungarian: Lajos), who came to the Hungarian throne in 1342. In exchange for Hungarian support of his claims, Kazimierz agreed that Louis would inherit his kingdoms should the Polish king die without siring a legitimate male heir.

Kazimierz's acquisition of Red Ruthenia, which became the southeastern corner of Poland, would have important repercussions. It opened up the Polish kingdom to the lucrative Black Sea trade, which apparently was worth making the above-mentioned concessions to Hungary. The region also would provide Poland with an outpost whence the Polish monarch could defend his kingdom from Tatar incursions.

With the new territory, the Polish state began to acquire a frontier mentality. Its own frontier with the "east"—with Lithuania, with what remained of Kyivan Rus', and with Moldavia—had lengthened significantly. Poland would increasingly see itself as a crusader of sorts, destined to convert the peoples of the East. This was also the foreshadowing of the idea of Poland as a bulwark of Christendom, as a power located on the border between East and West, fated to defend the West from any threats coming from the East.

At the same time, Poland also absorbed some of the same East. This expansion into the Ruthenian lands gained the Polish state a more diverse population. For here in the newly acquired territories were Orthodox Christians (the Ruthenes, today's Ukrainians) and Armenian Christians (members of the ancient Armenian Apostolic Church).

Both these populations could be found in the most important town of the region, Lviv (Polish: Lwów). The city is strategically located on the continental divide between the Baltic and the Black Sea basins, which made it a prime site for the transit trade. Already a multidenominational entity prior to Polish rule, Lviv would soon become even more so. Reorganized along the lines of Magdeburg Law in the 1350s, the trading town witnessed an influx of Catholics, particularly Germans. It also witnessed an influx of Jews.

The history of the Jewish presence in the Polish lands goes way back. The occasional Jewish community certainly could be found as early as the tenth century, its members engaged in long-distance trade. Some of these early Jews even spoke a Slavic tongue as their native language. Beginning in the twelfth century, though, they began to be outnumbered by the inmigrating Ashkenazi Jews, speakers of Yiddish (a Germanic language). From Western Europe, these Jews came to the Kingdom of Poland during a period when they were persecuted in the Holy Roman Empire. The Polish state welcomed them, even encouraged them to settle, and they became part of the colorful mosaic of foreign colonization. Jews ended up in the country's nascent towns, working for the most part as traders, merchants, bankers, even minters. With a background in commerce and trade, they helped to develop the circulation of currency; one curious early coin circulating in the Kingdom of Poland featured the name of a Polish monarch in Hebrew letters. Jews came to the Polish lands as free people—people who would be given their own corporate legal status, with rights and privileges, duties and obligations, just like so many of the other groups and/or estates (nobles, burghers, peasants, clergy) within the country. The earliest privilege was granted by Duke Bolesław the Pious to the Jews of Greater Poland in 1264. Among the privileges was their exemption from municipal court jurisdiction and the right to be judged by their own, Jewish, courts.

King Kazimierz III the Great encouraged Jewish settlement in the Polish lands. The recent incidence of the so-called Black Death in Europe's west had led Jews there to be turned into scapegoats, leading many to flee eastward. Kazimierz's reception of the Jewish communities led some even to label him "king of the Jews"—and led Jews to revere his name. In charters granted in 1334, 1364, and 1367, Kazimierz made it clear that Jews were subjects of the Crown, and as such they were protected by it.

Kazimierz was a nearly model medieval monarch. He did more than consolidate and make secure the country's expanding borders and provide for further economic development. He truly established the *Corona Regni Poloniae*—the Crown of the Polish Kingdom. No longer were the Polish lands simply the property of the Piast dynasty. As the Crown of the Polish Kingdom, they existed independently, outside the person of the monarch. In this way, one can see parallels between the formation of other states in the region. The united Bohemian lands were also referred to as the Crown of Saint Wenceslas, which Charles IV declared distinct from the fate of the Luxemburg dynasty; a similar understanding took hold in Hungary, which was also known as the Lands of the Crown of Saint Stephen.

Kazimierz drew up a number of statutes that would help shape the administration of the state, especially insofar as laws and the functioning of a judiciary were concerned. He also upheld the country's defense. Even today, any Polish child can recite the ditty (unpoetically rendered here) that Kazimierz "inherited wooden towns and left them fortified with stone and brick" (Kazimierz miasta zastał drewniane i zostawił murowane). The country underwent a great program of construction. It was funded in part by a land tax paid by peasants (who nonetheless had a favorable view of the monarch, who was also known as "king of the peasants"), in part by income that came from the rich salt mines of Wieliczka and Bochnia in the south of the country. (Even today, the salt mine at Wieliczka—quite a tourist destination—is a testament to the technological feat undertaken in this early period.) Growing exports and tax revenues funded the construction of some fifty castles, and fortification walls were supplied to nearly another thirty towns.

Another major and far-sighted achievement of King Kazimierz the Great was his establishment, in 1364, of a *studium generale* (variously titled an academy or a university) in his capital of Kraków. Pope Urban V gave his permission for instruction to be provided in canon and civil law and all other faculties except for theology. Nonetheless, Kazimierz's academy was a secular institution, like the universities of Padua and Bologna. Its establishment boded well for education in the Polish lands. Furthermore, it was a rare distinction in this part of the world: in Central Europe, only Prague can boast of having obtained a university earlier.

Poland's International Stature

Under Kazimierz the Great, Poland was becoming an important Central European power. One event that encapsulates this new distinction was the great Congress of Kraków in 1364, convened the same year the university was founded. It amassed a magnificent cast of royal characters. Present were the Holy Roman Emperor Charles IV, King Louis of Hungary, King Peter of Cyprus, King Waldemar of Denmark, King Wenzel of Bohemia, and other lesser dukes and princes along with all their retinues. All assembled to garner support for a crusade against the Turks, who at the time were threatening Cyprus. Although no such crusade ever materialized, other negotiations ensued among the participants. These included a peace between Charles, the Holy Roman Emperor, and Louis of Hungary, as well as negotiations between the latter and Kazimierz regarding issues of succession.

The event is more notable for its reflection of the stature of Kazimierz and his Corona Regni Poloniae than for any diplomatic agreements. Kazimierz entertained his guests magnificently—truly in royal fashion, in his capital city that was also becoming a city of stone and brick, in keeping with the heaven-bound Gothic style found throughout Europe. Heads of state were housed in the new royal castle on Wawel Hill, while other guests took lodging in the city proper. Reportedly Kazimierz was liberal in his bestowal of gifts upon his guests, who were entertained—with tournaments, feasts and the like—for three weeks in September 1364.

The site of the international event, Kraków was growing into a respectable capital as well as a thriving city of trade. It had long profited from the overland transit trade connecting east and west. Kraków enjoyed staple rights, which meant that merchants traveling via the city had to exhibit their wares, thus allowing Cracovians to purchase them. Hugely important to the city's economy was the highly lucrative export of Polish lead from Olkusz and of salt mined in nearby Wieliczka and Bochnia. Kraków, incidentally, profited from north–south trade as well. It was a member of the Hanseatic League, which was comprised mainly of port cities along the Baltic and North Seas.

During the reign of Kazimierz the Great, the city was taking on the shape so familiar to tourists today. Leveled following the devastation of the Mongol invasion, Kraków had been reestablished by a regional duke, Bolesław the Bashful, in 1257. It boasted an immense market square (some two hundred yards square), with the grand Gothic structure of Saint Mary's Church at one corner and a Gothic cloth hall in the center. The town's earliest fortifications were built in 1285; the main entrance to the city, the Florian Gate, was begun in 1298. The medieval city even possessed a water supply system.

Further construction came during the reign of the great monarch. In the fourteenth century, a new district called Kazimierz—named after the king, nota bene—was springing up across the Vistula, with synagogue, church, and other buildings underway. Construction was proceeding apace of yet another royal cathedral on the limestone rock that was Wawel Hill, overlooking the meandering Vistula River.

The capital's long-standing location on the axis of both north–south (Baltic–Hungary) and east–west (Bavaria–Ruthenia) trade routes raised its stature. In 1306, Władysław Łokietek bestowed on Kraków the staple right, which meant that all merchants traveling through the town had to exhibit their wares for sale. Kraków was already known as a place where one could buy lead, silver, and cloth. Now, with the staple right, its inhabitants were able to purchase gold and copper from Hungary; fancier cloths, spices, fruit, and various finished goods from the West; as well as other goods. This improved access significantly strengthened the economic position of Kraków's merchants, in turn increasing the wealth and prosperity of the town.

A French poet, Guillaume de Machaut, penned some verses regarding the Kraków Congress, including his impression that those assembled were entertained—certainly they were fed—with true largesse. That was no exaggeration. Perhaps Kraków's richest citizen, the burgher Mikołaj Wierzynek, a municipal councilor and owner of a large townhouse on the market square, invited all the guests to dine with him there. His townhouse still stands, long since turned into a restaurant that bears his name; for years it was the finest place to dine in all of Kraków.

According to Kazimierz's deputy chancellor and author of a chronicle of his rule, Janko of Czarnków: "It is not possible to describe the extent of delight, magnificence, glory and abundance that there was in this 'convivium,' not even if it were given to everyone to report as much as they wished. The kings and princes promised and affirmed great friendship for one another, and were given many gifts for themselves by King Kazimierz of Poland."* Kazimierz's star—as well as that of the Crown of the Polish Kingdom—appeared to be on the rise. The son of Łokietek had brought the country much needed stability. He had secured the country's frontiers with some of its more troublesome neighbors and had won the respect of other European rulers. He consolidated his hold over various lands (both Polish and Ruthenian) and provided for his increasingly diverse subjects by improving governance and rule of law, shoring up the state's defenses, and even providing his people with new educational possibilities. The former "lands of the princes

---

* Ibid., 217.

of the Poles" were united into a strong and (for medieval times) modern hereditary monarchy, the Corona Regni Poloniae.

Yet the Polish king, the country's only "great" ruler, had a major personal fault, related to his taking care of dynastic business. Kazimierz had no legitimate male heir. Not that there had not been occasion—Kazimierz had two legitimate marriages, and two marriages that might not be seen in so favorable a light, given that his second (barren) wife, Adelheid of Hesse, had not died. Rather, he had incautiously fallen in love with a widow from Bohemia. Then Kazimierz used the ruse of a papal dispensation (never granted) to marry his fourth wife. His love life was indeed messy: it was rumored that he had a Jewish mistress, Esther, as well. Would all his work—all his efforts to reunify and strengthen the country, reestablish a hereditary monarchy, even elevate Poland to pride of place in Central Europe in 1364—have been for naught?

CHAPTER 2

Embracing the East

The Lithuanian Connection

The End of a Dynasty

In the year 1370, King Kazimierz was busy taking care of affairs of state in the region of Greater Poland. As did all medieval kings, he made the rounds of his kingdom, rendering justice and strengthening relations with the local population. The month of September found him at Przedbórz, in the vicinity of Sieradz. He had just begun his return trip to the capital, Kraków. As we will see, this would be his last journey through his country. And what a journey it was!

The fateful date was September 8, the feast of the Nativity of the Virgin Mary—perhaps not an auspicious day to undertake other than pious pursuits. Yet, that day Kazimierz was persuaded to go hunting by "some knave"—according to the chronicler, deputy chancellor and great admirer of Kazimierz, Janko of Czarnków. Kazimierz did enjoy the pleasures of life, and he seemed to be well enough, even in the seventh decade of his life, to undertake one of his favorite activities—an activity that, taking him away from the royal castle, doubtless had also given him recourse, in the past, to other pursuits of the flesh. Despite the voices of reason (expressed by some of the king's advisers—perhaps even including Janko himself), the king hurried away in his carriage and headed to the forest, but his pleasures at the hunt would be short-lived. The following day, while chasing after a deer, the king fell off his horse and sustained a not insignificant wound to his left leg.

Kazimierz was seized by fever—a fever that, although soon to pass, would come back to haunt him for the remainder of his journey, for (as Janko relates) the king once again eschewed reason and dined immoderately on foods and availed himself of the baths forbidden him by his court physician,

Master Henryk of Cologne. He appeared close to death, but the ministrations of the doctors had some effect. His faithful courtiers went so far as to harness themselves to the carriage like horses and lead the ill king to the Cistercian monastery in Koprzywnica, where he recuperated over the next eight days. In gratitude for this return to health, Kazimierz vowed to rebuild the church in Płock, at that time in ruins.

Yet was he truly recovered? Apparently not, for his fever returned after, while at the Osiek manor, he took a drink of mead. This he had been allowed by Master Matthew, yet another physician of the king's—perhaps giving in to the king's strong desire for the drink. After all, this physician's approval went counter to the advice of the afore-mentioned Master Henryk and the royal courtiers present. Taken to the beautiful—and new—royal manor at Nowe Miasto, he was treated again. Once again the king made enough of a recovery to travel further on to Opatowiec, where he once again recuperated. Feeling well, he set off once more for Kraków. En route he was beset by fever. The way the medieval doctors perceived it, he was suffering from several types of fever—the "everyday fever as well as three- and four-day fevers"—at once. The king was a very sick man indeed.

The remaining days of his life were spent in traveling back to Kraków—an arduous journey indeed, as the motion seemed to make him worse—and subsequently undergoing treatment there. In Kraków he was to live some ten days more—this despite the protestations of his physicians that he would yet live a long time. (Clearly it did not matter how powerful one was: the medical profession in medieval times—in the rest of Europe as well as Poland—was woefully inadequate.) At one moment the king was not even sure whether he had already arrived at the castle. This prompted renewed ministrations on the part of his doctors.

Kazimierz was so ill that, after arriving in Kraków, he composed his last will and testament in order to secure the future of his household as well as his soul. The king clearly had a better sense of his condition than did his physicians: for the following week—on November 7—he died. The last of the Piast kings had been generous with his belongings and his properties, although his successor would not allow things to stand as written in Kazimierz's will.

Southern Detour

The same Janko of Czarnków, witness to the scenes of Kazimierz's last days (and much more), had no love of the king's successor. His distaste led the former deputy chancellor and archdeacon of Gniezno to go so far as reportedly to steal the royal insignia from the tomb of the dead king—one imagines, in the hopes of passing on the royal torch, so to speak, to yet another possible candidate for the Polish throne. Yet the succession to the Piasts proved to elicit no crisis—Janko's purported theft notwithstanding. (That deed led him to be banished from the country in 1372, although the elderly Janko was back in Gniezno and composing his chronicle of the times of Kazimierz the Great and the memoir of his own times only four years later.)

But how was a succession crisis sidestepped? How did the country of Władysław Łokietek and—even more—of Kazimierz the Great withstand the challenge posed to the hereditary monarchy they had just reestablished by the fact that the latter produced no legitimate male heir? (Kazimierz had a daughter Elżbieta, whom he much loved, as well as illegitimate sons, to whom he bequeathed properties.)

That the Corona Regni Poloniae would prove indivisible is due to the care taken by King Kazimierz the Great in providing for a successor. True, it would not be one sired by him. After the death of his beloved first wife, Kazimierz wanted to ensure that there would be a male heir lined up to succeed him, should ensuing wives not provide him with the longed-for son. No question: the inability to produce a legitimate male heir was a destabilizing factor in an age that tended to view monarchy as hereditary.

Kazimierz was all too cognizant of his failure to sire his successor. It led him to action. He did two things. First, as early as 1339 Kazimierz set as his heir someone from the illustrious Angevin dynasty in Hungary. Who would succeed—as so often was the case in medieval times—depended on who outlived whom. With time it was determined that this person would be Louis of Anjou. Louis (Hungarian: Lajos) ruled Hungary from 1342 to 1382 and subsequently became known among Hungarians as "Louis the Great." The son of Kazimierz's sister Elizabeth and Charles Robert of Anjou, Louis was clearly part-Angevin, part-Piast. Such a succession would further the Hungarian alliance initially forged by Kazimierz the Great's father, Władysław Łokietek, with Charles Robert of Hungary, the first Angevin king to sit on that throne. Second, the Polish king hedged his bets by adopting another relative, Kaźko, in 1368. Kaźko was duke of Słupsk, hailing from Pomerania, along the Baltic Sea coast. His succession to the throne might have been considered a northern connection of sorts. But, in this case, the southern connection prevailed. As it turns out, the part-Hungarian nephew proved acceptable to the Polish nobility.

The original negotiations regarding the Angevin succession in Poland came after the death of Kazimierz's first wife. Charles Robert of Hungary initiated the discussion of this possibility—a possibility that the king and the Polish nobility found intriguing. The line of succession would be drawn through Kazimierz's sister Elizabeth, with either her husband (Charles Robert) or one of her sons gaining the Polish throne. Ultimately, it worked out that Elizabeth's long-lived son Louis was destined to be king of Poland.

It should be noted that Kazimierz made his nephew Louis his heir on one condition: should Louis die without legitimate male issue, the choice of his successor would revert back to the Poles. After all, this option too might be a dynastic dead end (for Louis had not yet sired a son). Might this not have been why, late in life, Kazimierz positioned yet another relative, Kaźko, in such a way as to be seen as a legitimate successor—if not to him, then to Louis?

Although it appears that the matter of succession was relatively straightforward, it was not as simple as it seemed. The Polish nobles needed to give their assent—and they were not willing to do so without a sweetening of the deal. Among the original stipulations for the Angevin succession in 1339 was that the new king would seek to return lands, such as Pomerania, that had been lost to Poland; that Poles and not Hungarians would be given governmental appointments; and that all existing privileges would be respected. And this was not all. To make his future ascent to the throne more palatable, in 1355 Louis granted privileges in his capital of Buda, where the succession was confirmed. Among other things, no new taxes would be imposed without the consent of the Poles affected, nor would the nobility be required to fight outside of the country's own borders (and thus could not be pressed into fighting Louis's wars outside of Poland), but only to fight in defense of Corona Regni Poloniae. Also important: the succession of the Angevins in Poland would encompass only Louis, his nephew John, and their male offspring. (John died in 1360 and figured no further in the calculations of succession.)

Indeed, Louis was not loath to give privileges to secure the succession for himself. In this he was following precedent: privileges had already been granted to a segment of the Polish population by Václav II, king of Bohemia (whose brief, five-year rule as king over Polish lands interrupted Łokietek's push for the throne). Through promises made to Lesser Poland's nobility, knights, clergy, and towns in the Privilege of Litomysl of 1291, the foreign monarch from Bohemia had sought to garner enough support to gain control over Kraków. This facilitated Václav's coronation as king of Poland in 1300.

Poles, thus, had already had experience in dealing with foreign monarchs—as well as wresting privileges from them. They clearly anticipated that, once Louis ascended to the Polish throne (he ruled Poland from Kazimierz's death until his own death in 1382), he would be an absentee ruler. His mother, Łokietek's daughter Elizabeth, would act as regent for him. (An influential woman, she had acted as regent of Hungary for her son once, when his ambitions took him west to Naples.) His focus would lie not on the Polish lands but, rather, on his extensive Hungarian holdings—although part Piast, part Angevin, Louis would go down in Polish history as "Louis the Hungarian" (Ludwik Węgierski).

This doubtless had less to do with blood and more with Louis's own personal ambitions, which did not necessarily dovetail with those of the second country he came to rule. He had various designs that sat ill with the Polish nobility and in part undid some of the hard work of his Piast predecessor. For example, he renounced all Polish claims to Silesia—to the benefit of the Luxemburgs of Bohemia. This move posed no problem for him, as his elder daughter, Maria, was betrothed to one of the Luxemburgs. Likewise in 1377 Louis incorporated the Ruthenian lands into Hungary, leaving the Poles without direct connection to lands that had lain within Kazimierz's sphere of influence, Podolia and Moldavia.

But the Hungarian and Polish king found himself in the same situation as had Kazimierz. He too had no male heir—only daughters, and these were born to him late in life. They included the previously mentioned Maria and her younger sister, Hedwig. (An older sister, Catherine, also figured in the picture until her death in 1378.) As already noted, Maria was betrothed to Sigismund of Luxemburg, whose father was king of Bohemia as well as Holy Roman Emperor. Hedwig—born only in the year 1374—also awaited a princely husband, having been promised in marriage since early childhood to Wilhelm of Habsburg.

How to convince the nobles to allow a woman—let alone a young girl—to ascend to the Polish throne? Louis knew how to proceed: he would have to promise them more privileges. The nobles saw it coming and drove a hard bargain. What resulted was the so-called Privilege of Košice (Kassa) of 1374. The pact greatly benefited the nobility in particular. Taxes owed on land worked by the peasants on noble (and later church) estates would be reduced from 12 to 2 *grosze* (Latin: *grossi*, the basic unit of coinage in medieval Poland) per tenant. The nobility would not be required to fight outside of the country's own borders. Even the towns profited some from Košice: they would have more liberties, while Kraków was given the right of storage of goods brought into the city, which strengthened the position of its merchants. Still, these were ad hoc privileges, not extended to all municipalities.

All of this might have been enough to inspire a degree of friendliness between Hungarians and Poles. Historically they were on good terms. They did not figure as much of a threat to each other, as they were both just one step removed from Bohemia and the Holy Roman Empire. The Carpathian Mountains served as a boundary between the two countries, but it was a porous one. There was much contact across that border. Furthermore, it is important to note, the clanlike structure and the substantial role played by the nobilities in the two countries were similar. It is not for nothing that, even today, Poles know the ditty "Polak, Węgier dwa bratanki—tak do szabli, jak do szklanki" (The Pole and the Magyar like brothers stand / Whether with sword or with tankard in hand), whereas the corresponding Hungarian rhyme affects the same brotherly affection for the hard-fighting—and drinking—Poles.* (The verse, however, dates from a much later period.)

The Poles had anticipated that one of Louis's daughters would succeed him to the Polish throne—but which one? After Catherine's untimely death, Louis decided that Maria would reign in Poland. The Polish nobility balked, however: most Poles could not countenance a Luxemburg prince on the Polish throne. Things got so bad that in 1379 Louis forbade a delegation of Polish nobles at Košice to leave the city before they recognized Maria as his successor. Their persistent opposition, however, did not bode well for Maria in Poland.

But the situation changed—and changed dramatically. Five days after the death of Louis in 1382, the Hungarians proclaimed not Hedwig but Maria as "king." This veritable coup d'état would have life-changing consequences for her younger sister. The youngest of Louis's daughters, Hedwig had been betrothed to Wilhelm of Habsburg several years earlier. She was not yet old enough to consummate a marriage (the minimum age at this period was twelve for girls, fourteen for boys); however, it was anticipated that she would inherit Hungary and that Wilhelm, thus, would become king of Hungary. Now everything was up in the air.

And how things changed for the young princess! The final resolution provided Hedwig with a new destination—Kraków—and a new life. In October 1384, at the tender age of ten, Princess Hedwig of Hungary (henceforth known in Polish as Jadwiga) was crowned king of Poland. She was, of course, no less Polish than her elder sister. Both of them had two Polish grandmothers and even more Polish great-grandmothers, making them essentially more Polish than Hungarian. This, of course, was beside the point in an age that cared little for ethnicity and much more about blue blood. Jadwiga was of unquestionably royal lineage. And she behaved like the well-bred princess and later king/queen that she was.

Jadwiga had been brought up to believe she would marry into the House of Habsburg. She had even spent two years in Vienna, from the age of four to six. What could a child of four have understood of the symbolism of such medieval rites as the *sponsalia de futuro*, which involved having the young

---

*   Translation of the verse from Davies, *God's Playground*, 1:114.

girl (in this case, the four-year-old Jadwiga) and the eight-year-old Wilhelm lie down in the same bed—especially as there could be no talk of consummating the marriage for eight more years?

Vienna was the place where the young girl was expected to become queen. It was a destination fitting for a well-educated and cultured princess, one who demonstrated a facility for languages as well as piety. All these qualities—and more—would prove necessary to this girl-child, thrown before her time into the maelstrom of national and international politics. And there was drama in the ensuing years, before Jadwiga ascended to the Polish throne: not the least of which was an attempted kidnapping of the princess that nonetheless backfired (Jadwiga had not yet set off for Kraków, reportedly because floods in the Carpathian Mountains had made them impassable). She more likely remained at home, as news of the expected "welcome" reached Hungary. Besides, Poland proved an inhospitable place at that moment: civil war was being waged by a desperate Mazovian Piast, eager to win the throne for himself. Even Sigismund of Luxemburg saw fit to invade Poland. These were trying times, and great challenges faced the Poles. Would the succession ever be determined?

The nobles finally reached an important decision during this painful *interregnum*. In March 1384 they gave the princess a kind of ultimatum: only if Jadwiga came to Poland within two months would her claim to the throne be respected. So Jadwiga came. On October 16, 1384, she was crowned "king" of Poland—the accepted title for a monarch of Poland at that time, even if that monarch happened to be female.

The life of the young Hungarian princess turned Polish king was to take on a completely different character than she had grown up expecting. At the tender age of ten she was ruler of a different country, one she knew infinitely less well than Hungary or even Austria. Doubtless she took a crash course on Poland after the coup that placed her sister on the Hungarian throne, and she likely evinced greater interest in her Polish heritage. Jadwiga must have made progress. After her coronation the situation in Poland calmed down dramatically.

Jadwiga was considered lovely by such partial sources as Polish historian Jan Długosz but also by those who had no reason to exaggerate her beauty, such as the envoys of the Teutonic Knights. Most certainly she was stately and well built. More importantly, she was accepted by the Polish nobility as the legitimate heir to the throne. There was no reason to believe she would not be an appropriate person to facilitate the continuation of the Piast-Angevin dynasty. That such was not to be the case only underscores the tragedy of this young girl's life.

Jadwiga had been betrothed to Wilhelm of Habsburg, and the two seemed to get along well—at least, as childhood playmates in Vienna. Doubtless the princess's designated future father-in-law, Leopold III, was disappointed that she was not to rule Hungary. Already then, Habsburg interests lay in that more southerly direction. Poland was situated not only further to the north but separated from the Habsburg lands by the Luxemburgs' landholdings. The prospect of a king from the House of Habsburg left the Polish nobility in a quandary, seeing that such a marriage would dash the nobles' chances of becoming big players in East-Central Europe. Yet Leopold—and by extension, Wilhelm—did not sense any real threat to the marriage agreement entered into so many years earlier.

This meant that the reaction to the arrival of Wilhelm of Habsburg in Kraków in 1385 was all the more unexpected. When the dashing young Habsburg duke arrived in Kraków the following year to claim his bride, the scene was dramatic. Wilhelm was barred from the castle and ultimately forced to leave Poland and Jadwiga behind.

Why such a violent reaction? The Polish nobles did not want a Habsburg on the Polish throne. They had more ambitious dynastic plans—plans that would win over to the state a whole new region and people to the east.

The Eastern Connection

You may recall that Władysław Łokietek forged more than one alliance with his neighbors during the trying times of his rule. To be sure, he married his daughter Elżbieta /Elizabeth to Charles Robert of Hungary. We have seen what good that brought to Poland: Hungary provided an acceptable male heir after the death of Kazimierz the Great, thus saving the country from a succession crisis, at least for the moment. But this last of the Piasts had originally been offered as a kind of olive branch—in the form of a husband—to one of Poland's eastern neighbors, Lithuania. And the olive branch was accepted. Not only was a formal Polish-Lithuanian treaty signed in the fall of 1325; the fifteen-year-old heir to the Polish throne, Kazimierz, gained for his first wife Aldona, daughter of the ruler of Lithuania, Gediminas (c. 1316–1342). Anna—she would be known in Poland by her baptismal name—was a person who reveled in the delights of the world, in games, music, dancing, reportedly quite a contrast to the more subdued Polish court of that period. The passionate Kazimierz loved her deeply and mourned her greatly when she died in 1339.

It is this eastern connection that now would become important for the Poles. It had surfaced as an important region already during the rule of

Władysław Łokietek, who was married to a descendant of the Ruthenian dynasty that had ruled over the kingdom of Halych and Volodymyr from the late twelfth century. These were the Romanovichi, named after Prince Roman (1199–1205), who had united the two Ruthenian territories. The land had not escaped the notice of the West, most notably Pope Innocent IV. He sent a crown in 1253 to Roman's successor, Daniel, in the hopes that the latter would convert from Orthodoxy to Roman Christianity and become part of the Western world. Furthermore, a Polish duke (whose mother had been a Romanovich) named Bolesław—a distant relative of Łokietek—ruled over the Ruthenian lands (where he was known as Yuri) until his murder in 1340. Following this, as we know, Kazimierz laid claim to the territories and ultimately ended up controlling Galicia, the so-called Red Ruthenia.

After the death of Kazimierz's first wife, Aldona/Anna, relations between Poland and Lithuania grew strained, and Ruthenia—or more precisely, the question of who would rule there—proved a major stumbling block to improved relations, then as well as later. Witness, for example, the sudden invasion of Lesser Poland by the Lithuanian prince Kestutis in 1376: he penetrated well into Poland, all the way to Tarnów (less than 50 miles from the capital), burning, looting, and taking captives. The situation between the two countries had become anything but friendly . . .

There was a distinct possibility that Lithuania might choose—nay, might even prefer—an Eastern orientation. For this period marked the rise of Dmitrii Donskoi (1350–1389), the ruler of the principality known as Muscovy, after its capital of Moscow (Russian: Moskva). While the town of Moscow was originally built in the mid-twelfth century (to be burned down two decades later), only as of the second half of the thirteenth century did a separate family of princes come to dominate the principality and really begin to develop it. Dmitrii Donskoi (meaning "of the Don") was particularly notable in that he won an important victory in 1380 over the Golden Horde (the Mongols) at the battle of Kulikovo Pole, near the upper reaches of the Don River (hence his sobriquet Donskoi). This battle marked the turning point, the beginning of the end of Mongol dominance over what today we call Russia. The same grand prince was striving to gather up" all the Russian or East Slavic lands—and he was making headway in doing so.

The ruler of the large multiethnic Lithuanian state, with its majority of Orthodox East Slavs, Jogaila (he became Władysław Jagiełło only with his baptism and ascension to the Polish throne) might well have figured in this project. His mother—princess Juliana of Tver, from yet another Russian province whose ruler was now recognizing Dmitrii Donskoi as his "elder brother"—wanted her son to marry the daughter of Donskoi. Of course, marriages had long been contracted between Lithuania and Muscovy. The son of the enterprising Moscow prince Ivan Kalita, for example, had married the Lithuanian Anastasia. Kalita was the Muscovite who acquired the lucrative right to collect the tribute owed the Tatar khan by the princes of the Rus' lands. Yet, given the present upward trajectory and ambitions of Muscovy, this marriage alliance would be different.

A Lithuanian-Muscovite marriage alliance would have been of significance for the whole of Europe, for this would have resulted in Jogaila being baptized publicly into the Orthodox faith. The enormous Lithuanian state would have come under the direct influence of Muscovy, strengthening that increasingly strong entity. The borders of the East would have come right up to the eastern border of Crown of Poland. The development of any greater Central-Eastern European power would have been stalled, if not rendered impossible.

Yet fourteenth-century Lithuania was not to fall under the sway of Muscovy. The preliminary arrangements with Muscovy notwithstanding, negotiations were soon under way with the Crown of Poland. This was a momentous decision. At the time it may not have appeared so, but hindsight has shown this carried enormous repercussions for Polish and Lithuanian history. It resulted in a true regional revolution: the pagan grand duke of Lithuania would marry the young heir to the Polish throne, Jadwiga of Anjou, and in the process add King of Poland to his other titles.

After so many centuries (and despite the spilling of enormous amounts of ink), the chicken-and-egg question will likely never be answered: that is, was it the Polish power brokers who sought out Jogaila, or did he or his representatives seek them out to ask for the hand of Jadwiga in marriage? Regardless, the mere fact that both parties—Poles and Lithuanians alike—pursued this arrangement suggests that there was something in the deal for everyone.

The arrangement is presented in a bit of paperwork that has gone down in history as the so-called Union of Kreva (Lithuanian: Krėvo; Polish: Krzewo), dating from August 14, 1385. Prior to this meeting, it is likely that some representative of Jogaila was present at Jadwiga's coronation as king of Poland the previous year. This encounter—again, whether initiated by Poles or Lithuanians is not known—convinced a Polish delegation to travel to the town of Kreva (in present-day Belarus) to work out the details with the Lithuanian grand duke. The document—the act of union—essentially represented the dowry that the suitor Jogaila brought to the negotiating table.

How could the staunchly Catholic Poles of the province of Lesser Poland who were involved in the arrangements take so seriously the offer of a pagan ruler? Well, for one thing he promised to deliver. Among his promises were the traditional offers to place his wealth and army at the country's disposal and to reclaim the territories of Pomerania, Chełm, Dobrzyń, and Silesia as well as other lands previously lost to the Crown of Poland. Both states, furthermore, faced the same threat from the Teutonic Order; presenting a united front could have its benefits.

More intriguing were two larger issues, of greater importance for Central-Eastern Europe as well as Europe as a whole. The first was that pagan Jogaila promised to facilitate the conversion of Lithuania. The grand duke would lead the way, bringing to the faith not only himself but his brothers and, if possible, the entire territory of Lithuania. He also promised to set free any Christian captives that had been taken by the pagan country previously. The second, no less important, issue was the promise of union of the Lithuanian lands with Poland.

The true nature of this union has also been debated. The Latin verb *applicare* (apply) was the term used. Was it—according to Lithuanians—meant to signify a union of equal partners (the ambiguity of the Latin term conveniently covering a Lithuanian strategy to attain Jadwiga's hand for Jogaila)? Or have Polish historians been right to counter that *applicare* implied subordination of the territory of Lithuania to Poland—essentially forming a larger, Polish or Polish-dominated state?

It seems quite possible that the ambiguity of the chosen term served the purpose of Jogaila. He had to tread a fine line negotiating with the Poles (here, with the influential nobles of Lesser Poland as well as Elisabeth of Bosnia, mother of Jadwiga) while not wishing to complicate relations back home in Lithuania (his life was complicated enough there, as we shall see). More important, however, this proposal, with all its problems, suggests that the other option, closer unity with Muscovy, was less palatable. And indeed: in dealing with the West (that is, with Poland), Jogaila had the prospect of becoming king; it is unlikely that a marriage alliance with Muscovy, even one (or perhaps especially one) led by the ambitious and effective Dmitrii Donskoi, would have offered the Lithuanian rule over anything comparable. And could marriage to a nubile young princess bearing an attractive dowry—the Crown of Poland itself—be so bad?

A Young Girl's Dilemma

Jadwiga's personal reaction to this new and unusual marriage proposal was likely one of panic. Such a development would literally turn her life upside-down. The prospect of marrying a heathen much her senior (Jogaila was three times her age) instead of a cultured duke more or less her own age cannot have sat well with the poor princess. She had already been through much by this point. Being herself a minor, Jadwiga insisted to the Poles that her mother give her approval. Yet her mother deferred to her daughter and to the Poles in this matter. The nobles needed to convene that summer to decide what to do. Ultimately, as chronicler and historian Jan Długosz wrote, those "more sensible" in favor of the radical new Lithuanian project prevailed. How did they see it? This greatest medieval Polish historian wrote:

> Some, however, find it distasteful to promote to royal degree a foreign, pagan duke over the heads of their own Catholic dukes [clearly Wilhelm of Habsburg had already been rejected by the Polish nobles], but the majority of the more sensible, having regard to the good of Christianity and the peace this would bring to Poland, consider they should choose J[ogaila], Jadwiga's dislike of the idea being outweighed by the glory this extension of Christianity would bring to Poland.[*]

The Poles ultimately agreed to Jogaila's proposal.

In the interim, word reached the Habsburg court of the impending settlement between the Poles and Lithuanians. Wilhelm was dispatched to Kraków to consummate his marriage to Jadwiga, arriving a day before the Kreva agreement was signed. He learned upon his arrival that he was to be barred from the royal castle. Somehow, a meeting took place between the betrothed at a monastery at the foot of Wawel Hill, at which it was decided that the two would proceed to consummate the marriage as soon as Wilhelm managed to enter Wawel Castle. Doubtless Wilhelm could see the castle from the site and had to figure out how to evade those who sought to keep him out or trick those who previously had not let him in to renege. It was a formidable task—yet one that the Habsburg duke succeeded in accomplishing on August 23.

What followed next would cast a long shadow upon Jadwiga's all too short life. Having learned of the Habsburg's plans, a group of knights came upon the pair that evening in Jadwiga's chambers. Thus surprised, Wilhelm found it necessary to escape. The door was locked after him and orders were given not to let his former betrothed out. The young Jadwiga wanted desperately to follow him, even asking for an axe—according to Długosz—so that she might break down the locked door herself.

What does this signify? Generations of historians have debated whether

---

[*]   Jan Długosz, *The Annals of Jan Długosz; Annales seu cronicae incliti regni Poloniae; an English Abridgement*, trans. Maurice Michael (Charlton, West Sussex: IM Publications, 1997), 345.

the two were discovered before or after the consummation of the marriage. It depends on whom you believe. Jadwiga claimed right before she was wed to Jogaila that she had never been married to Wilhelm, whereas the latter, back home, later boasted to the contrary. Even the pope eventually took an interest in this question and investigated, in the process exonerating the young girl (doubtless a salutary development for this future saint).

Regardless what happened that fateful night, Jadwiga was in a terrible predicament. The young Hungarian princess had been brought up in a cultured court, was well educated, and grew up expecting marriage to a young man of similar background and upbringing. She was now compelled, for the good of her new country, to marry a man thirty years her senior, a heathen, illiterate, one lacking in basic hygiene (even in a less than hygienic age). Her personal sacrifice was indeed great—so great that legend has it the desperate young girl contemplated the situation in prayer before a crucifix in Wawel Cathedral before she would agree to the marriage.

Nonetheless, the accomplishment was also great. This union brought about the baptism of pagan Lithuania. Whereas Poles had accepted Christianity from the Bohemians, the Lithuanians were baptized through the intermediacy of the Poles.

On February 15, 1386, Jogaila was baptized, together with many other Lithuanians from the grand prince's family and retinue, at Wawel Cathedral. He assumed the Christian name Władysław (in honor of Jadwiga's Polish great-grandfather Władysław Łokietek) and was henceforth known—as he shall be known here—as Władysław Jagiełło, Jagiełło being the Polonized version of his Lithuanian name.

From Pagan to Pole?

The baptized Jagiełło and young Jadwiga were married on February 18, her twelfth birthday. Several days later, the former heathen was crowned king of Poland. According to the historian Długosz, "He then inscribe[d] Lithuania, Samogitia [Lithuanian: Žemaitija] and Ruthenia, territories over which he ha[d] complete sway, to the Kingdom of Poland, to be united with it and incorporated in it."* While several aspects of this medieval account can be debated, the deed was done—and personal union between Poland and Lithuania was accomplished. Yet another part of Jagiełło's proposal had been realized.

---

* Translation after ibid., 347.

Within the next year, Lithuanians back in the Grand Duchy were being converted, not by force (and most certainly not at sword point) but by education and example—both facilitated by the entrance into Lithuania of numerous Polish officials and clergymen. Jagiełło himself translated some Christian prayers—the Lord's Prayer and the Apostles' Creed—into the Lithuanian tongue for his subjects. They soon could worship in the new faith at the cathedral built at the Lithuanian capital city of Vilnius (Polish: Wilno), atop a pagan site where it was thought an eternal flame had burned. Vilnius now became the seat of a Roman Catholic bishopric, one so lavishly endowed that it was wealthier than any secular lord in Lithuania. Parishes were established for the expanding church throughout the country. Jadwiga also took an interest in the spiritual welfare of her newly converted subjects. She contributed to Vilnius Cathedral and many churches all the rich appurtenances so associated with Roman Catholicism: chalices and crucifixes, monstrances and prayer books, chasubles and robes. The easternmost part of this newly united entity, the Grand Duchy was taking its first tentative steps in a Western direction, under Polish guidance.

Poland's East

So what was this Lithuania that came into union with the Crown of Poland? It was very different from the present-day state of Lithuania, a tiny entity in northeastern Europe. The Lithuania of the early fourteenth century was second in size in Europe only to the Holy Roman Empire, an enormous entity stretching from the Baltic to the Black Sea. The core Lithuanian territories lay in the north, in the region of the Neman River (Polish: Niemen). Given their stony, muddy, swampy homeland, which hardly facilitated a life of ease, the six Baltic tribes that came to comprise Lithuanians (in a manner not unlike the early unification, under Polanians, of Polish tribes) came to make their living via conquest and looting. They raided territories to their west and to their east, gathering booty of various kinds. The favored booty was captives, who would be turned into slaves.

The Lithuanian leader Mindaugas assumed power in 1230, not long after the invasion of Europe by the Mongols. He was quick to profit from the disorganization the Mongols brought to the Ruthenian lands. Within several years, Mindaugas had annexed the nearby territory historically known as Black Ruthenia (the region of Grodno and Nowogródek—today's Hrodna and Navahrudak, in Belarus). Although he had converted to Roman Catholicism at the hands of the Teutonic Knights in 1251 and subsequently was given a crown

Map 2.1: Poland-Lithuania, ca. 1386

from Pope Innocent IV, this connection with the West was dashed with his renunciation of the faith only ten years later. It does not seem that Roman Catholicism made further advances in Lithuania at that time.

The pagan Lithuanians had managed to conquer the western Ruthenian territories (roughly today's Belarus and Ukraine) at the time of these lands' greatest weakness. In a relatively short space of time, they made huge advances. Lithuania gained control over Polatsk in 1307, over Minsk in 1340, over Smolensk (a mere 230 miles from Moscow) in 1356, and even over the far-distant Kyiv—the former, great capital of Kyivan Rus'—in 1363.

This tremendous expansion was in part facilitated by the protoplast of the great Lithuanian dynasty, Gediminas (1315–1341). He was ably assisted by his numerous sons, the most important Kestutis and Algirdas. While Kestutis's presence could be felt in the Polish southeast in 1376, it was Algirdas who earlier defeated the Golden Horde at Syni Vody (Blue Waters; Polish: Sine Wody) and gained control over Kyiv. The two formed a sort of diarchy—a kind of dual rule that would be inherited by their sons, Jogaila (Algirdas's favorite son) and Vytautas.

In the process of conquering this large swath of Eastern Europe, the Lithuanian Gediminid dynasty inherited a sizable population that was Slavic and Orthodox—a population that outnumbered the Lithuanians themselves eight to one. The Lithuanians figured mainly as rulers and elites. Most of the East Slavic inhabitants—most notably, the boyars (nobles) of Ruthenia to the south—were members of the Orthodox faith. In other words, they were Christians, but not followers of the Church of Rome. The pagan Lithuanians within this large multiethnic entity were the nobles and villagers of the north—that is, residing in the core Lithuanian territories, before the decline of Rus' allowed the Lithuanians to gain control of a good chunk of the Ruthenian lands. This was a small but not insignificant population, especially as it included members of the ruling family, such as the future king of Poland. This expanded Lithuanian state was a completely decentralized entity, with descendants of Gediminas ruling over various sections of the state (and often quarreling among themselves).

Although Lithuanians ruled, the rapid expansion of the state left the initial population, which had yet to establish a written language, with real challenges. How could they rule over Christian, and lettered, peoples? In part this imbalance was ameliorated by the Lithuanians availing themselves of a ready-made state language—the language of the conquered Ruthenes. Intermarriage with Ruthenian princes led to the spread of Ruthenian culture within the Grand Duchy. Many Gediminids became converts to Orthodoxy and otherwise found the culture of the conquered Slavs to be attractive. Some went so far as to ally themselves with the Muscovite state to the east. This most certainly was true of the numerous sons of Algirdas and his first wife, Maria, all of whom embraced Orthodoxy and ruled in the eastern section of the Grand Duchy. (Their half-brother Jogaila long remained a pagan, as did the other children of Algirdas and his second wife, Juliana of Tver—this notwithstanding her Orthodox provenance.)

The pull in the direction of the Eastern Church apparently came with time. Like Mindaugas before him, Gediminas had actually flirted with conversion to Catholicism in the early years of his rule. He received a letter from Pope John XXII in 1317 exhorting him to join the Catholic faith; some six years later Gediminas seemed inclined to do just that, though nothing ever came of the subsequent correspondence. That period was followed by the marriage of his daughter Aldona to Kazimierz the Great, and she was baptized into the Roman Catholic faith after she came to Poland. Still, it is unlikely there were many Catholics in the Lithuanian lands even after that.

Despite the country's amazing trajectory, these were trying times for Lithuania proper. In the north, the pagan Lithuanians were under constant pressure from the crusading Teutonic Knights, ever eager to convert at the point of a sword, who advanced into Lithuanian territory. For example, in 1394 the Knights laid siege to the castle at Vilnius, but ultimately they were frustrated by the boggy, forested terrain to which the Lithuanian forces had retreated nearby. More significant, the Knights had conquered the key Lithuanian "low country" territory of Žemaitija (Polish: Żmudź; Latin: Samogitia), possession of which was confirmed by the Peace of Salin in 1398. Henceforth it would be only a short trip for the Teutonic Knights—with the Livonian Knights of the Sword, their crusading allies along the northern reaches of the Baltic coast—to attack Vilnius.

By this time, the crusading knights had long been a threat to the Poles. As early as the Polish-Lithuanian treaty of 1325, Władysław Łokietek had hoped the alliance would serve him in his conflict with the Teutonic Knights. In ensuing years, he fought continuously against the Knights, who sought to isolate the Poles through diplomatic means. To them he lost Pomerania, Cuiavia, and Dobrzyń—all significant losses for the reuniting Polish state. Even a seeming victory over the Knights at Płowce in 1331 had brought the Poles no territorial gains.

Łokietek's son Kazimierz sought via diplomatic means if not to solve then at least to ameliorate the tense situation along his country's northern borders. One of his first moves was to sign a truce with the Teutonic Knights. The Treaty of Kalisz in 1343 gave Dobrzyń and Cuiavia back to the Poles, thus shoring up the northern border of Poland. Yet the Knights still held the more valuable Pomerania with its crucial port at the mouth of the Vistula River, Gdańsk (German: Danzig). Such was the situation under the last of the Piasts. It worsened further under Louis of Hungary, who relinquished some disputed territories in the north to the German state of Brandenburg.

The unexpected new alliance between Poland and Lithuania and conversion of Lithuania to Christianity changed the balance of power in the region. Now the Polish Crown and Lithuania presented a united front, to be reckoned with if the Teutonic Knights continued to pester the Lithuanians (or the Poles, for that matter). The invitation to serve as godfather for Jagiełło must have hit the grand master of the Teutonic Order like a slap in the face. Indeed, even after the conversion of Jagiełło, the Knights sought to vilify him, claiming his conversion was superficial. (They allied themselves with poor Wilhelm of Habsburg, who as we know had lost his betrothed to the former pagan.)

Of course, this was a crucial matter for the Order, whose raison d'être would be undermined in the region if there were no one left to convert. They had subdued the pagan tribes of the seacoast out of all existence. Indeed, the term "Prussia" soon would come to refer not to the pagan tribe of yore but to the entity that had conquered its living space. As of 1309 the Teutonic Knights had as their headquarters the massive and nearly impregnable brick fortress at Malbork (German: Marienburg). Even today the fort's imposing size impresses riders who take the train northward to the seacoast. The Knights had become very ambitious and very hungry for land.

Gediminid Rivalry

Besides the problems at the international level, there were problems brewing back home in Lithuania as well. This can be seen in the wrangling and dissatisfaction of various Gediminids, many of whom envied Jagiełło's swift rise to power in the region, but the tension was most pronounced between Jagiełło and Vytautas. After Algirdas's death and the rise of his son Jagiełło to high position within the diarchy, Kestutis with his son Vytautas began to challenge Jagiełło's rule. In the course of the bloody conflict (during which, at one point, Jagiełło was imprisoned), Kestutis was murdered, and Vytautas managed to escape with his life only by dressing up as a woman. This left Jagiełło in charge of the Grand Duchy. The family infighting hardly improved relations between the cousins. Indeed, the love-hate rivalry between Jagiełło and Vytautas (Belarusian: Vitovt; Polish: Witold) would last as long as both men lived, although Jagiełło sought many times to placate his cousin.

For Vytautas had many virtues, not the least being the skill with which he rendered many of his Lithuanian cousins politically impotent (not for nothing have Lithuanian historians labeled him Vytautas the Great). While good at consolidating power within Lithuania, Vytautas more often than not proved a thorn in the side of his cousin in Kraków. He occasionally conceded not only peripheral lands but also even core Lithuanian territories such as Žemaitija to the Teutonic Knights. That said, it is impossible to speak of any sort of Lithuanian national interest at this point: each man did what was necessary to stay in power or to strengthen his position. While Jagiełło seemed to find a satisfactory solution in the Polish-Lithuanian union rather quickly (only several years into his rule alongside his cousin), Vytautas cast about time and again in search of how to wrest control of the Grand Duchy from his cousin.

In the process, Vytautas proved particularly opportunistic. Witness his inconstancy on matters of religion—a flirtation perhaps not unlike moves made by Lithuanian dukes before him. That said, this particular pagan truly explored the full gamut of religious possibilities in the region. In 1383 he accepted baptism at the hands of the Teutonic Knights, accepting the baptismal name of Wigand; then only a couple of years later, after aligning himself with Jagiełło, he abandoned Catholicism for Orthodoxy and accepted the new baptismal name of Alexander.

Vytautas wore his religion lightly. His choice of denomination seemed to be related to the moment's choice of tactical alliance. Indeed, keeping track of his moves—let alone predicting them—is no small feat. In his battle to change the power dynamics within the Grand Duchy in his own favor, Vytautas sided time and again with neighbors who were all too happy to use the alliance to gain control over territories that had been under Lithuanian rule, neighbors such as the Teutonic Knights, Muscovy, and the Golden Horde.

Vytautas's independent foreign policy made for strange bedfellows and a situation that did little to advance the Lithuanian cause. Indeed, the Teutonic Knights sought to profit from the enmity between the two Lithuanians, even to the point of making territorial gains in the north. The Polish garrison at Vilnius was compelled to defend the Lithuanian capital on more than one occasion (at least once with Vytautas storming the ramparts as well as the Teutonic Knights), although the Polish forces were able to hold the others at bay. This alliance with the Teutonic Order, incidentally, was something the quicksilver Vytautas abandoned and renewed with amazing alacrity.

In addition to the northwestern alliance with the Teutonic Order, Vytautas paid plenty of attention to Lithuania's neighbors to the east, especially Muscovy (the Lithuanian was the father-in-law of the Muscovite grand prince, Vasilii I), generally viewed as enemy and rival, not friend. He entered into alliance with the Golden Horde, even taking sides in its internal conflicts. Vytautas came to the aid of the Mongol leader Tokhtamysh, who had been ousted from the imperial throne by Tamerlane (his English name being a corruption of his name, Timur, and sobriquet, the Lame). Victorious in a battle on the Don, Vytautas pressed successfully into the Crimea, even winning papal support for his crusade. In this, however, the Lithuanian was not joined by Vasilii, who perhaps had not forgotten how Tokhtamysh once set fire to Moscow and who now awaited with interest the results of the battle. This time, the forces of Tamerlane, his famous limp rendering him no less fearsome, dealt the combined Lithuanian armies a blow at the battle on the Vorskla of 1399. This loss marked the retreat of the independent-minded Lithuanian from the Black Sea region.

It also prompted a renewal of relations with his cousin in Kraków. Over the course of a decade, Jagiełło—in more than one way seeming the elder statesman, although the men were relative contemporaries—had striven to placate his infuriatingly independent cousin, who, although returning to good graces in 1392, repeatedly tested the limits of loyalty and the terms of the Polish-Lithuanian union. Jagiełło repeatedly adjusted Vytautas's title and position within the Grand Duchy, both to keep him in line and to keep him managing things back home.

In 1401 the two Lithuanian princes finally seemed to resolve the matter between them. Vytautas became Jagiełło's plenipotentiary in Lithuania, with the title of Grand Duke—Jagiełło nonetheless topping that title with Supremus Dux Lithuaniae (supreme duke of Lithuania). Both Poland and Lithuania were considered to have equal weight within the union.

All this was important, as Jagiełło's rule in Poland had now come under increased scrutiny. This was a result of sad events in the year 1399. Queen Jadwiga, finally pregnant with her first child, died of complications in childbirth. Perhaps she sensed the end was near. Jadwiga eschewed the rich tapestries, curtains, and jewels that her husband encouraged her to hang around her bed, claiming that were she to meet her Maker in childbirth, she would rather He be impressed with the beauty of her soul than the beauty of her surroundings. It was an agonizing end to a saintly life. She died on July 17, 1399, with the knowledge that the daughter she gave birth to on June 12, christened Elżbieta Bonifacja (Elizabeth Bonifacia), died shortly before she did. In a fitting tribute to a later saint, Długosz praised at length the extreme modesty, piety, and religious devotion of this oft-called beautiful woman, clearly all the more beautiful—according to the chronicler historian—for having a beautiful soul.

Among many charitable gifts made by the queen both during her life and in her dying days, she earmarked a significant part of her jewels to benefit her charity of choice: the refounding of the university established by her great-uncle Kazimierz the Great. The next year, on the feast of Saint James the Apostle, Jagiełło officially founded the university that Jadwiga had championed. Doctors and Masters from the various faculties were brought from Prague to teach at the refounded university. Out of the money left by the deceased queen were built two colleges: the College of the Arts and Theology and the College of Law and Medicine. To this day ancient yet still imposing university buildings stand in those two locations: Collegium Maius on Saint Anne's Street and Collegium Juridicum on Grodzka Street. The university—now known as the Jagiellonian University—owes its very existence to the young Hungarian princess turned Polish king, who saw to it that the idea first hatched by her great-uncle, the last of the Piasts, was not abandoned.

The Teutonic Knights, Revisited

Let us return to the Poland that Jadwiga left behind in such sad and untimely fashion. The conflict between the Teutonic Knights and Poland-Lithuania that had been brewing for well over a century soon came to a head. The Teutonic Order declared war on the Poles on September 6, 1409, but after some initial moves on the part of both forces, they soon negotiated an armistice. This allowed the two parties to seek further allies and support abroad. Both sides went where they thought they would gain assistance. And volunteers were variously motivated. Some (for example, the Bohemians and the Hungarians, with Sigismund of Luxemburg) joined the Teutonic Knights for the money; others (such as Western Europeans) for the glory of the battle—ever important in an age of chivalry.

The Poles sought the support of the newly elected Pope Alexander V, which he lent—although to be sure he was not exactly influential as pope yet (not everyone recognized him, coming as he did on the heels of several pretenders to the papacy). A delegation to England turned up nothing, and thus the Poles and Lithuanians came to rely on forces nearby: the Mazovian princes and Muscovy, even some 300 Tatars as well as Swiss mercenaries. (Some of these Tatars would settle in the Lithuanian territories; mosques thus also became part of the Lithuanian landscape.) The Czech general Jan Žižka along with other Czechs and Moravians also fought on the side of the Poles and Lithuanians.

What becomes clear is that neither assembled army could be characterized as representing the forces of either Slavdom (Poland-Lithuania) or Germandom (the Teutonic Knights), which is how they were perceived in a much later period. Each army had "Westerners" on its side. The "Slavic" army had many important non-Slavic Lithuanians, not to mention Tatars. Nor was a win or loss of either automatically good or bad for the Church of Rome, or (in its broader form) Christianity, regardless of the arguments put forth either by the two different sides or by the descendants or heirs to the mantle of each side.

The truce negotiated in 1409 and an additional ten-day truce allowed the combined Polish-Lithuanian forces to assemble and cross the Vistula River near Czerwińsk with the help of a pontoon bridge. The innovative bridge—according to Długosz, "to be supported by boats, a thing never yet seen"—took all winter to build.* It was assembled on the spot and then removed to Płock for safekeeping. (When told of such a feat, the grand master of the Teutonic Order, Ulrich von Jungingen, apparently laughed it all off as lies and nonsense.) The Polish-Lithuanian forces under King Jagiełło and Grand

---

* Ibid., 373.

Duke Vytautas were well prepared in another way also, with not only cannons and the like. Barrel after barrel of salted meat (the kill from numerous hunts over the last months) attest not only to the easy availability of game in this well-forested country but also to the seriousness with which the Polish-Lithuanian forces were preparing for the coming battle.

Indeed, the underdogs (underestimated by the Teutonic Knights) proved a crafty and tenacious lot. As soon as the truce ended, Janusz Brzozgłowy of Bydgoszcz engineered a clever ruse that led a group of enemy knights into an ambush. This first minor encounter augured well for the pitched battle to come. In the days before the major meeting of the two multinational forces, the Poles and Lithuanians also captured the wealthy and well-supplied fortress of Dabrówno and left the inhabitants of the fortress bereft of their rich stocks and valuables. The Polish-Lithuanian combined forces certainly would not go hungry.

There were signs that these combined forces were a motley bunch, more so perhaps than the army of the Teutonic Knights, where at worst there could be problems with communication due to the numerous languages spoken. The Poles had to rein in the Lithuanians and the Tatars, some of whom acted like barbarians in the nearby villages, raping, pillaging, as well as desecrating religious shrines. Yet, after two Lithuanian instigators were ordered by the grand duke to hang themselves in front of the assembled troops, the bad behavior was curtailed.

Still, there were many more signs of piety than paganism or barbarism. Witness the support given to the cause by a certain Roman Catholic clergyman, whose sermon to the assembled soldiers proclaimed the Poles' cause to be a just one. The majority of the troops, together with the Polish king, took the last sacrament the Sunday before the battle. On the day of the battle, the Polish king heard two masses in a row and prayed for divine assistance. He seemed more willing to engage in diplomacy and conclude a peace prior to the battle. Even the Hungarian envoys of the grand master thought that Jagiełło and Vytautas's conditions—the return of Žemaitija to Lithuania and Dobrzyń to Poland—were just. Yet the komturs (the commanders of the Teutonic Order) advised their grand master that they would be victorious in battle, as they possessed certain holy relics. The strength of those relics would soon be tested.

The Battle of Grunwald

The fateful day was Tuesday, July 15, 1410. The troops woke up at dawn to winds so great that a tent could not be erected for the king's mass. This led the Poles and Lithuanians to move their encampment to the thickets and woods near the great level plain in the vicinity of Tannenberg and Grunwald, the two localities that lent their name to the battle. In German accounts it has been known as the battle of Tannenberg; in Polish, the battle of Grunwald.

The Polish and Lithuanian forces did not know that the grand master had just arrived at the village of Grunwald. Still, the Polish king bided his time, hearing his masses. Was this out of fear? Out of a hope for divine intervention on his side? Or was the neophyte—so often accused by the Teutonic Order of being an insincere convert to the faith—also demonstrating to the Teutonic Knights that he was indeed a true and pious Christian?

Whatever the reason, it also appeared to be a great strategy. Not only did the Polish-Lithuanian forces essentially dictate where the two heavily armed forces would meet. They dictated the hour at which the battle would begin, simply by not coming out immediately to fight. To be sure, the troops were at the ready, the fifty standards of Poles on the left wing and forty standards of Lithuanians on the right. But the king dallied.

The Teutonic Knights grew impatient. They stood in the scorching heat of day waiting for the enemy to engage them. Dressed in full armor, they must have found the wait agonizing. All the while, the joint Polish-Lithuanian forces were in the shade of the grove of trees, waiting for Jagiełło to signal it was time to begin.

But the signal did not come. The king did put on his own suit of armor, mount his horse, and ride up to a hillock whence he would have a good view of the entire battle. (It had been determined earlier that the king was too valuable a person to take actual part in the battle. The small but feisty Zyndram of Maskowic had been chosen to command the troops.)

At that moment, the king was approached by a group of Polish knights escorting two heralds from the enemy camp. Demanding to see the king, the heralds came bearing a gift and a message. The gift: two unsheathed swords. A nephew of the king translated the German of the spoken message. The grand master had sent them to Jagiełło and his brother, the heralds informed them, in case they did not have their own swords to begin fighting with, instead of hiding in the woods and postponing the inevitable battle. Continuing in the same impudent and boastful tone, the deputation added that the Teutonic Knights would fight them here, or if they found the site too cramped, on any other battlefield of their choice. (And at that moment, the Knights of the Teutonic Order were seen withdrawing some distance, to give the Polish forces more space—in that way attesting to the truth of the heralds' message.) They were willing to fight now, fight here, fight there, fight anywhere—only be on with it! The patience of the knights clearly had worn thin.

In the presence of his chancellor and other lords whose job was to protect the king, Jagiełło accepted the swords. He did so not in anger, although they were meant as an affront. Rather, he reacted with humility and sorrow (to the point of tears, wrote the chronicler Długosz, whose sources included his own father, who fought in the battle, as well as Jagiełło's secretary, the later bishop of Kraków, Zbigniew Oleśnicki).

Jagiełło was sad that Christian forces desired to spill his blood and that of his men. He replied patiently and calmly that he had swords of his own but would keep these to strengthen the support, protection, and defense being lent him in his just cause by God. Furthermore, the king said that he would turn to the Lord to avenge the unbearable pride and impudence of his enemy, and he would pray to the patron saints of his country—Stanisław, Adalbert, Wacław, Florian, and Jadwiga—for protection and help in defeating those who repeatedly sought recourse to violence when the king had striven repeatedly for peace. Even now, Jagiełło added, he would sue for peace, if such could be obtained in just fashion. This said, he was convinced that the heavens would be on the side of justice this time. Yet, as a Christian and a Christian ruler, the Polish king would leave the location, even the outcome, of the battle for God to decide. The relentless Teutons, he hoped, would be routed and their wickedness put to an end. These carefully weighed words of the king (certainly as reported by Długosz) suggest he was not a coward, as the knights had implied but, rather, a pious ruler, willing to leave matters in God's hands (having done his preparations conscientiously in advance).

Having dismissed the heralds, Jagiełło prepared for battle. He had the bugles sounded, a summons to the united forces to sing the religious hymn "Bogurodzica" (Mother of God). The most ancient of Polish songs resounded through the air:

> Mother of God, virgin, by God glorified Mary!
> Your son, the Lord, chosen mother, Mary,
> Win over for us, send to us.
> *Kyrie eleison.*
> Son of God, for the sake of thy Baptist,
> Hear our voices, fulfill man's intentions!
> Listen to the prayer that we bring.
>
> And deign to grant what we are asking for:
> On earth, a prosperous sojourn,
> After life, a place in heaven!
> *Kyrie eleison.*˙

---

*   From *Medieval Literature of Poland: An Anthology*, trans. Michael J. Mikos (New York and London: Garland, 1992), 65.

Buttressed spiritually by the ancient anthem, the Poles and their allies were now ready to fight.

The Lithuanians departed from the nearby woods, where they had escaped the heat of the sun, to fight the Knights. At the command of Vytautas (who, unlike Jagiełło, was in the thick of things all day), they galloped into the middle of the vast field. Not only the Polish king had a good view of the battle; there were people—hard to say, from which side—sitting high in the branches of six tall oak trees in the midst of the field. And the fighting was fierce. Salvos from the Order's cannons did not repel the Lithuanians. They valiantly fought the Teutonic Knights, lance against lance, then hand-to-hand; in the tangle of bodies it was hard to tell who was on which side. The lances and swords of the knights of both sides, clanging like hammers in a blacksmith's forge, could be heard for miles away. Such it went for the first hour. While the right flank of Poles made headway among the Knights, the left flank of Lithuanians was weaker. As the Order got wind of this, they pressed further on the Lithuanians and their Ruthenian and Tatar allies—to the point where the latter turned and ran. The Order pursued them, thinking the battle was won.

Rain began to fall, and the dust of the field settled down. Doubtless this was a godsend to the overheated knights on both sides. At one moment the Polish royal standard, with its crowned white eagle in the coat of arms, fell to the ground, then immediately (embarrassingly) was picked up by one of the Poles. That near loss of the standard inspired the Poles to redouble their efforts, and they routed their opponents.

Before long the Knights who had gone off in pursuit of the Lithuanians came back with their prisoners. They saw the fight in full force and once again joined in. It was they, however, who now felt the brunt of the fight. The Czech and Hungarian mercenaries weakened, with only the Knights of the Order remaining firm in their resolve to fight to the end. The battle raged fiercely.

All this was being observed by King Jagiełło, who was giving commands from a safe distance, perched atop a nearby hillock. Yet the safety of the hillock was deceptive, as the king would soon learn. For all of a sudden, sixteen fresh squadrons of enemy forces approached the place where Jagiełło, on horseback, followed the battle. A Lusatian knight charged forward toward the king, who at that moment was practically alone, barring a small group of bodyguards—all his soldiers being pressed into battle elsewhere. Would these bodyguards be able to defend their king, or would their king defend himself? Or would this mark the end of Jagiełło—and the beginning of the end for the Poles? With great presence of mind, the king's young secretary, Zbigniew of

Oleśnica, unarmed and wearing no armor, leaped forward and took on the Knight of the Order. Zbigniew grabbed a broken lance and parried the blow that would have knocked the king off his horse. The tables were turned, and the Lusatian knight fell, to be killed by the king's bodyguards. Need we say that the king owed his life to his secretary? Moved by the deed, Jagiełło wanted to knight his secretary then and there. However, Zbigniew demurred, claiming he would prefer to fight in God's ranks as a priest. (Zbigniew of Oleśnica was later made a bishop and even served as bishop of Kraków, having received papal dispensation for his contribution to the battle this once.)

Having witnessed the death of the Lusatian noble, their comrade in arms, the remaining German knights began their retreat. The Poles engaged them once more, in a true fight to the death. In all, the battle raged for seven hours. The grand master and his commanders entered the fray once it became clear the Polish forces were winning. They were cut down. Even the grand master Ulrich von Jungingen perished on the battlefield; his golden pectoral full of sacred relics provided no protection this time. Rather, the forces of heaven seemed on the side of the Poles: some men of that force reportedly saw a man in bishop's robes in the sky blessing their army throughout the battle. It was thought to be Saint Stanisław, bishop and martyr, patron saint of the Poles, who lent his help to his nation at this crucial moment.

In the end, the rout was complete. Thousands of knights perished, others were taken prisoner. A total of fifty-one enemy standards were taken.

We doubtless will never know the full count of soldiers who fought and perished. The Polish chronicler of the event, Jan Długosz, gave no numbers. According to the Teutonic Knights' own sources, there were some 202 fallen Knights of the Order and 18,000 others (mercenaries and knights from elsewhere in Europe) who died that day. This implies a sizable force on their side—although not so many that a nearby stream really ran red with blood, which is what some accounts concluded. (The locals later told of the stream of blood that flowed toward their village, but the color actually came from the Order's wine barrels, which the king ordered punctured so that his men would not get drunk and thus be unable to defend themselves.) Długosz reported a hard-to-believe number of only twelve eminent Polish knights perishing. Some historians estimate the size of the armies as twenty-one thousand men for the Teutonic Knights and twenty-nine thousand Polish troops, of which eleven thousand were under Lithuanian command. Whatever the actual numbers of troops and casualties, the Battle of Grunwald was undeniably one of the biggest battles of the Middle Ages.

The victorious Poles and Lithuanians plundered the Order's camp, which made them all much richer than when they had begun. In the camp they discovered wagons full of chains and wooden handcuffs. Originally intended for Polish prisoners, they were now used on the Order's own knights, a number of whom (representing many nationalities) had taken refuge in the camp.

Yet, with all the plundering, as well as the need to eat and rest (for they did not pitch camp until the sun was ready to set), the victorious forces won the battle but missed an opportunity to win the war definitively. Had they set off for the Order's headquarters at Malbork immediately, they might have taken the fortress without loss of life, as those in the castle hurried away at hearing news of the dreadful defeat. The capture of the fortress at Malbork would have meant the end of the Teutonic Knights in East-Central Europe—the ultimate goal. The Polish-Lithuanian forces did not manage to achieve this, having dallied to bury the dead of both sides and say masses for their souls. Internal disagreement (that is, between Jagiełło and Vytautas) likely also slowed down their progress. By the time the Polish and Lithuanian troops arrived at Malbork (nearly ten days later), Henry of Plauen had amassed another five thousand knights to continue the fight. Then, when Henry sued for peace, asking that the Poles not utterly destroy the Order but rather take back only the lands they traditionally laid claim to (and had now recovered), the Poles insisted that Malbork be surrendered as well.

From this moment, according to Długosz, the tide turned in favor of the Order. The siege of Malbork was abandoned in September. Henry of Plauen was elected grand master, and he sought to avenge the defeat of the Order's forces at Grunwald. As Długosz recounts, that year there were many more skirmishes and sieges, ruses and treachery—albeit nothing close to the magnitude of the Battle of Grunwald. The Teutonic Knights would never again be the same, although unfortunately they were not thoroughly trounced. The Poles and Lithuanians had lost the best chance they had to recover the lands for which they had fought for so long.

This became all too obvious the following year. In 1411 a peace between the Polish-Lithuanian state and the Teutonic Order was finally achieved at Toruń. At that time, Jagiełło managed only to secure Žemaitija for Lithuania and Dobrzyń for Poland. Thus, ultimately, Lithuania benefited much more than did the Crown of Poland—somewhat paradoxical in a state that purportedly was dominated by the Polish half. While Lithuania regained all that it sought, the Poles remained unsatisfied. Notably, however, these were the territories that the Order had refused to give Poland-Lithuania to keep the peace only a year earlier. Still, this left many formerly Polish lands along the Baltic coast in the hands of the Teutonic Order, including the important towns of Gdańsk and Toruń. And the Crown of Poland still had no outlet to the sea.

The Union of Horodło

However, in a way, the Battle of Grunwald did have an important outcome for Poland-Lithuania. The joint fight against a common enemy brought the subjects of the two halves of the state closer together, proving to Poles and Lithuanians alike that they had mutual interests. Together, they could accomplish much, even if separately each (especially Lithuania) was weak.

Within a couple of years, Poles and Lithuanians took another step on the road to becoming closer. This was in the so-called Union of Horodło, signed in the Volhynian town of that name in 1413. What had previously been a personal union cemented solely by the person of Jagiełło would now have a solid dynastic connection. To be sure, the position of grand duke in Lithuania would be hereditary (Vytautas agreed to be *dux* [no modifier], under Jagiełło), while the king of Poland would be elected. But the latter—that is, Jagiełło's successor—would come from the Lithuanian dynasty, to be elected upon consultation of Vytautas and the Lithuanian boyars.

One of the most interesting provisions of the tripartite document called for a special union of (Catholic) Lithuanian and Polish nobility and clergy. Some fifty years after their conversion to Roman Catholicism, forty-seven Lithuanian noble families were embraced by and included in Polish heraldic clans. In this way, the palatine of Kraków, for example, accepted into his Leliwa clan the palatine of Vilnius. The Polish castellan of Sącz would be united with the Lithuanian castellan of Trakai (Polish: Troki). The numerous Półkozic clan embraced a Lithuanian noble family, while the protoplast of the Lithuanian Radvila family (better known under their Polonized name, Radziwiłł) became part of the Sulima clan. In essence, a joint Polish-Lithuanian noble estate was established. Henceforth, there would be a single nation for the united state.

The Preamble to the Union of Horodło gives evidence of the lofty principles undergirding the union: "Whosoever is unsupported by the mystery of Love, shall not achieve the Grace of salvation. . . . For by Love, laws are made, kingdoms governed, cities ordered, and the state of the commonweal is brought to its proper goal."* The love between the Poles and Lithuanians would truly have a familial (clan) basis now. Yet the union was not complete. It did not include the Orthodox nobility—for the most part, Ruthenes. They were, in a way, second-class citizens—something that would not bode well for the future.

---

* English translation from Davies, *God's Playground*, 1:119.

CHAPTER 3

Spreading Southward

The Jagiellonian Moment in East-Central Europe

With its sentiments of brotherhood as well as newly established clan connections, the Union of Horodło provided a crucial further linking of the two states, which until now had been a purely personal basis. It was all the more crucial, as Władysław Jagiełło, king of Poland and grand duke of Lithuania, was now in his sixties. What would be the fate of this arrangement—the union he achieved between Poland and Lithuania—upon his death?

The Rise of the Jagiellons

Such moments of transition were often tricky in medieval Europe. As we have seen, the Piast dynasty experienced a roller-coaster trajectory: rising with Mieszko and the Bolesławs, declining during the period of "feudal disintegration," becoming refocused on a unified Polish state under Władysław Łokietek and Kazimierz the Great, only to meet an untimely end, yet one all too familiar to medieval ruling houses. The rule of the Hungarian Angevins (which some could interpret as Piast rule, given the intermarriage between the two dynasties) came to a quick end in Poland with the early death of the young queen Jadwiga, who left no progeny of her own to carry on either Piast or Angevin lines. What was to be the fate of the newest dynasty, the one that hailed from Lithuania? Can one even speak of a Jagiellonian dynasty?

Indeed one can. The Jagiellons—by whom we mean the descendents of Władysław Jagiełło, the pagan Lithuanian turned Roman Catholic king of a Poland united with Lithuania—were to rule Poland-Lithuania for several centuries. They managed to do this despite the fact that they had no automatic right of inheritance to the Polish throne, only to the Lithuanian. This in itself is noteworthy, although perhaps not hard to understand, given that Poles wished for the union with Lithuania to continue, and the Jagiellons were hereditary rulers there.

Even more notable was the fact that members of this ruling family still rather new to Poland (and new to Christianity) were to be offered the crown of other neighboring states. This is a historical thread worth pursuing—even if it (and it can be admitted up front) ultimately led nowhere. Nonetheless, despite the final outcome—with Jagiellonian rule to be long-lasting only in Poland and Lithuania—the very fact that Jagiellonian princes were seriously considered as potential rulers of other neighboring states tells us something. And indeed we should investigate why this might have been so.

The fates of dynasties, like monarchs, vary indeed, but there are various permutations of possibilities that might suggest why any given dynasty was able to make a name for itself internationally. One of the reasons undoubtedly is marriage politics. Some families simply manage to marry well—or better—than others. Another reason is more sinister. Some families are more ruthless, more Machiavellian (an anachronistic term in the fifteenth century, for Niccolo Machiavelli—born in 1469—did not write *The Prince* until early in the sixteenth century). Some families kill off their competition, and in that way rise to power.

Yet none of these truly explains the popularity of the Jagiellons. One could single out two important factors. The first is related to international opinion—the international stature of the Jagiellons, or of Jagiełło, rather. Ruling houses as well as the nobilities of the larger East-Central European space took note of the victory at Grunwald and noted also the new and energetic king on the Polish throne.

But another important factor figured here also. Call it the luck of longevity. Władysław Jagiełło lived a long life. This in itself provided an important degree of stability for the Polish-Lithuanian Union. More important, he outlived his cousin Vytautas, the Gediminid who had done the most both to serve and to subvert the king of Poland. However, when Vytautas died in 1430, the question of who would succeed him emerged. (After all, a country of this size and complexity needed someone to deal with issues in the field.) And indeed, there were further bumps in the road, further challenges to Jagiełło's rule over the Grand Duchy, mainly in the form of Jagiełło's younger brother, Svidrigaila, who on Vytautas's death made an attempt—ultimately unsuccessful—at seizing control of the Grand Duchy.

Jagiełło had another advantage over Vytautas. He had the great fortune, finally, to sire several sons in his old age (in his seventies, to be exact). His second wife, interestingly, was the granddaughter of Kazimierz the Great; while strengthening the sense that Jagiełło was the rightful king of the country, this marriage provided him with no sons. His third wife, the thrice widowed and hardly youthful noblewoman Elżbieta of Pilica, brought him happiness, but it caused a bit of a scandal. Not only was she merely a noblewoman (albeit a tremendously wealthy one); she was the daughter of Jagiełło's god-mother, which made the marriage incestuous according to canon law. Only his fourth and final wife—the much younger Ruthenian princess Sonia of Hal'shany (Sonka Holszańska), who also happened to be Vytautas's niece—was able to provide the king with the requisite heirs: two sons, to be precise.

It was hardly expected that the boys would be of age when Jagiełło died, aged eighty-three, in 1434. At that time Jagiełło's eldest son, Władysław, was only ten years old and the younger, Kazimierz, only six. But was that so much of a hurdle in a country desirous of dynastic continuity—not to mention seeking to continue the Polish-Lithuanian union?

Jagiełło, before his death, sought to convince the nobility to agree to elect his firstborn, Władysław, king of Poland. This proved more difficult than the king had anticipated. There was a series of congresses within the country, during which the Polish nobles repeatedly insisted that they had the right to elect a monarch of their own choosing. Yet they were ready to make a deal. In exchange for agreeing to elect Władysław to the Polish throne, the nobles demanded that the king affirm their privileges and that he extend those privileges to parts of the kingdom where Polish privileges had not yet penetrated, including Ruthenia. When Jagiełło balked at this agreement, the nobles assembled at Łęczyca hacked the previously prepared document to pieces with their swords. The king was forced to comply, on the terms set by the Crown nobles.

The Polish nobles had prevailed. Flexing their collective power, they extracted privileges from their monarch in exchange for this conditional succession to the throne. Jagiełło's son and namesake, King Władysław III Jagiellon, would rule after his death—by the grace of the Polish nobility.

Jagiellonian rule was good for the Poles, who knew how to use elections to their benefit. It would be good for other nations as well. Before long, the descendants of Jagiełło would garner further titles—titles that directed their attention in a new direction: south.

Turbulent Times in East-Central Europe

The situation of the Polish-Lithuanian succession was nothing compared to what was experienced, over the next century or so, in Bohemia and Hungary. In Bohemia, the question of religion and religious choice played a major destabilizing role, as seen in the movement inspired by Jan Hus (c. 1371–1415). The Czech preacher and professor (who ultimately was burned as a heretic during the church Council of Constance) criticized a number of aspects of the church, including the sale of indulgences and the accumulation of church wealth, not to mention church interference in politics. Hussitism gained footing not only in Bohemia but also in Silesia and the south of Poland, where it was especially popular among the lesser nobility. The more powerful nobles were supporters of Cardinal Zbigniew Oleśnicki, bishop of Kraków (the man who as Jagiełło's secretary, nota bene, saved the Polish king's life at the Battle of Grunwald), who had been appointed guardian of Jagiełło's two sons.

As usual, royal deaths made for political turbulence. This was true for the death of Sigismund of Luxemburg, who had been king of Bohemia and Hungary as well as Holy Roman Emperor. Although much younger than Jagiełło, Sigismund died only three years after the Lithuanian, in 1437. While he had no direct male heir, Sigismund had designated his son-in-law Albrecht Habsburg as his successor. Czech Hussites nonetheless decided to cast their vote for Jagiełło's son Kazimierz, Władysław's younger brother, if he agreed to uphold their religious rights. Kazimierz's decision to accept the nomination alienated the Austrians, the Hungarians, and the Catholic Czechs, who supported Albrecht, and the subsequent Polish military expedition was unable to seat Kazimierz on the Bohemian throne.

Things became further complicated after the sudden death of Albrecht Habsburg, who had assumed the Hungarian crown as well. This was the crown that Oleśnicki wanted for one of Jagiełło's sons, the Bohemian crown still carrying the taint of Hussite heresy. The bishop wished to seat Władysław III Jagiellończyk (meaning "the Jagiellon," the sobriquet denotes him as his father's son) on the Hungarian throne. As in the case of their Polish counterparts earlier, the Hungarian nobles were not opposed to Władysław, for as an elected king, he would have to give privileges. But it turned out that the Hungarian queen—the widow of Albrecht Habsburg—shortly gave birth to his son and natural heir, leaving Władysław to rule Hungary from 1440 (as Ulászló I) only until the child reached maturity.

The royal succession in Bohemia and Hungary was complicated, indeed. Nonetheless we see that members of the Jagiellonian dynasty were in demand in East-Central Europe. The young sons of the first Jagiellon on the Polish-Lithuanian throne were serious contenders for the Bohemian and Hungarian crowns. Indeed, the Jagiellons would become the dominant East-Central European dynasty in the late medieval/early modern period.

The Varna Debacle

Elevated status brought risk, as Jagiełło's firstborn learned all too soon. Władysław the Jagiellon—king of Poland, king of Hungary—could not long revel in the extent of his rule. Unfortunately for Poland, Hungary, and Europe at large, Władysław III came to an unfortunate and untimely end. While in his Hungarian capital of Buda (still many centuries before Buda and Pest were united into one city, Budapest), he was approached by the papal legate to lead a crusade against the Turks. The now twenty-year-old Władysław, only in his fourth year of ruling Hungary, was stirred by this call to defend Christendom.

Hungarian forces under János Hunyadi won a significant victory against the Turks in 1443. The following year, the young king of both Poland and Hungary personally led a foray against the infidel in the Balkans. Despite Turkey's offer of a truce on favorable terms, Władysław ambitiously, or indeed rashly, set off to capture Adrianopol (today's Edirne), the Ottoman capital. Few of the expected allies materialized, beyond Hunyadi's Hungarians, the Venetian fleet, and the Wallachian troops of Vlad Dracul, the father of the famous Dracula, leaving the twenty-year-old king facing bad odds. Apparently, Władysław perished in the catastrophic battle at Varna—whence his more common Polish sobriquet Władysław Warneńczyk (Władysław of Varna). The king's body was never found, the dual monarch having disappeared in a sea of janissaries, never to be seen again. The Turks reported that they cut off Władysław's head and preserved it in honey, making it hard—if not impossible—to identify. To make matters worse, the head they ultimately produced for inspection was dark skinned with light hair—not similar to the pale-skinned, dark-haired king. At any rate, doubts about his fate (among other things) kept the Poles from appointing a successor for several years.

All in the Family

Chosen to succeed Władysław in Poland was his younger brother, Kazimierz. Kazimierz had inherited the looks as well as the luck of his father, Jagiełło, thus truly deserving of the sobriquet "Jagiellończyk"—son of Jagiełło. However, the beginnings of his rule were not so auspicious—this despite the fact that, he, too, was sought after as a ruler elsewhere in the region. At the tender age of eleven, he had been advanced as a candidate for the Bohemian/Czech throne, although this elevation ultimately did not come about. Given his youth, Kazimierz was expected to be a pliable pawn in the hands of various power brokers in this part of Europe, including the clergyman Oleśnicki. The eighteen-year-old king, Kazimierz IV Jagiellon, proved both strong-willed and independent-minded, however.

The young Jagiellon's ascent had begun in the Grand Duchy. In 1440 Kazimierz had been appointed his brother's plenipotentiary in Vilnius. Lithuania had not weathered Jagiełło's death at all well. The country had gone through a period of civil war and upheaval, with an assassination ending the life of Žygimantas, whom the Poles had supported in his bid to run the Grand Duchy, in 1400. After the young Jagiellon's arrival in Vilnius in 1440, the powerful Lithuanian council of lords unilaterally declared him Kazimierz, grand duke of Lithuania. As this had been done without the approval of his brother the Polish king or the royal council, the Lithuanian lords were essentially violating the terms of union. However, all eyes of the Polish power brokers—that is, the regency council dominated by the powerful Oleśnicki—were so fixated on the south and on securing the Hungarian throne for Kazimierz's elder brother that they did not react as they might have done. The situation back home still required a good deal of diplomacy on the part of the influential Lithuanian council of lords, dominated by Jonas Gostautas (Polish: Jan Gasztołd) and Prince Yuri Semenovich Holszański; they needed to placate a number of Gediminids, all of whom lay claim to rule Lithuania.

Perhaps emboldened by its successes in this regard, after Władysław's death at Varna, the same council of lords encouraged the now seventeen-year-old Grand Duke Kazimierz, who had every reason to expect he would become king of Poland, to flex his muscle and demand that the Polish crown become hereditary in his family. However, this proposal so enraged the Poles who had been running the country that they prepared to offer the throne to a Mazovian duke. Alarmed by this state of affairs, Kazimierz and the Lithuanian council of lords met with a Polish delegation in Brześć (today's Brest-Litovsk) in the fall of 1446. The Jagiellonian grand duke helped to craft a workable compromise between the elective Crown of Poland and the hereditary Lithuania—a compromise that would last for the next 123 years.

Despite an early—and unsuccessful—attempt on his life, King Kazimierz IV Jagiellon was also blessed with longevity, although he did not live to be quite as old as his octogenarian father. His reign on the Polish throne lasted a full forty-six years, from 1446 to 1492—right up to what some would call the end of the Middle Ages (the early modern period being initiated by the discovery of America by the Genoese explorer Christopher Columbus). Given his lengthy reign, there is much one can write about Kazimierz, not the least of which would be his eminently successful dealings with the Teutonic Knights, to which we will turn in due course. First, however, let us return to dynastic issues within East-Central Europe as a whole—in particular, to Kazimierz's ambitions for his sons.

Dynastic Dealings

Kazimierz IV Jagiellon married Elizabeth, the daughter of Albrecht Habsburg and granddaughter of Sigismund of Luxemburg. She produced for him an abundance of heirs: six sons and five daughters. This situation was enviable in a world where dynasties so often died out but also challenging, in that all this royal blood cried out for distinguished posts. And indeed: the royal pair strove to find places for their children to rule, capitalizing on the still prevalent medieval idea that royal bloodlines were important. All their children were brought up for exalted positions, and many of them would rule on one throne or another (sometimes on several at once). They were given an excellent education under none other than Jan Długosz, former secretary to Bishop Zbigniew Oleśnicki and Kraków canon. His greatest and certainly most durable claim to fame came from his twelve-book Latin-language history of Poland, *Annales seu Cronicae Regni Poloniae* (Annals or Chronicles of the Kingdom of Poland), which covered the history of the country up to 1480. In addition to royal heads of state, the pupils of the royal tutor Długosz included a future cardinal (Kazimierz's son Fryderyk) as well as a future saint (his namesake, Kazimierz).

This time, the politics of marriage as well as that of the respective nobilities put the crowns of Bohemia and Hungary within the Jagiellons' grasp. The thrones of Bohemia and Hungary became conveniently vacant in 1458, which allowed Kazimierz to try to seat his sons. Despite the impressive Jagiellonian pedigree, this was not an easy task, for this time, each country sought to elect one of its own noblemen to the throne. In the case of Bohemia this was the Bohemian nobleman George (Jiři) Poděbrady. A leader of the moderate Hussite faction, Poděbrady was elected unanimously by the Bohemian estates that same year. Poděbrady's career proved relatively short, however, which afforded Kazimierz's eldest son, Władysław (the namesake of his deceased brother), the chance to rule in Bohemia. This he did from 1471, as Vladislav II. He would continue to reign in Bohemia for forty-five years, a period marked by reduced religious strife and a relative absence of war.

A longer period ensued before the same Jagiellon gained control over the Hungarian throne. In Hungary, it was the Transylvanian-born Matthias

Corvinus (son of János Hunyadi) who was chosen king in 1458, doubtless in part due to the memory of his father's military prowess, which he seemed to have inherited. Better known by a nickname taken from the raven (Latin: *corvus*) on his escutcheon, Corvinus was the first commoner to ascend to the Hungarian throne, and he was an outstanding ruler. He made inroads into what had been Poděbrady's holdings, annexing Moravia and Silesia as well as the Lusatias. At one point the Hungarian king even occupied Vienna, the Habsburgs' capital, which he retained control of until his death in the spring of 1490.

Władysław followed these developments closely. To strengthen his position as a candidate for the throne, that autumn the Jagiellon secretly married Corvinus's widow, and she sought to have him gain power in Hungary. Although it may seem paradoxical, there was opposition from Władysław's own father, who wanted to seat another son, Jan Olbracht, on the Hungarian throne. The men even fought two wars over the succession (so much for family unity). Yet, once the Habsburgs got involved, the tide turned against Jan Olbracht. To keep Hungary and Bohemia safely in Jagiellonian hands, Kazimierz IV Jagiellończyk threw his weight behind his eldest son, already seated on the Bohemian throne.

Personalities played no less a role in the Hungarian succession. Jan Olbracht had a reputation as a strong individual—unlike his more pliant elder brother, Władysław. This in a way explains the attraction of the latter for the Hungarian magnates, who preferred to remain influential within their own country. At this time, Hungary was an estates-based state whose parliament was dominated by the nobility—the magnates in the upper chamber (the house of lords) and the lesser nobles in the lower chamber. Jan Olbracht nonetheless gained some support from the lesser Hungarian nobility. Ultimately, however, the magnates prevailed, and Władysław became king of Hungary.

Although in Hungary he was officially hailed as King Ulászló II, Władysław came to be known there as King Bene—this, apparently, from always answering "very well" (*bene*) to whatever was asked of him. Among other things, in 1514 he allowed the Hungarian nobles to establish the so-called *Tripartitum*, a new codification of Hungarian law that gave them increased power over their peasants. Yet the Jagiellon was indeed the true ruler of the two countries, though he reconfigured them somewhat, restoring Moravia, Silesia, and Lusatia to the kingdom of Bohemia (they had come under Hungarian control under Matthias Corvinus). He also notably restored Vienna and eastern Austria, which had been occupied by Corvinus, to the Habsburgs—a move that, while keeping Habsburgs from conniving to unseat him, would nonetheless strengthen a future rival to Jagiellonian rule. Władysław lived until 1516, to be succeeded on both thrones by his son Louis (Czech: Ludvik; Hungarian: Lajos). In this way, Jagiellons came to control both the Bohemian Crown of Saint Wenceslas and the Hungarian Crown of Saint Stephen.

But this was only the near realm of Central Europe. All five daughters of Kazimierz Jagiellończyk fared well in the marriage game also. They demonstrated the potential impact of the Jagiellonian dynasty on the German-speaking world. Jadwiga married George the Rich, prince of Bavaria. Another daughter, Barbara, wed another George the Bearded, duke of Saxony. Two other sisters, Anna and Elżbieta, married the dukes of Pomerania and Legnica (German: Liegnitz), respectively; each of these husbands (Bogislaw X and Friedrich II) would be given the sobriquet of Great. Their other sister, Zofia, was the wife of Friedrich von Hohenzollern-Ansbach, elector of Brandenburg. Zofia would give birth to Albrecht von Hohenzollern-Ansbach, who (as we shall see) would be last in the long line of grand masters of the Teutonic Order on the Baltic Sea coast.

All this left the Jagiellons seemingly in a strong position. Men from the dynasty came to control all of East-Central Europe: from Hungary and Bohemia through Poland and Lithuania, putting them in a position to rule over vast territories and peoples. Kazimierz IV Jagiellon ruled Poland and Lithuania, while his son Władysław had ascended to the Crowns of Saint Wenceslas and Saint Stephen—that is, Bohemia and Hungary, respectively. Jagiellons would rule uninterruptedly over these four political entities for some thirty-six years: from 1490 to 1526, their power extended from the Baltic to the Adriatic and nearly all the way to the Black Sea.

That the Jagiellonian Moment in Central and Eastern Europe is so little known has to do with both the nature of Jagiellonian rule and the times in which they lived. With the exception of Lithuania, the countries they ruled—Poland, Bohemia, Hungary—were elective monarchies with relatively powerful, noble-dominated parliaments. In these countries, what was wanted was not an absolute monarch but, rather, someone who would work with the existing parliamentary bodies.

Not fully of either the medieval period or the modern one, these strong parliamentary traditions were reflected in such concepts as the Crown of Saint Wenceslas or the Crown of Saint Stephen. These were preexisting crowns for which rulers were to be found, and not the other way around. The implication was that, while rulers would come and go, the crown and the lands associated with it were eternal. Indeed, Bohemia equally well can be referred to as the Lands of the Crown of Saint Wenceslas, just as

Hungary was the Lands of the Crown of Saint Stephen. Even under Kazimierz the Great, Poland became the Crown of the Kingdom of Poland—Corona Regni Poloniae. Under the Jagiellons, these native traditions were respected. While some might thus see Jagiellonian rule as weak, in that its rulers were compelled to make concessions to its subjects, it represented a more palatable alternative to the absolutist rule that all too soon would muscle its way into parts of the region.

Kazimierz Jagiellończyk and His Legacy

Indeed, the reins of power in the region were not long to be maintained in the hands of Kazimierz IV Jagiellończyk and his first-born, Władysław. Only two years after winning the Hungarian throne in 1490, the second of Jagiełło's sons to sit atop the Polish throne died. His marble tomb in Wawel Castle would be carved by the famous Nuremberg artist Veit Stoss, whose stunning wooden altar in the Marian Church is perhaps the crowning glory of Gothic art in Poland.

During his long rein, which closed out the medieval period, Kazimierz IV Jagiellończyk accomplished a good deal. Some consider him to be one of Poland's greatest monarchs. He succeeded in wresting power from the cardinals and bishops who had essentially dictated policy to his underage elder brother, and he managed to extract himself from the clutches of the Lithuanian lords. These moves paved the way for the rise of the lesser nobles of the Crown, whom Kazimierz encouraged to participate in the overall governance of the country by sending delegates from the local political gatherings, known as seymiks, to meet when the royal council was convening. The Polish king likewise adjusted the balance of power between Poland and Lithuania to reflect the reality that Lithuania was stronger than a subordinate polity should be, setting the tone for over a century of stability.

The Creation of Royal Prussia

One of Kazimierz IV Jagiellończyk's major achievements, alluded to earlier, concerned the Baltic Sea coast. Recall that the 1410 Battle of Grunwald, although a decisive victory, had given little in the way of territorial gains to the Poles. Lands taken from the newly forming Poland under Władysław Łokietek still remained under the control of the Teutonic Order, despite further attempts at regaining them.

In 1454 the Poles profited from the revolt of Prussian Estates living under the Teutonic Knights, who were tired of being oppressed both economically and politically. The subsequent thirteen-year war between the Knights and Poland-Lithuania enabled the reopening of the Vistula River to Polish commerce and led to the signing of the historic Peace of Toruń (German: Thorn) in 1466, which resulted in the partition of the Teutonic Knights' territories along the Baltic coast. The Poles gained much of the Baltic Sea coast with its important cities—Gdańsk, Toruń, Elbląg (German: Elbing)—as well as the wealthy bishopric of Warmia (German: Ermeland). The fortress at Malbork had briefly come under Polish control in 1457, the Polish king having paid the mercenaries defending it the whopping sum of 190,000 florins, and the fortress was then regained in 1460. These territories would come to be known as Royal Prussia. In the terms of the agreement, Kazimierz IV Jagiellończyk "incorporated and reunited" these lands—the gateway to the Baltic—with the Crown of Poland. Nonetheless, the new and valuable lands would be given various privileges, including a separate parliament and treasury, the maintenance of Kulm Law (not Magdeburg Law), and the right for burghers to participate in the parliament.

The Teutonic Knights were left in control of eastern Prussia, and they would have to content themselves with the city of Kaliningrad (German: Königsberg) as their capital. To add insult to injury, they would henceforth be a political dependency—a fief—of Poland. The Knights of the Order were not happy with this settlement and did what they could to maintain what influence they still had in the region. This was the first major victory for Poland-Lithuania in the Baltic Sea region since the Battle of Grunwald.

The Next Generation

So much for one of the major accomplishments of Jagiełło's younger and long-lived son. According to a promise made by Kazimierz IV in 1478, rule over Poland and Lithuania was subsequently divided between his next two surviving sons. Jan Olbracht (1492–1501) was declared king of Poland (his younger brother Fryderyk, at that time bishop of Kraków, presided over his election), while Alexander was appointed grand duke in Lithuania. Although aged thirty-three and thirty-one, respectively, neither son was yet married—a tremendous oversight on the part of their father. Indeed, the elder would never marry. And his election to the Polish throne had not been assured: he had competition not only from Janusz of Mazovia but also from two of his own brothers: Władysław, king of Bohemia and Hungary, and a younger brother, Zygmunt. Interestingly, it appears that Jan Olbracht won the election thanks to the behind-the-scenes work of his brother Fryderyk, bishop of Kraków. For his pains, the latter was appointed primate of Poland.

As of 1492, thus, we have a situation with Jagiellons—this time in three persons, all brothers—ruling over not only Poland and Lithuania but also Bohemia and Hungary. Yet a fourth Jagiellon sibling, Fryderyk, would soon become a cardinal, giving him further influence. But did this mean that the Jagiellons were especially powerful? Were they truly a dynasty to be reckoned with in East-Central Europe? Unfortunately not. The four brothers did not all cooperate with each other.

Had they worked together, as had Jan Olbracht and Fryderyk, they might have been able to strengthen the family holdings even further. For example, Moldavia might have been wrested from the Turks for the younger brother, Zygmunt, in the process facilitating Polish access to the Black Sea trading routes once again. But this was not to happen, despite the efforts of Jan Olbracht. His attempts at forging a workable coalition with all his brothers, who convened in 1494, came to naught.

The subsequent Moldavian campaign of 1497 proved a disaster. After an unsuccessful siege of Suceava lasting three weeks, Jan Olbracht's retreating army was ambushed by a composite force of Turks and Tatars as well as Moldavians (Olbracht's ally, the Moldavian hospodar Stefan, had switched sides). The Turks, who had only recently conquered much of the Balkans, not to mention Constantinople, the very capital of eastern Christianity, would see this Polish aggression as license to begin raiding Poland's southern districts.

Fighting, and losing, such battles could be costly in more ways than one. In order to win support for his war in 1496, Jan Olbracht had been compelled to make concessions to the Polish nobility. Among other things, these concessions meant that the peasants were limited in their movements and townspeople were forbidden to own land. Neither of these developments ultimately strengthened Poland-Lithuania. While the nobles clearly profited, the peasants were becoming increasingly tied to the land (although they were not yet forced to provide labor dues) and the towns were not expanding economically like their west European counterparts.

Nonetheless, Jan Olbracht's short reign—only nine years—left their mark on the development of Poland. His contribution was the formal establishment of a parliament, the so-called Seym. Prior to 1493, there had been less formal Seyms, where concerned parties—attendance was not restricted—came to deliberate. The Polish Seym was unlike its counterpart in France, which was divided into estates, and more closely resembled the English ex-

Map 3.1: The Extent of Jagiellonian Rule in Central and Eastern Europe, ca. 1500

ample with its two bodies, the House of Commons and the House of Lords. Also bicameral, the Polish Seym consisted of the royal council, or Senate, the members of which had been appointed to high office, and the Chamber of Deputies—members of the latter representing the local seymiks, thus reflecting the broader will of the country's sizable nobility. This configuration of the Polish parliament would persist as long as Poland existed.

The Menace to the South

While Tatar raids were a constant threat to the southern reaches of Poland-Lithuania, the rising power of the Ottoman Turks in the Balkans was increasingly felt by the Jagiellons. The kings of Poland were pulled into the conflict by the desire to protect their trade routes along the Dniester and the Danube. Defending the mouth of the latter was Moldavia, which alternated between being a fief of Ottoman Turkey, Hungary, and Poland. While Jan Olbracht had had designs on the Ottoman fief of Moldavia, the last Jagiellons on the Polish throne would try to keep the peace and avoid the pitfall of another crusade against the Turks.

In part, this was the result of the family's devastating experiences in dealing with the Ottoman menace. Witness the fate of Louis II (Czech: Ludvik; Hungarian: Lajos), the last Jagiellon to rule Bohemia and Hungary. The son of King Bene, Louis became king of the two countries in 1517 at the tender age of ten. Louis was married to Maria of Habsburg, but at the time of his death, aged only nineteen, he had no heir. The young Louis proved no match for the great Ottoman sultan Suleiman the Magnificent (1520–1566). Having already seized most of the Aegean islands and other coastal possessions from Venice, Suleiman set his sights on territory further north—lands held by Louis. Trying desperately to fight the Ottoman forces of seventy-five thousand with a force one-third that size, Louis perished at the famous Battle of Mohács in 1526.

The year 1526 was a tragic year for Hungary. The Turkish victory led to the partition of that formerly large, strong state. By 1541 Hungary would be divided into three parts, each with a slightly different fate. The largest part—central Hungary—was occupied by the Ottomans. Another distinct entity was Transylvania, which became an Ottoman vassal state (similar, say, to Moldavia). That left a small strip of territory in the north and west that evaded Ottoman rule. Closest to Austria, this was so-called Royal Hungary; it included Croatia, which had not been lost to the Turks.

Felix Austria

Royal Hungary would have gone to Louis's son had he had one. And herein lay the problem. That he would eventually sire an heir was a gamble the Jagiellons ventured to make in 1515. That year the Jagiellonian rulers of Poland-Lithuania and Hungary made a trip to Vienna, the seat of the Habsburg ruler and Holy Roman Emperor, Maximilian I. The Jagiellonian brothers hoped to prevail upon Maximilian to cease interfering in the Baltic and in the east. The price of this agreement turned out to be a double marriage contract, which ultimately united two sibling pairs of Habsburgs and Jagiellons. Sister and brother of one family would marry brother and sister of the other. Louis would marry Maximilian's niece Maria, and her brother Ferdinand would marry Louis's sister Anna.

But this was not all. The double marriage was contracted not out of mutual love but with dynastic considerations at the forefront. A crucial part of the contract ensured that, if one of the couples produced no heir, the other would inherit the respective dominions. In other words, the double marriage contract was simultaneously a mutual inheritance pact. It was the House of Habsburg, thus, that profited in 1526 from the Jagiellons' loss. The lucky Ferdinand Habsburg took over Bohemia and rump Hungary.

This sudden transition to Habsburg rule over Bohemia and Hungary marked the end of the Jagiellons' domination of East-Central Europe. Henceforth, it was the House of Habsburg whose star was in the ascendant. Not for nothing was the following Latin phrase penned: *Bella gerant alii, tu felix Austria, nube!* (Let others fight wars—you, happy Austria, marry!). The Habsburgs ultimately made both Bohemian and Hungarian crowns hereditary. Nonetheless, the strength of the respective parliaments, consolidated during the period of Jagiellonian rule, meant that the Habsburgs' attempts to gain full absolutist control over both realms would take a very long time—over a century in Bohemia (to 1620) and some three centuries in Hungary (to 1850).

The Other Brothers: Inching toward Modernity

While the Habsburgs' marriage politics were met with stupendous success, marrying seemed something the Jagiellons did with less and less success in the sixteenth century. The two middle sons of Kazimierz Jagiellończyk, Jan Olbracht and Alexander (1501–1505), died without producing heirs—the former never having even married. While there had been talk of Jan Olbracht marrying a French princess, as his elder brother Władysław had done, the king died before anything was achieved in this respect.

Grand Duke Alexander's choice of a bride reflected Lithuania's perception of the rising force to the east. This was Muscovy under Ivan III (1462–1505)—Ivan the Great, according to Russian historians. Most readers may know him only as the grandfather of Ivan IV the Terrible—if at all; but there is much reason to consider his long and significant reign here.

An early Muscovite ambition was to "gather" what remained of the principalities that had once been part of Kyivan Rus' and subject them to Muscovy. By the end of the reign of Ivan III, this task was more or less accomplished. This was the period when Muscovy was first being discovered by the West. In 1472 Ivan himself facilitated this encounter by marrying Sophie Paleologue, a descendant of the emperors of Byzantium. The Byzantine connection led some Muscovite clerics to think of their country as inheriting the mantle of that great entity, whose capital, Constantinople, had only recently (in 1453) been conquered by the Turks. They had ambitions for Muscovy to become the "Third Rome."

These ambitions would have implications for relations with Poland-Lithuania. Relations had soured since Kazimierz IV Jagiellończyk came to the rescue of the father of Ivan III, Vasilii II the Darkened (the sobriquet refers to the fact that the Muscovite grand duke had been blinded by an enemy). The ungrateful Ivan asserted his "right" to rule all the Ruthenian lands—including those that were part of the Grand Duchy—immediately after Kazimierz IV died. The marriage contracted between the Lithuanian grand duke Alexander and Ivan's beautiful daughter Helena in 1494, thus, was more a sign of Lithuanian weakness than its strength.

Habsburgs, Tatars, and others were allying themselves with Moscow at the turn of the century, and this left Poland-Lithuania nearly encircled—a result, perhaps, of Jagiellonian overreach (the battle for Moldavia was but one obvious sign of this). The country was also smaller than it had been: Ivan III had managed to "gather" about a third of Lithuania by the time of his death in 1505. To be sure, these territories lay on the outskirts of the once enormous Polish-Lithuanian state, which held them only nominally. But it meant that Smolensk and Kyiv, both still very much part of the Grand Duchy, were now dangerously near the frontier.

This sad state of affairs and sense of encirclement reverberated throughout Poland-Lithuania, for Ivan III did not hesitate to inflict pain on Poland proper. This is evident in a devastating Muscovite-inspired invasion of southeastern Poland by the Crimean Tatars in 1502. Even the capital Kraków felt threatened and, to counter the threat, built the imposing Barbican that stands to this day in front of Florian Gate.

Alexander succeeded his brother Jan Olbracht on the Polish throne in 1501—although even here, he had competition from his brothers Władysław, king of Bohemia and Hungary, and Zygmunt. The Lithuanian grand duke turned Polish king reigned only until 1506. In the Crown of Poland, he bore the brunt of a backlash against the brash style of his predecessor, Jan Olbracht. The powerful Polish magnates furthermore sought to press their centralizing vision of Poland-Lithuania, one that would give the mightiest nobles more power.

Yet Alexander ultimately pushed back. He is most remembered for the path-breaking achievement at the Radom Seym in 1505, where Alexander issued a royal statute, commonly referred to as "Nothing New" (*Nihil novi*). In this he stated: "We have hereby affirmed for all time to come that nothing new may be enacted by us and our successors save by the common consent of the council and the representatives of the lands."* This meant that the king (and henceforth all his successors) had to reach agreement with the Seym

---

* Modified rendition of the English translation found in Davies, *God's Playground*, 1:119.

before enacting any new legislation. It was also agreed that the opinions of both houses of the Seym—the Chamber of Deputies as well as the Senate, with its powerful magnates—would be given equal weight. Parliamentarians would be aided in their deliberations by a compilation of historic statutes and privileges helpfully prepared by Alexander's chancellor, Jan Łaski the Elder, which was published in Kraków the following year.

The significance of the 1505 *Nihil novi* statute—alternately referred to as a constitution (that is, a law passed by the Seym) or cardinal law—is worth underscoring. It built upon the privileges granted to the nobility by a series of medieval rulers: Louis of Hungary, Jagiełło, and Kazimierz Jagiellończyk. (Kazimierz the Great had already recognized the nobility as an "estate," that is, as a distinct group within society.) Louis had given his assurance, at Košice, that the nobility would not be taxed further without their consent. In turn, Jagiełło granted to the nobility something along the lines of habeas corpus: that is, a nobleman could not be arrested or have his property confiscated except after due process. This, notably, took place some three centuries before the English Habeas Corpus Act of 1679. And several decades after the Polish nobility attained these rights from the first of the Jagiellons, Jagiełło's son and Alexander's father, Kazimierz IV Jagiellończyk, agreed, in the Nieszawa statute of 1454, to consult the seymiks before summoning the nobles to battle or promulgating laws.

Nihil novi further dotted the "i" of noble privileges within Poland-Lithuania and set the country on the road to modernity. According to this tripartite system of government, the monarch, the senate (his appointed officials), and the house of deputies (representing the entirety of the nobility) were all to work together to shape the laws of the land. The system constituted an effective limitation upon potential royal absolutism, thus making Poland-Lithuania distinctive in continental Europe in the early modern period, when the trend was toward absolutism. The statute of 1505 would be the basis of noble freedoms for nearly three centuries and would assist what some would term a process of democratization in the country. With time, this would contribute to a unique set of arrangements that would transform Poland-Lithuania, making the country stand out in the Europe of its day.

Poland-Lithuania and the West

Yet Poland also marched to the same tune as the rest of Europe—at least, up to a point. Despite the spread of Poland-Lithuania in an easterly direction and its preoccupation with Central and Eastern Europe, this does not mean that the West and Western trends were of little concern. Poland-Lithuania was in tune with developments in the West throughout much of this period.

In the economic realm, Poland-Lithuania was on an upward trajectory beginning around the time of the marriage of Jadwiga and Jagiełło. Early on, the country supplied naval stores (timber, including masts for ships, as well as pitch and potash) to western shipbuilders as well as the traditional goods of the north: wax, honey, furs, and skins. Lithuania participated in the trade of such northern goods. Much of this early trade was facilitated by the Prussians, who then shipped most of the goods from Gdańsk to Amsterdam and other destinations in the north and west. In the south, Ruthenes traded some of the same items (but also salt and cattle) with the Turks.

Improvements in agricultural techniques—including the use of the scythe, the rotation of crops, and fertilization of the soil with manure—helped the country of fertile plains develop into a major producer of grain. Although not quite as efficient as some countries in the west, Poland was more efficient at grain production than its German and Russian neighbors. Much of this grain was consumed at home, although (as we will see) the European maritime expansion to the New World would eventually make Poland-Lithuania an important source of grain in Europe. Its economy was, thus, increasingly integrated into the broader European—even world—economy.

The expansion of the country that began under the Piasts also increased the Poles' involvement in the transit trade. Located in the heart of Europe, the Polish-Lithuanian state profited from its location along east–west and south–north trade routes. Armenians, Jews, and Italians based in Lviv, for example, traveled to and from the Crimea and the Black Sea bringing silks, cottons, and spices from exotic sources to the west and north. Copper from the mines of Slovakia (part of Hungary) was an important transit good. Substantial profits accrued to local burghers, who had been given staple rights—that is, the right to warehouse and even sell the goods being transported further. Patricians of various cities were able to enrich themselves handsomely; some even became ennobled, often through marriage, and purchased landed estates.

Of course, not only raw materials were exported. Some were processed. For example, salt from Poland's mines made its way north to the region of the Baltic to preserve herring. Manufactured goods included textiles, as the existence (and flourishing) of the Cloth Hall in Kraków's main square will attest. Even in these centuries, Gdańsk was known for shipbuilding, and this major Baltic port provided ships to countries further west. There were guilds of all sorts in Polish towns, although these produced primarily for domestic consumption:

countless breweries and bakeries, cobblers and furriers. They were relatively well-off, especially for the period and for East-Central Europe.

The Golden Age: Cultural Revolution

Another important realm of development in Poland-Lithuania at this time was cultural. Here too the country did not lag far behind the West in embracing new intellectual trends and movements. These included the Renaissance and the Reformation, both of which had a significant impact on the free citizenry of Poland-Lithuania. In this, the lands of Poland-Lithuania marked the furthest reach eastward of these movements, thus placing these lands, intellectually and culturally, on the easternmost frontier of the West. These Western ideas never penetrated as far as Muscovy; the closest that rising region came to such emanations from the West in this period was restricted to a veneer of architectural construction done by Italians in Moscow.

Not only did these new ideas penetrate and percolate within the Jagiellonian realm. The sixteenth century has been termed Poland-Lithuania's Golden Age. The reigns of the last two Jagiellons (about whom more shortly) were a fruitful period for the country, and not only economically. These intellectual movements had their own unique resonance in this multiethnic and multidenominational part of Europe, with different aspects of particular significance.

Fertile soil for intellectual movements such as the Renaissance to take root in Poland-Lithuania was prepared by the university. It was a place where new ideas could be encountered and where the culture of the West, especially as expressed in Latin, could be explored. Historically even since early medieval times some Poles—mainly clerics—had traveled to the West to study at Europe's universities (especially in Italy and Bohemia).

As early as 1400, Jagiełło "refounded" the university in Kraków (which had been established by Kazimierz the Great in 1364), with the proceeds that came from his dead wife Jadwiga's jewels, donated expressly for that purpose. Not only did he found it again; he expanded it as well. According to the king, education was supposed to do more than prepare clerics who could, for example, aid with the Christianization of Lithuania—a not unimportant task, to be sure. (The refounding of the university had an important effect on the Catholicization of the Polish masses as well: a better education meant that more priests gave sermons.) Jagiełło also wished to educate officials for the enlarged state as well as raise the general level of education. And this was made possible as of 1400, when all four main branches of scholarship available for study at Europe's universities were represented: the liberal arts, medicine, law, and theology.

Some of the fruits of this new push toward education in Poland-Lithuania became visible only a few years later. Witness the noteworthy participation of Poles in the great church councils of the fifteenth century. During the Council of Constance (1414–1418), the Polish legal scholar Paweł Włodkowic (Latin: Paulus Vladimiri) publicly spoke against the right of Christians to impose their will on nonbelievers by force. This doctrine (among other things) had justified the crusading zeal of the Teutonic Knights, only just recently defeated by the joint Polish-Lithuanian force.

Włodkowic's views synthesized a potent mix of Western legal thought and Polish practice. Educated in canon law, he was no less familiar with the Poles' successful—and peaceful—conversion of the pagan Lithuanians, including his own monarch. This professor from Kraków saw a better way of winning converts to Christianity: no pretext of Christian piety justified the impious treatment of peaceable pagans who, like all people, should have the right to live in peace on their own lands. That this humane approach was not embraced by the church in the West does not diminish the correctness of his assessment.

Renaissance Poland

Such were some of the first fruits of the high quality of education Poles were now able to receive—an education without which the country would never have been able to produce so many scholars, politicians, scientists, and poets during this period. It has been suggested that contacts made at the Councils of Constance and Basel (1431–1449) helped to expose the Poles to the Christian humanism of the early Renaissance. Already part of the Latin-speaking world, they now became acquainted with the classical Greek and Latin culture that was being rediscovered at this time. And they, too, came to value the treasures of the ancient world, not only its literature but also its history.

An early, major figure of the Polish-Lithuanian Renaissance was an alumnus of the Kraków university, Gregory of Sanok. Well traveled (son of a poor burgher, he ran away from home at an early age), he nonetheless managed to study in Poland as well as abroad, where he amassed a library and made a name for himself. Influential in Polish magnate and royal circles, he had barely escaped with his life at the battle of Varna in 1444, where he had accompanied his former pupil, King Władysław III. (The latter's successor on the Hungarian throne, Matthias Corvinus, had also been taught by Gregory.) After becoming archbishop of Lviv, Gregory of Sanok built himself a palace on the Dunajec River, which became a salon of sorts for Renaissance thinkers, poets, and scholars.

The archbishop's palace at Dunajów also became a haven for more than one foreigner. The Italian Filippo Buonaccorsi (1437–1496) would come to play an important role in spreading Renaissance ideas in Poland-Lithuania. Thanks to him, incidentally, we know more about Gregory of Sanok (Buonaccorsi was his biographer). The Italian owed his life to his Polish mentor, who rescued him from certain death: Buonaccorsi was a fugitive from justice, having been part of a conspiracy to murder Pope Paul II in 1468. Gregory's patronage ultimately resulted in Callimachus—that was the Latin sobriquet of the poet and author—being appointed as secretary to King Kazimierz Jagiellończyk; he was also close to the latter's son and successor, Jan Olbracht.

A writer of elegant classical Latin, Callimachus penned many works: poetry, prose, as well as history and biography. Together with yet another foreigner who had traveled to Kraków, the German Conrad Celtis (1459–1508), the former renegade founded the influential Literary Society of the Vistula (Sodalitas Literaria Vistulana). Celtis—as poet, playwright, scholar, as well as University of Kraków student and teacher—helped to spread interest in Plato, Cicero, Horace, and Seneca. He even wrote verses about Kraków as well as his Polish lover, Hasilina. All of this helped to spread knowledge of the ancients and their history as well as of pure, classical Latin among the educated elites of Poland-Lithuania, whether of burgher or noble extraction. (And this was a time when education—even in more remote towns and villages—was proceeding apace.)

Many Poles came to write excellent classical Latin, and indeed Poles were known far and wide for their command of this universal language. Important Latin writers during this period included the globetrotting diplomat Jan Dantyszek (John of Gdańsk; known in Latin as Iohannes Dantiscus); the poet, satirist, and (somewhat surprisingly) later primate of Poland Andrzej Krzycki (Latin: Andreas Cricius); and the poet Klemens Janicki (Latin: Clemens Ianicius, 1516–1543). Janicki was so skilled at writing Latin verse that, while in Italy, he gained the title of Poet Laureate from Pope Paul III, who was loath to see him return to Poland.

Study Abroad

Despite the existence of the University of Kraków, numerous Poles during this period traveled abroad to study. Their knowledge of Latin and other languages allowed them to embark on studies anywhere in Europe. Many began their studies in Kraków and then made the rounds of other European universities in a sort of educational Grand Tour, as it were—and as such, no less eye-opening. Poles both rich and poor engaged in Renaissance travel to places such as Rome and even to the Holy Land. And let us not forget that artisans made their way about Europe, perfecting their craft, while merchants had their own set of international connections.

Nonetheless, of foreign universities the august university of Padua figured most prominently in the education of sixteenth-century Poles. Padua was part of the Venetian Republic, and the city and region held many charms for the international student body. Over a thousand students from Poland-Lithuania entered through those doors in this period, many of whom made noteworthy careers back home afterward, fulfilling various diplomatic and political functions. A significant number of government officials in Poland-Lithuania studied in Padua, including fourteen palatines, twenty-four castellans, and three vice-chancellors. Graduates of the university served as Polish diplomats, and the number of graduates (at least some of them bearing letters of recommendation to the king from the University of Padua) who ended up serving as royal secretaries in the 1500s was legion. Even highly placed clergymen had the experience of humanistic study at this wealthy university, as attested by the thirty-seven bishops and twelve abbots who also figured in this mix.

In a slightly later period, destinations for study abroad varied in accordance with one's religion. While Padua and Bologna were perennially popular, they were destinations for the Catholic faithful. With the advent of the Reformation in 1517, newly minted Protestants might travel to places such as Heidelberg, Leipzig, Marburg, or Wittenberg, where they could not only educate themselves but also forge contacts with fellow believers. At around the mid-century and beyond, counter-reformation Catholics headed to places like Vienna, Graz, or Freiburg for theological reinforcement. By this later date, the university of Kraków was no longer on the cutting edge of scholarship. It had reached its zenith by around 1525, after which time it became a much more conservative institution. But in its heyday, classical Latin, Greek, and Hebrew were taught, as well as law and medicine and the natural sciences.

Lest one think that this humanistic education was only for nobles or for the well-to-do: this was a period in which those of the lower classes also strove to educate themselves. Many burghers took an interest in the ideas of Erasmus. At one point, half of the students at Kraków University were the sons of burghers. Education helped them advance, whether into royal service or in the clergy. It thus should come as no surprise that many humanists—king and nobles, bishops and patricians—had their own courts and circles, where they served as patrons of the arts and of knowledge. Even some peasants were exposed to all kinds of new ideas and were taught to read in this age of the printed word.

Yet, even the enlightened age of the Renaissance had its limits. Women were forbidden from stepping foot on the university grounds. Legend tells us of a young woman from Greater Poland who disguised herself as a man in order to be able to study at Kraków University. Apparently the young student was assiduous, even well liked by both peers and professors. When she/he became ill, however, the doctor discovered the truth. Nawojka was not only expelled; she was also forced to take monastic orders—thus exchanging university walls for those of a convent. Clearly having profited from her studies, Nawojka became a model mother superior.

Renaissance Men

So much for the all too short experience of a budding Renaissance woman. Those who attended universities during the efflorescence of the Renaissance were not content to specialize in one narrow field. Indeed, they were "Renaissance men" in all meanings of the phrase—men who probed a wide range of different fields of knowledge.

Many of them took an interest in public affairs. A case in point was Andrzej Frycz Modrzewski (Latin: Andreas Fricius Modrevius, 1503–1572). One of the most illustrious of Kraków university alumni, he is considered to be the most important political writer in the Golden Age. In 1551 Modrzewski authored a treatise entitled *De Republica Emendanda* (On the reform of the republic), in which he addressed the role that education should play in improving governance. This was not a popular view among the nobility. Nobles saw high office as a means of enrichment, something they were entitled to by birth, not by talent—but education did ultimately improve the preparation of those who played a role in the affairs of state.

Such Renaissance men were both conversant with and appreciative of ideas percolating in the West. During his travels abroad, Modrzewski made arrangements for the transfer of the library of Desiderius Erasmus, the famous Dutch humanist, to Poland. Erasmus's library had been purchased much earlier by Jan Łaski (John à Lasco—not to be confused with his uncle Jan Łaski, who had been primate of Poland), who generously allowed Erasmus to keep it until his death in 1536. (Indeed, during his lifetime Erasmus had many Polish visitors as well as correspondents, not to mention legions of admirers.) But Modrzewski was no stranger to controversy. He eventually got in trouble for criticizing aspects of the church, which resulted in some of his works being put on the Index—the list of prohibited books prepared by the Roman Catholic Church, itself a product of this new age of printing.

The most perfect example of a Polish Renaissance man is the most illustrious former student of the University of Kraków, Nicolaus Copernicus (1473–1543). Who has not heard of the man who determined that the Earth revolved around the Sun—or perhaps heard him claimed as a national by both Germans and Poles alike? Notwithstanding modern debates concerning his nationality—a deceptively anachronistic concept when applied to the premodern period—his life trajectory was very much intertwined with Poland-Lithuania, his country.

The path-breaking author of the heliocentric astronomical theory was born in Toruń in Royal Prussia, the former part of the Teutonic Knights' territory that transferred its allegiance to the Crown of Poland in 1466. We have no proof that he knew Polish, as he wrote only in Latin and German; nonetheless he was not only a local, Royal Prussian patriot but also a loyal subject of the Polish crown.

While Copernicus would travel and study widely, he would make important contributions to his home region. His education spanned several countries: he studied not only in Kraków, which at that time was on the cutting edge of astronomical scholarship, but also in Padua, Bologna, and Ferrara. The astronomical observations that convinced him to write the famous book in which he questioned the belief that the Sun orbited around the Earth were made in Frombork (German: Frauenberg), in the bishopric of Warmia, part of Royal Prussia. That is where Copernicus spent the last forty years of his life, serving in the Warmian church as canon.

Yet Copernicus was a real Renaissance man, doing much more than just changing the way people would view the world. In addition to being an astronomer, he earned degrees in medicine and canon law. Copernicus had considerable engineering skills, which he put to use designing a water supply system for Frombork. He notably led the defense of the city of Olsztyn (German: Allenstein) when it came under attack from the Teutonic Knights in 1520–1521. Copernicus made and published economic observations, explaining what in economics was later to be known as Gresham's Law: that good coinage is pushed out of circulation by bad (or less valuable) coinage. And he was the first scholar in Poland to translate an obscure but newly discovered Greek literary work into Latin, demonstrating that he was very much a part of the humanism of his day.

As a man of the cloth, Copernicus had no delusions about the impact his revolutionary heliocentric theory might have. While he began to write his famous *De revolutionibus orbium coelestium libri VI* (Six books on the revolutions of the heavenly spheres) in 1510, the book was not published until 1543, the year of his death. This said, he and other scholars, for whom the pursuit of the truth was paramount, believed it was a very important book that had to be published. Copernicus decided to dedicate the book to Pope Paul III, explaining to the humanistically educated pope in his dedication how he came to conclude that such a view of the universe, in which the Earth moved, was possible. This logical explanation aside, Copernicus hoped that the support of Pope Paul III would defuse any opposition to his book. Interestingly, among the first to protest against Copernicus's heliocentric theory were Protestant theologians, who based their claims on the Bible. Copernicus's magnum opus was not put on the Index until 1616.

The Renaissance Revolution

Copernicus may have helped to place Renaissance Poland on the map, but other developments, of an architectural and urban-planning nature, situated the Renaissance permanently in the landscape of Poland-Lithuania. Anyone who ever climbed Wawel Hill in Kraków has seen the wonderful Renaissance detailing of the castle, most notably the several stories of arcades lining its large courtyard. Its overall design was credited to King Zygmunt I, whose fascination with Renaissance art and architecture dated from the period he spent at the court of his older brother Władysław in Hungary. Upon assuming the Polish throne, Zygmunt demanded that similar work be done in Kraków—work that took years to accomplish but whose effects are still admired to this day.

The reconstruction of the castle in Renaissance style was completed by a truly international team. It included a series of Italian architects, the most famous the Florentine Bartolomeo Berecci, and German artists such as Hans Dürer (the brother of the more famous Albrecht) and Hans Sues, who painted the friezes. The work of woodcarvers graces the splendid (extant) ceiling of the Hall of Deputies, comprised of a checkerboard with 194 sculptured heads of contemporaries, each individually framed. Likewise dating from this period is the splendid Zygmunt chapel abutting the side of Wawel Cathedral. Designed by Berecci, with an imposing interior of light-colored marble, it is a true Renaissance jewel. (See Figure 3.1.)

Yet not only Polish royalty delighted in the riches of the Renaissance. Even within Kraków, many buildings—including the large Cloth Hall in the center of Market Square—got a Renaissance facelift. Tombs and mausoleums dating from this period can be found across the Polish lands. Given the country's increasing prosperity, not only nobles and clergymen but also patricians saw fit to imitate royalty and serve as patrons of the arts.

Another noteworthy, if somewhat later, jewel of the Renaissance was an entire private town. Zamość was the beautiful brainchild of Jan Zamoyski, in whose honor the town was named. Zamoyski began his life as a noble of middling means. Educated in Padua, he began his career back home as a secretary to the king but catapulted to prominence in the last third of the sixteenth century, eventually holding the top offices of chancellor and grand hetman (that is, commander in chief or leader) of the Crown (that is, the Crown of Poland, or the Polish kingdom). His great ambition led him to enter into alliances with the rich and powerful, marry into their families, and put his legal education to effective use as he set about gaining title to the lands of indebted nobles. In sixteenth-century Poland-Lithuania, high offices tended to bring with them uncommon access to wealth and control over the rich royal landholdings. Zamoyski would become the richest man in the entire country.

The wealthy and influential magnate commissioned Bernardo Morando of Padua to build for him, from scratch, a Renaissance-style "ideal city"—one that would have numerous functions. The Italian architect proved an inspired choice. He designed a fortified town in the shape of a pentagon, with Zamoyski's castle on one side and commercial buildings for the town's burghers on another. Indeed, the presence of merchants and traders was much desired: Zamość lay on the important trade route linking western and northern Europe with the Black Sea, and as such attracted both Armenians and Jews, the historic traders in this part of Europe, whom Zamoyski welcomed to his town (with privileges dating from the 1580s). Armenians built their townhouses on the north side of the main market square; Jews (originally Sephardic Jews, coming to Zamość originally from Lviv, although later Ashkenazim would take their places) constructed theirs along the smaller market square known as Salt Square. Zamość became a veritable microcosm of Polish-Lithuanian society: also resident in the town were Ruthenes, Greeks, Italians, Scots, Englishmen, and Germans. It was, thus, a place where people of various ethnicities and religions could live in harmony.

Zamość's central public space contained an expansive town square, a hundred meters square, with an imposing town hall. This "ideal city" lacked neither houses of worship (including a Roman Catholic cathedral, a Greek Orthodox church, an Armenian church, and a synagogue) nor a university

Figure 3.1: Wawel Cathedral with the adjoining Wasa and Zygmunt Chapels. The gold-domed Zygmunt Chapel of the Jagiellons is in Renaissance style (both interior and exterior); the later Wasa Chapel to its left is in Baroque style. Each reflected the spirit of its age and patrons.

of its own, the Zamość academy. Again, everything was done in Renaissance style, with an admixture of central European architectural styles (seen, for example, in the townhouses built by the burghers who settled there). It is the best example in the Polish-Lithuanian lands of a noble's private town, of which there were many during this period, though they were not put together with as much thought (nor constructed all at once) as was Zamość. Even today, Zamość retains its uniquely homogeneous, exquisite, and innovative style and has been designated a UNESCO World Heritage Site.

The Last Jagiellons

Much of this spread of Western ideas, art, and architectural styles took place during the reign of the last two Jagiellonian monarchs. The first of these was Zygmunt I (1506–1548). Although not the youngest of Kazimierz Jagiellończyk's sons (Fryderyk, the cardinal, was younger than he was), Zygmunt was the youngest sibling to ascend to the throne. It is somewhat paradoxical, thus, that he is referred to as Zygmunt the Old—a sobriquet that reflected the longevity of his rule as well as his life, not to mention the fact that his son and heir was his namesake.

Whereas his predecessor (and elder brother Alexander) took as his bride the daughter of a Muscovite grand duke, Zygmunt first turned his sights southward and married a Transylvanian Zapolya. (This, after all, was the brother who had hoped to rule nearby Moldavia.) This did not mean, however, that the king was embroiled in the battle with the Ottomans. Rather, he made peace with these fearsome neighbors, thus putting an end to any sort of Jagiellonian imperial overstretch in the south. After his first wife died, the nearly fifty-year-old Zygmunt was persuaded to look westward for a bride. Bona Sforza of Milan became queen of Poland in 1518.

The Milanese princess facilitated the Poles' embrace of major culinary as well as cultural contributions, provided by her Italian contacts and retinue—from Renaissance architectural ideas through to the introduction of Italian vegetables. Even today, the bouquet garni that goes into soup—comprised of carrots, parsnips, onions, celery root, leeks, parsley—is referred to in Polish as *włoszczyzna* (meaning "something Italian," *Włochy* being the term for Italy). Yet she did much more than that. Brought up in the heady world of Italian politics, Bona not only bore her husband the requisite children (including a son and heir); she also proved tenacious in her efforts to strengthen both her husband's position within his kingdom and that of the dynasty. Her perceived interference in the politics of Poland-Lithuania, naturally, was not appreciated by the rank-and-file Polish nobility, who thought her husband allied too closely with the state's powerful magnates. An increasingly vociferous movement for the "Execution of the Laws" (by which they meant the implementation of previously enacted legislation that would benefit the lesser nobility) shows that rank-and-file nobles feared the rise of absolutism in the country.

Still, Queen Bona was a force not always reckoned with, even by her weak-willed and indecisive husband (who, as one of the youngest sons of Kazimierz, had not been groomed to rule Poland-Lithuania). For example, instead of pressing for control over part of Silesia in 1522, Zygmunt demurred. The reason: the duchy of Głogów (German: Glogau) was in the family: Zygmunt's nephew Louis II of Hungary was in control of it. Clearly the thought that it might soon pass from Jagiellonian to Habsburg control did not cross his mind.

Zygmunt's reign did bring many positive developments, however. One important accomplishment was the ultimate incorporation of Mazovia (with its ducal capital of Warsaw) into the Crown of Poland. Regardless how odd this may seem to contemporary readers, Warsaw—despite its central location and later claims to fame—was not yet fully a part of the realm. Since the fourteenth century, Mazovia had been a fief of Poland, controlled by a branch of the old Piast princely dynasty. Bit by bit, the Crown of Poland had acquired pieces of that territory; yet it was only after the death of the last Mazovian prince, Janusz III, in 1526 that the process of incorporation was completed.

For a Polish province, Mazovia was in many ways atypical. The duchy had long eschewed battle with the Teutonic Knights to its immediate north and even maintained good trade relations with them. As of the late fourteenth century, Mazovians had played an important role in facilitating the trade of timber and naval stores coming to Baltic ports via the Narew, Bug, and Vistula Rivers. The duchy likewise assisted the transit trade of furs, wax, and honey from Lithuania as well as cattle from Volhynia. After 1500, Mazovians expanded their activities to include the grain trade. As for the social composition of the duchy, it boasted a preponderance of nobles—certainly vis-à-vis Poland-Lithuania as a whole. Some 20 percent of the population claimed a noble patent—quite a large number, though to be sure most of these were impoverished soldier-nobles. Warsaw had a provincial feel, although in the sixteenth century it was beginning its ascent, in part thanks to trade.

Although King Zygmunt managed to incorporate the remaining pieces of Mazovia into the Crown, he was less successful in pressing state and dynastic interests in the region of the Baltic Sea, this despite a very real occasion to do so. For a war fought against the Teutonic Order in 1519–1521 brought the Knights to their knees—literally. One of the most famous images in Polish history dates from 1525, the so-called Prussian Homage. A triumphant view of this grand event was painted in 1882 by the nineteenth-century Polish artist Jan Matejko, whose colorful brushstrokes lavishly rendered the scene of the former grand master of the Teutonic Knights, Albrecht von Hohenzollern, kneeling before the Polish king and publicly swearing his fealty.

Yet such a rosy view of the event—although attractive to Matejko's contemporaries, who took especial pleasure in seeing Prussians bowing down before the Poles, even if only in the deep historical past—was misleading. Much more could have been achieved than simply having Albrecht von Hohenzollern kneel before the Polish king (who was, after all, his uncle) and resign himself to the status of subordinate. What could have marked the end of Prussia as an independent entity—had Zygmunt pursued the fight further—instead gave little Prussia a new lease on life. Recall that part of Prussia had already been incorporated into the Crown by Zygmunt's father. This was the so-called Royal Prussia, which had sought to break away from the hold of the Teutonic Knights and turned to the Polish king for help.

What went wrong, then? Although it was a Polish fief, in this moment Prussia was permitted to undergo a notable change. No longer to be run by the Teutonic Knights, it was transformed by Albrecht von Hohenzollern-Ansbach (the aforementioned nephew of Zygmunt) into a secular state. Henceforth the last grand master of the Teutonic Order would be known as Duke of Prussia, and his successors would have hereditary rights in the lands formerly held by the Order.

Not only that: the Prussia of Albrecht von Hohenzollern simultaneously embraced the views promulgated by Martin Luther, who by nailing his ninety-five theses to the door of a church in Wittenberg in 1517 initiated a movement that would forever change the face of Christian Europe. This was the Protestant Reformation. Close to Martin Luther himself, Albrecht became—with Zygmunt's permission—the first territorial Lutheran ruler and Prussia became the first Protestant state in Europe.

That this should occur without bloodshed or upheaval was in part due to Zygmunt the Old's willingness to approve this amazing transformation of the former arch-Catholic polity—in part to keep Ducal Prussia from moving into the orbit of the Holy Roman Empire. To be sure, in the Treaty of Kraków of 1525—the first European treaty between a Catholic and a Protestant state—Zygmunt and Albrecht agreed that Ducal Prussia would come fully under Polish control on the extinction of Albrecht of Hohenzollern's line. That only a generation later a different king would, in a pinch, exchange his hereditary rights to succession for military assistance is but one of the fateful missteps that would haunt Polish history for centuries to come, even if it could not be foreseen in 1525.

The Wisdom of Stańczyk

That Zygmunt may not have been good at anticipating the potential consequences of his actions is suggested by an incident that followed some time after the Prussian Homage. A royal hunt organized by the king took place in the great forested area outside of Kraków known as Niepołomice. For this occasion an enormous bear was brought all the way from Lithuania in a large crate. Let out from the crate and baited by dogs, it began to charge in all directions, causing those gathered to scatter. In the process, the court jester Stańczyk fell from his horse—bruised perhaps, but not hurt. Later on the king joked with his jester, claiming that, in running away from the bear, Stańczyk had behaved like a fool, not like a knight. To that the jester replied, "The greater fool is the one who, having a bear in a crate, lets him out, to his own misfortune."

This tale—and the all too apt retort made by the wise jester, who well may have been referring to the Prussian bear—would perhaps have been more humorous, had the queen, also in attendance at the hunt, not fallen from her horse as well. This caused her—some five months pregnant—to give birth prematurely. The baby—a son—did not survive. He would have been yet another Jagiellon, able to carry on the dynasty should anything happen to his elder brother. Bona was to bear no more children after that accident.

"Poles Are Not Geese . . ."

This wry account of the hunting excursion comes down to us from Marcin Bielski, a chronicler who wrote not in Latin but in Polish. With the Renaissance and the increasing numbers of educated Poles came a demand for publications not only in Latin but also in the vernacular.

This was a period when the publishing industry was taking off in this part of Europe. Paper mills in Poland-Lithuania dated from the end of the fifteenth century, and the first printing press was set up in Kraków in 1474, by the Bavarian Kasper Straube. Naturally, Latin books were the first to come off the press, only later to be followed by Polish-language books. The first Polish-language book to be typeset (of course, much earlier there were manuscripts laboriously written out by hand), was the popular *Paradise of*

Souls, which appeared in 1513. It is interesting to note that a Cyrillic-alphabet book was printed in Kraków even prior to that, in 1491, and the first Hungarian-language book was printed in the same city, in 1533. The first Polish grammar book did not come out, however, until 1568.

The sixteenth century proved the Golden Age insofar as the development of writing in the vernacular was concerned. Behind the move to turn Polish into a fully developed literary language was Mikołaj Rey (1505–1569). His famous ditty proclaimed to the world (or certainly, at least, to the Polish-speaking world): *iż Polacy nie gęsi, iż swój język mają* (that Poles are not geese, that they have their own language). Rey himself had not received a strong classical education, which may explain why he opted to write exclusively in Polish. Still, he penned many works, especially polemical ones, with juicy anecdote and ribald humor.

Rey helped to pave the way for the preeminent poet of the Polish Renaissance, Jan Kochanowski (1530–1584). Unlike Rey, Kochanowski was well educated and more than just conversant in Latin, yet he switched to writing in Polish sometime around 1560, while serving as secretary to King Zygmunt August. Clearly well connected, Kochanowski wrote, among other things, a play for the wedding of Chancellor Jan Zamoyski in 1577. A pure Renaissance drama, *The Dismissal of the Greek Envoys* boasted a message of pacifism as well as the elegant Polish for which Kochanowski was to become known. He did a magnificent job of translating the biblical Psalms, published in 1579. But Kochanowski will forever be remembered as a loving and doting father—in particular of his daughter Ursula, who died at the tender age of two. Heartbroken, Kochanowski wrote a moving series of nineteen poems lamenting her death, aptly called *Laments* (Polish: Treny). Here is a translation of the fifth Lament:

As when an olive sapling under an orchard tall takes flight,
In the tracks of maternal love from the soil to an elder's height.
As yet, with neither leaf nor budding twig,
Just a sprouting slender sprig.
Then as the fruit grower weeds the nettle and thorn,
His haste causes the little sapling's shoot to be shorn.
In no time it fades, drained of its natural sap,
Collapsing dead at her sweet mother's lap.
To this fate befell Ursula, so dear,
Burgeoning before her parents' eyes, providing warm cheer.
Short time of the earth, Death's cruel enveloping bane,
Before her pensive parent tree, caused her life to wane.

Oh, evil Persephone! How could you consent
For so many tears to be so spent?*

Kochanowski's touching verses demonstrate that Poles of this age could truly be attached to their families and home life—such as the idyllic life the poet enjoyed at his rural estate in Czarnolas (Black Forest) with his wife and seven children.

The Polish Reformation

This interest in the vernacular was bolstered by yet another important movement of the sixteenth century, the Protestant Reformation. The prevalence of Roman Catholicism in today's Poland notwithstanding, Poland-Lithuania actually experienced a very noteworthy period in which traditional beliefs were questioned and—in numerous cases—jettisoned.

A number of developments facilitated the penetration of Reformation ideas into Poland-Lithuania. The Poles' perception of the Roman Catholic Church was becoming increasingly negative. Although other nations might have decried various aspects of the church (as demonstrated by the outcry over the sale of indulgences and the like), Poles perhaps had more reason than most to complain. The Roman Catholic Church had consistently taken the side of the Teutonic Knights, the great foe of the Poles and Lithuanians, and also persecuted Poland's neighbors, the Hussites of Bohemia.

Poles also decried the sometimes ostentatious wealth and privilege of the church hierarchy. For example, the see of Gniezno owned 292 villages and 13 cities, while the Kraków episcopate owned over 225 villages and 11 cities. The Vilnius archbishopric was so well endowed that, when it was established, it immediately became the largest landowner in the Grand Duchy. The great clergymen of Poland-Lithuania, in other words, were wealthier than the wealthiest of nobles—practically competing with the monarch. Given this situation, doubtless many a noble was galled by the fact that, for a spell in the sixteenth century, two of the above-mentioned offices were held by one individual, Piotr Gamrat, simultaneously bishop of Kraków and archbishop of Gniezno.

That this same clergyman was known for his extravagance (his own court amounted to some 180 individuals) and debauchery clearly did not help matters, although Gamrat was also a patron of the arts and education. Nonetheless,

---

* Translation by Barry Keane. Original found at http://info-poland.buffalo.edu/web/arts_culture/ literature/poetry/Koc/wv/link.shtml, last accessed June 8, 2012.

Poles of this period were often taken aback by the corruption of the clergy and their lack of religious commitment. Consider the statement attributed to one highly ranked clergyman that he did not care if the people believed in goats, as long as they paid the tithe . . . Perhaps, indeed, the time was ripe for change.

Poles naturally were already familiar with the unorthodox ideas of their former neighbor, the Bohemian Jan Hus, who had burned at the stake as a heretic a century earlier (in 1415). No less were they to be exposed to new ideas emanating from the west, from Germany and beyond, especially given the flow of people as well as ideas. Some of the ideas advanced by the Protestant Reformation attracted more than passing interest.

This does not mean that they embraced all denominations of Protestantism equally. Social status seemed to influence the choice made by any given citizen. While Lutheranism advanced where there were Germans in Poland-Lithuania (such as the burghers dominant along the seacoast or in a number of cities), most nobles interested in the new ideas eventually opted not for Lutheranism but, rather, for Calvinism. Perhaps it was the doctrine of the "elect," those chosen by God to be both spiritual and temporal leaders, that appealed to the nobility. The idea of the laity having some control over the church was also a draw, as was the fact that Protestant nobles would not have to pay the tithe. The nobles of Poland-Lithuania were Calvinists more out of pragmatism than out of dogmatic conviction. They were motivated more by anticlericalism and a wish to reduce the influence of the church hierarchy on their lives. Yet even some church hierarchs were taken with the new doctrines: the head of the Roman Catholic Church in the Ruthenian lands, Bishop Mikołaj Pac, abandoned his flock to convert to Calvinism.

The geography of Protestantism in Poland-Lithuania is also instructive. While in Poland proper the lesser nobility were more attracted to the new denominations (perhaps in the face of dominance by Catholic magnates), in the Grand Duchy it seemed that Protestantism spoke loudest to the highest and mightiest. The Lithuanian magnates—a tiny but influential group—seemed particularly attracted to these new ideas; of the Grand Duchy's twenty-two senators in 1572, a full sixteen (that is, nearly three-quarters) were Protestant.

The Reformation was a time of endless possibility—a period when the Polish-Lithuanian nobility was amenable to trying out new things. As a contemporary wrote in 1564, "We are as ready to pick up a new faith as a new dress."*

Yet Protestantism in Poland-Lithuania was not a slavish following of fashion. Poles also developed their own, even more radical, religious movement,

---

* Cited in Janusz Tazbir, *A State without Stakes: Polish Religious Toleration in the Sixteenth and Seventeenth Centuries*, trans. A. T. Jordan ([New York]: Kościuszko Foundation, 1972), 27.

called the Polish Brethren. The Polish Brethren went under various names. They were often referred to as Arians; and, as they denied the existence of the Holy Trinity, they were also known as Antitrinitarians. The Arians were unique in their nonviolence (some of them wore wooden swords) as well as in their calling for a return to the old ways of the church, with equality for all its members. While they had a relatively small following, in Raków they ran a famous academy.

This efflorescence of Protestant ideas within Poland-Lithuania did not make for unity among the so-called Dissenters (non-Catholics). Members of various Protestant denominations could not agree even to be tolerant of each other entirely. For example, the major denominations labeled the Antitrinitarians as heretics, finding their views beyond the pale.

Toleration of Difference

At the same time, however, something in Poland-Lithuania set the country apart from many other lands at this time, and this was its religious toleration. Here we must agree with the historian Janusz Tazbir, who wrote of a "state without stakes." The country simply tolerated religious diversity to a degree that was unheard of elsewhere. This was due in part to the experience of life in Poland-Lithuania. As one contemporary acknowledged in 1592, "There is nothing new about diversity of religion in Poland. Aside from the [Orthodox], which is Christian, pagans and Jews were known for a long time and faiths other than Roman Catholic have existed for centuries."[*]

The religious toleration in Poland-Lithuania led many foreign Dissenters (as non-Catholics were called) to flood into Poland, once other countries started to persecute them. German Anabaptists, Dutch Mennonites, Bohemian Brethren (a distinct Protestant sect that arose in the Czech lands), all came and settled down, some such as the last, in their seat in Leszno, founding schools and publishing books—and not only their own. Antitrinitarians escaped to save their lives from the Palatinate (in the Holy Roman Empire) and elsewhere. Yet other Protestants abandoned their French, Scottish, and Irish homelands for this distant country. Jews fleeing the Inquisition in Spain, as well as those coming from the German and Bohemian lands, found a haven here in this part of East-Central Europe. The Polish Reformation movement was strengthened by the presence of Italian intellectuals such as Faustus Socinius (Italian: Fausto Paolo Sozzini) of Siena, whose writings provided the theoretical underpinnings for the Polish Brethren.

---

[*]   Cited in ibid.

In the same period, foreign Catholics made their way to Poland-Lithuania's hospitable shores, coming from countries such as Sweden and England where the doctrine of *cuius regio, eius religio* ("Whose realm, his religion," meaning that the religion of the ruler dictated the religion of the ruled) worked against them. Indeed, Polish and Lithuanian noblemen saw the religious wars abroad as a way to attract skilled labor and artisans to their own villages and towns. While some new immigrants established agricultural settlements, many artisans and traders became part of the urban fabric, some even making their fortunes and/or entering the king's service, all thankful for the asylum offered to them. Although this high level of toleration would ebb with time, it did survive well into the seventeenth century and was noteworthy in creating the sense, for many of the immigrants, that the Polish-Lithuanian lands were truly a haven.

While these newcomers tended to become part of the lower and middle classes, the spread of Protestantism among the nobles resulted in a degree of religious toleration not found elsewhere in sixteenth-century Europe. Religious differences notwithstanding, there was one thing on which all nobles in Poland-Lithuania agreed: each nobleman—whether Calvinist, Lutheran, or Antitrinitarian—must be treated on par with the Catholic nobles. Thus, while they might disagree on matters of doctrine, they would not disagree on matters of estate rights and freedoms, including the freedom of religion. This toleration among the nobility was reflected in the not infrequent incidence of intermarriage. To cite one notable example: while Chancellor Jan Zamoyski early on made the transition from Calvinism to Catholicism, two of his four wives (a Radziwiłł and a Báthori) were Calvinists.

This level of toleration ultimately led to a situation where, after the death of Zygmunt the Old, the number of Protestants in the Seym was unusually high. At the height of the Reformation in Poland-Lithuania, a majority of members of the Seym were Dissenters—perhaps no surprise, as such individuals tended to be particularly well educated, activist types. Things were so skewed that, in 1564, reportedly only two noblemen followed the king to church to attend mass for the opening of the Seym. And indeed, despite the Polish kings' endorsement of Roman Catholicism, during the rule of the last of the Jagiellons, one-quarter of all nobles were Protestants.

The regional distribution of Protestantism in Poland-Lithuania was nonetheless uneven. Half of the nobles in Lesser Poland, a full two-thirds in parts of Greater Poland, and 15–20 percent in Lithuania embraced Protestantism, with (once again) most of these Protestants being among the more influential and the wealthier nobles. By contrast, Protestantism held little appeal in Mazovia, a land inhabited by a particularly dense collection of poorer nobles, who eked out a living on small plots.

Perhaps we should be more amazed at these numbers, given the fact that, under Zygmunt the Old, legislation was introduced that could lead to the persecution of heretics. But the king took a more tolerant stance, even if he remained a staunch Catholic himself. And this was true also for his son Zygmunt August, the last Jagiellonian king of Poland-Lithuania—indeed, the last king of the old Poland-Lithuania, to whose reign we now turn.

CHAPTER 4

Crafting a Center

The Commonwealth of Both Nations

The Golden Age of Poland-Lithuania reached its apogee under the rule of the last of the Jagiellons. The reign of Zygmunt II August would bring a remarkable transformation to the country. The system of government that had evolved under Piast and Jagiellon rule would be changed in new and creative ways, leading to a phenomenon that can only be described as sui generis. Designed to thwart yet another succession crisis, this creative resolution would set the polity apart from the rest of sixteenth-century Europe, lending it an air that in many ways seems surprisingly modern.

The Last Jagiellon

Zygmunt II August's regnal years are generally listed as 1548–1572. Yet, while correct in essence, they were actually different in fact. The young prince was crowned king in 1530, in the twenty-fourth regnal year of his father, who was still very much alive. Little Zygmunt was a mere ten years old at the time. (Henceforth Zygmunt I—who had been the one of the younger sons of Kazimierz IV Jagiellończyk—somewhat paradoxically became known as Zygmunt the Old.) The only example in Polish history of a king being crowned during the life of his predecessor, this unusual situation was attributed to the scheming of Zygmunt August's mother, Bona Sforza—something that did not sit well with many nobles, who resented what they saw as her interference in the politics of Poland-Lithuania. For the Seym was not asked to give its consent. The situation even led to something called the Hen War—on account of all the poultry eaten by the belligerents. Not a real war, this military mobilization of the nobility against royal abuse of power, led by nobles affiliated with the Execution of the Laws movement, was ultimately resolved through negotiations and a renewed commitment of Zygmunt the Old to the privileges of this Polish parliament. Still, this election *vivente rege* was a precedent that the Poles were loath to see repeated.

Thus, thanks to his Italian mother, Zygmunt August grew up knowing not only that he would become king, but that he, in fact, already was king. (Not that it was likely that the great-grandson of Jagiełło would not have been chosen to rule the country after the death of his father; there clearly had been much precedent set since Jagiełło ascended to the throne.) Zygmunt August took a keen interest in preserving the prerogatives of power that came with his being hereditary ruler of Lithuania, and thus he preferred to retain the distinctiveness of the two halves of the country. All the more paradoxical, thus, was the fact that during his reign agreement was reached between the monarch and those behind the Execution of the Laws movement, which led the last of the Jagiellons ultimately to opt for a greater, more permanent union between Poland and Lithuania.

Yet clearly all this was not in the mind of a boy-king aged ten, especially given his somewhat unusual education. He was brought up by his strong-willed Italian mother rather than by his phlegmatic Lithuanian father. This arrangement resulted in the young future ruler of Poland-Lithuania being kept distant from important affairs of state and much closer to affairs of the heart—to life in court, with all its carnal distractions. And, to be sure, Zygmunt August was Bona's son. He was raised to be fluent in Italian and Polish, if not in Ruthenian (as his father was) nor in Lithuanian (a language that even his father likely did not know). And indeed: hot Italian blood coursed through the brooding young Zygmunt's veins.

Yet young Zygmunt was not lucky in love. Rather, there was much tragedy in his personal life—in his conjugal life in particular. Zygmunt had a total of three wives. Two came from the power to the west, the Holy Roman Empire. He married the first, Elizabeth of Habsburg, in 1543, but she died a mere two years later—perhaps by poisoning (it was rumored), as her death came not long after her rich dowry was paid. (Zygmunt August ultimately gave back some of the dowry.)

Not yet king in his own right, Zygmunt August spent a good deal of time far from the capital, Kraków. He had been sent to Lithuania, where he served as his father's representative. There Zygmunt fraternized with the Lithuanian magnates, the richest and most influential nobles. Key here was the powerful Radziwiłł family (Lithuanian: Radvila). The Radziwiłłs first appeared in this narrative as one of the Lithuanian families to benefit from the Union of Horodło of 1413. Since that time, the family had risen to great prominence, profiting from the export of grain—among other things. Indeed, pocketing the proceeds from over twelve thousand peasant farms, the Radziwiłł family was among the wealthiest of noble families. Members of the Radziwiłł family also belonged to the elite council of lords, which originally was a rather unstructured vehicle for holders of high office in Lithuania as well as the magnates, yet one that importantly allowed them to exert influence on the grand duke. This was not a body that relished the idea of becoming subordinated in any way to Polish influences.

In a way, the Lithuanian magnates were fighting an uphill battle. Polonization—in the cultural, if not always the political sense—was proceeding apace within Poland-Lithuania. This was seen most notably in the grand ducal family itself. The last Jagiellon to speak Lithuanian was likely Kazimierz Jagiellończyk—only a generation removed from the dynastic protoplast, Jagiełło. Nor was the Lithuanian language gaining any ground within the Grand Duchy proper, which was populated more heavily by East Slavs than by ethnic Lithuanians, most of whom occupied the small northern region we know as Lithuania today. (Recall that the lands of the Grand Duchy of Lithuania comprised not only this core ethnic Lithuanian territory but vast swaths of what earlier had been part of Kyivan Rus'—lands that today comprise Belarus and Ukraine and parts of Russia.)

This strong presence of Ruthenes was reflected in the very choice of official language for the Grand Duchy. Indeed, the so-called Lithuanian statute of 1529 (a compilation of laws) was written not in Lithuanian but in a language often referred to as Chancery Slavonic or Old Belarusian. (This language would be the official language of state in the Grand Duchy until 1697, by which time Polish had overtaken this East Slavic tongue to become the unquestioned lingua franca of the nobility.) The East Slavic element within the Grand Duchy of Lithuania, thus, was not only palpable but—one might say—dominant, at least numerically. This reality is further underscored by the fact that even many ethnic Lithuanians came to understand this East Slavic tongue or Polish (or perhaps both).

This is not to say that the Lithuanian half of Poland-Lithuania did not remain in many ways distinct. Whereas Poland (as we have seen) was pulled in various directions (west, south, east), the Grand Duchy fit even more squarely between west and east. In some ways it was more like Poland, in others more like its neighbor to the east, Muscovy. Take, for example, the above-mentioned Lithuanian statute. The statute—revised in 1566 and 1588—was a compilation of legal codes for the Grand Duchy, a systematization of the laws and rights that were in effect, but which, according to the Grand Duchy's boyars (the rank-and-file nobles), were not always observed. Their compilation, in a way, was a "Western" development—one akin to a similar process that had taken place in the Crown of Poland under Kazimierz the Great. In some ways, the statute of 1529 put the Lithuanians ahead of the Poles in the Crown, who were still relying upon the so-called Łaski statutes from the first years of the century. The very vocal Execution of the Laws movement had been lobbying Zygmunt the Old for a true compilation of laws and rights that would weed out irrelevant outdated parts, and this was still quite an issue in the Crown during the 1530s.

Despite this development, Lithuania still seemed more "Eastern" than "Western." In this as in other ways, the Grand Duchy was shaped by the legacy of Kyivan Rus', that is, by the Orthodox population of the lands that Lithuania had come to control earlier. The Lithuanian statute, please note, was written in Chancery Ruthenian. The grand dukes had inherited a stratified society, with a clear hierarchy at the top. This is seen in the persistence of Gediminids, of the Ruthenian princes and the rank-and-file boyars. It is also reflected in the tiny percentage of truly influential individuals gathered in the council of lords. Their power and wealth was way out of proportion with that of the rest of society.

It was to this unique, diverse, hybrid land that Zygmunt August was sent in 1544. Lithuania clearly held attractions for the young grand duke. Amazingly enough, despite the wonders of the Renaissance—architectural, cultural, intellectual—in the capital of Kraków, Zygmunt came to dislike the city intensely and contrived to spend as little time there as possible, even once he became king. Likely this had something to do with reactions to his Lithuanian adventure. While in Vilnius, the young grand duke fell in love with the lovely Barbara Radziwiłł, the daughter of Jerzy Radziwiłł, grand hetman of Lithuania, and widow of the phenomenally wealthy Stanisław Gasztołd (Lithuanian: Gostautas). Zygmunt August was so enamored of the beautiful Barbara that he even had a gallery built to connect his Vilnius palace to that of the Radziwiłłs. Clearly he could not get enough of her—or simply wanted to keep their trysts secret.

Barbara and Zygmunt August were secretly married in 1547, much to the chagrin of his mother, who entertained hopes of a royal marriage for her son. (Blue blood, not money, was clearly Bona's object, as the noble Barbara had inherited great wealth upon the death of her husband.) Nor did much of the Polish-Lithuanian nobility take kindly to the marriage of the future king and grand duke to one of its own—that is, with the exception of the Radziwiłłs themselves. The latter thought they could benefit from the situation, according to some accounts even tricking Zygmunt August into marrying Barbara. After all, the Jagiellons—like the Piasts before them—were not against dalliances with people beneath their station; the grand duke and soon-to-be king in his own right could have held out to marry royalty. Several years passed before Barbara Radziwiłł was crowned queen. She did not live much longer. Barbara died in 1553—according to legend, she was poisoned by Zygmunt August's own mother.

Regardless whether there is any truth to the poisoning, the two hot-blooded Italians—mother and son—subsequently became estranged. Bona departed for Italy in 1556, taking much in the way of money and precious jewels with her—items that were never recovered. Although her son was supposed to inherit her Neapolitan landholdings as well as these items, when Bona was on her deathbed, her will was mysteriously changed in favor of Philip II of Spain, thus benefiting the Habsburgs and not the Jagiellons. When today Poles speak of Neapolitan sums, the reference is to money frustratingly beyond one's reach.

Nor was that the end of Zygmunt August's personal misfortune—although it should be noted that he was an extremely wealthy monarch. The papal nuncio Ruggieri estimated the king's wealth to be a million ducats, a sum that could have bought him a nice kingdom in the West. He detested his third wife, Katharina of Habsburg, and kept his distance from her. The king preferred to spend time hunting in the virgin forests of the Białystok region, his court based at his favorite palace of Knyszyn. There he also had a royal stud with thousands of horses, including the Arabians for which Poland would become famous. The king's estrangement from his wife did nothing for his chances at fathering a son and heir—one of the key responsibilities of any dynast. To the consternation of his subjects, Zygmunt bedded numerous mistresses while still married to Katharina but had no luck in producing an heir with them, either. After Katharina died in February 1572, the king resolved to marry one of his mistresses. Yet nothing came of that: before six months passed, this last of the Jagiellons was dead.

Polish Peculiarities: The Creative Synthesis

The king may have died unexpectedly but, already earlier, he knew that the chances of his dying without legitimate male issue were great. And with this knowledge, in his last years, Zygmunt August changed his tack on the matter of Lithuanian separatism. Someone had to provide for the country as a whole after the death of the childless king, and Zygmunt August took it upon himself to ensure that his death would not result in utter chaos or the severing of bonds between the two halves of Poland-Lithuania, which had been united, in the person of the monarch, for nearly two centuries. The resulting, more permanent union (to which we will turn in a moment) was the crowning achievement of Zygmunt August's reign.

It likewise represented a development found nowhere else in Europe—this despite its European lineage. A creative synthesis of ideas, the new arrangement built on traditional Polish parliamentary politics, enriched by elements that came courtesy of the Renaissance and Reformation.

The Renaissance had opened the eyes of the educated public to the classical world, the ancient heritage left to the world by the Greeks and Romans. In Poland-Lithuania, this classical heritage figured as much more than window-dressing. Not limited to artistic or literary realms, it informed the political worldview of the country's inhabitants. In fact, one might venture to say that educated Poles embraced classical literature (as seen through the tremendous development of Latin poetry) and politics above all, in many instances leaving the artistic trappings—for example, architectural design—to foreigners, including all the immigrants escaping persecution elsewhere.

The Renaissance influence on politics is seen in the potent political ideas developed by Wawrzyniec Goślicki in his *De optimo senatore libri duo* (On the perfect senator, two books) of 1568. Goślicki was an alumnus of the Kraków Academy who, like so many other Poles of the period, continued his education in Western Europe (Padua, Bologna, Rome), where he published the work. It is of the same genre as Macchiavelli's famous *Prince*, which provided both theoretical and practical advice for said prince, Cosimo de' Medici. By contrast, Goślicki addresses the ideal senator and sets out his concrete vision of a proper state, as well as the place in it for said senator. Although the ideal state in this work was in some ways similar to ancient models, Goślicki presents concrete examples from his homeland, the Kingdom of Poland.

So what did this ideal state, the Kingdom of Poland, look like according to Goślicki? Within the tripartite power structure of the kingdom, comprised of the monarch, a senate, and a parliament, all pieces were shown to be interlocked, with no one force dominating the other. Indeed, Goślicki maintained that the source of all power resided in society, not in the monarch. The monarch was not permitted unbridled power—far from it. The king was obliged to adhere to the laws established in parliamentary fashion as well as to heed the advice of the senate. He was to be held accountable to his subjects, responsible for their welfare. To ensure that tyranny did not develop, it was the job of the senate, a small group of wise citizens dedicated to the common weal, to mediate between the virtuous citizenry (the nobles) and the king. Goślicki's titular senator was to play a key role in this system of checks and balances: the king's inclination to tyranny would be checked, while the citizenry's inclination to anarchy would also be held at bay.

While today Goślicki's ideas hardly raise eyebrows, this was not at all the case in sixteenth-century Europe. The reaction in the land of the Tudors and the Stuarts is particularly noteworthy. There *De optimo senatore* was perceived to be so incendiary that each time the book was translated into English during Goślicki's lifetime (and this happened twice, in 1598 and 1607), the print run was confiscated.

Compare this to his reception in Poland-Lithuania. When he returned from abroad not long after the book first came out, the author was appointed secretary to King Zygmunt August. Clearly what was incendiary abroad was merely "the way things worked" (or, ideally, were to work) back home. Such attitudes outside of Central and Eastern Europe would change with time, of course. American readers may be interested to note that Goślicki's ideas were not unfamiliar to the Founding Fathers.

That Poland-Lithuania was able to rein in the natural inclination of monarchs to seek absolute power was partly the result of the country's unique political heritage and traditions and partly the result of a unique period of efflorescence, one reflected not only in the degree to which Renaissance ideas penetrated the polity but also in the economic well-being that accompanied the Golden Age.

The Golden Age: An Age of Enrichment

This Golden Age was no misnomer. Not that Polish miners had suddenly discovered a rich vein of gold. The market for gold and silver bullion was dominated by Spain, whose recent penetration of the New World had uncovered vast new supplies of these precious ores. Poland-Lithuania turned out to have ample reserves of a resource that was in great demand elsewhere in the world: grain.

The particular world conjuncture of the late fifteenth century suddenly upped the ante for the grain trade. The Black Death of the mid-fourteenth century (which, incidentally, never made its way to Poland) had a significant effect on the economy of the countries in Western Europe, which upon rebounding shifted from agricultural production to animal husbandry. The population increase in the growing cities of the West, combined with the conscious decision to raise sheep for wool instead of planting seeds for grain meant that food was at a premium—a situation reflected in the so-called price revolution, which suddenly made it exceedingly profitable to engage in the export of staple foods.

It so happened that Poland-Lithuania was perfectly poised to take advantage of this situation. Not only did these lands have ample fields of grain. They now could profit in full from exporting their grain surplus via the Baltic. How? Because Poland-Lithuania now had an outlet to the sea. In earlier centuries, the Teutonic Knights had dominated the Baltic Sea coast and, with it, all sea-bound trade. This changed in the mid-fifteenth century when the population of Royal Prussia—including cities such as Gdańsk and Elbląg—opted for Polish rule. One long (thirteen-year) war and peace treaty later, Royal Prussia became part of Poland-Lithuania. After the mid-fifteenth century, the Teutonic Knights had to content themselves with the less fertile and less developed lands to the east; and even those lands, known after 1525 as Ducal Prussia, became a fief of the Crown of Poland.

In exchange for their allegiance, the inhabitants of Royal Prussia were given several important political and economic privileges. These included the right to their own regional parliament (the Prussian estates), municipal self-government for the cities, the right to trade everywhere in the vast country, and exemption from any additional tolls on the Vistula. The region's incorporation into Poland-Lithuania, thus, had the potential to bring much benefit to the state. Gdańsk merchants could contract for Polish grain, and those supplying the grain had recourse to the growing world market for their staples, the easiest commodity for a large lowland country to produce.

The result was that in the sixteenth century Poland became the main supplier of grain to Europe. Each fall, tons of golden grain—oats and rye, wheat and barley—were shipped to markets far and wide. Whereas in the year 1490, around twenty thousand tons of rye were exported, for example, nearly a century later (in 1587), the figure had risen to around seventy-one thousand tons.

Some of the grain went to destinations within the Baltic region—to places such as Lübeck or Copenhagen, Stockholm or Riga. The other (larger) half sailed through the sound. Some of the grain ended up not only in Amsterdam but also in places such as Setubal or Faro in Portugal, or even all the way to the Mediterranean.

Among the greatest consumers of Polish grain were the Dutch. Those mighty world traders hailing from a tiny waterlogged flatland could no longer feed themselves. Gdańsk itself was responsible for half of Amsterdam's Baltic trade. But the Dutch were hardly the only foreigners present in the port Gdańsk. Germans, Frenchmen, Flemings, Englishmen, Spaniards,

Portuguese, all traveled to this Baltic entrepôt in search of what Poland-Lithuania could supply. They found a sea of warehouses bursting with rye, wheat, and other grains as well as fibers (flax and hemp), forest goods (wax, honey, potash, lumber), even salted beef.

All this earned the Gdańsk merchants and their Polish suppliers a pretty penny. In the early years of this increased Baltic trade, a foreigner noted what he observed during the annual two-week long fair in Gdańsk, which began on Saint Dominic's feast day (August 4). He saw over 400 ships arrive in the port. Yet their holds, albeit awaiting the harvest of grain, were hardly empty. They had brought to the shores of Poland-Lithuania all manner of luxury items: French wines; Spanish olive oil, lemons, preserves, and fruits; silks and other fine cloths; Portuguese spices; English cloth and tin. Reportedly the first eight days of the fair were spent loading the boats of the foreigners with Polish-Lithuanian wares, the next eight with selling luxury items (some clearly of global provenance) to the Poles. Business was booming. By mid-century, the historian Marcin Kromer was reproaching his compatriots in the Kingdom of Poland for being obsessed with luxury and splendor, and for adorning themselves in foreign fabrics and exotic leathers, in silks and purples, silver, gold, pearls, and gemstones.

The Grain Trade's Impact on the Social Structure

Here we need to consider the social and economic conditions in Poland-Lithuania that led to this accumulation of wealth. Who benefited so richly from the grain trade?

For the most part, these were the nobles—the nobles of Poland-Lithuania. In part this was the result, during this period of relative peace, of a trans-formation of the military caste of *szlachta* (nobility) into an increasingly powerful caste of landowners. Formerly accustomed to the military way of life, in the fourteenth and especially the fifteenth century the nobles became increasingly accustomed to a settled life on their estates. And these estates over the same period—certainly for the wealthier nobles in the core Polish lands, further removed from the front lines of the country's vast frontiers—began to look less like fortresses and more like Renaissance palaces.

Yet even lesser nobles paid more attention to landed endeavors, above all agriculture and animal husbandry. This period witnessed a revolution in education that percolated through the nobility into the other estates. Renaissance men such as Mikołaj Rey sought ways to make the best of their (often limited) landholdings. With rational management, someone like Rey could go from owning a mere two villages to owning seventeen villages and a town, increasing not only his agricultural output but also adding further to the national economy and his own revenues by establishing breweries or digging fishponds.

While Rey himself might be held up as an example of the Protestant ethic, it is clear that the nobility across the board, regardless of religion (and these were numerous in the Golden Age), increasingly became convinced that it was destined to feed the West. The grain trade proved the only trade that nobles saw fit to engage in, trading generally being seen as beneath their status. In this, incidentally, they patterned themselves after the ancient Greeks, who saw paid employment as getting in the way of a man's objective view of the world—a view that was necessary for those whose job it was to govern the state. This view was reinforced by legal limitations placed on noble engagement in trade mid-century—limitations that, incidentally, reflected the desire of the country's merchants to keep the nobles from seizing control over the rest of the country's trade. Not that this worked to the detriment of the noble estate: nobles would hold a monopoly in providing grain for the foreign export market.

The benefits of the country's competitive advantage were not limited to the nobility. Numerous players figured in the grain trade. Merchants traveled about the country to negotiate with the various noble producers, securing the golden grain for export. Yet all those oats and rye had to reach the Baltic Sea coast. Generally it was the responsibility of the producer to ensure the delivery to Gdańsk. Here, river transport was crucial. And here Poles had a distinct advantage: the main tributaries of the Vistula were all navigable, meaning that their goods could be shipped this way—the most efficient way during this period. This extensive river system, thus, became the economic life-blood of the country.

The very means of shipment provided income to more individuals. Many nobles entrusted their precious cargo to members of a specialized guild of master boatmen, skippers, or to freighters. They in turn transported the grain downstream to Gdańsk on massive shallow rafts, each equipped with a silo atop as well as a lean-to for the crew of raftsmen. Many flotillas included the freight of more than one nobleman, which was cost-effective.

While the wealthiest noble doubtless had his subordinates make these arrangements, lesser nobles often took a hands-on approach to the grain trade. The seventeenth-century noble memoirist Jan Chrysostom Pasek wrote of his first experience sailing in this fashion downriver to Gdańsk. The trip to this Mecca of consumption, this veritable Babel (certainly during the main trading season), was an education in itself. The negotiations over price proved the bane of more than one noble. In his diary, Pasek himself boasted of his good fortune: on his very first trip to Gdańsk, he managed to get a higher price for his grain than did some more seasoned shippers, who had warned him that he would get fleeced.

From the nobleman's colorful memoirs, one gets the sense that such trips to Gdańsk were a lark. Indeed, even for a noble of middling means like Pasek, these expeditions were viewed as an adventure, not a risky business. How so? This was the result of the unique conditions of Polish agriculture. The noble manor economy was essentially autarkic: between his fields, villages, and towns, the nobleman had everything he needed for his daily consumption. He did not need to earn money to get along. Any money he was able to earn in the grain trade was icing on the cake—it was all profit.

This explains why the Polish-Lithuanian nobility had no qualms about earmarking these earnings for luxury consumption. Even if the Gdańsk merchants got the better of him, a noble like Pasek would still be flush with cash, still hear coins jingling in his pocket—coins that could be spent on anything his heart desired. The only thing at this time that limited his export capability was crop yields, a variable more dependent on the weather (for grain yields were higher than in the German lands, if still not at the level of Britain, France, or the Netherlands). Changes in price simply did not factor in the way they would have elsewhere. It is easy to see how initial competitive advantage might, with time, be recast as destiny.

Paying the Price: Peasants

Yet the Polish noble's seemingly carefree life came at the expense of another segment of society: the peasants. Costs were low because the labor was provided free of charge, a result of a new development. This was related to the land/labor equation. Poland-Lithuania was a vast country, still lightly populated by Western European standards. In 1500, the population was 7.5 million, whereas the smaller France boasted twice that many inhabitants. In the Polish-Lithuanian case, the population density was only 6.6 persons per square kilometer, although regions varied widely: the central Polish lands were slightly more densely settled than the corresponding Lithuanian territory, while the Belarusian and Ukrainian lands were much less populous.

Once the export of grain started proving so lucrative, there was more incentive to increase production. Given the abundance of arable land and scarcity of labor, nobles had incentive to keep their peasants on the land— that is, to tie them to the land and make them work their lord's land. Decreasing mobility and increasing labor obligations marked the beginnings of the enserfment of the peasants of Poland-Lithuania.

Serfdom began to make its way through the Polish-Lithuanian economy (as well as other lands east of the Elbe) at the end of the fifteenth century. It was the first experience of serfdom in this region—even though it is sometimes (confusingly) referred to as the "second serfdom." The "first serfdom" was that found in the West in medieval times.

This qualification notwithstanding, serfdom (whether primary or secondary) was a phenomenon that had tremendous ramifications for the rural population—and one must remember that peasants comprised some 60 percent of the population circa 1569. It marked a change in relations between noble and peasant, rendering the latter much more dependent on the goodwill of the former. The peasant increasingly was obliged to render labor—forced unpaid labor dues, known as the corvée—to his lord. He had limited (if any) recourse to due process should the latter be unreasonable in his demands.

Serfdom was a pillar of the manor economy. The manorial estate physically transformed the vast part of the country that was rural. Peasant cottages were clustered near the great manor house and barns. The path to the manor house—the central feature of the manorial estate—was often lined with a long row of trees. This rendered what could be relatively simple wooden dwellings more imposing. (Only the wealthiest nobles built their manors—or, rather, palaces—of brick.) Properties were acquired in various fashions: by inheritance, by marriage, by purchase, by leasing, which meant that a wealthy noble could have a constellation of properties throughout the country. The manorial estate was a place of culture as well as coercion; it was the court of the noble as well as his source of income.

Mediating between Two Worlds: The Jewish Contribution

Being a coercive system, serfdom relied upon supervision. Peasants had to be watched in the fields and told what had to be done on the lord's land. While a lesser noble might well watch over his own serfs, those more well-off hired someone else to do the job. In many instances, this job was entrusted to Jews.

The Jews of Poland-Lithuania were an estate unto themselves, with their own charters and privileges. They had traditionally figured in a limited range of professions, primarily in commerce and the economy: they were traders, innkeepers, toll collectors, moneylenders; with time, they would also figure in other capacities, including freighters involved in the river trade. The persecution of Jews elsewhere in Europe had led many to immigrate to Poland-Lithuania. As a result, the Jewish population surged from about 30,000 in 1500 to 150,000 in 1576 (about 2 percent of the country's total population). Their presence in Poland-Lithuania was remarked upon by many a foreigner, such as the Venetian envoy Pietro Duodo, who summed up their position within the country in a very stereotypical fashion:

> There are many Calvinists and Lutherans, but most numerous are the Jews; because the nobility is ashamed of trade, the peasants are too backward and oppressed, and the burghers too lazy, the entire Polish trade is in Jewish hands. The aristocrats treat them with respect, because they have profits from them, the government treats them so, because when in need, it can extract great sums from them.*

The Jews' traditional residence in urban environments and facility with accounting made them prime candidates for the job of *faktor*—enough so that Faktor would later become a typically Jewish surname. The faktor was the lord's right hand in a given locale, the plenipotentiary. He was a middleman of a different kind. Instead of facilitating trade, he was employed by the nobleman to facilitate dealings with the peasants. Thousands of Jews thus came into noble employ. In a way, the faktor often became the face of serfdom to the peasant, who saw him on a much more regular basis than he saw the lord—and thus might conceivably hold a grudge against him.

It is worth noting that the peasants of this age did not put up any protest—no revolts, as were seen in countries elsewhere in Europe. Despite the changes that took place in the village, their situation was not all bad. In the fifteenth century, yeoman peasants—those who had enough land and animals to produce their own surplus—were still in the majority. Labor services owed the lord were on the order of one or two days a week, leaving ample time for a given peasant family to tend to its own fields and plot—and perhaps sell some surplus in the nearby town. There were free peasants as well—millers, innkeepers, and the like—as well as peasants who had been settled on so-called Dutch law (that is, they owed rent instead of labor).

In the Lithuanian lands, the sixteenth century witnessed a noteworthy rationalization in agriculture. This was initiated by Queen Bona, who had the royal lands resurveyed. Once they were more rationally subdivided, the plots could be worked more productively. Perceiving the advantages that would ac-

---

*   Pietro Duodo, quoted in Eva Hoffman, *Shtetl: The Life and Death of a Small Town and the World of Polish Jews* (Boston: Houghton Mifflin, 1997), 49.

crue with such a move, the magnates of Lithuania soon followed suit. All this led to improved village organization and increased economic output. Those peasants who did not like their lord may have had little recourse legally, but they could vote—with their feet. There was always another clearing, or at least another lord (kinder, gentler, perhaps) down the road. Still, thanks to the Baltic trade, one could say that all boats appeared to be rising.

Urban Renewal

Then there was the option of moving to the towns, although the relatively easier upward mobility of the earlier period was increasingly complicated by the tendency (from the end of the fifteenth century) to reinforce distinctions between the social estates, not break down barriers between them. Cities—rising in this period—must have been huge draws. In the sixteenth century, there were hundreds of chartered towns, if the vast majority were on the small side: somewhere between five hundred and two thousand inhabitants, with a blend of urban and rural features. Still, there were larger centers: regional hubs such as Lublin and Lviv, Poznań and Toruń. The population of some of the Baltic towns amounted to some twelve to twenty thousand inhabitants.

Despite signs of relative prosperity in these urban centers, none of them could hold a candle to Gdańsk. Poland-Lithuania's economic capital was in a league of its own. Gdańsk boasted some fifty thousand inhabitants—over twice as many as the second-biggest city, the Polish capital of Kraków. Although full of merchants, Gdańsk also was rich in artisans, who provided luxury goods for broader consumption within Poland-Lithuania. The urban patriciate was led by councilors who served lucrative life terms. The city was known for its independent streak—it did not always like the policy established by the monarch. Yet, buttressed by their rights and privileges, the inhabitants of Gdańsk and the rest of Royal Prussia were loyal citizens of the country. That a region dominated by German Protestants could identify with the mainly Catholic, heavily Slavic population of Poland-Lithuania suggests that the Jagiellonian state had a strength of attraction that has long been underestimated by those unfamiliar with its history.

Freedom of Conscience

All of this—the increasing wealth and prosperity, the recognition of the rights and privileges of various regions and estates—helped to shape the

Polish polity. Another factor in the country's development was its unique experience of the Reformation.

Modern man ignores confessional divides at his own peril. And it was precisely new confessional divides that were arising in the early sixteenth century, as witnessed by the birth of the Protestant Reformation and the subsequent proliferation of variants of Protestantism, from Lutheranism through Calvinism through the even more radical reforms of the Antitrinitarians. In nailing his soon-to-be famous theses to a door, Martin Luther opened a door, as it were, to thoughts of church reform, even among the staunchly Catholic faithful.

For a moment, at the height of the Reformation in Poland, there was a distinct possibility that the country would move in the direction of a national church. Calls rang out for a national synod, the abolition of ecclesiastical courts, and complete freedom of religion. And these were but the most mild of proposals: more radical suggestions extended to doctrinal matters such as the marriage of the clergy (something, incidentally, found in the Eastern Orthodox Church as well as the new Protestant sects) and the giving of communion in both kinds (which, incidentally, has today recently been reintroduced by the Roman Catholic Church).

If there were ever an auspicious moment to break with Rome, this may have been it. Consider the trials facing Roman Catholicism in the sixteenth century. Not only had Protestantism emerged to splinter the Western church. One of the Medici popes, Clement VII, was for a spell imprisoned in the Castel del Angelo while his opponents sacked Rome and the Vatican. As physical center as well as spiritual capital of Christendom, Rome suddenly seemed extremely vulnerable. And there was the precedent of Henry VIII's Church of England to consider as well, which came on the heels of that debacle.

Of course, Henry's break with Rome was occasioned by his desire to divorce his Spanish wife and marry Anne Boleyn. Despite his marital woes, Zygmunt August was not pulled in this direction. He remained loyal to the faith of his fathers. Protestantism made advances among his subjects, yet he did not impress his own faith on his subjects. Although staunchly Catholic, the last Jagiellons were hardly Crusaders, either beyond their country's borders or within them. In particular, Zygmunt August seemed to recognize the danger that religious fanaticism in any shape or form represented to his large, multiethnic, multidenominational state. Faced with the increasing religious heterogeneity among the nobility, the king famously declared, "I am not the ruler of your consciences."

Thus, perhaps as a result of the country's historic toleration (not to mention diversity), two things were avoided. The first was that a drastic step—of a Polish national church breaking away from Rome—was not taken. The Catholics of Poland-Lithuania remained firmly within the orbit of Rome, and the plan of creating a national church was abandoned by 1570. The second was that, at the same time, the nobles of Poland-Lithuania—led by their monarch—agreed to disagree about the virtues of one or another means of worshipping God.

This acknowledgment of the sixteenth century had repercussions for the Orthodox nobles of Polish-Lithuania. In 1563 and 1568 Zygmunt August granted the Orthodox nobles of the Grand Duchy the totality of civic and political rights that were had by Roman Catholic nobles—for the first time allowing the Orthodox to vie for state offices, titles, and membership in the council of lords. It was fitting that the last of these acts was affirmed in Horodło, as it undid the damage wreaked in 1413 when the otherwise laudatory Horodło union, while bringing the Polish and Lithuanian nobles closer together, expressly addressed only those of the Roman Catholic faith. The wording of these two sixteenth-century acts (in places referring to all "of Christian faith") seemed to suggest that Protestant nobles were to enjoy the same rights and privileges.

That said, the religious scene in Poland-Lithuania hardly represented some kind of parity. The most radical Dissenters (as Protestants were often referred to) managed to offend the sensibilities of members of other religious denominations, even fellow Protestants. The latter seemed particularly incensed by the Arians, whose noble members carried wooden, not metal, swords to emphasize their passivism—a stance that did not sit well with the noble ethos as defender of the country. This was one of the reasons—in another, more trying century—the Arians would end up expelled from the Poland-Lithuania. More important for developments in the sixteenth century, the inability for the various Protestant denominations to agree upon even the most basic doctrinal issues meant that they never were able to present a united front, notwithstanding the 1570 agreement of Sandomierz among some of the major Protestant denominations. This lack of Protestant unity ultimately left the door open for a resurgent and reform-minded Catholicism, one that would bring many Dissenters and their descendants back into the fold.

The Northern Diversion

But this would happen only later. In the interim, Zygmunt August went from expressing his intent to respect the beliefs of Protestants to ruling over new Protestant populations. The king of Poland's nominal sovereignty over

Ducal Prussia has already been noted. Here, Zygmunt August maintained the position his father had won for his office as Polish king; after his father's death, he inherited this special relationship with his cousin Albrecht von Hohenzollern. Under the son, however, the Polish king's influence would come to extend over populations lying even further east.

Toward the end of his life, Zygmunt August came to rule new territory along the Baltic Sea coast. The territory in question was Livonia (modern-day Estonia and Latvia, known in Polish as Inflanty). Boasting the Baltic ports of Reval (today's Tallinn) and Riga, the region had an old Hanseatic connection. Much as the Teutonic Knights had long dominated the central Baltic coast, to the east and north a different crusading order ruled. These were the Livonian Knights—more precisely known as the Knights of the Sword. This territory had many parallels with the lands of the Teutonic Knights—including its ultimate secularization.

Zygmunt August got involved in the process, in part as a result of the machinations of his cousin and vassal, Albrecht von Hohenzollern of Ducal Prussia, who wanted to gain influence in the region. Livonia would turn out to be a hornets' nest. Not only were there conflicts within Livonia between Catholics and Lutherans; the neighboring countries of Sweden and Russia also sought to make inroads into this part of the Baltic Sea coast. In the course of the Livonian wars, Zygmunt August ended up fighting on both sea and land, having built up a seventeen-ship fleet. The country's sea adventure would nonetheless be short-lived, on account of trouble with Gdańsk (which did not want privateers in its harbor) as well as Danish interference.

In the end, Livonia was divided up among various parties. Its northern section, Estonia, came under Swedish control. Southern Livonia, known as Courland, became a Polish fief ruled by Gotthard Kettler, the last grand master of the Livonian Knights, now a secular ruler. Other parts of Livonia would end up as a separate duchy under joint Polish and Lithuanian control.

This northern diversion would carry a higher price tag than Zygmunt August doubtless imagined, although the true cost to the country would be evident only after his death. Back home he already had been obliged to make concessions to the Executionist deputies, who wanted him to reclaim royal lands from magnate control, in exchange for their support of the war.

The rule of Poland-Lithuania over Livonia led to two developments in the international realm that Poles would rue in later centuries. On the one hand, Zygmunt August ventured into a remote region that ultimately was of little economic value to Poland-Lithuania but of much greater interest to the powers emerging to the north and the east, Sweden and Russia. Inadvertently making enemies of one's neighbors—here, by the big Poland-Lithuania picking up, more for political than for economic reasons, territories that had a greater intrinsic value to dirt-poor Sweden or port-poor Russia (peripheral players in the European scheme of things, but countries that increasingly were making their presence known in the region)—would prove dangerous.

The other mistake (again, its huge cost evident only in hindsight) was to give away too much in the long term for short-term assistance. In exchange for timely (and, indeed, much needed) military assistance in Livonia, Zygmunt August acquiesced to the request of the Hohenzollerns of Brandenburg (Albrecht's cousins to the west) for the right to succession in Ducal Prussia, should Albrecht's line die out.

Such mistakes at the margins suggest a degree of imperial overstretch. It would require concentration and care on the part of future rulers to keep the peace—and to keep the Hohenzollerns of Brandenburg from pressing for further advantage. Could such careful attention be expected after the Jagiellons ceased to rule the country?

From Dynastic Crisis to Uncommon Solution

These diversions along the Baltic notwithstanding, the most pressing issue for a childless monarch ultimately had to be what would happen after his death. And indeed, Zygmunt August is more remembered for this accomplishment than for his marital foibles or other deeds. What would become of the union, under Jagiellonian rule, of the Crown and the Grand Duchy after the Jagiellonian glue that held it together dried up?

The Poles behind the Execution of the Laws movement had come up with the idea of a more perfect union for Poland and Lithuania as early as 1538. At that time both the Lithuanians and their hereditary dynasts, the Jagiellons, opposed this, as it would make the joint throne elective. (The Polish throne was elective—and had been elective since the death of the last Piast, Kazimierz the Great, even if it had long made a habit of choosing the next in line from among the Jagiellons; that said, sometimes assent was given rather grudgingly—or, as in the case of Kazimierz IV Jagiellończyk, with a delay.) Nonetheless, toward the end of his life Zygmunt August had a change of heart, given that the odds of his producing an heir were dwindling. He did not want to see Poland-Lithuania torn asunder after his death, which was a distinct possibility.

At the same time, there were those within the Lithuanian camp who came to realize the benefits that increased union could bring. Many admitted that they themselves were not up to the challenge of defending their tremendously long border, extending from Livonia in the north along the border with Muscovy down to the historic frontier with the Tatars and Ottomans. Were union to be strengthened, the Poles of the less threatened Crown might feel more obliged to come to the Lithuanians' assistance. Of course, there were bound to be tradeoffs, including giving Poles rights to acquire territories in the Grand Duchy. This was one of the reasons that the powerful magnates of Lithuania—literally loath to share the wealth—were more inclined toward separatism than unification.

Their behavior stood in contrast to that of their less well-to-do noble neighbors in the Grand Duchy, who sought Polish-style rights, in part a result of their increasing exposure to important aspects of Polishness: while these included the Polish language, they also included the language of politics. Zygmunt August made some strides here by providing the Lithuanian nobles with their own Seym and seymiks. In this, it seems, he actually radicalized them. As early as 1562, the lesser Lithuanian nobility appealed to the king for Polish-style rights and a real union. At that moment, however, the king was not yet ready to give up his hereditary claim to the Grand Duchy.

Under the last Jagiellon, thus, the two halves of Poland-Lithuania were nonetheless inching closer—in terms of political culture, even in terms of administrative structure (subdivided into palatinates, kingdoms, and counties and staffed with the appropriate hierarchy of state offices)—if they still were not in agreement on how they might come to comprise a single entity.

Discussions ensued over a number of years as to how the states might be joined. It is worth underscoring that the ultimate settlement was negotiated. This was no project of imperialism, no military conquest, no imposition of one side upon another. Union could not be accomplished by fiat—even by the last of the Jagiellons. It was to be accomplished voluntarily, not by force—just as it had been in 1385, when the prospect of marriage to Jadwiga brought Jagieło and the Grand Duchy into the Polish orbit. Yet this time, the voices of a larger body of nobles had to be taken into consideration. The nobles of both halves sought to preserve the traditional rights, immunities, and freedoms that had accrued to them over the centuries—nor did they wish to allow one side to subjugate or dominate the other. Given the existing configuration of power that gave nobles a say in the outcome and the enormous size and diversity of the combined states, which even themselves were hardly homogenous, a creative solution was required.

And this is precisely what resulted. The solution to yet another dynastic crisis—which, as we have seen in the Polish case, repeatedly inspired creative solutions—boldly surpassed all previous solutions to the lack of a legitimate male heir. It proved so creative, so unique, so different from the forms of government elsewhere in the Europe of that age, that many were at a loss of how to understand it. As subjects of increasingly absolutist rulers, how were they to perceive the new entity in the center of Europe, one that established a contractual relationship between the ruler and the ruled? Without much exaggeration, one could consider it the most modern of early modern states. A new era in Polish history was initiated by the bold moves initiated by the Union of Lublin of 1569.

The Road to Union

That this union was ultimately agreed upon was in part miraculous. Given the relative strength of the nobility within Poland-Lithuania, not every nobleman was keen on the idea of forming a joint commonwealth—and those who were opposed to the plan made their displeasure known. The proponents of closer union, which would mean more equality among the nobles of the country, had to convince the wealthiest Lithuanians and the powerful Radziwiłł family, in particular, to sign on. They were not easily moved. In fact, the Radziwiłłs—first led by Mikołaj the Black, then after his death by his cousin Mikołaj the Red—did what they could to win over rank-and-file Lithuanian nobles to separatism. The elder Radziwiłł proposed that union be limited to a common ruler and military alliance for the two countries. Contrast this to the other extreme of those Polish nobles, especially those from the capital of Kraków, who agitated for complete incorporation. They were even inclined to drop all references to Lithuania and to rename the Grand Duchy—to be demoted to the status of a province—New Poland.

Such was the situation preceding the lengthy negotiations that began at the end of December 1568 in the border town of Lublin. The relative accessibility of the historic city (capital of a palatinate, Lublin was a convenient location for both states) may have brought Lithuanians to the table, but it did not make the most influential of them any more amenable to the idea of greater union. Mikołaj the Red in particular was determined to counter the move toward greater unification. Unable to secure Polish support for their proposal of limited union, at the beginning of March the Lithuanian magnates walked out. They expected the rest of the Lithuanian deputies would follow them and that this would put an end to talk of union. But they were mistaken.

The ploy of the magnates backfired—and in ways they could not have even imagined. Their absence allowed the king to alter the political and cartographical balance of power between the two halves of Poland-Lithuania. Using his prerogative as grand duke, Zygmunt August made a present of certain Ruthenian lands to the Crown of Poland. In a series of decrees, four eastern palatinates—first Podlachia, then Volhynia and Bratslav (Polish: Bracław) and finally Kyiv (Polish: Kijów)—were removed from the jurisdiction of the Grand Duchy of Lithuania and awarded to the Crown of Poland.

What seemed to be mere sleight of hand on the part of Zygmunt August (after all, was he not, in one person, both Polish king and Lithuanian grand duke?) had important repercussions, both short-term and long-term, for people and polity alike. First and most notably, the Grand Duchy lost nearly half of its territory. Lithuanian nobles who owned territories in the incorporated palatinates found themselves subject to the laws of the Crown—and were now forced to swear allegiance to Zygmunt August as their king or else lose their offices and landholdings.

This cartographical reconfiguring of the two entities, the Crown of Poland and the Grand Duchy of Lithuania, also divided the predominately Ruthenian population of the Grand Duchy. Lands we associate with modern Ukraine came directly under Polish rule; lands we associate with modern Belarus remained under Lithuanian jurisdiction. In a way, this made sense for reasons of orientation and interest: the Grand Duchy had been much more focused on its interests to the north (Livonia) and east (Muscovy), whereas these southernmost provinces—like other parts of the Crown of Poland, such as Red Ruthenia and Podolia—were more cognizant of the threat from the south (Tatars and Ottomans). The king doubtless could not imagine that this reconfiguration, which resulted in the new acquisitions being folded into the Crown rather than given a separate status, would have serious repercussions at a later date for the entire country.

The bold move by Zygmunt August also spoke to another party to the negotiations: the representatives of the Royal Prussian Diet. They had been loath to join the Polish Seym, preferring to deal with their own, Prussian matters themselves. Now the Prussian senators and councilors—perhaps fearing a backlash such as met their Lithuanian counterparts—felt compelled to take their seats in the Seym and acquiesce to the new closer union that ultimately emerged. In the end, Royal Prussia would be permitted to maintain its own parliament back home, although it would be treated on par with the other regional seymiks of the Crown of Poland.

Last but hardly least: the loss of nearly half the territory of the Grand Duchy finally jolted the Lithuanian magnates into returning to the negotiating table and acquiescing to union. Terms acceptable to both sides were worked out by June 28, and the swearing by representatives of both sides took place on July 1, 1569.

Map 4.1: The Commonwealth of Both Nations, Polish and Lithuanian, ca. 1569

The working out of terms of union in Lublin marks a satisfying symmetry. Lublin had been the city where, in 1386, Polish nobles had put their stamp of approval on the beginning of Jagiellonian rule and officially elected Jagiełło king of Poland. In a sense, thus, the Union of Lublin—for that is how this new arrangement has gone down in history—was a fitting conclusion to Jagiellonian rule.

To be sure, the document also has its asymmetries. The act of union begins with an enumeration of those present in Lublin representing the Grand Duchy of Lithuania. It records a range of figures, from the highest and mightiest princes, lords and bishops, castellans, marshals, palatines, and bailiffs all the way through lesser deputies, scribes, and even several representatives of the city of Vilnius. Notably present were some of the great noble families of Lithuania: Mikołaj Krzysztof Radziwiłł, Jan Chodkiewicz, Mikołaj and Paweł Iwanowicz Sapieha, all signed the document. There is no comparable list of representatives of the Crown of Poland in the act, which suggests that it was much more crucial for the names and offices of the Lithuanians to be recorded for posterity, together with their affixed seals—in order to attest to the fact that they, in the name of themselves and their noble brethren back home, swore the oath of union.

Yet, lest it be thought that Zygmunt August, allied with the nobles of the Crown, ran roughshod over the Lithuanian opposition to more permanent political union, even his cleverness had its limits. Both extremes were brought to a more central place of compromise. Room was made for both commonality and distinctiveness. There would be no relabeling of the Grand Duchy as New Poland, as some Poles had wished. Although he would be crowned as monarch in Kraków alone, the king of Poland would retain the full gamut of historic titles. The existing rights of the Lithuanian nobility would be retained, and the Lithuanian statutes would remain in effect. Even the monetary union would allow for separate, if equivalent, currencies. Despite the establishment of an overarching commonwealth, this was not incorporation but federation.

The powerful magnates of the Grand Duchy ultimately derived no small benefit from the new arrangement. After all, Lithuanians desperately needed help in defending their borders from Muscovite incursions—and such aid would be forthcoming with a closer union. While the most powerful Lithuanian nobles ultimately agreed to political unification, they were not about to lose economic ground in the process. Zygmunt August was persuaded to make an important concession to the Lithuanian magnates—one that may have sealed the agreement. They were allowed to retain control over the grand ducal demesnes in their possession—something their contemporaries in the Crown of Poland had been denied earlier in the century, as a result of the Executionist movement.

This meant that the powerful within Lithuania would stay powerful—and rich. The two halves of the Commonwealth would not be perfectly even: the wealthiest of Lithuanians would have larger landed estates than their counterparts in the Polish lands. This new development did not please rank-and-file nobles, who criticized Zygmunt August for not upholding the principle of equality of the two halves. Still, it appeared to be the price that had to be paid for the new and closer union.

Thus, despite the various tactics employed, the creation of the Commonwealth truly represented a negotiated settlement, a creatively achieved compromise between the various parties that doubtless represented the best that could be achieved at the time. While Zygmunt August strove to create a more perfect union, he achieved not true centralization but, rather, federalization (as we will see), one that respected regional differences. This creative consensus building would become the framework of a union that would remain the standard for centuries to come.

Republican Poland

The act of the Union of Lublin of 1569 created a new entity, one that reflected a "real" union, not a personal or dynastic one. In its main point, the act reads, "The Kingdom of Poland and the Grand Duchy of Lithuania are one inseparable and indistinguishable body, as well as an indistinguishable and single united commonwealth, which has been created and joined out of two states and two nations into one people." The entity, thus, came to be called the Commonwealth (Polish: *Rzeczpospolita*).

The name of the entity is telling—if also somewhat confusing. Etymologically the Polish term, *rzeczpospolita,* comes from the Latin *res publicae*—which can also be rendered as "republic." The Latin connection is crucial not only linguistically but also conceptually. Not only the vocabulary of the ancients but also critical concepts such as *societas, civitas,* and *res publica* had come to shape the mind-set of the educated citizenry in Poland-Lithuania. Important Renaissance thinkers such as Andrzej Frycz Modrzewski and the famous writer Stanisław Orzechowski were enamored of the ancients, whom they saw as providing models worth emulating. It gave them a context in which to view their own polity, which could be compared to the ancient Sparta or even the Venetian Republic of their own time.

As such, it should come as no surprise that the newly established Commonwealth would be thought of as a true Roman republic. The Poles regarded the republic as the most perfect form of government. Yet not just any republic: they favored the mixed form first laid out by the Greek historian Polybius, which shared characteristics of monarchy (king), oligarchy (senate), and democracy (nobility), yet by combining bits of them all managed to avoid the dangers of each. As Goślicki noted, "This kind of state not without reason was regarded as the most just," as it combined (and here I borrow his metaphor) sounds representing these three entities into a harmony that would be "the strongest and tightest knot of security for all."[*] Thus, what to the reader might seem a curious mixture—a monarchic republic—represented the embodiment of the golden mean to sixteenth-century Poles.

When speaking about the republic, sixteenth-century Poles (certainly those mentioned above) had in mind their existing state, the Crown of Poland under the Jagiellons. It was, according to them, a prime example of a mixed-form republic (in other words, a republic with a small "r"). One can think of the new, post-1569 Commonwealth as a palimpsest, one in which the heritage of the Crown of Poland underlay understandings of the new state.

---

[*] Goślicki, cited in Włodzimierz Bernacki, *Myśl polityczna I Rzeczpospolitej* (Political thought in the first commonwealth) (Kraków: Arcana Historii, 2011), 118 (author's translation).

In this case, what was truly novel about the new Commonwealth? Clearly it was not the republican aspect alone, although with time this would seem increasingly at odds with the fashion for absolutism that was increasingly conquering Europe. Rather, what represented a real revolution in politics was its broader application—that is, its extension eastward (for Lithuania had been a hereditary monarchy)—and further, unique evolution.

The Commonwealth of Both Nations

Hinting at part of this uniqueness is the name often given to the Commonwealth. Perhaps paradoxically, the authors of the Union of Lublin had not provided any more specific term for the new federative state than "Commonwealth" or "Republic" (again, either term being perfectly appropriate). They clearly had been more focused on achieving union than on supplying a formal title for the union. This left the door open for the state to be referred to in various ways—including, incidentally, Poland (this last usually for foreign consumption). More often, however, various qualifiers were added to the name "Commonwealth" that would make it clear that one was talking of a real existing state and not a generic republic. The particular republic/commonwealth that came to dominate East-Central Europe, thus, has often been labeled the Commonwealth of Both Nations, Polish and Lithuanian.

Here it may be helpful to think of the implications not only of this title but of the actual wording of the Union of Lublin, which notes that the new state has been "created and joined out of two states and two nations into one people." Who and what were parties to this new union?

That the Commonwealth was comprised of two states is clear enough: the Crown of Poland and the Grand Duchy of Lithuania were two separate political entities that were now being joined together into one of the largest states in Europe. The territory of the Commonwealth—some 815,000 square kilometers—made it the biggest state in Europe proper (that is, excluding Muscovy and the Ottoman Empire, both of which extended into Asia as well). Yet it was decidedly unlike the average large European state of its time, which increasingly sought to downplay diversity. The duality of the state was reflected in the emblem, which incorporated both the Polish crowned eagle and the Lithuanian "chase," a figure on horseback brandishing a sword. Perhaps its motto should have been "Unity in Diversity"?

What Union? Unity in Diversity

This anachronistic borrowing of the slogan of the European Union is no accident. First and foremost, the Commonwealth of Both Nations was a kind of federation. While there would be a single monarch and one Seym (Diet) for the entire country, distinctions between the two halves would persist. There would be separate armies and judiciaries, separate currencies (if of equivalent value) and finances; and each half would be administered separately. The Union of Lublin even allowed for each half to carry out its elections to the joint Seym, or Diet, in accordance with its own traditions. The Commonwealth was, thus, truly a union of two distinct halves—two political halves.

But the document (as well as the long version of the name) also mentions two nations, Polish and Lithuanian. What, then, does "nation" mean? This can give the English-speaking reader a headache, as we tend to use the two terms—"nation" and "state"—somewhat interchangeably. The state, in the European context, is best thought of as the political entity—the one that, in the definition popularized by sociologist Max Weber, has a monopoly on the legitimate use of violence. A less ambiguous English-language equivalent for "state" would be "country."

The idea of nation stands in direct contrast to that spatial, geographical, and political dimension. Clearly nation was not to be equated with state (given the above quotation, which distinguishes between the two). Rather, the idea of nation concerned the human content of each half—the people of the Commonwealth. Here it may be useful to think in terms of citizenship. Whose Commonwealth was it? It was a political entity belonging to the two specified nations.

The mention of only two nations should raise eyebrows. The careful reader will note that, almost from the very outset, the population of the country that is the focus of this book has consisted of more than one nation or ethnic group. German burghers, Armenian merchants, Ruthenian boyars, Jewish traders and moneylenders, all have made their way onto these pages—as have all the Europeans fleeing persecution in the West during the age of the Reformation and the wars of religion. Nobles and peasants reflected a regional patchwork. Why, then, are only two nations invoked in the Union of Lublin, which established one united Commonwealth out of two states and two nations?

Clearly each half of the Commonwealth—the Kingdom of Poland, and the Grand Duchy of Lithuania—had its own "nation." Yet the sixteenth-century definition of "nation" does not exactly match our contemporary understanding of the word. Indeed, it would be anachronistic to equate the two nations with modern-day "Poles" and "Lithuanians." Neither nation circa 1569 was ethnically or even linguistically homogeneous (although to be sure, the lingua franca was increasingly Polish), nor did they represent the entirety of the population whom today we would see as Polish or Lithuanian.

Instead, the nation was conceived in political terms. In the case of both Poland and Lithuania, the nation consisted of the warrior caste, the nobility (Polish: *szlachta*), those individuals who by their virtue of defending the country had the rights of citizens. In this part of early modern Europe, these were the people who mattered politically, who could play a role in affairs of state: participate in the local seymiks, hold regional and national offices, and serve as deputies to the Seym. The szlachta was the active citizenry, if you will, of the Commonwealth.

This concept of nation was, thus, a civic nation par excellence. The corporate identity of the szlachta had little or nothing to do with ethnicity, religion, language, or culture. After all, languages—our means of dealing with the outside world—could be acquired, as we have seen from the increasing linguistic Polonization of the nobility of the Grand Duchy that proceeded over the centuries of personal union. The same could be said for religious affiliation, which—especially during this period of flux known as the Protestant Reformation—was a less permanent marker than was one's estate. Many inhabitants of the Polish-Lithuanian lands experimented with various denominations. Burghers in many cities along the Baltic Sea coast became Lutherans. Christian nobles from across the large country (whether originally of Catholic or Orthodox faith) opted for any of an array of Protestant denominations.

While at a certain (later) point it becomes easy to draw facile equivalents (Protestant means German, Catholic means Pole, Orthodox means Ukrainian), such equivalences would have confused the inhabitants of the Commonwealth of Both Nations, as they hardly reflected the reality they knew. And even one's religious affiliation need not have become a permanent marker for a person or that person's descendants. Consider the 1592 marriage of the scions of two wealthy noble families, Orthodox Prince Alexander Ostrogski and his Roman Catholic wife, Anna née Kostka. The five children of this reportedly happy union were baptized in the faith of their parents, with a twist: the boys were raised as Orthodox, the girls as Catholics. This practice, like so many other things within the Commonwealth, represented a compromise: one that shrugged off lesser differences (here religion) while not yielding where more important questions were concerned (noble status). It should thus come as no surprise that the three daughters of this multidenominational family would end up marrying into the most powerful noble families, with names like Chodkiewicz, Lubomirski, and Zamoyski.

What in part enabled such marital unions was the way the idea of nation developed in the new Commonwealth. It elided differences of region and religion and emphasized a corporate identity. No longer would there be a separate Polish or Lithuanian nation. There would be one, overarching noble nation—a nation of the Commonwealth nobility.

Creating a Nation for the Commonwealth

But how to achieve such a unity of purpose—such an overarching identity? The regional differences were all too visible in the official title of the joint monarch, King of Poland and Grand Duke of Lithuania, Ruthenia, Prussia, Mazovia, Samogitia, Kyiv, Volhynia, Podlachia and Livonia. (Those familiar with the complex geography will note that some of these lands fell under the jurisdiction of the Crown of Poland, others under that of the Grand Duchy.) In other words, was it possible to acknowledge the rich regional diversity of both the Crown of Poland and the Grand Duchy of Lithuania—and yet, somehow, transcend it?

It was. But this required a certain creativity on the part of those most concerned—the citizens of Poland and Lithuania as well as those who would develop this new concept.

It would take no small creativity, for barriers to a common identity were all too real. Not only were there two political nations—the Polish nation, the Lithuanian nation (which, as we have noted, had different definitions than our modern notion of the term). Reflecting the rich layers of half a millennium of history, regional variations within these two states were further complicated by ethnic, linguistic, as well as religious diversity. Consider two extremes: the densely populated Baltic region of Royal Prussia—heavily German, heavily urban, with Protestantism and Catholicism both strongly represented—was a world away, geographically, geopolitically, and culturally, from the lightly populated, heavily rural, black earth territories of Ruthenian Podolia, inhabited primarily by East Slavs, adherents of the Orthodox faith, that bordered on the Ottoman Empire. And, although both regions entered into the Commonwealth as part of the Crown of Poland, neither had a large ethnic Polish component—yet another paradox of Polish history. All of this made for an extremely diverse experience of life in the "indistinguishable and single united commonwealth" promised by the Union of Lublin.

Ancient Sarmatia as Polish Homeland

Given such vast discrepancies in an even vaster federalized state, what might counteract the centrifugal tendencies, pulling—for example—one region eastward, one westward, one toward the Baltic, the other to the Black Sea? An opportunity presented itself, in the form of a national genealogy.

With its interest in antiquity, the Renaissance had spawned an interest in the lineages of states and peoples, causing many national groups to devise their own stories of national descent. While the Italians looked to ancient Rome and the Germans to the Vandals, the French, English, as well as some Germans (for instance, the Habsburgs) all claimed roots in the ancient Trojans. By contrast, the Poles looked not to classical Greece or Rome for their own myth of ancient descent but rather to the east—to ancient Sarmatia.

The Sarmatians were a warrior people who lived in the vicinity of the Black Sea during the third century. This made them attractive as a national progenitor for two reasons: geographic proximity and national disposition. It did not require much of a stretch of the imagination to conclude, as did the Renaissance clergyman and historian Marcin Kromer, that the inhabitants of Poland-Lithuania were descended from that people. And indeed, the connection between Poland, Slavs, and the Sarmatians was first suggested in the medieval period.

The myth of Sarmatian origin had further, more significant ramifications for those in Poland-Lithuania. In distinction to the myths devised by many other peoples elsewhere in Europe, it was not mere window-dressing. Rather, it served in a way as justification for the very existence of the Commonwealth, as well as an explanation of its unique position within Europe.

Sarmatian Nation

While at the outset the myth of Sarmatian origin was applied to the entirety of the Jagiellonian state's population, as time went on the idea of a Sarmatian nation increasingly carried noble connotations. It became the myth of common origin of the Commonwealth's diverse nobility. Either way, this myth of origin was patently false: how could one attribute common origins to such a heterogeneous population, of differing ethnic, linguistic, even cultural heritage? It proved a tremendously useful fiction, nonetheless. It provided the nobility as well as anyone else who bought into the myth with a sense of overall unity, purpose, even mission, within this unique country, the Commonwealth of Both Nations. Thus, one can speak interchangeably about the noble nation, comprised of the noble estate (szlachta), and the Sarmatian nation. Although each was equally heterogeneous in origin, the fact that the nobles of the Commonwealth embraced this common identity of a noble brotherhood meant that it took only one more step for them to agree to make common cause and accept common basic principles—that is, they were simultaneously the political nation, the citizens of the Commonwealth. Together with the king, they were the source of political authority.

The arrangement that emerged in the Commonwealth, thus, was truly unique. Nobles—whether Calvinists, Catholics, or Orthodox, and regardless of the region from which they hailed—all felt themselves to be part of the Commonwealth. And not only were they a part, they were the part that truly mattered: its active citizenry. Together, in the process of compromising and consensus building, they were developing a unique political culture— aspects of which would eventually percolate down and across the estates, provinces, and ethnicities.

One feature of the new system worth underscoring was the Polish tradition of reaching unanimous decisions in the legislative process. Dating from the fifteenth century, this stress on reaching consensus demonstrated a respect for the diverse voices in the provinces of the diverse state. Regional seymiks often gave their deputies concrete instructions before the latter set off to participate in the national Seym, and these had to be taken into serious consideration, not ignored or silenced. The principle of unanimity reflected the sense that legislation was to serve the common weal, and all parties should reach agreement that what was being implemented was, indeed, serving the interests of the nation as a whole. The Commonwealth's citizens were to be, in the words of Cicero, "slaves to the public interest." In this way, the union would not disintegrate; in the hope-filled words of the act of union, "with God's will this union will last until the end of the world."

It was one thing to create the Commonwealth: to get members of both powerful nations to agree to a basic framework. Yet further decisions would need to be made—and fast, once the last of the Jagiellons was no more.

Commonwealth Creativity: From Confederations to Consensus

When Zygmunt August suddenly died in July 1572, it was feared that chaos would ensue. It did not, however, because of the concerted efforts of numerous individuals who worked together, stepped into the breach, and fleshed out the framework given them by the Union of Lublin. Well over a dozen congresses and so-called confederations (ad hoc organizations of concerned citizens, a tradition that dated from medieval times) formed throughout the Commonwealth to take care of business, both regionally and nationally, during this time of transition. It was a dangerous moment for this unusually large and now headless state.

The moment required a degree of creativity on the part of the Commonwealth's citizens, whose Renaissance education, exposure to religious diversity, and profound knowledge of Poland-Lithuania would help them set the ground rules for the first royal election. Their success or failure would have huge ramifications for this part of Europe.

From these congresses and confederations emerged the idea to convene a Seym in Warsaw in January 1573. The importance of the so-called Warsaw Confederation cannot be overstated. If the Union of Lublin formed the skeleton for the Commonwealth, this important convocation of nobles crucially put the flesh on the bones. It would need to countenance different views of how to proceed, acknowledge the voices of various regional and political factions, and ultimately strengthen and not sunder the only just crafted union.

The Warsaw confederation was the first of three Seyms that would take place in the period of transition between rulers. This first one, the Convocation Seym, provided the occasion to work out the details for the election and established some precedents. The confederation came up with some carefully crafted compromises. One of these was that the archbishop of Gniezno, the Polish primate (that is, head of the Catholic Church in Poland), would serve as interrex during the interregnum and run the election. The archbishop selected the village of Kamień, near Warsaw, as the place where the election of the monarch would take place.

In these two matters of organization, a certain group of nobles based in Greater Poland were able to get their way. The heavily Catholic senatorial camp pushed for the primacy of the primate during the interregnum as well as for the environs of Warsaw and not Lublin as the site of the election. After all, Mazovia (of which Warsaw was capital) had been the province of Poland least interested in Protestantism. Closer to the farthest reaches of the Commonwealth (making it more accessible to nobles coming from the Lithuanian and Ruthenian lands), Lublin was part of Lesser Poland, where there was a strong Protestant base—which is why it had been proposed by the Protestant/Executionist camp.

Were the Executionists and Protestants to be marginalized in the Commonwealth? Their candidate for the position of interrex—the man holding the highest senate seat in the land, the grand marshal of the Crown, the Calvinist Jan Firlej—had not gained that distinction. Yet issues of importance to the rank-and-file nobles as well as to the non-Catholics found their champion in a former Calvinist, Jan Zamoyski. As a royal secretary to Zygmunt August, Zamoyski had been privileged to have access to state documents, from which he learned a good deal about Poland-Lithuania through the ages. He now put this knowledge to good use.

A deputy at the Convocation Seym, the former secretary proved to be a charismatic orator and persuasive voice even in writing (he published a brochure entitled *Modus electionis*). Zamoyski advocated a novel way to run the royal election: this was the idea of free election *viritim* (in person). Whereas in earlier times the Polish king had been elected by parliament, now any nobleman living anywhere within the Commonwealth would be allowed to come to the Election Seym and participate in the electoral process. This right would soon become the hallmark of the Commonwealth noble: be he rich or poor, influential or unknown, he could be a kingmaker.

Procedural matters of the interregnum were also set. The transition period was to be characterized by a three-part legislative process. The Convocation Seym would take care of preparations for the election. It would set the date for the second, key assembly, the Election Seym—an opportunity not just for the Seym's deputies and senators but also for any nobleman who choose to participate in this important dimension of Commonwealth politics: the royal election *viritim*. The final step in the process of electing a new monarch was the Coronation Seym.

Enshrining Freedom of Religion

Those most supportive of the Catholic stance in 1573 did not get their way in one more important matter, which eventually became the claim to international fame of the Warsaw Confederation. For, in addition to fleshing out the details of procedure for the new state, the Protestant/Executionist camp pushed for a proviso guaranteeing religious toleration. The religiously heterogeneous nobles of the Commonwealth would not allow religious differences to upset the political balance. On January 28, 1573, some 206 nobles affixed their seals to the so-called Act of the Confederation of Warsaw. It was to become part of the official core tenets of the Commonwealth of Both Nations.

This legal enshrining of religious toleration in the Commonwealth was a move way ahead of its times, an anomaly in an age of religious upheaval in Europe. The miscellaneous German states of the Holy Roman Empire had taken a very different step in 1555. Their Peace of Augsburg led to a situation—expressed in the Latin phrase *cuius regio, eius religio*—in which the monarch of a given state would determine the religion of his subjects. In the

Commonwealth, citizens could profess the faith of their choice and not suffer any political or other consequences for it.

The nobles in Warsaw doubtless understood that they would have to make clear to any elected king the scope of his rights, duties, and restrictions. The religious toleration specified in the Act of the Confederation of Warsaw as well as other key tenets were enshrined in a list of non-negotiable conditions that the king-elect would have to swear to uphold in order to become Polish king. Often referred to as the Henrician Articles (the reason will become clear next chapter), these conditions would also go down in history as the Golden Freedom(s)—the foundation of the republic.

Polish historical memory helped to shape these non-negotiable demands. Perhaps given the memory of how Queen Bona had (successfully) lobbied for the coronation of the underage Zygmunt during the life of his father, the Henrician Articles clearly spelled out that no elections vivente rege (during the life of the king) would be tolerated in the Commonwealth. As per the 1569 Union of Lublin, all existing noble privileges, rights, and immunities would be preserved. The 1505 principle of *Nihil novi* (nothing about us without us) was echoed in the insistence that the nobles have the last word in the running of the country. Not only was the monarch to call for a six-week session of the Seym—now the joint assembly of the Commonwealth—every two years. He could not impose taxes or declare war by himself but, rather, needed the approval of the Seym. And, in accordance with the Act of the Warsaw Confederation of 1573, the king was obliged to preserve the principle of religious toleration. To underscore the importance of these demands, Commonwealth nobles reserved to themselves the right to rebel against their elected king if the latter did not abide by them.

In addition to the non-negotiable Henrician Articles, a special *pacta conventa* would be negotiated with each ensuing ruler. This would allow the nobles to make adjustments to what was expected of their king-elect as well as countenance the strengths of a given candidate, in keeping with the needs of a given age. Thus, a degree of flexibility was built into the system.

Europe's Creative Center

The establishment of the Commonwealth of Both Nations put the Poles, Lithuanians, and other peoples of the federative state in a position unique for its time. The fact that each noble citizen could participate in the election of the king, that he had the right to worship as he chose, and that his voice would be heard when it came to determine how best to govern the country rings surprisingly modern.

To be sure, the political influence of these noble Sarmatians far exceeded that of the rest of the inhabitants of these vast lands: the economically thriving but politically insignificant towns, the numerous but all but invisible peasantry (that is, invisible to all but those who oversaw them in the fields), the distinct Jewish population. The nobility amounted to some 8–10 percent of the population of the Commonwealth, a country of some 7.5 million, which still makes for a respectable number of genuine citizens.

In the past, this disproportionate influence of the nobility in the overall political scheme of things was often held against the Commonwealth—as if any sixteenth-century European polity had better political representation. (Likely the only other society that had a disproportionate number of nobles at this time was Spain.) Even at a much later date, the voting population elsewhere was miniscule by comparison, even in countries that are considered infinitely more advanced. Sixteenth-century England awarded the franchise to only 5 percent of its population. Well into the nineteenth century, Western powers—such as Louis Philippe's France, in which only 1.5 percent of the population could vote—were stingy in extending these rights of citizenship that were enjoyed by the sixteenth-century Sarmatian noble. Nor did these small percentages of citizens in the West have the right to elect their monarch; they were not kingmakers, like the nobles of the Commonwealth.

Rethinking the "Rise of the West"

In the sixteenth century and for a long time afterward, the political nation of the Commonwealth expressed very different views concerning the proper role of the monarch and the necessity of the rule of law. The general belief was that the true seat of authority in the state resided in the people and not in the ruler. Bearing elements of a federal system, their monarchical republic was based on ideas and values that seem surprisingly modern: personal liberty, the right to resist, the social contract, the principle of government by consent, the value of self-reliance.

This acknowledgment of rights and freedoms as the foundation of the state hardly reflected the situation emerging to Poland's west, however. The emergence of the doctrine *cuius regio, eius religio* out of the bloody experience of the sixteenth-century wars of religion has been the starting point for many a textbook on European history. The traditional trajectory of "the rise of the West" builds on this development: once able to dictate the religion of

their subjects, Western monarchs could move in the direction of centralization and consolidation of power in their own hands. Yet, as we have seen,
this narrative of *absolutum dominium* (absolute power) hardly encompasses
the totality of European experience.

Look a little further east, and the situation was strikingly different. Were
we to use the experience of the Commonwealth of Both Nations, Polish and
Lithuanian, to set the benchmark, what would emerge would be a constitutional, anti-tyrannical, tolerant, consensus-building, empowering civic
narrative. It represented an attempt to transcend historical and regional
differences by establishing a common identity for the citizenry. This civic
brotherhood of modern Sarmatians was convinced that the best form of
government was one in which the rule of law trumped the whim of the monarch. The messy and often time-consuming process of consensus building in
the legislative process was seen as more respectful of divergent views within
a heterogeneous state than a mathematically simple majority rule could ever
be, let alone the peremptory dictate of an absolute monarch.

Such was the atmosphere in which the two halves of Poland-Lithuania
would develop a bond based not upon the person of the monarch (king of
Poland and grand duke of Lithuania) but upon a sense of a common political and civic culture and a shared fate. They began their journey as the
citizens of the new Commonwealth of Both Nations, Polish and Lithuanian,
building on a shared heritage as well as a shared set of expectations. This
novel solution to the dilemma of yet another succession crisis was informed
by native traditions of governance and peaceful coexistence interacting
with the intellectual stimulation provided by the encounter with Western
trends such as the Renaissance and Reformation. At its apex—for this was
the country's Golden Age—we find a fascinating, creative synthesis of ideas
and approaches.

Part II

THE EUROPE OF POLAND

CHAPTER 5

The Commonwealth, Part I

Sarmatia Ascendant

The combined efforts of the last of the Jagiellons, Zygmunt August, and the country's diverse nobility had created a new political entity, the Commonwealth of Both Nations, Polish and Lithuanian. A series of steps had forged a closer union between the two federated halves, the Crown of Poland and the Grand Duchy of Lithuania, as well as between the noble citizens resident in each. An overarching federal framework provided for a common existence and allowed for the maintenance of local distinctiveness. Thus, the country that many still called Poland had room for local and regional allegiances that were anything but ethnolinguistically Polish. Being "Polish" was a matter of shared political culture, not ethnolinguistic homogeneity, let alone dominance of one ethnic group over another. This is one reason that it is simpler to favor the use of the term Sarmatian, after the myth of common origin.

This maximization of freedom in a heterogeneous country demanded a certain sophistication on the part of each major political player. Various constraints on the monarch, Senate, and Chamber of Deputies, not to mention the diversity of views within the parliament itself, resulted in a situation where cooperation, concessions, and compromises were required in order for the system to function. A center of Commonwealth consensus had to be crafted, time and again. In the process, this creative consensus building could help consolidate a new political culture and create a sense of community—an overarching Sarmatian identity. This was how the system looked, in theory.

The First Royal Election

The Union of Lublin and the Confederation of Warsaw had set the basic principles that were to govern the Commonwealth, this new and unusual political entity in the heart of Europe. The time had come to put the new system into practice. While the legislative branch—the joint Seym, with its feeder seymiks—was already in place, the executive branch of the government had to be activated. The Commonwealth needed to choose a monarch.

The Commonwealth's first royal election, scheduled for the first days of April 1573, would be no trifling affair. There was no precedent for what was to happen. In the course of its deliberations in Warsaw, the nobility of the Commonwealth had decided that the king would be elected *viritim*, thus instituting what today one might call universal suffrage—with one important caveat: the right to elect the king was the monopoly of the szlachta, the acknowledged citizenry of the state. Would the heterogeneous nobility of the federative state manage to come together and settle on a single candidate? Could the election be achieved in expeditious fashion? Or would it lead to a prolonged fight, which would destabilize the Commonwealth, still taking its first (shaky) steps?

The stakes were high. Any period of transition anywhere in Europe invited foreign interference. A state of this size had a sizable number of neighbors, any of which could choose to make trouble. Not counting the countries that were fiefs of the Commonwealth (Ducal Prussia, Courland), these neighbors ranged in size from tiny Estonia (under Swedish rule) and the Hohenzollern elector's state of Brandenburg, both in the north; the kingdoms of Bohemia, Hungary and Silesia (all under Habsburg sovereignty) to the west and south; the Ottoman vassal states of Transylvania and Moldavia as well as the Crimean Khanate along the long southern border; to the growing Eurasian power of Muscovy. The monarchs of any of these might take advantage of the interregnum to profit at the expense of the vulnerable Commonwealth.

Yet might not the novel configuration of the Commonwealth of Both Nations confound such intentions? Perhaps this time, the potential threat of foreign interference in a state in the throes of a succession crisis would be transmogrified into something more constructive. Instead of conniving to carve out chunks of territory for themselves along the state's long borders, neighboring heads of state were invited to channel their energies into vying for an incomparably bigger prize: control over the entire Commonwealth. A true coup, indeed!

The interest in the election of 1573 was palpable. This was not only an opportunity to become king of the largest country in Europe. Freed of all dynastic constraints by the death of the last Jagiellon, the nobles of the federative state could elect any ruler they chose. The playing field, thus, was as level as it might ever be. This moment in Polish history represented an unparalleled opportunity for an ambitious royal foreigner to expand, in exponential fashion, his influence in Central and Eastern Europe.

Thus, instead of a military campaign, there was a political campaign to be fought. And what a campaign it was! The curiosity factor itself must have been great, given that this was the first election of its kind. To borrow a metaphor from a Polish nobleman who would participate years later in the election process, the period of interregnum was a courtship dance: the Commonwealth the attractive bride, and the candidates from various countries her suitors. Each strove to make a positive impression on the father.

The Rules of the Game

Yet the matter was not that simple. Making a good impression was not entirely under the control of any given suitor, and the choice of ruler was not a personality contest. The foreign candidates for Polish king were not even to enter the territory of the Commonwealth, let alone campaign. Nor could domestic candidates be present at the election field. This was a move introduced by Jan Zamoyski during this first election—a move that resulted in the elimination of conniving magnates from consideration. Envoys would campaign, as it were, on their behalf.

There nonetheless were various ways to make an impression—some within the control of the individual candidate, some beyond. Some candidates in 1573, such as the Habsburgs, were not above trying to buy votes— nor were some nobles above benefiting from this; "wining and dining, and making promises" would become part and parcel of Commonwealth elections. In contrast to past elections elsewhere in Europe, however, it would not suffice to win over the most influential individuals, the senators—each of whom represented powerful interests within the country as a result of the offices held—or even the parliamentarians/members of the estates. Those could be numbered in the dozens—or at most, hundreds. Here (thanks again to Zamoyski, who pushed for the king to be elected *viritim*), one had to make an impact on a much larger, fluid assembly comprised for the most part of rank-and-file nobles. These were nobles who cared to exercise the right bestowed on them and help decide who would rule the country, but who may or may not have had much experience in governance outside of the local seymiks.

In a way, the noble collectivity that convened during the interregnum resembled more a whole front porch's worth of shotgun-wielding relatives than a genteel father. The prospect of an election drew some forty thousand nobles to the environs of Warsaw in April 1573. Astride their steeds, they assembled on and around an enormous field, resembling nothing more than the site of a medieval chivalric tourney. The central field, where the palatine and regional delegates convened, was marked off by a ditch and a stockade fence. The masses of noble electors gathered along its perimeter; information was relayed back and forth between center and periphery, allowing those gathered to hear the various reports on the candidates. A large wooden building stood at the end of the field. Its purpose was to protect from the elements the collected paper results of the electoral process.

While the ballot papers might be kept high and dry, the noble electorate was forced to rough it. To be sure, these warriors were used to the privations of military campaigns. Having no residence in Warsaw, most nobles ended up camping out in smaller tents nearby. Yet the weather could hardly put a damper on the event. Nobles came sumptuously dressed and armed to the teeth (the saber was perhaps the most visible mark of nobility, and the wealthier nobles' sabers were encrusted with jewels). The noble voters tended to move around in regional groups, veritable squadrons, listening to the pitches made by the candidates' representatives and weighing the options. If, over the course of several days, tempers rose, the sabers could be put to use, which is one of the reasons it was probably salutary that the responsibility for the course of the election fell to none other than the highest church dignitary, the Polish primate.

Most numerous on the fields outside of Warsaw were Mazovians—a fortuitous accident of geography, one that benefited these by-and-large impoverished nobles (who likely otherwise could not have afforded to make the trip to vote). These Mazovians were men who by virtue of their own or their ancestors' participation in the wars of the past had become ennobled, nearly en masse, to the extent that an unheard-of proportion of the population of this Polish province—some 20 percent—claimed noble status. In addition to being relatively new to the Crown of Poland (incorporated only as of 1526), Mazovia had proved the province most resistant to Protestantism. Less educated, less politically savvy, with no magnates to direct them, the nobles of Mazovia tended to take their cues from the church. One might thus expect that a candidate who stood staunchly on the side of the Catholic population would be victorious.

These considerations notwithstanding, the nobility—certainly its leaders—realized that the election had a much broader, international significance for the Commonwealth and its inhabitants. The choice of king essentially boiled down to a choice of alliances—not an inconsequential consideration for a state in flux. Which way would the Commonwealth lean—north, south, east, west—and what were the implications of each possible permutation?

In the case of this inaugural election, interest in the Commonwealth crown came from all directions. However, the pursuit of alliances with the north and the east—the first represented by Sweden's king, Johan III, and his underage son Zygmunt; the second by Fedor, the younger son of Ivan IV—did not amount to much, for various reasons. The candidates whose names were brought up most often during the interregnum came from a different direction: from the west. The two favored candidates were Archduke Ernst, of the Habsburg dynasty, and Henri Valois, duke of Anjou, the brother of Charles IX, king of France.

Which alliance promised the most? Which entanglements were most dangerous? Electing a Habsburg would have involved the Commonwealth in the battle with the Turks. This might appeal to Crown magnates, who could salivate at the thought of eventual spoils (read: territory) in the region of the mouth of the Dniester and the Dnieper Rivers, spoils that might give them greater access to the Black Sea trade routes. By contrast, a French alliance would keep the Poles and Lithuanians away from that imbroglio as well as improve relations between France and the Commonwealth. A greater degree of French interest in Central Europe, however, could inspire the Habsburgs to renew their alliance with Muscovy.

The electors were divided. Catholic senators tended to favor a Habsburg connection, while the strong Protestant contingent among the deputies favored the French connection. This second connection made for strange bedfellows: the knee-jerk anti-Habsburg (read: anti-absolutist) stance of the rank-and-file nobles caused them to consider Henri Valois—this despite his recent role in the ignominious Saint Bartholomew Massacre in August 1572, which amounted to the wholesale killing of French Huguenots. Valois's plenipotentiary was the bishop of Valence, Jean de Montluc, who nonetheless facilely claimed his candidate had little part in the murder of these French Protestants—and that the Valois would embrace the religious toleration dictated by the Confederation of Warsaw.

Indeed, the bishop of Valence seemed ready to promise the moon, if that is what it would take to win votes for his candidate. Yet perhaps the perspective of encroaching Habsburg absolutism—something the Poles witnessed in the neighboring kingdoms of Bohemia and Hungary—proved decisive. Montluc took no chances, made a strong case for his candidate being one who would respect the laws of the Commonwealth, and had some fifteen hundred copies of his speech distributed among the nobles. It likely did not hurt that Jan Zamoyski, who had been making a name for himself as a defender of noble rights in the deliberations of the last year, came out in favor of the Frenchman.

A week of debating ensued. On May 11, 1573, the nobles on horseback finally elected their first joint monarch. Their first choice of king for the Commonwealth of Both Nations, Polish and Lithuanian proved to be the one most removed from the country—geographically, genetically, and perhaps temperamentally: the French duke. Several days later, after certain formalities were completed, Henri Valois, duke of Anjou, was proclaimed king-elect.

Chalk one up for the Commonwealth: the first mass noble election went amazingly smoothly. The peace was kept during the interregnum, and the desired result was produced: a king was chosen by the nobles who assembled near Warsaw. The new system was shown to work.

This is not to say that the election of 1573 did not have rough spots. The first of these was the absence of Lithuanian nobles, who boycotted the election—although certain magnates had not been above negotiating with the Habsburgs to seat the archduke on the throne of the Grand Duchy as a return to the status quo ante of the Union of Lublin. They nonetheless put up no resistance when presented with the results and accepted the new king as their own ruler; apparently a gift of a hundred thousand ducats was enough to convince several influential Lithuanians to agree to support the Frenchman. The second—and, in this case, more damning—drawback was related to the Poles' choice of monarch: the man Poles would come to know as Henryk Walezy.

The King Who Ran Away

To be sure, none of the assembled nobles had actually seen Henri. All impressions of the duke of Anjou came refracted through the rosy prism provided by the bishop of Valence, Jean de Montluc. A delegation from the Commonwealth traveled to Paris, where negotiations as to the terms of Henri's rule ensued. Henri Valois acquiesced to the demand to recognize the existing privileges of the nobility as well as various limitations on his power contained in a document of non-negotiable principles that would henceforth be called the Henrician Articles. Henri also swallowed many of the excessively generous promises that Montluc had made in his name. These had been put into the second written document, the pacta conventa, that the king-elect was required to sign. A bad sign: Henri balked at the—no surprise—religious toleration. Only with the greatest reluctance did he swear he would observe it.

Despite the best-laid plans, the competently run election, and the negotiations in Paris, Henri Valois proved a disastrous choice. He made a bad impression at his coronation, which was wracked by controversy. At that event, he refused to renew his oath to abide by the Henrician Articles and pacta conventa. Henri clearly did not like the limitations on his power, nor did he like being told what to do by the Commonwealth nobility. The twenty-four-year-old balked at marrying the fifty-year-old sister of Zygmunt August, Anna, who reportedly was so excited by the prospect that she had fleur-de-lis embroidered on her garments. It seemed that Henri was partial to boys . . . or at least was happiest in the company of the men in his own entourage, which did nothing to win over the nobles in the capital. Doubtless he felt out of place, and alien, and this despite the fact that the Polish delegation to France had impressed the French court with their mastery of his native tongue.

Although—in accordance with the Henrician Articles—he was watched over by a group of senators who resided in the capital, Henri clearly was not watched closely enough. In May 1573—not even a full four months after his coronation—news of his brother's death back in France reached the Polish king. Henri wanted to return home to secure his place as king of France. The senators in Kraków nonetheless forbade him to leave until a Seym could be summoned. His heart in Paris, where a hereditary kingship awaited him, the Valois surreptitiously planned his escape. Having donned disguise, on the night of June 18/19, Henri slipped out of the castle and made haste for the Silesian border.

Once news of Henri's escape reached the country, the Commonwealth went into crisis mode, its citizens unsure whether this was a period of rule or interregnum. The situation was exacerbated by the runaway king. Henri led his former country on, claiming he would rule the Commonwealth from abroad. In the end, Henri was given an ultimatum: return by May 12, 1575, or forfeit the throne. The king remained in France.

Despite the clarity imposed by the ultimatum, the whole situation still left the Commonwealth reeling—a situation that did not win over any converts among the nobles to the idea of a foreigner coming to lead them. News of his escape poisoned the minds of his former electors, the Commonwealth nobility. Even villagers near the capital came to demonize the French, as a foreigner who happened to cross their path learned (barely escaping with his life). To add insult to injury, the country would have to undertake the whole complicated procedure of royal election once more—much sooner than anyone could have imagined.

For the record, Henri was not an entire success upon his return, although he did sit on the French throne significantly longer than the Polish one and seemed to mature there. Yet King Henri III would be the last of the Valois dynasty to rule France. Unable to calm down religious unrest, his rule was challenged by (among others) the Huguenot Henri of Navarre, whom Henri Valois had to designate as his successor. As the situation escalated, Parisians revolted against his rule, and Henri III himself met a violent end: he was assassinated (stabbed) by a monk in 1589.

So much for this onetime king. Henri Valois was not a part of the fabric of the Commonwealth long enough to accomplish anything noteworthy, nor was his heart in the country. The next king, on the other hand, would prove lion-hearted.

The Triumphant Transylvanian

After the French debacle, it might not have surprised anyone if the citizens of the Commonwealth turned a jaundiced eye toward the prospect of yet another election. And, to be sure, the number of participants in this second election *viritim* was somewhat reduced. Yet the noble nation persisted, and to good avail. The system rebounded with alacrity, and the assembled nobles were able to surmount the various obstacles they encountered on the way to electing their second king.

This time, the noble electors would ultimately choose one of the best kings ever to rule the Commonwealth. He was István Báthori, palatine of Transylvania—known in his adopted country as Stefan Batory. Batory was the "southern" candidate, Transylvania sharing a border with the Ruthenian palatinate of the Commonwealth. Transylvania was the part of the Crown of Saint Stephen that had managed to gain some degree of autonomy from its Ottoman overlord, unlike further Hungarian territories to the west. It remained distinct from the so-called Royal Hungary, which had come under Habsburg control upon the death of the last Jagiellon to rule Hungary, in 1526.

Although Batory's candidacy was laughed off during the first joint election, the second time around, the palatine of Transylvania was given a closer look, particularly after news reached the Commonwealth of a recent military victory of his. Still, at the Election Seym near Wola, which took place on December 7–15, 1575, the Habsburg candidate and Holy Roman Emperor, Maximilian II, was a serious rival. Maximilian was the scion of the Habsburgs who had gained control over Royal Hungary—and thus, through his grandmother, boasted some Jagiellonian blood. This garnered Maximilian support not only from the expected Catholic quarters (including many senators) but also from the Lithuanians and Royal Prussians.

They were, however, outnumbered by the masses of Polish nobles with connections to the old Executionist/Protestant camp, who remained displeased by the thought of having another foreigner, let alone a Habsburg, as king. They were determined to elect a "Piast"—one of their own. How Batory came to be considered "their" candidate was through his promise (a promise that the first elected king of the Commonwealth had broken) to marry the fifty-year-old Anna Jagiellon, although clearly this would be a dynastic dead end for him.

What ensued might, at first glance, seem a veritable comedy of errors, had it not turned out so well in the end. Initially, the only candidate seemed to be the Holy Roman Emperor, Maximilian II, although behind the scenes others were sounding out Batory. Nobles gathered on one field (not the election field) elected Maximilian, while several days later, nobles on another field opted for the Transylvanian/Jagiellonian pair. This time, not only were swords unsheathed—a brief war was fought. No love was lost between the contending candidates (the Transylvanian considered himself the rightful ruler of Habsburg-occupied Royal Hungary). Batory proved his mettle, won the war—and with it, the right to rule the Commonwealth. In the interim, the assembled nobles convened to straighten out the matter of succession, which was done quickly and efficiently—a testimony to the fact that, indeed, this new system could work. The new king assumed the Polish-Lithuanian throne in May 1576, while continuing to rule Transylvania (leaving a brother there as viceroy).

The Hungarian connection proved infinitely superior to the abortive French one. At age forty-two Batory was a more mature candidate, and he made a much better impression on his new subjects. He had solid anti-Habsburg as well as pro-Jagiellonian credentials. He had fought on the side of Zygmunt August's sister Izabela, the wife of János Zápolya, when she tried to preserve the Hungarian throne for her son János Zsigmond. Batory would succeed the latter as palatine of Transylvania. Scrappy, battle-scarred, and hardy, Batory was, in his own words, neither "sculpted, nor painted" a king like his French predecessor. With his martial credentials and convivial demeanor, in many ways the Transylvanian proved a soul brother to the Commonwealth nobility.

Batory proved capable of dealing with diverse constituencies. His experience in ruling Transylvania, home to a mixed population of Magyars, Szeklers, Saxons (all three political nations), and Romanians, adherents of an even wider array of religious denominations, could be seen as a good training ground for a Polish king. Indeed, he managed to win over the Lithuanians, even if he did not fulfill all their wishes. Perhaps coming out best in that arrangement was Mikołaj the Red Radziwiłł (one of the Lithuanians who protested against the Union of Lublin), who ended up being elevated by the new king to two high positions: that of grand hetman of Lithuania and palatine of Vilnius. On the international front, the election of Batory led to an alliance with Turkey, which proceeded to order the Crimean Tatars to make trouble for Muscovy.

In contrast to Henri Valois, Batory was a man of his word. His swearing at his coronation on March 3, 1576, to uphold all the conditions laid out in the Henrician Articles and pacta conventa—now a non-negotiable condition of his becoming king—meant something and not only in his promise to marry the last of the Jagiellonian princesses. Batory's pacta conventa (this being the document enumerating additional obligations that the king-elect would assume, a document written specifically for each successful candidate to the throne) mandated that the Transylvanian deal with a thorny problem: Muscovy.

The "Polish"—"Russian" Rivalry

That Russia once figured as a peripheral irritation for the Poles is hardly self-evident to the modern reader. The contemporary map of Europe features only a tiny point of contact between the two states—so tiny that it is easily overlooked. The only border the two countries share lies in Europe's north. This is where Poland abuts the tiny Russian enclave of Kaliningrad, which Poland's eastern neighbor (in its Soviet incarnation) acquired only after World War II.

Even less evident is that Poland could ever have posed a real problem for Russia. Yet, as we shall see, it did—already in the early modern period, when the countries were known as Muscovy and the Commonwealth of Both Nations.

The conflict between these two states had been brewing for some time. Indeed, it long predated the existence of either entity. For this, we should take a step back to consider how it came about that one can speak not only of Polish-Russian relations but also of a Polish-Russian rivalry—one in which there was no preordained conclusion who would come out on top.

The Polish-Russian rivalry was the most pronounced national conflict within the world of the Slavs. Linguistically, Slavs are divided into three basic categories: West, South, and East Slavs. Like Czechs, Slovaks, and other Slavic peoples about whom the world has forgotten (Lusatians et al.), Poles were a part of Western Slavdom. Russia laid claim to hegemony over Eastern Slavdom, which—in modern linguistic calculations—also includes Ukrainians and Belarusians, as well as some smaller regional entities as well. (Falling for so long under Ottoman rule, the South Slavs did not figure in any power calculations in the early modern period.) The position of each was reinforced by denominational differences: Poles had embraced Latin Christendom, while the Russians took their religion from the Greeks—from Byzantium.

The earliest encounter of Poles with Eastern Slavs came at the expense of the defunct Kyivan Rus', which had broken up into principalities, all of which had been subjugated as of 1240 by the Golden Horde. During this period of Mongol Yoke, a young and dynamic Lithuania was the first to profit from the disintegration, incorporating a number of these principalities into the Grand Duchy. Even Poland, during the reign of Kazimierz the Great, had acquired Halych and Volodymyr in 1340.

At this point, Muscovy appeared only faintly on the horizon. It had not been a self-standing Kyivan principality but rather was part of Suzdal. Nonetheless, with a stroke of good luck, it began to emerge—an upstart in the east. At about the same time as Kazimierz was integrating Halych and Volodymyr into his Polish state, Ivan Kalita of Moscow had secured from the Golden Horde the right to collect the tribute that each old Rus' principality owed the Mongol overlords—profiting from the commission in the process. It still took another century before Muscovy would begin to figure in Polish calculations.

With the Polish-Lithuanian personal union in 1386, the Crown of Poland became embroiled in Lithuania's battles with its neighbor to the east. Here it is worth remembering how extensive the Grand Duchy's holdings were—how much of the old Kyivan lands had come under Lithuanian rule. It truly seemed to be the heir to Kyivan Rus', more so than the upstart Muscovy. In the west and south, Lithuania had absorbed the principalities of Volhynia, Kyiv, Pereiaslav, and parts of Chernihiv (Polish: Czernihów). Further to the east (that is, in the Kyivan lands closest to Muscovy), Lithuania controlled parts of the former principalities of Polatsk (Polish: Połock) and Smolensk and had a common border with the principality of Tver as well as with Novgorod. The border between the Muscovite state and Lithuania was hardly much larger than that between Poland and Kaliningrad today. At its greatest extent, Lithuania flanked Muscovy on both west and south—all the way to the source of the River Don. Simply put, Muscovy was dwarfed by its western neighbor.

The plucky little state nonetheless stood on the verge of expansion. Its first real calling card was delivered by Dmitrii Donskoi, who in 1380 defeated the Golden Horde at Kulikovo Pole. Donskoi announced his intention of "gathering" the Rus' principalities—which made him automatically an enemy of the Grand Duchy of Lithuania, which had incorporated the territory of the vast majority of them.

The Muscovite Menace

It was the great-grandson of Donskoi, Ivan III, who proved unrelenting in his quest for regional dominance. Ivan III finally managed to "gather" the important territories of Tver and Novgorod. The Muscovite grand prince and his successors engaged in almost continuous battle with the Grand Duchy of Lithuania, picking fights in 1492–1494, 1498–1503, 1507–1508, and 1534–1537. The skirmishes did not cease, even while Alexander was married to Ivan's daughter. In fact, the marriage allowed the father to renew his aggression, complaining that his daughter (who, incidentally, was very happily married) was being badly treated in Poland-Lithuania.

Ivan III made good use of marriage alliances—of his own as well as his daughter's. Having married a Paleologue princess, he came to have greater ambitions, ambitions worthy of the Byzantine connection. It was he who proclaimed Muscovy a tsardom (the word "tsar" being a corruption of the imperial title Caesar). During his reign, Orthodox clergymen began to talk of Muscovy as being the Third Rome. Ivan III tried to gain control over the territories of Polatsk, Vitsebsk (Polish: Witebsk), and Smolensk, which he claimed were part of his patrimony.

The Jagiellonian kings sought to defuse this destabilizing force on their eastern frontier. Zygmunt the Old allied himself with the Tatars of Kazan in the east as well as the Livonian Order in the north. His rival, Vasilii III (Ivan III's successor), upped the ante, allying himself with the Crimean Tatars as well as a defector from the Lithuanian side. This was Prince Mikhail Glinskii. The prince was a picture of paradoxes—a prominent and wealthy nobleman of Tatar descent, a close friend of King Zygmunt, educated in typical Renaissance style, and a Catholic to boot. Following a conflict with another noble, whom Glinskii contracted to kill, the Tatar escaped to Muscovy and joined the fight against his former friend. The two sides engaged in a long-drawn-out war. The conflict up north both enabled and emboldened the prince of Moldavia to run over the nearby Polish region of Pokutia in the south, even making his way toward Lviv before he was stopped. Although the southern incursion concluded with a peace treaty in 1510, it suggests how vulnerable Poland-Lithuania, with its long borders, could be.

As if this were not enough, assistance came to Muscovy from the west as well. The Habsburgs were all too happy to play the Russia card. They supplied Russia with armaments and the personnel to direct their use, leading to the capture of Smolensk in 1514. Even the victory at Orsha later that year by the Lithuanian grand hetman Konstanty Ostrogski could not win Smolensk back for Poland-Lithuania.

Ostrogski, incidentally, had also found himself on both sides of the Polish-Russian border. Not by choice, however: he had been taken captive during the fighting in 1500. Despite being a devout Orthodox prince, he repeatedly distinguished himself in battle with both the Tatars and with Muscovy, which earned him the title of grand hetman of Lithuania. An exception within the Grand Duchy, this Orthodox prince was given offices that had been reserved for Catholics, per the original Union of Horodło: the most notable of these were the chancellorship of Vilnius and the palatinate of Trakai.

This example suggests some of the tensions inherent in the Polish-Russian rivalry. There was always the chance that discontented nobles in Lithuania could vote with their feet. Glinskii went east; Ostrogski returned to the west. Under the next ruler of Russia, the Muscovite state was not only catching up to Lithuania in the competition for the lands of Kyivan Rus'. It would start muscling in on Poland ...

In 1547, a sixteen-year-old named Ivan was crowned tsar of Russia. Later that year, a great fire raged through Moscow—a sign from the heavens that the reign of Ivan IV, Russia's first tsar, would be out of the ordinary. And it was. The ruler crowned Ivan IV has gone down in history as Ivan the Terrible.

Whether one translates his sobriquet as terrifying or terrible is ultimately immaterial. Ivan was a terrible person to have as one's enemy—something to which his neighbors to the east would soon attest. He extended his hold over territories that had never been part of Kyivan Rus': the Khanates of Kazan and Astrakhan, in this way bringing Moslem populations under Russian rule and gaining control over the Volga.

Not satisfied with expansion to the east, Ivan set his sights on the north. The goal was to gain control over Baltic trade. Despite its increasing size, Russia had limited access to the Baltic. The tsar wanted to increase trade via Narva, the port town at the far eastern end of Estonia, which Muscovite forces occupied in 1558. In this, though, Ivan had to contend with two other forces not indifferent to the balance of power in the Baltic region, Sweden and Poland-Lithuania. Like hungry dogs, they all fought over the bone of contention: Livonia. The saga of Zygmunt August's northern diversion (described earlier) underscored the riskiness of the Commonwealth's involvement in this region.

Nor did Ivan ignore the traditional occupation of his ancestors, the "gathering" of the Rus' principalities. Having already eliminated other contenders, he now focused the battle squarely on territories under Lithuanian control. As a result, war with Russia was the underlying current within that polity during its process of unification. It served as a weathervane for the talks on unification. When Lithuania fared well, Lithuanian sentiments for union decreased—and vice versa. A sign of the encroaching danger, and impetus for formalizing a real Polish-Lithuanian union, was the loss to the Muscovites of the important fortress of Polatsk in 1563.

By the end of the Jagiellonian era, the Polish-Russian rivalry looked very different. Muscovy was transformed from a gadfly to a real thorn in the side of the Commonwealth. More and more Lithuanian territory had come under Muscovite occupation. Livonia was in chaos. And, to add insult to injury, in order to deal with these pressing wars on the Commonwealth's periphery, Zygmunt August was forced to seek outside aid, from the Brandenburgs—in the process conceding the line of succession in Ducal Prussia to the Hohenzollerns of Brandenburg.

Third Rome versus Sarmatia?

The final third of the sixteenth century witnessed a changed dynamic. On one hand, we have the emergence of the Commonwealth of Both Nations. On the other, we have Muscovite Russia—the Muscovy of Ivan the Terrible (the Commonwealth did not publicly acknowledge his self-elevation to tsar).

Over the course of the previous century, similarities between the two countries had multiplied. Both now comprised large, even unwieldy, states with at least a degree of diversity both ethnic and religious within their thin populations. Both lay claim to a large swath of lands inhabited primarily (although not exclusively) by people of Ruthenian stock—lands that had centuries earlier been part of Kyivan Rus'. Both countries stretched nearly from sea to sea: in control of the mouth of the Volga, Russia strove to reach the Baltic; in control of the mouth of the Vistula, the Commonwealth strained to reach the Black Sea. In some ways, thus, they were relatively comparable entities.

In other ways, however, they were diametrical opposites. Poland and Russia represented two opposite ends of the political spectrum. If the freedom-loving Poles sniffed out every whiff of royal absolutum dominium, Muscovy was the extreme case of what the Poles feared most—autocracy or absolute rule by a single individual, the tsar. Polish nobles exercised a huge degree of independence, as reflected in their most precious possession, the Golden Freedoms. Polish kings were obliged to uphold the laws of the land, which limited their own royal range of independent action. The citizenry of the Commonwealth were to be, in the words of Cicero, "slaves to the public interest."

Muscovy functioned in a completely different fashion. Realizing that one's position in life was a function of one's proximity to the tsar, Russian boyars termed themselves "slaves of the tsar," to whom they were indebted for everything they possessed. Dependent on the tsar's mercy, Muscovites had little comprehension of the rule of law or how a ruler might be bound to it. The Commonwealth was decentralized, with a strong tradition of local representation. In the emerging Russian state, the tsar held firm the reins of power and made decisions about who would do what where.

Even their approaches to growth were different. In its Commonwealth incarnation, Polish expansion relied upon the federative principle and was governed by respect for regional differences. The rulers of Muscovy had imposed their notion of "gathering" upon formerly independent principalities, choosing to conquer them militarily and subdue them. They had squelched the independent spirit of distinct entities such as Novgorod and subordinated them to control from the center. If the tsar would have agreed with (the later) Louis XIV, who famously claimed "L'état—c'est moi," the nobles of the Commonwealth saw themselves as the embodiment of the state, which in turn existed to serve them. It was a true clash of civilizations.

This was particularly evident in the shifting borderlands of the two states, a place where the conflict was clearly experienced. An example of this might be the receptiveness with which the idea of a Muscovite candidate on the Polish throne was greeted by certain rank-and-file nobles of the Grand Duchy. Already in 1573, there were nobles who were excited about the candidacy of a Muscovite grand prince. To be sure, some of these nobles nursed the hopes that the man who ruled with an iron fist back home might take care of their highly placed nemeses, the powerful Lithuanian magnates (by this time Ivan had ordered or participated in the murder of nearly all the members of his advisory board, the Chosen Council), in similar fashion. Yet the idea of being an elected monarch did not appeal to the autocrat. Unwilling to play by the new rules governing the balance of power in the Commonwealth, Ivan the Terrible set his own (unacceptable) terms: he demanded the incorporation of Lithuanian territories all the way to the River Dvina as well as the creation of a tripartite state, Poland-Lithuania-Muscovy, which would become hereditary in his family.

Transylvanian Travails

Such was the situation when, in 1576, the valiant Transylvanian assumed the Polish throne. Batory was obliged by his coronation oath (the famous pacta conventa, specially written for each ensuing elected king) to try to deal with the Russian menace—specifically, to regain territories along the Lithuanian and Livonian border.

The Transylvanian approached this task systematically. He began by reforming the army, introducing sensible changes at the level of the artillery, infantry, and logistics. His most famous change was when he transformed the former light cavalry of the nobles into a powerful fighting force known as the Hussars. The Polish Hussars were professional heavy cavalry—the ferocious "winged horsemen," known by the distinguishing feature of their battle gear, a curved wooden frame that sprouted a row of eagle or vulture feathers. Together with their arms (a saber, pistols, and a second long sword strapped to the saddle), the Hussars intimidated many an opponent.

No less crucial, Batory managed to raise funds to run a war. One of the faults of the system, from the point of view of a monarch on the warpath (if not from the Commonwealth noble, who was allergic to the thought of paying taxes), was that the king of Poland had no war chest. Instead, the king had to request the Seym to levy extraordinary taxes for each campaign—and Batory fought three. While this was a hindrance, the Transylvanian's prowess on the battlefield nonetheless had the desired effect, and taxes were levied for each campaign in turn.

With this new, more efficient, and fearsome military machine, Batory began chipping away at the advances made only years earlier by the Muscovites. With an army comprised of fifty-six thousand troops, he captured Polatsk in 1579. However, he magnanimously allowed the occupants of the fortress to depart with their belongings. This was not a usual approach during wars of this period, when armies plundered what they could. Livonia required greater expenditure of hard-won funds but still proved achievable. In this way, Batory managed to regain what had been lost during the reign of the last of the Jagiellons.

This was Batory's first campaign against Muscovy. In 1580 he proceeded to capture Velikie Luki, a fortress to the north of Vitsebsk. A sign that they were in Muscovite territory: the region had no roads, meaning the troops literally had to cut their way through forests and swamps. It is worth noting that Batory's chancellor, Jan Zamoyski, also fought at Velikie Luki. Following the battle Zamoyski was rewarded with the title of grand hetman of the Crown for life (the first ever nobleman to achieve this distinction).

The year 1581 marked Batory's third campaign against Muscovy. Tensions continued to mount between the two countries, expressed by each monarch in his own inimitable way. That year, Ivan the Terrible wrote a letter in which he questioned the legitimacy of Batory's election (by common nobles, no less)—to which Batory responded by challenging the Russian to a duel ... Both prepared for war. On the Polish side, delays (waiting for money) caused for a change of plans: instead of making their way to Novgorod, the Commonwealth forces (some forty-seven thousand strong) would attack Pskov—in the late fall. In this northern climate, this meant winter conditions.

Although a second choice, the well-fortified Pskov represented no small prize. An important center of trade for Muscovite Russia since Hanseatic times, it was essentially four fortresses in one—so massive it reminded some of the Poles of ... Paris. Note that the population of Pskov was over thirty thousand, and it was defended by a force of twenty thousand, making it larger even than the Polish capital of Kraków.

That year's siege of Pskov dragged on relentlessly to little avail: the massive walls withstood the onslaught, and the Commonwealth forces were unable to penetrate even where cannons had opened a breach. Short on ammunition, Batory's army was getting desperate from hunger and disease. Then, in what appears to be a stroke of genius, a Lithuanian cavalry unit led by a mercurial Radziwiłł with the nickname of Lightning Bolt set off a rash of fires in the vicinity. Caught off guard by the suddenness and the ferocity of the blaze, Pskov capitulated. Russia sued for peace. The Treaty of Yam Zapolski was negotiated in January 1582 and, while not giving the Poles Pskov, did confirm the country's possession of Livonia. It likewise set the terms for a ten-year truce—a period that could be used to regain strength for a future onslaught.

At this time, the Commonwealth, so ably led by Stefan Batory, seemed to have gained the upper hand. The Transylvanian went so far as to propose union with Muscovy at the beginning of 1586. Full of ambitions, he sought to regain freedom for the Hungarian lands under Ottoman rule and to reconstitute the Crown of Saint Stephen. Those ambitions would remain unrealized: by the end of that same year, Batory was dead from kidney failure.

The Union of Brest

The war with Muscovite Russia was hardly over. Despite the accomplishments of the valiant Transylvanian, Polish-Russian relations had yet to enter
into their most interesting—indeed, most incredible—phase. In the interim,
another development took place, one that would have important repercussions for the battle not only for territory but also for the hearts and minds of
the borderland inhabitants.

More precisely, this new development represented a war for souls. At the
same time that Poland-Lithuania and Muscovy were vying for control of
the Rus' principalities, questions of jurisdiction over the Orthodox population of Eastern Europe generated sparks. This was the world of the Greek
Church, adherents of Christianity in its Byzantine (that is, Eastern) rite.

Byzantine Christianity differed from the Church of Rome in a number of
ways, not all of them doctrinal. Whereas in Roman Catholicism the high
church language was Latin, there was no one single high church language in
the Greek world: the Slavic lands had been given their own church language
by the earliest missionaries to the Slavs, Cyril and Methodius. This language
came to be known as Old Church Slavonic. Distinct from the spoken ver-
naculars of the region, it was nonetheless for the most part comprehensible
to the population.

The relationship of the church and state in the East was also different
than in the West. Following the pattern of Byzantium, the Eastern Church
pragmatically subordinated itself to the authority of the state in which it
functioned. Another seemingly obvious distinction: the Eastern churches
did not owe allegiance to the pope in Rome but, rather, acknowledged the
patriarch of Constantinople. After the fall of Constantinople in 1453, the
position of the Greek Church was much diminished. This allowed for some
jockeying within Eastern Christendom, especially in the East Slavic lands,
where the majority of the faithful resided and the religion flourished.

To be sure, even before the Ottomans moved into Byzantium, not all was
well in the Eastern Greek world further north. This in part was the result of
the fact that, from its inception, the head of the Greek Church in the Rus'
lands had been the metropolitan of Kyiv. The shift of state borders that resulted in the Greek faithful residing in different states complicated the ecclesiastical picture and led various clergymen to vie with each other for influence
over the faithful of Eastern Europe. To give one example: the Bulgarian clergyman who was chosen as metropolitan of the Ruthenian lands in 1415 soon
found himself excommunicated by the patriarch of Constantinople, whose
mind had been poisoned by the metropolitan of Moscow, who wanted this

position for himself. Not until 1458 was Poland-Lithuania able to establish an independent Kyivo-Halych metropolitanate for its Orthodox population.

The church leaders of Muscovy became emboldened during the reign of Ivan III, who married into the Byzantine imperial family and began to entertain imperial pretensions. How could one talk of a "Third Rome" if Muscovy did not have its own patriarchate?

Not long after Batory's death, the Muscovite church got its wish. The patriarch of Constantinople, Jeremiah, traveled to Moscow. Desperately in need of financial support, he agreed to consecrate Boris Godunov's choice of candidate to the position. (At this point, Godunov was ruling in the name of Ivan the Terrible's son Fedor.)

This new development clearly had repercussions for the Orthodox of the Commonwealth. Their church was hemorrhaging. Its relatively low level of clerical education, with the married clergy essentially passing on its knowledge to its sons, left the Greek faithful at a decided disadvantage when it came to defending their beliefs against the challenges posed not only by the Roman faith but by the new and aggressive Protestant denominations. Many important Lithuanian/Ruthenian magnates and nobles abandoned the faith of their fathers for Calvinism or other Protestant sects. Some eventually converted to Catholicism.

The patriarch of Moscow aspired to be the leader of the Orthodox world. Could he make gains within the Commonwealth? The prize was a worthy one: nearly half the population of the Commonwealth of Both Nations belonged to the Greek faith.

Those in the Commonwealth realized that they needed to counteract such moves. Essentially there were two options. They could either establish an autocephalous Orthodox church for the country or bring about church union—here, union with what was still the biggest force in Christianity: the Church in Rome.

The latter option won out, in part because the Church of Rome had made similar efforts in the past. First attempted in Constance, union between the Roman and Greek Churches had been achieved at the Council of Florence (1439), although nothing ultimately came of it (it is this attempt at union, incidentally, that led to the formation of an autocephalous Orthodox church in Moscow). Yet another sign that union was the direction favored by the Vatican was that, as early as 1573, a Greek College was opened in Rome as well as a Congregation for Eastern Churches.

The Commonwealth, thus, was convinced to work toward union and capitalized on a desire among Commonwealth clergymen not to subordinate themselves to Muscovy—in particular, not to send their financial dues there.

This became visible in the synods that took place in the town of Brest, along the internal Polish-Lithuanian border, at the end of the sixteenth century. The Greek clergy decided to support the idea of union—with qualifications. While they would recognize the authority of the pope in Rome, they were not ready to make many changes that would affect the look and feel of their religion. They were allowed to retain their distinctive Eastern rite: the liturgy in Church Slavonic, as well as other traditions, including the marriage of the clergy. A selling point for the Orthodox bishops was a further advantage specified in the act of union: they were to be admitted into the Senate of the Commonwealth, on par with the Roman Catholic bishops.

This Union of Brest, as the 1596 agreement was called, produced a new phenomenon in the Commonwealth: so-called Uniates. These were Eastern-rite Catholics, in official parlance members of the Greek-Catholic Confession of the Slavonic Rite. In other words, while they retained their traditional Eastern rite and practices, they were part of the Catholic Church.

Despite the acceptance of union on the part of most Orthodox bishops, the union proved a much harder sell to the faithful masses, who did not want the faith of their fathers to change in any way, shape, or form. This adverse reaction was not a simple knee-jerk reaction of the peasants, however. Cossacks, urban dwellers, as well as at least a handful of highly placed Orthodox nobles were among those who balked at the idea. Many urban members of the Orthodox Church, furthermore, had been organized into lay brotherhoods, which played an important role in their social and religious lives. There seemed to be a geographical dimension to this: the inhabitants of Lviv and the Ruthenian Palatinate, the most densely populated centers of the Orthodox Church in the Commonwealth, were particularly adamant in their refusal to change anything. It is clear that some decried the fact that union would put them likely under greater Polish control.

The results of the Union of Brest were mixed. It rent the fabric of the Eastern Christian community of the Commonwealth, creating Uniates but also creating Disuniates—those who preferred to retain their distance from the West and the Polish church. Still, those who acceded to the union derived some profit from the connection with Rome. The Basilian monastic order provided the best-trained Uniate clerics, the order having been reformed after the Jesuit model. Their position contrasted with that of those who, remaining staunchly Orthodox, remained outside the union. Their position within the Commonwealth was tenuous as, after 1596, Orthodoxy was outlawed (although the Disuniates were not prosecuted).

Another serious drawback was that not all of the terms of the union were put into practice. Despite agreeing to affiliate themselves with the West, the Uniate bishops did not obtain what for them would be the main advantage:

membership in the Senate. The shortsighted Roman Catholic bishops refused to permit them into their ranks. In this way, the Uniate bishops had less to show for their efforts, something that doubtless weakened their ability to win over any of the Disuniate community. They and their flocks would continue to be treated as second-class citizens. This strained relations and may have made union with Orthodox Muscovy more attractive.

Russia's Time of Troubles

Although Batory worked valiantly to recoup territorial losses incurred during the rule of earlier kings, even his biggest military triumph had more symbolic than real value. Nonetheless, in many ways he prepared the ground for further encounters with Muscovy. Not only did he build up the Commonwealth army and create the fearsome Hussars. His eastern policy fueled the flames of noble ambition. The first to succumb to this temptation was perhaps Jan Zamoyski, his chancellor. In the course of his career, Zamoyski amassed not only titles but also enormous wealth—in part a result of owning numerous estates. Other Commonwealth magnates appear to have been on the lookout for opportunities that would propel them into the stratosphere.

One such opportunity presented itself in the early 1600s. This period of Russian history—known in English as the Time of Troubles—marked the most significant incursion of Commonwealth forces into Russian territory. Ominously named, this period lasted over a dozen years and represented Muscovite Russia's first crisis of succession, resulting in unbelievable chaos.

The last real ruler of the Rurik dynasty, Ivan the Terrible himself, is in part to blame for what was to follow. At his death in 1584, his country was reeling from the truly terrible consequences of his rule. Not only had his foreign policy of expansion into the Baltic region been countered by moves on the part of Sweden as well as the Commonwealth. His capricious and still poorly understood policies initiated the murder of numerous relatives and officials, the destruction of towns (the most important of which being the enormously significant trading entrepôt of Novgorod), and a state of general confusion. Some believe the tsar's insanity was probably the result of mercury poisoning, a side effect of the medical care he received for other ailments.

Whatever the reason, Ivan wreaked no less havoc on his immediate family. A fit of rage in 1581 led him to strike and kill his first-born son, also named Ivan, with a pointed staff. This left the middle child, Ivan's half-brother Fedor, next in line to succeed him, but Fedor was a half-wit and ill suited to rule. There had been a third son, Dmitri—but he died, under mysterious circumstances, in the small Volga town of Uglich in 1591. When Ivan the

Terrible died in 1584, he left no heir who was able to seize the reins himself, let alone continue the dynasty.

Marriage politics had always been a central factor in Muscovite politics, where so much depended upon one's literal proximity to the tsar-autocrat, who ruled by divine right like no other prince in Europe. In this case, the beneficiary of marriage politics turned out to be Boris Godunov, whose sister had been married to Fedor. Godunov served as regent during the reign of his brother-in-law. Fedor died, childless, in 1598.

Despite the dogged persistence, craftiness, and competence of Ivan IV and his Rurikid predecessors, who had done so much to expand Muscovy from a tiny appanage of the Golden Horde into a mighty state, none of them had thought to establish a law that would govern the issue of succession in Muscovy. As a result, the early seventeenth-century Muscovite elites had to scramble to place someone in power. And indeed, after the death of Fedor, his brother-in-law—who had served capably enough as regent—was elected in his own right.

Godunov's rule marked the end of the Rurikid dynasty in the Muscovite lands. This did not make the new tsar's job any easier. Envy bordering on hatred for this rank-and-file boyar having been elevated to tsar soon poisoned his rule. The Shuiskii family was particularly upset at his being made tsar and plotted his demise. Upon Godunov's death in 1605, the succession crisis escalated.

Who, now, would rule Muscovy / Russia? Was there no anointed one—no Rurikid? Was there no one who had a real claim to the throne? Doubtless many a subject sighed, if only Ivan's youngest child were alive. Memory of the third son, Dmitri, persisted—even if no one was quite certain how the nine-year-old met his death in 1591. Some thought that Boris Godunov had killed him, though this was unlikely. Banishing the boy to Uglich with his mother should have sufficed to keep Godunov's brother-in-law firmly in the seat of power.

Questions regarding the fate of the young Dmitri notwithstanding, crucial here is the sense that, within the Russian lands, a dynast who could claim a direct connection to the Rurik ruling dynasty was desperately needed. Such a conviction—perhaps wishful thinking?—led many to posit that perhaps Ivan the Terrible's youngest son, Dmitri, had not died after all.

The Saga of the False Dmitris

A certain gullibility, thus, underlay the polity—a gullibility that more savvy politicians could use to their own profit. Rumors began to circulate that in fact Dmitri had not perished but somehow, somewhere, had survived.

And indeed: in June 1605 word spread that Dmitri, son of Ivan the Terrible, had been found. The circumstances of his appearance were rather murky.

What is known is that this imposter—this man who claimed to be the son of Ivan the Terrible—had made his way from Lesser Poland to Russia already in 1604. In this he was aided by a number of Polish and Lithuanian nobles, including members of the Wiśniowiecki family. Most fascinating here is the role played by Jerzy Mniszech, the palatine of Sandomierz. Perhaps the meteoric (and somewhat suspicious) rise of Jerzy's father, Mikołaj (an émigré from Moravia who later became the chamberlain and a favorite of Zygmunt August), encouraged the son to have delusions of grandeur? Mniszech came up with a plan: he would marry his daughter Maryna to this Dmitri—and see what would happen. At any rate, Mniszech, the false Dmitri, and his newfound supporters (complete with their private regiments) crossed the border, where they drummed up support in famine-racked Russia—certainly on the part of peasants and Cossacks.

Thus, under the sponsorship of Commonwealth nobles, Dmitri was placed on the Muscovite throne—his purported mother, Maria née Nogay, having recognized him as her son. Yet the assistance that had been forthcoming from across the border was hardly disinterested. In exchange for the hand of his daughter Maryna in marriage, Jerzy Mniszech demanded a wedding present of territory: Dmitri would award his future wife and father-in-law the significant territories of Pskov and Novgorod, Seversk and Smolensk—territories that Poles had long coveted, even fought for—as well as a million zloty (a hefty sum of money).

Support for the false Dmitri—for that is what historians have labeled him—was forthcoming from another, less expected quarter: the Catholic Church. Dmitri had secretly "converted" to Catholicism, apparently while still in Poland. Not that those present at the coronation of Maryna Mniszech in Moscow would have had any inkling of this, the ceremony being as properly Orthodox as could be. This incidentally, was the first time a woman was crowned tsarina.

Alas for the new tsarina and her husband the imposter, the latter's reign as tsar was short-lived. Not even a full year into his reign (and literally weeks after Maryna's coronation) he was assassinated by dissatisfied boyars—men who had opportunistically supported the imposter but now found it opportune to rid themselves of him. This also seems to have been occasioned by the misbehavior of the Commonwealth nobles in their entourage, whose undeniable foreignness may have reminded the Russian boyars of the danger of having Poles in such close proximity to the tsar. They had full right to fear the use of marriage politics, upon which the Muscovite system was based—politics that might now give Commonwealth nobles unprecedented access to the lands and wealth of Holy Russia. Something that gives credence to this view: the real Dmitri's mother, Maria Nogay, now unmasked Tsar Dmitri as an imposter. His body supposedly was burned and the ashes fired off in the direction of the Commonwealth for good measure. In the course of the massacre, which touched other former supporters of Dmitri, one of the boyars, Prince Vasilii Shuiskii, assumed the throne.

Shuiskii's brief reign, as Vasilii IV, was also troubled. There was no end of opposition to the new tsar on the part of other Muscovite princes, doubtless envious of his sudden elevation. The death of the false Dmitri hardly put an end to the succession crisis. A False Peter paraded about, claiming to be the son of the childless Tsar Fedor. And, despite his being reduced to cannon fodder, Dmitri apparently rose, phoenix-like, from the ashes. Another flesh-and-blood Dmitri would come to haunt Shuiskii.

For the Polish adventurers had not given up. A new Dmitri—recognized by Maryna and her father, both of whom had escaped with their lives in 1606—stepped forward in August 1607. Once more, the Mniszech family stood to profit handsomely from recognizing the second imposter as the miraculously saved original. This said, they were dependent upon the help—military and otherwise—of other powerful Commonwealth supporters such as Jan Sapieha, son of Kyiv castellan Paweł Sapieha. Under the younger Sapieha, an army formed and fought its way to Moscow. The second Dmitri set up a parallel court in nearby Tushino. The raucous and ruthless behavior of the camp of the second Dmitri caused much of the original opportunistic support of aggrieved Russians—serfs, Cossacks, as well as boyars—to melt away. The disillusioned began to rally around Shuiskii.

Until this point, the succession crisis had fueled the fires of ambition of a handful of individual magnates, Polish and Lithuanian, who in a way were waging their own wars and conducting their own foreign policy. The Polish-Lithuanian Commonwealth had taken no official stance, although the activities of the false Dmitri were intimately known by both the court and the king. The Commonwealth had heard tales related by those who had been released from Russian prisons by the new tsar. Would the king involve the Commonwealth in these unsavory doings?

Shuiskii's signing of an alliance with Sweden in 1609 was all it took to prompt the new Polish king—that is, Batory's successor—to get involved. This is not to say that Zygmunt III, who ascended to the throne in 1587, had not been following the succession crisis in Muscovy. As early as 1598, there was thought of having the widowed Zygmunt marry Godunov's daughter, and two years later a Commonwealth delegation traveled to Moscow to broach the topic of succession with Godunov, offering something along the lines of a joint inheritance pact to the first non-Rurikid to rule Moscow. This would give the Polish king and his sons a shot at the Moscow throne should Godunov predecease him. Yet this proposal, which would have allowed for the practice of Catholicism in Russia and Orthodoxy in the Commonwealth, did not prove attractive to Godunov and the boyars.

With the eternal peace contracted between Russia and Sweden, Zygmunt was compelled to act. A Russian-Swedish alliance promised to challenge the Commonwealth's position in the northeast. And the new alliance personally cut him to the quick. Zygmunt was a scion of the same Vasa dynasty that ruled Sweden and a pretender to the Swedish throne. The king decided to invade.

Poles in Moscow

The Moscow campaign did not begin propitiously. Both the king and the Seym took their time—the first, vacillating as to whether to invade despite the fact that his own pacta conventa specified that he regain the territories lost to Moscow, and the second, as usual, being slow in supplying the cash to fund the army. This irritated to no end the man put in charge of the Moscow campaign, Field Hetman Stanisław Żółkiewski.

This well-educated and competent nobleman proved an excellent choice of leader. Hailing from the Ruthenian palatinate, Żółkiewski was a true Renaissance man, famous early on for his command of languages. While he doubtless put his French to good use as a member of the official delegation that traveled to Paris to meet the king-elect Henri Valois, the Pole's knowledge of Latin and the ancient authors Horace and Virgil was particularly fine. He was said to know all of Horace by heart. A later memoirist himself, he was capitivated by the writings of Julius Caesar, which perhaps served as inspiration as well.

Closely linked to the mighty Jan Zamoyski, by the early seventeenth century Stanisław Żółkiewski was a seasoned military man. Although he fought in battles along various parts of the Commonwealth periphery, he had proved his mettle and competence during the string of campaigns orchestrated by Batory, beginning with the Velikie Luki campaign of 1580.

He also served faithfully all the elected monarchs of the Commonwealth, who rewarded him with various offices: that of Crown field hetman (from 1589) and castellan of Lviv (from 1593). Nonetheless, his relationship with King Zygmunt III Vasa was fraught—something the noble's fascinating memoirs (published anonymously) demonstrate. In them, the hetman (Żółkiewski) figures (perhaps not unsurprisingly?) as the voice of reason addressing a monarch who could be difficult to deal with.

This becomes clear from the conduct of the Moscow campaign of 1610. Although summoned to command the combined Polish-Lithuanian forces, Żółkiewski was unable to get the king to commit to the campaign until late in the year. The hetman had wanted to start mobilizing the forces necessary to fight this foe in the spring, but the king and the Seym took their time. The delay caused Żółkiewski to fear—and rightly so—that this would leave little time for training as well as for transporting the troops to their distant destination. Having been a part of Batory's campaigns, he knew the price that fighting a war in the cold months could have on the troops as well as on the outcome.

Once he ceased vacillating, King Zygmunt III himself set off for Smolensk with the army in the fall of 1609. Its ostensible aim was to conquer the massive and near impenetrable fortress. The Poles and Lithuanians lay siege to Smolensk. However, well-fortified, -armed, and -supplied, Smolensk under the leadership of the competent commander Mikhail Shtein not only refused to surrender but also managed to repel the first siege.

Back in Moscow, troops loyal to Vasilii Shuiskii were finally able to put an end to the blockade of the city organized by the second Dmitri, forcing the latter to escape to Kaluga. Thus emboldened, the Russians made plans to deal with the Commonwealth forces near Smolensk. They assembled a huge army, estimated to fall within the range of thirty to forty-eight thousand soldiers. Thanks to the assistance of Zygmunt III's nemesis, Karl IX of Sweden, the Russian forces were augmented by some six thousand foreign mercenaries: Germans, Frenchmen, Englishmen, Scots, and Swedes. The combined forces were led by Prince Dmitrii Shuiskii.

Word of the approaching army reached Żółkiewski via a spy. The hetman had at his disposal a much smaller army: a little over five thousand Hussars, several hundred infantrymen, and a couple of cannon. How to deal with the approaching threat? Żółkiewski boldly decided to thwart the Russian move and meet the enemy army before it reached Smolensk. He and his army set off in the night of July 3/4 to surprise the Russian army—only to find the enemy forces already camped near Klushino, between Viazma and Mozhajsk.

The fateful following day, July 4, 1610, demonstrated that the outnumbered Hussars were up to the challenge. Setting fire to villages in the region, the Polish forces rushed head-on to meet the enemy, which had not yet fully assembled its battle lines. In the course of the battle, over five hours long, the Hussars charged time and again. They reduced the Muscovite forces to disarray and caused them to retreat. Then the Commonwealth forces proceeded to attack the foreign mercenaries. The latter—themselves a force numerically greater than the combined army under Żółkiewski at Klushino—lost some seven hundred soldiers, while two thousand Russians perished in the battle. Of the Commonwealth forces, a little over three hundred soldiers lost their lives.

Klushino proved a huge defeat for the Russian forces. For Żółkiewski, this victory against the odds was but the first step. He and his men pressed on farther—all the way to Moscow. There he learned that Vasilii Shuiskii had been deposed and forced to become a monk (a typical Muscovite way of removing one's enemy from politics). In his stead, a group of seven boyars were frantically trying to establish order. They desperately needed legitimacy but could find no way out—that is, beyond accepting the second Dmitri as tsar (hardly a palatable option, given his inflammatory behavior) or finding another, more suitable candidate.

In Moscow the boyars entered into negotiations with Żółkiewski. They proposed that the son of Zygmunt III, the fifteen-year-old Władysław, become tsar

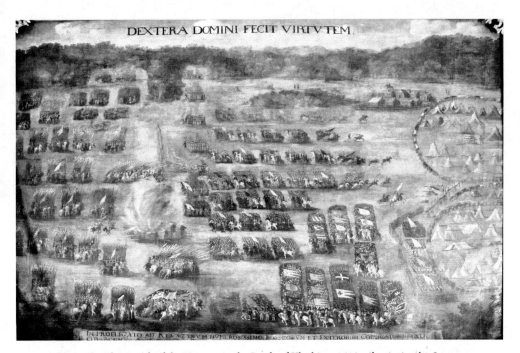

Figure 5.1: *The Attack of the Hussars in the Battle of Klushino, 1610*, oil painting by Szymon Boguszowicz (1620). The painting was commissioned by the victor, Stanisław Żołkiewski. The original painting hangs in the Lviv Art Gallery.

of Russia, and the two realms be united. The Vasa's election was nonetheless predicated upon several non-negotiable points. Not only would Władysław have to convert to Orthodoxy; the Commonwealth would have to undo the Union of Brest, thus removing Eastern rite believers out from under the control of the papacy. Żółkiewski agreed to the proposal in August of that year.

The boyars invited Żółkiewski and his army into the Russian capital, and they established a garrison in the Kremlin. Moscow, thus, came under Polish occupation. To be sure, this situation lasted for only two years. In the interim, however, the near impregnable fortress of Smolensk surrendered.

While it might seem odd today, Zygmunt III was more pleased by the capture of Smolensk (which his pacta conventa obliged him to try to regain) than by all of Żółkiewski's efforts on his and his son's behalf in Moscow. Zygmunt refused to countenance the terms of the agreement. Nor would he send his son to Moscow. Some believe the king himself wanted to be tsar, although not under those conditions. Zygmunt's crusading Catholicism had already proved a stumbling block in Protestant Sweden. Perhaps the Vasa monarch set his sights on converting the Russians to Catholicism, on bringing them—like the Orthodox of the Commonwealth—into union with Rome?

Such plans seem to border on the fantastic, for a number of reasons. The damage wreaked upon Russia during the Time of Troubles by so many wayward Commonwealth magnates, out to profit at Russia's expense, prejudiced the population against the foreigners. The arrest and imprisonment of highly placed boyars likely did nothing to improve relations either (at one point Żółkiewski paraded his captives, including Vasilii Shuiskii, before a session of the Seym).

More generous assessments of Zygmunt III give him credit for rejecting the conditions for the union with Russia, expecting that nothing would come of it. They argue that, far from being overly ambitious, the Polish king never entertained more than minimalistic ambitions for the Moscow campaign. He was more than happy to settle for the fulfillment of the terms of his pacta conventa: the reconquest of Smolensk and the winning back of other territories taken from his predecessor. And indeed, back in the Commonwealth, the Polish king commissioned a commemorative medal be struck in honor of the Smolensk victory.

In the interim, Russia continued to be wracked by upheaval. Swedes had entered the country from the north and were trying to seat the son of Karl IX on the Russian throne. These developments resulted in a popular backlash against the occupying forces—and against foreigners ("heretics") in general. Between famine and the tribulations of the preceding years, the countryside had been radicalized. Attacks on the capital took place in several waves.

In March 1611 the situation got so out of hand that the Polish-Lithuanian forces were forced, for reasons of riot control, to set Moscow on fire—which did not endear them, or their memory, to the Russians, in spite of the fact that it was the boyars behind the candidacy of Władysław who essentially advised Żółkiewski to set the city ablaze.

It took the accumulated dissatisfaction on the part of the Russian masses, led by a burgher named Kuzma Minin and a nobleman named Dmitrii Pozharskii, to push the Polish army out of Moscow. The occupiers of the Kremlin capitulated in the fall of 1612. Back home, the news was no more encouraging: the Seym adamantly opposed the union, blaming the Moscow campaign on the king's insatiable desire for personal gain for himself and his family, at the expense of the Commonwealth. The Poles' adventure in Moscow was over.

To be sure, Polish-Lithuanian forces maintained their control over the hard-won borderland territories, including Smolensk. In their pursuit of the bigger prize, however, they nonetheless lost control of some territories in the north. The Swedes availed themselves of the opportunity to make inroads into Livonia. Nor were Commonwealth forces able to repeat their earlier victories against the Russians. A fourteen-year truce signed with Russia in Deulino at the end of 1618 confirmed the Commonwealth's possession of Smolensk while restoring to Polish-Lithuanian control the Chernihiv and Seversk regions. In this way, the Polish-Lithuanian Commonwealth reached its zenith, insofar as territorial expansion was concerned. No mention was made of Władysław's claim to the Russian throne.

By that time, however, Muscovy was reemerging from its turmoil. The boyars had settled on a new tsar—one of their own. This was the young Mikhail Romanov.

The teenager was a safe choice, as he was for all practical purposes orphaned—at least, in the eyes of Russia's boyars. The ascension of Mikhail Fedorovich Romanov as tsar of Russia marked a return to influence of a family that, only a few years earlier, no one would have imagined would ever resurface. The father of the first Romanov to sit on the Russian throne had been a rival of Boris Godunov. When the latter came to power, he forced Fedor Nikitich Romanov to become a monk, taking the name Filaret, essentially removing his rival from the public sphere—if not for long. For good measure Mikhail's mother, Ksenia, was forced to take religious vows as well.

With the death of Godunov, the story becomes even more improbable. Although removed from politics, the monk Filaret saw his career as a religious leader take off—thanks to the False Dmitris. The first Dmitri appointed him metropolitan of Rostov; the second elevated him to the highest church position in the land, that of Russian patriarch. Patriarch Filaret fell into Polish hands in 1610 and spent the next nine years as a prisoner in the Commonwealth. After the Peace of Deulino, he returned to Russia, where he was officially (re)appointed patriarch, this time by the patriarch of Jerusalem. The crafty old clergyman essentially held the reins of power, serving as co-regent with his son. One can say, thus, that the entirety of the Romanov family ruled Russia (Fedor/ Filaret having been the first to use that surname).

The Time of Troubles proved a succession crisis of huge proportions. Russians would not soon forget this episode in history. Although they won the battle, without winning the war, Poles managed to do what neither Napoleon nor Hitler could achieve: they made their way to Moscow, occupied it, and even entertained the prospect of ruling Russia. Perhaps it is no surprise that, after the fall of communism, Russians chose to commemorate the moment of victory, the Russians' "Liberation of Moscow from the Polish Interventionists" in 1612, instead of the October (Bolshevik) Revolution of 1917. Heroes Minin and Pozharskii were memorialized in a monument erected on Red Square as early as 1818.

In a way, Russians can thank the Poles for serving as a concrete, easily identifiable enemy against which they could rally. Although the Time of Troubles was no small stumbling block (Muscovy was on the verge of imploding), the foreign intervention ultimately provided Russians with an opportunity to regroup and reconfigure their polity. Relieved that this costly and painful period had come to an end, Russians reunited under a new banner, that of the Romanovs. In dynastic terms, it turned out to be a good choice: the Romanov dynasty would continue to rule as long as there was a tsar in the realm, and this longevity would stand Russia in good stead. Within the space of a century, the country would be a very different entity from the Russia facing the Commonwealth in 1610. The saga of the Muscovite menace would continue.

CHAPTER 6

The Commonwealth, Part II

Sarmatia Besieged

The Commonwealth had weathered its first interregnums, both domestically and abroad. The first royal election *viritim* showed that, while the new system did work, it needed additional fine-tuning. Nor could the country be guaranteed a good outcome, even if the country's citizens managed to agree on a candidate. Additional—and quite practical—adjustments were made during the rule of Batory that placed further limits on royal power. For example, new tribunals established for the Crown of Poland and the Grand Duchy meant that, while the king would still be the court of last resort, he was not the sole arbiter within the Commonwealth. The system of noble rule, thus, seemed to be functioning—even thriving.

None of the interregnums of the sixteenth century proved anywhere near as devastating a transition as the succession crisis that wreaked havoc in Muscovy. Yet, despite the best efforts of wayward Commonwealth magnates as well as the state, the adventure of the Poles and Lithuanians in Moscow was not quite the triumph it might have been. Despite the singularity of the achievement of Poles occupying Moscow, the whole affair amounted to little more than just another big and inconclusive campaign for the Commonwealth. It did not help the Poles make any lasting gains within the disputed Ruthenian territories, let alone into Muscovy proper. Still, the Moscow campaign did demonstrate that the Commonwealth forces were a force to be reckoned with in Central and Eastern Europe.

Batory the Great?

It was the reign of Stefan Batory that raised the military profile of the Commonwealth. Let us take a step back to revisit the reign of the Transylvanian. Despite his valor and his virtues, not every move of Batory's reflected a golden touch. Even the tremendous Transylvanian had his faults.

One of them resulted from the fact that Batory was perennially strapped for cash—not a good situation for a monarch who needs to fight wars. The Commonwealth's constitution (the Henrician Articles) dictated that the king could not levy taxes without the approval of the Seym. To play on a phrase familiar to most Americans, in the Commonwealth the slogan was not "Taxation without representation," but "Representation without taxation" (at least, not regular taxation). In other words, the nobles deemed it their prerogative to determine whether a war was just or not—as well as whether they would agree to fund it.

Batory, thus, ultimately compounded a mistake made earlier by the Polish king Zygmunt August. Short on money to pay his troops, in 1577 he made a deal with the Hohenzollerns of Brandenburg. For the sum of two hundred thousand zloty, Batory permitted Georg Friedrich of Ansbach-Bayreuth to administer Ducal Prussia in the name of its ruler, the elector's cousin, who was mentally unstable. It is interesting to note that the Prussian Estates were vehemently opposed to this move; they were willing to pay the king, in perpetuity, an annual fee of a hundred thousand zloty to keep the Brandenburg Hohenzollerns out. Either Batory was bad at math, or he was truly desperate for cash.

Nor did the Transylvanian, terrific in so many ways, seem to realize the importance that secure control over the Baltic held for the Commonwealth. In gratitude for military assistance, the Polish king allowed the same Georg Friedrich to style himself Duke of Prussia (as opposed to Duke in Prussia). Although subtle, this change in title was nonetheless significant: it implied—if it did not guarantee—that the Brandenburg branch of the family would succeed Albrecht Friedrich (in whose name Ducal Prussia was being administered). Future Polish kings would have to exercise caution to keep this situation from escalating—to the disadvantage of the Commonwealth and the advantage of Brandenburg. Perhaps this is the reason that, despite his accomplishments as king of Poland, Stefan Batory was never awarded the sobriquet "the Great."

Magnate Highs, Magnate Lows

More likely it was that many nobles then were not nearly as fond of the Transylvanian as are contemporary Poles. Their dissatisfaction had less to do with his military exploits, more with domestic developments. Under Batory, the balance that the mixed monarchy represented—king, senate, nobility—began to be weighted more heavily on the side of the senate, the officeholders of the Commonwealth. In other words, the rich and powerful magnates began to become richer and more powerful than ever before.

Royal favoritism propelled a handful of individuals into positions of unheard-of power—Batory's chancellor, Jan Zamoyski, being only the most extreme example. He seemed to be approaching royal status himself: after the death of his first wife (a Radziwiłł), Zamoyski married into the family of the Transylvanian Báthoris. The king's niece Gryzelda became Zamoyski's wife in 1583. For all practical purposes, the tribune Zamoyski—the man famed for defending the rights of the average nobleman—seemed to be changing his skin from the senatorial to the quasi-royal.

Those who were displaced found themselves entirely out of favor—even when they, like members of the Zborowski family, had helped Batory get elected. The Zborowskis watched their fortunes wane as Zamoyski's rose. To make matters worse, they seemed to be punished out of keeping with their status. When one of the sons, Samuel, returned to the country after having being banished, he was unceremoniously beheaded—a fate considered unseemly by many nobles, who wanted him subjected to a court of his peers. His brother Krzysztof received the worst fate (barring death) that could befall a nobleman: infamy, banishment, and with that loss of nobility and confiscation of his property. Outraged, Commonwealth nobles claimed that their elected king was trampling their freedoms.

The largesse of Batory helped to elevate Zamoyski to the pinnacle of magnate status. At the end of his life, the chancellor owned 11 towns and over 2,000 villages, while controlling an additional 12 towns and 612 villages that were part of the royal demesne. This meant that, for all practical purposes, he was as wealthy as Bishop Gamrat (archbishop of both Kraków and Gniezno) had been during the Renaissance years of the sixteenth century.

Batory's chancellor nonetheless put some of his wealth to good use. It was he who commissioned the construction of a perfect Renaissance city, Zamość. A magnet for trade, the city also became a magnet for students. The chancellor established and endowed a school in his private town. The famous Zamość Academy provided students with a fine humanistic education and had links with Batory's alma mater, Padua, among other foreign universities. In a way, the powerful chancellor was helping to perpetuate the educational system that had thrived under the last Jagiellons and from which he had himself profited. In other words, Jan Zamoyski demonstrated that he was truly a product of the first flush of Sarmatia—Sarmatia as perceived with a Renaissance sensibility. The illustrious contribution of

Renaissance ideas to the shaping of the Commonwealth would soon be obscured by a different set of ideas, however.

Baroque Beginnings

While Zamoyski sought to create a Renaissance city, his monarch, Batory, boosted a new style known as Baroque. Although this style did not immediately displace the Renaissance in Poland-Lithuania, it would make itself at home. In its specific Polish incarnation, the Baroque would have an enormous and lasting impact on the life of the Commonwealth.

The Baroque is associated with the Counter-Reformation (dating from the Council of Trent in 1545–1563). This was the official response of the Roman Catholic Church to the Reformation, its answer to the rise of Protestantism in Europe. In the Polish lands, Counter-Reformation ideas were introduced by one of Poland's most illustrious churchmen, Cardinal Stanisław Hosius. Of burgher origin, Hosius made a stunning career in the church, rising to the position of prince-bishop of Warmia, a small but wealthy part of Royal Prussia.

Hosius was an active participant at the Council of Trent and an advocate of its crusading Catholicism. Upon his return, he saw to it that Poland-Lithuania did not go the way of England and establish a national church. Instead, the Roman Catholics of the Commonwealth were pulled more tightly into Rome's orbit. And not only the Roman Catholics: the Union of Brest had brought the Commonwealth's Greek Christians into union with Rome. The Counter-Reformation focused on establishing centralized control and initiating a return to religious orthodoxy; toleration and more creative solutions to religious problems were anathema.

While there were still plenty of Protestants in the Polish-Lithuanian lands, this did not mean that the Roman Catholic Church in its Tridentine mode was not working hard to regain souls and expand its influence. Key here was a new religious order—the Society of Jesus, more commonly known as the Jesuits. Brought to Poland-Lithuania by Hosius in 1565, the Jesuits helped to raise both the visibility and the authority of Roman Catholicism in the country. By the end of the seventeenth century, there were seventy Jesuit colleges in the Commonwealth.

The Jesuit mission gained significant support from Batory. The king founded various schools in the eastern borderlands, the most important being the university in Vilnius. Indeed, Vilnius would get its share of Baroque churches. The Jesuits and their program would also find favor with Batory's successor. In many ways, the ultimate winner of the third royal election in the Commonwealth of Both Nations would be the quintessential Counter-Reformation monarch, one who would try to realign his country in keeping with the trends emanating from the West.

Royal Election Number Three

The unexpected death, in December 1586, of the mighty Stefan Batory left the Commonwealth in need of another king. The Transylvanian died childless, his marriage to Anna Jagiellon not giving much hope to the thought of an heir. Whom would the noble electors invite to be the third king of their choice to head the Commonwealth?

Although four candidates were proposed, including the Russian Tsar Fedor and a Hungarian Báthori, the choice eventually came down to two. The ever-persistent Habsburgs quickly put forward the candidacy of Archduke Maximilian, the son of the Holy Roman Emperor who had previously sought the prize. One would imagine that he would garner support from the expected quarters—those who had considered voting Habsburg during the two previous elections, the Catholic senators.

But the political landscape had changed since the election of Stefan Batory. The election turned out to be a referendum on the king and some of his policies, and the opposition focused on one goal: to unseat his powerful chancellor, Jan Zamoyski. Those disillusioned with the chancellor (and these included a number of Protestants) joined his sworn enemies, the Zborowskis, who were still smarting from the ill treatment their family received at the hand of Zamoyski. They agreed to support the candidate that the anti-Habsburg Zamoyski could not stomach: Archduke Maximilian. It made for strange bedfellows all around. Not only was the archduke staunchly anti-Protestant; he was a member of the German Order of the Virgin Mary—more commonly known as the Teutonic Knights. This alone should have given the Poles and Lithuanians second thoughts—and it suggests the deep hatred many of them must have had for Zamoyski.

Other nobles were casting about for a candidate who could beat the Habsburg. The prospect of a "Piast" on the throne continued to tantalize. Zamoyski surely thought he was the man for the job of king. Was he not practically a king already in everything but name? Yet he proved a divisive figure—as seen from the motley camp that mobilized behind the Habsburg archduke solely to displace Batory's powerful chancellor. When it became clear that his own candidacy would not win over the Lithuanian magnates who might object to being ruled by a Polish counterpart, Jan Zamoyski ended up promoting a fresh face: the twenty-one-year-old Zygmunt Vasa, son and heir of the king of Sweden.

The Vasa's Jagiellonian connection was stronger than that of the Habsburg, who was the descendant of one of the two Habsburg-Jagiellonian matches arranged in 1515. Zygmunt was the nephew (and likely namesake) of the last of the Jagiellons, Zygmunt August, whose sister Catherine had married Johan Vasa. Johan's father had been King Gustav Vasa, the protoplast of the Vasa dynasty and Sweden's first monarch after gaining independence from Denmark. At the time of his marriage in 1562, Johan held the title of Duke of Finland, Finland being part of the Swedish kingdom.

Zygmunt's young life had been tumultuous—a result of Swedish politics. Sharing the fate of his parents, who were out of favor with Jan's elder half-brother, King Eric XIV of Sweden, little Zygmunt was born and spent the first years of his life imprisoned in Gripsholm Castle. Yet fate eventually smiled on this branch of the Vasa family. In 1568 his father, Johan, managed to depose the deranged Eric and assume the Swedish throne.

No longer a straightforward function of international alliances, this Commonwealth election of 1587—the third royal election in fifteen years—threatened to turn into a civil war. Some seymiks called for a noble levy—a true summons to fight. The warring factions of magnates came to Warsaw complete with their own private armies. Augmenting these were hosts of the magnates' clients, lesser nobles who allied themselves with the rich and powerful in exchange for assistance of various kinds.

The election field was fraught, with each group staking claims to a different spot. For six weeks, they took up their positions, like various parties to a war, unable even to initiate the election. Tired of the privations and running out of food, some nobles prepared to leave for home.

The primate, acting as interrex, found it impossible to execute his duties impartially. Declaring to the assembled nobles that he would never vote for a "German," he proposed they elect Zygmunt Vasa. This left Zamoyski no choice but to rally whomever would follow behind the Swedish candidate.

Now both sides set down to business—if not in the way foreseen by the rules. Instead of reaching agreement on a single candidate, each side elected its own king-elect. How to resolve the dilemma of a double election?

What resulted was a race to Kraków for the coronation. The first candidate to make his way to the capital and have the royal crown placed on his head would become king. It was not quite a literal race from the election field to Kraków: each side needed to prepare a pacta conventa with a list of conditions of rule that not only would satisfy the Commonwealth nobility (always desirous of extracting promises from the new ruler) but also would be palatable to the king-elect, who had to arrive from abroad. Time was of the essence nonetheless.

The geography of the solution favored the Habsburgs, whose Silesian territories were much nearer to Kraków than the faraway Sweden. Nonetheless, Zamoyski's forces (albeit without the king) reached the capital first. They were intent on rallying the Cracovians to their side and helping them repel the Habsburg king-elect, who was headed their way with his army of several thousand.

Leading an army of comparable size, Zamoyski engaged the Habsburg army as well as the forces mustered by the archduke's Polish supporters, defending Kraków in the process. He later pursued the Habsburg forces to the Silesian town of Byczyna (German: Pitschen), where a decisive battle was fought. Only the capture of Archduke Maximilian by Zamoyski's army was enough to convince his supporters finally to give up on him. The election—and the war—was over. After he arrived in the capital in December 1587, Zygmunt Vasa became the third Polish king of the Commonwealth period.

In many ways, the outcome seemed nothing short of miraculous. The newly crowned King Zygmunt III Vasa ultimately commissioned a painting of the scene of the victory for the royal castle to buttress his legitimacy. However paradoxical this may seem, for part of his reign, there were three men who had pretensions to the Polish throne: Zygmunt, Maximilian, and the still very much alive Henri Valois. Maximilian, incidentally, would soon be chosen as grand master of the Teutonic Order within the Holy Roman Empire, a position from which he could continue to criticize the Poles, who denied him the crown.

Looking at the outcome (yet another disputed royal election), the time seemed ripe to adjust the Commonwealth's election procedure. Zamoyski proposed to the Seym a number of changes that would simplify and straighten out some of the kinks encountered so far: foreign candidates lacking a Polish/Lithuanian connection would not be considered, landless nobles would not be allowed to vote, and private armies would be forbidden to enter the election field. Despite the fact that amnesty was offered to those who had fought on the losing side, there was enough bad blood to ensure that these changes were not accepted.

The royal election of 1587 nonetheless secured for the Commonwealth a long period of relative stability. King Zygmunt III Vasa (1587–1632) would reign for a full forty-five years. This period free of election turmoil allowed the Commonwealth of Both Nations to settle comfortably into what would later be called the Silver Age.

The Polish-Swedish Vasa

The first Vasa to ascend to the Polish throne, Zygmunt was the first ruler of the Commonwealth who could speak to his subjects in their native tongue. One would imagine that this could have won over—if not Zamoyski, who was likely still smarting from the fact that he himself would not be king—the average Commonwealth nobleman, so many of whom came out to defeat the Habsburg pretender. Paradoxically, this was not the case. The young Zygmunt did not manage to endear himself to the nobles who not only pressed for his election but actually fought for his coronation. This likely stemmed, at least in part, from the peculiarities of his own upbringing, which in turn suggested how times had changed since the last of the Jagiellons.

Although the son of a Jagiellonian princess, Zygmunt was nonetheless shaped by his youth in Sweden—if not always in the ways one might expect. After his rather inauspicious first years under lock and key, the little Zygmunt was groomed to be the successor to his father, King Johan III of Sweden. His education was to prepare him to rule Sweden, a cold and inhospitable land—in some ways not unlike Zygmunt, and quite different from the Commonwealth he was now to rule.

When Zygmunt addressed his new subjects in Polish at his coronation, he was merely putting to use one of the five languages he knew. Indeed, the Vasa was intelligent and cultured, a lover of music, the arts, and sport (supposedly he was quite a tennis player). Temperamentally, however, the young Zygmunt was hardly prepared to lead a country as politically volatile and differentiated as the Commonwealth. Not only did he not relate to typical noble pursuits: waging wars and hunting, immoderate drinking and eating, all done with unabashed gusto. He was as yet too young to have had any experience of leading men, in battle or in politics, and was far from the charismatic type of leader the Poles seemed to prefer. Despite his Polish blood, the Vasa from Sweden seemed foreign and aloof. He did share one important characteristic with many of his new subjects: his religious faith. Zygmunt, heir to the Swedish throne, was a Roman Catholic.

This was unusual for someone born and raised in the Lutheran state of Sweden. Zygmunt's Roman Catholicism came courtesy of his mother, Catherine, the Jagiellonian princess and youngest of Zygmunt August's three sisters. The young boy would lose his mother at a tender age, but not before she entrusted his upbringing to the Jesuits, who ensured not only that Zygmunt would be a pious young man but that he would be a newfangled post-Tridentine Roman Catholic. The Vasa was too young to have had the experience of Roman Catholicism in the age of the Renaissance, a Catholicism that was both less confrontational and less dogmatic—one that had helped shape the ideology underlying the new state. Zygmunt supported the Counter-Reformation and the Jesuit Order, even was an honorary member of that order.

It is easy to see that Zygmunt III Vasa was not likely to be a ruler who would wish for his son to convert to Orthodoxy, even to gain the throne of Muscovy—something we saw in his reaction to the unprecedented Russian proposal during the Time of Troubles. If anything, he probably harbored ambitions of converting the Orthodox East—that is, of bringing it into union with Rome. Was it not this king who had been persuaded by the Vatican to press for the Union of Brest, which brought the Commonwealth's Catholic and Orthodox populations closer together (if not entirely successfully)?

Northern Entanglements

Nonetheless, his fervent Catholicism would prove a stumbling block elsewhere as well. This was in the Vasa's relationship with Sweden. For Zygmunt was the heir to Johan III. His father's death led to Zygmunt III Vasa being crowned king of Sweden in 1594. His dual reign over the Commonwealth and Sweden would be short-lived. Also fervent in their faith, the Swedish Lutherans were ultimately convinced—in part by Zygmunt's uncle Karl of Södermanland, who would subsequently rule Sweden as Karl IX—that they could not abide a Catholic ruler. This led to war on Swedish soil, which the Commonwealth forces lost. Zygmunt was dethroned in Sweden in 1599.

This did not mean that the Swedes had given up on the dynasty. The Swedish parliament offered the throne to Zygmunt's son Władysław, if the latter would agree to convert to Lutheranism. This development was not acceptable to Zygmunt, and he responded by handing Estonia over to Commonwealth control.

War ensued in Livonia. Despite not having even half as many forces at his disposal, the valiant grand hetman of Lithuania, Jan Karol Chodkiewicz, decimated the Swedish army at Kircholm (today's Salaspils), near Riga, in 1605. The victory, although impressive, did not decide the overall outcome of the conflict, however. It led only to a series of locally agreed–upon truces. Zygmunt III Vasa remained firm in his conviction that he was the rightful ruler of Sweden. Although put on the back burner, the Swedish problem continued to simmer—indeed, as long as a Vasa sat on the Polish throne.

Yet the little country that suffered defeat at Kircholm in 1605 would soon become a more formidable force. Sweden made significant progress under its new leader, Gustav Adolf. He not only solidified the position of Lutheranism within the country but also built up its army, having learned a thing or two from the Poles on how to fight. These lessons stood him in good stead in the Thirty Years' War, a terribly destructive war of religion fought in the lands to the west of the Commonwealth in the years 1618–1648. During lulls in that conflict, the Swedish king renewed his battle with the Commonwealth, taking Riga and making his presence known in Livonia.

Even worse for the Commonwealth, in 1626 Gustav Adolf attacked not only Livonia but also Royal Prussia. While he could not take Gdańsk, he levied a duty on all ships that came through that port. Although the Poles would pull off a victory at sea (like the uncle after whom he had been named, Zygmunt III had built up a navy, if only on a small scale), the battle of Oliwa in 1627 was not decisive. Once again, the two countries could only agree to disagree—that is, on a truce. Nonetheless, even this truce had a sting: one of the conditions imposed in Oliwa was that Sweden could collect a 3.5 percent tariff on all trade that went through Gdańsk.

The Baltic region continued to be an Achilles' heel of sorts for the Commonwealth. In the midst of the various conflicts of the early seventeenth century, Zygmunt III Vasa followed the precedence set by Batory and, against the wishes of the Commonwealth nobles, allowed the Brandenburg Hohenzollerns to continue to administer Ducal Prussia in the name of Albrecht Friedrich. When the latter died in 1618, the Brandenburgs were allowed to assume hereditary control over the duchy, in exchange for military assistance as well as annual payments (which nonetheless ceased in 1620). Although Ducal Prussia was still a Polish fief, the Brandenburgs were increasingly putting their own stamp on this part of the Baltic.

The Rise of Warsaw

Zygmunt's fixation on his Swedish claims (often at the expense of domestic concerns) had other ramifications for the Commonwealth of Both Nations, not all of them deleterious. The Vasa king contributed to the geographical refocusing of the Commonwealth by using Warsaw as his royal base. Indeed, he is the ruler who is traditionally credited with transferring the capital of the Commonwealth from Kraków to Warsaw in 1596. While this statement is incorrect in a number of ways (there was never any official transfer of function, nor was there any kind of royal exodus that year), the outcome was nonetheless palpable. The locus of political life shifted north.

In a way, Zygmunt III Vasa was only adding to the rise of Warsaw that was initiated by the Union of Lublin, which established little but centrally located Warsaw as the site for sessions of the Seym. Kraków, incidentally, had long been too small for this: most Seyms during the period of Jagiellonian rule had been held in Piotrków. Kraków would nonetheless retain certain important characteristics of a capital—among them, it remained the site of royal coronations and funerals.

Zygmunt's wish to be closer to his other ancestral homeland led to the rise as well as the reconfiguration of the former capital of Mazovia. Increasingly Warsaw was not a town of burghers anymore, the picturesque medieval Old Town and New Town notwithstanding. Instead, it gained all the trappings of a capital. In addition to being the legislative heart of the country (as the site of the Seyms), it would serve as the permanent site of the royal court. This led Zygmunt III to have the castle—built on the spot where the Mazovian dukes had once ruled—both overhauled and expanded. The Italian architect Giovanni Battista Trevano was entrusted with this task. Other construction came at the instigation of the royal family. Vasas would build other palaces in the Warsaw suburbs later, such as the so-called Villa Regia, designed by Trevano.

The importance of Warsaw led the Commonwealth's nobles to set up residences in its suburbs, that is, outside the fortified medieval burgher town. These residences—many of them built along the Krakowskie Przedmieście (the Kraków suburbs, the road leading in the direction of the capital)—originally consisted of wooden constructions in a distinctly Italianate suburban pattern, set back from the street and boasting stately grounds and extensive gardens. The nobility, thus, became the prime engine of change in the city of Warsaw. Palace after palace was built so as to give the noble residents comfortable accommodations during royal elections and parliamentary sessions. Poland's main clergymen would also build residences in Warsaw: the primate's palace on ulica Senatorska (Senators' Street) was built on land where previously breweries and small houses had stood.

The Specter of Absolutum Dominium

Still, Zygmunt's Swedish and dynastic obsessions as well as his desire to do things his own way did little to endear him to the Commonwealth nobles. Notwithstanding the visceral anti-Habsburg sentiment that resulted in his gaining the Polish throne, the Vasa demonstrated his political tone-deafness by entering into alliance with . . . the Habsburgs. Among other things, he repeatedly chose to marry Habsburg archduchesses. After his first wife, Anna, died, he promptly married her sister Constance. The specter of royal incest shocked many Catholics, despite the fact that Zygmunt had secured a dispensation from the pope.

And this was not the worst of the king's doings. Early on in his reign, it was rumored that Zygmunt (perhaps anticipating the Swedish succession) was willing to relinquish the Polish throne on behalf of Ernst Habsburg. This news incensed the nobility, in particular Jan Zamoyski, who in so many ways had played kingmaker for the Vasa. No longer the king's righthand man (Zygmunt clearly felt the chancellor was already too powerful), the influential Polish magnate rallied the nobility in defense of their rights and against royal abuses of power. In the process he managed to polish his formerly tarnished reputation as defender of the Golden Freedoms of the nobility, who continued to see themselves, and not the king, as the repository of power in the country.

Zamoyski was not the only powerful magnate to take on the king, fearing Habsburg-inspired centralism and absolutism. Not long after Zamoyski's death in 1605, the Kraków palatine Mikołaj Zebrzydowski led a revolt to overthrow the king. The revolt resonated broadly among the nobility—the anti-Habsburg crowd, republicans, Protestants, so many of them alienated by the king, who disregarded their opinions and (in the case of Protestants) passed them over for offices. This was a moment, incidentally, when the idea of the Sarmatian nobility and their need to defend their Golden Freedoms was popularized. Nonetheless, the rebellion was handily defeated by Jan Karol Chodkiewicz and Stanisław Żółkiewski. While the rebellious nobles were given amnesty, they still remained deeply unhappy with the direction the king was taking the Commonwealth.

In part this stemmed from the fact that Zygmunt had little understanding of the realities of the large multiethnic, multidenominational country he had come to rule. By propelling the country into a Habsburg alliance and pursuing the Swedish throne, he made concessions where they should not have been made (for example, with the Hohenzollerns in Ducal Prussia) while involving the country in wars that it should not have had to fight—or fight as often as it did.

Southern Entanglements

Witness the Commonwealth's relations with its neighbor to the south, the Ottoman Empire. Historically the southern frontier had been vulnerable to incursions, whether on the part of the Tatars or the Turks. After 1450 the Crimean Tatars essentially lived off the slave trade, raiding the Commonwealth lands to the north for slaves, whom they would then sell to the Moslem world. Yet the lightly populated lands of the south, not to mention the

Ottoman fiefs of Moldavia and Wallachia, had long been considered prime lands for expansion. At times it was the state that sought to expand, at times ambitious border magnates sought to gain influence there.

While the Jagiellons had been on good terms with the Ottoman Porte, the Habsburg alliance of Zygmunt III Vasa led to renewed conflict with the Turks. In the course of lending a supporting hand to the Habsburgs during the Thirty Years' War, Polish forces made incursions into Moldavia and hampered the actions of the Porte's vassal, the prince of Transylvania. This resulted in Hetman Stanisław Żółkiewski being sent to Tutora (Polish: Cecora), where he would engage the Moldavians in battle.

Żółkiewski was the model of a Commonwealth noble who, although he might disagree with his ruler, would do his best to serve him faithfully. This he did for Zygmunt III from the very outset, suffering a leg injury during the victory at Byczyna that put the Vasa on the throne. Żółkiewski suffered repeatedly from the king's capriciousness, vacillation, and ingratitude, all of which were visible in the 1610 Moscow campaign. While accomplishing the seemingly impossible—defeating the Muscovites despite unfavorable odds and making his way all the way to Moscow—he was still criticized by the Polish king for his efforts. As a result, the military leader was promoted to grand hetman of the Crown only as of 1618. Of course, Żółkiewski had several advantages over the king: he not only knew the art of war but also was well familiar with the vagaries of the Commonwealth's borderlands, from which he himself hailed.

And indeed, Żółkiewski had already been to Tutora. In 1595 forces led by Zamoyski won a victory there, which allowed the Commonwealth to place Jeremiah Mohyla on the Moldavian throne as a joint Commonwealth-Ottoman fief. Part of a string of victories in the south, Tutora was followed by a victory in 1600 against the Wallachian palatine, allowing Zamoyski to seat yet another Mohyla, Simeon, on that throne. These moves had strengthened Commonwealth control, albeit temporarily, over its southern neighbors.

Autumn of 1620 would be Żółkiewski's last trip to Tutora—and the last battle of his long career. A much larger Ottoman army comprised of Tatars and Turks defeated the Poles and caused them to retreat as best they could, while being pursued. As they approached the Commonwealth border, the Tatars attacked again. Melee ensued in the Polish ranks, leading them to scatter. Abandoned by his troops, Żółkiewski persisted in fighting, preferring to die in battle than in retreat. His wife was forced to collect what remained of the hetman—his body left on the field, his head ransomed from the Turks, after having been displayed on the gates of the sultan's palace in Istanbul. These patriotic relics were placed in the church in Żółkiew (today's

Zhovkva, in Ukraine), the hetman's fortified residence, to remind later generations of the Turkish threat and to inspire them to defend their homeland.

The Poles would have their revenge the following year. The Lithuanian
grand hetman Jan Karol Chodkiewicz orchestrated an important victory
over a Turkish and Tatar army of 120,000 at Khotyn (Polish: Chocim) on
the Dniester. He too paid with his life.

Sarmatian Solidarity

Men like Żółkiewski, who put national interests and faithful service above
private gains, were becoming more rare. Nobles—especially the wealthy
magnates—had few reasons to put up with what they saw as unreasonable-
ness on the part of the king. Instead, they embraced a new idea that would
knit the diverse Commonwealth nobility even closer together.

This represented an adjustment to the myth of Sarmatian origin. Already
in the sixteenth century, Kromer and others had concluded that the inhabitants of Poland-Lithuania were descended from this ancient warrior people.
Increasingly, this origin myth was limited to the Commonwealth's nobility,
however. The divisions between the estates solidified and became firmer—as
the nobles maintained that, while they themselves were descended from the
Sarmatians, the country's commoners were not and thus were inferior in
status. Already a brotherhood of privilege, the noble nation (the diversity
of religious faiths and ethnic origins notwithstanding) came to be seen as a
brotherhood of blood.

Sarmatian descent was seen as a distinction of another kind—a sign that
the noble nation was a chosen nation, one destined for greatness. This sense
of Sarmatian uniqueness had three components: economic, cultural, and
political. First, that the Commonwealth was the Granary of Europe had
been made amply clear to the owners of manorial estates, who in the period
of peace that ensued in the 1620s promptly settled back into that still lucrative occupation. Their mission was to feed Europe, to help it thrive and, in
the process, to help themselves thrive.

Second, their battlefield encounters with the infidel—here, understood
as the Muscovites to the east as well as the Tatars and Ottomans to the
south—had bolstered their vision of the Commonwealth as being the Bulwark of Christianity (*antemurale Christianitatis*)—a vision that the Baroque
Church was all too happy to reinforce. This aspect of the Sarmatian myth
was expanded to depict the nation as being under God's special protection.
Despite this fervent Catholicism, Commonwealth nobles increasingly em-

braced Eastern elements of dress and adornment. Witness the trend of having shaved heads—or heads with just a wisp of hair, just like the Moslem
warriors they repeatedly fought. Thus, while the Commonwealth nobles
defended Western values, their encounter with the East also shaped their
identity—if only superficially.

Third, the sense that the Commonwealth's mixed form of government,
which provided the nobility with their cherished Golden Freedoms, was
seen as infinitely superior to absolutist rule elsewhere. The myth of Sarmatian descent, thus, gave the nobles a sense of superiority, even invincibility,
vis-à-vis the rest of Europe.

Sarmatian pride percolated down to even the poorest of nobles. Despite
the exponential growth of magnate wealth during this period, the Sarmatian brotherhood was posited on noble equality. As the saying went, "The
nobleman on his plot is equal to the palatine." The thought that a landless
noble might fancy himself as the peer of a magnate with his estates, court,
and private army (practically a kinglet himself) nonetheless suggested that
there was no glass ceiling: the possibility of upward mobility was always
present, if not always likely. All it took was a happy accident of luck or patronage—an advantageous marriage, an appointment to a state office—and
a clever nobleman could rise in stature. It was possible to become instantly
wealthy if one married the heiress to a magnate family fortune that had
been established as an indivisible inheritance (*ordynacja*). After all, even
magnate families died out, to be replaced by new beneficiaries of the Commonwealth's system. And even the magnates had to take care that their less
wealthy noble clients—the men who hoped for that comfortable job, an
education for their sons, and a decent marriage prospect for their daughters—retained their allegiance.

The Silver Age—and Chosen Nation?

This positive unifying myth of Sarmatian origin of the nobility was buttressed by the sense that times were good. The reign of Zygmunt III Vasa, after all, initiated the Commonwealth's Silver Age as well as a period of peace.
No longer were nobles forced to spend much of their time defending the
country's borders or beefing up the fortifications surrounding their estates
and private towns. This lull allowed them to undergo something of a transformation. Increasingly the nobles were becoming landed gentlemen, not
warriors, and their concerns more economic, not military. Since the transfer
of the Ukrainian lands to the Crown of Poland in 1569, more Crown nobles

had been able to profit from control of those fertile lands. And the economic boom was not limited to the Crown of Poland. The trading towns of the Grand Duchy of Lithuania—places such as Mahilioŭ (Polish: Mohylew) and Slutsk (Polish: Słuck), which dealt in fur and hides—also prospered.

Let two examples, each involving precious metals, serve to emphasize the perception of the Commonwealth's wealth during this period. Poland's economic capital of Gdańsk became known for an aromatic herbal liqueur with flakes of gold suspended in it, the so-called gold water (German: Goldwasser; Polish: złota woda). No expense was too great, no ingredient too exotic to be included in the recipe—as seen from the fact that even sandalwood and rosewood were used to impart flavor. If gold could be consumed in this fashion, clearly it was not in short supply . . . especially as, in the year 1642, some 2,052 seafaring vessels were counted in the Gdańsk harbor.

A no less golden image of the Commonwealth was conveyed by Chancellor Jerzy Ossoliński. Sent on a delegation to Rome in 1633, Ossoliński made such an uncommonly splendid entrance that paintings of it have been preserved for posterity. Between the gold horseshoes of some of the steeds, the silver dress of the retinue of riders, and the camels bedecked in silver and covered in silks, it was truly a memorable—and exotic—sight, blinding in its unalloyed wealth and splendor. While some Western observers remarked that the golden procession smacked of barbarism (even in an age accustomed to Baroque gilt), it is worth noting that the same Ossoliński also owned paintings by artists such as Titian, Raphael, and Dürer. Baroque Sarmatian splendor now overlay the Renaissance foundations of the nation—much as Baroque interiors increasingly displaced other styles in the Commonwealth's churches.

The Silver Age, indeed, had a distinctly Baroque lining. It spawned a triumphalist vision of the noble nation, the excesses of unbridled luxury (its reward for fulfilling its mission of feeding and defending the West) and a sense of Sarmatian superiority vis-à-vis the outside world. Few seemed to heed the words of Zygmunt III Vasa's court preacher, the fiery Jesuit Piotr Skarga. He was critical of the Commonwealth's system and in his sermons had been foretelling national misfortune of this self-styled "chosen nation." (His book *Lives of the Saints* was much more popular than his predictions.) Skarga's words would nonetheless come back, as if from the dead, to haunt later generations of Poles, for the Silver Age was fast winding down. Despite its promising beginning, much of the seventeenth century would prove a nightmare for the state and its inhabitants.

The Most Popular of Polish Monarchs

Unimaginable to the Sarmatians of the early seventeenth century, that period was ahead of them. Upon Zygmunt III's death in 1632, his son Władysław was elected king. No other candidate came forward, and for good reason. Władysław was infinitely more popular in the Commonwealth than his dour father had ever been. Not only was he born to rule, he was ready to rule, having been brought up to do precisely that.

Władysław was destined to sit on a throne somewhere, although for quite some time it was not clear where. It is not that he lacked opportunities. Recall the Muscovite election of Władysław as Russian tsar during the Time of Troubles. The first-born Vasa was likely considered a substitute for his father, who had inherited the crown of Sweden. Both instances would have required the young Vasa to change his religion: to Russian Orthodoxy in the first case, to Lutheranism in the second. This may not have sat well with a prince who was the son of the fervent Roman Catholic Zygmunt and his no less Roman Catholic mother, the Habsburg Anna, although, before his election to the Polish throne, he had been sounding out various other options—perhaps not knowing whether he would be outmaneuvered ultimately by supporters of his younger half-brother, Jan Kazimierz.

None of this came to pass, and Władysław assumed the Polish throne. Great things were expected of the new ruler—one who, despite being the product of a staunchly Catholic Vasa-Habsburg union, had been brought up in the Commonwealth and knew the lay of the land. He also knew the lay of Europe, having had occasion to travel widely in the West as well as to gain an appreciation for the cultural side of life.

More reminiscent of Batory than his father, Władysław was a military man at heart. This was a good thing as one of his first tasks as king was to fight the Muscovites, who took advantage of the interregnum to invade. With an army of twenty-five thousand the former commander of Smolensk, Mikhail Shtein, laid siege to the fortress he had defended in the Time of Troubles. To counter the Muscovite offensive, the Commonwealth's new king set about reforming and modernizing its forces. Among other things, he augmented the cavalry of the Hussars, so well suited to the types of battles that typically took place on the periphery of the country. Now, a modern infantry in German style ("foreign style") was added, as well as engineers used to construct fortifications. The reforms had an effect: the Commonwealth forces turned the tables on the Muscovite army and forced it to surrender. The Muscovite authorities were incredulous that their army had not been able to defeat the

Poles. When the defeated Shtein returned to Moscow, he was labeled a traitor and sentenced to death.

Although incomplete, Władysław's reforms stood the military in good stead. As we will see, this was a very good thing. It would allow the country somehow to withstand what it was to encounter midcentury.

More like his great-uncle Zygmunt August than his father, Władysław Vasa came out on the side of religious toleration—an idea that had taken a direct hit under his Jesuit-educated father. During Władysław's reign, the position of both Protestants and Orthodox was strengthened.

Getting the Protestants to rally around him was a political necessity for the new king. The powerful Calvinist Krzysztof Radziwiłł had considered proposing a Lutheran Vasa, Gustav II Adolf, for the Polish throne. Protestant nobles had been frustrated for decades by Zygmunt III's treating them like second-class citizens; and the situation looked even worse for Protestant communities within cities dominated by Roman Catholics. In a number of deft moves at the outset, Władysław made it clear he would not tolerate the persecution of Protestants. Changing his father's discriminatory policies, he nominated Janusz Radziwiłł for high positions within the Grand Duchy, including the title of field hetman. Let us not forget that such toleration could improve his position within Sweden as well—and Władysław had not given up the idea of gaining a kingdom he could call his own, whether that be Sweden, Finland, Livonia, or something else. His ambitions were nonetheless stymied by the Commonwealth nobles, who sought peace with Sweden.

Even more significant were the concessions King Władysław made to the numerically significant Greek Orthodox fringe. Recall that, with the establishment of church union in 1596, the Commonwealth's Greek Orthodox were to become part of the new Uniate Church. Many simply had refused—this despite the fact that the Greek Orthodox faith was now outlawed. Instead of decrying this fact, Władysław accepted it. While the Orthodox hierarchy had been officially reinstated in 1620, it was the new king who gave the church a chance to flourish in the Commonwealth. With Władysław's permission, the newly appointed Orthodox metropolitan of Kyiv (who was also the archimandrite of Kyiv's Caves Monastery), Petro Mohyla, officially established an academy for Orthodox students in the city.

Mohyla's academy, the first institute of higher learning specifically for the East Slav Orthodox, proved to be a fascinating synthesis of East and West. Patterned after the Jesuit model, the program at the Kyiv academy consisted of the liberal arts. The languages studied were not only the expected Slavonic and Greek but also Latin and Polish—the last of these proving the delivery vehicle for many Renaissance ideas. This exposure to Western ideas and intellectual trends would help a new generation of educated Ruthenian Orthodox to situate themselves more broadly in the world—a good thing, as the world they knew was about to change.

In the 1640s Władysław took on a warmongering position vis-à-vis the Islamic world. His dreams of military glory included the capture of Constantinople. Yet again, his ambitions were frustrated by the Commonwealth nobility, who were not willing to provoke war with the Ottoman Empire. Their lack of support led the king to bypass the traditional channels and make plans in secret.

It was only his death on May 20, 1648, that stopped those plans. It was a death that came tragically upon the heels of the death of his seven-year-old son, Zygmunt Kazimierz. (Władysław had been not very happily married first to the Habsburg Cecilia Renata, the mother of his son, and then to Louise Marie Gonzaga de Nevers.) The man who might have ruled three countries—Muscovy and Sweden as well as the Commonwealth—left the last of these. Unfortunately for the Commonwealth, the country was forced to hold an election at the worst moment possible.

The Third Vasa Dynast

Władysław's half-brother, Jan Kazimierz, was the next Vasa elected to the Polish throne. The son of Zygmunt III and his second wife, Constance Habsburg, he had a rather uneven education in all the affairs related to ruling a country. The young man did manage to imbibe what was now passing for a more traditional Polish noble upbringing, that is, little attention paid to intellectual matters, much more paid to the knightly side of things: how to wield a sword, ride a horse, pass time in good company. Portraits depict him as a traditional Polish nobleman. Still, his life and reign turned out to be anything but typical.

Jan Kazimierz's trajectory demonstrates that life is sometimes much odder than fiction. Seemingly best prepared for the military life, he fought in various campaigns under his father and brother and even joined up with the Habsburgs to fight France in 1635. Taken prisoner by Cardinal Richelieu and held in France for a period of time, he later unexpectedly demonstrated an interest in religion and eventually traveled to Rome and became a Jesuit. This clearly did not please everyone. The next step seems even more improbable. After only a handful of years in the order, Jan Kazimierz was made a cardinal, while simultaneously being freed from his religious vows—likely on the urging of his half-brother, the king. Yet his period within the church hierarchy lasted no longer than did his religious vows. He was out of Rome and hunting for a bride when he heard of his nephew's death.

Jan Kazimierz hurried home, sensing that the future held something different for him. And indeed, he was to be the next king of Poland, for by the time he arrived his half-brother Władysław was also dead. The only other real competition this time came from the two men's youngest brother, Karol Fryderyk, who had made a career entirely in the church.

The title Ioannes Casimirus Rex (Latin for King Jan Kazimierz) was already at the time given a different twist. At the time of his election, the king's Latin initials I.C.R. were ominously predicted to stand for something else: the Beginning of the Calamity of the Kingdom.

The predictions we recall tend to be those that are fulfilled. This certainly proved true in the case of the third, and final, Vasa on the Polish throne. The reign of King Jan Kazimierz would be subjected to a barrage of challenges unlike anything the Commonwealth had ever experienced before. Given the sheer elemental force that would rock the country, it was no wonder that the era of I.C.R. has been remembered as the Deluge.

The Cossacks and the Commonwealth

The first great wave to crash over the Commonwealth came from the southeast. It was not another Tatar raid, the likes of which had been regular features of borderlands existence. Rather, this borderland business was an internal problem, one emanating from the remote borderland region known as Ukraine.

The Ukraine of the seventeenth century was an integral part of the Commonwealth of Both Nations. While at this point it is hard to speak of a compact Ukrainian territory, most certainly the enormous Kyiv palatinate was its focal point. The southeastern borderlands of the Commonwealth had long been lightly populated—due in part not to low birth rates but, rather, to a high captivity rate. Tatars and Turks made regular incursions into the region for Christian slaves, whom they sold all over the Moslem world. Perhaps one of the most famous slaves ever taken was a girl called Roxolana who was captured in the early sixteenth century. Taken to the harem of the sultan known as Suleiman the Magnificent, she became so beloved by the Sultan that he made her his wife (and not just his concubine, as was the rule). Roxolana bore the sultan several sons. In that part of the world she was known as Hurrem Sultan. Although the sources are light insofar as her heritage is concerned, Roxolana was probably of Ruthenian origin. Today she is considered one of the most famous and admired of Ukrainian women. How this came to be is in part explained by the Cossack debacle of the mid-seventeenth century.

The trouble for the Commonwealth began in the far southeast corner of that palatinate. This was in lands labeled the Wild Fields and Zaporizhia. *Za porohamy* means beyond the rapids, and the rapids here are those of the Dnieper River, at the place where the river bends before flowing into the Black Sea.

Within this borderland region lived a population that has gone down in history as the Cossacks. The word "Cossack" comes from the Turkic for "free man." This was a population truly shaped by geography and destiny. As early as the fourteenth century, the distant steppes and region near the Dnieper River became a haven for those who had reason to run far away: runaway serfs, individuals who had gotten into trouble with the law, as well as the occasional adventurer. In their new home beyond the Dnieper rapids, the settlers formed self-contained military communities and became adept at defending themselves and their borderland home.

With time the Zaporizhian Cossacks, this community beyond the rapids, assumed control over a fortress below the Dnieper rapids known as Sich. The barracked units of Cossacks who resided there had their own form of self-government, complete with a hetman and his staff. Officers of the Sich were elected by the Cossack host. It was a fluid group with members coming in and out of service as the situation required (some settled down in the nearby region). Nonetheless, it was a brotherhood of arms—and of interests. While these hardy, armed, freedom-loving peasants had escaped from the more structured life elsewhere in the Commonwealth, they seemed to have imbibed a desire for self-rule not unlike that of the Polish-Lithuanian nobility.

In contrast to many other parts of the Commonwealth, where the Union of Brest had made inroads among the Orthodox community, Uniatism did not penetrate the Ukrainian steppe. The Cossacks retained the faith of their fathers, the Slavic rite of Greek Orthodoxy, and their distance from Roman control. Doubtless a role was played by their proximity to the holiest shrines of their faith: Kyiv, with its great church of Saint Sophia that was patterned after the Byzantine Hagia Sofia, or the Monastery of the Caves. Defenders of the Orthodox faith, the Zaporizhian Cossacks en masse joined the lay brotherhood of the Monastery of the Caves in 1620.

The Cossacks' demonstrable ability to keep outsiders at bay came to the attention of the Polish and Lithuanian authorities. In the fifteenth and sixteenth centuries the Cossacks were occasionally employed as specialized infantry troops to defend the Commonwealth's southern borders, ever plagued by incursions of Tatars and Turks. Already under Stefan Batory there were five hundred Zaporizhian Cossacks on payroll. These were placed on the so-called Cossack register. When not paid regularly they revolted—but they did fight in the Commonwealth's armies, and often to fine effect. During the Russian Time of Troubles, some thirty to forty thousand Cossack troops fought on the side of the Commonwealth. Also noteworthy was the group of some thirty thousand Cossacks, led by their able leader Petro Sahaidachnyi, who helped the Polish and Lithuanian forces defeat the Turks at Khotyn in 1621.

Back in their own backyard, the Cossacks helped to defend cities in the Kyiv and Bratslav palatinates against Tatar raids. This made it possible to bring in settlers to work the land, well irrigated and fertile, but which constant attacks had left depopulated. Many of the towns and settlements of this most remote part of the Commonwealth were parts of vast estates belonging to magnate families, both Polish and Polonized, such as the Wiśniowiecki, Ostrogski, Zamoyski, and Potocki—for it took wealth, a considerable upfront investment, to take full advantage of the natural riches of the region.

This region—the least densely populated palatinates of the Crown of Poland—encapsulated the extremes of the manorial system. Its heterogeneous population was highly differentiated according to function. The fertile lands were controlled by big noble landowners, defended by a mix of Cossacks and private and state armies, farmed by Ruthenes, staffed by Jews. The role of the last was crucial. Thousands of Jews had been brought into the region by the magnates to serve as the grease that kept the machine going. Jews mediated between noble and peasant, serving as estate agents, tax collectors, and moneylenders.

The Cossacks fell between the social cracks. It is understandable that they should seek to regularize their relationship not only within borderland society but also within the Commonwealth as a whole. Ostensibly peasants (and thus subject to serfdom), they nonetheless defended the country's borders, just like the nobles. These rough-and-ready, undisciplined, colorful fighters wanted recognition of their warrior status—the same status that had created the Polish nobility, after all. For was not a noble a member of the citizenry, by virtue of his willingness to put his life on the line for his country?

Although the Cossacks were treated like peasants, in numerous ways they behaved more like the Polish-Lithuanian nobility. They had their own corporate organization, with a distinct esprit de corps—even an elective leadership. As to their military prowess, not only did they help to defend the country's borders. As a group they could be just as unruly as the Polish magnates, who on occasion conducted their own "foreign policy" in the hopes of amassing further wealth. Such developments could have consequences for the country at large. It was the Cossacks' incredible raiding of the Istanbul harbor, for example, that led the Commonwealth into war with the Turks in the 1620s. They had an independent streak, these Polish-Lithuanian subjects.

At times coexisting with the regular military forces of the Commonwealth, the Cossacks wanted to ensure their position within the Commonwealth military and retain their freedom. Reaching an agreement that would satisfy both sides was a tricky business. Although the Cossacks served, the nobles were not keen on endlessly funding the force. Thus, as of the time of Batory, the idea of a Cossack register—a list of officially recognized Cossacks in the pay of the Commonwealth—had been introduced. The problem was that the number of Cossacks allowed to be on this list never quite met the expectations of the Cossacks themselves. They demanded respect.

This, incidentally, was a position that Władysław IV Vasa understood. The new Polish king both knew and liked the Cossacks. He was willing to acknowledge the Cossack contribution to the military campaigns of the Commonwealth, especially on its far fringes, always under threat. Cossacks had contributed to the king's own victory at Smolensk. At the same time, Władysław realized that their elemental force needed to be controlled.

The Seym was less enamored of the Cossacks—perhaps seeing in the Zaporizhian Host a force too similar to themselves . . . After peace was achieved with the Ottoman Empire in 1635, for example, the Seym tried to ensure that the Zaporizhian Host would make no more unauthorized "sea incursions" of its own. It could not prevent the Cossacks from rebelling repeatedly in the 1630s, however, rebellions that were put down by the royal army.

Only as of 1638 did the Seym and Cossack host reach a modus vivendi. A certain number of Cossacks (six thousand, divided into six regiments) would be admitted to the Cossack register. This select group would be acknowledged not as peasants but, rather, as free men. The price of this arrangement: the Cossacks would no longer be allowed to elect their leaders, who would be appointed by the king—just as was done in other parts of the Commonwealth military. Those numerous Cossacks who were not registered were to be considered burghers or peasants.

This limited acknowledgment of the Cossacks as a genuine military force was only a partial solution. Perhaps it reflected the cash-strapped situation of the Polish king, who could not afford either to put or to keep all the Cossacks on the payroll. Still, it marked an improvement over complete uncertainty—and it managed to keep the peace for a decade. After all, it was infinitely better to be a free man than a peasant liable to be enserfed.

Of course, even those Cossacks fortunate enough to be admitted to the register would have preferred to gain further rights and privileges—to be rewarded for their contribution to the national defense. However, the Polish nobility did not want to grant the Cossacks the same estate freedoms, and the corresponding political rights, that they themselves cherished. The Commonwealth nobles doubtless objected for various reasons—among them their Sarmatian conviction that they were biologically distinct from the Commonwealth's commoners. This could be seen from the reaction of the nobles to a Cossack delegation that appeared during the 1632 Convocation Seym. Demanding to participate in the election, they were laughingly told that they were members of the Commonwealth just like fingernails—and, like fingernails, needed to be trimmed on occasion . . . Clearly there was not much in the way of support for admitting the Cossacks into the ranks of decision-making citizens.

Nonetheless, while plotting his anti-Turkish campaign right before he died, King Władysław opened the door to Cossack thoughts about further privileges. More exactly, in exchange for support, he promised to double the size of the Cossack register and reinstate the privileges the Cossacks had lost in 1638. This was beginning to sound like what the Cossacks sought: they wanted the privileges of a military force along the lines of that which nobles cherished, to have the Golden Freedoms that made them not only free men but citizens.

From Incivility to Civil War

With ballooning expectations, the Cossacks were ready to fight. However, they would end up fighting not the dead Władysław's war but, rather, the Commonwealth itself. And this would not turn out to be yet another small-scale Cossack revolt, of which so many had been put down without too much trouble by the Polish forces. In 1648, the latter would not be so lucky. Paradoxically, it would take "only" an indignity suffered by a proud Cossack nobleman to set the Wild Fields alight.

In 1648 the Zaporizhian Cossacks were led by an Orthodox noble named Bohdan Khmelnytsky. Fighting as a Cossack officer as of the early part of the century, even suffering captivity at the hands of the Turks, the Ruthenian Khmelnytsky had been distinguished by his loyalty to the throne. It was he whom Władysław IV placed in charge of the Zaporizhian Cossacks.

It was not relations with the king but with fellow nobles that soured. A quarrel between Khmelnytsky and a Polish neighbor left the Cossack leader both livid and on the lam. Abandoning his homestead, he raced off to the Sich and rallied the Zaporizhian Cossacks, whose numbers were already swelling in anticipation of the approaching war with the Turks. The personal quarrel between an Orthodox and a Catholic noble thus morphed into an uprising against injustices both personal and communal. Augmenting his forces with Tatar cavalry, Khmelnytsky—now as Cossack hetman—took on the Commonwealth forces. The message resounded in the Ukrainian borderlands. Registered Cossacks deserted to Khmelnytsky's side in a battle with the Poles at Zhovti Vody in May 11–16, 1648. On his deathbed, King Władysław learned of the defeat of his army at the hands of one who had been the epitome of a loyal Cossack.

The Cossack rebellion gained strength. It struck a note with the Ruthenian populace of the region, who swelled the Cossack host and rallied in support. Some forty thousand Cossack regulars augmented by another forty thousand warriors proved a formidable foe. This was civil war. The traditional borderlands society of the Ukraine was in danger of disintegration.

Civil war, of course, is an oxymoron; but this civil war was as uncivil as they get. The Cossacks and their new allies, the Tatars, savagely attacked not only the military forces but also those civilians whom they saw as enemies: Catholics, Poles, and Jews. Two targets of Ruthenian enmity were singled out for especially harsh treatment. Given the religious nature of the dispute, the Polish Catholic clergy fared badly. Yet even worse was the fate of the region's Jews, who, while religiously distinctive, were doubtless attacked primarily for being the face of serfdom in the region. At least ten thousand perished, although many Jews also rose to the occasion to defend themselves and fight the Cossacks as best they could.

This led to reprisals against the Cossacks forthcoming from the Polish-Lithuanian army, which to some extent regrouped under the leadership of the enormously wealthy Jeremi Wiśniowiecki. This Catholic scion of an Orthodox Ruthenian magnate family proved as ruthless and savage as the Cossacks and the Tatars he sought to defeat.

In the midst of all this, the Commonwealth needed to select a new king. During the interregnum, the reinforced Commonwealth forces, ineptly led, proved no match for the Cossacks. This elemental force swept through the region like a hurricane, laying waste to the countryside while exacting tribute from cities such as Lviv and Zamość, which desperately sought to avoid being besieged. To help the Polish nobles make up their minds which Vasa brother to select, Khmelnytsky weighed in on the side of Jan Kazimierz, who took a more moderating position vis-à-vis the Cossacks than did his younger brother Karol Fryderyk, who appeared to advocate an anti-Cossack crusade. This "vote" of the Cossack hetman for Jan Kazimierz was no small factor in the nobles' ultimate decision.

Although King Jan Kazimierz sought to reach agreement with Khmel-nytsky, war continued. Clearly being a power broker went to the Cossack's head, and the hetman decided to keep on fighting, setting his sights on greater gains. In the 1649 campaign, Khmelnytsky's force, comprised of Crimean Tatars as well as Cossacks, overwhelmed the Poles at Zbarazh. The king himself fought subsequently, and valiantly, at Zboriv (Polish: Zborów); more importantly, however, after the battle, Jan Kazimierz managed to convince the Tatars, who had no interest in creating an autonomous Cossack country on their borders, to leave the war.

The departure of his Crimean Tatar allies led Khmelnytsky to enter into negotiations and settle on terms that might be acceptable to both his Cossacks and the Commonwealth. An agreement was reached with the Commonwealth at Zboriv, which would have significantly improved the situation of the Orthodox within the country. Neither party to the agreement was really keen on it, however. Khmelnytsky dreamed of achieving more, while the Commonwealth nobles balked at making the planned concessions to the Cossacks. Each side viewed the arrangement more as a pretext for a temporary truce than as the foundation for a lasting peace. And indeed, war resumed in 1651.

The growing ambitions and sundry preoccupations of both major players resulted in a stalemate, which nonetheless cost each dearly. Jan Kazimierz was distracted by negotiations with Sweden and unable to take advantage of victories such as the one at Berestechko (Polish: Beresteczko) in 1651, where he himself led the troops. These, incidentally, were huge clashes: at this time the Commonwealth was able to muster some seventy thousand soldiers. At Berestechko, despite the fact that Khmelnytsky had to be whisked off the battlefield by his Tatar allies (some of whom came back after the resumption of war), the Cossacks did not give in, and Khmelnytsky quickly rebounded. After the Cossack/Tatar victory at Batih (Polish: Batoh) the next year, the Cossack hetman ransomed the Polish prisoners of war from his Tatar allies and then made sure the men who had defeated him at Berestechko would never fight again . . . This wholesale slaughter of Polish officers and career soldiers literally decapitated the Polish forces. Yet Khmelnytsky, too, was sidetracked as well as stung by dynastic issues. While trying to place his son Tymish on the Moldavian throne, he conquered Suceava, only in the process to lose his son, who was felled by a cannonball there.

As if there were not enough trouble in this part of the world, that same year an epidemic of plague hit the Commonwealth. Emanating from the Ukrainian lands, it swept westward, causing deaths in the hundreds of thousands.

Nor was the disaster in the Commonwealth limited to elemental forces. Tensions mounted between King Jan Kazimierz, who sought to augment the power of the king, and the nobility. Among other things, the nobles did not like the idea that he wished to concentrate control over the military in his own hands, instead of appointing new individuals to the offices of hetman that were now vacant. The king clashed with his vice-chancellor, Hieronim Radziejowski, a former royal favorite who subsequently was forced to flee the country. Jan Kazimierz would come to rue the day he made the unprecedented move of sentencing Radziejowski to death and infamy and land confiscation.

There was plenty of bad blood to go around, as other magnates were also in conflict with the king. The first Seym of 1652, unable to reach agreement, dissolved. Things got so bad that the nobles in opposition secretly approached György II Rákóczi of Transylvania for assistance, letting him know that they were ready to dethrone Jan Kazimierz if the latter persisted in seeking changes to the government of the Commonwealth.

Secession

Throughout this period, the ambitious and resourceful Khmelnytsky continued to explore his options. Instead of looking south to the Tatars or Turks for help, he turned north—to Moscow. At the beginning of 1654, an agreement was reached in the border town of Pereiaslav between the Cossacks and the envoy of the Muscovite tsar. The Cossacks under Khmelnytsky would secede from the Commonwealth. Instead, in exchange for a promise of autonomy, Cossacks would swear allegiance to Tsar Alexei Mikhailovich and become part of the tsarist empire.

Those who conclude that this alliance was inevitable, on account of the shared religion of both entities, ignore one very important dimension: the very real differences in political culture. Raised in the Commonwealth, the Cossacks had imbibed the elixir of freedom and notions of self-government. Viewing themselves as a corporate entity on par with the Polish nobles, they expected to be treated as an equal partner. Although Muscovy under the first Romanovs had regrouped and reformed, its reforms took the country in the opposite direction from that of the Commonwealth: the autocratic rule of the tsar over the entire population was confirmed and strengthened. This was no brotherly reunion. In the minds of both parties, the Pereiaslav Agreement of 1654 was a tactical move—a temporary alliance, designed to further their respective causes. Nonetheless, the son of Mikhail Romanov seemed to be (re)gaining at least a modicum of control over territories that his Muscovite ancestors—claiming the title of Tsar of All Rus'—had considered their patrimony.

The Muscovites' intent becomes clearer in the next phase. The realignment of alliances agreed upon at Pereiaslav clearly meant war with the Commonwealth, which had now seen a significant swath of territory secede from the union. While the Polish forces headed to Ukraine to try and recoup their losses, both Cossack and Muscovite forces headed north: Muscovy had its eye on the Grand Duchy of Lithuania. Formerly limited to the south, the civil war was beginning another, more ominous phase.

The Swedish Problem

To this point, the problem facing the Commonwealth had been an internal problem, one essentially of its own making—the result of years of lack of recognition for a distinct part of the population. That it looked to be escalating into the international arena was a by-product of that conflict. The next phase of the mid-century debacle had an external component, one that seemed to accompany the reign of each Vasa dynast elected king of Poland. This was the conflict with Sweden.

Like their father, both sons of Zygmunt III cherished illusory hopes of some day gaining the Swedish throne—or, if that were impossible, gaining something nice in exchange for relinquishing their claim to the throne. While perhaps laudatory insofar as dynastic concerns were concerned, their dogged preoccupation with Sweden not only infuriated the Commonwealth nobility but also exacerbated relations with the country's neighbor to the north.

The ramifications of this stubbornness took on a new and ominous shape in 1655. The previous year, a new and energetic ruler assumed the Swedish throne. Karl X Gustav was not a Vasa but, rather, a member of the Wittelsbach family. The nephew of Gustav Adolf, he inherited the Swedish throne upon the abdication of the last of the Vasas, Christina. In a move that put her closer to her Polish relatives, Christina had decided to embrace Catholicism and thus was no longer considered a suitable ruler for that Lutheran country.

The new king of Sweden watched the Commonwealth thrashing about like a shark excited by the taste of blood in the water. It took little to convince Karl X Gustav that the moment was ripe to intervene. King of a relatively poor and lightly populated northern country with a harsh and unforgiving climate (although also with some good reserves of iron and, more notably, copper), he already entertained ambitions of gaining a bigger share of the lucrative Baltic Sea trade, and even of controlling the Baltic. More urgent, the new king needed to improve the state of his treasury—if only to be able to maintain his military garrisons on both sides of the Baltic. The best way for the king to do this was to wage war.

Given the salience of the Baltic, the watery moniker given this northern war by the Poles—the Deluge—was perhaps apt. It was the Polish king's brazen use of the title King of Sweden that ostensibly caused Karl Gustav to cross the Baltic in July 1655, this time engaging the Poles not in the remote northeast region of Livonia but on their own home turf. There, in the heart of the Commonwealth of Both Nations, he and his men would seek influence, territory, and booty, the likes of which were not to be had back home. This Swedish Deluge literally inundated the Commonwealth, washing away many cherished noble illusions in the process.

The Deluge

Karl X Gustav had a real military machine at his disposal. His superbly trained, professional, and experienced soldiers had proved themselves in the Thirty Years' War. The king proceeded to put them to effective use. He planned a two-pronged attack, coming in not only from the north (which would have been expected from the Swedes), but from the west as well (via Pomerania, which Sweden acquired as a result of the Thirty Years' War). In this way, the Commonwealth forces, already engaged in Ukraine and Lithuania, now had to cope with military advances on two more fronts.

And advance they did. The situation was particularly embarrassing in the Commonwealth's western region of Greater Poland. This area, so remote from the traditional theaters of war for the Commonwealth in the north, east, and south, had no memory of war. Its local military commanders and noble levy were untried and unsure. They quickly capitulated, in part encouraged to do so by none other than Hieronim Radziejowski, for the exiled noble had gained the ear of the Swedish king and was exacting his revenge on Jan Kazimierz.

In the course of a mere six weeks, facing limited resistance, the Swedish forces, together with Karl Gustav himself, marched across Greater Poland all the way to the undefended capital, Warsaw. Nor was Lesser Poland, although more ably defended, able to stop the Swedes. Kraków fell under Swedish control. With no prospects of the relief promised by the king, the valiant Stefan Czarniecki was not able to withstand a siege lasting three weeks long, and he capitulated, albeit under terms that would allow him and his army

Map 6.1: The Commonwealth in the Seventeenth Century

to exit the city. Jan Kazimierz was nowhere to be found: he had abandoned the country and escaped to Silesia. Radziejowski's revenge seemed complete.

That there had been no love lost between the Polish king and many of his subjects, including a number of magnates, influenced the turn of events in the east. They were already having trouble repelling the Muscovites and the Cossacks, in the face of which even subordination to Sweden was looking good . . . Still smarting from his contretemps with Jan Kazimierz and desperate for military assistance, Lithuanian grand hetman Janusz Radziwiłł recognized the Swedish king as Grand Duke of Lithuania—in this way, breaking the Polish-Lithuanian Union.

Given this unprecedented and unanticipated state of affairs, a flurry of negotiations took place with various neighboring powers. The noble citizens of the Commonwealth had lost hope that their country would emerge in the same configuration it had entered the war, and the powerful sought to realign themselves as best they could. The Lithuanian grand hetman's cousin Bogusław Radziwiłł joined ranks with the Swedes. Yet other magnates sought the assistance of Elector Friedrich Wilhelm of Brandenburg, who opportunistically decided that alliance with Sweden would give him greater advantage. A group of Commonwealth senators literally pleaded with the Holy Roman Emperor, Ferdinand III, to suggest a Habsburg candidate who could be placed on the Polish throne in exchange for help in expelling the Swedes. As if this offer were not enough, the desperate senators were willing to sweeten the deal by offering the emperor control of the engine of Poland's economic boom, Gdańsk and Royal Prussia.

The situation had denigrated into chaos. With Poles and Lithuanians fighting on both sides, it was truly civil war. And, while in the case of the Cossack conflict one could at least tell who the enemy was, in the Polish heartland the enemy was much less easily identified. This led to a growing suspicion, on the part of Poles, of anyone who might be seen as different. Not only Swedes but also the Commonwealth's own Protestants came under attack. Jews were fingered as agents of the enemy and accused of treachery. While some in both groups collaborated with the Swedish invader, so did many Catholics. The fabric of Commonwealth society, never tightly knit to begin with, was rent.

Or was it? Little by little, the situation began to turn. It began on a small scale, with partisan warfare in various places—including the previously cowardly Greater Poland. The Polish forces there found that Swedes requisitioning food and monetary contributions from the local population were easier targets. Nobles in various parts of the Commonwealth began to form confederations. The great Ruthenian magnate Paweł Sapieha's enmity for his Lithuanian rival Janusz Radziwiłł put the former, and his private army, solidly on the side of the Polish king. Even non-nobles began to join in the fight, as witnessed in the Carpathian foothills.

The Siege of Częstochowa: The Miraculous Madonna

A symbolic turning point was the nearly six-week-long defense of one of Poland's holiest shrines, the monastery on Jasna Góra (Bright Mountain), in Częstochowa, in late 1655. Run by the Pauline Order, a religious order of Hungarian origin brought to Jasna Góra during the reign of Louis of Anjou, the well-fortified monastery housed a miraculous icon of the Mother of God, the so-called Black Madonna—black and visibly scarred from a fifteenth-century Hussite incursion. Devotion to the Mother of God in the Polish lands came early, as witnessed by the hymn "Bogurodzica," which the Polish-Lithuanian forces had sung while going into battle with the Teutonic Knights in 1410. In more recent times, the cult of Mary was promoted by the Jesuits. The image of the Black Madonna had been embroidered onto military standards that flew at the battles of Khotyn in 1621 and Berestechko in 1651 as well as featured on the pectoral of many a Hussar. Like so many things in Poland, the Black Madonna icon itself was a palimpsest—of Italian origin, the icon was repainted in Byzantine/Orthodox style around 1430, to become the most famous, and most recognizable, icon in Poland.

The legend of Our Lady of Częstochowa grew when, from November 18 to December 27, 1655, the Pauline monks and their lay defenders not only refused to capitulate to the greedy Swedes, who had set their sights on the monastery's treasures; they actually managed to force the Swedish forces to retreat. Contemporaries believed that the Mother of God had interceded on behalf of the Poles, repelling the Swedish cannonballs with supernatural means. While not a true turning point in the war, the 1655 victory at Częstochowa surely represented a new and empowering model for the Poles. Religion—here, the defense of their Roman Catholic faith— could serve as a potent rallying cry. After weathering the long siege, could Poles be blamed for believing that, perhaps, the heavens had changed their opinion of the Sarmatians?

Polish piety notwithstanding, it was not a figment of the imagination that the war against the Commonwealth was also a war against Catholicism. The average Swedish soldier, hardy and certainly not wealthy, would have found the wealth of the Commonwealth utterly bedazzling—as did the Swedish king himself. And a sizable amount of that wealth was found in the places of worship. The first thing the king did—upon entering Kraków and making his way to Wawel Hill—was demand a contribution of a hundred thousand Swedish silver talers from the Kraków episcopate.

The sacrilegious Swedes showed no respect for the religion of the conquered. Their previous wartime experience had come from the religiously motivated Thirty Years' War, and this experience had taught them no respect for any faith that was not their own. The occupying army often took over churches and monasteries, levied heavy contributions from them, and used them as barracks, hospitals, ammunition depots, even stables for their horses.

These religious sites were also systematically and repeatedly looted. The occupying Swedes could not keep their hands off the fabulous wealth of the Catholic Church, for centuries the beneficiary of generous gifts and votives from the faithful: bejeweled gold chalices and monstrances, silver crosses and candlesticks, copes and chasubles embroidered with pearls and jewels, and countless smaller votive gifts of silver or gold. Nor were they above laying their hands on the religious. It was no wonder that the clergy of the Commonwealth incited the population to expel the heretics.

News of the growing anti-Swedish sentiment of the population encouraged King Jan Kazimierz, who returned to the Commonwealth in late 1655. In a way, he needed to provide a counter-focus for his subjects. Somewhat surprised at the easy progress he and his men had made, Karl X Gustav's appetite had grown with the eating. Instead of contenting himself with a generous slice of pie (Royal Prussia, say, or Livonia), he now wanted the whole pie—the Commonwealth—for himself.

As Karl Gustav and the Swedish army headed in the direction of the city of Lviv (to which Jan Kazimierz had gone), the Polish king made several pronouncements that are noteworthy for their symbolism. On April 1, 1656, he gave an oath that he would improve the lot of the peasants, who had been rallying in support of their king. Taking a cue from the Black Madonna's miraculous intercession for the Poles at Jasna Góra, Jan Kazimierz entrusted the country into Mary's care. She would henceforth be known as Queen of the Crown of Poland. Whether via divine intervention or through the efforts of those who defended the city, including military reinforcements from Lithuania, Lviv escaped capture.

Indeed, when word reached Karl Gustav that he would be facing a larger army than he had anticipated, he decided to retreat with his forces, whose progress through the terrain was already made laborious by the spring muck. The fate of the Swedish army began to turn. The Polish-Lithuanian army had its first big victory in battle at Warka. Polish forces then spread out in various directions, freeing parts of the occupied territory. They reconvened near the capital, Warsaw. After weeks of fighting, Swedish-occupied Warsaw surrendered.

Threatening Partition

Yet the Deluge was not yet over. A final phase truly internationalized the war, giving the population of the Commonwealth even more reason to believe they were surrounded by enemies, intent on divvying up whatever spoils were available.

Exhausted by their efforts in 1656, the Commonwealth and Sweden each sought to augment its forces with fresh soldiers from new allies. Each made all kinds of promises—some genuine, some not. An example of the latter would be the Polish promises of the Polish crown to both Habsburgs and the Russian tsar. An example of the former would be Swedish promises to share the loot, that is, to distribute shares of the Commonwealth, with those who helped Karl Gustav put the nail in its coffin. A number of Poland's neighbors expressed more than a passing interest in the Swede's offer: at the negotiations in Transylvania at the end of 1656, not only György II Rákóczi of that country but also Friedrich Wilhelm of Brandenburg and Bohdan Khmelnytsky signed on to the plan. Even the Lithuanian magnate Bogusław Radziwiłł, who had cast his lot with the Swedes, was promised rule over the little Navahrudak (Polish: Nowogródek) palatinate, where the Radziwiłł family's seat of Niasviž (Polish: Nieśwież) was located. It would be a Swedish fief.

Thus, paradoxically, Poland could have been partitioned in the seventeenth century. Yet this was not the right time—the right century—for such a move.

Not that the new alliance did not try. Assisted by some Cossack troops, the Transylvanian Rákóczi invaded in 1657 and wreaked havoc across a broad swath of the country. Nonetheless, his defeat at the end of the year meant the end of his dream of being the king of whatever was left of the Commonwealth after the others had taken their shares.

News that Denmark and Holland had declared war on Sweden and that the Holy Roman Emperor was sending in his troops convinced the clever Friedrich Wilhelm of Brandenburg to reconsider his alliance. Not labeled the Great Elector for nothing, he played both sides for all they were worth. Earlier in the war, the Swedes had promised him the prince-bishopric of Warmia as well as territories in Greater Poland and Royal Prussia for his efforts in the field as well as for transferring Ducal Prussia from Polish to Swedish suzerainty. While the prospect of these territorial gains fizzled out, the turncoat Hohenzollern still profited immensely from his participation in the Deluge—for, incredibly, it was Friedrich Wilhelm and not Jan Kazimierz who gained the upper hand during the negotiations at Wehlau (today's Znamensk, in Russia) in 1657. That treaty, unfavorable to the Commonwealth, made several concessions to Friedrich Wilhelm, the most important of which represented a huge victory for the Hohenzollern: Ducal Prussia advanced from Polish fief to sovereign country. That said, Poles importantly retained the right to regain control over the duchy, should the male electoral line of Hohenzollerns die out.

Thus, while the pact of partition had failed, not all the signatories ended up faring badly. Still, the involvement of the big players to the west—Denmark, Holland, and the Holy Roman Empire—helped put a nail in Karl Gustav's own coffin. Nearly literally: for the Swedish king died during the negotiations at Oliwa in 1660 that finally put an end to the Deluge. Nonetheless, a degree of parity was restored. Sweden relinquished the territories it had conquered during the Deluge, though it confirmed its hold over Livonia. Jan Kazimierz relinquished his claim to the Swedish throne as well as to Swedish Livonia.

Catastrophe Continued

Yet this was not the extent of the war experience by the Commonwealth mid-century. In the midst of the Deluge—that is, right after the Swedish invasion of July 1655—came more trouble from the east. The Cossack catastrophe was not yet over.

The Pereiaslav Agreement of 1654 led to the civil war between the Cossacks and the rest of the Commonwealth being transformed into a war of international dimensions. As a result of the agreement, the Cossacks had gained a new ally or, more precisely, Russia had gained a new territory and belligerent subjects. A joint Russian and Cossack attack on Lithuania ensued. In the late summer of 1655, the invaders, led by Tsar Alexei Mikhailovich himself, besieged Smolensk for a full three weeks (ultimately forcing the fortress town to capitulate) and succeeded in taking other cities of the Grand Duchy, including Vilnius.

The capture and burning of Vilnius was particularly tragic. Vilnius had long known peace, and the capital of the Grand Duchy was a flourishing city, full of life and abounding with riches. It is worth noting that the inhabitants of the city—burghers as well as nobles, and representing the full gamut of religions: Catholics, Protestants, Uniates, Orthodox, and Jews—all put up a good fight. This they did under the rallying cry of their corporate rights and freedoms.

The crusading nature of the Russian attack—to reclaim the region for the Orthodox world—meant that not only Catholics but also Uniates and Jews were to be eliminated. The only path to temporal salvation was conversion to Orthodoxy. Many did not find that option palatable. Refusing to give up the faith of their fathers, the Jews of Smolensk were herded into wooden buildings and burned. Noteworthy is the fact that, even after their town capitulated, the Orthodox nobles of Smolensk sought to have the religious rights of their Catholic brethren—Roman Catholics and Uniates alike—restored. The inhabitants of Mahiliou similarly appealed to the tsar to protect the rights of its citizens of varied faith.

Knowledge of the ruthlessness of the joint Cossack/Russian forces must have helped inspire the residents of other towns of the Grand Duchy to resist. Places such as Slutsk and Stary Bykhou (Polish: Stary Byków) managed to keep the Russians and Cossacks at bay for the duration of the war. Slutsk was a multiethnic and multidenominational trading town, the property of the Calvinist Bogusław Radziwiłł. While there were Jews and even Scots among the population, the majority of the population was Orthodox—precisely the people that Tsar Alexei Mikhailovich wanted to return to the fold.

However, the inhabitants of Slutsk, proud of their civic rights as burghers subject to Magdeburg Law, did not see the foreign incursion as a blessing. They fought to ensure they would remain citizens of the Commonwealth and not become vassals of the autocratic tsar.

Although the fate of the inhabitants of the Grand Duchy during this period is not well known, it gives the lie to those who might assume that devotion to the freedoms provided by the Commonwealth—to burghers as well as to nobles—was weaker in the Grand Duchy than in the Crown of Poland. Even territories that had long served as a bone of contention between the Commonwealth and Russia seemed to prefer being part of the former. Witness the fact that members of the nobility of the palatinates of Smolensk, Vitsebsk, and Polatsk moved to safer territory, where they continued to convene their traditional seymiks for the next century.

Other inhabitants of the Grand Duchy were not fortunate enough to escape. Many were either deported to Russia, which needed new serfs to farm in the place of those who had died in the recent plagues, or sold as slaves to the Turks. Many craftsmen, whose services were sought by the tsar and his nobles, ended up being taken in Moscow, significantly raising the population of the Russian capital. As a sign of their "otherness," these Orthodox artisans were even often obliged to sign an act of conversion before being allowed to work. Belarusian historians have seen these deportations as an enormous and unprecedented demographic loss for this East Slavic people, the Ruthenes of the Grand Duchy. Even after the armistice of 1667, they were not allowed to return to the Commonwealth. Altering the demographic mix of the region further, Tsar Alexei Mikhailovich awarded land grants for the now depopulated territory to military men.

As the Swedes had demonstrated, foreign occupation of these wealthy territories of the Commonwealth of Both Nations led to the systematic plunder of their riches. After the invading Russians and Cossacks entered Vilnius, the city burned for seventeen days. Some six hundred buildings were destroyed. Some twenty-five thousand townspeople were massacred—a full third of the inhabitants of the capital of the Grand Duchy. Palaces, churches, and monasteries were plundered. Works of art, libraries, and archives belonging to the state, the nobles, even the wealthy burghers were shipped back to Moscow and were never returned to their rightful owners or country of origin. Contemporaries wrote of the countless silver treasures found in the streets and markets of Moscow—a testimony to the fact that not only the tsar's coffers were enriched by the looting of the capital of the Grand Duchy.

Unfortunately for Vilnius, her famous Marian icon, Our Lady of Ostra Brama, worked no miracles that summer. The Virgin Mary, Mother of God, came to the nation's aid only later that year, during the siege of Częstochowa. But still, the city would rebound, after the Deluge had come to an end, when its ranks were augmented by people—burghers, nobles, clergy, Jews, some of whom returned to the city from exile—who felt themselves to be loyal citizens of the Commonwealth.

Toward a Commonwealth of Three Nations?

The population of the Grand Duchy had demonstrated its commitment to the Commonwealth, of which they considered themselves citizens. Perhaps a creative extension of citizenship was the answer to the Cossack debacle? Not relying on divine intercession, the nobles of the Commonwealth strove to put an end to the civil war with the Cossacks via diplomatic means. They entered into negotiations with the new leader of the Cossacks, Ivan Vyhovsky.

Already earlier it had become clear that his predecessor Khmelnytsky was not entirely satisfied with the outcome of Pereiaslav. Centralizing and humiliating Russian rule proved very different from the genuine autonomy the Cossacks had expected. After all, not all Cossacks were uneducated; whether they had studied at the Mohyla Academy, elsewhere in the Commonwealth, or even in the West, they had been exposed to ideas at great odds with the autocracy they now encountered. Even the Orthodox clergy of the Cossack lands, especially Kyiv, were unhappy at being subordinated to Moscow. Among other things, this dissonance and the resulting dissatisfaction led Khmelnytsky to join the other potential partitioners of Poland—Sweden, Transylvania, and Brandenburg—at the end of 1656.

After Khmelnytsky's death in 1657, Vyhovsky reached agreement with the Commonwealth. The two parties convened in a town of the Kyiv palatinate near the border with Russia. Although lying to the east of Pereiaslav, Hadiach (Polish: Hadziacz) notably marked a move westward. The Treaty of Hadiach established the terms of the Cossacks' return to the Commonwealth—terms that were far better than the Cossacks had ever been offered before.

Signed in 1658, this treaty has been compared to the Union of Lublin, and for good reason. The Commonwealth of Two (Both) Nations would be transformed into a Commonwealth of Three Nations—the third being a newly established Duchy of Ruthenia. Consisting of the former palatinates of Kyiv, Bratslav, and Chernihiv, the Duchy of Ruthenia would be an autonomous entity, on par with the Grand Duchy of Lithuania. Under the leadership of the common king, the Duchy would share a common foreign policy and send its own citizens to the Seym. A certain number of Cossacks would be accepted into the Commonwealth nobility.

The new Duchy would also retain its distinctiveness: executive power would be wielded by the hetman of the Ruthenian army, some thirty thousand strong. The Uniate Church would be disallowed on the Duchy's territory, where the Orthodox Church would be the favored religion, its higher clergy members of the Senate. The Mohyla Academy would be treated on par with other institutions of higher learning in the Commonwealth.

In short, the Cossacks appear to have successfully won the rights and privileges they had long sought. No longer to be looked down upon, they were to be treated as an equal partner. The Cossacks would be the third "nation" of the Commonwealth—a Ruthenian/Cossack/Orthodox one.

The Seym ratified the Treaty of Hadiach the following year, marking a sea change in the mentality of the Commonwealth's citizenry, the Polish-Lithuanian nobility. For many Cossacks back in the hetmanate, however, it was too little, too late—at least a decade too late. To be sure, power politics within the hetmanate likely helped to determine the rejection of the proposal. Vyhovsky had been acting in the name of the underage son of Khmelnytsky, Yuri, who now displaced Vyhovsky at the top of the hetmanate. Yet, might the deal still go through—be pushed through? For a moment it looked as though the Poles, who now amassed the largest army in their history—a force of some seventy to eighty thousand, and one that had a string of victories over the Russian and Cossack armies in 1660—would be able to expel the Russians from the Grand Duchy and implement the new arrangement with the Cossacks.

Ultimately, this was not to be. As a result of internal political problems, the Commonwealth was not able to profit from this impressive surge. The terms reached between Russia and the Commonwealth in the armistice of 1667 at Andrusovo were by Commonwealth accounts devastating. The armistice confirmed the Commonwealth's loss of both the Smolensk region in the north and the Cossack lands to the south, albeit in a novel configuration. The Cossack Hetmanate itself was partitioned between the two states—the dividing line being the Dnieper River. Territories on the right bank of the Dnieper (that is, in the west) were awarded to the Poles, while the left (east) bank came under Russian rule. The Russians also reserved to themselves control over Kyiv, on the right bank of the Dnieper, ostensibly for a two-year period (see Map 6.1). The city would never again be part of the Commonwealth. As the famous mathematician and philosopher Gottfried Wilhelm Leibniz observed at the time (albeit from his comfortable vantage point in the west), the "barbaric East" was on the rise.

After the Deluge: Assessing the Damage

After the debacle that was the Time of Troubles, the Muscovites somehow managed to rebuild their country, installing a new dynasty and shoring up a system of government—autocracy—that would last until the Revolution of 1917. Might not the Poles, reeling from the Deluge, be able to work a similar miracle?

A miracle, indeed, seemed to be necessary. The events of 1648–1667 had taken their toll on the Commonwealth—demographically, physically, and psychologically. The overall population of the country is estimated to have dropped by 25 percent, although the numbers were not spread evenly around the territory. It has been reckoned that the Swedish wars and their aftermath alone led to a decline of the urban population by some 60–80 percent, a stunning figure. In some cities, even a greater percentage of the buildings were destroyed. Many municipalities could not make up for the losses. Some would never again rise to their previous state. Many smaller towns degenerated to almost village status, with burghers now planting crops to make up for lost revenues.

Part of the reason for this huge hit was the multifaceted nature of the destruction as well as its unrelenting nature. In certain parts of the country, the depopulation came on the heels of the devastating plague of 1651–1652, which had already left the urban centers, from Kamianets-Podilskyi (Polish: Kamieniec Podolski) in the east to Kraków in the west, significantly weakened.

The history of Kraków during 1651–1657 gives a sense of the catastrophe. The devastating "black death" of 1651–1652 was compounded by the flooding of the Vistula River in 1652, which left at least thirty thousand dead and many houses empty. The ranks of the guilds were depleted, meaning that goods of all kinds were in short supply. Still recovering from the natural disasters, Kraków was subsequently subjected to the man-made disaster of the Swedish invasion. The city was thrice occupied—by Polish defenders, then the Swedes (later joined by Transylvanian troops), then Poles and Austrians—and thrice besieged. The prosperous suburbs were deliberately set on fire twice: first by the Polish defenders so that the Swedish attackers would be vulnerable, and later vice versa. In the city proper, Cracovians suffered frequent requisitions, enforced contributions, terror and intimidation, as well as hunger, inflation, physical endangerment, and death. At the end of the Deluge, the city was a wreck, scarcely habitable in places. And this was a city that had been one of the Commonwealth's best. Other locales would not fare so well.

The geography of the demographic disaster is instructive. Take the Commonwealth's Jewish population, which in 1650 exceeded half a million, for example. Most Jews lived in the eastern part of the country, primarily in urban or semi-urban areas. Within the space of a mere eight years, the Jewish population had declined by 10 percent. The missing fifty thousand Jews either were dead or had emigrated. Given how they were targeted by the Cossacks, Jews in the east (previously estate agents, tax collectors, tavern owners, and moneylenders) were probably in the first category. At least some Jews in the west and north (more often merchants and traders), located closer to more hospitable borders and with some making their exit with the Swedes, had a chance to flee.

The Commonwealth's villages were hit hard as hungry troops crisscrossed the country. Many villages were leveled. Others suffered tremendous losses in population, crops, buildings, and farm animals, leaving those who survived no resources with which to begin anew. A huge number of farms were simply abandoned. Figures for the region of Mazovia suggest that only 15 percent of the fields previously sown were planted in 1660–1661, after the official end of the Deluge. This also meant that many urban dwellers were forced to take up farming in order to feed themselves.

The devastation naturally extended to the lands in the southeast. The fight for Cossack rights did little for the inhabitants of the Ukrainian lands. The entire Ukrainian region was essentially depopulated, leading the ensuing period to be termed, simply, "ruin." Black earth or no black earth, new settlers would not move into the territory until after the Peace of Carlowitz (now Sremski Carlovci, in Serbia) of 1699.

There were other kinds of losses, related to the physical reshaping of the urban and rural landscape. Whatever was movable had been moved: looted, plundered, removed. We have already seen how municipal wealth had been the target of the invaders from the north as well as the east. Anything that glittered was fair game—but not only.

Swedes demonstrated an interest in art and the printed word. They cleaned out the vast libraries in the Prussian and Warmian territories and decimated the libraries and archives in Greater Poland. While those targets were closer to the Baltic and thus easier to empty, the Swedes did not leave other cities untouched. Warsaw lost its royal library and irreplaceable Royal Office Archive (Archiwum Metryki Koronnej). While the crown jewels, which had been evacuated from Kraków, eluded them, the Swedes consoled themselves by absconding with a treasure of a different kind—the Royal Treasury Archive (Archiwum Skarbca Koronnego). These losses still sting today.

Post-Deluge Reconstruction

What may seem amazing is that the Commonwealth was able to rebound after this desecration. Numerous cities dug themselves out of the rubble, some faster than others. Two factors proved important: geography and wealth. The areas closest to the Baltic—in particular important cities such as Elbląg and, especially, Gdańsk—rebounded most quickly. The renewal of the grain trade, which had been interrupted by the war, would aid in their recovery. Yet, although impressive, even this recovery was only partial. After the Deluge, the grain trade was no longer as lucrative it had been earlier in the century. Given that war on such a scale had made the transport of Polish grain to Gdańsk impossible for years on end, the English and Russians had stepped into the breach. Neither country was willing to relinquish its newfound position. The level of exports from the Commonwealth, thus, fell by half.

Elsewhere in the country, the situation looked grimmer. Greater competition meant that earnings from the grain trade were insufficient to cover the costs of the lesser players. It became harder for the rank-and-file nobleman to get his grain to market unless his estate was in easy proximity to the Baltic Sea or the Vistula River system. The Commonwealth's magnates were much better positioned to take part in the grain trade. And indeed, cities where magnate influence could be felt were among the first to rebound. These included private cities such as Zamość, where the magnate owner could be counted on to invest in reconstruction and take an interest in the city's resurrection. The burghers and municipalities were otherwise too poor and too weak to make good progress by themselves. Even in a city as important as Kraków, it was not the traditional heart of the city—its burghers and artisans—who recovered fastest but, rather, the church and the nobles, who came to own more of the historic capital than ever before.

This relative rise of the nobility (and the magnates, in particular) was also visible in the recovery of Warsaw, which had suffered heavy losses during the Swedish occupation. The royal castle had been systematically looted and the city's numerous noble residences ransacked. Not unexpectedly, the large collection of paintings amassed by the Vasas, including a Rembrandt or two, were taken back to their ancestral homeland in the north. Nothing was seemingly too big or bulky to be taken away: the Swedes even ripped out the elaborately carved wooden decorations on the ceilings of Warsaw's royal castle.

That Warsaw's burghers had fallen upon hard times is evident from the difficulty with which they rebuilt their properties. Take, for example, the stately residence of an armorer, Wawrzyniec Feffus, adjacent to the royal castle. It had been destroyed during the Transylvanian occupation of Warsaw in 1657, part of the Deluge. By 1687 the residence still languished, uncompleted—which ultimately led to the property ending up in the hands of a Lubomirski prince.

That it should end up in noble hands is not surprising. It was Warsaw's function as the heart of the Commonwealth political system that caused it to rise more quickly than most other towns. Given the city's parliamentary functions and its proximity to the election field, magnates would continue to desire residences constructed in the vicinity. Even after the Deluge, they could afford to build palaces and to commission foreign architects to design them.

The most prominent of the architects working in Warsaw during this period was Tylman van Gameren of Utrecht. He was brought to Poland by the magnate Jerzy Lubomirski right after the Deluge, where he worked for the next forty years, even being admitted into the ranks of the Commonwealth nobility in 1685. In Warsaw, Tylman designed a lakefront property, known as the baths, for Lubomirski's eldest son, Stanisław Herakliusz, as well as a palace for the Radziwiłłs. The Gniński family hired the Dutchman to build a new palace atop the fortifications of the former palace of the Ostrogskis, demonstrating that, while magnate families might die out, another one was always ready to jump into its place. The primate of Poland availed himself of Tylman's services to rebuild his palace, which had been destroyed during the Deluge.

Architects of Italian descent also figured prominently in the post-Deluge building boom in Warsaw. Stanisław Koniecpolski had a pair of Italian and Polish architects rebuild the former residence of the Mniszech family into a palace. In nearby Wilanów, Jan Sobieski commissioned himself a palace, built by Agostino Locci; it would grow in size and importance by the end of the century.

Perhaps the most magnificent late seventeenth-century construction was the late Baroque palace of Jan Dobrogost Krasiński. It too was the work of Tylman van Gameren, under whose direction Italian master builders worked. The elaborate sculptural decorations and allegorical painting for the ceilings and elsewhere were done by Andreas Schlüter and Michelangelo Palloni, respectively. The walled-in palace complex contained not only the impressive several-storied building made of stone, marble, and sandstone. It also included a two-story annex (where the kitchen was situated), various buildings housing exotic plants, even an arsenal. The Krasiński palace surpassed in magnificence even King Jan Kazimierz's

Renaissance-style Villa Regia, which was rebuilt after the Deluge.

The magnate-funded recovery of Warsaw demonstrates the importance of this small section of the Commonwealth's society of nobles. The wealthy and well connected had advantages that the lesser nobleman simply did not have. Owning estates all over the territory of the Commonwealth, the great magnate families were best positioned to recoup their losses. There was still plenty of wealth in the country: in terms of estates and land, naturally, but even in terms of riches.

Consider the above-mentioned Jerzy Lubomirski. During the Deluge, Swedes plundered his imposing Baroque palace of Wiśnicz in the south of Poland, reportedly needing 150 wagons to cart away all the loot. Still, while the loss of Wiśnicz's movables doubtless was a blow, the Lubomirski family owned other palaces, still perfectly intact. One of them—the palace in Łańcut—even served as residence for Jan Kazimierz upon his return from Silesia during the Deluge. Not only did the Lubomirski family rebound; by 1739, it had increased its total landholdings to a whopping 1,050 properties. This came about as a result of enviable marriage connections, royal favors, and the ability for the family to remain players in the grain trade. At the top, then, if not elsewhere, the Commonwealth proved it had the resources to rebuild and rebound.

Political Quagmire

It was much harder for the Commonwealth to rebound psychologically. Here the conflicts during the reign of Jan Kazimierz are instructive. Much more heavy-handed than his half-brother, the second son of Zygmunt III had managed to alienate the nobility in numerous ways. Nobles rich and poor were upset at the king for his treatment of Radziejowski, sentenced so harshly for lèse majesté. Even quite early in his reign, many magnates wanted to dethrone him.

Things had become so bad that a new and ominous precedent was set in 1652. During a session of the Seym, a nobleman named Władysław Siciński made a motion that ended up dissolving the Seym: he exercised the right, held by every noble deputy, of *liberum veto*—the right to veto the proceedings. Never before implemented, the right to wield the liberum veto was nonetheless a pillar of the noble republic—one of the Golden Freedoms. Given the regional diversity of the Commonwealth, it had been decided early on that parliament was not only to aim for but also to attain consensus during its deliberations. This was the only way to ensure that no one's rights would be trampled by the "tyranny of the majority," which might be manipulated (perhaps even by the king, who might be able to muster a majority). In other words, a single dissenting voice was allowed to be significant.

In 1652, the session was dissolved at the discretion of the speaker of the Seym, Andrzej Maximilian Fredro—himself a later defender of the practice. In his view, the nobles of the Commonwealth were bound to work for the common weal, to work out differences if at all possible. If that could not be accomplished, then they were justified in availing themselves of this powerful tool.

Fredro doubtless assumed that Siciński had good cause to state his objection. But the liberum veto could also fall prey to manipulation. Was this noble—whose sole claim to fame came from this first-ever use of the liberum veto—acting on the orders of his powerful patron, Janusz Radziwiłł? While historians are divided on this account, they nonetheless agree that the privilege was ripe for abuse. In future years, the liberum veto would be seen as an easy way to interrupt the functioning of the Seym (between 1582 and 1762 the Seym was dissolved nearly 60 percent of the time). Instead of crafting consensus (a task that required dogged persistence and often even creative measures from the parliamentarians), it allowed the noble parliamentarians to avoid doing their duty, while still appearing patriotic: they could dissolve the parliament, crying that the Golden Freedoms were being trampled . . . This was not a good precedent—for parliament, state, or king.

As one might imagine, Jan Kazimierz's efforts at governmental reform, which included a proposal to jettison the liberum veto in favor of a two-thirds majority vote, fell on deaf ears. Then again, the Polish king himself appeared to be politically tone-deaf. Both in the midst and after the war, he doggedly sought to line up a successor—in part on the instigation of his French wife, who favored a French candidate. The very idea of an election vivente rege (during the life of the king) was rejected by the nobility, although it had the interesting side effect of leading to the publication of Poland's first newspaper, *Merkuriusz Polski Extraordynarijny*, in 1661. Yet the timing of the proposal was unfortunate. It came on the heels of the Commonwealth's stunning new military successes in the Ukraine. The country seemed to be rebounding, which led many rank-and-file nobles to assume there was no need to change anything. Instead of consensus, the king got confederations, which sought to unseat him each time the issue was raised. In these Jerzy Lubomirski figured prominently—and repeatedly. His leadership of anti-monarchical confederations earned him accolades from those who sought above all to protect the Golden Freedoms.

Ultimately, Jan Kazimierz had enough. In November 1668 he notified the Seym that he was abdicating the throne, and he left the country. The king was deep in debt—and indebted to Louis XIV, king of France, who provided him with the income from a handful of abbeys to live on. He died in 1672, after learning that the Turks had captured the major southern fortress of Kamianets-Podilskyi.

Thus ended the period of rule by the Polish Vasa dynasty. The Vasa monarchs' concerns about their dynastic future led them to lose sight of the overall position of the Commonwealth, which had serious consequences for the country. The one Vasa raised to rule the Commonwealth—Władysław—was the one allotted the shortest time to do so. And he left the stage at a crucial moment. His half-brother was nowhere near as talented. Jan Kazimierz would see the country through decades of unrelenting war and occupation. And before the population eventually rallied behind the king, the damage had been done. The Commonwealth of Both Nations had lost its chance

Figure 6.1: Fortress at Kamianets-Podilskyi. This is what remains of one of the great borderland castles that for centuries helped to keep the Turks and Tatars at bay.

to be the Commonwealth of Three Nations when the Orthodox Cossacks chose to remain outside its structure. This was a true blow.

Sarmatian Retrenchment

All this led to what one might call Sarmatian retrenchment. After the Deluge, the nobles returned to their estates and set about recouping their losses. This was done increasingly at the expense of the peasants, whose labor dues increased, in some cases to as much as six or eight days a week (eight days meaning that more than one member of the household had to work for the lord). Jan Kazimierz's oath to improve their lot turned out to be a dead letter. While the glory days of Sarmatia's being the granary of Europe were over, the manorial system remained the basis of the Commonwealth's economy.

The peasants' serfdom and increasing impoverishment denied the towns their normal markets, which meant the nobles were hurting for the lost revenue, particularly as the terms of the grain trade were no longer so favorable. The nobles increasingly profited from the demoralization of their peasants—as seen in the abuse of the alcohol monopoly (*propinacja*). Nobles had a lucrative monopoly on the production and sale of alcohol, and surplus grain that was not exported via Gdańsk could be turned into vodka, which peasants could be forced to purchase. Serving once again as middlemen, Jews often owned the taverns and were obligated to pay the noble owner of a given town or village a certain annual amount for the liquor license. In the seventeenth century, the nobles in the Ukrainian regions of the Commonwealth, where innkeeping was an overwhelmingly Jewish occupation, made more money off the sale of vodka than off the export trade. The alcohol monopoly would be an important source of income for nobles all over the country, however.

The religious dimension of the Sarmatian mission (as the bulwark of Christianity) degenerated into xenophobia along with a growing intolerance of diversity with the country. Years of Jesuit education had their effect. Toleration was increasingly seen as a vice, a sign of religious indifference that was unacceptable in an age of emotive Baroque Christianity, and no longer as a civic virtue. The Jesuit-led Counter-Reformation triumphed in a period when the enemy had been identified as Protestant (the Swedes) or Orthodox (Muscovy). This led to the expulsion of the Arians (Antitrinitarians) from the Commonwealth in 1658. The appeal of Protestantism among the nobles continued to contract, although "dissenters" still prevailed in Royal Prussia and among German settlers elsewhere. Protestants were tolerated more grudgingly than before, however, and were less and less accepted as being fully of the Commonwealth.

Politically, the Sarmatian nobility remained contemptuous of the absolutism found in the West. The period of Vasa rule had given the nobles even less reason to believe that their Golden Freedoms were not threatened by a looming absolutum dominium. They laid the blame for the Commonwealth's trials squarely on the king—not on the system, which they still considered to be the perfect form of government. There was, however, increasing imbalance in the mixed system: the republican (noble) elements consequently gained at the expense of the royal powers. This as well as other distortions of the Sarmatian system would be visible in the next election.

The Saga of the Piasts

Fed up with foreigners in their country, the nobility of the Commonwealth proceeded to try a new approach. They chose a Polish king from among their own ranks, a "Piast," in the parlance of the day. Such an approach had merits. In this way, the country would get a king who was fully conversant with and committed to the system of governance of the Commonwealth, understanding the special position of the noble citizens within it as well as entirely committed to its welfare, as the source of his own personal gain. At the same time, it meant that the nobles and, especially, the magnates would have to swallow the elevation of a peer to the highest office in the land, which thus dealt a blow to pretensions of noble equality.

As in the early days of the elective monarchy, the results of the elections of the first non-Vasa candidates in the space of a century were mixed. The only claim to fame of the first of the two Piasts to be elected, Michał Korybut Wiśniowiecki, lay in his pedigree. His father was one of the military men who figured prominently in the Cossack wars, the Ruthenian Prince Jeremi Wiśniowiecki, and his great-grandfather was Jan Zamoyski. Indeed, both modern-day Piasts would represent the diverse heritage of the Sarmatian nation. Although they had Lithuanian, Ruthenian, as well as Polish forbears, they were now held up as the quintessence of what was noble and Polish.

To read the account of a participant in the election of 1669, Jan Chrysostom Pasek, the election of Wiśniowiecki was in part accidental. A nobleman who had settled in the southern region of Lesser Poland, Pasek reported how the primate, the traditional interrex, had hoped to speed up the procedure by limiting the voting to delegates, in the hopes they could be persuaded to select the French candidate, Philipp Wilhelm. (Obviously, not everyone was set on a Piast.) He did have a Polish connection, although it was tenuous: the first wife of the duke of Neuburg had been the daughter of Zygmunt III Vasa. Other foreign candidates included the sons of Tsar Alexei Mikhailovich as well as Duke Karl V of Lorraine, the Habsburg candidate.

The seymiks did not agree to these proposed limitations of their voting rights and summoned their nobles to travel to Warsaw, armed and on horseback. Tensions between the average nobleman and the high and mighty senators on the election field led to shots being fired. Terrified, the senators raced off in their carriages, and still shaken, not all of them returned in later days for the deliberations. Still, the nobles were supported and even emboldened by the bishop of Kraków, who reminded them that their participation in the voting was necessary if they wished to defend the freedoms for which their ancestors fought.

Although Pasek and others found the arguments of the envoy of the duke of Lorraine persuasive, the nobles from Greater Poland were calling for someone of noble blood—a Piast. They did not need someone related to foreign monarchs, just a "strong man, a military man." The wining, dining, and bribing done by the foreign envoys seemed to be targeted at the more illustrious nobles—the senators and deputies. They proposed one Polanowski (according to Pasek; it seems more likely that the person they had in mind was Alexander Janusz Ostrogski-Zasławski). Pondering the possibilities, the Lesser Poland group countered with Wiśniowiecki, a young man with an impeccable patriotic pedigree. They began to shout, "Vivat Piast" (Long live the Piast)—and the other group of nobles joined in, thinking it was their candidate who was being cheered. Still, no one protested when Wiśniowiecki was brought forward: rather, they embraced him with spontaneous fervor. Pasek attributed the Piast's election to divine inspiration—the assembled nobles, who had made the effort to come to Warsaw and influence the outcome, were bound to settle on the right candidate.

Wiśniowiecki had other characteristics that allowed his candidacy to appeal to a wide range of voters, the powerful magnates as well as the rank-and-file nobles. That his family had lost its fortune with the loss of the Ukrainian lands meant that Wiśniowiecki posed no real threat to the magnates. Pasek noted the alacrity with which presents of all kinds were lavished on the victor, claiming rather naively that "the Lord God [had] so inclined people's hearts to him."[*] More likely, many were looking for future favor. At any rate, election to the Polish throne brought with it instant wealth and influence, not only in the Commonwealth but abroad. In

---

[*] Jan Pasek, *The Memoirs of Jan Chrysostom z Gosławic Pasek*, trans. Maria Swiecicka (New York: Kościuszko Foundation, 1978), 215.

Wiśniowiecki's case, he was immediately offered the hand of the sister of Emperor Leopold I in marriage.

If blood truly made kings, Wiśniowiecki should have been a memorable one. Unfortunately, the scion of this illustrious Ruthenian/Polish family proved underwhelming—even passive. The colorful election of Wiśniowiecki proved the most interesting part of his reign. An inauspicious sign: Wiśniowiecki's Coronation Seym was dissolved by the use of the liberum veto. Not the most impressive of rulers, it may be a blessing that he seemed unable to father a child. This had one advantage: it meant that the Commonwealth would elect someone other than a Wiśniowiecki upon his death.

The biggest news of the Piast's reign was the resurgence of the Turkish threat, and to a lesser extent of the Cossack threat, which came to engulf the right bank of the Dnieper—the Cossacks were unhappy about the terms of Andrusovo, which had partitioned their territory. Most notable here was the Ottoman invasion of Podolia in Poland's southeast and (a true blow) the capture of the formerly impregnable fortress at Kamianets-Podilskyi in 1672. The news of the loss of Kamianets-Podilskyi apparently so shocked the exiled Jan Kazimierz (who, for all his faults, had been an effective military leader) that he died of apoplexy. To add insult to injury, the Treaty of Buchach (Polish: Buczacz) confirmed not only the cession of Podolia and Kamianets-Podilskyi to the Turks but also control over right-bank Ukraine.

The only good to emerge was that Wiśniowiecki's mercifully short reign (he died in November 1673) came to an end just as a new potential Piast candidate was making headlines. That same month, Crown Hetman Jan Sobieski, who had been occupied with keeping the Turkish forces from making further inroads into the Commonwealth, pulled off a magnificent victory against the Turks at a site all too familiar to earlier generations of Poles: Khotyn.

Sobieski to the Rescue?

The victory at Khotyn in 1673 ultimately catapulted Jan Sobieski into the royal castle as the successor to Wiśniowiecki, the Commonwealth nobility still reacting allergically to thoughts of the French or the Habsburgs using the Polish election field to ratchet up their own positions in Europe. Only the Lithuanians, dominated by the powerful Pac brothers, Krzysztof and Michał, required further convincing to abandon the French candidate, Karl V of Lorraine.

The king-elect Sobieski could not immediately occupy the royal castle, because, when elected king, he was still on the battlefield, working to regain

control over territories threatened by the Turks and the Tatars. His coronation was only to take place in early 1676. As tradition mandated, it was immediately preceded by a royal funeral—this time, a double funeral, for the
first elected Piast was buried simultaneously with the last of the Vasas, the
king who abdicated. Jan Kazimierz's body was brought back to the Commonwealth to be buried in the royal crypts of Wawel Cathedral. A telling
sign was that, while the bishop of Kraków, who gave the funeral eulogy,
found words of praise for Jan Kazimierz, he dispatched with Wiśniowiecki
in short fashion.

After the young and ineffectual Wiśniowiecki, Sobieski represented a welcome change of pace. Although Sobieski likewise had a fine pedigree—Hetman
Stanisław Żółkiewski was one of his grandfathers, and his mother was descended from the Ruthenian Danilovich princes—he was elected king of Poland not out of any familial pietism but entirely on his own merits. Here was
a mature man who, in the course of his forty-five years, had experience in
politics as well as in battle. The new king appeared ready, and eager, to rule.

Indeed, Sobieski had availed himself of all the opportunities that being a
wealthy noble had given him. He was well educated, a product of not only
the Jagiellonian University but also several years of private study abroad,
in the company of his elder brother Marek. In a way he was something of a
Renaissance man, if already after that period had come to an end in Poland.
He spoke five languages—and he put them to good use, whether in his vo-
racious reading (in which the Latin, French, and German served him well)
or in his fighting (he also knew Turkish). The level of culture found at the
family residence at Wilanów was remarkable—and it was remarked upon
by those who visited him. Sobieski had amassed one of the most extensive
private libraries in the country, while also proving himself a connoisseur
of art and onetime collector of Rembrandts. Perhaps in his cultural tastes
he was assisted by his beloved wife, Marie Casimire Louise d'Arquien, who
had come to Poland as lady-in-waiting to Marie Louise Gonzaga, Jan Kazimierz's wife. Although Sobieski, too, shared the typical magnate's insatiable
appetite for estates and ultimately acquired as many of them as he could for
his heirs, he ran them rationally and, it appears, humanely.

Early in his career, Sobieski had mixed luck in the theater of war, if an extended period of experience in it. He fought against the Cossacks, beginning
with the Cossack wars, fighting at Zboriv and Berestechko. That he was seriously wounded at that latter victory saved him from the fate of his brother,
who went on to fight at Batih. Marek was one of the prisoners of war whom
Khmelnytsky bought from his Tatar allies, only to have them massacred.
One of the Poles who switched sides during the Deluge, Jan Sobieski fought

first alongside the Swedes and then later alongside the Tatars (at that time, allies of the Commonwealth). Those experiences—as well as his service under Hetman Stefan Czarniecki—helped him to broaden his knowledge of the art of war. Still, his greatest victories would involve Poland's neighbor to the south, the Ottoman Empire.

The Turkish threat obsessed the new king of Poland, who shared some of the Sarmatian views of his day—certainly insofar as the crusading spirit and fascination with the East was concerned. After the victory at Khotyn, Sobieski was able to regain control over the more distant right bank of the Dnieper, which the Cossacks (now under Russian rule) had been trying to regain for themselves. Nonetheless, the region of Podolia remained in Ottoman hands. This put the Turks within easy striking range of the major city of the Ruthenian palatinate, Lviv. The threat was very real.

Sobieski Saves the West

In a way, the concern with the Ottoman threat propelled Sobieski closer to the Habsburgs, for whom the threat was equally palpable if not more so. A truce between Russia and the Ottoman Empire allowed the latter the freedom to focus its attentions on a different, and potentially more lucrative front, Royal Hungary, the gateway to the Holy Roman Empire's capital of Vienna.

At this time Leopold I, king of Hungary and Holy Roman Emperor, ran into trouble. His abuse of absolutist power in Hungary led that proud people to rebel. Under Imre Thököly, the rebels occupied Upper Hungary (today's Slovakia), which under Thököly's rule was turned into an Ottoman fief in 1682. While this loss was bad in many ways for the Habsburgs, it also meant that the Ottoman threat now extended across almost the entirety of the Commonwealth's southern frontier.

Only now was the proud emperor convinced of the need for an alliance with Sobieski. In part, the new alliance helped both sides to set aside old differences. It most certainly obliged them to stand united against the Turkish threat. While each would be responsible for defending parts of the threatened frontier (the Commonwealth in the east, the Habsburgs in the west), each was in turn obligated to come to the rescue of the capital of the other—here, the agreement specified Vienna and Kraków—were it under direct threat.

Military reforms initiated by Sobieski had strengthened the Commonwealth's forces. He sought to move away from reliance upon the noble levy, not always reliable or well trained, toward a professional army. To the ranks of the tried and true Hussars he added more and better trained infantry and dragoons, into which numerous peasants from royal and ecclesiastical demesnes were drafted. In a sense, thus, while the nobility of the army was being diluted, its overall effectiveness was being bolstered.

The agreement, reached in the spring of 1683, came none too soon. In July 1683, the Ottoman forces, commanded by Grand Vizier Kara Mustafa, had reached the gates of Vienna. It seemed that it was only a matter of time before the Viennese would have to capitulate.

Vienna was not only a tremendously wealthy city and the seat of the powerful House of Habsburg. The traditional election, since 1440, of the head of the House of Habsburg as Holy Roman Emperor meant that the rest of the German imperial princes—by this time, Protestants as well as Catholics—acknowledged him as their superior. This distinction made Vienna the capital of Western Christendom. The emperor styled himself the "head of universal Christianity." Were Kara Mustafa able to pull it off, the conquest of Vienna would be an unprecedented coup for the Turks.

First, however, the grand vizier would have to contend with the forces of the Commonwealth. In the space of eight days, Sobieski and his Polish troops made their way to meet up with the other forces assembling to relieve the Vienna siege. As the most experienced in fighting the Turks, the Polish king assumed the leadership of the coalition forces that had been supplied not only by Emperor Leopold I but also by various other princes of the Holy Roman Empire. The imperial forces were commanded by Karl of Lorraine, with other German forces led by Georg Waldeck. In addition to Sobieski, the Polish forces would be under the command of Crown Grand Hetman Jabłonowski and Crown Field Hetman Mikołaj Sieniawski. Altogether, the relief forces amounted to some sixty-five to seventy thousand, of which twenty-six thousand were Polish troops (the Lithuanian forces were stationed too far away to make the battle). It was Sobieski's plan to break up the Turkish army.

The Relief of Vienna

From the vantage point of Kahlenberg atop the Vienna Woods, the view was not encouraging. A cowed and crumbling Vienna stood to be overwhelmed by the infidel. To the west, the eye was met by another city. No real city, it was the Turkish camp of Kara Mustafa. A veritable sea of enormous tents, it had room enough to house the Ottoman army, here comprised of over a hundred thousand troops. In the tents were huge supplies of ammunition, copious amounts of food, and all manner of luxuries. The grand vizier had come fully prepared for what he anticipated would be his crowning glory: the taking of the capital of Christendom. What he did not realize is that, this time, he would be up against more than the municipal defense system or imperial army. Sobieski was on the way.

The Polish king set the offensive for September 12. In the early hours of the morning, the combined army under Sobieski's command made its way down through the hilly and densely forested Vienna Woods, demonstrating his signature masterful command of difficult terrain. Karl of Lorraine's troops were positioned closest to the Danube, Waldeck's to the right of him, and the Polish forces on the extreme right—closest to the Turkish and Tatar camps. Karl was commanded to engage the Turks first with his heavy troops. The Turkish forces countered by shifting in that direction, to keep Karl from breaking through to Vienna, which nonetheless resulted in a weakening of the Turkish front on the right.

This provided the opportunity Sobieski had anticipated. He ordered his infantry to clear the route of Turkish defenses and got his Hussars into position. At five in the evening, the Polish forces charged the Turks. They broke through the Ottoman defense and galloped straight into the Turkish camp, aiming for the grand vizier's tent. Kara Mustafa made a hasty retreat—according to Sobieski, escaping with only one horse and the clothes he had on his back. Abandoning camp and everything in it, the rest of the Turkish army fled in confusion and consternation. The carnage was great. Some ten thousand Turks perished, five thousand were taken prisoner, but there were also casualties on the victors' side. Over four thousand were killed or wounded.

The victors had a field day in the Turkish camp. In addition to enormous supplies of powder and ammunition (obviously the grand vizier knew the siege of such a great city would not end quickly), the camp held all kinds of booty, among them bags of mysterious black pellets that would soon become familiar to this part of Europe as coffee beans. According to legend, an enterprising soldier named Kulczycki got his hands on these and soon set up a coffeehouse in the Habsburg capital. Sobieski wrote his wife that anyone who wanted a tent could help himself and estimated it might take them over a week to pull them all down. He himself came into possession of some of the grand vizier's possessions: military equipment studded with precious jewels, as well as the grand vizier's horse with its rich caparison. As proof of his victory, Sobieski sent the green Islamic banner that had been bestowed upon the grand vizier by his sultan to Pope Innocent XI, with a terse message: *Venimus, vidimus, Deus vicit* (We came, we saw, God conquered).

Sobieski did not tarry long in Vienna. He set off in pursuit of the Turks and eventually caught up with them at Párkány, in Upper Hungary (today's Štúrovo, in Slovakia). Victory did not come easily or immediately. At one point the coalition army, traveling in unfamiliar territory, was caught unawares by the Turks. But victory did come, with the help of imperial reinforcements.

The Ottoman Empire's push into the heart of Europe, the seat of the Holy Roman Empire, had come to an end. Sobieski went down in history as the defender of Christianity—the man who kept the Moslem menace at bay. The Relief of Vienna has been remembered as a battle of world significance—one of the eighteen most decisive battles in the world, according to d'Abernon, writing in the early twentieth century. And none other than the famous nineteenth-century Prussian general Clausewitz considered Sobieski one of the best military leaders the world had seen.

Western Ingratitude

While the inhabitants of Vienna as well as Sobieski's cohort of foreign comrades in arms expressed their appreciation at the time, the victory over the Turks at Vienna was not decisive in any way that served the narrower interests of the Commonwealth, which unfortunately gained little, if anything, from the victory. It was unable to recapture the fortress of Kamianets-Podilskyi, and Tatars moved into the Ukrainian lands. Only after Sobieski's death would Podolia be returned to the Commonwealth.

All too happy to avail themselves of Sobieski's assistance in 1683, his erstwhile allies did nothing to help him out back home. Although the Polish king was part of the anti-Turkish Holy League established the following year, his allies—the Holy Roman Empire, Venice, and the papacy—repaid his deed with . . . thanklessness. They did nothing to help the Commonwealth regain Podolia, let alone place Sobieski's son Jakub on the throne. Worse, the lack of support even forced the Polish king to make a humiliating "eternal peace" with Russia—a move that finalized the partition of the Ukraine and possession of Smolensk that had been established at the truce of Andrusovo.

This last move brought him only criticism back home. While acknowledged for his military prowess at home and abroad, the savior of Western Christendom proved less effectual in the realm of domestic politics. Even before Vienna, a group of magnates had tried to dethrone him, for this second Piast king—perhaps under French influence and most certainly under the influence of his French wife—had been suggesting reforms similar to those proposed by Jan Kazimierz. Those were rejected by the nobility, and Sobieski's efforts met with same fate.

In a way, the enmity was even greater in the case of the hetman turned king. Jan Kazimierz, just like Wiśniowiecki after him, had been childless. Sobieski fathered numerous children, including four sons. The latter were being groomed to rule—and were the reason why the Polish king also advocated election vivente rege.

Such attempts at electoral reform remained anathema for the Commonwealth nobility. The nobles feared the impact that kingship had on individuals, even those who had credentials as impressive as Sobieski's. And they were not pleased by the queen's conniving, whether with foreign powers or powerful magnates back home, to assure positions for her children. The Sarmatian nation had already had its fill of dynasties putting their family interests above those of the Commonwealth. The Sarmatian nobles continued to sniff out the first whiff of inclinations toward centralization, consolidation, even bureaucratization, anything redolent of their biggest fear—absolutist rule. In short, they did what they could to diminish Sobieski's powers as king of the Commonwealth of Both Nations.

Sobieski would end his days a sick and weakened man, resembling more and more just another incredibly wealthy magnate, dividing his time between his estates at Zhovka and Yavoriv (Polish: Jaworów) as well as in his lovely Baroque palace in Wilanów. Although attacked by his enemies (the Sapiehas in Lithuania were preparing a revolt), Sobieski remained unwilling to take extraordinary measures to clamp down on them, suggesting that accusations of the king abusing his power were exaggerated. He died in 1696.

It would take several generations before Sobieski's accomplishments would be fully appreciated by Poles. This second Piast king would go down in history as the best monarch to rise from the Commonwealth nobility, a model of patriotic virtue and military valor, the unrelenting defender of Western Christendom as well as his country.

CHAPTER 7

The Commonwealth, Part III

Sarmatia Transformed

The seventeenth century had proven a mixed bag for the Commonwealth. It began on a relatively high note, with the reign of Zygmunt III Vasa that ushered in the so-called Silver Age. Mid-century, however, the Commonwealth nearly imploded, wracked by devastating invasions, civil war, and the loss of left-bank Ukraine. The country's recovery from the Deluge, although noteworthy, was only partial. The nobility clung ever more tightly to its cherished Golden Freedoms and rejected anything that smacked of political reform, particularly if it might lead to a strengthening of the monarch's position within the country. Even the triumphant, world-historical victory of Sobieski and his forces at Vienna—the high point of the century—did more for Western Christendom than for the Commonwealth itself.

Royal Election Number Eight

The final election of the seventeenth century did not lead to the confirmation of a new Piast (or native Sarmatian) dynasty. Despite his efforts, King Jan III Sobieski proved unable to secure for his sons the Polish succession. To the contrary, the election of 1697 would mark a reversal of recent policy, which since the Deluge had given preference to candidates of noble Piast heritage.

From the vantage point of hindsight, an interesting pattern emerges. Consider the elections both preceding and following the triplet of Vasa reigns. The first two elections, limited to foreign candidates, put one regrettable (Valois) and one memorable (Batory) candidate on the Polish throne. The anti-foreign backlash following the abdication of Jan Kazimierz Vasa (which marked the end of the Polish Vasa dynasty) put two Piasts (native candidates) on the Polish throne: once again, one regrettable (Wiśniowiecki) and one memorable (Sobieski) candidate.

Despite the fact that Sobieski not only had significant military victories under his belt but also had fathered sons who could contend for the throne, the electoral pendulum swung once again—out of their reach. In part, one might blame Sobieski's eldest son, Jakub, for this state of affairs. The young man had been groomed to rule, and he doubtless assumed the throne was within his grasp. To buttress his position, Jakub had been making the rounds of Europe, seeking support for his candidacy abroad. Yet he managed to neglect one thing—the all-important domestic audience, his noble electorate. The reputation of the eldest Sobieski plummeted among the Commonwealth nobility, which could not help but note the very public and acrimonious quarrel between Jakub and his mother over the inheritance of the king's fortune. At the Convocation Seym of 1697, the nobles decided against accepting native candidates, thus preventing Jakub from placing himself in the running.

This clear rejection of the Sobieski heir—and, by extension, all candidates of Polish/Sarmatian noble descent—opened the doors wide to foreign involvement. This time, the results of the election ended up demonstrating to what extent the Commonwealth elections could be used in the power struggle between the various major European players.

That the field was wide open once again raised the stakes, giving candidates lacking any Polish connection a chance to make advances into this part of Europe. They were likely to be from further away; candidates representing the countries that had been so instrumental in wreaking havoc in the Commonwealth—the parties to the Deluge—would be not be viewed kindly. An additional condition for consideration set by the Convocation Seym was that the candidate be a Roman Catholic.

This final qualification clearly did not limit the field enough—at least, not enough to ensure a smooth transition of power. Once again, the Commonwealth faced the double trouble of a double election. François Louis de Bourbon, the duke of Conti, won the vote of the assembled nobles and was proclaimed king-elect—only to find another group of nobles subsequently declared a different candidate king-elect. The latter were influenced by foreign powers that did not want the French, who under Louis XIV seemed to be fighting the rest of the West, to gain a hold in this part of Europe. Their candidate was Friedrich August I Wettin, elector of Saxony.

The outcome of the election once again came down to the wire: who would get himself crowned in Kraków first? Inexplicably, the duke of Conti dallied in France, setting off by sea with a month's delay. By this time, the Saxon contender had long since made his way to the Polish border, where he swore to uphold the pacta conventa that had been devised for him. He was crowned King August II in mid-September. While it seemed that the disputed outcome was now settled, it still had some unfortunate repercussions, though not of a military nature as had been the case with the election of the first Vasa a century before. Recognizing the Wettin as king, the city of Gdańsk refused to let the French king-elect, whose ship had finally arrived at the Baltic Sea coast, disembark there. Although Conti accepted the fait accompli and called off his supporters, this lack of welcome in Gdańsk led France to sever its relations with the Commonwealth as well as to sequester the contents of its ships in France.

August II "the Strong" Wettin

The newly elected Polish king would go down in history as August the Strong. The sobriquet stemmed from the Saxon's exceptional physical strength: he is said to have straightened horseshoes with his bare hands. While it remained to be seen whether the new Polish king's physical strength would be an asset of any value to his new country, one thing was certain: August II Wettin was as opportunistic a ruler as they came, willing to do whatever it took to win the election. In order to become a contender for the Polish throne, he had secretly converted from Lutheranism to Roman Catholicism in 1697, mere months before his election. Reportedly this confessional change gave him papal support as well as the much-desired support of the Habsburgs. The Wettin's conversion to Catholicism, incidentally, ruined his married life. His staunchly Lutheran wife separated from her husband and remained in Dresden, wanting nothing to do with either him or his reign over the Commonwealth. Perhaps this is why August II Wettin is remembered as an inveterate womanizer, with many mistresses and illegitimate children.

Such was the price to pay for the Polish throne. The new arrangement resulted in yet another personal union: Saxony and the Commonwealth of Two Nations were united in the person of the king/elector, while retaining their distinctiveness. The situation, thus, in some ways echoes the novel arrangement of the Union of Kreva, which brought another new convert to Roman Catholicism, the pagan Jagiełło, to the throne. Nonetheless, this time there was no act of union, no promise of any state being "joined" to another. Neither the Commonwealth nor Saxony would be joined by any firmer bonds than the person of the monarch.

All the same, there was potential benefit to even this weak linkage of the two states. Saxony during this period figured quite respectably within the sovereign countries of the Holy Roman Empire. Separated from the Commonwealth by Habsburg-ruled Silesia, Saxony was relatively densely populated, and it boasted a certain level of economic development, even industrialization. The country was perhaps most famous for the fine porcelain produced in Meissen. Positioned on an important east–west trading route, the city of Leipzig was a bustling major trading center, the site of many trade fairs. The capital of the country was nonetheless Dresden, where the Wettins maintained a cultured court. Saxony's population—a mix of German/Saxon and Lusatian Sorb (a West Slavic people)—was Lutheran.

That August II converted to Catholicism to have a chance to win the Polish throne suggests that he calculated on further benefit from the new arrangement. It should be noted that nowhere was he an absolutist monarch. Even in Saxony he had to take into consideration the opinions of the local parliaments. His rule over the Commonwealth might have seemed even more straightforward at this period: the Election Seym that had limited the field to Roman Catholics had also decided that, in the Grand Duchy of Lithuania as well as in the Crown of Poland, Polish would henceforth be the language of governance. Interestingly enough, the Wettin candidate had expressed interest in Poland's development even before his election: he had prepared a memorandum entitled "How to Transform Poland into a Country Flourishing and Enjoying the Respect of [Its] Neighbors."

Thus, despite the uneven road to the Polish throne, the reign of August II Wettin as king of Poland and elector of Saxony held out promise. Might not the military and economically minded elector be what the country needed? Perhaps this is what some Cracovians thought when, during the events that preceded his altogether elaborate coronation (much more splendid than that of Sobieski before him), they erected a triumphal arch in his honor with the inscription, "The Golden Age Returns to the Crown of Poland."

The Saxon Night

It is one thing to hope for a Golden Age. Poles likely would have been happy to settle for a Silver Age—for a ruler who could bring back the prosperity experienced under Zygmunt III Vasa and his son Władysław. Yet August II Wettin brought the Commonwealth neither of these, despite the golden promises. The period of Wettin rule came to be labeled in the darkest of terms. It has gone down in history as the Saxon Night.

Not that August II began badly. His first and perhaps major accomplishment concerned the Poles' relations with their most recent foes, the Ottomans. August's task upon assuming reign over the Commonwealth was to regain the territories his predecessors had lost. The terms of his pacta conventa dictated that the new king was obliged to try to regain control over Kamianets-Podilskyi, Livonia, even Moldavia. In this he was partially successful. A military victory over the Ottomans at Pidhaitsi (Polish: Podhajce) in 1698 led to negotiations at Carlowitz in 1699. In accordance with the terms of this long-awaited peace, both Kamianets-Podilskyi and the right-bank Ukrainian territories were returned to the Commonwealth.

Unfortunately for the Wettin, he was not able to make any territorial gains in Moldavia, which might have satisfied his land hunger. In many ways, the attitude of August II mirrored that of the Vasas in power who, while serving as kings of the Commonwealth, felt the loss of the Swedish crown like the proverbial severed limb that still hurts. In the case of the Wettin, his attention was divided between Saxony and the Commonwealth. In the former country, he would encounter more opposition on account of his conversion to Catholicism, which clearly was no longer veiled in secrecy. As seemed true of nearly all the Commonwealth's rulers, August concluded that his new position as Polish king could be utilized to gain personal (that is, hereditary) control over new territories, which would further bolster his international stature. If not Moldavia, why not try to secure Livonia?

Livonia had long been a bone of contention in Northern Europe. And now that the king had settled matters in the south, it was probably time to turn his attention northward, if for no other reason than that, at the turn of the century, this swath of the Commonwealth was a weak spot. The elector of Brandenburg, Friedrich III von Hohenzollern, had occupied the Royal Prussian city of Elbląg, as the Commonwealth had not repaid a debt incurred in 1657. Furthermore, the Grand Duchy of Lithuania was in the throes of conflict. Magnates and nobles combined were battling the powerful Sapieha family, which would soon get its comeuppance in a spectacular defeat in 1700. In the interim, however, other Lithuanians reached out to the Russian tsar, Peter I, who agreed to support them—especially as they gave him permission to bring his troops onto the territory of the Grand Duchy. Two neighbors, thus, had a foothold in the Commonwealth, which seemed a recipe for disaster.

A more prudent king might have tried to defuse these two potential tinderboxes before proceeding any further. August II was not a prudent king, however, and certainly not if prudence meant keeping to heart the interests of the Commonwealth. Instead of ensuring that Elbląg was returned to

Commonwealth control, August II had secretly given the elector his permission to take over the city, in exchange for a sum of 150,000 thalers. With the foreign troops of the Hohenzollerns and Romanovs on his periphery, as well as Saxon troops in the Commonwealth, the new Polish king prepared to declare war . . . on Sweden.

To be sure, he did not plan to wage war all by himself. August II entered into alliance with Denmark and Russia, each of which also had pretensions to territories in Sweden's possession. The Polish king also entered into a secret agreement with the Livonian estates unhappy with Swedish rule. In exchange for his support, he would gain hereditary title to Livonia, which would then become a fief of the Commonwealth.

The new king was making light of the restrictions placed on him by his coronation oath. While entering into negotiations as the king of Poland, August II had no guarantee that the Seym would support him in any of these warmongering endeavors. And it did not. Tired of war and uninterested in fighting the Wettin's war, the noble citizens of the Commonwealth would demand that their monarch fight Sweden as elector of Saxony and not as king of Poland.

Unfortunately for the Commonwealth, this subtlety was lost on the target of all these negotiations and alliances, Karl XII, king of Sweden. Of course, one could blame it on his youth. Only fifteen at his coronation in 1697, Karl clearly had no experience in affairs of war and state. This made the new king of Sweden appear an easy target—easy enough to bring Denmark and Russia into a coalition with the elector of Saxony and king of Poland. What the world did not yet realize but would soon learn was that the young Swede possessed will, aggression, and talent in abundance. What had promised to be an easy victory would turn out to be nothing of the sort. Instead, a victory over Karl XII, king of Sweden, would require more from the belligerents than they ever could have expected. Not only would it be costly for August II and his allies, it would be another devastating period for the Commonwealth and its inhabitants.

The Great Northern War, 1700–1721

Although untried and inexperienced, Karl XII surprised the coalition by turning out to be quite the warrior—perhaps the best military leader Sweden ever produced. He had inherited a strong professional army and a cadre of service nobles to lead it. His force was superior to the one that had wreaked havoc in the Commonwealth some fifty years earlier. Northern Europe would soon turn into Karl's playground. From Copenhagen and Dresden in the west, through Estonia and Livonia in the north, and all the way to the heart of Ukraine, all these territories would come to feel the wrath of the young, underestimated king of Sweden. As, of course, would the Commonwealth, which lay in the center of this enormous theater of war.

From the Swedish king's first military foray in 1700, it became clear that he was no pushover. For example, an inauspicious sign for the coalition, Karl forced Denmark's Frederik IV out of the war with a single move. He surrounded its capital, Copenhagen. Next the valiant Swede traveled to the eastern side of the Baltic, where he handily defeated the much more numerous Russian army of Tsar Peter I (the same Peter who would later be labeled "the Great") at Narva. What was in store for the remaining belligerent, August II, the monarch who had instigated the war?

The Commonwealth had wanted another warrior-king, and the nobles thought that they had got one in August II. The Wettin was hardly another Sobieski, however, and proved much weaker on the battlefield than expected. Perhaps he was unnerved by the Swede, who had already wreaked so much havoc. At any rate, the elector of Saxony and his Saxon troops were unable to take Riga. The tactics of the young Swedish king proved spectacularly successful. To make matters worse, the Sapieha family, defeated in its own private battle for control of Lithuania, decided to join forces with the Swedes, in the hopes that the alliance would help them to rebound.

The Commonwealth nobles watched, utterly unhappy about what they saw and about what their own king, August II, had done. They disapproved of his alliance with Russia, and they did not want Saxon troops making their way across their country. The desire of the citizens of the Commonwealth to stay neutral—to let August fight his own battles as hereditary elector of Saxony, not as king of Poland—was not respected by Karl XII. And indeed, why should the young Swedish king care that the Wettin officially was fighting him in his capacity as elector of faraway Saxony? Karl XII could get at him much closer to home, in Commonwealth territory. In response to a delegation of Commonwealth nobles who implored the Swedish king to put an end to the war, Karl demanded that they first dethrone August II.

The king of Sweden did not wait for the Poles to move on this suggestion. He and his army forged ahead, moving out of Livonia in 1702 in the direction of the Commonwealth. Karl XII led his army from Courland to the Lithuanian palatinate of Žemaitija and straight into the heart of the Crown of Poland. For the second time in half a century, the Swedes took an essentially undefended Warsaw. Other cities also were captured that year, among them Hrodna (Polish: Grodno) and Kraków.

This time, the Swedes moved about the country with even greater freedom. The pattern of serial occupations, requisitioning, and contributions established a half-century earlier by Karl XII's grandfather, Karl X, was resurrected—even perfected. Certainly it was déjà vu for the Commonwealth's inhabitants, both urban and rural. Still ruthless and exacting, the Swedish machine was even more efficient this time around. Special expeditions were organized to keep the forces supplied and the cash flow positive. From a winter expedition in 1702–1703 to Ruthenia and Volhynia, they collected a full six barrels of gold as well as other supplies. When their demands were not met, the Swedes were not above plundering and then burning whatever was left of a given locale. Those who put up resistance were killed.

All this meant that Karl XII did not endear himself to the inhabitants of the Commonwealth. They proceeded to form confederations—assemblies of concerned, armed nobles—in various parts of the country, each trying to deal with the Swedish menace. To oppose the Swede, they had to work with their Saxon king. In 1704 the Seym agreed to summon up an army of forty-eight thousand and also approved the king's alliance with Peter I at Narva. All the assembled armies—Swedish, Commonwealth, Saxon, Russian—traipsed across the Commonwealth, wreaking havoc but not resolving the conflict. To make matters worse, Cossacks revolted in the Polish-controlled territories on the right bank of the Dnieper. Peter of Russia ultimately took advantage of the armies' preoccupation with the Commonwealth to make his famous move north: the tsar seized the mouth of the Neva River, where he would build the city that was to bear his name—Saint Petersburg.

It was all too much for some in the Commonwealth to bear. In Warsaw, a small group of confederated nobles, tired of the occupation, disgusted with their king, followed Sweden's orders and, on May 6, 1704, dethroned August II Wettin. In his stead, they elected a Piast: Stanisław Leszczyński.

The Puppet King

This was not a typical election, even by Commonwealth standards. Karl XII, whose heavily armed troops hovered over the electors, forced the candidacy of Leszczyński on the nobles in Warsaw.

The choice of Leszczyński came as a surprise, even to the candidate. Certainly the young palatine of Greater Poland could not have imagined he would be king. The most obvious Piast candidates would have been the sons of Sobieski. Yet, sensing his luck might take a turn for the worse, August II had "removed" them to Silesia, just in case ... Stanisław Leszczyński happened to be one of the few Polish nobles that Karl XII had actually met (he had been one of the delegates sent to deal with the Swedish king). Poor Leszczyński was in over his head—a feckless pawn in a game he did not fully comprehend.

Even the coronation of the puppet king was a travesty. The primate refused to be party to the coronation: reportedly the pope (firmly on the side of the Catholic convert, August II) forbade the clergy from taking part. With little in the way of domestic support, Leszczyński ended up being crowned in Warsaw. This in itself was an inauspicious first—a break with long-standing tradition. As the historic Polish insignia were in Kraków, Karl paid for a new set of royal insignia for Leszczyński. It was but a small price for all the concessions he wrung out of his puppet. In the Treaty of Warsaw of 1705, Leszczyński was forced to agree to eternal peace between Sweden and the Commonwealth, hand over control of the Baltic trade (which would now be centered on Riga and Szczecin, ports controlled by Sweden), relinquish Livonia and Courland, and promise more favorable treatment of Protestants in the Commonwealth.

In the interim, the uproar against the illegitimate election of Leszczyński was huge. This was an affront to the most cardinal of cardinal laws in the Commonwealth: the nobles' right to choose their king freely. It actually won the not exactly beloved August II more support. Warsaw ended up changing hands several times (the royal castle was destroyed in the process), while supporters of the Wettin wreaked havoc in Greater Poland, taking their revenge on Leszczyński's landholdings and property. Both Swedes and Russians were happy to plunder what they could. Demonstrating his continued control over the Commonwealth, Karl XII made a special trip to the wealthy city of Lviv, from which he demanded an enormous contribution.

The peace that was promised to follow the dethronement of the Wettin seemed nowhere in sight. The Polish confederates entered into agreement with Peter of Russia at Narva, which the tsar had finally captured. As the price for alliance against Sweden, Peter could fight his enemy on the territory of the Commonwealth. Although both Saxons and Russians prepared to battle the Swede in 1706, with admirable aplomb Karl XII put their plans to naught. Not only did he destroy the Saxon army: his attack on the Russian army led Peter I to call his troops home.

The indefatigable Karl XII was not finished. That same year he and his army marched across Silesia to get to the source of the original trouble, Saxony. August II was forced to relinquish the Polish crown, while wealthy Saxony, his hereditary dominion, was compelled not only to feed the Swedish army but to fill its coffers as well.

While the period of dual monarchs in the Commonwealth was ostensibly over, the trouble was not yet halved—not by far. Leszczyński was king, but neither by the grace of God nor by the will of the Commonwealth nobility. Instead, the wobbly puppet was propped up by Karl XII. One certainly could not call the Commonwealth of this period a fully sovereign state. Peter I, who was dealing with the Commonwealth confederates, considered whether to put his own man on the Polish throne—and, if so, whom. The primate declared an interregnum, although the clergyman decided he would not call for a new election right away but, rather, would rule until conditions changed.

The Russian Campaign, 1707–1709

This state of affairs hardly seemed to hamper Karl XII. The young king had taken on all those who had conspired to defeat him and had emerged victorious. Emboldened, he plotted one more victory, one that would put an end to the war and seal his position as master of Central and Eastern Europe. Karl XII set his sights on Moscow.

In 1707, the Swedish army, well stocked and reinvigorated after its stay in Saxony, made its way back to the Commonwealth. The Polish lands now figured as a place of transit for the troops. The Swede secretly made overtures to a new force he thought could help guarantee him a victory in the east. This force emanated from what Karl XII hoped was Russia's soft underbelly: the ever fractious and elemental Cossack Hetmanate, led by Hetman Ivan Mazepa.

The prospects of adding Russia to his conquests were tantalizing; but could the Swede pull this off? For the first time since 1700, Karl XII's luck began to ebb. Supplies and food were not so easily obtained in the Polish or Lithuanian territories. The further east he went, the worse it got. The Swede soon saw that it would be difficult, if not impossible, to make his way to Moscow, as the Poles had done a century earlier. He abruptly changed his plans and headed south into the more fertile Ukrainian lands—hurrying off before his supplies met up with him from the north. They would never make it to the Swede and his army.

Although he had anticipated military reinforcements coming from both the hetmanate and the forces around Leszczyński, Karl was disappointed. Mazepa had not been able to round up the Cossack host, bringing to battle a force of only several thousand Cossacks; the Russians would lay waste to the Zaporizhian Sich, in that way preventing stragglers from joining up. Nor was help forthcoming from his allies within the Commonwealth. The Polish confederates were able to defeat an army comprised of Swedish and Leszczyński's forces at Koniecpol in late 1708; while the Swedish allies managed to occupy Lviv and make trouble in the region, they nonetheless were prevented from traveling further east.

Karl XII, thus, had to deal with the Russians nearly by himself. His army experienced great hardships in the winter of 1708–1709, which happened to be a particularly cold one. Having begun the Russian campaign in 1707 with some thirty-five thousand soldiers, he now was hemorrhaging men— in part from cold and hunger, in part from skirmishes with Russian units, who found foraging Swedes easy prey.

To make matters worse, this was no longer the Russian army that Karl had encountered and overpowered in Narva. In the interim, Peter the Great's army had gained in confidence and prowess from fighting the Saxons in the north. The turn-of-the-century Russian army was increasingly comprised of professionals, enrolled in modern-style regiments. Formerly reliant on the help of foreign commanders, by this later date Russians were developing their own style of fighting, one informed by both Western and Eastern methods. It was the Russians who ultimately had decided to draw the Swedes into their home territory—and they laid waste to the areas through which the hungry Swedes would have to pass.

The alarming shortage of supplies—of ammunition as well as food—made the Russians' unsparing treatment of Mazepa's headquarters at Baturyn the more painful. The Swedes had set their sights on the supplies they would find there. But the Russian army massacred the population and took the supplies themselves.

Ultimately, in July 1709 Karl XII and his remaining twenty-five thousand troops would lay siege to the fortress at Poltava, by the River Vorskla, once again hoping to seize whatever supplies could be had. This was the opportunity that Tsar Peter had been waiting for. He and his much larger Russian army (over forty thousand strong) had already crossed the Vorskla, thus exerting pressure on the Swede. Still, the outcome of the battle was by no means predetermined. It was the loss of a disoriented infantry corps, which failed to pass through the Russian defenses and ended up surrendering, that led the Swedes to lose their momentum. By the time they pressed on, the Russians were ready for them. Karl, who lost nearly half his troops, was forced to escape with Mazepa across the Dnieper River, ending up in exile in Moldavia for the next five years. The Russian campaign was over.

Emerging Powers on the Polish Periphery: Russia and Prussia

If the giant Peter of Russia had not been noticed by the world earlier, now he most certainly was. His victory at Poltava marked the changing of the guard. After Karl's death in 1718, Sweden would retract its formerly mighty military claws into the northern reaches of the Baltic and relinquish its reputation, established in the previous century, as a dynamic and aggressive northern power.

Ready to fill in the void left by the departing Swedes, Peter's forces would go on to conquer Estonia and Livonia. The rest of the world would come to forget that Muscovy had once been a state where raucous Commonwealth magnates could wreak havoc. When speaking of "Russia and the West," they would overlook the role played by Russia's near west—by the Commonwealth.

Circa 1709, Poland felt the difference as well. This can be seen in the fate of Gdańsk. Poland's window on the Baltic trade did not escape the ravages of the Great Northern War. Saxon troops had been stationed nearby; the Swedes exacted a contribution of a hundred thousand thalers and forced the city to accept the puppet Leszczyński as king. Nor did Danzigers escape pressure from Peter the Great, who demanded from them not only a contribution of sorts but also—more ominously—the right to have a Russian commissar in the city and allow the Russian fleet into its harbor.

Peter's improved position after the Great Northern War also forced the Commonwealth finally to acquiesce to changes in the southeast. Only now did the Polish Seym finally ratify the Andrusovo Treaty of Eternal Peace of 1686. Russia's possession and control of the left bank of the Dnieper that had been the Cossack Hetmanate was confirmed. In turn, the hetmanate would be weaker for its onetime alliance with Sweden. Having secured control over the south, the Russian tsar would be free to refocus his attentions on the north, on his new capital of Saint Petersburg, with its precious access to the Baltic and beyond.

Also benefiting from the woes of both the Commonwealth and Sweden was yet another Polish neighbor, Friedrich III, since 1688 elector of Brandenburg and duke of Prussia. Friedrich sought to build on the success of the opportunistic pendulum policy of his father, the Great Elector, who in the wake of the Deluge had managed to extract Ducal Prussia from its vassal status vis-à-vis the Commonwealth. While this was already quite an accomplishment, by the turn of the century Friedrich was not satisfied with the gains made by his father. Having witnessed the elevation of a fellow elector of the Holy Roman Empire to royal status in the person of the Saxon elector

turned August II, king of Poland, this Hohenzollern from Brandenburg aspired to figure among the crowned heads of Europe. Thus, at the beginning
of 1701, with so many neighbors preoccupied by what was shaping up to be
the Great Northern War, Friedrich had himself crowned king. No longer
would he style himself duke of Prussia: henceforth he would be Friedrich I,
king in Prussia.

This self-coronation was a risky business, one in part reflected in the new
and unusual title. As an elector within the Holy Roman Empire, Friedrich
sought permission from the Holy Roman Emperor, Leopold I, with whom
he had recently become allied and to whom he showed the requisite defer-
ence—if not going so far as to let the emperor put the crown on his head—
for he chose not to style himself king of Brandenburg but, rather, to relate
his new title to his Prussian landholdings. Recall that Ducal Prussia was not
part of the Holy Roman Empire; until the reign of Friedrich's father, it had
been a fief of the Crown of Poland. This unusual phrasing—King in Prussia
(Latin: *in Borussia Rex*)—was devised to sidestep international objections.
For there already was a king of Prussia: the duchy's former overlord, the king
of Poland, who was still the unquestioned king of Royal Prussia.

Friedrich, thus, found it expedient to assign himself the official title of
King *in* Prussia. His self-coronation in Kaliningrad (German: Königsberg)
took place in an elaborate and extravagant ceremony that cost 6 million
thalers, thus indicating to the other crowned heads of Europe that, at least
in wealth, he was in their league. He counted on the fact that the subtleties
of his new official title—the "King in" distinction—would be lost on most of
his contemporaries, who soon enough would call him and his descendants
king of Prussia.

This illegitimate (if creative) transformation of Friedrich III, duke of Prussia, to Friedrich I, king in Prussia, did not go unnoticed by the country with
the most at stake: the Commonwealth. The noble citizens remembered all
too well that the dukes of Prussia had been required to swear an oath of allegiance to the Polish king, the real king of Prussia, as well as that the duchy
was to revert to Poland, should the Hohenzollern line die out. They saw this
move as brazen self-promotion—although, with war looming on the horizon,
their objections were not backed up in any way that threatened the self-styled
king. And, to make matters worse, their own king, August II, had no qualms
about accepting his fellow elector's self-promotion, doubtless sensing in him
a kindred spirit. The Commonwealth's Seym nonetheless refused to accept
the Hohenzollern's new title until 1764, and under very different conditions.

The citizens of Royal Prussia felt doubly threatened by Friedrich's new title.
It verged dangerously close to encroaching on their own Prussian identity

as loyal members of a diverse, multiethnic Commonwealth. They were the greatest opponents of the move, for Friedrich also saw fit to rewrite the ancient Prussian history shared by both Ducal and Royal Prussia. The new king jettisoned the trajectory of historic Prussian republicanism—the bane of any aspiring absolutist monarch—in favor of a focus on the mythical figure of Waidewuthus, Rex Borussorum. How long would it be before a Hohenzollern aspired not only to the title of Prussian king but to gain control over the entirety of the Prussian lands—the Commonwealth's Royal Prussia included?

Poland after Poltava

Saxon rule was not yet over. With a huge sigh of relief occasioned by Peter the Great's defeat of the Swedish menace, August II returned to the Commonwealth. The Wettin was reinstalled as king, this time with the "protection" of the man of the moment, Peter the Great. Demonstrating that his dynastic and personal interests continued to take precedence, August II traded his rights to an independent policy in the Commonwealth for hereditary rights to Livonia—which was what he had been after all along. Once again, he demonstrated an utter disregard for the ways things were done in the Commonwealth. Nor had he managed to get Russian troops out of the country: they were still to be found in the Ukrainian lands.

Indeed, while a triumph for Peter and Russia, the 1709 victory at Poltava hardly marked the end of troubles for the Commonwealth. The battle to the east took place during a period when an epidemic of plague once again decimated the population of major Polish cities such as Gdańsk, Toruń, and Kraków. Russian forces had destroyed Hrodna, Vitsebsk, Mahilioŭ—all major trade towns in the Grand Duchy. When the ravages of war, endless occupations, requisitioning, famine, and plague are all taken into account, the country had lost perhaps a full quarter of its inhabitants. The population had declined to less than 6 million. While the country would once again endeavor to rebound, it was an uphill battle. The one exception to the rule was the lands of Royal Prussia, which reconnected quickly to the international market. Territories dominated by the traditional Commonwealth nobility were slower to rise.

Nor were those nobles who had survived reconciled. Like the Deluge before it, the Great Northern War was not only a war fought by foreign armies but a civil war as well; the latter did not end just because a powerful neighbor reinstalled the former king. While the Wettin had his supporters, so did Leszczyński. The ensuing decade witnessed further conflicts, political (among other things, August's plans for reforms were tarred as absolutist) as well as military (including war with the Ottomans, who had recognized Leszczyński as king—leading Saxon troops to enter the country again). In the course of these clashes, which took place throughout the country, alliances were fluid. Unhappy about the return of Saxon troops, some noble confederates who had previously sided with Sweden actually prevailed upon the tsar, their former enemy, to help them get rid of the Wettin. Given that both Swedish and Saxon soldiers were Protestant, this led to the Commonwealth's Protestants' becoming scapegoats, with the Seym now limiting the number of places where they could worship.

Things did not start to settle down until 1717. August II reached an agreement with the confederates: Saxon troops would leave the country, and the relationship between king and Commonwealth was regularized. The Seym approved the arrangement, if under unusual conditions. In order to ensure that no one was able to use the liberum veto to break up the Seym, Russian troops kept order. Forbidden from deliberating in its usual manner, the one-day "silent" session of the Seym nonetheless resulted in the introduction of some long-needed reforms. Most notable was the one that concerned the Commonwealth's army. A permanent standing army of twenty-four thousand was to be established, and it would be funded by regular taxes. While this could be seen as an improvement or perhaps a first step, it was far too little. The actual tax allotment would not support even such a small army. This kept the Commonwealth at a disadvantage with its neighbors, whose own standing armies were massive by comparison.

Russian interference in the parliamentary doings of the Commonwealth set a bad precedent. The nobles of the Seym saw that their voices could be stifled, not by the absolutum dominium of its own monarch but by a foreign one. One of the only things they seemed to agree upon in this fractious century was their increasing dislike of non-Catholics, the product of years of fervently Catholic Jesuit instruction as well as bad memories of foreign invaders. Witness the Toruń affair of 1724, in which a Lutheran attack on a Jesuit college led to several Lutherans being beheaded in that city. When both August II and the Seym upheld the verdict, the non-Catholic European states of England, Prussia, and Russia took the formerly tolerant Poles to task. The protection of so-called dissidents (non-Catholics) in the Commonwealth would become a cause in a Europe that, by the early seventeenth century, had lost its religious crusading fervor of just a century earlier.

The Russian army did not leave the territory of the Commonwealth until 1719. When the Great Northern War came to an official end in the Treaty of Nystadt of 1721, the Commonwealth proved no less a loser than Sweden: Russia annexed Livonia (which Peter had formerly promised to August II).

The Polish king's own power over the country was weakened: he was not even able to seat his illegitimate yet acknowledged son Maurice as duke of Courland, due to Russian opposition. On his deathbed in 1733, August II would admit that the Polish throne was more trouble than it was worth.

Election Number Nine

No longer master of its own fate, the Commonwealth was figuring increasingly as a pawn in the larger European power struggle, although the states that took the greatest interest in its fate were its closest neighbors: Prussia, Austria, and Russia. This becomes clear from the fraught election that followed the death of August II Wettin. It would prove contested as well as internationalized—a true War of the Polish Succession.

Having emerged, not entirely unscathed, from the Saxon nightmare that was the reign of August II Wettin, the nobility of the Commonwealth wanted to seat a "Piast" on the throne. Perhaps to guarantee that they would get their wish this time, they decided to exclude non-Catholics from the Convocation Seym as well as from all future Seyms, a discriminatory move that boded ill for the country.

Despite all the grief he had brought earlier, the former puppet king Stanisław Leszczyński was not only considered a serious candidate but elected, fair and square—some thirteen thousand nobles coming out to vote in his favor. To be sure, his stature had risen since the Great Northern War. Leszczyński's daughter Maria had won the international marriage lottery, becoming the wife of King Louis XV in 1725. This put the French as well as a strong cohort of Commonwealth nobles and magnates on the side of Leszczyński, who was proclaimed king in September 1733.

The election once again became a field for international interference. Not pleased with the prospect of a Polish-French alliance, which clearly was built into Leszczyński's candidacy, the Commonwealth's neighbors Russia, Prussia, and Austria instead endorsed the son and heir of August II Wettin, Friedrich August. In return, the Wettin happily promised concessions. He would support the Pragmatic Sanction, Emperor Karl VI's unprecedented attempt to ensure that his daughter, Maria Theresa, might inherit the Habsburg throne. Russia would be allowed to seat its own candidate as duke of Courland. A small cohort of Commonwealth nobles was persuaded, in November 1733, to elect the Wettin, to be known in the Commonwealth as August III, as king.

Despite this uneven support (some 13 to 1 in favor of Leszczyński), this time it was not votes but armies that would prove decisive. The Commonwealth's neighbors had an advantage here. The Russian army literally chased Leszczyński out of Warsaw; the second Wettin was crowned king in Kraków in January 1734, not by the primate of Poland—as was custom—but by the bishop of Kraków. The Cracovians were more mournful than welcoming—with some reportedly even wishing he would fall from his steed and break his neck . . . Their mood seemed at odds with the music that followed the coronation: the Wawel choir director conducted a performance of Johann Sebastian Bach's joyous cantata, *Eolus Pacified*. Bach, incidentally, dedicated his Mass in B-minor (the Kyrie and Gloria) to the Saxon elector turned Polish king.

In the meantime, the lawfully elected Leszczyński raced to Gdańsk, which recognized him as king and managed to keep the Russian army at bay for five months. The expected French military support proved disappointing: it was slow in coming as well as totally inadequate to take on the Russians. Leszczyński ultimately escaped to Prussia, where he was rather naively willing to make territorial concessions to the Hohenzollern for support. Confederations supporting both candidates sought both diplomatic and military means to ensure their candidate's victory.

All this—and more—resulted in the agony of dual (or rather, contested) monarchy, which lasted for three years. In the end, Louis XV pressed his father-in-law to abdicate. In emigration in France, Leszczyński took consolation in the estates he was given in Lunéville and Nancy. Once again, he had not been able to do more than serve as a pawn in a game that was now dominated by Poland's neighbors.

The Second Saxon and Sarmatian Republicanism

If the Poles saw the reign of August II as a Saxon nightmare, the reign of August III was for them merely the soporific blackness of night. The next Wettin to sit on the Polish throne was not one to make waves. Pressed as a youngster by his father to convert from Lutheranism to Catholicism, before assuming the Polish throne he had married the Habsburg princess Maria Josepha, with whom he would have fifteen children. Had the Commonwealth's neighbors wished it, the fertile pair could have provided for an endless Saxon night in the country.

August III was an absentee king, preferring to remain in Dresden and rule from afar via his ministers and appointees, at least until the Seven Years' War (1756–1763), which forced him to take refuge in Warsaw for six years and, unfortunately, turned parts of the Commonwealth into an international barracks once again. Not that such royal inaction particularly bothered the generation of nobles who had weathered the Great Northern War and the recurrent conflicting claims to the throne. Not only did they gain peace and some breathing space, they increasingly saw the monarch as irrelevant to the running of the Commonwealth.

This led to a situation where the wealthier of the Commonwealth nobles were able to do pretty much what they wanted. They recuperated from years of war, set down to the work of running their estates and (where possible) increasing the profitability of their landholdings, and enjoyed the luxurious lifestyle their wealth afforded.

Even less well-to-do nobles considered their disengagement from the larger world to be the epitome of the Sarmatian idyll, one in which the Cincinnatuses of the Commonwealth hung up their swords and, having returned to their estates or plots, retreated into blissful private life. This, after all, was to be the Sarmatian's reward for being part of the system that provided grain to Europe: a static, peaceful, rural, provincial, isolated, undisturbed, self-centered life. At best, these noble Sarmatians indulged in the pleasures of noble society, of sumptuous feasts and gatherings that allowed them to demonstrate their hospitality and enjoy the company of friends and family. There is a Polish saying that sums up the mentality of the era of August III: "Under the Saxon king, eat, drink, and loosen your belt."

Despite the fact that this second Saxon king remained uninvolved in the doings of the Commonwealth (no push for absolutum dominium under August III), the nobles did nothing to change the way their country functioned. Perhaps this was because they liked it the way it was. The mixed form of government had tipped in favor of the noble masses. The noble estate saw itself, alone, as embodying the Commonwealth. Nobles easily could have modified the dictum of a famous French king to read, *L'état—ce sommes nous* (We are the state). To be sure, on his own estate or plot the noble truly was king, not subject to any higher authority. The proper forum for noble political activity was increasingly seen as the local or regional seymik, which dealt predominantly with issues of provincial, not national, importance.

Unruly Nation?

The decentralized republicanism of the nobility was encapsulated in the saying "Poland stands by unrule," which (it should be noted) the Poles saw as a virtue, not a vice. While it is easy to equate this with anarchy, it was not lawlessness that Poles advocated. Rather, they believed there was no need for new laws; if the laws they had were respected and executed as originally designed, all would be well. It was the vagaries of rule—of governance—that made things worse, in their opinion, not the other way around.

This attitude in part resulted from the ossification of the Sarmatian ideology. Whereas early on it had reflected a creative, unifying concept and a useful myth of common origin of the nobility of the entire Commonwealth, aspects of it had now degenerated into what would become known as Sarmatism. Perhaps this was in part a result of its success in giving the entire nobility a sense that they were the Polish nation, the active citizenry, the people who counted in the Commonwealth. From this original sense of inclusiveness and emphasis on shared responsibility for the fate of the country, the idea became an unquestioned dogma, emphasizing noble exclusivity, privilege, and megalomania. Sarmatism was characterized by its steadfast belief in the nation's God-given destiny and mission as granary of Europe, bulwark of Christianity, and unique land of freedom—a mission and status that the rest of the world failed to appreciate and even tried to undermine. The original mission of feeding the West had fostered a rural parochialism and license to exploit the peasantry for personal enrichment; the belief in the country's mission to protect and spread Christianity led to religious intolerance both within and without; and each perceived threat to its hard-won liberty, the Golden Freedoms, pushed the nation further in the direction of anarchy and xenophobia.

This had grave consequences for the Commonwealth and its ability to adjust to changes in its neighborhood. There was a sense that the existing rights and freedoms—which their noble forbears had fought so hard for—were perfect and thus needed no adjustment. Even though their ancestors, certainly at the outset, had nonetheless been willing to tinker with these rights and freedoms, by this time, Sarmatism had become a conservative, even reactionary, ideology. Those nobles who tried to pass reform measures invariably saw the measures defeated. Not even one session of the Seym managed to pass legislation under August III: each was broken up by the (ab)use of the liberum veto or filibustered.

This abuse of the right of the individual nobleman to break up a session of the Seym and nullify all its doings undermined a foundational notion of the Commonwealth of Both Nations—the idea that its active citizenry was obliged to do what was necessary for the common weal, for the prosperity of the entire country. Even after the liberum veto began to be used, the Seym was still able to accomplish a good deal; there were thirty-three successful Seyms between 1652 and 1736, which suggests that the system was not unredeemable. Increasingly, however, the Golden Freedoms of the nobility became used not to construct a happier future for the still large and potentially prosperous country but, rather, to enrich individual nobles or, conversely, to ensure that their opponents could not enrich themselves.

This particular Golden Freedom was abused as much by foreign powers as by the Commonwealth nobles themselves. Foreign interference in Commonwealth affairs came cheap: buy off one petty nobleman, who could declare his lack of assent, and the parliamentary proceedings, no matter how advanced or extensive, would be annulled.

Yet such interruptions did little for the career of an individual nobleman. A more effective way to gain in stature was to gain the attention of the monarch. Odd as it may seem, given the nobles' proverbial mistrust of their king, it was to him they were beholden for offices and for control over lucrative royal lands. This situation, incidentally, was exploited by both Saxon kings. They bestowed offices on certain lesser nobles, with the assumption that their appointees would be grateful for this favor and serve them loyally. This explains the rise, during the rule of August II, of members of the Poniatowski and Czartoryski families, who were destined to play an important role in future doings of the Commonwealth.

The Rise of the "Family"

In the case of the Poniatowski and Czartoryski families, a combination of royal favor and stunningly successful marriage politics catapulted them into top positions within the Commonwealth nobility. Although the Czartoryskis descended from the Lithuanian princely line, the family had long languished until it found favor with August II Wettin. This was the work of two brothers, one talented, one rich. The talented elder brother, Michał Fryderyk, was promoted early on by August II to the post of Lithuanian vice chancellor; he also married into the politically influential family of the Flemmings. This success was nonetheless dwarfed by that of August Aleksander Czartoryski. The younger brother hit the jackpot by winning the hand of the Commonwealth's most eligible heiress, Maria Zofia Denhoffowa née Sieniawska, the Commonwealth's greatest landowner and one of the richest individuals in Europe.

Daughter of a hetman and the widow of another hetman, Stanisław Denhoff, Sieniawska held in her lovely capable hands fortunes acquired over the centuries by the Sieniawski and Lubomirski families as well as that of her first husband. At the time of the young widow's marriage to August Czartoryski in 1731, these amounted to over twenty entire complexes, containing some thirty towns and hundreds of villages, in various parts of the Commonwealth. Had these territories been assembled in one place, it would have been a totally respectable kingdom in its own right. Naturally, these landholdings did not lack for palaces; one relatively new possession was the former Sobieski residence at Wilanów, which reportedly Sieniawska declared would do as a place to stable her horses while she attended sessions of the Seym . . . All these palaces, towns, and territories were owned outright; Sieniawska had also been granted lucrative leases of numerous royal lands.

The repercussions of the Sieniawski-Czartoryski marriage were enormous. In one stroke, the Czartoryski family acquired tremendous wealth and, as a consequence, the ability to gain tremendous influence. The brothers joined forces with their brother-in-law, Stanisław Poniatowski. A talented and influential politician and military leader, Poniatowski held many offices under the Wettins, among them palatine of Mazovia and castellan of Kraków. His brother-in-law August became the Ruthenian palatine.

In this powerful configuration, this family alliance became known throughout the country simply as "the Family" (*Familia*). The various members had the wealth as well as the political clout to have their own extensive noble courts, which proved an attractive alternative to the mostly absent royal court of the Wettins. Like little kings themselves, magnates such as the Poniatowskis and Czartoryskis (as well as their rivals) held sway over lesser nobles around them, who in turn profited from economic and political opportunities under magnate patronage. While their rivals embraced the extreme version of the Sarmatian ideal and opposed anything that smacked of change (a stance of "*Nihil novi* period"), the Family was intellectually and temperamentally open to new ideas and trends emanating from the West that might improve the functioning of the Commonwealth. In this way, in addition to playing an influential role under Saxon rule, they would make a name for themselves in debates about the future of the country.

Enlightened Ideas

For there were rays of light, even during the Saxon Night. As in the period of the Renaissance, new ideas began to emanate once again from the West. They came in various forms, some—perhaps most potently—through education. And indeed, there was a thirst for knowledge of varying sorts, a thirst satisfied in part by the existing schools of the Commonwealth. Schools were run not only by Catholics (generally Jesuits, with a traditional scholastic approach) but also by Protestant denominations; for example, the Gdańsk

Academy introduced elements of the German Enlightenment in the north.

The desire to get ahead in the world—to gain insights and skills that would assist with various aspects of life, whether in the economic or political realm—caused some young nobles to study abroad. During the period of Saxon rule, some were already receiving a military education in Saxony. Others soon acquired similar knowledge from the Wettins' rival, Leszczyński, in France. In 1737, the onetime Polish king founded a Cadet Corps in his seat at Lunéville. These options were available to the fortunate, and fortuned, few.

The education level of the Polish noble masses had plummeted since the Golden Age in the sixteenth century. It is estimated that in the mid-eighteenth century about half the Commonwealth nobles were functionally illiterate. If they had any schooling, it took the form of a smattering of Latin and religious instruction that favored rote learning and Baroque piety. Such an upbringing hardly provided pupils, whose horizons were already parochial, with a way to improve their own lives, let alone deal with the problems and challenges faced by their country.

At a time when the reading of most nobles was limited to calendars or religious materials, some still found inspiration in books—enough to establish significant libraries. Here notable are the efforts of the Załuski brothers—both serving the Commonwealth as bishops, yet both influenced by ideas of the Enlightenment that first began to reach the country via the German lands. Andrzej Stanisław Załuski, bishop of Kraków, served as chancellor of the Jagiellonian University, where his efforts to introduce major changes to the curriculum were stonewalled. His brother Józef Andrzej, bishop of Kyiv, sought to further knowledge of the Commonwealth's parliamentary history through the publication of *Volumina Legum*, a compilation of the decisions reached by the Seym. The brothers amassed a library comprised of some three hundred thousand titles and some ten thousand manuscripts, one of the largest collections in Europe. Housed in a Warsaw palace redone in the fashionable rococo (late Baroque) style, the Załuski Library opened to the public in 1747. It was willed to the Commonwealth and came into its possession in 1771.

Yet another clergyman would have an even greater impact on Polish noble society than the Załuski brothers. He was Father Stanisław Konarski, a member of the Piarist order. Konarski founded a boarding school for young well-to-do nobles in Warsaw, the Collegium Nobilium. Based on what Konarski had seen in Italy and France, its curriculum included the study of modern foreign languages as well as the natural sciences. Latin—a familiarity with which long was seen as the mark of a noble—would still be taught,

and pupils were exhorted to speak both Latin and their native Polish properly, without the undue mixing of the two that had been characteristic of
the Baroque period. In place of the bombastic rhetoric characteristic of the
Baroque, pupils learned in mock parliaments to speak and argue in a more
reasoned and logical way. Having helped Bishop Załuski publish the *Volumina Legum*, Konarski made sure that his pupils were taught Polish political
history. The overarching purpose of the Collegium Nobilium was to educate
future citizens, to expose young nobles to ideas that would help them steer
their country in the future. Attendance at the Collegium Nobilium was limited to those who could afford to pay for such an education, but this effort
would bear fruit in the decades to come.

Other clerical orders involved in teaching the youth of the Commonwealth were influenced by the college's success, most notably the Jesuits.
They too began to introduce changes into their largely scholastic curriculum, and they extended their reach by founding new colleges. Jesuits were
instrumental in teaching astronomy in Vilnius, where they constructed an
observatory, and they worked to further the knowledge of the Commonwealth through cartographical studies of their homeland.

Polish society, religious as well as secular, was nonetheless divided as
to the merit of these newfangled developments, which infused the Commonwealth with new and often provocative ideas. Konarski did not limit
his reform efforts to the education of young nobles. In his 1761 tract, *On
the Effective Means of Counsel*, the Piarist sought to improve the efficiency of the Seym by advocating that the nobles abandon the liberum veto.
This attack on one of the Golden Freedoms resulted in a backlash among
the most diehard Sarmatian types, who would not countenance any limits placed on their liberties. Nor did all clergy agree that reforms of any
kind were necessary, preferring to place the fate of the Commonwealth
firmly in God's hands. In his book of 1764 entitled *The Happy Continuity
of Kingdoms or Their Sad Fall*, the Jesuit Szymon Majchrowicz reassured
readers that only the genuine religious piety of the country's inhabitants
would guarantee that nothing befell their country. Despite this pious yet
politically passive stance, Majchrowicz nonetheless sounded a note that
had been reverberating within the Commonwealth: the need for moral
and civic virtue. In this way, works such as Konarski's elicited a discussion
of the efficacy of the form of government that so long had gone unquestioned in the Commonwealth.

The idea of reform became a lightning rod for the most ambitious party
within the Commonwealth, that of the Family. They first attempted to introduce reforms during the waning years of the nearly thirty-year reign of

August III Wettin. Not that the Czartoryskis and the Poniatowskis were in complete agreement as to what needed to be done. Their attempts nonetheless met with opposition on the part of other powerful magnates, most notably the Radziwiłłs, Potockis, and Branickis. Led by Hetman Jan Klemens Branicki (who, incidentally, was married to Izabela Poniatowski), these Sarmatian republicans had an advantage, in their control over the army, should matters come to a head militarily.

Although the members of the Family owed the Saxon kings for their uncommonly swift elevation to magnate status, this did not mean they remained loyal to the Wettins. As August III's health was failing in 1762, the Family decided not to support another Wettin in the next election (recall that the Saxon king had sons galore). Instead, Family members sought to promote one of their own as an authentic Piast candidate. In order to make this dream a reality, the Czartoryskis and Poniatowskis sought an ally among the European powers in the vicinity of the Commonwealth. Themselves concerned about the rise of Prussia under the warmongering Friedrich II, the Family reached out, not north but east, to Russia.

"Great"-ness in the Neighborhood

Perhaps this was a logical choice. Russia had already been meddling in the internal matters of the Commonwealth since the reign of Peter the Great and likely would continue to do so. The Russian army had ensured that the Silent Seym of 1717 would pass uncontested. And it had experience with Polish elections. Recall that the presence of the Russian army in the Commonwealth had allowed August III to be crowned king some thirty years earlier.

In 1762 a new monarch with new ideas came to rule Russia. Neither Russian nor Orthodox by birth, Sophie Friedericke Auguste began her life as princess of the principality of Anhalt-Zerbst. She left it famous as Catherine II of Russia, that is, Catherine the Great. The German princess was dispatched to Saint Petersburg at the tender age of fifteen to become the wife of the heir of the Russian throne, the mentally ill grandson and namesake of Peter the Great. Yet she was not one to sit quietly while her husband, Peter III, ruled Russia. Indeed, in the summer of 1762 she initiated a coup d'état, only a half year after he became tsar. Peter died soon afterward, leaving Catherine free to run the country herself.

Catherine styled herself an Enlightened monarch. Her French was much superior to her Russian, and she corresponded with Voltaire and charmed members of the French *Encyclopédie* such as Diderot. It has been said that Montesquieu's *Spirit of the Laws* was her Bible. It is more certain that Catherine believed in enlightened absolutism; its emphasis on the absolute nature of sovereignty fit quite well with traditional Russian autocracy. At the same time, certain aspects of her policies appealed to the Enlightened thinkers of the West; one of these was the alacrity with which she came to the defense of non-Catholics in predominantly Catholic states, even in France itself. This and other policies associated with enlightened despotism would bring Catherine closer to another monarch whose reign would be perceived as great, Friedrich II of Prussia.

We have already seen how Prussia was gaining ground at the expense of the Commonwealth. The Polish fief known as Ducal Prussia had come under the control of the Berlin Hohenzollerns toward the end of the sixteenth century. It became independent of the Commonwealth after the Deluge of the mid-seventeenth century. At the beginning of the eighteenth century, the Hohenzollerns (who ruled over Brandenburg as well as Prussia) began to style themselves king in Prussia.

The grandson and namesake of the first king in Prussia, Friedrich II, made even more stunning advances. The latest Hohenzollern monarch built on the achievements of his ancestors, whose single-minded pursuit of power and status had elevated them to royalty and increased the size of their dominions. Friedrich's first major move came at the expense of the Habsburgs, who were undergoing their own succession crisis. Emperor Karl VI had no son to inherit his hereditary landholdings, let alone retain the imperial title within the Holy Roman Empire. Not only did Friedrich contest the Pragmatic Sanction, which was to provide for an exception that would allow the emperor's daughter, Maria Theresa, to rule over the Habsburg dominions. In what came to be known as the War of the Austrian Succession (1740–1748), Friedrich invaded Silesia and wrested it from the Habsburgs.

Friedrich's military victory also marked a change of ruler for a territory we encountered early in Poland's history. After more than two centuries of being held by the Habsburgs, Silesia now came under Hohenzollern rule. Silesia was inhabited in part by Polish speakers whose ancestors had in medieval times been part of the Polish state. By the last third of the seventeenth century, however, the Piast dukes had all died out. The population's Catholicism helped to maintain its Polishness, however. The acquisition of prosperous Silesia was a coup for Prussia, as the populous kingdom had a strong industrial base in mining and metallurgy as well as in textiles and trade. Disciplined Prussian rule of Silesia would look very different from the more diffuse rule of the Habsburgs: as the saying went, Prussia was more army than state, the electors having transformed their population into soldiers.

It is worth noting that the belligerent Friedrich was hardly the only European monarch to seek to profit from Habsburg vulnerability circa 1740. The Wittelsbachs of Bavaria had set their sights on Bohemia, and the Poland's own do-nothing king, August III Wettin, in his more active role as elector of Saxony, had designs on parts of Silesia and Moravia. Only the Great Hohenzollern, however, had the military might needed to achieve his goals. Chipping away at Habsburg dominance over the German lands, Friedrich's Prussia was now moving into the ranks of the major European powers. This made him a valuable ally for Catherine of Russia.

Like their seventeenth-century predecessors, albeit both more enlightened and more despotic, Friedrich and Catherine agreed that a weak—or, at least, subservient—Commonwealth was in the interests of both countries. They would soon be given an opportunity to increase their influence over the Commonwealth and its inhabitants.

The Last Royal Election

King August III Wettin died in 1764, just before celebrating the thirtieth anniversary of his reign. The Commonwealth had experienced a period of relative peace, yet not one that augured better times in the future. Not an unintelligent man, the Saxon ruler had no less intelligently concluded it made no sense to fight to change things in the Commonwealth. His long stint as elective monarch had its purpose: it elevated the second Wettin (as the first) into the realm of European royalty and gave him some economic benefits. August III's initiatives on the international or domestic political scene, such as they were, were channeled into gaining ground within the Holy Roman Empire and strengthening his position in electoral Saxony, areas where he might lay the foundations for the continuation of his dynasty. These initiatives remained irrelevant for the vast majority of the inhabitants of the Commonwealth who paid little attention to what transpired on a day-to-day basis in Warsaw.

The prospect of a royal election was another matter altogether. Poland might proverbially stand by unrule, but its citizens still prided themselves on having the right to elect their own king. Faced with an election in 1764, the assembled nobility could take the path of least resistance—that is, settle on one of dead king's sons—or find someone new. Before his death,

August III had tried to strengthen the standing of his sons by placing one of them, Karl Christian, on the throne of Courland, the remaining piece of Livonia that was a fief of the Crown. Would this be the latter's stepping-stone to power?

A century earlier, this might have been the case: witness the election of ensuing Vasa heirs to the throne until the abdication of the childless last king of the dynasty. However, the outcome of Polish elections in the eighteenth century had hardly been a matter of domestic choice. The second Wettin himself owed his election to the heavy hand of the foreign coalition that saw fit to back him.

In this regard, the election of 1764 would be similar to the election of 1734. Russian troops would once again facilitate the promotion of the candidate favored by Tsarina Catherine II. The tsarina's interference in Commonwealth affairs would come at a higher price this time, despite the fact that the other candidates put forward—the aged Hetman Branicki and an underage Wettin—were hardly attractive. Still, Catherine would have to finance the purchase of votes so as to overcome the opposition of the republicans. Taking no chances, August Czartoryski organized an armed confederation that, disallowing the use of the liberum veto, would guide the Convocation Seym to completion and even introduce some reforms. Ultimately these developments caused the leaders of the opposition, including Branicki, to flee the country.

Who was Catherine's candidate? Like the candidate advanced by the magnate-led republicans, he was a Piast, if one with a rather unusual major qualification. Stanisław Poniatowski was the son and namesake of the recently deceased former leader of the Family. Yet his claim to fame was not solely—or even primarily—because he was related to the rich, powerful, and influential Czartoryski brothers, his uncles, who had allied themselves with Russia to secure the succession. Rather, Poniatowski attained the crown thanks to what turned out to be a happy accident: when he was in Saint Petersburg in the years 1756–1758, he had been the lover of the young wife of Grand Duke Peter—Catherine, herself.

Nearly a decade later, Catherine saw him as the perfect pawn in her game of controlling what happened in her increasingly impotent and unruly neighbor: any reforming to be done was to come at her instigation. She envisaged the Commonwealth of Both Nations as a vassal state, a well-run vassal state. The tsarina's selection of Poniatowski was supported by Friedrich II, who nonetheless preferred to keep the Commonwealth the way it was, weak and ineffectual. It was thought that Poniatowski, who incidentally had no wealth of his own (after his father's death he was supported by his cousins) and who held only the amusing title of Lithuanian Master of the Pantry, would be a malleable and subservient Piast.

Figure 7.1: This is what Polish royal elections looked like. The final Polish royal election *viritim*, painted by Canaletto, the Italian artist who immortalized on his canvases the Warsaw of the late eighteenth century. The original hangs in the National Museum, Warsaw.

The Enlightened Polish Monarch and His Impact

Having helped scare away the opposition, the Russian army withdrew discreetly (if not very far) to allow the actual election to proceed without the benefit of Russian bayonets. Nonetheless, the scheduling of his coronation for November 25, 1764, the name day of Empress Catherine, seemed to give a subtle message. Breaking with tradition, Poniatowski's coronation, as King Stanisław August, took place not in Kraków but in Warsaw. Shades of Leszczyński's ignominious coronation at Swedish insistence, this hardly seemed an auspicious beginning.

Yet all did not evolve as Catherine expected. Not content to profit from the Commonwealth's impotence, she wanted to serve more actively as the Commonwealth's protector. Russia's enlightened despot would be its source of enlightenment, select elements of which would be introduced at her command, so that the country might evolve in ways useful to the tsarina. Her former lover had his own ideas, however. Poniatowski wished to be his own man, although neither his dire personal finances nor his powerful protectress would afford him as much room for maneuvering as he would like—or, perhaps, as befit his own image of himself and what he might accomplish.

Unlike the masses of barely literate nobles, Poniatowski had received an excellent education and, for a man barely in his thirties, possessed many qualities that should have made him an exceptional king. His foreign travels (an atypical Grand Tour that included places such as Paris and London) had given him extensive exposure to the West and Western ideas. Unusual for a Pole, Poniatowski was something of an Anglophile; he knew English, in addition to the more standard French and Italian. He had met the English diplomat Charles Hanbury Williams in Berlin; it is thanks to Williams that he traveled, as the Englishman's secretary, to Saint Petersburg, where clearly he had both the requisite status and opportunity to come into very close contact with the future tsarina. In addition to his diplomatic contacts and experience, Poniatowski also had some acquaintance with the workings of the Commonwealth. His tenure at the treasury and the Lithuanian tribunals informed his perception of the rank-and-file Sarmatian noble as a half-literate reactionary. It also convinced him of the need for real reforms—a conviction that his stint as a Seym deputy only reinforced (he had been part of a Family effort to break up the 1760 Seym).

Neither Poniatowski nor the Family was interested in placating the republican opposition. Instead of donning traditional Polish dress at his coronation, the king appeared in Spanish garb. Given Poniatowski's penchant for historical symbolism, it appears he was trying to conjure up images of a king from an earlier age, Zygmunt III Vasa, whose rule had initiated the Silver Age of Polish history. Even more visible a sign of the new king's vision of his reign was his addition of the name August to his title. That Stanisław Poniatowski was crowned as "Stanisław August" had nothing to do with his Saxon predecessors. Rather, the August (Latin: Augustus) of his name was a classical reference—and a telling one at that. Stanisław August saw parallels between himself and Augustus Caesar. The latter had saved the Roman Republic by transforming it into the Roman Empire. This Polish Piast saw his role as transforming a Commonwealth wracked by unruly republicanism into a well-functioning and stable constitutional monarchy.

The king's education and predispositions inclined him to take an active and Enlightened approach to rule—Enlightened with a capital "E." Although Enlightenment ideas had been making their way to the Commonwealth for several decades, Poniatowski's reign marked a huge upswing in their propagation and reception. The new king undertook to reform the aspects of governance that fell within the competency of the monarch as well as provide a breath of fresh air to a society that had long stewed in its Sarmatian juices.

Poniatowski helped establish the newspaper *Monitor*, patterned after the English *Spectator*, which over the course of its twenty-year history would propagate Enlightened ideas. To create new Enlightened cadres for the future and give opportunities to those less fortunate, in 1765 Poniatowski established a Knights' School. Housed in the Kazimierz Palace in Warsaw and run by Prince Adam Kazimierz Czartoryski, the king's cousin, the school provided deserving yet impoverished young nobles with a solid modern education. Perhaps its most famous pupil was a young man named Tadeusz Kościuszko. Stanisław August sought to fix the country's economic woes. A mint was built to provide new coinage, the old having been debased by his Saxon predecessor; and the king introduced measures designed to foster municipal development, which led to a veritable urban boom.

The king thus shared the reformist bent of the Family. Their combined use of the rare opportunity to effect change was visible already at the Convocation Seym of 1764, when the confederation organized by August Czartoryski enacted a significant series of reforms. While a number of these were of a political nature (such as the introduction of majority voting on budgetary matters—quite a change for the Commonwealth), others added important corrections to the current state of the economy. Most crucial for the state of the treasury was the introduction of import and export duties to give the Commonwealth an important revenue stream.

The Anti-reform Backlash

Neither the reforms nor the means by which they were pushed through by the Family pleased various other constituencies. In addition to objections voiced by the republicans, the inhabitants of Royal Prussia were unhappy at the new centralizing efforts that threatened to subordinate to Warsaw their stubbornly independent region. Nor were the country's neighbors enamored of the reforms. Friedrich of Prussia became so incensed at the new trade duties that he responded in kind, starting a tariff war. Asked to mediate between the Prussian and the Polish kings, Catherine of Russia sided with the former, thus indicating that her true interests lay not in making the Commonwealth financially secure (what Stanisław August wanted) but in keeping it docile (what Friedrich wanted). The Polish reformers were forced to cease collecting what even in a short time had represented a huge increase of revenue for the country.

At the same time, the king exhibited what some would consider an alarming desire to strengthen the monarchy. It has already been noted that King

Stanisław August seemed to have an affinity for Zygmunt III Vasa—to the extent that he also sought to marry a Habsburg archduchess. However, his former lover Catherine would not allow her protégé the luxury of such an alliance—not out of jealousy (she continued to have lovers and favorites of her own) but, rather, out of political concerns.

Personally acquainted with the workings of diplomacy, Stanisław August also strove to place his own representatives abroad, which would enable the Polish king to deal directly with foreign powers instead of going though Saint Petersburg. Catherine was displeased by her former lover's attempts to gain some independence from Russia. Her vision of the functioning of the Commonwealth revolved around the king's every move being approved by the Russian ambassador in Warsaw, who took his instructions from Catherine herself.

The Polish king, strapped for cash and lacking his own royalist constituency, was in a predicament. He was already out of favor with the woman who put him on the throne. The coalition that had facilitated his coronation back home, the Family of the Czartoryskis, soon split with their nephew over differences of approach. Unable to see Stanisław August as anything but the arm of the reformist wing, the republicans and others in the opposition (for the opposition leaders had returned home) continued to despise and distrust him, despite certain conciliatory overtures made by the king. Members of the opposition were all too happy to keep the Russian ambassador informed as to the reformers' plans—a situation that led to a stand-off on the liberum veto in 1766. The Russians forced the king and the reformers to accept a bill that reinstated this pillar of Commonwealth freedom.

Russia's defense of the liberum veto led some republicans to see Catherine as the champion of the Commonwealth's Golden Freedoms. They hoped the tsarina could be counted on to help repeal the reforms and, perhaps, even dethrone the upstart Piast, thus bringing the country back where it had been under the Saxons.

Yet the all-powerful autocrat of Russia did not desire a return to the status quo ante. Rather, she wanted a free hand to mold the Commonwealth to suit her own interests. Catherine undermined the goodwill that the support of the liberum veto had secured her in some quarters by rather irrationally insisting on defending the rights of the Commonwealth's non-Catholics (here, the remaining Protestant nobles). She demanded that they be accorded not only freedom of worship but also the right to hold any Commonwealth office, barring that of king. While the move looked Enlightened to the West, it did not sit well with the rank-and-file nobles of the Commonwealth, who had come to see their pious and patriotic Catholicism as the guarantee of Sarmatian liberty. They had come to suspect the Protestants within their midst of being inclined to side with the foreigners who sought to profit from or dominate the Commonwealth. Still, some of the Sarmatian opposition might have overcome their objections to Catherine's initiative, their hatred of Stanisław August trumping their religious sensitivities, especially if her initiative had been enacted with proper preparation and tact. Given the centrality of Catholicism in the Sarmatians' world, it would take a skilled and subtle touch to pull this off.

Subtlety, however, was not the autocratic Catherine's strong suit. Instead of working the Commonwealth's idiosyncratic system to achieve her goal, she rammed her reforms down the nobles' collective throat. Her heavy-handed approach to reforming the Commonwealth only widened the chasm between traditional Commonwealth republicanism and Russian absolutism. Indeed, Catherine was not content to let Russian bayonets do the talking, although her army did serve to enforce acquiescence in Warsaw and elsewhere. Prior to the vote, four ringleaders of opposition to the proposed legislation, two noblemen and two bishops (one of whom was Bishop Załuski of Kyiv), were arrested and exiled to Kaluga, in the Russian interior. Also lacking in subtlety, the message *à la Russe* was clear: those who opposed the tsarina's wishes would share their fate.

Directed more at foreign opinion than at the Poles, Catherine's Enlightened pose as the defender of religious freedom in the Commonwealth was a sham, a veneer of Enlightenment covering an autocratic essence. The ostensibly tolerant tsarina was not above humiliating the Poles' own revered Catholic faith. As if to demonstrate the extent to which her wishes dictated the fate of the Commonwealth, she had chosen the most outlandish candidate to head the Roman Catholic Church in the country. Threatening to create a Polish National Church if he did not comply, Catherine forced Stanisław August to appoint a corrupt cleric—one who egregiously embraced atheism as well as a Protestant mistress—as primate of Poland. Even the pope watched helplessly as Gabriel Podoski assumed leadership over the country's Roman Catholics, joined the Senate, and did the tsarina's bidding. If this were not enough to raise hackles, other reforms were enacted in the Seym of 1768 that not only altered the country's Fundamental Laws but also would make it difficult for further changes to be made by the country's citizens. Could no one stand up to the autocratic tsarina?

The Confederation of Bar, 1768–1772

What Catherine did not count on was that even her seemingly limitless power within the Commonwealth did in fact have limits. She may have been able to get some opposition ringleaders, such as the Potockis, to support her by establishing a confederation in the summer of 1767; and, using the methods described above, she was able to intimidate the Seym into approving her slate of reforms, religious and otherwise, the following spring. However, the Russian army could not control every last provincial gathering, let alone every last nobleman, for whom the defense of the Commonwealth's Catholicism might be a crusade worth fighting. These last of the tsarina's humiliations struck a raw nerve among a large segment of the country's citizens.

Indeed, while the Russians were pushing through their slate of selected reforms in Warsaw, discontent was taking on a new shape in the distant palatinate of Podolia, near the Turkish border. In February 1768, a group of middling nobles formed a confederation in the town of Bar. They resolved to come to the defense of their religious and political rights that were being trampled by the Russian interlopers. While the confederation may have seemed quixotic (taking on mighty Russia) and old-fashioned (desiring a return to the Sarmatian status quo), its organizers nonetheless demonstrated that they were willing to shed blood for what was most important to them: a Catholic vision of the Commonwealth. These and other facets of the Confederation of Bar have led some scholars to label it the first (modern) Polish national uprising intent on liberating the country from foreign domination.

The confederation aroused various constituencies, not only in ways that promoted the aims declared at Bar. The confederates in that remote locale soon learned that their own backyard was unreceptive to their idea of rebellion. Egged on by Cossacks from across the Russian border, peasants unleashed a terrifying revolt in the Ukrainian region of the Commonwealth. Twelve thousand nobles and Jews were murdered at the enormous Potocki complex of Uman (Polish: Humań) alone. The militantly Orthodox Cossacks and Ruthenian peasants were obviously not on the same wavelength as the militantly Catholic Polish nobility.

While the original confederates were soon defeated, the ranks of Polish discontents were swelling elsewhere in the Commonwealth. The news of Bar spawned a host of confederations, some of which found support among a new constituency, the country's Catholic commoners. Over three-quarters of the prisoners taken during the conflict were not nobles, which suggests a greater anti-Russian, pro-Catholic resonance. Even the nobles in the confederacy tended to be of the rank-and-file variety, not the magnates—the traditional leaders of confederations.

Fighting mainly a partisan war, confederate armies were more nuisance than danger to the Russian forces. They nonetheless won a patchwork of victories in the Grand Duchy as well as in the Crown of Poland. Son of one of the founders of the Confederation of Bar, a young and brash Kazimierz Pułaski ably defended Częstochowa in 1771. Pułaski, incidentally, would later make a name for himself fighting in the American Revolution, perishing on the battlefield of Savannah in 1779.

That the Confederation of Bar lasted over four years without being squelched was the result of a new party to the conflict, the Ottoman Empire. Having watched with dismay as Catherine and her ambassadorial henchmen ran roughshod over the Commonwealth, in October 1768 the Turks declared war on Russia. Russian troops were hastily pulled out of the Commonwealth to confront Catherine's most feared foe.

Other European powers, such as the Catholic powers of France and Austria, sympathized with or even lent military assistance to the confederates. The confederacy brought the Commonwealth to the attention of influential individuals in the West. There it found notable support in the figure of Jean-Jacques Rousseau. Briefed on the state of the Commonwealth by the ideologist of the Bar confederacy, Michał Wielhorski, Rousseau wrote a passionate and powerful defense of Polish freedoms in his 1771 *Considerations on the Government of Poland*.

Yet could the confederacy, with its idiosyncratic ideology so out of step with the rest of Europe, truly win over the West? A decentralized, quintessentially Sarmatian movement, the Confederation of Bar long lacked overall direction and coordination. When finally established in October 1769, its general council hurt more than helped the situation. The council, unwieldy and undisciplined, functioned more as a venue for its vainglorious leaders to try to settle personal scores and formulate improbable scenarios.

Instead of focusing on the main threat, Russia, this motley crew of inveterate and aggrieved Sarmatians was obsessed by a shared hatred of the king and of reform. Their declaration of an interregnum in 1770 backfired: it only pushed Stanisław August back into the arms of Russia, which hardly furthered the cause of the confederation. The confederates' brief capture and inept attempt on the life of the king left absolutist Europe aghast at this treatment of a monarch. Still, Stanisław August refused to head a new counter-confederation under Russian aegis, and the conflict continued to rage.

The "Unscrambling of the Polish Chaos"

The raucous, vainglorious, Sarmatian nation—now riled, vexed, stubborn—could not, would not, be pacified. The solution to the four-year-long conflict turned out to be catastrophic for the Commonwealth, one that would require Russia to give up its plan of dominating its unruly neighbor all by itself.

The conflict of 1768–1772 had already led to nonbelligerent foreign troops encroaching upon the territory of the Commonwealth, the country's other neighbors being concerned about the spread of the Polish contagion, literal as well as figurative (the plague was once again wreaking havoc in the war-torn land). Taking advantage of the confusion, the Habsburg empress Maria Theresa annexed a tiny piece of land—the region of Spiš (Polish: Spisz), high in the Carpathian Mountain borderland. Spiš had once belonged to Hungary, and thus in the view of the Habsburg empress who also wore Hungary's Crown of Saint Stephen, she was merely reclaiming what was rightfully hers.

This opportunistic land grab may well have put ideas in the minds of the Commonwealth's other absolutist neighbors: could not this be the way (borrowing the later phrase of Voltaire) to "unscramble the Polish chaos"? Historians are divided as to who ultimately was to blame for the ensuing partition. The ambitious Friedrich consulted with Catherine of Russia, who was the party who had the most to lose (by sharing any part of the Commonwealth with other European powers). Nevertheless the tsarina seemed poised to partition: in the course of the confederacy (once she had dispatched the Turkish threat), her troops occupied a swath of Lithuania. The Prussian army likewise cordoned off part of the adjacent "infected" Commonwealth territory. News of their discussions and fears that they would act without her prompted Maria Theresa to order her troops further into Lesser Poland. By the time all three parties came around to discussing partition, it was more a matter of the extent of annexation than the fact of annexation that needed working out. In August 1772, the three enlightened absolutists—Catherine, Friedrich, and Maria Theresa—signed an act of partition.

The First Partition and Its Repercussions

In the Act of Partition, the three monarchs confirmed and sanctioned each other's claims to a sizable chunk of Commonwealth territory. Catherine seized the eastern borderlands of the Grand Duchy as well as Polish Livonia; Friedrich moved into the long coveted territories of Royal Prussia, including the prince-bishopric of Warmia, and parts of Greater Poland; and Maria Theresa extended her claim to encompass the entire Carpathian region and Lesser Poland south of the Vistula River. With the stroke of a pen,

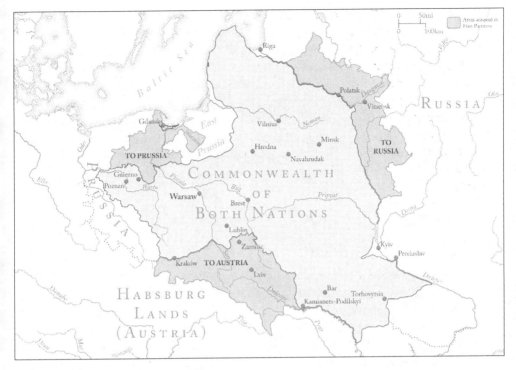

Map 7.1: The First Partition, 1772

the Commonwealth had lost nearly a third of its territory and over a third of its population.

The three partitioned zones were important additions to the empires that bordered on the Commonwealth. Each party to the partition appropriated a piece of land that promised to bring it further economic gain. Russia gained access to the Dvina River up to its Baltic port of Riga as well as control over the network of trading towns to the east of the river. Prussia profited immeasurably from the partition: the inconvenient and long-standing gap between the Hohenzollerns' Prussian and Brandenburg dominions was now bridged. And, despite the fact that the Carpathian Mountains provided more of a barrier to the integration of the new swath of territory by the House of Habsburg, Austria would take consolation in the lucrative salt mines and other natural riches of Lesser Poland.

The partitioning powers' gains were the Commonwealth's losses. Although Friedrich hesitated to annex Gdańsk itself, the river trade henceforth would flow through Prussian-controlled territory. Gdańsk would be a small and vulnerable island in the larger Prussian sea. The former capital of Kraków teetered on the edge of the truncated Commonwealth, while the important cities of Lviv and Zamość were now on the wrong side of the border.

As if the loss of these territories and populations were not bad enough, the enlightened despots expected—nay, demanded—that the Commonwealth officially acquiesce to the partition. A confederated Seym was organized for this express purpose under the leadership of Adam Poniński. The ceremonious charade was disrupted by the dramatic protest of the nobleman Tadeusz Reytan, who famously used his own body to block the entrance to the hall where the ratification was to take place. Delaying tactics only stayed the verdict: the confederated Seym ratified the Act of Partition on September 30, 1773.

Shocked . . . into Action

The confederated Seym was allowed to continue working for another year and a half, after the humiliating ratification, to try to stabilize the country. Like a patient with a brutally amputated leg, the Commonwealth was in shock. The loss of the annexed territories and people was all too palpable. Measures had to be taken swiftly to restore some kind of equilibrium to what was left of the country.

While reactions to the loss were varied, many Commonwealth nobles sought to make the best of the situation. To be sure, some found parts of their extensive landholdings under foreign rule—a situation that in some cases made them at best circumspect, at worse sycophantic vis-à-vis a given partitioning power or powers. Yet others sought pragmatic solutions to the new dilemmas posed by the lack of these peripheral territories.

Some solutions concerned the country's economic situation. The lifeblood of the nobility was its income from agriculture, which traditionally was exported via the Vistula River and Gdańsk. A project of the Lithuanian grand hetman, Michał Kazimierz Ogiński, provided an alternate route, should Prussia block the Commonwealth's access to the Baltic or impose unfavorable terms of trade. Trained as an engineer, Ogiński (who incidentally had led Bar confederates in battle in the Grand Duchy) built a canal fifty-four kilometers long linking the Neman and Dnieper River systems. Completed in 1784, the Ogiński Canal would allow grain to be transported through the Grand Duchy of Lithuania, whose grain output was rising, south to the Black Sea. To be sure, this alternate route had its disadvantages; it made the noble exporters—including Ogiński—dependent on the goodwill of Russia, through which the Dnieper flowed.

Nobles across the Commonwealth worked hard to improve the efficiency of their estates, some even experimenting with transforming the peasants' labor duties into rents. First planted in western regions, the potato entered the Polish diet during this period. More ambitious nobles also dabbled in manufacture, centers of which sprung up across the Commonwealth. All manner of textiles, porcelain, armaments were all part of the king's Enlightened program, which also facilitated the development of stock companies to fund the investments. While the vicinity of royal cities such as the Lithuanian Hrodna witnessed much of this early industrial development, it could also be found in the private towns and estates of wealthy nobles. Industrial development was also facilitated by the explosion of banking in the country's capital, Warsaw.

The initial reforms of the reign of Stanisław August had paved the way for the further development of Warsaw. During this period, Warsaw grew in size and population. Beginning at a meager 30,000 when he assumed power, by 1792 its population topped 115,000. Now Europe's tenth largest city, Warsaw was transformed into a modern metropolis worthy of the name, with not only magnate palaces but also much civic construction. Streets were paved and lit; all manner of shops and businesses, hotels as well as apartments for rent were added as the city expanded in all directions. Industry also made its way to the city, which became a multiethnic cultural center. After 1768 Jews settled in the city, amounting to some 10 percent of the population by 1792. Numerous foreigners such as Germans, Frenchmen, Italians, and others found niches for themselves in the growing capital. Among these immigrants was the painter known as Canaletto, who documented the city's development during his thirteen-year stay in Warsaw; his paintings provided such fine detail that they were used to assist, some two centuries later, with Warsaw's postwar reconstruction.

Much of the construction that characterizes Warsaw to this day dates from the late eighteenth century. The city's newest buildings tended to be designed in the architectural style known as Classicism. Magnates' residences were built or remodeled in the new style, which was also favored by the king, a great lover of the classical period. His projects included the expansion of the royal castle and his elegant summer palace, all of which were completed during his reign. Situated picturesquely on an artificial lake and surrounded by a beautiful park, Poniatowski's charming summer palace came to be known as the "Baths" (Polish: Łazienki). The complex was a harmonious if imaginative mix of styles, with various buildings situated in the surrounding English-style garden taking their inspiration from Chinese, Turkish, and Italian motifs as well as classicism and baroque.

Stanisław August proved a cultured and Enlightened royal patron as well
as monarch. He initiated and supported numerous endeavors that would
benefit the truncated Commonwealth. Among these were the intellectual
and cultural pursuits that would bring his countrymen into contact with
new and stimulating ideas. After the partition, the king resumed his famous
Thursday dinners, begun in 1770. These opportunities for intellectual and
cultural exchange were held at the castle or the Baths. A favorite guest was
the poet Ignacy Krasicki. An original editor of *Monitor* and prince-bishop of Warmia before the partition, he entertained the king and those assembled with his wit as well as his writings, whether critical, comical, or
patriotic. Theater performances of all kinds flourished, especially after the
National Theater was completed; it flourished under the director Wojciech
Bogusławski, whose sense of the political moment was keen. This was also
the period in which the dance and musical genre known as the Polonaise
was popularized.

While some of the Enlightened developments of the age were similar to
what one could find in the West, the post-partition Commonwealth initiated some truly innovative moves. On October 14, 1773—only months after
the ratification of the partition—it established the first education ministry
in Europe. While building on the experience of Konarski and other Enlightened educators, the Commission of National Education was in part enabled
by the abolition of the Jesuit order by the pope earlier that year. Moving into
the void, the Commission established a new and ambitious program of education for the schools of the Commonwealth, which were divided into districts and supplied, where possible, with new textbooks. Reformers sought
to extend education not only to the nobility but also to all the estates and all
the religious denominations of the Commonwealth.

The Commission of National Education did much to prepare its pupils
and students to be good and patriotic citizens. The study of the entirety of
Polish history was introduced, and the schools were to foster the students'
civic development. The king demonstrated his interest in the work of the
commission. He attended the public school pageants that took place in the
capital annually at the end of the school year, which included declamations
by students on subjects such as on the development of freedom in the Polish
lands or the lives of great patriotic Poles of the past.

A favorite Polish son of this period—certainly of Poniatowski—was Jan
III Sobieski. To mark the centenary of the 1683 Relief of Vienna, a marble
sarcophagus was fashioned for Sobieski and placed in Wawel Cathedral in
Kraków. The victor at Vienna was also honored with a bronze monument
in Warsaw. Historical paintings and works of history—including Narusze-

wicz's *History of the Polish Nation*, which in six volumes reached only the year 1386—furthered citizens' knowledge of their past. Might not this increased understanding of the past help the nation to ensure its continuity in the future?

The Great Four-Year Seym

Even without the loss of territory, the reign of the Enlightened Stanisław August would likely have been stormy. The ideas of the Enlightenment spread by the king, segments of the clergy, and the nobility came into contact with traditional perceptions of governance, the economy, and society promoted by the Sarmatian view of the world. With the help of new publications, a growing number of societies as well as salons, a true sense of civil society, the formation of public opinion, began to emerge. The new public sphere transcended the local magnate courts, the provincial spaces of the seymiks, the halls of the Seym, and the election field. It was a heady period, if one that also held new promise. Could not the human gift of reason, so valued by Enlightenment thinkers, be utilized to find a happy synthesis between these new ideas and valuable aspects of the past? The partition of 1772 made it all the more imperative that citizens contemplate changes that would ensure a future for the Commonwealth.

Even if the Commonwealth's citizens were to agree upon measures (something unlikely to happen in a country as differentiated as the Commonwealth), the road would not be easy. Catherine's ambassador, Otto Magnus Stackelberg, served as her "proconsul" in the Commonwealth. Like a modern-day Cerberus, he was determined not to let any reformist initiative pass.

A rare opportunity nonetheless provided itself in 1787, when war broke out once again between Russia and the Ottoman Empire. Preoccupied with the war and wishing to keep the Commonwealth out of the way, Catherine gave her permission for a confederated Seym, which was to be convened in 1788. Members of this crucial Seym nonetheless contrived to keep it going beyond its mandated length. Lasting a full four years, the Seym of 1788–1792 gave the assembled nobles the chance of a lifetime—to legislate with only limited foreign interference. The parliamentarians seized the initiative, in the process elevating this historic Seym to the status of Great, a singular distinction.

A number of nobles were prepared to act. Over the last years, and particularly since the partition of 1772, the ground had been prepared for more radical political ideas by Enlightened individuals. Some of them were men of the cloth, such as Hugo Kołłątaj and Stanisław Staszic, who published pamphlets with titles such as *Warnings for Poland*. Polish thinkers held up the Enlightenment mirror and did not like what it reflected back at them. Vis-à-vis the West, the Commonwealth in their view was not simply out of step with the West, it was backward. In the memorable, if painful, words of Staszic, "Poland is only in the fifteenth century, while all of Europe is finishing the eighteenth century."* Such reformers saw only one way out: to set the country on the road to modernization, utilizing the ideas of the Enlightenment that were prevalent in the West. Still, ideas on how to do this were legion. Some reformers advocated a gentle transformation. Others, such as the men who came to be known as Kołłątaj's Forge, sought more radical solutions. These and other ideas made their way into the extensive pamphlet literature of the period.

Naturally, not all nobles were convinced of the country's backwardness, despite the veritable onslaught of Enlightenment ideas that assailed anyone who came to Warsaw. Within the Seym, parliamentarians represented the full spectrum of views, from reactionary Sarmatian to radical Westernizing. They nonetheless all agreed on one thing: the standing army needed to be better funded and greatly enlarged, to a hundred thousand troops. Other reforms took much longer to achieve, especially as individual nobles spent more time thinking through their own positions rather than simply following the lead of a magnate. Clearly the Enlightenment's championing of human powers of reason was having some effect. The most ambitious task undertaken by the Great Seym was to work on a new constitution for the Commonwealth.

Yet this was not all they worked on. In the year 1789, so bloody and revolutionary in France, the burghers of the Commonwealth also made their wishes known. On the invitation of Warsaw's mayor, Jan Dekert, representatives from 141 royal cities came to Warsaw. All dressed in black, they processed from the town hall to the royal castle to present the Seym with a petition that Hugo Kołłątaj had helped them prepare. Perhaps relieved that the burghers' demands were presented in such a civilized fashion (news of France's revolution traveled fast) as well as convinced of the righteousness of their demands, in April 1791 the Seym passed a law that gave the townspeople of the Commonwealth more rights, including the right to send a number of plenipotentiaries to the Seym. While burghers as a whole were still not admitted to full citizenship, the door was opened for those who came into possession of landed estates, which they would now have the right to pur-

---

*   Cited from Tazbir, *Kultura szlachecka w Polsce: Rozkwit—upadek—relikty* (3rd revised edition) (Warsaw: Wiedza Powszechna, 1983), 152 (author's translation).

chase. Each subsequent Seym would ennoble an additional thirty burghers. These were steps in the right direction. The Commonwealth was moving in the direction of an expanded citizenry, one that would be defined not by estate but by property qualifications.

The Creative Challenge, the Coup, and the Constitution

The reformers had to be careful. While Varsovians had been exposed to the ideas of the Enlightenment, there were still plenty of nobles in the provinces for whom little, if anything, had changed. It became clear to those committed to reform—the king as well as Enlightened parliamentarians— that getting the collective nobility to agree to anything as revolutionary as a new constitution would require not only significant compromises but also a creative touch.

Prepared in secret, a draft of a new constitution for the Commonwealth was ready as early as March 1791—but how to get it past those who were bound to raise objections? Even under conditions of majority voting, this would be a challenge. Nonetheless, the reformers came up with a plan. Advantage was taken of the fact that most parliamentarians went home for the Easter recess. Parliamentarians of reformist bent were secretly instructed to return to Warsaw early.

On May 3, there were a mere 182 parliamentarians in the capital. The reformers knew they had about a hundred votes in their favor. Taking no chances, Stanisław August ordered his nephew Prince Józef Poniatowski to surround the palace with soldiers. Clued in as to what was happening, Warsaw burghers came out into the streets. The tension of the moment was underscored by an announcement to the Seym that the country's freedom was once more under threat. Asked about the prospects of saving the Commonwealth, the king proceeded to pull out a copy of the Constitution, read it to those assembled, and asked that it be enacted by acclamation. That same exhausting day, it was accepted.

This unorthodox procedure—a genuine, if parliamentary coup d'état— succeeded, and the Constitution of 3 May 1791, Europe's first constitution, became the law of the land.

News that the legislation had been passed electrified the city. The king and parliamentarians made their way from the royal castle to Warsaw's Church of Saint John, where those present solemnly swore obedience to the newly acclaimed Constitution. Leaving the church, they were greeted by cries of "Long Live the King! Long Live the Constitution!" The rejoicing crowds carried the Polish king through the streets of the capital.

Those behind Europe's first constitution recognized the significance of this historic attempt at reform, which they hoped would set the country on a new, more orderly path. No longer would Poland stand by its proverbial un-rule; rather, it had reformed itself and subjected itself to a new, more modern set of rules. Above all, the Constitution of 3 May 1791 demonstrated to the world that the country was capable of reforming itself. It deserved the right to independent, sovereign existence.

All this was worth commemorating. In a Declaration of the Assembled Estates, the Seym resolved to hold an annual celebration of the Constitution as well as construct a Temple of Providence in the capital in perpetual remembrance of this deed.

Part III

EUROPE WITHOUT POLAND

CHAPTER 8

Sarmatia Dissolved

"Poland Has Not Yet Perished . . ."?

The Constitution of 3 May 1791 was a portentous achievement. The shock of the partition of 1772 had led various inhabitants of the Common-wealth of Both Nations to conclude that reform was imperative. Long leery of change, the nation nonetheless had to change its priorities. As the reform-er Stanisław Staszic observed and the Constitution's preamble gently echoed, the fate of the nation had to take precedence over the Golden Freedoms; its continued existence should trump any considerations of individual comfort.

With Russia—and the Russian army—preoccupied elsewhere in 1788, the Commonwealth was able to avail itself of an unprecedented window of op-portunity. The Great Seym not only provided stimulating years of dogged discussion of the country's fate. It also enabled reform-minded national activists to flesh out a new framework—the framework that was pushed through that fateful May day in 1791.

The May 3 Constitution as Enlightenment, Polish Style

Presented as an emergency measure, Europe's first constitution was craft-ily constructed. The tone of urgency that sounded in the Seym on May 3 was echoed in the preamble of the document, which declared that the new constitution was the only way to provide "for the general welfare, for the establishment [*ugruntowania*] of liberty, [and] for the salvation of our Fa-therland and its borders." Comprised of eleven articles, the Constitution first enumerated the country's social framework, before elucidating the new shape of the government. In the process, centuries of native tradition were laced with innovations redolent of the Enlightenment, with elements based on the French, English, and American examples.

The innovations were seen above all in the altered nature of the government. While the will of the people was declared to provide all authority, there was no talk of a classical republic, as there had been in the sixteenth century. Rather, the focus was on the modern three powers of government: the legislative, judicial, and executive. (In this it was not unlike the U.S. Constitution, promulgated only several years earlier.) Set to meet every other year, the traditional bicameral Seym remained the locus of legislative authority. However, it would rely upon majority vote: the liberum veto and confederations were outlawed.

No less radical from the Sarmatian perspective were changes concerning the "supreme executive authority," that of the king. There would be no more royal elections viritim. The monarchy was to become hereditary, not in the (non-existent) family of Stanisław August Poniatowski but in the Saxon Wettin dynasty. Furthermore, the king would have a small royal council (the so-called guardians of the laws)—essentially a cabinet of ministers—to aid with the execution of the laws as well as countersign the king's actions. The competency of individual members of the royal council would extend to education, the police (here understood more as a ministry of the interior), war (defense), and the treasury; and each of these realms would have its own commission in the Seym. The new form of government was, in essence, a modern constitutional monarchy.

Redolent of the Enlightenment from which it derived its inspiration, its innovations were nonetheless tempered by tradition. With memory of the Confederation of Bar doubtless in their minds, the reformers chose to begin the Constitution proper by affirming and, indeed, enshrining the leading role of Roman Catholicism in the country. While Roman Catholics were forbidden from changing their faith, non-Catholics were nonetheless to be allowed full religious rights. Nor did the strengthening of the executive give the monarch license to absolutism. In a procedure reminiscent of bygone centuries, each new monarch would be required to swear an oath to God and nation to uphold the pacta conventa. Provisions were made for the proper preparation of subsequent monarchs; an entire article of the Constitution was devoted to the education of the sons of kings—the idea being that they would be brought up not only as devout Catholics but also to love "virtue, the Fatherland, liberty and the state constitution."

Toward a Modern Poland—and a Modern Polish Nation

With a nod to the Commonwealth's peculiarities, the Constitution clearly moved the country in a more modern direction. This was visible in the subtler changes that concerned the country's social structure. Articles 2 through 4 covered the three fundamental estates of the country: nobles, burghers, and peasants. Each was tweaked, if some more gently than others. The peasants fell into that last category. While acknowledged as supplying the "most plentiful source of the country's wealth" and comprising the most numerous estate, the peasants were merely placed under the protection of the law and the state government. Thoughts of peasants' gaining more rights were left for the future, although the Constitution made it clear that anyone who settled in the country henceforth would be considered a free man.

The inhabitants of the country's royal towns were also dealt with briefly. Their fate had already been described by the Law on the Royal Cities, passed in late April 1791, which was to be considered part and parcel of the May 3 reforms. In accordance with this law, not only were cities to have representation in the Seym. The chasm separating burghers from nobles was being bridged in various ways. Nobles were allowed to become municipal citizens, and burghers were permitted to acquire land. Burghers who owned an entire village or town and paid the proper tax could be ennobled automatically.

The idea that taxpayers should comprise the country's citizenry was yet another Enlightenment innovation visible in the May 3 Constitution. The authors of the Constitution wished to transform the noble republic into a "nation of property owners." No longer was a noble patent sufficient to be part of the political community. This point is delicately reflected in the title of the article on the nobility, "The Landed Nobility." Yet the social revolution had been initiated by another recent piece of legislation, the Law on Seymiks of March 24, 1791, to which the Constitution also refers. In accordance with that recently passed law, only persons eighteen years of age and older who owned land on which a state tax was paid were qualified to participate in the seymiks. Thus, while nobles were still declared equal, only the propertied—seen as having a vested interest in the running of the country—were to be counted among the active citizenry (this concept, incidentally, came from Rousseau).

Another subtle but important change concerned the nature of the country. Barring the listing of the long historic title of the king, who together with the nation brought forth the Constitution, there was no mention of a federal arrangement. Distinctions between the Crown of Poland and the

Grand Duchy of Lithuania are nowhere to be found. The country is now properly labeled Poland—a modern, Enlightened Poland.

This transformation was in keeping with the views of reformers such as Hugo Kołłątaj, who saw the Polonization of the entire population as something desirable. Kołłątaj had defined the nation as "millions of people speaking Polish." It was thought that such cultural homogeneity could embrace even the country's Jews, who might assimilate to Polishness in all matters but religion. (To be sure, the position of Jews was not satisfactorily addressed either in the Constitution or the other legislation of the Great Seym.) In other words, the definition of who was Polish was no longer restricted to the nobles but was expanding to embrace the entirety of the population. A radical change, thus, transformed the Sarmatian Commonwealth into something approximating a modern Poland: truncated, under threat, yet espousing a more modern sense of nationhood.

For those who were dissatisfied with the new Constitution, the document also had an answer. This culmination of the Four-Year Seym's reforms was not seen as inherently perfect. Rather, it was acknowledged to be a work-in-progress, something that ought to undergo periodic amendment and modification. To this end, the farsighted framers of the Constitution made provisions for a constitutional Seym to be summoned every twenty-five years to review it.

Reactions to Reform

The Constitution of May 3, 1791, has gone down in history as one of the most crucial and most significant documents in Polish history. It demonstrated that the country was neither ungovernable nor unreformable, thus giving the lie to any thought that the partitions were justified. No longer an exotic outlier, the new Poland was in the European avant-garde. Witness the stunned response of a contemporary Prussian minister, who assessed this Polish achievement and considered its implications for his own country: "The Poles have dealt a fatal blow to the Prussian monarchy, by bringing in a hereditary throne and a constitution better than England's ... Sooner or later, Poland will take West and perhaps even East Prussia from us. How can we, exposed from Teschen to Memel, defend ourselves against a populous and well-ruled nation?"* The May 3 Constitution—Europe's first—seemed

---

* The words of Ewald Fridrich von Hertzberg, chief minister of Friedrich Wilhelm II, from Jerzy Lukowski, *Liberty's Folly: The Polish-Lithuanian Commonwealth in the Eighteenth Century, 1697–1795* (London: Routledge, 1991), 253.

to promise a new and impressive dawn for the country, truncated yet transformed. While one can quibble with the reforms, their extent, not to mention the methods used, it is clear that the Constitution represented a major step in the direction of bringing the Polish polity into conformance with the ideas percolating about the enlightened West.

The Polish Constitution nonetheless alarmed as well as impressed. The quotation above suggests that at least some Prussian officials felt threatened by a reforming Poland. Armed with an enlightened, modern constitution, the new Poland could conceivably undo the strides made by earlier generations of Prussian Hohenzollerns, who had built up their dominions from their East Prussian base, the old lands of the Teutonic Knights with their far eastern edge at Memel (Lithuanian: Klaipėda), all the way to Silesia, with Teschen (Polish: Cieszyn) being the one part of Silesia still in Habsburg hands. Of the three partitioning states, Prussia clearly had the most to lose. Nonetheless, both Prussia and Russia had previously sought to "protect" the liberties that the reformist wing under Stanisław August sought to jettison.

Nor were the Polish reformers and their Constitution assured of support back home, either from the magnate-led Sarmatian opposition or from the noble masses. Could one expect these unruly Sarmatians to relinquish, with good grace, the cherished freedoms that were the essence of their noble identity: the right to elect their monarch, the right to have the last word on legislation, and the right to express their dissatisfaction in public fashion (vocally or militarily) and still be considered patriots? Furthermore, the measure had been pushed through during the absence of many of them from the capital.

The popularization of the Constitution proceeded apace. Not only reform-minded nobles but also enlightened clergymen, burghers, and Jews rallied to its support. Slogans of national unity—of the king with the nation, of nobles with the townspeople—became part of a new patriotic mood. The wearing of noble Sarmatian garb (as opposed to Western dress) became fashionable among supporters of the Constitution, who styled themselves defenders of the country. In this way, the reformers placed themselves squarely within Polish tradition. The effect was tangible: practically all the seymiks held in February 1792 swore to uphold the Constitution—thus legalizing the coup d'état—with some even sending delegations to the king to thank him for bringing it about. This somewhat surprising outcome—could it be that easy to win over the noble masses?—encouraged some reformers to make plans for further economic and social change.

Targowica Treachery

Yet gaining the support of the seymiks was but one—and hardly the most daunting—hurdle facing the reformers and their constitution. Danger was brewing. A handful of Poland's wealthy and connected magnates reacted to the Constitution with indignation. Ksawery Branicki, Szymon Kossakowski, Szczęsny Potocki, and Seweryn Rzewuski proved a colorful—if confused—quadrumvirate. All four magnates were influential and wealthy; they had little love for their monarch, who nonetheless had elevated them to positions of authority. Szymon Kossakowski had gone from fighting the Russians as a Bar confederate to joining the Russian army in 1790. Hetman Ksawery Branicki's Russian sympathies may have evolved as the result of his marriage, in 1781, to Alexandra Engelhardt. His wife was not only known as the niece of the Russian field marshal Grigorii Potemkin, Catherine II's close associate and lover; she very likely was the natural daughter of the tsarina.

The most literary of the lot, Hetman Seweryn Rzewuski had gained fame in republican quarters from his five-year exile in Kaluga (he had accompanied his father in 1767) as well as from his writings. This makes his about-face—from Russian prisoner to Russian supporter—less understandable, perhaps, but for the fact that he had been in Paris when the Bastille was stormed. Then again, his pleas for assistance in Vienna (his estates at Olesko and Pidhirtsi had come under Habsburg rule in 1772) had gained little traction, leaving Rzewuski little option but to turn elsewhere for help.

Rzewuski joined forces with another magnate who also had some estates under Austrian rule, Szczęsny Potocki. The not-very-bright ringleader of the quadrumvirate, Potocki could be considered a tragic figure—were the fate of those he professed to love not infinitely worse than his own. Son and heir of the enormously wealthy Franciszek Salezy Potocki, palatine of Kyiv, even the child's given name was redolent of good fortune (Szczęsny is the Polish rendition of Felix), which, from the vantage point of the historian, seems terribly ironic.

Szczęsny was taught early on that wealth and status were everything, and that he should settle for nothing but the best. As a nineteen-year-old, he incautiously fell in love with, impregnated, then married in secret a young noblewoman, Gertruda Komorowska. Although boasting an ancient noble lineage, the parents of the beautiful Gertruda were only of middling means. Having learned of the mésalliance, Szczęsny's parents contracted to have their pregnant daughter-in-law abducted on a winter's night; suffocated in the sleigh by her captors, Gertruda's lifeless body was cast into a hole in the ice-covered river, not to be found until the spring. Her erstwhile husband was still forced to finalize divorce proceedings.

The young Potocki quickly learned the value of being ultra-rich and connected. In the 1780s, his casual gift to the state of a four-hundred-strong infantry regiment plus cannon—a trivial expense for him—resulted in Szczęsny being acclaimed as a true patriot. His ego on overdrive, this scion of the Potockis came to entertain dreams of someday becoming king—or at least of gaining control over some discrete piece of the country. Those dreams were cruelly dashed by Poland's transformation into a hereditary constitutional monarchy with the promulgation of the new constitution in 1791.

Seeing their cherished republican ideals trammeled, and even more resenting what they saw as a royalist coup, the four opposition magnates made the rounds of the neighboring countries seeking help in the restoration of the status quo ante. Poland's neighbors were themselves preoccupied with other matters. Much had changed in both Prussia and Austria since the first partition. In Prussia, the devoutly Protestant but otherwise unremarkable Friedrich Wilhelm II had succeeded his accomplished yet childless uncle, Friedrich the Great. As the new king entered into an official alliance with Poland, he was not one likely to come to the aid of the disgruntled republicans. The Habsburg lands had seen even more flux at the top. First under the control of Maria Theresa's able son Joseph II, the quintessential Enlightened monarch, after his death in 1790 Austria was ruled in quick succession by Leopold II and Francis II. These monarchs were more concerned with the French Revolution to their west than anything that was happening in Poland.

This left the Tsarina Catherine, the only surviving partitioner, as the monarch of the moment. Once the peace treaty with the Ottoman Empire was signed in January 1792, Russia was free to interfere again in Polish affairs. The opposition magnates gave her a fine pretense for this. Undeterred by still being in the employ of the Polish state, both Rzewuski and Potocki corresponded and met treasonously with her and her advisers (beginning with Potemkin), first in Jassy (today's Iasi), then in Saint Petersburg. The plan that emerged was a typical Polish one: the magnates would respond to what they saw as the king's reneging on his pacta conventa with a traditional confederation—the type that had been outlawed by the Constitution. This would go down in history as the Targowica Confederation, after the small Podolian border town (today's Torhovytsia) where the confederation would be proclaimed. That the Targowica Confederation's manifesto had been forged—and preapproved—in Saint Petersburg a month earlier only demonstrates the extent to which this spontaneous outbreak of opposition to the constitution was actually stage-managed by Catherine and the extent to which such opposition was under her thumb.

In the interim, the elevation of the May 3 Constitution as national symbol continued in Warsaw and elsewhere. Varsovians commemorated the one-year anniversary of the document's signing on May 3, 1792, with Poles coming even from outside of the truncated state to take part in the festivities. Among other things, King Stanisław August Poniatowski laid the cornerstone for a commemorative Temple of Providence. Nonetheless, rumors of the forming opposition, the possibility of foreign intervention, even an attempt on the life of the king disquieted those who hoped this deed of 1791 would be a turning point for Poland.

Instead of a turning point, 1791 turned into a point of no return. Some fault the reformers and/or the king for pushing things too far (or not far enough) and making it easy for opposition to the Constitution to coalesce. Nonetheless, it is hard to believe that Poland's powerful neighbor to the east truly needed the invitation of the Targowica confederates to interfere, once again, in Polish affairs. Catherine hardly needed the Targowica confederates to legitimate Russia's continued "protection" of traditional Polish rights. To be sure, the confederates' eagerness to undo both the reforms and the king allowed her to justify her interference to the world. Yet the West was preoccupied with France's recent declaration of war on Austria. The confederation in Torhovytsia/Targowica was officially proclaimed on May 14, 1792. Two days later, Catherine sent in close to a hundred thousand Russian troops to defend the "true" Commonwealth.

From there, the situation deteriorated in depressing fashion. The Prussian king refused to honor the terms of the alliance with Poland and would not come to the country's defense. Although built up in recent years, the Polish army was still only three-quarters of the size of this Russian force—and this only on paper. Despite some Polish victories, with military commanders Prince Józef Poniatowski and Tadeusz Kościuszko distinguishing themselves, the army was still no match for the Russian forces, whose military experience was fresh from the recent war with the Ottomans. There seemed no way for the Poles to win, especially as the confederates were able to sway some republican-minded nobles. Catherine demanded that Stanisław August join the confederation. Even the king's most reform-minded ministers advised him to do so, in the hopes that Poland's territorial integrity could be preserved. Yet this move was insufficiently explained to the king's supporters at home and disillusioned many. Worse, it led his best military commanders to tender their resignation. The king found himself isolated.

Nor was he, or anyone else, able to save the country from further partition. At precisely this time, the French Revolution was raging to the west. This led the alarmed Friedrich Wilhelm II of Prussia to push for territorial gains in the east. Despite her assurances to Stanisław August that the country's borders would be respected, Catherine, too, saw the advantage of seizing more territory: she had many military officers who had distinguished themselves in battle in the Ottoman Empire and Poland, and they needed to be rewarded with land grants. The two monarchs agreed to a second partition on January 23, 1793. Poor Stanisław August was not even informed of this decision until April of that year.

The Targowica confederates—the four magnates who had originally pressed Catherine for assistance—were themselves caught off guard by the second partition. They had hoped for greater control and influence, not for further truncation. Together with the Russians, they had been intimidating Poles into joining the confederation and had taken pleasure in seeing the king forced to submit to them. Shamelessly used by Catherine, they finally discovered that they had no influence over her doings in their country. The names of these four delusional, misguided, megalomaniacal, reactionary magnates would go down in infamy. The very word "Targowica" has come to be a Polish synonym for treason.

In an ironic twist, by the outbreak of the actual confederation, the Targowica ringleader, Szczęsny Potocki, had lost interest in Polish political developments. At Jassy he had fallen head over heels in love with Potemkin's mistress, Zofia. A Greek courtesan, Mrs. Józef Witt was universally acknowledged as the most beautiful woman in Europe of that age. Szczęsny took advantage of the death of Potemkin to make his move. This time, there was no one to stop Szczęsny from making the beautiful Greek his mistress or even marrying beneath his station. He spent millions of his vast wealth on an enormous landscape park, Zofiówka (named in his wife's honor), at his estate in Uman (which came under Russian rule with the second partition). In Szczęsny's case, treasonous activity (the trip to Jassy) seemed to have had its benefits. Other Targowica confederates would not fare nearly so well.

The Targowica Confederation and the subsequent second partition brought new humiliation to Poland as well as the hapless confederates. As with the first partition, Catherine demanded that the Seym give its stamp of approval. Summoned in June to Hrodna, which had been a periodic site of Seyms, the Seym was increasingly dominated by a new opportunistic layer of confederates at the helm. The parliamentarians nonetheless resisted for weeks—this despite arrests and intimidation, as well as their silence at one particularly long session being taken as a sign of approval. In the fall of 1793, the ratification of the second partition was completed.

The results of the second partition of Poland were not pretty. It was no consolation that, this time, there were only two countries involved, Prussia and Russia (Austria, preoccupied with France, was excluded from the agreement).

Both made off handsomely. Friedrich Wilhelm II of Prussia gained a million new subjects as well as control over cities as economically important as Toruń and Gdańsk, in this way turning his dominions—in his words—into a "coherent monarchy."* The inveterate Protestant monarch also came to control places of symbolic importance: the religious center of Częstochowa as well as the cradle of the Polish state, Greater Poland. Russia's portion of the former Poland was even larger: Tsarina Catherine boasted three million new subjects and the hugely profitable black earth farmlands of Podolia and the right bank of the Dnieper.

What remained of the rump Polish state made little sense: physically, economically, or psychologically. Nor would its government look anything like the Targowica confederates had imagined, let alone the reformists behind the May 3 Constitution. A Permanent Council would rule the humiliated country, with the king essentially nothing more than a figurehead. Reformers faced persecution, causing many Poles to leave the country. How much longer would it take for the remaining large and historic cities—Kraków, Warsaw, and Vilnius—to be swallowed up?

The American-Style National Rising

The last third of the eighteenth century had initiated an increasingly painful spiral of action and reaction. Catherine's trampling of Polish religious sensibilities led to the Confederation of Bar, which in turn resulted in the first partition. That shock propelled Poles to contemplate the series of reforms that culminated in the Constitution of May 3, 1791. The reaction to this was the Targowica Confederation and the second partition. Despite the Russian terror and intimidation, however, not all Poles were resigned to this fate.

One of these Poles was Tadeusz Kościuszko. Hailing from the region of Polesie (in the vicinity of today's Belarus), Kościuszko was one of the poor but deserving young noblemen who received an education from the reform-minded Piarists, as well as at the Knights' School in Warsaw. After a brief period spent in France (where he studied further) and elsewhere in western Europe, Kościuszko headed across the Atlantic in 1776. The Pole offered his services to George Washington and the Continental Congress. Kościuszko's arrival was timely, and his services were both needed and appreciated by the Americans fighting for their independence. The Pole was given a com-

---

* Cited in Jerzy Lukowski, *The Partitions of Poland: 1772, 1793, 1795* (London: Addison Wesley Longman, 1999), 154.

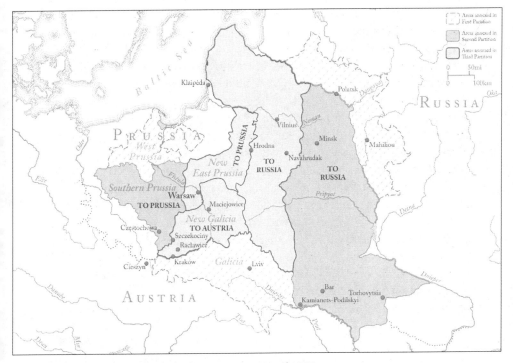

Map 8.1: The Second and Third Partitions, 1793 and 1795

mission and put to great use his skill as both a military engineer and a field commander. Among other things, Kościuszko fortified and defended places such as Philadelphia, Saratoga, and West Point, thus enabling these locations to withstand British attack. For his contributions to the American victory, the Polish nobleman was given United States citizenship and was promoted to the rank of brigadier general in the U.S. Army before returning home in 1784.

Having secured a position in the Polish army as of 1789, he fought on the side of King Stanisław in August 1792. However, upon learning the summer of 1793 that the king had acceded to the Targowica Confederation, General Kościuszko resigned his commission and left the country. France awarded him honorary citizenship. While in emigration, he was prevailed upon to return to rump Poland to lead a national insurrection.

With his eye-opening experience in America as well as Poland, Kościuszko was the right person for the job. He was convinced that the Poles had to fight a new type of war, one in which the entire citizenry rose to defend their country. In other words, he sought to mobilize the entire population of Poland—all estates, all regions. The challenge of getting burghers and peasants as well as nobles to join the fight did not escape Kościuszko. He admitted himself, "we must awaken love of our country among those who hitherto have not even known that they have a country."* Kościuszko, thus, was a man with a mission. Although given dictatorial powers to lead the national rising, the general was not one to abuse them. This is seen from the oath he gave in Kraków on March 24, 1794, when he took control of the rising that would bear his name. Kościuszko swore he would use the dictatorial powers invested in him "only for the defense of the integrity of the frontiers, the gaining of sovereignty for the nation, and the establishment of universal freedom."† He truly was an anti-magnate.

The all-powerful military commander set about gaining support from all sectors of society. An important source of manpower had to be the numerous peasantry. While in Kraków, Kościuszko conscripted local peasants, who—given their lack of other weapons—turned their scythes into bayonets and joined the battle for Polish freedom. (A lack of arms and ammunition was a big problem for the insurrectionists.) Fighting alongside what remained of the Polish army, such peasants—it was hoped—would be the mainstay of Kościuszko's insurrectionary forces. Having over the course of several weeks assembled an army of some four thousand regular troops and two thousand peasant scythe men, Kościuszko set north to engage the Russians in battle.

The two forces met near the village of Racławice on April 4. The Russian army was in for a surprise. The first battle of the Kościuszko Insurrection would look like nothing the Russians had ever fought. The Polish military commander employed tactics inspired by his experience in America. While the regular troops engaged the Russians, the fearless peasant scythe men raced out from behind them and toward the Russian cannons. They captured a dozen cannon and caused disarray and dismay among the Russians, who hastily retreated—if not before taking heavy losses. The Russians also left behind much-needed ammunition and arms.

Kościuszko's secret weapon—the Polish peasant—proved decisive at the battle of Racławice. After the battle, the military commander famously ennobled several peasant scythe men, the most notable of whom was Bartosz Głowacki, for their bravery. Kościuszko also donned the traditional peasant cloak as a sign of recognition of what this new and vital part of the nation had achieved. Still, for numerous reasons this did not result in an influx of peasant scythe men. The following month, Kościuszko would issue a proc-

---

*   Quoted from Emanuel Halicz, *Polish National Liberation Struggles and the Genesis of the Modern Nation: Collected Papers*, trans. Roger A. Clarke (Odense, Denmark: Odense University Press, 1982), 22.

†   Translation loosely based on Davies, *God's Playground*, 1:539.

Figure 8.1: Fragment of the Racławice Panorama, by Jan Styka and Wojciech Kossak (1894). This fragment shows Kościuszko summoning his peasant scythe men (on the right) to battle. The noble leader of the insurrection is anachronistically depicted wearing the peasant *sukmana*, which he did not put on until after the battle had been won. On view in Lviv before World War II, the Racławice Panorama finally went back on display—thanks to Solidarity activists—in 1985, this time in Wrocław (whence much of Lviv relocated).

lamation at Połaniec that gave the peasants personal freedom and reduced their labor dues for the duration of the insurrection. Like the potent image of peasant scythe men defending their country, the picturesque symbolism of a nobleman in peasant garb was but a first step in breaking down the barriers that had separated the two estates.

Kościuszko embraced the peasant out of conviction, not out of convenience. This, after all, was the man who had freed his own peasants upon his return to Poland and later would bequeath the property and money he had in the United States to free as many American slaves as was possible, charging his friend Thomas Jefferson to execute this, his last will and testament. Not for nothing did Jefferson famously call Kościuszko "the purest son of liberty."

In the interim, news of the victory at Racławice quickly electrified the rest of Poland. The insurrection gained momentum, as other segments of society took an active part in the country's defense. Tens of thousands of Warsaw townspeople and artisans, led by the shoemaker Jan Kiliński, initiated an uprising in that city, on April 17, 1794. Within the space of two days, the Russians—tremendously outnumbered—had all fled. In Warsaw, the rising was radicalized by the shoemakers and the butchers, the last in literal fashion. Indeed, events in the Polish capital in some ways echoed the type of bloody violence found in revolutionary France. Not only was there no mercy shown the Russian forces, but enemies of the insurrection—Russians, traitors (including a host of second-tier Targowica leaders)—were summarily murdered or hanged.

The rising of Warsaw burghers under Kiliński hardly reflected the full extent of the insurrection that spring and summer, either socially or geographically. Noteworthy was the role played by a Jewish regiment of light cavalry, created on the initiative of Berek Joselewicz. The insurrection spread to other regions as well, most notably to Vilnius, where Colonel Jakub Jasiński seized power. Also a revolutionary poet of note, that same year Jasiński called upon his compatriots to unite and rally to the nation's defense. Not unlike their bloodied counterparts in Warsaw, radicals in the Lithuanian capital sentenced to death and hanged the Targowica confederate Szymon Kossakowski. His brother Józef, bishop of Livonia, was met by a similar fate, albeit in Warsaw. Those Targowica ringleaders who could not be located (some had the presence of mind to stay out of rump Poland) were hanged in effigy.

Yet the insurrection, although spreading in the Polish lands (even those under foreign rule), was to face a growing foe. The French threat in the west worked against the insurrection. Fearing territorial losses at France's expense, both Prussia and Austria threw in their lot with Russia, hoping to recoup lands in the east. Also preoccupied with France, the rest of the West was unable or unwilling to come to the Poles' aid.

A combined Prussian-Russian attack, some forty-thousand strong, on Kościuszko's army at Szczekociny at the beginning of June proved costly for the insurrectionists: among the casualties were several Polish generals as well as the ennobled peasant, Bartosz Głowacki. The Prussians and Russians proceeded to besiege Warsaw—unsuccessfully. Under Kościuszko's leadership, Warsaw held out until news of insurrection in Prussian-controlled Greater Poland forced the Prussians to withdraw at the beginning of September.

Yet Poland's enemies could dig deep. A second Russian army, led by the fearsome Alexander Suvorov, ran over Vilnius in August and then headed toward Warsaw. Kościuszko desperately sought to keep the two Russian armies from uniting. The ensuing battle on October 10 was anything but even: Russian forces at Maciejowice outnumbered Kościuszko's two to one. In the course of the battle, Kościuszko was wounded and taken prisoner.

Although devastating, the removal of the insurrection's leader did not put an end to either the insurrection or the bloodshed. Suvorov continued his determined march from Vilnius to Warsaw. He decided to bring Warsaw to its knees in a most effective—if terrible—manner. On November 4, his troops attacked the outlying district of Praga, on the right bank of the Vistula. The Russian army proceeded not only to dispense with what there was in the way of defense; its soldiers set about killing the civilian population. Those Russian troops that had suffered significant losses at the hands of Varsovians only months earlier happily took their revenge. Some twenty thousand people were reportedly massacred that day, including much of the Jewish regiment formed by Berek Joselewicz. The sight and sounds of the massacre from across the river had the desired effect on the Varsovians; not wishing to suffer a similar fate, Warsaw surrendered. Within two weeks, the insurrection was over.

The death knell of the Kościuszko Insurrection of 1794 was also the death knell of Poland. A third and final partition was all but inevitable. Given the fact of foreign occupation, the armies of all three of Poland's neighbors staking their claims, it was merely a question of time before the deed was done. And it did take time. The three rapacious partitioning powers of Russia, Prussia, and Austria spent months quarreling about where to draw their new common border. (Prussia actually contemplated fighting the other two for a bigger portion of the spoils.)

Russia did not wait to see whether it would gain control over Warsaw (it did not). Once Suvorov's forces occupied the Polish capital, the takeover began—at least, the extractive side of it. Both the royal archive and the extensive Załuski Library were spirited off to Saint Petersburg, the collection of the latter becoming the basis for a new imperial public library in the Russian capital. While the occupying forces engaged in the traditional looting (there was still much in the way of European art), this time much of what had been gold, silver, or bronze in Warsaw had already been sacrificed to finance the failed insurrection. Nor was the population spared. Those Poles who had found themselves under foreign rule as a result of the first two partitions yet had joined the Kościuszko Insurrection had their estates confiscated. Some twelve thousand Polish officials and patriots, including the Warsaw shoemaker Kiliński, were exiled into the depths of Russia, while others languished in Prussian and Austrian prisons.

The border separating the three partitioning powers—and thus obliter-
ating the Polish state—was finally set in a final act of partition, signed on
October 24, 1795. Also eager to profit from a city they would not themselves
come to possess, the Prussian occupation forces in Kraków removed some
170 carts' worth of loot from Wawel Castle, including the Polish royal insignia, before they relinquished the city to the Austrians.

A month after the partitions were finalized, King Stanisław August Poniatowski, who had been forced to leave Warsaw for Hrodna at the beginning of
1795, was forced to abdicate. Poniatowski knew full well that abdication was
not a legal option for the Polish king: only the Seym could release him from
his duties. His ultimate acquiescence to Russian demands demonstrates
the degree to which the partitioning powers truly ran roughshod over both
Poniatowski and Poland—an ironic demonstration of how an enlightened,
reform-minded king and polity fared at the hands of their "enlightened"
neighbors. Hoping to be able to travel to the West to finish his days, the last
Polish king would instead be "invited" to Saint Petersburg. He died there,
suddenly, in February 1798.

The invitation to Stanisław August to relocate to the Russian capital came
from Tsar Paul of Russia. Only days before, unknown to the king, his former
lover Tsarina Catherine the Great had died. Not that her death had any impact on the final outcome for Poland: the third and final act of partition was
arranged as she wished.

Poland was wiped off the map of Europe.

The partitioning powers furthermore resolved to keep the country from
ever reappearing. Meeting at the beginning of 1797 to take care of some
remaining matters, the rulers of the three partitioning powers likewise
signed a secret protocol, in which they concluded: "In view of the necessity
to abolish everything which could revive the memory of the existence of the
Kingdom of Poland, now that the annulment of this body politic has been
effected . . . the high contracting parties are agreed and undertake never to
include in their titles . . . the name or designation of the Kingdom of Poland,
which shall remain suppressed as from the present and forever."*

After the Partitions: Finis Poloniae?

As odd as it may seem, the end of the Polish state did not mean the end
of Poland—and certainly not the end of Polish history. Some contemporaries clearly thought it might. Even Kościuszko is reported to have given

* Ibid., 542.

in to despair: lying wounded on the battlefield of Maciejowice, the general who fought so valiantly on two continents apocryphally exclaimed: *Finis Poloniae*—the end of Poland.

The valiant Pole (if he did say these words, which is debatable—indeed it has been considered the work of Prussian propaganda) was in part correct. Kościuszko understood that the end of "Poland" was nigh. With the defeat of his insurrection, further—complete—partition was inevitable. Poland as a territorially integral and independent sovereign state was coming to an end.

That there is more to this story is suggested by the secret protocol of 1797, which was written three years after the Kościuszko Insurrection, two years after the disappearance of Poland from the map of Europe. If this were really the "end of Poland," why should the three partitioning powers be so intent on suppressing even mention of the former country's name? Why should they feel compelled to do so—furthermore, to compel each other to agree to this, in secret? Kingdoms, after all, have been known to vanish from the map. Recall also that, by 1797, these three powers had been in possession of parts of the former Commonwealth—the lands taken in the first partition—for a quarter century already.

Each of the partitioning powers had taken pains to justify its acquisitions. Prussia renamed the lands it seized as if they were integral parts of a Prussian state. The lands of the first Polish partition—Royal Prussia—were restyled West Prussia; the former Ducal Prussia of the Hohenzollerns became East Prussia. Located to its south, the lands of the second partition were labeled, logically, Southern Prussia. The Hohenzollerns' last slice of Poland, the one including Warsaw, was also given a geographic moniker. Lying in a curving arc to the south, east, and north of the original Brandenburg (East) Prussia, it received the not very original but essentially correct name (geographically) of New East Prussia. In sum, the Prussian approach to the 141,400 square kilometers of territory it gained at Poland's expense was an eliding and integrative one—one that would play down regional diversity in favor of Prussian standardization.

Whereas Prussia expanded by multiplying "Prussias," the Habsburgs took a different approach to justifying their new possessions. The House of Habsburg ruled over a motley collection of kingdoms and principalities acquired over the centuries, often by marriage. The Habsburg empress Maria Theresa claimed to be "revindicating" the 81,900 square kilometers of territory acquired in the first partition. The basis for her claim came via the Hungarian crown: it had ruled over the Ruthenian kingdoms of Halych and Volodymyr for a brief moment in the fourteenth century. Subsequent rulers of Hungary never bothered to remove their claim from their title, which meant the Habsburgs retained it as well. The territorial amalgam acquired by Maria Theresa in 1772 was thus christened the Kingdom of Galicia and Lodomeria, these being the Latin forms of the historic name of the Ruthenian territory. Like a Procrustean bed, the title fit the lands of the first partition only with some stretching and contracting: parts of the new "Galicia" had never been subject to Hungarian claims, while the real "Lodomeria" eventually ended up under Russian, not Austrian, rule. The additional lands acquired in the third and final partition (Austria's second portion of Polish territory—an additional forty-seven thousand square kilometers) were designated, even more improbably, as Western or New Galicia—neither term reflecting much in the way of imagination. Such began the invention of Galicia by the Habsburgs.

Only Russia seemed uninterested in contriving new labels for its hefty territorial acquisitions. The Russian appetite for Polish territory far surpassed that of the other parties. In the three partitions, Russia bit off chunks of first 93,000, then 250,200, and 120,000 square kilometers. The sum total (of 463,200 square kilometers) is just about the size of the state of California plus one-sixth of Oregon. Russia's portion of the second partition alone—larger than today's United Kingdom—dwarfed the entire territory gained by either Prussia or Austria. Tsarina Catherine not only claimed she had "recovered what had been torn away"; she had a medal struck in honor of her achievement after the second partition. Clearly Catherine took credit for the completion of Russia's "gathering" of the Rus' lands begun centuries earlier. Yet she also annexed parts of the Grand Duchy of Lithuania and Livonia that had never been part of the Russian patrimony, however defined.

Such were the imperfect, if accepted, justifications for the incorporation of the Polish territories—the physical state that had been the Commonwealth of Both Nations prior to the Constitution of May 3. This truly had disappeared from the map. Henceforth the lands and their wealth were to be physically exploited by the expanding empires. Prussia would profit from its now complete control over the Vistula River grain trade. The Habsburgs quickly sought to investigate the extent of Galicia's natural riches, which in addition to fertile farmland and extensive forests included its salt mines and mineral deposits (the most lucrative and strategic of which—certainly for a spell—would be petroleum, soon to be discovered and exploited). The black earth lands seized by Russia provided Catherine with plenty of estates with which to reward her generals and diplomats.

Yet these territories, although in some ways terra incognita for the three empires, were scarcely uninhabited. They contained populations of varying density as well as ethnic and denominational makeup—populations that had not, all of a sudden, moved. Rather, it was the borders that had moved. The population, thus, was left disoriented, thrust into a new and very different state from the one they and their ancestors had known. Indeed, it was not the natural wealth of each newly acquired territory that would prove problematic for the three partitioning powers but, rather, the newly acquired population. Furthermore, the population was hardly a tabula rasa—definitely no blank slate on which Russia, Prussia, and Austria could write.

National Memory and National Existence

Is it not precisely this that bothered the partitioning powers in 1797? Russia, Prussia, and Austria resolved to "abolish everything which could revive the memory of the existence of the Kingdom of Poland." The fact they felt compelled to take a united front in this matter (if in secret) suggested that something still existed and, as a consequence, had to be suppressed.

Perhaps they had read their Rousseau. Prompted to write by Bar confederates, the famous philosophe from Geneva had been persuaded to write his *Considerations of the Government of Poland*. It was written in 1772, on the cusp of the first partition. It was clear to Rousseau that the country was an anomaly in Central Europe, and that its despotic, greedy, and aggressive neighbors sought to take advantage of it. At the same time, he was impressed by the fact that the anarchic Commonwealth had managed to hold Russia at bay and strengthen national sentiment during the four-year-long confederation.

Sensing that Poland's neighbors would press for further influence and control over the country, Rousseau gave the Poles advice. There was a way, he insisted, to "maintain [Poland's] existence in spite of all the efforts of her oppressors." The solution was to infuse the population with the national spirit he had seen during the Confederation of Bar. The country's defense would lie in "the virtue of her citizens, their patriotic zeal, the particular way in which national institutions may be able to form their souls." In short, what would keep Poland alive would be its firm establishment in the hearts of its citizens. As he presciently—and memorably—observed: "You may not prevent them from gobbling you up; see to it at least that they will not be able to digest you."[*]

What would make the Poles indigestible would be the persistence of memory. We have already seen how memories of past deeds were used to good effect by the National Education Commission and Stanisław August himself,

---

[*]   Jean-Jacques Rousseau, *Considerations on the Government of Poland and on Its Proposed Reformation, April 1772*, http://www.constitution.org/jjr/poland.htm, accessed October 7, 2009.

with an eye to shaping the new generation of Poles. Now they would have to nurture the memory of Polish distinctiveness, of language and culture as well as history. This is what made various initiatives in the former Polish lands so important—including the creation of a Polish dictionary by Samuel Bogumił Linde, the establishment of the Society of Friends of Learning in Warsaw, the nurturing of Polish art and traditions at noble seats such as Puławy, where Princess Izabela Czartoryska set up the first Polish museum.

In addition to looking backward toward their history, Poles would look forward—to the future of the nation. They could not embrace entirely the state-led modernizing trajectory of Central Europe, in fear of denationalization or transformation into passive imperial subjects within enlightened absolutist states. As a result, the Polish nobles would be maligned by the partitioning powers, which sought to paint them as backward, as reactionary, as opposed to progress. Henceforth one would have to choose, self-consciously, to be Polish. The country may have disappeared; yet the people remained. Some still felt themselves to be Poles. Perhaps the "body politic"—the Polish nation—was not really "annulled," as the partitioning powers claimed?

Yet the former inhabitants of the Commonwealth were in the process of reimagining themselves. Who is a Pole when there is no Poland? Remember what it meant to be a Pole prior to the partitions. It meant that one was a noble, a member of the noble nation, the true rulers—if one may say so—of the Commonwealth. At best, certain members of the patrician elite were inching their way toward citizenship. They still needed to incorporate the peasants. Future generations would have to see whether they could convince the entirety of the population of its Polishness. In the memorable phrase of Rousseau, "If you see to it that no Pole can ever become a Russian, I guarantee that Russia will not subjugate Poland."*

Dissonances

How tragic, thus, that the country should be partitioned precisely at this point of national reimagining. Even memory had already started to diverge—had been interrupted. Perhaps most disoriented was the population of the original partitions of 1772. Their contact with the fatherland had been severed much earlier. Many inhabitants of those lands, thus, missed out on the additional signs of national vitality expressed in the course of the Great Seym, the May 3 Constitution, and the Kościuszko Insurrection.

By contrast, the inhabitants of the lands seized in 1793 and 1795 had be-

---

*   Ibid.

come nationally mobilized: they had experienced life in a country that was ready to countenance change and effect modernization on its own terms. Furthermore, they had witnessed or even participated in an insurrection in which not only representatives of the noble estate but also peasants and townspeople fought for Polish independence—a very good sign, if again one that still had only a limited impact. The events of the Kościuszko Insurrection became important in a peculiar, symbolic dimension. They produced new Polish national heroes, of a type never seen before. Bartosz Głowacki, Jan Kiliński, and Berek Joselewicz were new role models demonstrating the realm of the possible in the new Poland. The definition of citizen—of Pole—was expanding.

The Poles' Dilemma: A Nation without a State

No matter how you look at it, the Poles were still a nation in 1794—a nation in transition, to be sure, and evolving from the old, premodern noble nation into something more modern. All the same, it was taking on some of the trappings associated with our contemporary vision of the nation. The most important of these for the Poles, who had long thought of themselves in corporate terms as a well-defined group, was the inclusion in the nation of more than the old nobility. The deliberations of the Great Seym, the May 3 Constitution, as well as Kościuszko's proclamation at Połaniec, all demonstrated the beginnings of a broader inclusiveness. Poland's peasants, townspeople, and Jews (even if they did not yet possess the fullness of political rights) could also be Poles. They could rise to the defense of their country—even die for it. This was the historic recipe for Polishness, here understood as membership in the body of active citizens: "he who defends, governs."

However, the Poles' national development was interrupted by the partitions. These came at a most inopportune time, for the world was changing. A new modern Europe was being born, and the Poles' attempt at moving into it was being pushed to the side. In the second and third partitions, they were punished for making the kinds of reforms that might leave other countries envious . . . or, as we saw in the case of Prussia, even threatened. In 1791, they had presented a model of transition: careful, cautious, creative.

Yet now they were to become a revolutionary people. If Europe accepted the fait accompli of the partitions, then it was imperative that they rebel. Their fate propelled the Poles from being perhaps the most reactionary people in Europe to being the most progressive. After the partitions, the nobles had taken a big step backward; instead of being proud citizens of a country that they dominated, they became mere subjects of absolutist emperors.

Furthermore, despite the partitions, Poles continued to see themselves as a great nation, their history as one of a large European state—once the largest in continental Europe. Their loss of independent statehood helped to usher in the birth of modern nationalism. By denying the Poles their independent existence, it made the body politic—the nation—that much more important. Poles already had a rather well developed sense of estate identity. With the reforms of the late eighteenth century, increasingly it became possible to countenance the inclusion of other estates—burghers, even peasants— within the Polish nation. They, thus, went from being a precocious nation to being a provocative one—one that in its desire for existence went against the prevailing winds of Europe. Those who took up the Polish cause after the partitions would continue to demand to be reunited in a state of their own.

Yet visions of a future Poland were numerous. Was the country to return to its Sarmatian heritage? Or might it opt for the reforms of the May 3 Constitution? None of this was clear. Despite the Constitution's overwhelming symbolic value today, at the time there were many willing not only to criticize but also to reject it outright—and these were not just the reactionary Targowica confederates and their ilk. The Constitution had already been revoked by Tadeusz Kościuszko. It would also be rejected by Polish democrats (for example, Joachim Lelewel) for being monarchical. The idea of reform, thus, was considered acceptable by some—but it had to be the right reform, taking the country in the right direction. And here there were differences of opinion as to how to proceed.

Kościuszko had his own dream about the future, which was shared by his associate Józef Pawlikowski. In a pamphlet anonymously published in emigration, *Can the Poles Win Through to Independence?* Pawlikowski saw a new and improved Racławice: peasants with scythes in hand, fighting for Poland and making it a "sixteen million–strong nation."* Given these figures, it was clear that Kościuszko and Pawlikowski saw all peasants of the former Commonwealth as joining in this effort. Yet they and their ideas would percolate with difficulty through the partitioned population of the former Poland. The birth of the modern age saw them as subjects of different empires.

Facing the New Reality: A Nation without a State

Indeed, the various inhabitants of the partitioned lands responded differently to the partitions. One's reaction depended not only on where one was

---

* Cited in Andrzej Walicki, *Poland between East and West: The Controversies over Self-Definition and Modernization in Partitioned Poland* (August Zaleski Lectures, Harvard University, April 18–22, 1994; Cambridge: Harvard Ukrainian Research Institute, 1994), 15.

but who one was. On the whole, the magnates, who had the most to lose (in landholdings, territory, not to mention political influence), generally tried to adjust to the new centrifugal forces pulling them in the direction of Saint Petersburg, Berlin, or Vienna. They felt it necessary to maintain their positions, their land, their lifestyle. The "Family," that is, the Czartoryskis, found it imperative to send their two sons, Adam Jerzy and Konstanty, to Saint Petersburg in 1795. The boys were, in a way, hostages: they were placed in Russian service so as to remove the Family's extensive landholdings under Russian rule from sequestration. (And none too soon: for many a nobleman's estate ended up in the hands of Catherine's servitors.) Their experience in Saint Petersburg—certainly that of the eldest, Adam Jerzy, had echoes of former Family members. They were installed as members of the Guards as well as Gentlemen of the Court. The Czartoryskis, thus, had access and influence in Saint Petersburg—and conditions infinitely more comfortable than in the Petropavlovsk prison, where Kościuszko (and others) were detained. Like his uncle before him, the young Czartoryski would bed yet another neglected and underappreciated grand duchess—this time Louise of Baden, who was rechristened Elizabeth—albeit this time with the approval, even encouragement, of the husband . . . Nor did the partitions stop Poles from playing the marriage game. With his estate at Nieborów (in "South Prussia"), Prince Antoni Radziwiłł married a Hohenzollern princess. Even the father of the Czartoryski boys, Adam Kazimierz, who situated himself within his Galician landholdings, had become a *Feldmarschall* under the Habsburgs and was accepted into the aristocratic circles within the empire.

For others, the response depended more on the way they were treated by the partitioning powers. Life under the three empires took on distinctly different forms. If regionalism was a problem earlier, it now threatened to become even more intractable. Although the three partitioning powers prided themselves on being enlightened states, each approached the new territories and new subjects differently. Thus, a new layer of regionalism was superimposed on the old ones.

The newly acquired population was incorporated into each of the partitioned territories in different ways. Each empire was further diversified and internationalized—perhaps in ways even the partitioning powers had not anticipated. Likewise recall that, although the final partition of Poland came only in 1795, already since 1772 certain parts of the country had come under foreign rule, which left the territories further differentiated.

Prussia became a much more heterogeneous entity, although it sought to dilute the concentration of Poles in the newly acquired territories. The Prussian state took over the Crown lands, which it sold to German landowners;

German bureaucrats took the place of Polish officeholders. No municipal self-rule or noble assemblies were allowed under Prussian rule. A Protestant power, Prussia also took over properties belonging to the Roman Catholic Church. Religious issues complicated the picture. Prussia truly became a multiethnic and multidenominational state. It was faced with either dealing with, or doing away with, diversity.

Prussia eventually undermined the Polish nobles by taking away their privileges. The position of their peasants was strengthened. The position of Jews was changed beyond recognition, their corporate rights undone. Rather, Friedrich the Great delineated two types of Jews: those who were to assimilate and in the process receive civil rights and those who did not have these rights and would be expelled from the province. This facilitated a relatively rapid Germanization of the first group—certainly compared to the two other Central and East European empires.

The situation in Austria looked quite different. Under Maria Theresa and especially Joseph II, various reforms were implemented—reforms that could be considered enlightened. But under Francis I, scarred by the events of the French Revolution and the Napoleonic periods, reaction ensued. Seeking to centralize power, the Habsburgs took away various privileges of the Galician nobility. Indeed, many nobles suffered dreadfully under Austrian rule: if they were not able to provide proof of nobility—something that was difficult for many an old noble family fallen on hard times—they were reduced to the status of peasants. This déclassé nobility was clearly the worst off, although the burden of taxation reduced further nobles to penury. The peasants came to fare slightly better, as they were protected by legislation and the amount of time they spent working for the landlord was regulated. Jews were obliged to take German surnames and serve in the military (like members of all the estates), but their communities still had jurisdiction over religious matters. Although a staunchly Catholic power, Austria clearly did not trust its own population: witness the strong censorship of newspapers and other printed materials in the empire. The province would remain backward, socially as well as economically.

The territories that came under Russian rule—the most extensive of the lot—were the most ethnically diverse. The easternmost lands were inhabited by people we would now call Belarusians and Ukrainians (but which then were most likely termed Ruthenes or even Russians), Lithuanians, Tatars, and Jews. Poles were mainly noble landowners. It was Polish (Sarmatian) culture that had long radiated out through the entirety of the Commonwealth and that still carried weight.

Paradoxically, these lands witnessed little initially in the way of reforms. Even the old courts and laws were maintained. The nobles within the Russian Empire initially were not as inconvenienced as were nobles under Austrian and Prussian rule, except for the fact that Crown lands were taken over. By contrast, peasants found Russian rule more onerous: now classified as serfs, they were the chattel—that is, the personal property—of the landholders, who could do with them as they wished. Furthermore, they would eventually be subjected to Russia's onerous military service: recruits were taken for a period of twenty-five years.

The biggest problem for the Russians related to religion. The imperial authorities would do away with the Uniate (Greek Catholic) religion in the 1830s, forcing Uniates to convert to Russian Orthodoxy. As the partitions provided Russia with her first real encounter with large Jewish populations, she decided to restrict them to a region that would become known as the Pale of Settlement; this swath of land was more or less coterminous with the boundaries of the former Commonwealth. Unlike their coreligionists elsewhere, Jews, thus, could not penetrate further into the heart of the empire, that is, into Russia proper.

Such was the starting point. It would not be the ending point. The arrangement ratified in 1795, and reaffirmed in 1797, proved less permanent than the partitioning powers might have imagined.

"Poland Has Not Yet Perished . . . "

Poles were increasingly making a transition from a bunch of died-in-the-wool reactionaries (our Sarmatian types) or somewhat timid modernizers (the Polish Jacobins) to revolutionaries, regardless of their political orientation. Why? They wanted to upset the status quo of partitions and regain their independence. The Polish Question would soon come into its own.

It should come as no surprise that these revolutionaries ended up looking for support in the West, that is, outside the borders of the empires that had so unceremoniously partitioned them. Different conspiratorial groups were established, both at home (in Lviv, Warsaw, and elsewhere) and abroad. The very same month that Russia, Prussia, and Austria secretly resolved to suppress the very name of Poland, Poles in western Europe were establishing Polish Legions.

At the same time, the French Revolution was entering into a new phase. Robespierre's Reign of Terror was coming to an end. From all this, Napoleon Bonaparte would emerge, originally as a general, then as first consul.

In 1797 Polish Legions formed in Italy, that is, in the Republic of Lombardy (a new French creation), out of émigrés as well as prisoners of war (many of peasant stock) taken from the Austrian army. The legions were founded and led by General Jan Henryk Dąbrowski. That Dąbrowski should come to be a universally acknowledged symbol of national defense among the Poles is somewhat paradoxical. Son of a Pole who had served in the Saxon army and a Protestant woman of Scottish and German heritage, Dąbrowski took a rather improbable national trajectory. He joined the Saxon army in 1771 and fell under German cultural influence, even styling himself Johann Heinrich de Panna Dąbrowski. Yet in 1792 he had occasion to fight for his Polish fatherland and, as a Polish general, fought against the partitioners in 1792 and 1794; he was, indeed, a most capable defender of Warsaw during the Kościuszko Insurrection. Dabrowski had been in Saxon employ, with a Saxon wife, but chose to be Polish—this, despite the fact that his command of the Polish language was not particularly fine. He and his legions were immortalized in the song, written in 1797 by yet another Polish patriot, Józef Wybicki. This "Song of the Polish Legions" in Italy is also known as "Dąbrowski's Mazurka"; today it is more commonly known as the Polish national anthem.

Over the next years, as part of the revolutionary French fighting force, the Polish Legions not only provided an important training ground for a national army; they brought former inhabitants of the Commonwealth— peasants from Galicia as well as upper-class volunteers—into closer communion. These Polish peasants (and they were of both Polish and Ruthenian descent) received a patriotic instruction and education in the legions, which emphasized their common citizenship as Poles and the more radical social goals of the Enlightenment and Kościuszko.

This generation of Poles was still trying to comprehend what had happened to them and to their country. Did either Poland or Poles still exist? Here opinion seems divided. The Legions famously, defiantly, sang, "Poland has not yet perished while we are alive." Yet the lyrics of the same song also suggest some fuzziness about what it means to be Polish. After leaving Italy, according to the song, "under your [Dąbrowski's] command, / we will join up with the nation." But did the soldiers of the Polish Legions believe they could be Poles while abroad? or without a Poland? Perhaps not, or not yet, if one reads carefully the words of yet another verse: "We will cross the Vistula, we will cross the Warta, [then] we will be Poles." Perhaps it is fitting that this song—expressing determination to keep Poland alive, but somewhat unsure who exactly or under what conditions one could be a Pole—should in modern times become the Polish national anthem.

Given the legionnaires' high hopes and lofty aims, Napoleon's original use of them was appalling. The Polish Legions had to prove themselves by fighting in Italy, for the French cause. Yet the Italian campaign of 1799 did not allow them to bring to life the lively refrain of "Dąbrowski's Mazurka": "March, March, Dąbrowski, from Italy to Poland!" Instead, the Poles' march—and fighting—was brought to an end with the 1801 Peace of Lunéville. Negotiated between France and the allied parties of Austria and Russia, which had invaded French-controlled Italy, the peace essentially obligated all parties not to give support to those who were intent on undermining the present order.

Napoleon then found it expedient to remove the Polish Legions from the scene. His solution proved devastating for the Polish troops—literally and figuratively. Napoleon augmented his French troops with some six thousand Polish soldiers, all of whom were sent across the Atlantic to suppress revolution in San Domingo. The irony of Polish freedom fighters being sent to fight against the Haitians, who sought freedom from French colonial rule, was not lost on those concerned. Reportedly Toussaint L'Ouverture and the Haitians treated the Poles differently from the French, whom they massacred. Some Poles joined the Haitians in fighting for independence from France. This ultimately led to the phenomenon of *nègres blancs* or "white negroes"—that is, the Haitian descendants of these Polish soldiers. That may have been a happy ending for some. Still, a full two-thirds of the Polish troops sent to San Domingo either died from yellow fever or were killed on the island. Only three hundred made their way back to Europe.

That should have been enough to sour Poles on Napoleon. Yet many Poles abroad persisted in wanting to fight the partitioning powers. Wishing to restore the map of Central Europe to its pre-1772 state, they saw no other way than to side with the man who himself was reshaping the map of Europe. Further legions were created after the debacle of San Domingo. These finally got a chance to make their way eastward with Napoleon, whose Grand Armée took on the Prussians. Victories such as those at Jena and Austerlitz in 1806 opened the door for Poles to make inroads under Prussian rule. Napoleon famously challenged them to prove that "Poles are worthy of being a nation." Needing no more prompting, Polish forces set about liberating Polish lands, beginning in Greater Poland, then making their way to their former capital of Warsaw. Individuals such as Dąbrowski and Wybicki were involved.

This time, the Poles' hopes were not dashed. In the 1807 Treaty of Tilsit between France and Russia, Napoleon rewarded Polish military efforts by finalizing the establishment of the so-called Duchy of Warsaw. Yet another Napoleonic puppet state, the duchy was created out of Polish lands that had come under Prussian control in the second and third partitions, as well as the southernmost part of the first partition. A mere decade after the secret protocol, thus, there was once more a Polish state, if not in name.

Encouraged and emboldened by their new semi-independent status under Napoleon, Polish forces soon augmented the original territory of the Duchy of Warsaw. As with other Napoleonic puppet states, the Duchy established a draft and built up an army; peasants, townsmen, and nobles all bore arms. Some of the Duchy's troops were compelled to fight Napoleon's wars elsewhere, as seen in their participation in the Spanish campaign, with battles taking place at places such as Somosierra and Saragossa. Yet the Polish army was also able to achieve military victories closer to home, in the partitioned lands. It was put to the test in 1809, when an Austrian army of thirty thousand invaded. Austria was trying to help its ally Prussia, which had lost most of the partitioned lands to the Duchy of Warsaw.

The military efforts of the nephew of the last king of Poland, Prince Józef Poniatowski, proved decisive. Leading an army of only twelve thousand, Poniatowski defeated the Austrians at Raszyn. The dashing Polish general then decided to move into Galicia, where Poles under Habsburg rule rallied in insurrection. Territories gained by Austria in the third partition as well as the historically and economically significant region of Kraków and the Wieliczka salt mines were incorporated into the Duchy of Warsaw at the Peace of Schönbrunn of 1809. It now contained several major historic Polish centers: Warsaw, Poznań, Kraków, with significantly more land as well as more people under Polish rule.

The strides made by the little but growing Polish state in 1809 were hugely significant, in territorial, demographic, and psychological terms. The Poles, under Napoleon, seem to be gaining momentum. It no longer seemed farfetched to imagine a different future for the nation than that promised by the three acts of partition. Might not the Poles manage—bit by bit—to undo the partitions?

While Poles may have dreamt of restoration, the ensuing years—and ensuing influences—meant that it would be impossible simply to turn back the hand of time: to 1772, 1791, or some other moment in the past. Each new development resulted in new experiences that shaped both the land and the people inhabiting it. How difficult it might be is suggested by the Napoleonic innovations introduced into the Napoleonic puppet state, this new nucleus of Polish statehood. The Duchy of Warsaw hardly represented the restoration of Poland—either in its earlier republican or its later constitutional form. Its form of government was based on the French revolutionary template, the famous Napoleonic code. In the case of the Duchy, some concessions were

Map 8.2: The Duchy of Warsaw, ca. 1809

made to the model of the May 3 Constitution. These included the establish-ment of the ruler of Saxony, Friedrich August, as hereditary ruler, as well as a bicameral Seym. Yet other innovations marked a sharp break with the past. Equality under the law was proclaimed. Serfdom was abolished, although the nobility retained control of the land; and various other innovations, such as civil marriages, demonstrated the French influence.

Yet another Western trend had an impact on both Poles and the new Pol-ish state. This was freemasonry. While Masonic lodges, serving as conduits for Enlightened ideas, had penetrated the Commonwealth in the eighteenth century, only with the Duchy of Warsaw did Freemasons become dominant in Polish politics. Even the country's military leaders—including Prince Józef Poniatowski and Jan Henryk Dąbrowski—had embraced freemasonry.

For these and various other reasons, not everyone was happy with the Duchy of Warsaw and the way it was developing. For some—such as many members of the Roman Catholic clergy—it was too radical. Yet even the radical Kościuszko retained his antipathy toward Napoleon and refused to stand by the French emperor, believing that the Poles should ally with other European powers. Other Poles took a "wait and see" stance toward the recent developments.

The fate of the Duchy of Warsaw and further Polish revindication of territory and population was closely intertwined with that of Napoleon. This could be a good thing—as it was for the Poles in 1807–1809, with the creation and expansion of the Duchy of Warsaw. It could also be a bad thing. For Napoleon's European exploits were not over.

CHAPTER 9

Poles in Arms

"For Our Freedom and for Yours"

Napoleon created an empire of unimaginable proportions. His French Empire proper came to include, in the north, even Holland and the port provinces of the now defunct Holy Roman Empire, all the way to Lübeck. He established a host of satellite states, in essence reconfiguring the map of Europe. In addition to Napoleon's creation of the Duchy of Warsaw, an undeniably Polish state, this reconfiguration was most notable in the Confederation of the Rhine. This confederation represented an amalgam of newly promoted kingdoms (including the former electorate of Saxony) that had swallowed up lesser independent entities—kingdoms, duchies, margravates, free cities, prince-bishoprics, and the like—from the former Holy Roman Empire. Yet the Duchy of Warsaw remained territorially separated from the rest, surrounded by the somewhat reduced partitioning states, which nonetheless had also been compelled, one after the other, to enter into alliance with the Corsican dynamo.

The only partitioning power that had not lost territory due to Napoleon's interference was Russia, which from the outset had been the biggest beneficiary of the partitions gaining, as it did, over 80 percent of the territory of the former Commonwealth. In fact, the Russian Tsar Alexander had managed to swipe a piece of formerly Prussian-controlled Polish lands—the Białystok region—in 1807. It was Russia that most notably competed for the hearts and minds of Poles. Although there had been various overtures made to Prussia and Austria proposing that a greater Poland would be under one or another of those scepters, the idea of linking Poland to Russia gained the most traction.

This is in no small part a happy accident of the partitions (if any aspect about the partitions could be considered happy). Various magnates had sought to ameliorate the threat of dispossession by ingratiating themselves with the partitioning powers. In 1795 the Czartoryskis had felt compelled to send their two sons to enter tsarist service in Saint Petersburg. This move not only allowed the family to retain most of its estates. Already the following year, the elder of the Czartoryski sons, Adam Jerzy, gained an influential friend. This was the nineteen-year-old Russian Grand Duke Alexander, heir to the throne. In private, Alexander professed to Adam his unhappiness with Poland's treatment at the hands of his grandmother and expressed interest in the ideas of the French Revolution.

This friendship between Russian and Pole would develop in various ways. Perhaps most unusual was the romantic connection between Adam and Alexander's wife, Elizabeth, an affair initially sanctioned—even encouraged—by the grand duke himself. The love lives of these two friends underscore the unabashedly international nature of aristocratic and royal affairs (and their love children): while the Pole (not unlike his great-uncle, the last king of Poland) was attracted by a former German princess, the heir to the Russian throne preferred the charms of a Polish Princess Czetwertyńska.

Of infinitely greater significance for Polish history, however, was the intellectual collaboration of the two men. Already the blow of the partitions had been softened somewhat by Catherine's successor, Tsar Paul. He had not only allowed the Polish nobility to retain its status but kept a good deal of the administrative system native to the partitioned territories in place. Still, Russia under Catherine's son proved a mixed bag. While some Poles, such as the aristocratic Czartoryski brothers, were given promotions within the service ranks, those who chafed under Russian rule, such as the members of secret conspiracies in Vilnius and Volhynia, felt the tsar's wrath upon them. After Paul's untimely death in 1801 (he was assassinated by a conspiracy of disgruntled Russian officials, who also found their tsar capricious and cruel), the new tsar—Alexander—sent for his friend Adam. The Pole had been dispatched on imperial business to Italy by Tsar Paul several years earlier, once the latter learned of his affair with the grand duchess. (Surely it was a better destination than Siberia, which the tsar had first thought more appropriate.)

While in Italy, Czartoryski had witnessed firsthand the results of Napoleon's doings, in particular, its effects on the ruling houses on the Apennine Peninsula. He did not like what he saw. This experience convinced the Pole all the more that his compatriots were wrong to place their faith in the Corsican who soon would style himself emperor of the French.

Upon Czartoryski's return to Saint Petersburg, he became part of what was known as the Unofficial Committee. In the years 1801–1803 the committee functioned as a tiny think tank for Tsar Alexander. Together with the tsar, the half dozen committed individuals—including men such as Nikolai Novosiltsev and Mikhail Speransky—spent hours discussing ways to reform Russia. Czartoryski was the only Pole in the group. Their goal, over time, was to transform the country into a constitutional monarchy. Their solution to Russian backwardness seemed to echo the path taken by the Commonwealth a decade earlier. With some crucial differences: for example, there was no talk of doing away with the tsar's autocratic powers, which were reaffirmed in 1803. Rather, the aim of the reforms was to introduce a degree of rule of law to the country and cut down on the level of corruption. The establishment of a series of ministries in 1802 provided official government posts for the reformers, and Czartoryski was among them. He was appointed assistant minister of foreign affairs, later to become minister of foreign affairs: quite a distinction for a Pole under Russian rule.

A realm in which the highly placed Pole could do the most for his compatriots was that of education. From the outset, Czartoryski shared with the appropriate people the efforts of the National Education Commission of the Polish-Lithuanian Commonwealth, in which his own father had played an important role. He also submitted his own memorandum, "Principles of National Education in the Russian Empire," to the Russian minister of education. Ultimately the entire education system within Russia—the establishment of education districts, in which there was a hierarchy of schools ranging from university level down through the parish schools—came to be based on the Polish example.

Poles were also engaged, from the outset, in running important parts of the system. In 1803 Czartoryski was appointed the curator of the university in Vilnius. Vilnius stood at the head of the educational district that encompassed nearly the entirety of the Polish lands gained by Russia through the partitions. Another Polish nobleman, Seweryn Potocki, became curator of the new university at Kharkiv. In the realm of education, he had jurisdiction over the former Cossack lands, whose autonomy was increasingly weakened under Catherine the Great, only to lose any vestiges of autonomy in 1782.

His Vilnius appointment gave Czartoryski control over the education of these lands and ensured that the education system for the region's pupils and students retained its Polish character, including use of the Polish language. The University of Vilnius was the largest school of higher education in Russia at this time. There did exist universities in Moscow and Dorpat (today's Tartu, in Estonia), and new universities were planned for Saint Petersburg, Kharkiv, and Kazan. The Vilnius educational district was particularly well served. In 1805, a lycée was founded in Kremenets (Polish: Krzemieniec), in Volhynia. Run by Tadeusz Czacki, the lycée proved a dynamic southern counterpart to the more northerly located University of Vilnius. Progressing through the feeder system of parish and district schools, pupils and students of this former part of the Commonwealth could continue to feel Polish in language, culture, and outlook. The region was a window on the west for Russia.

These developments suggest the kind of synergy that Adam Czartoryski and Tsar Alexander thought might be achieved in the realm of Polish-Russian relations within the empire. The Polish experience could serve as a model for Russian modernization. One could introduce reforms in the Polish kingdom, then let them radiate out to the rest of the empire. Given the promise of this arrangement as well as their long-standing friendship, Czartoryski remained not only a loyal subject of the Russian tsar; he continued to entertain hopes that his friend would reunite the Polish lands under the Russian scepter.

In the early years of the nineteenth century, thus, Russia was competing for the hearts and minds of the Poles, the Slavic giant representing an alternative to Napoleon. Before long, Russia would free itself from its enforced alliance with France. In the Corsican's books, this was tantamount to declaring war. And it was war he sought. The year was 1812.

On June 22, 1812, Napoleon and his army crossed the Neman River, intending to fight, in the French emperor's words, the "Second Polish War." The goal was not unlike that of Stanisław Żółkiewski in 1610—to march on Moscow. Yet the Corsican general turned French emperor would not meet with the same spectacular success achieved by the Polish hetman two centuries earlier.

Napoleon's multinational Grand Armée contained a significant number of Poles: some hundred thousand troops were fielded out of the population of the former Polish lands. To underscore their support of Napoleon as well as their historic existence, the Poles formed a confederacy. Czartoryski's aged father, Adam Kazimierz, served as marshal of the confederacy, thus serving as a link to the Polish past. The elder Czartoryski had been based in Austria, which, like Prussia, was still in the French alliance, if not enthusiastic about it.

The lands beyond the Duchy of Warsaw—that is, the former Grand Duchy of Lithuania—themselves provided Napoleon with only twenty thousand troops. Many in Lithuania took a "wait and see" attitude to the war. They had been less enthusiastic about Napoleon and more eager to gain concessions from this surprisingly liberal Tsar of all Russia. For a brief moment it appeared that Alexander was ready to grant the Grand Duchy a constitution, and he even contemplated bringing the Grand Duchy of Lithuania into political union with Russia. Only two months before Napoleon's invasion, the tsar had confirmed such plans in Vilnius, thus raising hopes among his subjects.

When Napoleon invaded, talk of new permutations of Lithuanian union—with the Duchy of Warsaw, or somehow under Napoleon—percolated. Yet in vain. The war did not go Napoleon's way, despite the determined fighting of his Polish troops, who did not hesitate to lead the charge. Napoleon proved victorious at Borodino, though he paid a high price for that victory. The determined Corsican even made his way to Moscow in September. Could he repeat the feat of Polish hetman Stanisław Żółkiewski? Yet the capital burst into flames and burned. It soon became clear that the city would not provide the shelter that Napoleon and the Grand Armée needed. And winter was around the corner.

This image of a frozen, inhospitable Russian landscape soon burned into the brains of the retreating French forces, unaccustomed to such utter brutality. The very elements seemed to conspire against the Grand Armée, which was becoming increasingly less grand. In truth, it was hemorrhaging men, beset by cold, disease, and the indignity of continued Russian forays. To give a sense of enormity of the losses: while the Polish general Prince Józef Poniatowski entered Russia with 37,000 soldiers in his Fifth Corps, not even a full 2,000 of them made it out of Russia in December 1812. All told, the Grand Armée of Napoleon Bonaparte was originally 611,000 strong, but some 400,000 perished, and another 100,000 were taken prisoner.

To make things worse for Napoleon and his supporters, the year 1813 witnessed a reconfiguration of alliances. Both Prussia and Austria abandoned the French alliance and sided with Russia. The tide was turning against the French emperor and his push for total European dominance. Napoleon raced back to France from Moscow in record time to build a new army. This too was defeated.

The decisive battle of the so-called War of Liberation took place at Leipzig in October 1813. The battle was later referred to by the Germans as the Battle of the Nations—here, the "nations" referring to the peoples who rose up against Napoleon. (As is often the case in history, the winners have the last word.) Still, Napoleon managed to evade capture. He escaped, to be pursued further to the west—all the way to Paris. At Leipzig the contribution of the nephew of the last king of Poland, Prince Józef Poniatowski, proved key, if also fateful. One of Napoleon's most loyal generals (actually, just promoted to French marshal), the dashing Polish prince covered Napoleon's retreat from Leipzig. Ultimately Poniatowski perished in the waters of the Elster, choosing to remain faithful to Napoleon rather than surrender to Tsar Alexander I of Russia.

Russians occupied the Duchy of Warsaw for the rest of its brief existence. Yet the occupation did not resemble the occupations of old. The Poles were treated not like enemies but like people with whom Russia might be dealing in the future. Would this augur well for the postwar settlement?

The Congress of Vienna and the Polish Question

The Napoleonic implosion meant the moment was ripe for restructuring Europe—the Europe the Man of Destiny had done so much to change. Despite his defeat, Poles entertained hopes for the future. With their willingness to take up arms to undo the partitions, Poles—with Napoleon's help—had managed to resurrect the Polish question, to place it on the European stage. The fact that a state had been created, even one without the name Poland, appeared to be significant. Poland truly had not perished, as the Legionnaires sang . . .

And this was not solely Napoleon's doing. Poles had been able to contribute to the fight for independent existence, and even themselves, under Poniatowski's leadership, had won more territory for the Duchy of Warsaw at the expense of Austria. Thus, Poles were learning that their military efforts could pay off: they were of some value in recasting the face of Europe, even if only briefly.

The post-Napoleonic restructuring was to be effected not militarily, however, but diplomatically. Much ink has been spilled about the Congress of Vienna that took place from September 1814 to June 1815. Representatives of the European Great Powers—Britain, Prussia, Austria, France, and Russia—gathered in the Habsburg capital to reconfigure Europe according to their own ideas. That they took nine months to reach agreement suggests that the principles underlying the work of the congress were muddy. The difficulty of reaching agreement nearly led the various parties to war. While there was much talk of establishing "a lasting peace founded on a just division of strength" and restoring a "balance of power" to the continent, the Great Powers' sense of justice—certainly insofar as the fate of the Poles was concerned—seemed hampered by their main goal: to keep each of the others from gaining more than his fair share of the spoils.

Indeed, the fate of Poland left the representatives in a quandary. Despite the valor exhibited by Poles in the conflict, there was no talk of resurrecting the Commonwealth of Both Nations or any other former permutation of the country. Alexander I was keen on creating a Polish kingdom out of all the former partitioned lands, which would be united with Russia, under his scepter.

This proved a stumbling block to the negotiations, as little was made of the distinction between kingdom and empire: Russian rule was, in the eyes of the other representatives, Russian rule. All the same, the European great powers had to contend with Alexander's desire to retain control over the former Duchy of Warsaw as well as the fact that Russian boots were on the ground in those lands. Prussia would agree to relinquish its Polish landholdings only if compensated with the Saxon lands. Austria was horrified at the thought of Prussia taking over all of Saxony, as this would make its northern neighbor a much stronger player within the German lands. Britain feared that Russia was gaining too much power. France (restored to the Bourbon monarchy) sought simply to reassert itself and took advantage of the discord to ally itself with Austria and Britain against Russia and Prussia.

Poles themselves were not admitted to the negotiation table, although Alexander's friend and collaborator Adam Czartoryski did what he could to influence the various players. Pleas for an undoing of the partitions—if only by bringing the Poles all under one of the partitioning powers—fell on deaf ears. None of the other big players would countenance giving Russia so much power. Thus Alexander had to scale back his proposal.

Token Statehood, Two Variants

Ultimately, the Congress of Vienna created two new states out of the Duchy of Warsaw. The more significant—certainly the larger of the two— was the Kingdom of Poland, also often referred to as the Congress Kingdom (after its origins in the Congress of Vienna). However, lost to this new entity were parts of the former Prussian holdings (Poznań and Toruń regions). In this way, the new kingdom was smaller than the Duchy of Warsaw had been. An even smaller (indeed, tiny) state was the Free City of Kraków, comprised of the city (once Poland's capital) and its immediate environs. Strategically located near the border of all three partitioning powers, the Free City was required to be neutral; it was subject to the tender ministrations of the so-called custodial powers (Russia, Prussia, and Austria).

Neither newly established entity was totally independent, although both profited, at least initially, from a certain degree of autonomy. The Kingdom of Poland did appear to be a sovereign state in many ways. It had its own army as well as its own laws. It even had its own constitution, which Tsar Alexander granted his Polish subjects. The legislative body of the kingdom was the traditional Seym. Yet there was one peculiarity that bears underscoring: the king of the new state was no longer the ruler of Saxony (as with

Map 9.1: The New Creations of the Congress of Vienna, 1815: The Kingdom of Poland and the Free City of Kraków

the Duchy of Warsaw) but none other than Alexander I, tsar of Russia. Thus, as envisaged by Alexander, the kingdom was united, in perpetuity, with the Russian Empire.

Russia also returned the borderland district of Ternopil (Polish: Tarnopol) to Austria, where it became part of Galicia. Per the Congress of Vienna, all the newly acquired Polish lands were to be given the requisite "representation and national institutions" by their imperial overlords. The above-mentioned Poznań and Toruń regions, thus, were organized into the Grand Duchy of Poznań (German: Posen), under Prussian rule. The Prussian king adopted a conciliatory tone vis-à-vis his Polish subjects and vowed to allow them to retain their distinct identity and language, and even, as of 1827, to have a provincial diet. Prince Antoni Radziwiłł—the magnate who had married into the Prussian ruling house—was appointed *Statthalter* (viceroy). In

Galicia, Habsburg officials appeared to be uniformly appalled by the low level of civilization evinced by the empire's new subjects, whether nobles, clergy, burghers, or peasants. They thought it would be necessary to remake them into Galicians—and, perhaps with time, into Germans/Austrians.

Poles, Russians, Slavs

Poles of this period placed their greatest hopes in Russia, in particular in the person of the so-called Savior of the West from Napoleonic "despotism," Alexander I. Alexander began as a liberal tsar—a seeming oxymoron, given the historic autocratic approach of Russian tsars to their subjects. Indeed, Alexander treated the Poles who came under him with a disarming magnanimity. Among other things, he allowed the Polish troops that fought under Napoleon—that is, against his tsarist Russia—to return home and become the core of the new Polish military. From the very outset of his rule he had considered various types of reform, although his vacillation led to few real reforms being made. Still, his gentle reformism could appeal to those who preferred a conservative but constitutional approach, men such as Adam Czartoryski. Given the proclivities of his Russian friend, Czartoryski had long hoped that Alexander might see fit to establish a Polish kingdom, which could be ruled separately from Russia. This the Russian tsar did, in 1815.

Yet the situation left something to be desired. To be sure, Czartoryski got what he wanted for his nation (the Polish prince penned a constitution for the Kingdom of Poland that was more liberal than that of the Duchy of Warsaw), if on a decidedly smaller scale. And there was always the prospect of enlarging the Kingdom of Poland. Alexander had intimated to the Poles that he might someday reunite them with the lands further east that had been integrated into the Russian empire proper, lands that later would be referred to as the *Kresy*, or the borderlands. Such a prospect made fervent Slavophiles out of many Poles, who saw cooperation with the tsar—their king—as desirable, in that it could lead to a reunification of the bulk of the old Commonwealth lands.

Even Poles who had been fervent stalwarts of Napoleon, and very much involved in the running of the Duchy of Warsaw, came around to this new Polish Slavophilism. Having been disillusioned by the West, many came to place their hopes in the East. As Stanisław Staszic exclaimed, "Western Europe permitted the partition of Poland, and so she must serve one more powerful; she neglected to find an ally in the Poles, and she will have them, incorporated in Slavdom, as lords. The die is already cast. Let us unite with

Russia. We will take might from her, and let her take enlightenment from us." In a way, this seemed to be a new mission for the Poles: to bring enlightenment to the great Slavic power, Russia.

Yet the relationship became not as congenial as had been hoped. To be sure, the first five or so years of Russian-Polish coexistence in the Kingdom of Poland passed without incident. Things might have gone even better had Alexander not appointed his brother Constantine as unofficial viceroy. Constantine also served as commander in chief of the Polish army. Unlike his vacillating brother, Grand Duke Constantine was known for his violent temper. The fact that he had a morganatic Polish wife did little to endear Varsovians to him. Neither did he and Alexander always see eye to eye.

At any rate, there was an inherent fault in this clever arrangement that united the Polish kingdom with the Russian Empire. How could Alexander reconcile his two positions? He was all-powerful tsar in Russia, where every word of his was the people's command—a true autocrat. But he was only king of a constitutional kingdom in Poland, where he would have to deal in the legislature with the Polish nobles, who were unused to being subservient to any monarch. In the mind of an autocrat, the Russian crown of Monomakh far outweighed the crown of Poland, especially now that the historic royal insignia had been relegated to the dustbin of history or, rather, likely smelted down by one of the partitioning powers, in order to remove all vestiges of the former Polish state. The tendency might be for even a tsar as reform-minded as Alexander to slip into old, familar Russian ways—to act like an autocrat in the kingdom of Poland.

Despotism clearly would not sit well with the Poles, who valued the existence of their constitution and expected the spirit as well as the letter of the law to be observed. That some of them had more Slavophile inclinations at this point did not mean they were content to be humble subjects of the tsar. Not that long before—certainly within recent memory—many of them had played active roles in the governing of a Commonwealth in the process of reforming itself. They and others expected their king to reward them with the return of the lands to the east of the Kingdom of Poland—the former Grand Duchy of Lithuania as well as the southeastern, heavily Ruthenian lands that had been part of the Crown of Poland. These two territories had become Russia's western provinces: the northwest guberniia, and the southwest guberniia. All this, combined with the heady new ideas that had emanated from the French Revolution—*liberté, égalité, fraternité*—made for a potent mixture within the Congress Kingdom.

And indeed, before too long there were signs that not all Poles—whether

---

* Cited from Walicki, *Poland between East and West*, 24.

within the Congress Kingdom or outside of it—were enamored of the current situation. This was manifested primarily by a resurgence of secret societies, of the type that were all the rage in the West. These formed at the Polish universities—institutions of learning that were in the lands of the former Commonwealth, whether in the Kingdom of Poland proper (where in 1816 Alexander had permitted the establishment of the University of Warsaw) or in the western provinces of Russia (the University of Vilnius). Many young Poles chafed at the increasing restrictions and sought to introduce further French-styled reforms. As of 1821 these secret student societies were declared illegal. The members of such societies were repressed, and many were sent into exile far within the Russian Empire.

One such participant was a young poet named Adam Mickiewicz, who hailed from the old Lithuania, from a town called Nowogródek (today's Navahrudak, in Belarus). The young Pole came from the lesser nobility, from a family that had been beset by hardship. Although there are rumors of him being of Jewish descent on his mother's side (some of these rumors fostered by the poet himself), this has not been proved. Nonetheless, Mickiewicz would later marry into a family of Frankist ancestry. (The Frankists were a late eighteenth-century Jewish sect, led by one Jakub Frank, who claimed to be the messiah; Frank and his followers ultimately ended up converting to Catholicism.)

Later to be hailed as Poland's greatest Romantic poet, Mickiewicz was a graduate of Vilnius University, where his poetic talent gained attention. Early on, he wrote works after the fashion of the German poet Schiller, one of the most noteworthy of Europe's Romantic writers. In 1819, the impoverished Mickiewicz took a teaching job in the town of Kaunas (Polish: Kowno). Yet he maintained the close friendships made during his college years. Mickiewicz had belonged to a secret society called the Philomats. This is what got him into trouble—and propelled him into the larger world, far from the provincial Lithuanian north.

Arrested in 1823, Mickiewicz was exiled into the interior of Russia. His exile was nowhere as onerous as that of some of his friends, who ended up literally in the middle of nowhere, under harsh conditions. The promising poet was treated much less harshly. Mickiewicz was able to spend time in places such as Saint Petersburg and Moscow, where he made the acquaintance of people who were interested in his poetry. He also gained further inspiration for his work. Mickiewicz completed his play *Forefathers' Eve*—in many ways an anti-tsarist work, yet a work in which he also addresses, in bittersweet fashion, his "Muscovite friends." The Polish poet also managed to travel to the Crimea, where he wrote a lovely series of sonnets.

Despite his favorable reception in Russia, Mickiewicz found inspiration for more than sonnets in the interior of the Russian Empire. He penned a work that would soon have an enormous impact on his compatriots. This was a narrative poem entitled *Konrad Wallenrod*. The titular hero was a grand master of the Teutonic Knights who, having learned of his Lithuanian roots, decided to lead the knights to defeat. While *Konrad Wallenrod* emboldened early nineteenth-century Poles to think they might subvert the Russian Empire from within, later critics would see the poem as a paean to treason, not a virtue upon which one might wish to build a country or nation. Such were the beginnings of Polish Romanticism.

The words of Mickiewicz's latest major work, published in 1828, reached receptive ears. In the late 1820s it was the deed—and not the moral consequences—of the poem that excited Polish readers. We have seen how the incongruity of the tsar of Russia as king of Poland was already felt under Alexander I, who had established the little kingdom and even (important) hinted at the possibility of an eventual reunification of the multiethnic western guberniias with the Kingdom of Poland. Under Alexander, influential Russians such as the writer and historian Nikolai Karamzin had already expressed their dismay at the idea of giving up to the Poles any of these former Commonwealth lands, which they considered their patrimony.

The dual role of tsar and king was even less comfortable for Nicholas I, Alexander's successor and youngest brother. Nicholas became tsar because his elder brother, Constantine, had taken himself out of the succession by marrying a Polish noblewoman. This fact was not, however, public knowledge. Nicholas ascended to the imperial throne in 1825 at what proved to be a rocky moment within the empire—for revolutionary ideas had penetrated the heartland. A number of young, liberal-minded Russian officers were seeking to incite a revolution at the very moment when they were supposed to swear allegiance to the new tsar, Nicholas. They decided they preferred the elder brother, Constantine, instead. A sign of how ill prepared most Russians were for reform: legend has it that some soldiers in the capital understood the cry for "Constantine and [a] constitution" to be a cheer for Grand Duke Constantine and his wife. This abortive attempt at revolution has gone down in history as the Decembrist uprising.

The new tsar was chagrined to learn that these Russian revolutionaries had had contact with Poles in the kingdom. Nicholas demanded that their contacts be put on trial back in the kingdom. He fully expected that the Polish accomplices would be sentenced for treason. Yet this was not to be, as the judge ultimately determined they were innocent. The Poles were not getting off to a good start with their new king—certainly not according to the man whose despotic character suited him infinitely better as autocratic tsar of Russia.

Many Poles in the Congress Kingdom came to chafe under Nicholas's rule. The kingdom's Poles understood what "constitution" meant. They also understood that their constitutional monarch was running roughshod over their constitution. And there were various other reasons for dissatisfaction as well. Before much longer, a conspiracy formed among a group of military cadets in Warsaw. They prepared themselves for the eventuality of an armed uprising.

Such was the domestic situation within the kingdom. The international situation was no less fraught. The Bourbon king, Charles X, was having his own troubles reconciling factions within France. In his efforts to strengthen the old aristocracy in France, Charles alienated the liberals. Revolution broke out on July 27, 1830. Faced with barricades in his capital of Paris, the Bourbon abdicated and set off for the relative safety of England. The duke of Orleans was offered the throne in his stead. The new king, Louis Philippe, styled himself king of the French and did more to appeal to his subjects, even calling himself not king of France but king of the French.

Yet this was not the end of revolution in Europe. Disturbances broke out that summer in Brussels. The Belgians were not happy with the fate determined for them by the Congress of Vienna, which had united the former (Catholic) Habsburg province with the (Protestant) Dutch Netherlands. Originally the Belgians asked only for local self-government. Once the Dutch king set his army on them, however, they proclaimed independence and produced a constitution for themselves.

This had repercussions further east. Back in the Kingdom of Poland, in the fall of 1830 a rumor reached Poles that Nicholas was preparing to send troops westward to clamp down on the Belgian uprising. Given their relative proximity to western Europe, the Polish soldiers were the ones most likely to be sent. The young Polish officers who had earlier formed a conspiracy naturally wanted no part in squelching a war of liberation. They took matters into their own hands. On November 29, 1830, they resolved to assassinate their nemesis, Grand Prince Constantine.

Their efforts were not met with success. Constantine managed to escape from the palace, reportedly dressed in a skirt . . . Nonetheless, the brother of the tsar was not facing much of an attack: a mere handful of conspirators had set out to kill him. Acting more on inflamed impulse than with judicious foresight, they furthermore had not put in place anyone to lead the insurrection. The young officers' assumption that their higher-ups would step in and direct what they had begun proved unrealistic.

All the same, the insurrection did manage to gain some support among the Warsaw populace. The younger generation had been reading Mickiewicz's *Konrad Wallenrod* and embraced the Romantic notions of the conspirators, out to defeat the tyrant. The older generation, including the generals and officers of the Polish army, were much less enamored of the new developments—and some of them paid for their disdain of the insurrection with their lives. Certainly at the early stage, the insurrection was more civil war than war of Poles against Russians.

Despite their lack of initial success, the conspirators and their allies' efforts triggered a series of events. In the first phase of the insurrection, Poles manifested their protest against Russian autocracy, which just did not seem capable of either keeping to the Polish constitution or keeping promises. The situation was exacerbated by the tsar. Nicholas categorically rejected any resolution to the problem in the Kingdom of Poland other than the unconditional surrender of the insurgents. This led the Polish Seym to produce a two-point rationale for the insurrection in December 1830. It maintained that the fact a despot could be a constitutional monarch was a "political monstrosity." It also decried the fact that the western guberniias, formerly part of the Commonwealth, had not yet been reunited with the kingdom. In the eyes of the Polish Seym, these were valid complaints that could be lodged against their king, the Russian tsar. Yet soon the insurrection would evolve in a more radical way.

The turning point came on January 25, 1831, when the deputies of the Polish Seym dethroned their Polish king, Nicholas I. In this the deputies appeared to be following the lead of the Belgians, who had recently dethroned the house of Orange-Nassau. It was a risky move. Like the Belgians, the Poles were now clearly breaking with the Vienna system. Unlike the Belgians, the Poles would be forced to pay for this sign that the insurrection had become a national struggle for independence—for the Poles had severed the relationship that lay at the basis of the deliberations at the Congress of Vienna, which—despite its imperfections—had made room for a Polish kingdom.

"For Our Freedom and for Yours"

The dethronement proved the last straw for Nicholas. The tsar and former Polish king sent Russian troops in, and war began in earnest. Everything had been so confused at the outset of the insurrection that reactions on both sides, Polish and Russian, had been quite mixed. Even Grand Duke Constantine—the object of the initial attack—had not seen fit to attack the Polish insurrectionists, realizing that they themselves were divided and unclear about their objectives.

At this point a national government was formed under Adam Czartoryski. While he played the same role his father had played in the Duchy of Warsaw's contribution to the Russian campaign, Czartoryski did so with a heavy heart. This conservative supporter of the Polish-Russian union had been devastated by the act of dethronement, realizing that the foundations of the kingdom as established by the Congress of Vienna had crumbled. He feared the repercussions, not only at the hands of tsarist Russia but also in European opinion.

Left-leaning insurrectionists sought to internationalize the war. During the conflict, they popularized a slogan ascribed to Polish historian Joachim Lelewel: "For our freedom and for yours." It was a powerful message, if it spoke not to the powerful but, rather, to the disenfranchised. Indeed, the Poles, wielding a red-and-white flag, won some sympathy abroad. The battle against tyranny spoke to those who cherished republican, democratic, or revolutionary ideals. Several thousand Poles came from across the Prussian or Galician border to join up. Yet sympathizers in the west—as seen from large manifestations in parts of France, Belgium, Piedmont, Switzerland, and elsewhere—did little more than start selling "eau de Pologne" instead of "eau de Cologne." The sweet smell of sympathy could not replace the lack of military or diplomatic help. Czartoryski's fears were founded. The Great Powers were wary of helping those who rebelled against the world order they had established.

The insurrectionists received no help from any of the great European powers, whose balance of power they were upsetting. Thus, they had to fight the war both outnumbered and alone. Battles at places such as Stoczek and Grochów in February nonetheless demonstrated to the Russians that the Poles knew how to fight. The Polish army had a number of victories in March and April before their major loss to the Russians at Ostrołęka in May 1831.

Already before that, the war had spread from the Congress Kingdom to Russia's western guberniias. While shots were fired and a battle won in Volhynia, much more activity took place in the north, in the former Grand Duchy of Lithuania. Even some Lithuanian-speaking peasants joined in the fight, singing a new version of "Dąbrowski's Mazurka," with the words, "Poland is not yet lost while the Samogitians live." Unfortunately, the military leadership of the insurrection was unable to come to the aid of the Lithuanians; their insurrection was put down by the Russians that summer.

After the defeat at Ostrołęka in May, Poles progressively lost their confidence in the insurrection's chance of victory. Attacked at the beginning of

September, Warsaw was brought to its knees. In October, the Polish forces occupying the fortresses in Modlin (near Warsaw) and Zamość capitulated. The war had lasted nine months.

Repercussions for the Kingdom of Poland

Given that the Poles had seen fit to undo the system established by the Congress of Vienna, Nicholas concluded he had no reason any longer to honor the arrangement made by his brother. He did away with the bothersome Polish constitution, Seym, and army. The royal insignia used by the Kingdom of Poland were taken to Russia, never to return. Many Poles were imprisoned, exiled to Siberia, or drafted into the Russian army, where they were obliged to serve for twenty-five years. Many others fled to the west, in particular to France, where they were known in republican circles. Given that the Russian army was needed in Poland, it never made it to Belgium. Both the Belgians and the French were thus spared the fate of the Kingdom of Poland.

Unfortunately, Poles did not do enough to get the masses of peasants to join them in this effort, the example of the Lithuanians being an exception to the rule. The insurrection was crushed. Could the Poles have acted otherwise? Would the Poles of the Congress Kingdom have been better off if they had let the Russian tsars run roughshod over their constitution? To be sure, they still would have had a constitution, at least on the books, as opposed to the Organic Laws that replaced it. They would still have had the University of Warsaw and the Society of Friends of Learning, both of which were closed after the insurrection, as well as the Seym and an army of their own. Certain Poles would not have had their lands confiscated for their fight against tsardom. Other nobles would not have been treated like peasants, with many even deported from the Polish lands, when they could not provide legal proof of nobility after 1836. The entire country would not have had to experience martial law for the next quarter century.

Yet could the Poles have expected an autocratic tsar such as Nicholas to be consistent in his dealings with them? His distrust of the Poles may have been tinged with national envy: Nicholas was well aware that there were Russians under his rule who resented the fact that Poles in the kingdom had it better—economically as well as politically—than the Russians did within the empire. In some ways, the insurrection did strengthen national consciousness. In their oppression, Poles became more like other oppressed peoples in the long nineteenth century. And oppression, while depressing, was not overwhelmingly so after the November Insurrection. Polish was still the language of the kingdom, although Poles beyond the Bug River to the east were forbidden to use it (they also witnessed the demolition of the Polish educational and cultural infrastructure that was the Vilnius educational district). The independence of the Polish bank and treasury was maintained. And the doors were not closed to Poles insofar as making careers in the tsarist administration was concerned (there was always a shortage of qualified people in the empire). Poles continued to serve as judges in the courts of the Kingdom of Poland. So, not all was lost.

The Great Emigration

Not all Poles stayed around to see how matters would develop after 1831. Already during the insurrection, some insurrectionists abandoned the Kingdom of Poland and made their way to the west. After the November Insurrection, a mass exodus of Poles ensued to France, Belgium, and Britain. There were so many Poles in western Europe that this came to be called the Great Emigration (Wielka Emigracja). The term *wielka* can mean large— which it was. Somewhere in the vicinity of ten thousand Poles became political émigrés in Paris and elsewhere. But *wielka* also means great. It was a great generation, comprised of the leading Polish intellectual lights as well as dedicated cadres of insurrectionists. Among those former were the great Romantic poets—the so-called Bards: Adam Mickiewicz, Juliusz Słowacki, and Zygmunt Krasiński. Mickiewicz, incidentally, had managed to escape from Russia to the west right before the November Insurrection.

Also in emigration was a young composer from Warsaw, Fryderyk (French: Frédéric) Chopin. Son of a Polonized emigrant from France, Fryderyk was in Vienna when the insurrection broke out and made the reverse journey. The young Chopin, whose musical genius would (among other things) popularize Polish dances such as the polonaise, the mazurka, and the krakowiak, channeled his anguished reaction to the loss of the November Insurrection into his famous, and moving, *Revolutionary Étude*.

Only in emigration did Polish Romanticism—in literature even more than in music—develop to its full potential. Polish literature of this period is interesting not only for its intrinsic value but for what it represented to Polish society in that period. When politics failed (as they clearly did in 1830–1831), poetry took its place. Poland went from being led by generals wielding sabers to generals wielding pens.

These newfangled generals led a cultural campaign. Their task was to produce a vibrant literary culture that would unite all the lands of the former

Commonwealth as well as enrich the Polish spirit. Here the Polish Romantics were influenced by thinkers like Herder, famous for his conception of
the *Volksgeist*, which can be translated as the spirit of the people or nation
or as national character. In this vision, the people or nation was viewed increasingly as the common man.

This proved to be one of the most important periods of Polish literature, if not
the most important (which surely could be argued). And Adam Mickiewicz—
the young poet introduced earlier—is the most famous of the Polish Romantic poets. Indeed, he is the most famous literary figure in all of Polish history.
Thus it is interesting to consider the opening line of his most famous work, the
epic poem *Pan Tadeusz*. Expressing the longing of the émigré for the country
he has left behind, it begins with the invocation, "Lithuania! My fatherland!"
Writing in Polish, this poet who hailed from the territory of today's Belarus,
considered Lithuania his homeland. This suggests that this quintessentially Polish poet reflected ideas of Poland and Polishness that were hardly straightforward—ideas more redolent of the former Sarmatian, Commonwealth realm.
Polish and provincial culture (brought to life in the Lithuanian landscape) were
one in this depiction of a soon-to-be-lost Sarmatian idyll in its encounter with
the transformations of the Napoleonic era. Indeed, it is a Polish peculiarity that
national self-definitions were often forged at its margins—in the borderland
realm increasingly referred to in the nineteenth century as the *Kresy*.

Paris proved a seedbed for all kinds of ideas about Poland's past, present,
and future. The émigrés were obsessed with "the Polish question," a question
not limited to the regaining of national sovereignty. Lacking independent
statehood, Poles had to answer some other crucial questions as well. They
increasingly had to choose, consciously, to be Poles, as this was no longer a
choice of state identification. But what, then, was Polishness? How was one
to define Poland, or who was a Pole? How to justify being—let alone becoming—Polish, in a world of imperial dominance?

Again, the poet spoke. Or, rather, wrote—although it should be added that
Mickiewicz also spent the period from 1840 to 1844 lecturing on Slavic literature at the Collège de France, his lectures often electrifying his audience.
Consider his *Books of the Polish Nation and the Polish Pilgrimage*. Mickiewicz believed that the Poles had a mission of universal significance. In his
messianic vision, Poland was the Christ of Nations, suffering for the rest of
the world. "But on the third day," he wrote in true biblical style, "the soul
shall return to the body, and the Nations shall arise and free all the peoples
of Europe from slavery."* Mickiewicz also saw a special role for his nation in

---

*   Cited from Peter Brock, "Polish Nationalism," in *Nationalism in Eastern Europe*, ed. Peter F.
Sugar and Ivo J. Lederer (Seattle: University of Washington Press, 1969), 318–19.

the Slavic world. The future of Europe lay with the Slavs—and the Poles, not the Russians, were Slavdom's natural leaders, who would fight against the perceived evils of civilization.

Despite his liberal use of biblical phrasing, Mickiewicz's Roman Catholicism was hardly orthodox. The Pole was conflicted in his relationship to the See of Peter. He, like many others, was outraged that the Vicar of Christ should side with the partitioning empires and condemn the Polish insurrection. Furthermore, Mickiewicz fell under the spell of Andrzej Towiański, a leader of a mystical cult; this experience did little to strengthen his connection to the Roman Catholic Church of his day.

Mickiewicz and the Romantics focused their attention, in exile, on the Polish nation, seeking to determine what in the Polish past was significant, and whether the nation had a historical mission. Theirs was an ideal vision of the nation, focusing more on the body politic—the potential masses of Poles—than on any future territorial incarnation. The Poland of the Romantics was one of the mind. They believed that their nation did have a mission, which was to bring universal freedom to Europe. In this mission lay all hope for Poland. Only if Poles fought for universal freedom could they be considered worthy of regaining independent statehood. Their national stance, thus, was an active and engaged one. The purpose of Polish Romantic literature, furthermore, was to embolden and inspire the nation as well as strengthen national consciousness, without which there could be no gains. In an age when generals wielding sabers had failed, the Romantics saw themselves as generals wielding pens.

Émigré Politics

While aware of the work of the Romantic writers many Polish émigrés remained absorbed by more traditional politics. Polish organizations proliferated abroad, most notably in France. That over a hundred periodicals were published by Poles in emigration in these years suggests there was no lack of ideas—if perhaps a lack of consensus on how to proceed.

Two main orientations attracted the bulk of the émigrés. The first was the constitutional-monarchical camp of Adam Jerzy Czartoryski, who left Poland after the abortive insurrection. His camp was known as the Hôtel Lambert group, after the building on the Ile-de-la-Cité in Paris where it was headquartered. Perhaps it should come as no surprise that Tsar Alexander's former minister of foreign affairs should seek to gain influence in the West through diplomatic channels. Czartoryski's vision of Poland continued to be the May 3 option—that is, a constitutional monarchy, yet now, one fully independent of Russia. Indeed, he and his camp underscored the citizen Poles' superiority to the Russians, who remained subjects of an autocratic tsar. Czartoryski and his followers saw Poland as vying with Russia for influence in the Slavic world. They contrasted Russian Panslavism (with Russia as unquestioned hegemon) with a Polish version of Panslavism, in which Poles would recognize the Slavic nations as equals.

The other main orientation, the Polish Democratic Society, stood to the left of Czartoryski's camp. It espoused more radical republican and democratic ideas, more in keeping with ideas espoused by fellow European revolutionaries such as Giuseppe Mazzini. Instead of expecting salvation from the West, members of the Polish Democratic Society placed their faith in the Polish masses, especially the peasantry, whose contribution would be crucial in the fight for Poland's liberation. They also argued that the Polish nation had no right to independence if it did not proceed with the emancipation of the peasantry. These democrats saw the nation in much broader terms than did the more conservative, noble-based Hôtel Lambert. For a future insurrection to be successful, according to the democrats' manifesto of 1836, it must include peasants, townspeople, and Jews, as well as nobles.

It is worth noting that the Polish left of the early nineteenth century was diverse. In England, Polish Romantic socialists of the 1830s such as Stanisław Worcell and Tadeusz Krępowiecki founded the Communes of the Polish People. Their vision of the nation gave pride of place to the peasant masses, the *lud* (people or folk), and expected that the nobility would subordinate itself to this new national force. Such a view literally turned on its head the old Sarmatian conviction that the nobles were everything and the peasants nothing.

Insurrectionary Initiatives

Poles in emigration were not content to twiddle their thumbs. These were for the most part dedicated military and political cadres, who had actively striven to re-create an independent Polish state. In emigration, unlike back home, they could discuss the fate of the nation, of Poland, with abandon. They laid many a plot in emigration. And there were attempts at engaging in conspiratorial-revolutionary activity back home. Take, for example, the case of Captain Szymon Konarski. His conspiracy network reached from Kraków and Galicia to the Kingdom of Poland and the Russian guberniias to the east. Yet in 1839 he was arrested and executed. This suggests that any sense that the November Insurrection was followed by a period of quietude would be incorrect.

A more novel—and potentially more successful—approach to winning over the masses back home was taken by a priest, Father Piotr Ściegienny, who had the right idea of what it would take to convince the peasantry to join in the Polish fight for freedom. What would spur them to action was a blessing—nay, a command—emanating from the very pope in Rome, the true source of authority for the pious folk. Indeed, religion more than anything else was a true marker of peasant identity. Most nineteenth-century peasants would be aghast if someone labeled them Poles. Poles were the nobles, their overlords, for whom they had little love. Rather, peasants saw themselves as Christians. This understanding of the mind of the peasant led Ściegienny in 1844 to fabricate a false papal bull that incited the peasantry under Russian rule to armed revolt. News of the bull produced some results; yet the revolutionary priest and his peasant followers were caught and subdued, putting to an end this seemingly fruitful approach.

Annus Horribilis—1846

There seemed to be no end of plans hatched by the Polish émigrés to ignite revolution back home. They sought to change the course of Polish history in 1846. That fateful year marked the attempt of a group of Poles to bring about a national and social revolution. This ambitious double revolution aimed to capitalize both on the general desire of Poles for national freedom and on the peasants, the yet unconscious national masses, without whose help the battle could not be won.

A combination of émigrés and local Poles hatched plans for revolution. Revolution was to break out on the night of February 21/22, 1846, simultaneously in Poznań and Galicia—that is, under both Prussian and Austrian rule, respectively. But things started going wrong almost immediately. Even before this date, the insurrectionists were denounced by a conspirator who got cold feet, and many were arrested not only in Poznań (at the center of conspiratorial activity) but also in various locations within Galicia. While insurrection in Prussia and Russia was nipped in the bud, the year 1846 is memorable for what transpired in Galicia and the Free City of Kraków.

The revolution began on February 18 in western Galicia. News that organizers of the revolution had been apprehended in Poznań prompted the earlier date. The noble activists were adamant: they would go ahead with the revolution. They chose to begin the insurrection in the city of Tarnów.

Simultaneously the noble revolutionaries declared an end to serfdom.

These developments (and rumors that something was in the air) set what might have been construed as "intranational" relations (that is, relations between nobles and peasants) on edge. Although the noble insurrectionists proclaimed peasant emancipation in Galicia, making this the most democratic of the Polish uprisings to date, the peasants did not respond to the nobles' overtures as had been anticipated (the nobles must have been expecting open arms). This may have been too much to expect in a province where relations between the peasants and their overlords were already strained. In addition, it appears that Austrian officials had gained the ear of some peasants first. We will never know exactly what the peasants were told: were they informed that the noble Polish revolutionaries were the enemies of the emperor (after all, some peasants thought of themselves as "the emperor's people")? Or that they meant harm to the peasants (nobles in Galicia were not exactly known for being kind to their serfs)? Or were the peasants even promised rewards for fighting—and killing—the revolutionaries, who sought to destabilize Galicia?

The agitation of the noble revolutionaries backfired. It resulted in a veritable bloodletting—but not against Austrian rule. Not only were the peasants suspicious of the activities of the noble revolutionaries in their territory; they actually attacked the revolutionaries—and by extension, other nobles.

One of the ringleaders of the peasant attackers in the Tarnów region was a fellow named Jakub Szela. He had long complained about the way the owners of his village treated him, even to the extent of seeking justice not only in Tarnów but even in the Galician capital of Lviv. Szela was summoned to Tarnów several days before the outbreak of the insurrection. On February 19, the day following the declaration of the insurrection, the alarmed peasants began attacking their noble landlords. Not only were the insurrectionists unable to gain support for their movement among the target group, the peasantry, but their activities managed to disquiet the peasants of the Tarnów region, who then went on a rampage, killing their overlords, the region's nobility. Over a thousand nobles were killed and over five hundred estates destroyed in the course of February and March, after which the Austrian authorities tried to contain the unrest.

All told, the peasants managed to massacre almost 90 percent of the Tarnów nobility. This peasant reaction to the beginning of insurrection in 1846 has gone down in history as the Galician jacquerie, that is, a popular revolt of the peasants. Rumors later spread that the killing was done not by Polish-speaking peasants but by Ruthenian peasants, but this was not true. The Tarnów region was peopled by Polish-speaking peasants. It is they who tragically massacred their Polish lords.

So much for the expected noble-peasant brotherhood. Despite the words of a later Polish song about the tragedy, which noted that "there were lots of Cains among us," the nationally conscious Polish elites of this period found it hard to blame the peasants—illiterate, uninformed, wary of advances made by the estate that had oppressed them for centuries—for their actions, however reprehensible. Instead, they blamed the Austrian officials for leading the villagers astray.

The Free City of Kraków and Its Reaction

The events of 1846 took a slightly more encouraging turn in the Free City of Kraków. One of the liberal enclaves of Europe of the post-1815 period, the tiny Free City had been given its own constitution, penned by Czartoryski. It was also given a chance to develop economically, given its strategic position at the place of intersection of the three partitioning powers.

The influence of educated citizens—whether in the Senate or in Kraków's ancient university—in the Free City was palpable. They took a more enlightened, if still cautious, approach to the peasants of the region. Kraków's peasants were given their personal freedom and owed rent instead of labor dues to their lords. In addition, each village within the tiny territory was able to send its own delegate to the local assembly. This meant that some peasants—doubtless the most well-off among them—had some experience of taking part in political affairs. In other words, the peasants of the Free City of Kraków were not oppressed nearly as much as the proverbial Galician peasant, such as those in the Tarnów region to Kraków's east.

Furthermore, the tiny Polish enclave had a symbolic status completely out of proportion with its physical size. As the medieval capital of Poland, Kraków still housed the remains of the country's royalty. Wawel Hill, with the castle and cathedral, was a place of national significance. Poland's kings and queens were buried in the crypts of Wawel Cathedral, making this a national sacred space of great import as well.

This national importance was further magnified during the period of existence of the Free City. Despite the city being subject to the whims of the custodial powers, it managed to gain approval for new national burials in the crypts of Wawel Cathedral. None other than Alexander I of Russia, in his capacity as Polish king (if across the border), gave permission for the remains of Prince Józef Poniatowski, who died at the battle of Leipzig in 1813, to be interred there. (That Poniatowski had been fighting Alexander's Russian troops indicates the magnanimity of that particular tsar.) Poniatowski's burial in the Wawel crypts in 1817 would quickly be followed by that of another Polish military hero. Tadeusz Kościuszko died that same year, and his remains were ceremoniously reburied in the Wawel crypt—again, with the permission of Tsar Alexander I—in 1818.

Cracovians so revered Kościuszko that they resolved to build for him a more visible monument: an earthen mound, much like the prehistoric mounds honoring Krakus and Wanda surrounding the city. These events gave Cracovians and visitors to the Free City a chance to act patriotically, at least for a period. The custodial powers eventually reined in such activities, occupying the Free City in 1836. Henceforth, the independent functioning of this tiny state would be limited.

Not that this kept the noble revolutionaries of 1846 from setting their sights on the Free City. The leader of the revolution in Kraków was Edward Dembowski. Called the "soul of the Kraków revolution," this noble radical democrat sought to elevate the peasants to pride of place in the Polish nation. He advocated an agrarian revolution.

Led by Dembowski, the revolutionaries managed to seize control of the city. Beyond Dembowski's ability to rally Poles in the Free City of Kraków to the cause (within the space of a few days, he gained about six thousand insurrectionists from among the artisans, urban poor, and petty bourgeoisie), his major achievement was the proclamation of the Kraków Manifesto of February 22, 1846. The manifesto called for social equality (that is, the removal of estate differences) and the end of serfdom, and it even promised land to landless peasants who fought in the uprising. (Dembowski took matters much further than Kościuszko had done a half century earlier.) The revolutionaries declared they would punish anyone who forced the peasants back into serfdom, and they planned to create national workshops with better pay than at present for the workers. They also announced to the Jewish residents of Kraków that they would have equal rights with the Poles.

Despite gaining some support in town, what the insurrectionists/revolutionaries really wanted was to win over more peasants. On February 27, 1846, Dembowski organized a procession out of town, with the permission and participation of the local clergy, some thirty of whom carried crosses and banners in the procession. Altogether some five hundred persons took part, with only a small group of thirty bearing arms. Dembowski was dressed in the traditional peasant coat, the *sukmana*. This was the same article of clothing that Tadeusz Kościuszko had donned after the victory against the Russians at Racławice in 1794, a victory that was made possible by peasant participation. Alas, this sign of respect for the Polish peasant did not protect Dembowski from the bullets from the Austrian troops. He perished that same day, during the procession, as he led his group with a cross in his hand. The following day Russian and Austrian forces occupied Kraków.

In sum, the revolution of 1846 completely backfired. The Galician peasant jacquerie was the last thing expected by that particular group of revolutionaries, who were reaching out to the peasantry. Ironically, the massacre was of Poles by Poles (although the latter would not see it that way): Roman Catholic peasant speakers of Polish massacred Roman Catholic noble speakers of Polish. Whether the former were egged on by Austrian officials does not change the tragic outcome.

The Free City of Kraków gave revolutionaries some small hope. The revolution lasted nine days in Kraków, only to be put down militarily by the Austrian authorities. Despite his best efforts, Dembowski was unsuccessful

Figure 9.1 Woodcut of Edward Dembowski during the Kraków Uprising, 1846.

in bringing his vision of a future democratic Poland, one that truly would have room for the peasant, to fruition. His plan also backfired.

Not only did the Austrians kill Dembowski; in November 1846 they incorporated the formerly Free City of Kraków into Galicia proper. The tiny state lost its independence. This little island of Polishness was swallowed up in the larger imperial sea. Under the Habsburgs, Germanization of the formerly Polish institutions, including the university, proceeded apace, and Kraków lost its position as a free trade entrepôt. The city was soon demoted to the status of a provincial garrison town. Garrison troops even occupied the royal castle on Wawel Hill. Kraków was relegated to the status of a border outpost in the larger multiethnic Habsburg state, which at the time was perhaps the most depressing and depressed of the partitioned lands.

The massacre of 1846 was a shock for the Polish revolutionaries and intelligentsia—a term invented by the Pole Karol Libelt in 1844 and later (and more famously) adopted by the Russians. The massacre set back relations between noble and peasant in Galicia for quite some time. The conservative Galician nobility was especially frightened of the peasants and wanted nothing more than to keep them in their place. Still, there were others within Polish society who saw this as a challenge: one had to educate the peasants, teach them that they were not "the emperor's people," as some had come to see themselves, and show them that they actually did have something in common with their noble landlords.

The European Revolutions of 1848

In a way the events of 1846 meant that Poles were in a worse position in 1848, a year often referred to in European history as the Springtime of Peoples. This was not a springtime for the Poles—certainly not as a nation in its entirety. In 1848 Poles in each of the partitioning lands had to deal with the specific circumstances of the empire in which they found themselves.

While unrest in 1848 began on the Apennine Peninsula and spread to France (where it gained a revolutionary cast) and elsewhere, the events of that year were perhaps most notable in the German lands. From May 1848 to May 1849, it appeared that the motley German states that had once been part of the now defunct Holy Roman Empire might reunite in one German superstate. An all-German assembly convened in Frankfurt to ascertain the possibility of unification; however, their cautious plans for unification ultimately met with a gruff rejoinder by the Prussian king, Friedrich Wilhelm IV, who disdained to accept a crown, even an imperial one, from the gutter.

While not participating in the Frankfurt assembly, Poles in Prussia were cognizant of events taking place in Berlin. Having wrung concessions from the king for a Prussian assembly, Prussian radicals proceeded to give autonomy to the Poles of West Prussia and the Grand Duchy of Poznań. The swift reaction from Germans in Poznań was quite different: the reactionary Prussian army vetoed any such move in the province. All this led to a brief uprising in the Poznań region. Thus, although initially there seemed to be a degree of German-Polish solidarity in 1848, when push came to shove, the Germans of Prussia could not countenance the loss of those territories to the Prussian state.

In the Austrian Empire, the situation evolved more threateningly, even leading to a change at the top. As of December 1848, the eighteen-year-old Franz Joseph would rule. Events grew heated in the Hungarian lands as well as in Vienna, although ultimately the empire would be pacified. A number of Poles, most notably the general Józef Bem, joined in the Hungarian fight for independence in 1848–1849, demonstrating again the relevance of the slogan "for our freedom and for yours."

Cognizant of what was happening in Vienna and elsewhere in the monarchy, the inhabitants of Galicia also sought to avail themselves of this opportunity to press for more rights in 1848. Revolutionary fervor encompassed the Galician capital of Lviv. A memorandum expressing the Poles' still rather timid desires was prepared and dispatched to Vienna, where it languished. In the end, cities such as Lviv and Kraków would be bombarded by Austrian forces. The city of Prague—where a pan-Slavic congress (attended by representatives of various Slavic nations, including the Polish) was being held—was also bombed. All this left no doubt as to who was in power.

Still, two developments make the events of 1848 in Galicia noteworthy. The perspicacious governor of Galicia, the Habsburg loyalist Franz Stadion, saw ways in which to take some of the sting out of these Polish endeavors. The governor moved preemptively to emancipate the Galician peasantry even before peasants in the rest of the Habsburg lands won their freedom. He acted quickly, in order to prevent the Poles from doing the same. Thanks to Stadion, the peasants of Galicia now had Emperor Franz Joseph to thank for the end of serfdom.

Stadion also sought to counter growing Polish patriotic sentiment by supporting the political emergence of the Ruthenes. The eastern part of Galicia was thoroughly multiethnic: peasants tended to be Greek Catholic Ruthenes while the towns were filled with Jews as well as Poles. Stadion assisted the formation of the Supreme Ruthenian Council in Lviv, which addressed the grievances of Ruthenes within Galicia and sought to split the province in half. This greatly alarmed the Galician Poles, who saw this as an attempt to use divide-and-conquer tactics in the province. Polish activists in Lviv countered by establishing the so-called Ruthenian Assembly, dominated by the Polish nobles of the region.

These moves by Stadion did not go unnoticed. Some Poles went so far as to credit him with creating the Ruthenes as a national group, as the vast majority had not given much evidence of national consciousness previously. Yet, in this, were the Ruthenian peasants so different from the Polish-speaking peasants of western Galicia, who (as was evident in 1846) hardly saw themselves as Poles? All the same, many nationally conscious Poles tended to see the Ruthenian peasants as part of the larger Polish national body, as potential Poles. They could be compared to Bretons in France, a distinct group with its own dialect yet still very much part of the French nation. In the case of Polish and Ruthenian, the languages were much closer, making this connection easier to argue. Nonetheless, the events of 1848 would have serious repercussions for Galicia in later decades.

The Crimean War and Its Unexpected Impact

Yet another major international conflict would set the tone for another series of events. This was the Crimean War of 1854–1856. Whereas readers may associate this war with the figure of Florence Nightingale, who nursed the victorious British troops, the conflict spawned various Polish initiatives. The elderly Prince Adam Czartoryski continued to make diplomatic overtures to the Western powers of Britain and France, the two major players fighting Russia. He strove to get them to use Polish resources and knowledge of the region, in the hopes of re-creating a Polish state. Czartoryski proposed the formation of legions of Poles in exile in Turkey after 1848 (some Poles had fought for Hungarian independence that year, later to escape south and spend time in emigration in Turkey). Polish officers might lead units of "Ottoman Cossacks." And indeed, Michał Czajkowski, a convert to Islam who subsequently took the name Sadyk Pasha, created a Cossack regiment comprised of Poles and Balkan Slavs.

Yet these were not the only Poles to avail themselves of the opportunity to get involved. Poland's aging poet-prince, Adam Mickiewicz, set off for Istanbul. Mickiewicz sought to rally Jews to join his legion and fight. The revolutionary poet was to die from cholera in the Ottoman capital, at age fifty-seven.

Russian Reforms

The efforts of the Great Emigration had been for naught. The Polish question did not figure in the deliberations following the Crimean War. Despite the lack of Polish success, the war had repercussions for Poles under Russian rule. One of the belligerents, Russia had lost the war. There is something about being defeated in battle that changes one's outlook—even if one is a big empire. And indeed, the debacle of the Crimean War led to changes within Russia. Already, during the war, there was an unexpected change of ruler. Nicholas I died in 1855, to be succeeded by his son Alexander II.

The new tsar proved very unlike his father. Alexander II took a different, more reformist, tack within the empire. This period has been referred to as the post-Sevastopol Thaw—that is, the sense that something had to change for Russia to be able to regain its prominence within Europe. Russia under Alexander II countenanced a degree of liberalization. The agrarian question also gained some traction.

As regarded dealings with the Poles, Alexander thought a conciliatory approach might work better. He allowed for an amnesty to free Poles who had been sent to Siberia; and censorship was somewhat relaxed. At the same time, he made clear to the Poles that he was in charge. When he appeared in Warsaw, Alexander famously declared to the Polish nobles, "point de reveries . . ." French was indeed the language he used to speak to his Polish subjects, French being the foreign language favored by the upper classes since at least the Enlightenment. What did the tsar mean by this? His Polish subjects were not to engage in daydreaming. There would be no uniting of the Kingdom of Poland with the *Kresy*. There would be no independent Poland, ever.

Alexander II nonetheless opened the door to some initiatives from below. Perhaps the most notable of these was permission granted Count Andrzej Zamoyski to found an agricultural society. This dovetailed nicely with the tsar's interest in agrarian questions, and these were issues of great importance to Polish landowners as well. Being a legal outlet for discussion of agrarian as well as other matters, the society proved tremendously popular among the Poles. Within the space of several months of its establishment in 1858, some seventy branches were founded. Poles found occasion to discuss their future with their compatriots.

Life was made easier for upper-class Poles, and by extension, there was some trickle down of prosperity. Alexander II relaxed restrictions on the employment of Poles in the civil service. Under the new tsar, more Poles entered into the imperial bureaucracy. This surely had an impact on the middling nobility and intelligentsia, which had a hard time making ends meet.

One might joke that Poles now could dream, that is, dream of becoming civil servants under tsarist rule.

Even Polish entrepreneurism was now encouraged in new ways. The Russian-Polish tariff border had been removed as early as 1851. The construction of railways connecting the former Polish lands with major Russian centers promised increasing trade and contacts. The economic health of the core Polish territories increased. More Polish grain was exported eastward; more development of industry was forthcoming. All this put Poles in a novel position: if things continued as they were going, that is, if Poles continued to prosper under Russian rule, they might be dissuaded from further uprisings. They would have more to lose.

The Danger of a Little Reform

Nonetheless, the danger of only a little reform was that the door set ajar for limited initiatives might be blown off its hinges. Perhaps afraid that their national sentiments would be lulled by recent developments, some more radically minded Varsovians decided to do something patriotic—and controversial. They resolved to commemorate, in public, the thirtieth anniversary of the battle of Grochów. Fought on February 25, 1831, Grochów was one of the Polish military victories during the November Insurrection. In honor of the anniversary, they sang hymns that could be considered inflammatory: "Boże, coś Polskę" (God, protect Poland), the new refrain of which concluded with the nation imploring God to free their fatherland. Nor could the song of the Polish legions, "Jeszcze Polska nie zginęła" (Poland has not yet perished), be construed in any but a revolutionary manner. Several persons at the demonstration ended up killed by the tsarist police.

This happened to be the same period when the head of the Agricultural Society, the generally cautious Count Zamoyski, saw fit to prepare a petition for the tsar. He politely asked Alexander not only for more rights and freedoms for the Kingdom of Poland but also to reattach to it the eastern borderlands that had been taken away, the so-called western guberniias of Russia proper. With all these demands and demonstrations, the situation was in danger of getting out of hand. The tsar needed to find someone within the kingdom he could deal with—and this could not be Zamoyski.

Alexander found another Pole he hoped might be more amenable. The man was Margrave Aleksander Wielopolski, Zamoyski's rival. Wielopolski hailed originally from Galicia. The debacle that was the peasant jacquerie of 1846 left the margrave seething. He penned an anonymous and scathing criticism of Metternich and his policies (as seen in the jacquerie), which was published in Paris. In it Wielopolski laid the blame squarely at the feet of the Habsburg regime, which had demoralized the peasants and sought, in its hatred of the Polish nobility, to destroy the social order. Wielopolski was so enraged that he voted with his feet, opting for Romanov and not Habsburg rule. He declared that the Polish nobility would much "prefer . . . to march with the Russians at the head of Slavic civilization, young, vigorous, fully of the future . . . rather than be dragged along . . . at the tail of your decrepit, anxious, and presumptuous [Austrian] civilization."* Clearly this was a man who was willing to work with the tsar.

The following month, Alexander appointed Wielopolski to a new post, as head of the Commission of Religions and Public Enlightenment. Initially, it seemed a good move. Wielopolski provided his compatriots with increased opportunities in the bureaucracy and administration. Poles came to dominate the local administration, which was also Polonized (if not the military). The influential Pole nonetheless took a rather heavy-handed approach in dealing with his compatriots. In distinct contrast to the traditional Sarmatian view of public participation in the political process for all noble citizens, Wielopolski disparaged such efforts. In his own words, "much can be done *for* the Poles, but nothing with their participation."

Perhaps it should come as no surprise that the anti-Romantic Wielopolski was a polarizing figure. The radicals remained uninterested in such gains as the margrave could provide them and even claimed that those who took advantage of the new opportunities for employment in tsarist service were traitors to the national cause. They sought more—and they were getting less, although some of the reforms included the bestowing of legal rights on Jews, which surely was a step in the right direction.

Finding it difficult to deal with not only the radicals but also Zamoyski and his colleagues, Wielopolski responded by dissolving the Agricultural Society. Yet another adjustment to the procedure for crowd dispersal meant that the date April 8, 1861, became a bloody one: over a hundred unarmed men, women, and children gathered in Warsaw's Castle Square, some on their knees praying, were killed. The deaths led to a declaration of national mourning—with demonstrators wearing black, as if grieving for a dead relative—and protests being channeled into the churches, where special masses were ordered and patriotic songs sung.

Wielopolski responded by declaring martial law—in essence, banning all public gatherings. This did not prevent a demonstration on the anniver-

---

* Cited from Larry Wolff, *The Idea of Galicia: History and Fantasy in Habsburg Political Culture* (Stanford: Stanford University Press, 2010), 165.

sary of the death of Kościuszko on October 15. The demonstration resulted in some fifteen hundred arrests. The military went so far as to enter the churches of the capital while services were being held to make the arrests. Those fifteen hundred were imprisoned in the Warsaw citadel, a rather fearsome prison.

The breaching of hallowed ground by the military enraged the population. Churches and synagogues (for a number of Jews had also notably participated in the commemorations) all over Warsaw locked their gates shut to prevent further profanation. While Wielopolski managed to wring more concessions from the authorities, including permission to establish a school of higher learning in Warsaw, the so-called Main School, the people could not be placated. The situation worsened when, after a conversation with Grand Duke Constantine, Count Andrzej Zamoyski was exiled for his audacity in asking that the eastern borderlands be reunited.

The situation was tense. Not only Polish radicals (the Reds) but also more established (and thus more reluctant) notables (the Whites) began to prepare for a future insurrection. These two groups even began to collect a secret national tax to finance the insurrection. They established a secret National Government, which would come to be known only by its seal.

The January Insurrection

The straw that broke the camel's back came in January 1863. Wielopolski had decided to nip the burgeoning upheaval in the bud by calling up recruits to the Russian army. Some ten thousand were to be called up on the night of January 14/15, in the hopes that a lot of the young radicals who were making life hard for the margrave would be affected. Given the conditions of such obligatory service, which since 1857 lasted for "only" fifteen years, the young men—potential recruits—preferred insurrection . . . and escaped to the forests. In a way, thus, Wielopolski's move only provoked the response he sought to avoid—insurrection.

Alas, despite the preparations made the previous year, there was no unity as far as the approach to the insurrection went. (This is a perennial problem with insurrections.) Two distinct camps had formed: the radicals (Reds), and a camp that was more conciliatory toward the tsarist regime (the Whites). The Reds were radical democrats fighting not only for freedom from tsarist rule but also for the liberation of the peasant masses (à la Kościuszko). It was the young radicals who initiated the insurrection. They were joined by the Whites only after months had passed. The Whites sought to gain support in the West, but although some countries made some supportive noises, there was no help forthcoming for the insurrectionists, barring several hundred foreign volunteers who joined in the fight.

The provisional National Government (initially called the National Central Committee) that had been established in advance of the insurrection produced manifestoes. These underscored two aims of the insurrectionists. First, they were unequivocal about the need for the emancipation of the peasantry and made a declaration to this effect. And, although peasants reacted in various ways, more peasants joined the fight than in any of the earlier insurrections—the Kościuszko Insurrection included. The tsarist regime responded in kind, if after the Polish National Government. On March 2, 1864, the regime proclaimed the emancipation of the peasantry. Henceforth peasants would not only have personal freedom; they would gain ownership of the land they worked. This, incidentally, would weaken the Polish land-owning nobility under Russian rule, as the terms of compensation for the loss of land favored the regime, not the landowners.

The second aim was to reach out to the Ruthenes of the old Commonwealth. This reflected the insurrectionists' desire that the future Poland be a multiethnic state. In a way, they seemed to be trying to make up for the lost opportunity of the seventeenth century, when the Cossacks were not given full rights. In the propaganda for the insurrection in 1863–1864, a new coat of arms was devised for the future state. It was divided not into two but three parts: Polish (the eagle), Lithuanian (the chase, or knight on horseback), and Ruthenian (the Archangel Michael). In other words, they seemed to be looking for a new Hadiach. This does not mean they were able to achieve this ambitious aim, however. More support seemed to be forthcoming from the Belarusians, rallied by the Pole Konstanty Kalinowski, than from Ruthenes living further to the south and east.

In contrast to the November Insurrection of 1830, the January Insurrection of 1863–1864 was characterized by partisan warfare. Indeed, the soldiers relied heavily on the local population, although Poles came from other partition zones to fight as well. Although about two hundred thousand insurrectionists fought in the insurrection, there were never more than thirty thousand at any given time. This resulted in hundreds of small battles and the use of guerilla tactics.

Another distinguishing factor in 1863 was the establishment of the National Government, whose seal magically opened doors. The number of conspiratorial clergymen was also large. Not everyone could easily take sides. Civil servants—the bureaucrats and officials who had been gaining jobs and influence under Wielopolski—were in an unenviable position. They were damned if they did not support the insurrection, but damned if they did. Some officials actually hung in their offices two-sided emblems: on one side was the emblem of the insurrection, on the other the Russian imperial eagle. When someone approached, the official had to have the presence of mind— or the good fortune—to discern which side of the emblem should be visible.

Not until October 17, 1863, did the insurrection gain an effective leader. That is the date that Romuald Traugutt became dictator. Despite his good leadership, it was too late. The year 1864 witnessed the end of the insurrection. Those insurrectionists who managed to survive were now trying not to get caught.

Yet others soldiered on. Particularly persistent was a priest in the region of Podlachia, Father Stanisław Brzóska, who rallied peasants to the cause, fighting until April 1865. Nonetheless, the insurrection had been decapitated some eight months earlier. On August 5, 1864, Traugutt and four conspiratorial compatriots were hanged in Warsaw.

Repercussions of the January Insurrection

The largest of the Polish insurrections, the January Insurrection was a Romantic endeavor—and as such, it seemed fated to fail. There was limited peasant support, few Ruthenes embraced the insurrection, and the general population remained divided. For those on the losing side, there was the noose—or exile. Tens of thousands of insurrectionists (perhaps as many as twenty-seven thousand) were sent to Siberia. Although it may be hard to comprehend, some insurrectionists were sentenced to walk all the way there while others were allowed to ride. It was a hardship, regardless. Some insurrectionists were kept in shackles throughout the trip of between twelve and sixteen thousand kilometers.

All this—together with the fact that thousands more Poles emigrated to the West—resulted in a tremendous loss of Polish manpower (and womenpower, for some wives accompanied their husbands). The fate of insurrectionists in Russia tended to be inversely proportional to their social status. Those who fared best—a relative term, to be sure—were insurrectionists of peasant stock (again, the Russian assumption being that they did not know any better). Next came the nobles and the middle classes (educated types, who should have known better). Singled out for the worst treatment by the tsarist authorities was the clergy. Poland's priests, monks, and nuns were identified as carrying the distinctive marker of Polishness, as understood by the Russian authorities: their Roman Catholic faith. In the view of the Russians, the religious should not have meddled in political affairs.

Not only was human capital tremendously depleted. Many Polish estates were confiscated. Poles lost control over large swaths of land, which now came into Russian possession. No longer could one speak of the Kingdom of Poland under any guise. Following the insurrection, the former kingdom was renamed Vistula Land and incorporated into the empire proper. As of 1879, Russian became the sole language of instruction. The civil service was de-Polonized. As the equation of Pole with Roman Catholic was strengthened during the insurrection, the tsarist regime came down hard on the Roman Catholic Church in Russia. Confiscations of the church's landed property were legion, making the church utterly dependent upon the goodwill of the tsarist regime.

The Polish poet Cyprian Norwid once remarked that he was a member of a "nation which is undeniably great as far as *patriotism* is concerned but which as a society represents nothing. . . . We are no society at all. We are a great national banner." After 1864, the banner was in tatters. Was there no society to emerge from the conflagration?

CHAPTER 10

Poles Are Not Iroquois

The Nation at Work

The latter of the two great failed insurrections of the nineteenth century had brought little, if anything, in the way of progress to the Poles. So many insurrectionists hanged, so many others exiled into the depths of Siberia—so little to show for the sacrifice and dedication to the Polish cause. What was the nation to do when it was becoming increasingly clear that insurrectionism was not getting it anywhere? Surely some Poles must have been asking this question circa 1864. Not only had the near constant uprisings and conspiracies not helped the Polish cause; they had resulted in greater loss of Polish life and property. Was there no other way to maintain and expand the Polish national element without subsequently causing it to suffer?

Perhaps the Poles would be better off just giving up. Should they not make their peace with the partitions—embrace empire? Indeed, as after the third partition so too after the January Insurrection, this appeared to be one of the options. The subjects of each of the three empires would be loyal to the empire in which they lived. This option has been referred to as triple-loyalism.

There were Poles who chose this option, some more blatantly than others. The centennial of the first partition of Poland in 1872 inspired some defections on the part of individual Poles. Michał Czajkowski used the occasion of the anniversary to appeal to fellow Poles to return to Slavdom and subordinate themselves to the Russians. Yet another subject of the tsar, Kazimierz Krzywicki, outraged Polish patriots by advocating that they abandon Roman Catholicism and the Polish language as well as the desire for national independence. Was there no other option—no way for the Poles to maintain or even gain in strength without rising up to fight a more numerous and better armed foe? Surely not all moves had to be that drastic.

The Example of the Iroquois

The lesson of the failed January Insurrection was not lost on a certain inhabitant of the Polish lands under Prussian rule, who evidently had observed what had happened next door. In 1864, Ludwik Powidaj published an article in a Galician literary publication. Its title was "Poles and Indians." Not a new game for children to play outdoors, the title referred to a long-standing comparison between the two peoples. No less than Friedrich the Great of Prussia had called his new subjects from the former Royal Prussia—those gained in the first partition—"those poor Iroquois." Why Indians? Because he felt that he had to accustom them to European civilization.

Here King Friedrich was referring to a common trope: the civilizing mission of the Germans. Over the centuries, Germans had "civilized" Slavic peoples such as the Wends, Obotrites, and Lusatian Sorbs, most of whom had assimilated into the German majority, to the extent that they were no longer to be found. Those who were part of the Teutonic Knights (originally a multinational crusading order) had in some cases provided a cure (death by the sword) that was worse than the disease (paganism). Such was the fate of most of the original Prussians—the people who lent their name to those who came after them.

Was such to be the fate of the Poles after 1864? Were they fated either to meld into the respective imperial peoples and lose their Polish identity, or die from attrition after too many abortive uprisings directed against a much more numerous and better equipped foe? Powidaj cited a Prussian politician—a democrat—who publicly declared:

> Poles, like the American redskins, are sentenced by Providence to complete ruin. Just as in the New World the strong Anglo-American race pushes more and more impoverished and stunted generations of Indians into the everlasting wilderness where little by little they perish from hunger and misery, so Poles pushed out of the towns and the larger estates [and] brought to misery are to give up their place to Prussian civilization.*

Were the Poles truly like the Iroquois, a nation fated to die out?

Already it was noted that the Poles of Silesia—who, as you remember, had been transferred from Habsburg to Hohenzollern rule thanks to Friedrich the Great's invasion of Silesia in 1740—were losing their nationality. They were increasingly dominated by the German element and assimilating to it. The Polish population of the province was declining, having had essentially

---

* L[udwik] P[owidaj], "Polacy i Indianie" [Poles and Indians], *Dziennik Literacki* no. 53 (December 9, 1864) and no. 56 (December 30, 1864). My translation.

no connection with the Polish mainstream since the Middle Ages. Could theirs be the fate of Poles elsewhere?

It was perhaps premature to speak of the imminent demise of the Poles, whether in Silesia or elsewhere. There was another option. If a nation could not be victorious in battle, it could try other tactics. The Poles need not share the fate of the Iroquois in America. Yet, to keep this from happening, they would have to change their ways. They had to demonstrate that, as the old Polish proverb had it, "A Pole is wise after injury."

The solution was not to immerse themselves in the eastern sea but rather to take lessons from the west. Poles had to join in the civilizational race. Instead of wielding steel, Poles had to steel themselves for a different battlefield: an economic one. And indeed, Powidaj exhorted readers of his article to engage in industry and trade. Poles needed to put their capital to productive use and contribute to the greater prosperity of the nation.

This would be no easy task for a nation educated for a life of leisure (or, at best, warfare). The centuries had conditioned Poles, certainly those of noble birth, to disdain working for a living. They needed to change their approach to the acquisition of knowledge. The traditional Polish education served more as a finishing school than as a source of practical knowledge that would allow graduates to work in the trades or elsewhere. Under foreign rule, furthermore, there was an overproduction of the Polish intelligentsia, who had little scope for employment. The same individuals would have done much better had they gained concrete skills, a trade, or learned how to run a business. The road to a future Poland, according to Powidaj (and, as we shall see, others), lay not through insurrectionism but through hard work, savings, and industry. These venues may have seemed prosaic to the poetically inclined Poles, yet they promised greater returns in the end. Centuries of inaction and neglect had to be made up, if Poles were to match their foes in craftsmanship, industry, and the arts.

The comparison of Poles and Indians was Powidaj's colorful way of bringing home what he thought might be a painful message. Poles had to reform themselves as a people. First, they needed to abandon insurrectionism. Poles had to turn their efforts in a more productive direction. For the nation to survive, it needed to be pragmatic. A particularly hard message for the formerly proud noble nation was the one embraced wholeheartedly by Americans: working for a living is actually beneficial. Having a means of making a living—as opposed to an inheritance, which can dry up at any moment, should conditions change—was laudable. A man with practical skills had the means to make a living, regardless of what fate dealt him.

In sum, Poles needed to work at the foundations of society. They could no longer be Norwid's "great national banner." They had to focus on more prosaic skills, skills that could guarantee them a continued seat at the table of nations. Otherwise, there was no guarantee the Poles would not meet the same fate as the Iroquois.

Organic Work

While the thrust of Powidaj's article may have surprised readers of the Galician paper, it was hardly new to Powidaj's nearest neighbors. Under Prussian auspices, Poles had settled down to work already in the 1830s and 1840s—even earlier, if one considers the progressive model landed estate that Dezydery Chłapowski ran in Turwia. With the leadership of thinkers and writers such as August Cieszkowski and others, the value of forging a different route to a future Poland was becoming more accepted. This approach, in its Prussian Polish variant, was labeled organic work. Given the political nature of Polishness in past centuries, Poles found it hard to embrace fully an ideology that might be seen as apolitical or even selfish, yet they were implored to enrich themselves and, by extension, their nation.

Initiated in the Poznań province of Prussia, organic work was predicated on the recognition that a Polish native middle class was necessary if Poles were to compete with the Germans. This recognition led the Polish doctor Karol Marcinkowski to establish the Poznań Bazaar, a national commercial center of sorts, in 1838. The bazaar enabled other individuals to become successful in industry. To cite one example, Hipolit Cegielski went on to found a company that manufactured agricultural machinery. The 1860s witnessed a host of agricultural circles and industrial clubs that helped the Poles help themselves while serving also as a center for social gatherings and other endeavors. Reading rooms were established to improve Polish literacy, especially among the peasantry. Polish clergy were not only involved in many of these activities but occasionally initiated and led them.

While the developments of the 1840s and beyond were important, there were limits to what could be accomplished under Prussian rule. For example, the Prussian authorities would not allow the Poles an agricultural school of their own, let alone a university. This practical approach, then, was really all Poles could manage under Prussian rule in the later part of the century. Even then, there were roadblocks.

The Nature of the New Germany

And Prussian rule soon came to be German rule. The creation of a united German state was a major event in the second half of the nineteenth century. As we have seen, it was not accomplished in liberal fashion, from below, in 1848. Instead, German unification came in the wake of a series of wars (with Denmark, Austria, and France), wars won by Prussia. It was Prussia—here, primarily in the person of the Prussian king's chief minister and soon-to-be German chancellor, Otto von Bismarck—that executed the unification, from above, in 1871 that created the German Empire. The Prussian king became German emperor.

So Germany as such was a young country. At the end of the eighteenth century, even German writers as famous as Goethe and Schiller expressed their puzzlement: "Germany? But where is it? I do not know where to find such a country." There may have been Germans (though doubtless many of them thought of themselves as Bavarians or Prussians or Hanoverians rather than Germans), but there was no Germany. With the unification of Germany, those Bavarians and Hanoverians and Prussians increasingly came to think of themselves as Germans—as part of a larger German national brotherhood.

Yet the 1871 unification of Germany was at the same time a partition. Austria—that is, the German-speaking lands under Habsburg control—was not included. The unification achieved by Bismarck was the *kleindeutsch* (little German) variant, not the *grossdeutsch* (great German) one. In other words, it was an imperfect—an incomplete—unification according to those who thought Germany should be anywhere that the German language could be heard.

The unification of Germany had ramifications for the Poles under Prussian—now German—rule. Whereas, earlier, one might be considered a Prussian Pole or a Polish Prussian, did the preferred ethnolinguistic definition of Germanness now not exclude those subjects of Polish descent? In other words, there was little room for national diversity within the newly united German Empire.

This, as well as a degree of insecurity on the part of Bismarck, who feared that the Poles would come to ally themselves more closely with the Catholic Habsburgs, led to a new kind of war. Not for nothing did Bismarck call his new campaign the Kulturkampf—that is, the culture war. While ostensibly designed to strengthen the secular and progressive side of German culture, which could be viewed as a unifying thread for the empire, the Kulturkampf was a thinly disguised attack on Catholicism and Polonism within the empire.

Map 10.1: Central and Eastern Europe in the Late Nineteenth Century

Beginning in 1873, Poles began to bear the brunt of the attack. The Kulturkampf had repercussions across the board. The Jesuits were expelled, and Germany broke off relations with the Vatican. The training of Roman Catholic clergy had to include a new "culture" component, and the state reserved for itself the right to veto choices of priests to serve in the empire. Churches lost control over their lands. The age-old practice of church marriages was jettisoned in favor of civil marriage, which was now the only legally recognized form. German became the language of instruction in the schools.

The Polish clergy was essentially terrorized, with priests fined or imprisoned for every little infraction. Seminaries were shut down and monastic orders abolished. Even the head of the Polish church under German rule, Archbishop Mieczysław Halka-Ledóchowski, was mistreated, even though he had assumed a conciliatory stance to the German state (while nonetheless

being an unabashed ultramontane, that is, a fervent supporter of the Holy
See). Ledóchowski was imprisoned for several years before the authorities
let him depart the empire for Rome. Such was the fate of the clergyman who
had occupied the see of Gniezno, that ancient capital of Poland—a person
who by that office would have been interrex in the old days of the elective
monarchy.

Although painful for the Polish community, the anti-Catholic, anti-Polish
campaign of the 1870s nonetheless backfired. Persecution served only to
strengthen Polish identification with the Roman Catholic Church. Poles later quipped that they, and not the Germans, should be erecting monuments
to Bismarck, for they had Bismarck—and the persecution under the guise
of the Kulturkampf that he initiated—to thank for fostering national unity
among the Poles of Germany. In the new German Empire, Polish nobles (already few in number), the local intelligentsia, urban professionals, and burghers (these last two growing estates), the peasants (quintessentially Catholic and already emancipated at the beginning of the nineteenth century),
and clergy, all rallied in unity. This was unique among the partitioned lands.
What is more, the persecution of the Roman Catholic Church also helped
to bring the Poles of Poznań and the Pomeranian region closer to those of
Silesia, who had had so little contact with Polishness over the preceding centuries. In this way the Germanization of the Silesians was somewhat attenu-
ated. Even the German priests who were Roman Catholics (for there were
German Catholics as well as Protestants) saw the value of preaching to the
faithful in their native tongue, and many found it expedient to learn Polish.

While the Kulturkampf was soon concluded, discrimination against Poles
in the new united Germany did not cease. In 1885 migrant workers from
Galicia and the Kingdom of Poland were expelled from the country. The
following year, the government came up with a new tactic: to settle Germans in the lands formerly populated primarily by Poles. To this end, they
created a colonization commission, which would help coordinate and fund
this inmigration to the former Polish lands by purchasing land from Polish
landowners.

Despite this support from above, however, Poles fought back and created
their own Polish Land Bank. Germans ultimately were unable to make major inroads into the Polish-held lands.

In sum, the Poles of Prussia-turned-Germany found themselves under attack, not unlike the Iroquois in the New World. Yet the Poles managed to
rally not with sabers or even scythes beaten into swords. Instead, they took a
pragmatic approach, tried to deal in a concerted fashion with each new challenge as it arose, and created or fostered organizations that would allow the

Poles of Germany to strengthen their position in industry, agriculture, and other spheres. This was no less a Polish approach than the much touted Romantic insurrectionary approach, which tends to be more closely identified with Polishness. When the option was to fight a war they could not win or try to catch up (or at least hold their own), the Poles of this region took the latter route. It is thus paradoxical that Germans should speak disparagingly of Polish economic efforts: the term *polnische Wirtschaft* (Polish economy) was treated as an oxymoron, certainly not a compliment.

This was what life was like for Poles in the new and still somewhat insecure German Empire. The partition of Germany left even the Prussian-led German Empire concerned about the future. Nonetheless, the new Germany proved a mighty state within Europe, and Poles within it were constantly on the defensive.

Polish Pragmatism

Organic work was not unique to the Prussian or German lands. One can find examples of it even under Russian rule, though the term "organic work" was applied to these developments only later. In other words, certain Poles did exhibit a pragmatic streak elsewhere in the former Polish lands. Several of them could be found under Russian rule.

The Kingdom of Poland provides a fine, early example of political realism in the person of Ksawery Drucki-Lubecki, the minister of finance in the Kingdom of Poland as of 1821. As one interested in the development of the country, he had a good reputation among the Russians, and thus he had the flexibility to initiate a real economic program for the kingdom.

Drucki-Lubecki had no desire for insurrectionary upheaval. Rather, he calmly envisaged a series of concrete developments in the economic realm that would strengthen Poland's autonomy. He renegotiated a more advantageous tariff agreement with Prussia, improved the collection of taxes, and streamlined the administration back home. The Polish finance minister concluded that three things were necessary. First, the kingdom needed schools, for those would provide education and understanding. Second, it needed industry and commerce, which would bring prosperity and wealth. And third (last but not least), it needed armament factories. In his view, these three things would allow Poland, even one united with Russia, to maintain its independence.

Yet Drucki-Lubecki did more than work to establish or foster schools, industry, commerce, and arms factories. A university existed in Warsaw as of

1816; plans for a polytechnical institute were in the works in 1830. In 1825 Drucki-Lubecki established the Land Credit Society, which helped raise the level of agricultural output. In 1828 he also created the Bank of Poland, which allowed the state to support new investments such as the construction of the Augustów Canal, connecting the Neman River system with that of the Vistula, as well as major roads. Drucki-Lubecki used government funds to strengthen three pillars of Polish industry in the kingdom: the area of Łódź, and the Dąbrowa and Old Polish Basins. Łódź began to witness a growth in the textile industry, which would take off in later decades of the nineteenth century. The Dąbrowa Basin produced zinc and lead as well as coal; the Old Polish Basin's iron ore was not nearly as lucrative. A mining school in Kielce helped provide workers with the specialized training. Such measures were important in a country that had previously imported most of its industrial goods.

Drucki-Lubecki was the counter to the example of the typical Polish nobleman, who held an animus toward trade, industry, even employment, thinking it beneath his station to engage in such pursuits. His compatriots complained about the level of taxes and about his industrial dreams, but this did not stop Drucki-Lubecki from making important advances. It should be noted that such developments in the Kingdom of Poland left Nicholas I, Tsar of All Russia and King of Poland, rather envious of the Poles' economic progress, even prowess, vis-à-vis the rest of the empire. Imposed after the November Insurrection, a tariff barrier between Russia and the Kingdom of Poland hampered economic development over the ensuing two decades.

Few Poles in the Kingdom of Poland took any real interest in the beginnings of capitalist development in their lands, but a major exception to this was Piotr Steinkeller (1799–1854). A Pole whose family migrated from the Habsburg lands, Steinkeller in many ways exemplified the Polish entrepreneurial spirit. He enthusiastically engaged in all manner of investments. Early on, Steinkeller founded a bank in the Free City of Kraków. While the Polish entrepreneur also got involved in trade and agriculture, he is most famous for his investments in the construction of agricultural machinery, the mining of zinc, even in the establishment of railways and the postal service. Unfortunately, Steinkeller overstepped his capabilities and went bankrupt in 1851.

The second period in which one could see organic work at play in the Kingdom of Poland was during the brief thaw following the Crimean War. Even earlier, Jewish financiers and industrialists such as Leopold Kronenberg promoted development. Some of them founded newspapers such as Kronenberg's *Daily Gazette*. Newspapers naturally provided members of the

Polish intelligentsia with opportunities to publish. The Agricultural Society established by Count Andrzej Zamoyski flourished for a spell. The brief tenure of Margrave Aleksander Wielopolski (1861–1863) also witnessed further development. Wielopolski saw Poland's future as linked to that of Russia and made room for Poles within the civil service. This was likely for practical as well as national reasons: Russia proper provided a larger market with more job opportunities, which the generally better educated Poles could avail themselves of. Of course, some of these civil servants were referred to by less conciliatory types as "Catholics with a [Saint] Petersburg cold" or, worse, as traitors.

Polish Positivists

Still, these developments paled in comparison with what was to come. After the January Insurrection, more Poles under Russian rule saw fit to jettison insurrectionism for a new program. It was termed positivism. Positivism—which in the Polish case was more social movement than intellectual trend—sought to recalibrate the nation's relationship on the West–East spectrum. Whereas Romanticism had been more Eastern-oriented, even Slavophile, in nature, positivism embraced the West wholeheartedly. The new positivists took their inspiration from the West.

The timing could not have been better. The Kingdom of Poland was already at the forefront of Russian industry and development. The recent (1864) emancipation of the peasantry allowed for rapid industrialization in the former Kingdom of Poland. Now that peasants were not tied to the land, and there were many peasants who were still landless and impoverished, surplus population could work in factories—becoming a new Polish proletariat. This was the period when industry in Łódź began its rapid ascent. Known as the Polish Manchester, the city produced textiles for the whole of Russia. Łódź was a complex organism, a multiethnic city, with German capital, Polish and Jewish labor, the whole spectrum of society represented. Juxtaposing great riches and great poverty, Łódź was a place where fortunes could be made and lost.

Textiles were not the region's only industry. The Kingdom of Poland also became an exporter of industrial goods to Russia; important branches of the economy included mining and metallurgy as well as machine building. Polish beet sugar refining factories modernized and thrived. Industrial development (the so-called second industrial revolution) really took off after 1870. While in 1884 only 44 industrial enterprises in the Kingdom employed more than 500 workers, by 1913 that figure had risen to nearly 150. The economy and society were becoming much more differentiated.

The economy notwithstanding, positivism was even more an intellectual movement whose adherents strove to recast Polish attitudes. They preached "work at the foundations." By this they meant a focus on much neglected society. Here, society was to include not only the nobles but the workers and peasants as well. This bottom-up approach was to strengthen the nation in its entirety and even turn previously unconscious segments of society into conscious Poles. This was modernization, Polish style.

In contrast to the abstract love of the nation preached earlier by the Romantics, positivists saw the nation in tangible terms. They sought to uplift the formerly downtrodden peasantry and to work with concrete specific individuals to improve their lot. Here the intellectuals could help increase Polish literacy.

A certain vignette described by the Polish writer Stefan Żeromski indicates the degree to which the Polonization of the peasantry could fly under the radar of the Russian censor. He described an idyllic scene, in which a group of peasants were sitting under a tree and one of them was laboriously sounding out a piece of text. The fragment may have had no meaning to the censor, but any educated Pole would recognize the words as an excerpt from Adam Mickiewicz's famous epic poem, *Pan Tadeusz*. In other words, while learning to read, the peasants were also making the acquaintance of patriotic Romantic literature.

Polish writers would prove crucial for the propagation of positivism, for its percolation down through the various levels of society. Literary figures such as Eliza Orzeszkowa, Bolesław Prus, Aleksander Świętochowski figured most prominently. In their realistic novels as well as in their journalistic work, they addressed concrete problems within the Russian Empire. They sought to downplay the traditional values of the Polish nobility and moved sharply away from the ideas of Romanticism and Polish messianism that had fired the insurrections. In these new works, one sees no more disdain for industry and trade.

Another writer who made a name for himself during this period was Poland's first Nobel Prize laureate (who received the award in 1905). The historical novelist Henryk Sienkiewicz wrote realistic novels that nonetheless were designed to "uplift hearts," even though his famous trilogy dealt with events of the seventeenth century. Scenes from the Cossack debacle, the Deluge, and wars against the Ottomans came alive on the page, showing how Poles from earlier centuries had fought for their country. In reading his novels and those of other historical novelists such as the even more prolific

Józef Ignacy Kraszewski, many nineteenth-century Poles learned their own history, which they were not taught in the imperial schools.

In a way, positivists found it necessary to rethink what it meant to be Polish. This is visible, for example, in an essay by Bolesław Prus on patriotism. In contrast to the Romantics, he saw patriotism as something both practical and protective. Patriotism was halting the German colonization of Polish lands, clothing the poor, sympathizing not with the noble estate but with the rest of the population without which the Poles would not become a modern nation. Prus wrote, "Polish society is not the Christ of nations as its poets have maintained, nor is it so evil and incompetent as its enemies claim it to be. It is a society in part regenerating itself, and in the main young, not having as yet discovered its new civilizational role."* In other words, the modern Polish nation, comprised of the entirety of society, was a work-in-progress, and one the positivists set out to shape in a positive way.

Positivists also demonstrated an interest in the role Jews were to play in a modern Poland. Jews had long substituted for the middle class that had not developed within the Polish lands. The urban Jews were the individuals who were most engaged in trade, banking, moneylending, and even, with the passage of time, industry. Positivists took stock of the fact that Jews, like Poles, were changing; they sought to counter old superstitions with new realistic knowledge about this segment of the population. Orzeszkowa in particular wrote sympathetically about Jews and their growing impetus to change. What was clear to the positivists was that Polish-Jewish relations could not be made healthy until Poles came to understand their Jewish neighbors better.

It is worth noting that these positivists were not only writers but also scientists, industrialists, businessmen—and many of them were not particularly religious. While it is hard to speak for all positivists, some certainly used the church instrumentally, in their quest to reach the poor and uplift them. That is, they did this not out of their own religious convictions but out of their observations that it would do the peasants good. In other words, traditional religious faith was seen as something of value, if not necessarily for everyone.

The move toward positivism actually dovetailed with the increasingly pragmatic approach of many Poles during this period. They may have embraced this somewhat apolitical stance not so much by choice but out of necessity. After the failure of the January Insurrection, when many insurrectionists' estates were confiscated and other landholdings were parceled

---

* Cited from *For Your Freedom and Ours: Polish Progressive Spirit from the Fourteenth Century to the Present*, 2d enlarged edition, ed. Krystyna M. Olszer (New York: Ungar, 1981), 108.

out to peasants, many Poles simply had to make a living. This reality influenced their attitudes. It had become much harder to live off the land (were one fortunate enough to possess estates) after the emancipation of the peasantry. And industry was still in its infancy—as well as not providing the more comfortable jobs that the intelligentsia types would prefer. This left the realm of state employment, work in the service of the tsarist state.

Despite the stereotype of the staunchly anti-tsarist Poles, the patriotic, ever protesting intelligentsia, this relatively small if influential group was numerically outweighed by the masses of Poles who were not nearly as financially secure or able to live by the pen (writing and publishing in Polish). Many rank-and-file Poles within the Russian Empire were simply struggling to make ends meet, and thus they actively and eagerly sought out positions in the Russian civil service (as bureaucrats, teachers, doctors, technicians, and other professionals). It is worth noting that it proved easier for these well-educated Poles to find work within the empire proper, where they were not discriminated against, than in the core Polish lands or the Western Provinces. Thus, a number of Poles left the former Polish lands to seek their fortune elsewhere in the empire, in places such as oil-rich Baku (an example given in Żeromski's novel, *The Spring to Come*). Thus, instead of seeing a black-and-white dichotomy between mobilized Polish patriot and indifferent national apostate, perhaps it is better to view the two on a broader spectrum, with few at either extreme. There was life after insurrection, if not always the life that certain Poles imagined for themselves. The triple-loyalistic approach carried within it the threat that the allegiance to the imperial state would eventually override any vestiges of allegiance to the Polish nation and the Polish cause.

"Mother-Pole" and Emancipated Polish Women

One way in which positivism and triple-loyalism were tempered was felt not in the public sphere but on the home front. Here one needs to give credit to generations of patriotic women who brought their children up not only as Poles but as patriotic Poles, ready to sacrifice for the Polish cause. These women have traditionally been referred to as the stereotypical "Mother-Pole" (*Matka-Polka*), the women who set the tone for the coming generations.

Precursors to this generation of Mother-Poles were legion. Recall the seventeenth-century creation of a shrine to the fallen hero Stanisław Żółkiewski at Żółkiew (today's Zhovkva, in Ukraine), the hetman's wife bringing up their children and grandchildren to honor and emulate his patriotism. No less important was the work of noble women of the turn of the eighteenth and nineteenth centuries. Take for instance Izabela Czartoryska, whose estate at Puławy became a center of Polish culture and destination of national pilgrimages. Her Temple of Sybil, a pavilion in the park, contained numerous relics of a heroic national past. Czartoryska's amazing collection included the swords offered to Jagiełło before the Battle of Grunwald, banners from the battle, sabers that had belonged to Batory and Sobieski. At Puławy there was even a mausoleum in the lower level of the temple commemorating Prince Józef Poniatowski, her contemporary. A black marble obelisk decorated with the Duchy of Warsaw eagle bore the inscription: "To Prince Józef Poniatowski. He led Poles, perished for the Fatherland." Poles from all over the former Commonwealth lands came to visit Puławy.

The same Czartoryska showed herself to be a positivist *avant la lettre*. She penned a popular reader for village children. Included among the readings were tales of kings and famous Poles. Czartoryska's goal was not only village literacy; she strove to teach peasants to love the Fatherland above everything while also providing moral guidance via their shared Christian values.

Few of the gentler sex emulated yet another noteworthy Polish woman, Emilia Plater, who during the November Insurrection fought on the battlefield alongside the men. Nor did many take the route of one of the world's most famous Poles (more in line with the positivists of the previous generation), Maria Skłodowska-Curie. The young woman grew up under Russian rule but ended up studying in France (the first women were admitted into the Jagiellonian University in Galicia only as of 1894). In Paris Skłodowska conducted research into the radioactive elements radium and polonium, which she discovered in 1898. Maria Skłodowska-Curie was twice awarded a Nobel Prize: the first in 1903, with her husband Pierre Curie, for physics; then a second, in 1911, by herself for chemistry.

Not much of a mother to her own daughters, Skłodowska-Curie presented a different model than did her contemporary, the "Mother-Pole" who relied on her feminine, motherly characteristics. Such a woman tended to the national hearth, in her own home, and raised her own children and grandchildren in a Polish and patriotic spirit (however these were understood). So many men had been lost in battle, to the noose, or to frozen exile. The women who remained in the Polish lands felt compelled to rise to the nation's aid.

This is not to say that there was no women's emancipation movement in the core Polish lands. Many of the same women left to run households by themselves sought to make gains in the fields of education and the economy. While relatively few followed Eliza Orzeszkowa's early lead in the emancipation movement, with the passage of time many women took an active part in social, religious (Catholic), and patriotic activities in the public sphere. If there was no suffragist movement under Russian rule, it was because no one—whether man or woman—in Russia had political rights. On the whole, the concerns of women mirrored the concerns of a changing Polish society, one in which the déclassé nobility was increasingly moving to the cities and becoming radicalized. At the same time, Polish feminists were no less Polish patriots, seeking simultaneously to improve the lot of their society and nation.

Polish women of this period were all too aware of the role they could— even should—play in keeping the nation alive. In the last third of the nineteenth century, the Polish nation was increasingly under siege in the partitioning lands. This is true mainly of the Russian Empire and the new German Empire. Tsar Alexander II's heir, Alexander III, immediately reversed the policies of his father, who had paid for his relative liberalism with his life. (Alexander II was assassinated in 1881 by members of the Russian terrorist organization Will of the People.) In both Germany and Russia, the Polish language was discriminated against. It thus was incumbent upon the women of the upper classes to bring up their children speaking Polish, raise them as Polish patriots, instill in them a desire to work for an independent Poland. Like the Mother of God, who had been declared Queen of Poland by King Jan Kazimierz, the late nineteenth-century Mother-Pole had an important role to play in this changing environment. Such activism on the part of Polish mothers may have helped create the next generation of Poles.

Still, the essentially apolitical stance of the positivists—even if it was meant ultimately to strengthen society, to strengthen the nation, to strengthen the future Poland—ended up, after time, rankling in certain circles. With time, a new generation born after the failed January Insurrection would swing the pendulum in a different direction.

Polish Socialists, First Generation

Positivism and organic work were far from the only approaches possible during this period. One could learn other things from the West, or the East. The first stirrings of socialism in the Polish lands date from the years after the January Insurrection. With the creation of an urban working class in the Kingdom of Poland, there was a base for a party, such as were forming to the west (the new industrializing German Empire being fertile ground for socialists, this despite Bismarck's intense dislike of them) as well as to the east (the first Polish group of socialists became familiar with the doctrine while in the Russian capital).

The nascent Polish socialist party was nipped in the bud at this point. Some of its leaders were arrested in Warsaw in 1878–1879. Other socialists such as Ludwik Waryński fled to the west (Geneva), interacted with Western socialists, and became convinced that the future lay with the international working class. In 1882 the first Polish socialist party, the Proletariat, was founded in Warsaw. They expected the brave new world foretold by Karl Marx and Friedrich Engels some decades earlier.

Socialism would prove one of the new activist "-isms" to displace positivism. Some young Poles clearly were troubled by the juxtaposition of triple-loyalism and positivism. The latter's focus on economic and not political issues allowed a new generation to tar and feather the positivists as anational. Members of this post-positivist generation—a crucial generation in Polish history, as it was to set the stage for things to come—have gone down in history as "the defiant ones." They sought to take an activist political stance. With time, they formed multiple political parties and challenged each other for influence over the look of a future Poland and the values that would characterize modern Poles. Yet these new parties were first to emerge under Russian rule, where they were illegal. For Polish political parties truly to be able to function, they had to relocate or emerge elsewhere. By the last third of the nineteenth century, the most promising place turned out to be the partitioned territory that represented the Commonwealth's southern border: an entity that was renamed Galicia.

Galicia Felix

Perhaps the most peculiar set of conditions for Polish life existed in the Habsburg province of Galicia, most of which had become part of the Habsburg holdings in the first partition of 1772. As a consequence, its noble inhabitants had not been part of the heady experience of the Great Seym and its promising culmination, the Constitution of May 3, 1791. "Their" piece of old Poland, as it were, underwent modernization entirely within the Austrian system.

The early experience of Habsburg rule was disorienting and disconcerting for the Poles, who had been used to being full-fledged and autonomous citizens. The Austrian carpetbaggers who came to rule the these lands beyond the Carpathians showed the Polish nobles little respect, seeing social relations within Galicia as barbaric (even "half-Asian," to borrow the phrase coined by Emil Franzos). These emissaries from Vienna saw themselves as having a civilizing mission.

Austrian bureaucrats were bemused by the province's multiethnic and multidenominational status. Nonetheless, they proceeded to apply an enlightened template to this new land, introducing all manner of reforms: centralization and rationalization, bureaucratization, religious toleration of the Jews (including bestowing surnames on them and initiating their Germanization), educational reforms, linguistic standardization (the imperial language was German), and the ending of personal servitude, if not the ending of serfdom, for the peasants.

The Ruthenes' religious distinctiveness prompted the creation of a school in Vienna for the Uniate clergy, with Uniates now referred to as Greek Catholics (the Greek modifier referring to the Eastern rite, as opposed to the Roman rite of the Roman Catholics). Although this school, the Barbareum, functioned for only two decades from 1774 to 1794, it laid a foundation for better educated Ruthenian elites.

Some of the reforms reflected the peculiarities of the House of Habsburg. Unlike the Russian and German Empires, there was no push to create an "Austrian" nation. Rather, the Habsburgs preferred their traditional pillar: loyalty to the dynasty. Their multinational empire was comprised of a patchwork collection of territories, each of which retained a modicum of native distinctiveness. The Habsburgs had often acquired territories through advantageously arranged marriages—such as the marriage that led them to succeed the Jagiellons in Bohemia and Hungary in 1526. They sought above all to foster imperial patriotism and dynastic loyalty.

Unlike the Hohenzollerns of Prussia/Germany or the Romanovs of Russia, the Habsburgs were Roman Catholic monarchs—and this is an important distinction. Furthermore, Habsburg piety was proverbial. All this meant that there should have been more common ground between the Poles and Austrians. At the same time, the Habsburgs had historically been the rulers of the Holy Roman Empire of the German Nation (defunct as of 1806) and thus had a special relationship to the Germans of the rest of Europe.

As in all the partitions, the treatment of the new subjects was uneven. In the beginning, the Austrian authorities sought to civilize what they considered to be a backward land. Later, under the oppressive influence of Metternich, they sought to constrain what they thought was a revolutionary people—as witnessed in the debacle of the peasant jacquerie of 1846. (The incorporation of the Free City of Kraków into Galicia set the relatively thriving medieval capital of Poland back decades.) Metternich had seen fit to equate Polonism with revolution. Doubtless the new ruler of the Austrian Empire, Franz Joseph, felt similarly.

Only after a period of absolutism and Germanization did the tone change.

This was brought about by several Austrian military defeats. The loss to the French in 1859 led to reforms at home that ultimately resulted in constitutional rule in Austria as of the early 1860s. Notably for the Poles, they were allotted their own provincial Seym as early as 1861.

The defeat of Austria by Prussia in 1866 was even more significant. The defeat forced the Habsburgs to reach a new modus vivendi with the Hungarians, who had been chafing under Habsburg rule particularly since the end of their failed revolution of 1848–1849. In 1867, the two parties reached the famous compromise that led to the establishment of the Dual Monarchy. Henceforth, the country would be known as Austria-Hungary.

That the Habsburgs had been compelled to make concessions to one of their subject peoples was a fact not lost on the Poles. Already the failure of the January Insurrection under Russian rule led some important Galicians to reconsider their approach to the Habsburg monarchy. A new and influential group known as the Kraków Conservatives resolved to be loyal to the Habsburgs. Although initially skeptical, after several years the Polish elites of Galicia were won over to this idea. Even the defeat of Austria at the hands of Prussia did not shake their belief in the monarchy. To the contrary. On December 10, 1866, the Galician Seym made the following declaration:

> We conclude, most gracious lord, in the true and deep conviction . . . [that] Austria, in order to flourish with greater strength than ever, will be in its internal organization the shield of the civilization of the West, the rights of nationality, humanity, and justice. . . . Without fear, then, of abandoning our national idea, with faith in the mission of Austria, and with confidence in the decisiveness of change which your monarchical word has pronounced as an unchangeable intention, we affirm from the depths of our hearts that we stand with you, Your Majesty, and we wish to stand with you.*

These developments led to a third, and most fruitful, phase for the Galician Poles. Unlike the disgruntled Czechs of Bohemia, Poles decided to participate in the Reichsrat or imperial council, a two-chambered parliament in Vienna. Polish elites sought to recast Galicia as a conciliatory, conservative, loyal province. All this boded well for the position of Poles within the Habsburg Empire. Indeed, during the Dual Monarchy, a number of Poles actually came to hold important posts in the imperial government, including that of prime minister.

Given a degree of autonomy, Galicia became a haven for the Poles—a place where Poles could be Poles while still being loyal to the Habsburg dynasty. This dual identity was facilitated by Article 19 of the Fundamental Laws,

---

* Cited from Wolff, *The Idea of Galicia*, 116–17.

which specified that each people within the monarchy had the right to cultivate its own nationality and language. Poles, and especially the democrats who vied with the conservatives for influence within the province, availed themselves of this opportunity in various ways, including the celebrating of a series of national figures and historic anniversaries. Among the most noteworthy were the solemn reburial of the poet Adam Mickiewicz in the Wawel crypts in 1890 and the five-hundredth anniversary of the Battle of Grunwald in 1910, also celebrated in Kraków. The Polish pianist Ignacy Jan Paderewski had commissioned a massive monument commemorating that great medieval battle. These large public celebrations helped to bring Poles from all three partitioned lands closer together.

Thus, in the last third of the nineteenth century, the best place to be a Pole—certainly if one wanted to be politically active—and unlike in the Prussian or German lands, politically active in Polish—was Galicia. One could breathe Polish air there—or, as was also remarked, the very stones spoke Polish. To be sure, in Vienna (in the Reichsrat) Poles used German for their interpellations. However, back in the province, in the Galician Seym, the Polish language ruled (although it should be noted that Ruthenian interpellations during the proceedings were written down, phonetically, in Latin—not Cyrillic—script). Polish nonetheless became the language of government, the language of schooling.

Galician Poles had a high degree of autonomy—all of which allowed them to school themselves in the art of governance, to work in the bureaucracy, to develop scholarly institutes and universities where Polish would be the language of instruction, and the like. They lived in a country in which they had parliamentary representation and the rule of law. This, combined with the rights of nationalities, suggests that, as of the last third of the nineteenth century, one might think of Galicia as the closest thing to a Piedmont that the Poles had (Piedmont, meaning the Italian province that initiated Italian unification in the 1860s). Could these advantages within Galicia, thus, help propel the Poles to their own unification?

Galician Paradoxes

At the same time, Galicia proved a study in contrasts. On the one hand, it had a degree of political autonomy that the Poles of Germany and Russia could only envy. On the other, Galicia remained the least progressive part of the former Polish lands. It was undeniably, incontrovertibly backward, both economically and socially.

The social problem that had been fixed in Germany—thanks to Bismarck's oppression of the Poles, which brought all estates closer together—festered in Galicia. The trauma of the 1846 peasant jacquerie long remained vivid. Memory of the massacre led the provincial nobility to fear the elemental power represented by the peasantry should it become organized or simply unleashed, as it had in 1846. Galician nobles, thus, sought above all to keep the peasants in their place. They were not advocates of education, fearing it would give the peasants too much independence. Nor did they foster much in the way of agricultural advances; they had no incentive to do so, as the nobility was allowed to maintain some of its old monopolies, such as the lucrative one over the production of alcohol. Even elections to political office were done on the basis of estates (by the so-called curias, themselves set up disproportionately). The curia system essentially gave the propertied a much bigger say in the outcome than the masses.

At the same time, Galicia had to deal with the effects of the 1848 emancipation of the peasants. How could the peasants be kept down if they were now free? While this concerned the conservatives, more democratically or liberally minded Poles within the province saw this as an opportunity to turn the peasants into Poles. Democratic activists began their approach to the peasantry by emphasizing that both peasants and upper-class Poles shared the Catholic faith and thus had more in common than perhaps the peasants had thought. They also reminded the peasants of their own contribution to Polish history, as represented in the figure of Bartosz Głowacki and the other peasants who at Racławice helped Kościuszko defeat the Russians. Yet there were numerous barriers to a closer relationship between Galician peasant and noble, including the former's lack of education and the proportional disadvantage of the peasants in the political realm. Such issues would need to be addressed before real progress could be made.

And then there was the economic realm. Galicia remained a densely populated, heavily agrarian, relatively impoverished province. Its nickname says it all: instead of being called the Kingdom of Galicia and Lodomeria, the province was jokingly labeled the Kingdom of Golicja and Głodomeria—the land of the naked and the hungry. In his famous book entitled *Galician Misery in Numbers*, the Galician entrepreneur Stanisław Szczepanowski claimed that the average Galician ate half of what the average European ate, while he worked only a quarter of what the average European worked. The one safety valve for the excess population of Galicia appeared to be emigration to the Americas.

The exodus of the Galician masses seems paradoxical, as the province was rich in natural resources that awaited development. It had salt and coal, even oil. The Galician oil fields once produced a not insignificant percentage of the world's oil. Still, development was slow to cross the Carpathian divide, and few invested in the province. Only with time did better roads and, especially, railroads reach Galicia. Railroads were often for strategic rather than economic purposes and were also used to flood the Galician market with goods produced elsewhere in the empire, thus helping to perpetuate Galician backwardness.

The Ruthenian Question

Furthermore, the provincial leaders clung to an increasingly out-of-date view of the social composition of the province. Galicia was inhabited not only by Poles. While, in Western Galicia, Polish nobles, Polish-speaking peasants, and Jews could all be found (the Jews mainly in cities and towns, in both Western and Eastern Galicia), in Eastern Galicia the vast bulk of the rural population was Ruthenian/Ukrainian (the term Ukrainian reflecting a certain political-national outlook). The latter were speakers of a Ruthenian (or even multiple Ruthenian) dialect who were adherents of the Eastern rite of the Catholic Church. While it is true that most Poles would recognize the distinctiveness of Galicia's Jews, whether they lived in the western or the eastern half of Galicia, not all were quite sure what to make of the peasants who spoke Ruthenian and attended the Eastern rite services. Were they not, in essence, part of the large Polish nation, heirs to the Commonwealth no less than peasants who spoke Polish? After all, the latter, sometimes called Mazurians, were surely Poles. Why, then, were Ruthenes, who also had lived in these lands from time immemorial, not Poles? Was not a Ruthene—in the old Latin phrase—*gente Ruthenus, natione Polonus*: that is, a Pole of Ruthenian descent?

The province's Ruthenes—or surely some of them—thought otherwise. Before long, other identities were placed before the Greek Catholic peasants, identities that would lead them to see a future not with the Poles but with the Ruthenes/Ukrainians across the border, or even with the larger Russian nation.

Indeed, while some Poles were caught by surprise in 1848, when Ruthenes began to organize (to be sure, with the help of Governor Stadion), there had already been a growth in Ruthenian literature in the previous decade or so. In 1837 a patriotic circle known as the Ruthenian Triad (its members Markiian Shashkevych, Iakiv Holovatskyi, and Ivan Vahylevych) published a literary work, *Rusalka Dnistrovaia* (Dniester nymph) in the "peasant" language.

The same "peasant" language, bolstered by influences from across the Russian border (from the old Ukrainian lands), would soon be labeled Ukrainian. Not for nothing one of the politically influential Kraków Conservatives, Józef

Szujski, called the Ruthenian question "a social question with national aspirations." In the late nineteenth century, it was still hard for some Europeans to determine what was a language and who was a nation, and what was a dialect and who were peasants or regional folk. That the outcome in the Polish lands did not follow the French pattern, which assimilated so many smaller peoples into the larger French nation, was in part the effect of the partitions.

The idea of Galicia as not the Polish but the Ukrainian Piedmont was helped by the persecution of Ukrainian language and culture under Russian rule. The Valuev and Ems decrees of 1863 and 1876, respectively, prohibited the printing and distribution of Ukrainian-language texts in the Russian Empire as well as the promotion of a distinct Ukrainian culture. By contrast, at the University of Lviv in Galicia, Ukrainian chairs were established—if not a separate Ukrainian university, which nationally conscious Ukrainians were fighting for. This agitation came over time, as a new Ukrainian intelligentsia was being created within Galicia and abroad. Yet, one can safely say that, even into the twentieth century, the bulk of this predominantly peasant population had no clear national identity.

Of course, the idea of national identity was hardly uppermost in the minds of most nineteenth-century Europeans, whether Poles, Ukrainians, Frenchmen, or others. There were so many other characteristics that defined a person's life: religion, town of residence or origin, profession, status, just to name a few. One Polish historian calculated that, in the era of the birth of the modern Polish nation, which he dated from 1764 to 1870, the number of people considering themselves Poles rose threefold—from about 10 percent all the way to 30–35 percent of those speaking Polish or some version thereof.[*] This suggests that, even circa 1870, most speakers of Polish thought of themselves in non-national terms. Such conclusions caution us not to assume that people in past ages shared the same outlook on life as someone living centuries or even only decades later.

Personal Choices

One of the fascinating aspects of life under Habsburg rule in Galicia was that people could choose relatively easily what identity was important to them. There were no pressures from above to become Polish or Ukrainian or even Austrian. Many people spoke multiple languages. Hence we have the career of Mikołaj Zyblikiewicz (1823–1877), onetime mayor of Kraków, and

---

[*] Tadeusz Łepkowski, *Polska—narodziny nowoczesnego narodu, 1764–1870* (Warsaw: Państwowe Wydawnictwo Naukowe, 1967), 508.

later provincial marshal for all of Galicia. Zyblikiewicz was a trailblazer in more ways than one. He was the son of a furrier from Sambor, in the eastern half of Galicia, a Ruthene by birth and religion. The young man proved an excellent student and mastered German handily. This opened the door to his advancement in law and politics, both at the imperial and at the provincial level. Naturally, in Galicia he learned Polish as well. Zyblikiewicz was perhaps the most prominent example of *gente Ruthenus, natione Polonus*. He functioned in Polish circles and was a very popular figure in Kraków. He was the only Ruthene ever to be mayor of Kraków; and he was the only commoner and the only Ruthene ever to be provincial marshal, a position generally reserved for the Polish nobles. The famous Polish painter Matejko curiously portrayed Zyblikiewicz in noble Polish garb, lending just another layer of complexity to this fascinating individual.

Perhaps this had to do with Matejko's own personal choice of national affiliation. This son of a Czech immigrant not only identified himself as a Pole; he became the preeminent painter of Polish historical scenes. His giant canvases toured Europe, presenting in colorful fashion historic moments from the Polish past: the Battle of Grunwald of 1410, the Prussian homage of 1525, the Union of Lublin of 1569, the Relief of Vienna of 1683, and the Kościuszko Insurrection of 1794 being perhaps the most famous. Matejko's contribution to Polish art paralleled Sienkiewicz's contribution to Polish literature: he too brought the Polish past to life and taught new generations their history. This the Cracovian artist also did quite systematically through a series of twelve paintings entitled "The History of Civilization in Poland." All this demonstrates Matejko's commitment to the Polish nation—its past, present, and future.

Other inhabitants of Galicia made different choices. Given the multiethnic legacy of the old Commonwealth, it was possible for siblings within a single family to opt for different national identities. Take the notable noble family of the Szeptyckis in Habsburg-ruled Galicia. One of the Szeptycki brothers, Stanisław Maria (1867–1950), ultimately became a Polish general (that is, after having begun in the Austro-Hungarian army, where he attained the rank of colonel). He fought in the Polish Legions during World War I and then served in the Polish military in the interwar period. Such a patriotic Polish career was perhaps to be expected from the grandson of the Polish playwright Aleksander Fredro.

Yet another grandson took inspiration from a different quarter. Stanisław Szeptycki's elder brother also began his career in the Austro-Hungarian military but ended up moving in an entirely different direction. Roman Maria (1865–1944) took religious orders—and not in the church into which he

Figure 10.1: Portrait of Mikołaj Zyblikiewicz, oil painting by Jan Matejko (1887). Galicia's most prominent Ruthene, the commoner Zyblikiewicz is nonetheless depicted in noble Sarmatian garb. The painting currently hangs in the National Museum, Sukiennice branch, Kraków.

was baptized but rather in the Greek Catholic Church, the church of his more distant ancestors. As a priest he took the name Andrei (after Saint Andrew). In 1899 this convert to Greek Catholicism was appointed Greek Catholic archbishop of Lviv, making him the highest-ranking Greek Catholic clergyman in Galicia. Known to his flock as Andrei Sheptytskyi, the new head of the Greek Catholic Church in Galicia became a fervent supporter of the Ukrainian people—something that certain Poles hardly expected from a scion of the Szeptycki family. Thus we have one family, a pair of brothers, and two different choices of national identity.

Lest it be thought that such disparate choices of identity were possible only in Habsburg Galicia, there was also a famous case of three Iwanowski brothers living under Russian rule, each of whom chose a different national identity.

In this part of the world—certainly in the long nineteenth century—identities were perhaps unusually malleable. There are many stories of immigrants from France, Germany, Italy, and elsewhere, with names like Vincenz, Linde, and Zanussi, who became fully Polonized in subsequent generations. As of the late nineteenth century, many Jews chose to style themselves as Poles of the Mosaic persuasion; the numbers of Polish scholars, writers, and artists in this category are legion. Assimilation even struck the families of Habsburg officials who had come to rule Galicia, whose sons sometimes chose to become Poles or even fight in the Polish insurrections.

The choice, as we see, was theirs. It was not blood that ultimately proved important in determining one's ultimate identity—as any American should know—but, rather, the sensibility of a people that attracted new converts. Many foreigners liked the qualities they saw in the Poles and chose to embrace them. They too sought to work for the betterment of the nation and, perhaps, hoped for a future Poland both free and independent.

Toward a Modern Poland

The 1890s marked the beginning of a new and important era in Polish history. Despite the partitions, a true Polish mass politics began to emerge. But this did not happen overnight. It was a while in coming. In Galicia, the new mass political parties moved in on, and eventually displaced, preexisting parties of a more elitist nature, such as that of the Kraków Conservatives or even the democrats.

Here we return to the generation born after the January Insurrection—that is, with no personal memory of that debacle, which with time became romanticized in the literature or even in family reminiscences. These Poles grew up in the age of positivism. And, while perhaps secretly admiring some of the work fostered by the positivists at the foundations of society, they became the positivists' most vocal opponents. These "defiant ones" labeled the elder generation apolitical, even anational, and claimed that their program produced philistines, not Poles, individuals overly concerned with money and economic, not national, development. The positivists were decried as being both too passive vis-à-vis the authorities and not patriotic enough (obviously the "defiant ones" defined patriotism in different terms than had Bolesław Prus).

Two major movements emerged out of this camp of defiance. In the beginning members of both movements were hardly distinguishable one from the other. They were allies in the fight against positivism and the positivists. Only over the space of several years would their defiance be channeled in different ways. The first, and most differentiated, modern mass political group to emerge was that of the socialists. In the lands of the former Commonwealth, a number of distinct socialist parties could be found as of the 1890s. Each had its own profile. The two major approaches to the socialist question were that of the SDKPiL and the PPS.

Socialist Options

The Social Democratic Party of the Kingdom of Poland and Lithuania (SDKPiL) was a socialist party in line with the former Proletariat. Despite its name, it had no real interest in the fate of either the Kingdom of Poland or Lithuania as independent entities. Indeed, it thought such strivings to be harmful. Rather, the reference to the two political entities simply specified the territory in which the party functioned.

The most famous leader and activist of this party was Rosa Luxemburg (1871–1919). Of Jewish origin, Luxemburg and her compatriots sought to overthrow the tsarist government. Nonetheless, they had no concern for Polish statehood (although Luxemburg reportedly loved Polish literature). In her own doctoral dissertation, Luxemburg had made it clear that she thought it did not make sense to remove Poland from the larger Russian scene: the future was one of socialist consolidation, not of redivision into national entities. In other words, this was a classical Marxist stance.

Another famous member of the SDKPiL went down in history as Felix Dzerzhinsky (1877–1926). Like Luxemburg, this Pole hailed from the borderlands of the old Polish-Lithuanian Commonwealth and became a socialist with an internationalist bent. Instead of playing a role in restoring Polish independence, Dzerzhinsky cast his lot with those on the winning side of the Russian Revolution, the Bolsheviks. The Pole (born Dzierżyński) went on to become the first head of the Soviet secret police, the Cheka—the forerunner of the KGB.

Both these individuals hailed from the lands of the former Commonwealth. Yet not all socialists were of the internationalist ilk. Nationally minded socialists belonged primarily to the Polish Socialist Party (PPS), founded in 1892. It saw the future of Poland in the working class. While it adhered to a Marxist program, the PPS put the nation—that is, the restoration of a Polish state—first. The most significant long-term player in the PPS was Józef Piłsudski (1867–1935).

Piłsudski hailed from the eastern borderlands of the old Poland, from the old Lithuania (near Vilnius). The revolutionary nature of noble Polishness of the borderlands variety was definitely felt in his family, active in the January Insurrection. The young Józef was raised on Romantic literature and imbued with the idea of fighting "for our freedom and for yours." His elder brother was involved in revolutionary events in Russia; even his younger sibling was exiled to Siberia for five years for reported participation in a plot to assassinate the tsar Alexander III.

Józef Piłsudski returned from exile and became a socialist, and a particular kind of socialist, that is, a patriotic Polish one. The young socialist activist wanted a more democratic Poland, one in which workers would be included. Piłsudski was the most important figure in the PPS. He edited its newspaper and authored its programs and policies. When that party split into two in the early years of the twentieth century, he would head the half that was called PPS Revolutionary Fraction.

Although a socialist, Piłsudski thought it important to fight for Polish national independence. Piłsudski's approach to questions of socialism and nationalism can be summed up in a neat statement, when he later claimed he got off the socialist train at the stop marked "independence." The Poland of his dreams was a modernized reincarnation of the Commonwealth, a federation of peoples between Germany and Russia. Piłsudski sought to unite Poles, Ukrainians, Belarusians, Lithuanians, and others in one large state that could stand up to Poland's neighbors. The best outcome, according to fellow PPS member Bolesław Limanowski, would be if the future Poland became a Switzerland of Eastern Europe.

There were other socialist parties to be found in the region as well. Among them was the Bund, the Jewish Socialist Party, which functioned in the Russian Empire. Another socialist party functioned in Galicia, within the mosaic of socialist parties in Austria-Hungary. This was the PPSD (Polish Social Democratic Party), led by the fiery orator Ignacy Daszyński.

The Nationalist Option

While Piłsudski's PPS was certainly patriotic in the Polish sense, there were other parties on the horizon that placed the idea of the nation on a special pedestal. This type of party is often called nationalist. In the Polish lands, this iteration evolved from a party founded in emigration by Zygmunt Miłkowski, the so-called Polish League. It eventually was taken over by a young Varsovian, Roman Dmowski (1864–1939), who relocated it to Warsaw and revamped it into the National League. Like its predecessor the National League was a conspiratorial party. Ultimately, when the party became legalized, it was known as the National Democratic Party (ND; or Endecja, from the Polish for those initials).

The nationalists took a different approach to the Polish nation than did other activists who also desired Polish independence. From the very outset, Dmowski believed they had to prepare to assume power when the moment was ripe. An important part of their program involved peasant outreach. For the National Democrats, the Poles were a young nation. In Dmowski's own words: "We are a young nation, and if it concerns the spiritual freshness of the social mass—perhaps the youngest in Europe. Poland fell not because it aged as a nation, but because it became derailed in its development."* It was the peasants and the rank-and-file masses who were to set the tone, not the old Polish nobility, which Dmowski considered outdated and irrelevant, even harmful. As such, the National Democratic Party sought to be the party of the middle class, and it made great gains in this segment of the population.

Roman Dmowski was as secular as they came; he was a scientist by training and inclined toward ideas such as social Darwinism. When the biologist gave up science for politics, he took a real politician's stance. Dmowski realized his message would reach more ears among those he wanted to see in the Polish nation, the peasants (peasants were, in his mind, Poles, even if they did not know it yet), if he spoke of the Poles' Catholicism and identified Catholicism with being Polish (and vice versa). In other words, his approach to religion was more instrumental than genuine.

A controversial aspect of National Democracy, one most closely identified with the person of Dmowski, was its anti-Semitism. Unlike some other

---

* Roman Dmowski, *Wybór pism Romana Dmowskiego* [A Selection of Roman Dmowski's Writings] (New York: Instytut Romana Dmowskiego, 1988), 1: 74.

parties, National Democracy did not see room for Jews within the Polish nation.

In 1902 Dmowski wrote an influential book entitled *Thoughts of a Modern Pole*. His conclusions shed light on the nature of the beast we call modern nationalism—that is, integral nationalism. Above all, the party had to take a hard realist stance. There was no room in the political sphere for generosity of spirit—as in "for your freedom and for ours." Each nation had to take care of its own. This was related to the example of German nationalism, with its national antagonisms and national egoism that he thought worth emulating. Dmowski noticed that, under German rule, "a new, active type of Pole" was forced to stand up to the enemy. He also was hard on those Poles who did not share his nationalist views, labeling them "half-Poles," or "quarter-Poles," or the like.

That Dmowski was a rabid anti-Semite and that his new Polish nationalism embodied elements of social Darwinism had an unfortunate impact on the development of Polish integral nationalism. Still, this was the nationalist party that was to emerge in Poland.

National Democracy claimed to speak for all Poles in all partitions, to have its finger on the pulse of the nation. It claimed to defend Poles both against the Jews (which won over a certain constituency of anti-Semites), and against the rising nationalism of the Ukrainians (which won over the nobles of eastern Galicia, who were constantly at odds with their former peasants). Echoing what the Germans were perpetrating against the Poles in the German Empire (in trying to expel and expropriate and Germanize, when they could not be gotten rid of), the party's harsh methods were seen by the Poles in that part of old Poland as being absolutely necessary.

The Promise of the Peasant?

Other inter-national political parties (all within the realm of the former Commonwealth) included the populists, that is, peasant parties. One prominent example would be the Polish People's Party (PSL), whose leadership included peasants such as Jakub Bojko, Jan Stapiński, and Wincenty Witos. The PSL attracted throngs of peasants to its ranks. Like the other peasant parties, the PSL sought to defend and expand the rights of this most numerous segment of society. Most visible in Galicia, some of these parties were initially under the leadership of clergymen or the intelligentsia. Others were anticlerical. Each was hampered by the generally low level of education of the peasants of the former Polish lands, as well as the fact that peasants could equally well choose to belong to any of the other parties.

More than just members of a party or the object of attention of the National Democrats, peasants were truly popular at the turn of the century. The fin-de-siècle neoromantic literary and artistic movement known as Young Poland was fascinated by peasants as well as by the Tatra Mountains. Beginning in 1904, the writer Władysław Reymont would portray, in very realistic fashion, the lives of Polish peasants in his novel *Peasants*, which, like so many massive novels, first came out in serialized form. Reymont was awarded a Nobel Prize for literature—Poland's second—in 1924.

Yet the turn-of-the-century Young Poland writers and artists in Kraków took an even deeper interest in peasants. Not only did they paint them, but artists and writers often married peasant girls—something that earlier would have been labeled a mésalliance. At the turn of the century, such socially mixed marriages were all the rage, certainly in Kraków.

The painter, writer, and all-around national genius Stanisław Wyspiański was one of the young artists of Kraków to marry a peasant woman. In a way, such marriages seemed to prefigure the coming together of the modern Polish nation, with the unity of various social classes writ small within individual families. Or was the new peasant-noble union simply a fad? Might something amount from this fraternization (and more) of noble and peasant?

Here Wyspiański's famous play *The Wedding* is instructive. *The Wedding* is based on the real wedding of one of Wyspiański's colleagues. The playwright depicted the wedding party, which took place in the village of Bronowice, where all the guests—a cross section of Kraków society—congregated. The same night as the wedding party, the host was visited by phantasmagorical figures from history. Figures such as the blind Ruthenian lyre player and soothsayer Wernyhora or the bloodied peasant Jakub Szela came and went. Toward dawn, a young peasant was given a golden horn, to summon the peasants to join the fight for Poland. The young lad set off . . . and managed to lose the horn. The play ended with nothing happening—the message that the playwright left for his turn-of-the-century audience. Was this inaction or even inertia to be the fate of the Polish nation, even as it seemed to be expanding in new and promising ways?

Part IV

POLAND IN EUROPE AND THE WORLD

CHAPTER 11

Phoenix Reborn

The Second Republic

Despite the partitions, it was clear that there were Poles around the world who agreed at least on several things. The first was that they were Poles, and the second, that they ought to have a state of their own. Despite the centrifugal forces pulling Poles in the direction of Berlin, Saint Petersburg, and Vienna, they saw reason to focus on places like Kraków, Lviv, and Warsaw—not to mention the Poznań region, where the first conflict of the new century began.

A whole century of war and conflict began for the Poles in the locality of Września (Wreschen). In this town, pupils at the local school rebelled and went on strike when they were told their religion classes would now be conducted in German. This reaction of the Poles is worth noting. Since the Kulturkampf, instruction in most subjects had been in German. Now, in 1901, pressure was being put on the schools to remove the last impediment to education being wholly in the language of state: the instruction of religion in a pupil's native tongue.

Yet the Kulturkampf legislation several decades before did not lead to such an outcry as was raised in Września in 1901. That this might be the case only at the turn of the century is reflected in the lack of trust between the Poles under German rule and the German state. These local Poles protested at religion being taught in German in part because they understood the German language so poorly. Parents as well as pupils feared that they would be taught Protestantism instead of their Roman Catholic faith. Given the Kulturkampf (that is, the persecution of both Poles and their faith) of the 1870s, perhaps this was not an irrational fear. While the average village Pole may have cared little about education in German, it did not mean that he cared little about his prospects for eternal life. Such prospects, the Września Poles thought, might be threatened by the teaching of religion in German. This was a threat the fiercely faithful Polish Catholics in the German Empire could not countenance—hence their protest.

The protest struck a raw nerve. The striking pupils were punished for being disobedient. Their parents, who came to the school to defend their children, fared no better: they were beaten, put on trial, and given sentences that seemed way out of proportion, given the infraction.

News of the harsh treatment of these Polish families by the German authorities soon spread far beyond the locality. Famous Poles across the partitioned lands rallied in defense of these poor Poles under German rule. They conducted a public outreach "survey" (*enquête*) in the West. They wrote to famous Westerners about the plight of their compatriots and they sought letters of support for the Polish cause. The letters that were received were ultimately published.

This and other mistreatment at the hands of the Germans inclined Poles to view the relatively new German Empire as the heir of the Teutonic Knights, who in medieval times had made life so hard for the Poles and their allies, the Lithuanians. This medieval-modern parallel was strengthened by the fact that contemporary Germans, even the German emperor Wilhelm II, proved not only ready but even eager to take on the mantle of the former crusading order. At the rededication of the church at the former seat of the Teutonic Knights at Malbork (which was no longer a Catholic church), the emperor chose to depict the rebellious Poles as the problem.

This incident inspired Polish elites to even greater solidarity with ordinary Poles across the partitions. They had already been angered by the establishment, in 1894, of the German Marches Association, which attempted to Germanize the formerly Polish lands within the German Empire. Educated Poles followed the historians' debate in a Viennese paper between the German Theodor Mommsen and the Pole Oswald Balzer over the question of Slavic "barbarism" (Mommsen's contention), which Balzer brilliantly countered. Polish elites decried the fact that a Polish peasant named Drzymała was forced to live in a circus wagon on his newly bought property, as he was not given permission by the German authorities to build on his own land.

These contretemps were hardly a war, although they surely were a conflict. A similar conflict would repeat itself later in the decade, when school strikes would take place in the Kingdom of Poland as well as the Polish lands under German rule.

The Russo-Japanese War

Yet genuine war was also on the horizon. In 1904 war broke out between Russia and Japan. As odd as it may seem, the clash with its tiny Asian neighbor proved troublesome for the Russians. The war effort led to problems at home and provided new opportunities, and new challenges, for the Poles of the Russian Empire.

The hostilities provided impetus for the Poles (always on the lookout for opportunity in the international arena) to plot. Both Piłsudski and Dmowski made their way to Tokyo, independently of each other, and each with a different agenda. Piłsudski offered the Japanese Polish military services; his men would fight the Russians on their home front, thus helping Japan win the war. Dmowski came to warn the Japanese against taking up Piłsudski's offer; he expected that the war might compel the Russians to make concessions to the Poles. While the double visit might have been seen as a comedy of errors (the two men actually met while in Tokyo, discussed their respective views, and respectfully chose to differ), the fact that the bemused Japanese were willing to hear each side suggests the Poles were being treated as if they were genuine players in the international realm, and not subjects of Russia. And, although they declined to use the Poles to fight, the Japanese general staff did provide Piłsudski with some money and war matèrial in the hopes he might gather intelligence for them.

The Revolution of 1904–1907

In the meantime the Russo-Japanese War continued, increasingly showing the weakness of the eventual loser, Russia. This weakness had repercussions for the Poles of the empire. The diplomatic efforts of Piłsudski and Dmowski notwithstanding, the events of 1904 and beyond would be more noteworthy for the upheaval and bloodshed they engendered. In the fall of that year, a working-class demonstration broke out in Warsaw's Grzymułtowski Square in which Piłsudski's PPS fighters (some sixty strong) defended the crowds against the Russian police and mounted Cossacks. A number of participants were injured, while over four hundred were arrested and six lost their lives— as did one Russian policeman. This was the first armed clash between Poles and Russians since 1863.

Events in the empire escalated in 1905, after the debacle in Saint Petersburg called Bloody Sunday, when Russian soldiers fired on a peaceful demonstration of Russians bearing a petition to the tsar. The massacre had huge repercussions for both Russian state and society, unleashing a wave of turmoil and chaos throughout the empire. Back in the Polish lands, strikes in places such as Warsaw and Łódź raised the specter of revolution; martial law was declared. Poles were becoming radicalized, especially the Polish workers, many of whom lost their jobs as a result of the economic decline brought on by the war.

Yet Poles were not in agreement as to how to proceed. Piłsudski and his supporters fed the flames of this radicalization, egging on their compatriots as they went on strike and fought in the streets. Dmowski and his supporters were opposed to demonstrations and unrest. This led to a veritable civil war within the former Kingdom of Poland, and many people on all sides—Polish as well as Russian—lost their lives. The unrest spread further. Left-leaning students, pupils, and teachers went on strike, boycotting Russian schools. This ultimately resulted in a number of students from the Russian Empire emigrating at this time to Galicia, which further radicalized that previously more conservative province.

The respective stances of Józef Piłsudski and Roman Dmowski belied their different approaches to the Polish dilemma, caught as they were between the powers of Germany and Russia. Their respective stances also tell us much about each man's position—and the position each man would take in the near future. Poles' actions without allies had not brought them independence, as the various abortive insurrections of the previous century had demonstrated. But who should the Poles choose to be their allies?

The answer to this question was closely related to each man's answer to the question, whom should the Poles *not* ally themselves with? For Piłsudski, Russia was the Poles' main enemy; for Dmowski the German menace was paramount. To this end, Dmowski spent the early years of the twentieth century favoring pan-Slavism, but this move turned out to be a political dead end for him. The nationalist Dmowski preferred to bet that the Poles—with their stronger, more developed culture—could have an impact on the Russians, which is why he thought an alliance with Russia would be favorable to the Poles. By contrast, Dmowski was convinced that German culture was stronger than the Polish, and thus the Poles would have a harder time if they allied themselves with that power.

His rival, Piłsudski, saw a completely different picture of the future. He eerily predicted how World War I would unfold. In early 1914, while in the West, Piłsudski gave a talk in which he foresaw the collapse of Russia, to be followed by the defeat of the allied Austrians and Germans at hands of the West. Piłsudski eventually would position himself to take full advantage of this situation.

Polish Politics under Russian Rule

Yet this was still in the future. The conflict that raged in the heart of the former Kingdom of Poland in 1904–1907 was not without some effect. Some concessions were wrung out of tsarist Russia. These included the greater use of the Polish language (in the classroom, for example) and even the right to participate and vote in the elections to the so-called Russian State Duma, a national assembly that was to be established.

This proved a long-awaited opportunity for Poles under Russian rule finally to participate in politics. To this point, political parties had to be active in Galicia in order to gain both cadres and maximum political experience. In the elections to the First Duma, National Democrats secured a majority of the fifty-five Polish seats. (Piłsudski's PPS boycotted the elections.) Tsar Nicholas II had problems countenancing even as tame a reform as this— that is, establishing a national assembly, not a full-fledged parliament. Every time the Duma attempted to do something that did not pass muster with the tsar, he prorogued the Duma. This in turn led to new elections. In sum, it resulted in a total of four Dumas being called within the space of a decade, each with its own elections.

The events surrounding the elections to the Fourth Duma in Warsaw proved significant for the Poles' political development. In 1912 Roman Dmowski bid for a spot in what would be the final Duma. He had to contend with the Jewish vote in this large city, the third-largest in the Russian Empire. Warsaw's population approached 885,000, of which about 38 percent were Jews, 55 percent Catholics. In earlier elections, the National Democrats had managed to win the majority of seats by pointing out to the Polish electorate the looming threat of Jews who otherwise might decide the outcome in the polling booth.

The elections to the Fourth Duma proved a different matter. Changes to the Russian electoral system left Jews in a majority position within Warsaw. Furthermore, in addition to Dmowski's National Democrats, an anti-Dmowski nationalist alliance managed to garner some Polish support for their candidate, the historian Jan Kucharzewski, meaning that the Polish vote was split. Warsaw's Jews decided it would be too incendiary to send a Jewish candidate to the Duma, so they ultimately threw their support behind another alternative to Dmowski (not Kucharzewski who, if not exactly an anti-Semite, at least managed to alienate the Jewish voters). In this way the Polish socialist Eugeniusz Jagiełło became the "Jewish" candidate. Jagiełło won the election; Dmowski and Kucharzewski lost.

The disappointed supporters of Dmowski and Kucharzewski reacted with bad grace. In their view, it simply was untenable that Jews should be able to decide the outcome of an election in this way in the Poles' main city of Warsaw—even if they did not actually seat a Jew in the Duma. Dmowski in particular relished the opportunity to tar and feather the Jews as working counter to Polish purposes. His National Democrats came out with guns drawn (figuratively, in the press), calling for an economic boycott of Jewish businesses. An economic boycott campaign on the part of the anti-Semites raged from November 1912 to the outbreak of World War I in August 1914. Poles were exhorted to patronize only Christian businesses.

The campaign poisoned relations between Poles and Jews in Warsaw and the empire as never before. And, while anti-Semites did not speak for the entire Polish population, they did color the way Poles were perceived inside the Russian Empire at this moment. The Russian authorities saw all this as part of the general Polish "revolutionary" movement. They clamped down further on the Poles—a response that was not likely to improve relations. So, the situation grew increasingly tense.

Piłsudski in Galicia

In the meantime, Józef Piłsudski had moved to Galicia. In the wake of the revolution of 1905–1907, his PPS split into two parties: the PPS-Left and the PPS Revolutionary Fraction. The socialist leader saw more opportunities for a new kind of activity in Galicia. Under his aegis, several paramilitary groups were established. They built upon the tradition, in Galicia and elsewhere, of gymnastics and firefighting organizations. Even seemingly peaceable organizations such as the Falcons (Polish: Sokół), an influential gymnastics association organized into local groups called "nests," trained with lances, clubs, and rifles. One of their main aims was to improve the body national through education, strong healthy bodies, economic development, the defense of their native tongue, and national unity. (Incidentally, the Falcon "nests" of Galicia had come under the control of the National Democrats.)

In the first decade of the twentieth century, such seemingly innocuous organizations began to imagine a time when their skills would be put to more practical applications. International tensions had grown since the annexation of Herzegovina and Bosnia by Austria-Hungary in 1908. This had inclined the Galician viceroy to give permission for paramilitary organizations to be established in the province. Piłsudski himself already headed a secret Union for Active Struggle. Now of necessity it gave birth to two legal entities, the Riflemen's Union and the "Rifleman" Society. These were founded in the Galician capital of Lviv and in Kraków in April and December 1910, respectively. Once again, the riflemen's organizations were registered as sport and gymnastics organizations, albeit with expanded privileges—courtesy of the viceroy. They had the use of military shooting ranges, permission to hold exercises and offer lectures, even obtain stocks of arms and ammunition. Before long, other new organizations representing other political parties (such as the populists) followed suit, resulting in a plethora of paramilitary organizations marching about Galicia.

Nor were the paramilitary organizations limited to Poles. Ukrainians also saw the opportunity to organize in this way and sought to avail themselves of it. They already had a number of Ukrainian Sich clubs. The reference to the Sich harked back to the Cossacks of the early modern period. In its early twentieth-century Galician variant, the Cossack imagery of the Sich had been augmented with local Galician highlander elements.

Would the Ukrainians be allowed to establish a paramilitary organization in Polish-controlled Galicia? In order to get their application to pass muster with the Galician Polish authorities, in 1913 the head of the Sich, Kyrylo Trylovskyi, simply translated the application of one of Piłsudski's organizations, substituting the name of his own organization where necessary. There was no way the Galician authorities could decline the request. The Sich, thus, was transformed into a military youth organization, the Sich Riflemen. Both organizations began to train, Poles and Ukrainians alike setting their sights on greater things—on independence—with both potentially vying for some of the same lands. There was no time to lose.

Indeed, war was in the air. The Great War was just around the corner.

The Outbreak of the Anticipated: World War

On June 28, 1914, a shot rang out in Sarajevo, and its echo reverberated around the world for the next four years. The heir to the Habsburg imperial throne, Franz Ferdinand, and his wife were both assassinated. The date happened to be the Serbian national holiday, Vidovdan, the anniversary of the Serbs' monumental defeat centuries earlier (1389) at Kosovo Pole. It seems Franz Ferdinand had little understanding of Serb history, or he would not have ventured into the Balkans on that fateful day—the perfect day for Serbs to make a political statement.

But war would not have broken out in the wake of the assassination had there not already been a whole series of alliances undergirding both the

1908 annexation of Bosnia and Herzegovina as well as the recent Balkan wars of 1912–1913.

A significant development had taken place in recent years in the international realm. The alignment of international alliances pitted two of Poland's partitioners, Germany and Austria-Hungary (who would become the Central Powers), against the third, Russia (allied with the Entente, which included Britain and France). For the Poles, a door had been left ajar. If war were to break out, there would be no united front on the part of the partitioners to thwart any Polish attempts at gaining independence.

Yet could Poles simply walk through that door? On August 1, 1914, Germany declared war on Russia, and Austria soon followed suit. The Poles in Galicia were prepared—even itching—to fight. On the night of August 5/6, a group of Piłsudski's Riflemen departed from Kraków and set off for the Russian border. The first Austro-Hungarian troops to invade enemy territory, they made an incursion into the former Kingdom of Poland. In the region of Kielce, however, Piłsudski's cadre company, later known as the First Brigade of the Polish Legions, was not met with outstretched arms as it had imagined. The "Polish" peasants under Russian rule were suspicious of the foreigners, and contrary to Piłsudski's expectations, they did not join in the fight against Russia, the country that had ruled them for so long. One can judge the incursion a fiasco, but still, Piłsudski and his men had demonstrated that Poles were willing to fight for their independence. And soon they really would be fighting—in the ranks of the Polish Legions, established in Galicia by Piłsudski in mid-August.

All the same, Piłsudski and his Riflemen sensed that their dedication and sacrifices were not entirely appreciated by the Polish population for which they fought. This was reflected in the lyrics of the march "We, the First Brigade" that became Piłsudski's theme song during World War I. The song begins: "The Legions are a soldier's melody; / The Legions are a sacrificial pyre; / The legions are a soldier's pride; / The Legions are the fate of desperate men."[*] The song would remain Piłsudski's favorite march and would be forever associated with him.

But this was all in the future. In the interim, society had to organize. Back in Galicia, on August 12, a proclamation circulated, announcing: "The decisive hour has struck! Poland has ceased to be a slave. She wishes to determine her own fate, she wishes to build her own future, throwing her own armed force into the scale of events." Although signed and sealed by the National Government (shades of 1863), the proclamation was Piłsudski's. He

---

[*]   Translation from Robert A. Rothstein, "Piłsudski in Song," *The Polish Review* 16, no. 1 (2011): 11.

was imitating the actions of the insurrectionists of the January Insurrection, who had indeed established a secret National Government, with only a seal to identify its members. Piłsudski hoped that his proclamation would summon forth the same kind of dedication to the cause of Polish independence as some fifty years earlier.

All this played into the vision of the war that Piłsudski had presented in his Paris lecture of January 1914. There he had opined that in the forthcoming war Russia would succumb to the Central Powers, which in turn would be defeated by the West. Not that much note was taken of his prediction—at least, not in the West.

The Mobile Eastern Front

World War I was not only the mutual annihilation that characterized the trench warfare of the western front, where countless soldiers lost their lives in the attempt to move the front mere inches in one direction or another. The eastern front looked very different. It witnessed a near constant movement of forces back and forth across former Polish territories, which themselves became the bulk of the eastern front. Indeed, at its westernmost point, the eastern front nearly coincided with the western border of the former Kingdom of Poland. At its easternmost point, the line ran from the Dvina in the north through the town of Pinsk down to the vicinity of Ternopil in Galicia and from there into Bukovina.

Some of the early movement took place in the north. In the fall of 1914, the battle of Tannenberg, a German victory, was designed to wipe out the memory of the loss at Grunwald (in German accounts also known as the battle of Tannenberg) some five hundred years earlier. The Russians had more success in the south against the Austrians. The tsarist forces occupied eastern Galicia. The occupation was hard on the civilian population, which the Russians hurriedly sought to Russify. The Russian occupiers remained unconcerned about any casualties that might occur in the process. Yet even the Austrians treated the region's Ruthenes brutally, suspecting them of being Russophiles: many were arrested, shot, or imprisoned.

The Russian occupation did not mark the end of the war in this region. In 1915 the fighting in the Carpathian Mountains took place in the harsh, unforgiving conditions of winter, the movements of the troops hindered by deep snow. The Polish Legions there fought valiantly but also suffered heavy losses.

Double Indemnity

From the Polish point of view, World War I was a human tragedy on all sides. It was a tragedy that Poles were fighting in all the different armies (German, Austrian, Russian) and living in territories that would undergo occupation by one side after the other, for where was the eastern front if not in former Polish lands? Yet Poles entertained the hope that they might obtain at least autonomy for themselves within the partitioning powers for whom they fought—the Central Powers (Germans and Austrians) on one hand, the Entente (Russians) on the other. Essentially this meant that brother (whether drafted foot soldier or commissioned or career officer) fought against brother—but there was no way out of that.

Within the former Kingdom of Poland, the evacuation of whole factories to the interior of the tsarist empire, sometimes beyond the Urals, resulted in the uprooting of whole families and communities. What was left behind was rendered useless to the enemy.

Ultimately the German and Austrian troops came to occupy most of the Polish lands that had been under Russian rule. The partitioning powers refused to grant concessions until deemed absolutely necessary for the conduct of the war. Economic exploitation, the bane of all occupations, followed. The Germans seemed indifferent to the starvation of the local population. Germans also forced Poles to work in industrial factories for them.

Promises of Statehood, Promises of Change

In November 1916, some important concessions were made to the Poles. The Central Powers issued the Two Emperors' Manifesto, in which a future self-governing Poland was promised. Nonetheless, the territories to be included in the future self-governing Poland were left to be determined. This served the purposes of the Central Powers, which sought to gain more Polish manpower for the conduct of the war. The Central Powers dangled this carrot in front of the Poles, although it was not certain what, if any of it, would really belong to them in the end.

Given the circumstances of the war, Poles early recognized the importance of diplomacy abroad. A brilliant example of such diplomacy was the work of the internationally famous pianist Ignacy Jan Paderewski, who toured the United States and had contacts in high places in the Wilson administration. But the Poles fought an uphill battle in western Europe, where the hopes had been to get Austria to sign a separate peace. The Western powers did not want to promise concessions to the minorities within Austria-Hungary.

The Polish nationalist leader Roman Dmowski (an accomplished linguist) was particularly active in the West. He was a founder of the Polish National Committee in Switzerland, where earlier other Poles, such as the famous novelist Henryk Sienkiewicz, had actively sought to raise funds as well as awareness for humanitarian causes. These causes included the plight of the Polish population, which was suffering in the middle of the combat that raged on its home territory. (Sienkiewicz died in Switzerland during the war.)

In the midst of all this, an important event took place that altered the course of the war completely. This was the two-part Russian Revolution of 1917. The revolution brought down the mighty tsarist Russia faster than any Central (or any other) Power could. It took the Russian Revolution and the concomitant withdrawal of Russia from the war to focus minds in the West. After the February Revolution, the Russian Provisional Government allowed Austrian prisoners of war to form Polish military units, which would join up with the Entente on the western front. This move was supported by the French, as they were desperately in need of reinforcements. But to get the Poles to fight, the French needed to lend their approval to Dmowski's Polish National Committee as the rightful government of Poland. This recognition was one step in the right direction for the Poles.

Polish diplomacy continued in the West, with both Dmowski and Paderewski involved. During the period of the Conference of Brest-Litovsk (December 1917–March 1918), which was to determine the border between what had now become Bolshevik Russia after the Bolshevik Revolution in October 1917 and the Central Powers, Woodrow Wilson was prevailed upon to support Polish independence. His thoughts on this matter ultimately were presented to the U.S. Congress in his famous Fourteen Points of January 1918. The thirteenth point reads: "An independent Polish state should be erected that should include the territories inhabited by indisputably Polish populations, which should be assured a free and secure access to the sea, and whose political and economic independence and territorial integrity should be guaranteed by international covenant." Similar sentiments were declared on June 1918 by the Inter-Allied Conference of Versailles. To be sure, Wilson's wording left plenty of room for misunderstanding. Who was to determine what were "territories inhabited by indisputably Polish populations," and how might the Poles gain access to the sea without gaining territory along the Baltic Sea at Germany's expense?

Nonetheless, it did seem that a Polish state would come into being after the war. But not all went smoothly for the Poles back in the theater of war.

Piłsudski was imprisoned in the Magdeburg fortress as of late July 1917. The reason? He refused to let his legions continue to fight on the side of the Central Powers unless they declared Polish independence. Simply put, his Legionnaires refused to take an oath for the new Polish army, to be under German direction. The Central Powers sought to placate the Poles by creating a regency council in Warsaw in October 1917. It was to be followed by a state council and a council of ministers, all comprised of Poles. Although this was truly a significant move, insofar as the establishment of a Polish state was concerned, the bodies that came into being were heavily conservative and had little in the way of popular support. They were also heavily tied to the Central Powers.

Nor was all well on the diplomatic front. The Treaty of Brest-Litovsk and an earlier treaty with Ukraine promised to transfer the territory of Chełm, claimed by the Poles, to Ukraine. There were also rumors that Eastern Galicia might be ceded to Ukraine—a move that Poles recognized as a "fourth partition of Poland." Manifestations and unrest ensued.

In the interim, the Regency Council found itself in trouble. The situation on the ground in Warsaw was growing more radical by the day. In October 1918, the Regency Council tried to declare Poland's independence, but at the same time it was having a terrible time forming a government the Poles could trust.

The Creative Countdown to a New Poland

To the aid of the Varsovians came Józef Piłsudski. After his release from prison the Polish military leader made his way to Warsaw, arriving in the former Polish capital on November 10, 1918. The following day he was given control of the Polish military and several days later was declared head of a new Poland, both by the Regency Council. Piłsudski set about forming a provisional government.

Other state-building developments had preceded him in the Polish lands. After the sudden disintegration of Austria-Hungary at the end of October 1918, the socialist Ignacy Daszyński established a People's Republic in the city of Lublin, the site of the old Union of Lublin that had created the Commonwealth of Both Nations. Thus, the Poles had several governments simultaneously. And let us not forget Dmowski, with his Polish National Committee, to the west. What were Poles to do?

Ultimately the socialist Daszyński was prevailed upon to throw in his support to the socialist Piłsudski (although the latter, as you may recall, had decided to leave the socialist train at the stop marked "Independence"). This still left one Polish government to the west (Dmowski's) and one on home turf (Piłsudski's). The situation proved awkward. Recall, further, that Dmowski's Polish National Committee had been recognized by the Western powers. Now negotiations had to take place between the archrivals Piłsudski and Dmowski. Realizing that much was at stake, both sides managed to reach agreement, each making some concessions. In exchange for Dmowski's giving way to Piłsudski, who had popular support on the ground, Piłsudski would ask his original prime minister, the socialist Jędrzej Moraczewski, to resign in favor of Ignacy Jan Paderewski, whose presence in the government would placate the Polish right. (A representative at the Paris Peace Conference, Paderewski would later be present at the signing of the Treaty of Versailles and the opening of the League of Nations.)

A modus vivendi thus seemed to be reached, one that had the prospect of satisfying a broad swath of Polish society. The new Polish state had not only been born again—it had been creatively negotiated.

World war had done its job. The re-creation of a Polish state, more a function of the collapse of empires than the direct result of the efforts of Poles at home and abroad, may have been out of the Poles' control. Nonetheless, it did not hurt that many Poles of different political persuasions sought the same goal—a state of their own—and not only fought for it but also advertised this goal abroad. It took soldiers with boots on the ground as well as diplomats in the halls of Europe to gain support for the nascent Poland—a sovereign Polish state, the so-called Second Republic.

The Second Polish Republic

The birthday of the Second Polish Republic is generally considered November 11, 1918. As we have seen, that date—when Piłsudski assumed control over the armed forces in Warsaw—was but a part of a series of steps that had already been taken. It would require more work on the part of the Polish army to solidify the borders of the new state.

What also became evident was that there were conflicting and competing visions of the new state. Was it to be a people's republic, as the socialist Daszyński wished? or a more conservative and/or nationalistic state, as Dmowski and Paderewski doubtless preferred? Were the opinions of Piłsudski, who had been the glue to hold much of the war effort together, to gain traction, thus enabling the new Poland to become a large regional federation? Let us not forget the vast majority of the population, the peasants.

Might they not shape the new polity to their own liking? The real question was whether all, or any, of these visions could be reconciled in one state—a state that was to resume (at least, in the minds of some Poles) where another, very different one had left off 123 years earlier. If not, what would become of the nascent state?

After the initial creative compromises were made, the new Poland set about creating the requisite trappings of parliamentary government. Parliamentary elections were scheduled for January 1919. Noteworthy is the fact that women as well as men were given the franchise—two years before the United States, ten years before Great Britain, twenty-six years before France; the women of Poland could, and did, serve as deputies and senators. A "Little Constitution" was promulgated in February 1919, the same month that the West officially recognized the Polish state.

Interwar Poland

The period of existence for the Second Polish Republic, from 1918 to 1939, is often referred to as the interwar period, meaning the period between the First and Second World Wars. In some ways, to speak of interwar Poland is a misnomer, however. War did not cease on November 11, 1918, and certainly not in the Polish (Eastern) theater.

Peace came to the Polish state only much later. Initially, the country was wracked by wars and armed conflicts, wars that nonetheless helped shape the borders of the new independent Poland. These wars and their ultimate resolutions were for the most part the work of the Poles and not of the dignitaries of the Paris Peace Conference, who likely would have set Poland's borders differently.

A full six wars continued to be fought by Poles in 1918 to 1921. These concerned practically all the frontiers of the newly emerging state.

War 1: The Polish-Ukrainian War

A war was fought with Ukrainians over Eastern Galicia. Poles considered Lviv, the Galician oil fields, the mineral wealth of the Eastern Carpathians, and the fertile lands of the Podolian plain to be part of their patrimony. Their Ukrainian neighbors did not concur. In November 1918, the Ukrainian National Council was established in the former Galician capital of Lviv. This represented the Ukrainian/Ruthenian population of the former Galicia, which numerically dominated much of the region (certainly the villages, if not the cities and towns). The council proclaimed the existence of an independent West Ukrainian People's Republic, the borders of which would reach westward to the San River.

The matter of eastern Galicia was to be settled militarily. Polish residents of the Galician capital of Lviv, including a significant number of urban youth, prepared to defend their vision of the future. These children fighters, many of whom lost their lives during the conflict, became famous as the Lviv Eaglets. Polish armed forces also reached Lviv in November. The government of the West Ukrainian People's Republic was forced to flee the city, making its way first to Ternopil, then to Ivano-Frankivsk (Polish: Stanisławów). In the midst of the fighting in Lviv, the city's Jews—caught in the middle—suffered a pogrom. This was not an auspicious start to Polish rule over the city.

Yet the Polish-Ukrainian war was not over. Ukrainian units continued to fight for control over the city. Poles did not secure Lviv until March 1919. The war continued, with the forces of General Józef Haller, which had arrived from France, engaged in this theater. The fate of this region was complicated by the fact that Poles were dealing with yet another Ukrainian entity, the Ukrainian People's Republic, further to the east. The conflict with the west Ukrainians did not end until July 1919.

Ultimately the League of Nations awarded the Poles the right to administer the old east Galicia for the space of twenty-five years. This did not satisfy the Poles, who delayed acting on the decision, and the Ukrainians within the new Polish state were not happy with the outcome. After losing their chance at independence, they wished to be no part of interwar Poland. The conflict between Poles and Ukrainians in the former Eastern Galicia would continue to simmer through the years.

The Polish-Ukrainian resolution represented but one complicated front, settling the southeastern border of the new Polish state.

War 2: The Poznanian War

Another conflict took place in the Poznań region. The Poznanian War—really more an insurrection than a war, and a successful one at that—broke out December 27, 1918, when Poles of the region tried to secede from Germany. The situation was resolved by the Paris Peace Conference in the Treaty of Versailles of June 28, 1919. The region of Poznań as well as an important narrow swath of territory to its north that included cities such as Bydgoszcz (German: Bromberg) and Toruń and extended all the way to the Baltic was awarded to the Poles. This award gave Poland the desired outlet to the sea. Further territory (several villages in the north) was awarded Poland on the basis of a plebiscite that took place in July 1920, which nonetheless resulted in most of that region being awarded to Germany.

While the Poles did gain an outlet to the sea, they did not gain control over Gdańsk. In the interwar period, the city and its environs would become the Free City of Danzig, dominated by Germans but under the League of Nations—with a high commissioner in charge. This meant that Poles could not be assured of free access to the sea via this seaport.

War 3: The Silesian Uprisings

The rich province of Silesia was also a bone of contention. It had long been under Habsburg rule, only to pass to Prussian control in the mid-eighteenth century. Nonetheless, the population maintained a distinct identity. Both Germans and Poles claimed Silesians as part of their nation. It took a series of Silesian uprisings for several months in three consecutive years (August 16–24, 1919; August 19–25, 1920; May 2–July 5, 1921) on the part of Silesian Poles to convince the West that Poles might be given part of this valuable industrialized province. A Silesian Convention resolved the issue in 1922. Thus, the borders of the new Poland were still contested, still fluid, long after 1918.

War 4: The Lithuanian War

Two wars, thus, settled Poland's borders with Germany. Poles likewise had pretentions to parts of the old Commonwealth of Both Nations, territories found to its east. Here the city of Vilnius was key. Recall that Vilnius had been the capital of the Lithuanian half of the Commonwealth. By the early twentieth century, however, ethnic Lithuanians (the former peasants of the northernmost part of the old Grand Duchy) had come to see Vilnius as the capital of their own future Lithuania. They did not wish to be part of a greater Polish state. Their state aspirations had been supported by Germany during the war.

Ethnic Lithuanian claims to the region made the situation difficult for Józef Piłsudski, who hailed from this part of the old Commonwealth. He envisaged a federation of states between Germany and Russia, and Lithuania should have been one of them. In the immediate postwar period, the city of Vilnius was repeatedly occupied: by Soviet forces in early 1919, then by Polish forces in the spring of 1919, with Piłsudski himself appealing to the population of the former Grand Duchy of Lithuania to join him in a Polish-Lithuanian-Belarusian federation. The city was given back to the Lithuanians by the Soviets, only to be occupied once again in October 1920 by the ostensibly renegade Polish general Lucjan Żeligowski, who nonetheless had consulted with Piłsudski before making his move. That the Polish Seym reacted to this occupation of Vilnius by treating Żeligowski like a hero suggests that Poles would have gone to any lengths to retain this symbolically important city.

The border that ultimately emerged with Lithuania enraged the Lithuanians, who had fewer boots in the field. In the city, Lithuanians amounted to a mere 2 percent of the population, compared to the Poles and Jews, each comprising some 40 percent. Denied Vilnius, they had to settle on Kaunas as their capital. Although eventually a truce was reached, Lithuanians would consider Poles their grave enemies throughout the interwar period. The issue of Vilnius would continue to rankle.

War 5: The Czechoslovak War

Poles even had a conflict on their southern border. Poles and Czechs vied for the city of Cieszyn (German: Teschen), which was part of the tiny piece of Silesia that had remained in Habsburg hands. In January 1919, the Czechoslovak army invaded Cieszyn. In July 1920, Allied arbitration ultimately settled the matter in the Czechs' favor. The Allies were not keen on giving the Poles (who seemed so set on settling border disputes through military means) control over even this tiny territory. Nonetheless, there were skirmishes between Poles and Czechoslovaks in the mountains until 1925.

War 6: The Polish-Soviet War

The outcome of the war with Czechoslovakia was colored by the biggest of the six wars to determine the new Poland's borders. This was the Polish-Soviet War. It was a war of much greater significance than merely where to draw the Poles' eastern frontier (as if that were not important enough).

Conflict between the independent Polish state and the rising Bolshevik Russia to its east was all but inevitable. The ideology of the Soviets, who had forced through their proletarian revolution in Russia despite its tiny working class, required the revolution to spread to the industrialized states of Western Europe. Only then would world revolution be possible. The Bolsheviks began to amass an enormous military force along the new Poland's eastern border and hoped that the Poles would blink first. On their part, Poles had no illusions about Soviet aims and realized that no Russian state—whether White or Bolshevik—had any interest in allowing Poland the borders it wanted. Both sides prepared for war.

The war was precipitated by the withdrawal of German forces from the borderlands, leaving Poland and Bolshevik Russia to vie for the territory. One might count the Red Army offensive that took Vilnius on January 1, 1919, as the first move of the war. It was followed by skirmishes in the borderlands, with the Poles taking back Vilnius and Minsk later that year. The following year, the Bolsheviks began to assemble a million-strong army running the length of the contested territory.

Despite these early moves, the Bolsheviks placed the blame for the war on a concrete step taken at the end of April 1920 by the Polish army, which was allied with the Ukrainian army of Ataman Symon Petliura. Petliura was part of the Kyiv-based Ukrainian state, not to be confused with the even shorter-lived West Ukrainian People's Republic that had fought for Lviv earlier. Petliura importantly supported Piłsudski's idea of a multinational federation.

Aware of the Bolshevik forces massing along Poland's eastern border, the alliance made its plans to invade to the south of the Pripyat marshes (a major obstacle to movement). The Polish army pushed quickly eastward in May, marching triumphantly all the way to distant Kyiv. The triumph was nonetheless illusory. Petliura's Ukrainians were unable to muster enough forces to protect the position of their Polish allies. The Poles were far from their supply lines and were compelled to retreat.

The summer of 1920 witnessed a turn of fortunes. The Poles were attacked by the Soviet Red Army, ably led by generals such as Semen Budenny and Mikhail Tukhachevsky. The two generals availed themselves of different routes to the Polish heartland. Budenny attacked to the south of the Pripyat marshes, reaching Galicia. Tukhachevsky took the favored route to the north of the Pripyat marshes. The latter's famous words encapsulate the Bolsheviks' real goal: "To the West! Over the corpse of White Poland lies the road to worldwide conflagration."

And indeed: by August the Poles were in grave danger. Five Soviet armies were approaching the Polish capital, Warsaw. Would Lenin's Red Army truly be able to overpower the Poles and spread revolution further west—to Europe and beyond?

Piłsudski managed to come up with a daring plan, after he sought the support of Poland's peasant prime minister Wincenty Witos, who was asked to rally the country's peasants to fight. Every able-bodied man was asked to defend Warsaw, and amazingly, they managed to stop Tukhachevsky's forces from crossing the Vistula.

Piłsudski's plan staked everything on a counterattack, one so risky that the Soviets did not believe the plan when they found it on a captured Polish soldier. They saw it as a decoy. Subsequently Piłsudski's cavalry-led assault force hit Tukhachevsky from behind, in the process cutting him and his troops off from possible Soviet reinforcements. The Soviets were routed, and the rest raced home as fast as they could. The "Miracle on the Vistula" of August 1920 proved a success. (It should be noted that the dedication of clergy as well as the masses of Poles was thought to have secured divine intervention for the besieged country.)

Yet the war was not yet over. The final great cavalry battles in European history took place near Zamość, to which the Soviets had retreated. The Poles proved victorious.

Polish forces had prevailed against the mighty Soviet hordes intent upon bringing about world revolution. The victory has been seen as comparable

Figure 11.1: Color postcard of the "Miracle on the Vistula" (1920), painted by Jerzy Kossak. The intercession of the Mother of God is visible, not simply felt by the Polish troops and the people.

to other major world-historical victories: Charles Martel's stopping of the Saracens at the medieval Battle of Tours, or the stopping of the Ottomans by Jan III Sobieski at the siege of Vienna. Like the Polish forces of Sobieski in 1683, their Polish descendants had played a key role in stopping a world-class danger. As a result, Lenin sought to cut his losses and sued for peace. He would have to settle for socialism in one country . . .

The Treaty of Riga, signed in March 1921, set the final terms of the peace as well as the eastern border of Poland. It proved an imperfect outcome for Poland. The Polish delegation had to settle for the border running from the Dvina River in the north to the Dniester River in the south. The restoration of the entirety of the Polish-Lithuanian Commonwealth proved impossible to achieve.

The outcome of the Treaty of Riga would have repercussions for the inhabitants of both twentieth-century states. It resulted in Belarusian and Ukrainian populations finding themselves split between Poland and Bolshevik Russia. The hundreds of thousands of Poles left on the opposite side of the Polish-Soviet border would suffer terribly under Stalin in the late 1930s, when it was decided the Polish population must be wiped out. More than 110,000 Poles perished at the hands of the Soviet secret police, the NKVD, in the year 1937 alone.

Whose Poland?

The problem with the new borders is that they matched no one's vision of Poland. The new Poland was not a pure Polish nation-state, such as Dmowski and the National Democrats wanted. Over 30 percent of the population consisted of non-Poles—people whom the nationalists would consider undesirable, for the most part unassimilable, at best second-class citizens. According to the census of 1921 (and readers should know that the numbers are not fully accurate, as parts of the country were still in flux), 69.2 percent of the country's citizens identified themselves as Poles, 14.3 percent as Ukrainians/Ruthenes, 3.9 percent as Belarusians, with 0.2 percent insisting they were "local" people. Jews amounted to some 7.8 percent of the population, 3.9 percent belonged to the German minority, and there were tiny fractions of a percentage each of Lithuanians, Russians, Czechs, and others. This would prove problematic for those who embraced the Wilsonian idea of nation-states in this ethnically and religiously heterogeneous part of the world, for the problem was not unique to interwar Poland.

Map 11.1: The Second Polish Republic, ca. 1924

The territory of the new Polish state, particularly as drawn by the Treaty of Riga in the east, was also not large enough to enable Piłsudski to cobble together the federation he had dreamed of, his East European Switzerland. Too much of the eastern lands lay outside the country, in the neighboring Soviet republics of Belarus and Ukraine; and neighbors such as Lithuania wanted no part of a Polish-led federation. In short, the new state did not fit anyone's expectations, nationalistic or federalistic. Any dream of Poland in its new incarnation being a modern nation-state was just that—a dream.

Nor was the state as stable as the outcome at Riga might have led one to believe. Given all the wars that were fought to secure Poland's borders, the country was insecure on many fronts. The Western Powers were slow to acknowledge the finalized shape of the Second Polish Republic, and some countries did so only grudgingly. The country did not have many allies. Poland sought to enter into alliance with the Baltic countries to counterbalance the threat from Russia, but Lithuania remained aloof, upset that Vilnius had been taken over by the Poles. Poland ultimately allied herself with France and Romania, while seeking to improve relations with

Czechoslovakia. As to her two most dangerous neighbors, Germany and the Soviet Union, Poland sought to reach a modus vivendi; the Poles eventually would sign non-aggression pacts with each of them, although Polish leaders realized these were stop-gap measures.

Still, the fact that Poland initially had been able to take care of her border issues through military not diplomatic means allowed many Poles to overrate the country's military. In the process they overlooked the fact that it had fared well only because both Germany and Russia were still weak at this time (recall that the Soviets had still been fighting White Russian forces, while the belligerent Germany had been brought to its knees by Versailles). If those two countries were to rise, then Poland would truly find herself in between a rock and a hard place.

Thus we have some paradoxes. Poland managed to attain independence, if a somewhat shaky one (shaky domestically as well as internationally). The definition of what it meant to be Polish was not universally agreed upon. Was the criterion of ethnicity to determine Polishness, thus favoring ethnolinguistic or religious (Roman Catholic) affiliation? Or could any citizen of the Second Polish Republic consider him- or herself a Pole? That, of course, was further dependent upon the goodwill of some of Poland's citizens: they may not have wanted to be Poles.

We should underscore, once again, the fact that neither national identity nor national unity was uppermost in many people's minds. This held true for those who by any account (religious, ethnolinguistic, citizenship) would be identified as Poles. Consider the problematic relationship of the peasants to Polishness. Even those peasants who spoke Polish were hardly convinced that their interests were the same as those of the large landowners.

Given the country's demographics as well as its overwhelmingly agrarian nature, peasants could have been a true force to be reckoned with in interwar politics. To be sure, peasant parties proliferated. Yet this was the problem: the peasants did not function as a united front but instead splintered into numerous smaller parties. To give but one example, three different parties went under the name Polish People's Party (PSL): PSL Piast, PSL Liberation, and PSL Left.

Yet even those who ostensibly should have been closer to a Polish national identity did not necessarily see the national idea as particularly relevant in their lives. Not every nobleman easily made the adjustment from being first and foremost noble to being just another Pole—for the new state did away with noble titles. Many noble-born landowners continued to live, much as they had for centuries, on their estates, their conservative mentality still very much in evidence.

Creating Poland

The first task facing the new state was to recover from the devastation of the war, which had been enormous. Much of the infrastructure of the country had to be rebuilt from scratch. Industry needed to be developed, as there was huge unemployment. And agriculture, which had been disrupted and ravaged by the war, needed to be put back on its feet. The country was impoverished; it was also experiencing a food crisis. To boot, some four hundred thousand Poles had died fighting in the Prussian, Austrian, and Russian armies during World War I, which meant a depletion of the best patriotic forces.

Another enormous challenge concerned the knitting together of disparate pieces of territory and peoples who had experience of very different imperial regimes—different legal systems, educational systems, forms of national and local governance, and the like. The enormity of the physical task of bringing together the previously partitioned lands, after 123 years of belonging to states other than Poland, was reflected in the network of railways. The railways all led to the imperial hubs, thus being a centrifugal not a unifying force. New railway branches had to be added to facilitate travel to the capital of Warsaw as well as to cross the breadth and length of the state. Even today one still notes a particular denseness of railway lines in the west (the former Germany), light coverage in the east, and the south best served by the Galician west–east line connecting Kraków with Lviv and beyond.

Those businesses that were able to resume operation relatively quickly now faced a different domestic market. No longer were they able to export to Berlin, Vienna, or Saint Petersburg. And if they had relied in part on inputs available elsewhere in those empires, they would need to find new suppliers within the borders of the new state. The country experienced a painful bout of hyperinflation in 1923: at one point, one U.S. dollar was worth 20 million Polish marks. The replacement of the mark by the zloty in the spring of 1924 and the concomitant currency correction essentially wiped out the savings of the country's middle class. This did not augur well for the economic well-being of the citizens of the young Polish state.

As the history of partition suggests, not all Polish citizens were equally prepared for national independence. Regionalism became pronounced, as inhabitants felt they had more in common with those who came from their partitioned zone than with those from other partitioned zones. Few had any real experience of self-rule, making Galicians the most likely candidates to move to the new capital, Warsaw, to help run the new government. This in turn rendered Lviv, the former capital of Galicia, a remote provincial backwater. At the same time, there must have been a clash of cultures in the new Polish capital. The earlier inhabitants of Warsaw (as we have seen) had a very unpleasant experience in the elections to the Russian State Duma. Would these experiences carry over to Polish politics in an ostensibly Polish state?

Indeed, few Poles knew what to expect from the new Poland. In a novel by Stefan Żeromski, *The Spring to Come*, the reality of life in a state experiencing growing pains is brought to life. A Polish industrialist in what was then the Russian imperial port of Baku tries to interest his son (the main protagonist of the novel), who had lived his entire life outside of the homeland, in moving to Poland. The father weaves a beautiful story of Poland as a land of glass houses and does convince his son to try his luck in the new Poland. However, this useful fiction of glass houses—a place of perfection, a promised land—proved but a bubble that soon would burst. There were no glass houses. Rather, the reality of life in the young state proved challenging at best.

Of course, no one in 1924 knew what a normal nation-state was to look like, let alone how to create one in this heterogeneous part of the world. There were various ideas as to Poland's future shape as well. Various political camps had their own visions and mobilized their constituencies to fight to turn them into reality. The Roman Catholic clergy most decidedly had its own ideas of the role the church was to play in Polish life. Peasants sought improved conditions for farming, as well as greater access to land—something that was more easily accomplished by expropriating non-Poles than by doing the same to Polish nobles.

Seeing Spring and Not Poland

Yet other inhabitants of the new Poland simply breathed a sigh of relief. Independence had been achieved. Now they could settle down to normality. Such a view was visible in the rich artistic world of interwar Poland. Perhaps it is most famously encapsulated in the phrase of poet Jan Lechoń: "and in the spring, let me see spring and not Poland." In other words, poets and painters no longer needed to infuse their work with national symbols. Lechoń might choose to depict the emergence of fledglings from their nest or crocuses breaking through the snow, with no hidden Polish agenda whatsoever.

The interwar period witnessed a plethora of new trends both monumental and modernist in literature, poetry, and art. Take, for example, the poetry of the Skamander group, represented by poets such as Antoni Słonimski, Julian Tuwim, and Jarosław Iwaszkiewicz, or the avant-garde poets and writers such as Czesław Miłosz, Julian Przyboś, Józef Czechowicz, or Stanisław

Ignacy Witkiewicz (usually called by his nickname Witkacy). This, after all, was a period in which not only theater but also cinema and radio broadcasts took off. The relative calm of interwar Poland provided Poland's composers such as Karol Szymanowski with opportunities to create: Szymanowski was famed for religious compositions such as *Stabat Mater,* for his opera *King Roger,* and his highland ballet *Harnasie.* Young performers were given the chance to shine. During this period, the International Chopin Competition and the Henryk Wieniawski Violin Competition were initiated. While non-vocal music clearly transcended linguistic differences, the wealth in the arts in interwar Poland extended beyond the Polish-language segment, as witnessed by the well-developed Yiddish theater, cinema, and literature.

It should be noted that Polish Jews made their mark not only on Yiddish but also Polish literature; indeed, they were among Poland's leading literary lights. From the poets listed in the previous paragraph, one can single out both Słonimski and Tuwim as well as Bolesław Leśmian (whom some consider the greatest Polish poet of the twentieth century) as assimilated Jews who wrote their outstanding poems in Polish—many of which remain beloved by Poles today.

Yet another Jewish artist and writer who made his mark on Polish literature was Bruno Schulz (1892–1942). An assimilated Jew, Schulz spent his life in the town of Drohobych (Polish: Drohobycz). With a population of thirty-two thousand in 1931, the town was hardly a shtetl. The wealth of the nearby oil fields had seen to that. Other cities in its environs, including Boryslav (Polish: Borysław), the center of the oil industry, and the spa city of Truskavets (Polish: Truskawiec) had about eighty thousand inhabitants total. At any rate, Drohobych had a vibrant Jewish community.

Young Bruno exhibited talent as an artist as well as a writer. He made a living as an art teacher, but his claim to fame was his short stories, which he began to publish to acclaim in 1933. Schulz is known for telling expressionistic, dream-like tales, each accompanied by his own illustrations. He published short stories with names such as *Sanatorium under the Sign of the Hourglass* and *Cinnamon Shops.* Bruno Schulz was but one of many Polish Jews, writing in Polish, who made significant contributions to Polish literature of the interwar period.

No less significant were the contributions of a wealth of women writers. They wrote on a wide variety of subjects, many of them topical. The poet Kazimiera Iłłakowiczówna (who also happened to be Piłsudski's secretary) featured Lithuanian folklore in her work, while the writer Pola Gojawiczyńska presented working- and middle-class life in Warsaw. One of the country's outstanding novelists, Maria Dąbrowska famously chronicled the last half century of Polish life before World War I in her historical novel *Noce i dnie* (Nights and days). Other notable writers such as Zofia Nałkowska and Maria Kuncewiczowa dealt in realistic or psychological fashion with the burning women's issues of the day, such as renegotiating motherhood or sexuality. In sum, the interwar period was a particularly fruitful one for Polish women in literature.

Polish Achievements: Toward a Normal State?

Interwar Poland needs to be credited with many important endeavors. The national education system and the introduction of compulsory education provided a relatively uniform point of departure for the country's pupils and students. By the end of the period, some 90 percent of children attended school, and a plethora of new institutes of higher learning also were founded.

Some land reform was initiated, although not nearly enough to satisfy the numerous peasants with small plots or no farmland for whom this was a crucial issue. Given the country's national imbalances, Poles did the land reform in a way that disadvantaged its minorities. While Poles eagerly redistributed former German and Russian state lands, wealthy Polish landowners had to be compensated for their land. Relatively little land was redistributed in the east, where Polish landowners were in charge, and when it was redistributed, available plots often went to Polish settlers. So the needs of land-hungry peasants—particularly but not only the Belarusians and Ukrainians—remained unmet.

There were also some important construction projects. The poster boy for these was the port and city of Gdynia, built in the 1920s. Recall that Gdańsk had been turned into the Free City of Danzig, dominated by Germans but ostensibly under the control of the League of Nations. Opened for business in 1926, the port of Gdynia was a proud Polish counterweight to the Free City of Danzig. Furthermore, a railway line was constructed, connecting the coal-rich Upper Silesian Basin with the port. It should be noted that these governmental projects required significant investment from a dirt-poor state. Regular (non-state-driven) economic development was haltingly slow, given the lack of native capital. Little foreign investment was forthcoming to finance Polish reconstruction.

So Poland had to pick its projects carefully. Yet another major governmental project was the creation of the Central Industrial Region (the COP). This industrial region was strategically located in the heart of Poland. Its rectangular shape reached nearly to Łódź in the northwest, Brest in the northeast, and from both of these southward to the Polish Carpathian frontier (see Map 11.1).

The COP was where Poland's production was concentrated. Part of the military-industrial complex, it contained armaments factories and heavy industry, while also containing some of the country's still functioning oil wells. It could draw on a relatively cheap workforce, in this way relieving overpopulated villages. Indeed, the region was developed in the 1930s in an attempt by the state to escape the funk brought on by the Great Depression, which had been a tremendous blow and a huge burden for its inhabitants.

One other major development was the rise of Warsaw as the modern capital. Recall it had last been capital of the Kingdom of Poland in the early nineteenth century (although the city still held significance in the later period, even within the so-called Vistula Land). A veritable building boom took place in Warsaw, the true heart of the country and a concentrated seat of political power. The capital's influence trumped all of Poland's regional hubs.

In the interwar period, Poles began to add to Warsaw's classical buildings dating from the end of the Commonwealth as well as from the first half of the nineteenth century, as well as the neoclassical, neo-gothic, and neo-renaissance styles favored in the second half of the century. Already during the First World War, Germans allowed the boundaries of Warsaw to expand significantly to nearly 150 square kilometers. This provided ample room for the new capital several years later.

One of the first moves made in the early 1920s was to tear down and not build. The object of loathing was the mammoth Russian Orthodox Cathedral named after the Russian Alexander Nevsky at Saski Square, a prominent reminder of the hated tsarist regime. Still, there was an enormous need for new housing, given the growth of the city as capital. Much of this was done in innovative fashion. Warsaw's avant-garde architects proved the equal of those to the west. Yet other construction integrated Polish folk motifs. Despite the Great Depression, private construction witnessed a boom in the 1930s. Many new apartment buildings had reinforced concrete skeletons, stone-faced elevations, and luxurious apartments; their halls and stairways featured marble and alabaster as well as chrome and glass. Poland's first skyscrapers were constructed during this period, and the city's main arteries were modernized. In addition to a modern airport, an innovative Main Railway Station was being constructed. All of this was turning Warsaw into a modern metropolis.

These and other developments suggest that a degree of normalization was taking place within Poland. The state made some major investments in infrastructure (Gdynia, railroads) and industry (the COP). Passenger planes flew to five Polish cities. Poles were free to engage in all kinds of pursuits. Wealthy Poles, many of them civil servants, were able to pay for nice apartments and villas in the country's capital as well as elsewhere. While many Poles worked hard to turn the country into a well-functioning parliamentary democracy, others took advantage of independence to pursue their own apolitical dreams. Or one might assume as much—were it not for the fractious character of so much Polish politics. The country was far from being nationally demobilized. To be sure, the admirably democratic March 1921 Constitution spoke of "We, the Polish nation" while nonetheless guaranteeing "complete protection of life, liberty and property to all, without distinction of origin, nationality, language or religion." How hollow this promise turned out to be can be seen in the election of Poland's first president.

Electing Poland's First President

On December 9, 1922, a close friend and cousin of Józef Piłsudski—the scientist Gabriel Narutowicz—was elected the first president of interwar Poland. The election was not an easy one. It took five ballots and the help of minority parties in the parliament to get Narutowicz elected over the other candidates, the conservative aristocrat Maurycy Zamoyski (supported by the National Democrats), the socialist Ignacy Daszyński, another former socialist Stanisław Wojciechowski, as well as professor and linguist Jan Baudouin de Courtenay, the so-called national minority candidate.

That the deadlock was ultimately broken by both the peasants and the minority parties throwing their weight behind Narutowicz proved a death sentence for Poland's first elected president. The nationalist camp immediately began to attack, calling him unpatriotic for winning with minority help, labeling him an atheist and a mason, and blaming the outcome of the election on a Masonic conspiracy.

Inflammatory words inspired no less inflammatory deeds. On December 16, two days after Narutowicz had been sworn in, the president attended the opening of an exhibition in Warsaw's main gallery. It turns out he was surrounded not only by friends. A fanatical right-wing nationalist named Eligiusz Niewiadomski shot Narutowicz. Niewiadomski objected to the man for his socialist convictions, his friendship with Piłsudski, and the fact that Jews and others had supported him. A mere week after his election, Poland's first president was dead. Niewiadomski had acted alone, but this act widened the gulf between Piłsudski and the National Democrats, many of whom treated Niewiadomski as a hero.

The assassination also helped to marginalize minority parties within the new Polish state, keeping them from playing any significant role in the ruling of the country. The minorities' political fate was sealed in 1923 by the so-called Lanckorona Pact of the parties of the right. They agreed that the (Polish) national nature of the country had to be maintained and advocated *numerus clausus* (quotas) in the realm of education (although the latter were only introduced in 1937).

Such outcomes were hardly normal. Clearly there were some Poles who found it difficult to accept "normal" democratic outcomes if they did not favor the Polish nation—or their particular understanding of it. What the debacle surrounding this first election boiled down to was a clash of ideologies. Despite the establishment of universal franchise, some Poles believed that only genuine ethnic or Catholic Poles (or however they defined them)—the so-called Polish majority—had the right to elect the president of the Second Polish Republic. In many ways, this approach calls to mind the disastrous election in Warsaw to the Fourth Russian State Duma in 1912—the election lost by Roman Dmowski to a non-Jewish candidate supported by the Jewish minority. Ten years later, *plus ça change . . .*

Piłsudski's Poland

These were not the only signs of trouble in the political realm. The prewar divisions spawned a huge number of political parties, which the French-style parliamentary system established by the March Constitution of 1921 did little to reduce. Since no party was strong enough to win a majority, multiple parties had to cooperate to form governments, which neither were created nor functioned with any real degree of success. By 1926 there had been a total of fourteen different cabinets. All this left Poles with a perception of corruption and lack of integrity at the top. Furthermore, in 1922, hyperinflation had wiped out the savings of Poland's middle classes and intelligentsia.

In the interim, Piłsudski watched from the sidelines. After Narutowicz's assassination, he had retired from his military functions and even moved out of Warsaw, to Sulejówek, so as not to be involved in Polish politics. By early 1926 the former military leader was disgusted with the system. In recent years he had been giving signs that he thought Poland was ripe for drastic change. The change he had in mind became evident in May 1926, when—following the establishment of a yet another center-right government—Piłsudski engineered a coup d'état. For three tense days, he faced off with President Stanisław Wojciechowski. The support of railway workers made it possible for Piłsudski's side to win this brief but painful civil war, in which nearly four hundred people lost their lives. Piłsudski himself had hoped, in vain, that the coup would be bloodless.

So Poland ended up with a military-based dictatorship of sorts. Yet Piłsudski was hardly the dictator one might have expected. For a man who effected a coup, Piłsudski was a strangely apolitical leader. He did not seek the presidency or position of prime minister—indeed, he turned down the first of these when elected at the end of the month. Rather, he styled himself Minister of Defense and General Inspector of the Armed Forces, the armed forces being his bailiwick. (He also took a great interest in foreign policy.)

Instead, Piłsudski had come to power to introduce a new program for Poland. The program was known as Sanacja, which may be thought of as a kind of restorative cleansing. Yet this program was too vague: it allowed both the Piłsudski camp and their opponents, the National Democrats, to speak of the need for cleansing. Piłsudski was much better at winning independence than at establishing a form of rule that fit the country he was given to rule.

Poland's first marshal was not keen on parliamentary democracy, but neither did he want to abolish it. This led to the formation in 1928 of a party of sorts, the awkwardly if accurately titled Non-partisan Bloc of Cooperation with the Government (BBWR). The BBWR was the work of Piłsudski's "Colonels," that is, former Legionnaires in the first marshal's inner circle. In a way, the organization was rightly labeled a bloc, as Piłsudski strove to be above partisanship and hoped his fellow citizens would be so as well.

What really concerned Piłsudski and his followers (besides military issues) was the relationship of the citizenry to the state. The first marshal was not a Polish nationalist who thought Poland to be for only ethnolinguistic Catholic Poles. Rather, Piłsudski expected the population of interwar Poland, regardless of nationality or social standing, to be loyal to the state. His was a state-building program, not a nation-building one. While he required loyalty, Piłsudski did not expect the population to be engaged in politics on a day-to-day basis. Hence his BBWR was more or less a rubber stamp for the government's program. Furthermore, he tried to establish a technocratic, not a politicized, government: witness his choice of the chemistry professor Ignacy Mościcki as candidate for president.

Despite the coup, Piłsudski could not breach the gaping divisions within society. Those who hated him outright detested him. And this group tended to include much of the Roman Catholic hierarchy, which preferred the right-wing program of Dmowski's National Democrats. In part they disliked

Piłsudski for the company he kept. His Legionnaires became his righthand men, although President Ignacy Mościcki served him loyally to the end. And whereas Piłsudski was respectful of the Roman Catholic Church and realized it was bound to have a special place in any Polish state (as the various constitutions and the Concordat with the Vatican made clear), his political base was keen to curb the influence of the bishops. To add insult to injury, some of his colonels were freemasons. On the other hand, in the first years of the Second Republic, Piłsudski had charmed the papal nuncio to Poland, Achille Ratti, who in 1922 became Pope Pius XI. The first marshal had friends in high places.

All the same, Piłsudski had a hard time dealing with political opposition. It was as though he expected the country to rally behind him in unity after the coup. When it became clear that not everyone did, Piłsudski could be more than petulant. Opposition leaders of the center and left alliance (Centrolew) felt his wrath. Many were imprisoned in Brest in 1930 and Biaroza (Polish: Bereza Kartuska) in 1934. These names—the locations where the opposition leaders were imprisoned (Bereza Kartuska was an "isolation camp")—carry connotations of injustice and the blatant abuse of power. Other limitations were placed on civil liberties in the early 1930s.

Nor did Poland's minorities fully embrace Piłsudski and his regime. Ukrainians continued to make trouble in eastern Galicia. Destruction wrought on infrastructure and the houses of Polish neighbors led to the so-called pacification of the region in 1930, a "pacification" carried out by the military that was anything but peaceful. During the 1930s Ukrainians became ever more mobilized against their neighbors (and for all practical purposes rulers), the Poles.

The majority of Poland's Jews tended to ally themselves with the powers-that-be, in this case, with Piłsudski. Like many others within interwar Poland, they saw him as the beloved Grandpa (his nickname) who could potentially help them in time of crisis—and the Jewish community was particularly hard hit by the Great Depression. Still, the first marshal did not do much to ease their pain. Among the general public, nationalistic Poles thought nothing about mistreating these fellow citizens or exhorting fellow ethnic Poles not to do business with the country's minorities.

After Piłsudski

After Piłsudski's death in May 1935, the situation within the country deteriorated. In a ceremony that brought together the man's supporters as well as many who had been his adversaries, the first marshal's physical remains came to lie in state in the Wawel crypts. It is worth noting that his staunch opponent, Prince-Bishop Adam Stefan Sapieha, nonetheless gave permission for Piłsudski to join the rarified ranks in the national pantheon, as one could indeed mourn the man who gave the country independence and stopped the advance of the Red Army. This cooperation between church and state seemed encouraging.

After the burial, however, the gloves of Piłsudski's closest supporters came off. What followed in the Second Polish Republic was the rule of the "Colonels," further empowered by the new constitution they had written for Piłsudski only a month before his death. Despite having held various offices in recent years, these military men were hardly prepared to rule. The colonels were better cheerleaders than leaders. Piłsudski's successor at the helm, Edward Rydz-Śmigły, seemed less intent upon ruling the country as it needed than upon exacting signs of loyalty from the public and nurturing a cult of Piłsudski in order to buttress his and his fellow colonels' position.

Among other things, the colonels lost sight of Piłsudski's toleration of minorities. They allowed further abuses of Jews, including Jewish "ghetto" benches at the universities, and this was at a time when Hitler's influence was reaching Germans in Danzig and elsewhere. The colonels tried to convert to Roman Catholicism those Ukrainians whose forebears had been impoverished nobles, although this was at a time when Ukrainians were beginning to engage more fully in conspiratorial groups. The Camp of National Unity established by the colonels in 1937 was grossly misnamed—or, more ominously, it was properly named, if by "national" one meant "Polish ethnic." Minorities could not count on any sympathy from the coterie of colonels ruling the country.

Furthermore, Poland had few committed allies, despite Piłsudski's robust, even muscular, diplomacy. The country had signed an agreement in 1921 with France, according to which each would come to the aid of the other in the case of German attack. Poland signed a Polish-Soviet Pact in 1932 and a non-aggression pact with Nazi Germany in 1934, essentially to bide time. But the writing was on the wall, as seen in the lead-up to the events of September 1939—something that Britain surely appreciated, having in March of that year agreed to guarantee Polish independence. Poland did not wish to follow in the footsteps of Czechoslovakia. Poland was to pay dearly for her intransigence.

Figure 11.2: The funeral procession of Józef Piłsudski in Kraków. Note the participation of the clergy as well as the armed forces. The marshal's remains would ultimately join those of Poland's royalty and other illustrious Poles here in the crypts of Wawel Cathedral.

CHAPTER 12

Phoenix Ablaze

Under Hitler and Stalin

Poland should not be blamed for the outbreak of World War II. The country had done her best to arrange non-aggression pacts with her neighbors the Soviet Union (1932) and Nazi Germany (1934). Poland also had managed to get France to agree to come to her aid, should she be invaded by Germany (1921), and Britain to guarantee Poland's borders (1939). What more was the country to do?

Perhaps she was expected to go the route of Czechoslovakia: appeasement. The Munich Agreement of 1938, instead of resulting in Neville Chamberlain's naive "peace in our time," seemed to give Hitler free rein. The frustrated Austrian-born artist turned all-powerful Führer of Germany proceeded to take over Czechoslovakia bit by bit: first the Sudetenland, then the rest of the country. Poland's demand for Zaolzie (the region of Silesia around the city of Cieszyn) from the Czechoslovak government in the midst of all this was apparently an attempt to keep the territory out of German hands—if one broadly appreciated by the Poles.

And Hitler threatened Poland: he demanded Danzig. On the point of appeasing Hitler, Poland stood firm. The Poles had faith that her Western allies, France and Britain, would not abandon her. Britain's guarantee of March 1939 was not signed until August 25. How ironic it was that, only two days earlier, on August 23, the signing of the Ribbentrop-Molotov Pact took place. This non-aggression pact between Nazi Germany and the Soviet Union may have seemed innocuous enough, but it had a secret codicil in which the division of Europe into spheres of influence of both powers was laid out to the satisfaction of both parties. Although the alliance between

Hitler and Stalin would be short-lived, it would have important—and trag-ic—consequences for the inhabitants of the Second Polish Republic.

Within another week or so, war broke out. On the night of August 31/ September 1, 1939, Germans dressed as Polish soldiers pretended to attack the German radio station in Gliwice, near the Polish border. The Germans proceeded to blame the Poles for crossing the German border—for invading Germany.

Within the space of hours, early in the morning of September 1, the sky over Poland was lit by bombing—the bombs coming from the west. The first target of the Nazi carpet bombers, the little town of Wieluń with its popula-tion of 1,200 was annihilated. More than 150 nearby settlements soon met a similar fate.

Further north that same day, the Poles defended their post office in Gdańsk, an extraterritorial piece of Poland. After surrendering, the remain-ing defenders were sentenced to death and executed. The ironclad ship the *Schleswig-Holstein* mercilessly pummeled the small Polish outpost at West-erplatte, another extraterritorial piece of Poland; despite all odds, the troops nonetheless managed to defend themselves for seven days. News of the de-fense, which was broadcast on Polish radio, emboldened Poles elsewhere.

Nazi Germany never bothered even to declare war. Perhaps this should come as no surprise, as the Nazis blamed the Poles for the first (faked) attack in Gliwice. Nor did the German forces attacking Poland act as though they were fighting a real war—a war in which one does not target civilians, in which captured prisoners of war are treated fairly, in which human beings, even if they speak a different language, are still considered human beings.

Poland's schoolchildren traditionally began school on September 1. This particular day in 1939 would begin a school of mourning, for the country's adults as well as children—one that would last for years and take decades to overcome.

Polish forces fought the Nazi intruders valiantly, attacked from the air and the land, but clearly they were no match for the Wehrmacht. Still, Poles did not surrender in the face of the powerful German Blitzkrieg (in this way, Poland's response was different from that of France in 1940). Nonetheless, hostilities came to an end on October 6. At this point, some ten thousand Nazis had lost their lives; some seventy thousand had lost their lives fighting the Nazis.

Yet this was but one part of the story. The Poles faced a two-front war—still undeclared. Nazi Germany invaded on September 1; the Soviet Union proceeded to do the same on September 17. Another fifty thousand Poles lost their lives battling the Soviet incursion. The Soviets justified their action (doubtless expected by the Nazis) as designed to protect Poland's mistreated East Slavic minorities in a time of chaos. (Minorities clearly were not faring well, if the treatment of Jews by the Nazis already by this date was any evidence.) Poland was being portrayed as helpless, even harmful, inept as well as inexcusable. After September 17, Poland was once again partitioned: the fourth partition.

One could say what one wanted about the Second Polish Republic. While the young Polish state clearly had had its problems (problems that hardly could be addressed within the space of a mere twenty years), it still did not deserve the aspersions cast on it, at various times, by foreigners. These came from the west as well as from the east. The Soviet diplomat Vyacheslav Molotov applied to Poland the moniker "the monstrous bastard of the Peace of Versailles." The British diplomat David Lloyd George was particularly unkind on the subject of Poland, the country he loved to hate. Poland, he opined, "had won her freedom not by her own exertions but by the blood of others" and served as an example of tyranny. Now, in 1939, Lloyd George went so far as to declare that interwar Poland "had deserved its fate."* How ironic, from the representative of a country that, although it had agreed to guarantee Poland's borders, did nothing after September 1, 1939, to make good on that guarantee. The Poles fought hard through the month of September, expecting that assistance would soon be forthcoming from France and Britain, both of which declared war on Germany. But nothing came. So much for the promises of allies.

Members of the Polish government, the High Command, and the primate of Poland managed to escape the once-again partitioned country via a southern route, through Romania, on September 17. The same escape route was used by a number of Polish citizens. There, to their surprise, their Romanian friends imprisoned the Polish government officials. Themselves helpless, President Mościcki nonetheless managed to deputize another politician, Władysław Raczkiewicz, as his successor; the latter called on General Władysław Sikorski, who at that time was in Paris, to form a government-in-exile. This direct line of continuity would prove crucial. The government-in-exile would have to be both flexible and mobile: established first in France, after the Nazi invasion of that country it moved to Great Britain.

The two belligerents proceeded to carry out the terms of the secret codicil to the Ribbentrop-Molotov Pact. The territory of the Second Polish Republic was amicably divided. The original line of demarcation between the Nazi

---

* The famous quotations of Vyacheslav Molotov and David Lloyd George are taken from Norman Davies, *God's Playground: A History of Poland*, vol. 2, *1795 to the Present* (New York: Columbia University Press, 1982), 393. Davies cites no sources.

spoils and the Soviet spoils ultimately shifted to the west of the earlier proposed line, leaving the territory between the Vistula and Bug Rivers under Nazi control.

Hitler incorporated numerous parts of Poland into Germany proper. These territories included the large industrial city of Łódź and the Poznań region. They became part of the region of Germany known as the Wartheland, after the Warta River. Recall the lyrics to "Dąbrowski's Mazurka": "We will cross the Warta, we will cross the Vistula, we will be Poles"? Now the river, which had been the border between the Second Polish Republic and Nazi Germany, would lend its name to yet another administrative district of the Third Reich. The Poles within would mostly be expelled eastward, to make room—Lebensraum—for German settlers.

Other formerly Polish territories also ended up as part of the Third Reich. The northernmost tip of the country, with its proud port of Gdynia, would be incorporated into the administrative district known as Danzig–West Prussia. A small region immediately to Warsaw's north and Suwałki in the northeast were appended to East Prussia. Last but not least, the region of

Map 12.1: The Fourth Partition of Poland by Nazi Germany and the Soviet Union, 1939

Upper Silesia that had been Poland's in the interwar period now rejoined the German region of Silesia. Readers unfamiliar with the geography of this part of Silesia may be interested to learn that the town of Oświęcim was part of this region. The town is better known by its German name, Auschwitz. Again, this town and the surrounding territory were incorporated into the Third Reich proper.

The remaining Polish territory occupied by the Nazis was turned into a new entity, the Generalgouvernement. It was distinct from the Reich, and under the control of General Governor Hans Frank, who would make Kraków his capital. This, incidentally, is why Poland's medieval capital managed to survive the war essentially intact.

German Occupation: Beginnings

The experience of most of the former inhabitants of the Second Polish Republic was occupation. In this part of the world, in this time and place, in Eastern Europe, the front was everywhere . . . That said, where you lived determined how you were treated—at least, to a certain extent. Already it became clear that the Nazis did not value the lives of human beings they found in conquered territories. Poles fared badly, soldiers and civilians alike. The Germans had no qualms about killing POWs or using them as human shields. Regarding civilians, any revolts were punished with reprisals, always out of proportion with the damage done by the Poles. An example of this was a killing in Bydgoszcz in the first days of September, which resulted in tens of thousands of Polish civilians being slaughtered in reprisal.

Jews in the Nazi-occupied territories fared even worse. Traditional Jews, with their long beards and sidelocks, were a novel sight for the Germans. They were easily enough identified as Jews. Doubtless the occupiers had a much harder time distinguishing the assimilated Jews of Poland from the rest of the population. At any rate, Jews already accounted for seven thousand of the forty-five thousand civilians killed by the end of 1939. And much worse was yet to come.

The Nazi approach to the occupation was conditioned by Nazi ideology. Hitler was bent on rearranging the map of Europe to suit the purposes of the German "master race." The Slavs were considered inferior. Hitler himself was unconcerned with the fate of territories not formally annexed to the Third Reich (here, such as the Generalgouvernement). He was not afraid of his men making mistakes, for the overall goal was to Germanize the acquired territories as rapidly as possible. What he sought, thus, was a radical transformation, one with both racial and colonial overtones.

To this end, a new category was created for peoples who might be Germanized: the *Volksdeutsche*. They were considered potentially part of the future Third Reich that would dominate Europe, as Hitler imagined it. Some Poles were included on the Volksdeutsche list, while others were forced to sign on. Whether someone was on the list determined how he or she was treated, and where he or she was allowed to live. Those who did not fit the profile were forced to migrate further east, to the Generalgouvernement or other territories—or to the concentration camps. They were treated like slaves. By the end of 1941, some eight hundred thousand Poles had been expelled from the territories incorporated into the Reich.

Many Poles expelled from the Reich fled to, or were herded into, the Generalgouvernement. Not that their position was any better there. Much Polish property was taken over even in Hans Frank's kingdom. The Nazis took over factories, even church property. Until January 1940, according to Hans Frank, the Generalgouvernement was considered fair game for plunder. Only with time did he see the usefulness of establishing and/or running munitions factories there. Yet employment, like life, in the Generalgouvernement was neither certain nor stable. Well over a million Poles were sent to forced labor in Germany.

The Poles of the Generalgouvernement were considered expendable cogs in the Nazi machine. All Poles above age fourteen were forced to work. As a result, this also marked the end of higher education and even most of primary education in the Polish lands.

The Nazis showed no respect for the Polish intelligentsia. The most infamous example of this is seen in what came to be called Sonderaktion Krakau. On November 6, 1939, the Nazi authorities summoned all the professors of the Jagiellonian University in Kraków for a meeting. The professors, old and young, dutifully came to meet and discuss the future of their university with the occupying powers. Instead of discussion, however, they were accused of subverting the Generalgouvernement and shuttled off to Sachsenhausen and Dachau, where many perished.

Germans had long prided themselves on being a civilized race, but Hitler turned this idea on its head. They would now be the only civilized race. In a speech of October 2, 1940, he declared: "For Poles there must be only *one* master, the German. For this reason, all members of the Polish intelligentsia are to be killed. That sounds brutal, but it is simply the law of life." This statement demonstrates to what extent even foreigners such as Hitler understood the historical importance of the Polish intelligentsia, which in past times of trouble had managed to keep hope alive for the nation. Hitler concluded that the Germans could not afford for this to happen again—hence his call for their annihilation.

With life having so low a price, it should come as no surprise that Polish society under such a harsh occupation was demoralized. Questions of life and death loomed large, as families tried to feed themselves. Under German occupation, Poles received low rations—and these were reduced even further in 1942.

Nor were normal human relations "normal" any longer. Poles were in a different category than the German master race. As such, a Polish laborer could be executed for having sexual relations with a German woman. The opposite—even if the relation was coercive—was rather the norm, if also illegal.

Soviet Occupation

The Soviet occupation was in some ways more straightforward. The territories east of the Bug as well as Lithuania came under Soviet control. (The addition of Lithuania was in exchange for the Nazi possession of all territory on the right bank of the Bug—that is, on the western bank.) The territories of eastern Poland were incorporated into the adjacent Soviet republics, its inhabitants forced to become Soviet citizens. A Lithuanian Soviet Socialist Republic was created. It, incidentally, would gain the long-desired Vilnius for its capital—some small consolation for the Lithuanians. The first fruits of the Ribbentrop-Molotov Pact had been harvested.

It would be a harvest of sorrow for many of the inhabitants of the region. The Soviets destroyed the fabric of social and political life in the territories they occupied. They terrorized the population, which was subjected to arrests, even deportations. At least four hundred thousand people were deported deeper into the Soviet Union.

Poles tended to be discriminated against. In the eastern borderlands, they had generally been the wealthier peasants or—even more likely—the landlords or civil servants. None of these were happily countenanced in the new Soviet paradise, whether the Lithuanian Soviet Socialist Republic (in which Vilnius lay), the Belarusian Soviet Socialist Republic, or the Ukrainian Soviet Socialist Republic (where the inhabitants of Lviv and the rest of former Eastern Galicia found themselves). As a result, many Poles—especially people of standing in their communities—were either killed or deported into the Soviet Union proper, with many dying en route. The landed estates of Polish landowners and settlers were confiscated.

Not only Poles from the eastern borderlands were so treated. Members of other nationalities who opposed the communists also met a similar fate, with many imprisoned and killed. On the other hand, some of Poland's former national minorities must have been happy to see an end to Polish rule and to be reunited with their national brethren—whether Belarusians or Ukrainians—across the border. They too were discriminated against, however, with people generally brought in from outside to rule.

Operation Barbarossa and Its Impact on Poles in the Soviet Union

Despite the Nazis' best laid plans, however, there was a problem. The nation that was supposedly a "people without space" was conquering a space for which it did not have the people. Incidentally, this led the Nazis to abscond with some two hundred thousand Polish children who looked Aryan; they were sent back to the Third Reich and turned into Germans. Only some thirty thousand of these children were recovered after the war.

Perhaps more crucially, Nazi Germany did not have food enough or manpower enough in the fields to feed its people. The Soviet Union now loomed large in Hitler's mind, having gone from being an ally to becoming an "exterminatory agrarian colony"—that is, Hitler's breadbasket. Here he valued in particular the black earth of Soviet Ukraine.

This is why on June 22, 1941, Hitler's army invaded the Soviet Union, which marked the beginning of Operation Barbarossa. This new stage in the war raised the stakes even further, with tragic consequences for countless Europeans.

While certainly—and particularly—tragic for the Soviet Union as well as for the entirety of interwar Poland (with the Nazi invasion of the USSR, all of interwar Poland was now occupied by the Nazis), the Nazi invasion had some positive outcomes for Poles who had been deported into the depths of the Soviet Union. Now some Poles were allowed to leave the country. This was thanks to Stalin, who allowed Polish military units to be created out of the Polish manpower found in the country's camps and prisons. The manpower was amassed in the Central Asian republics of the Soviet Union, under General Władysław Anders. From there, in 1942, the Poles traveled to Iran and into British service. Some hundred thousand soldiers and about forty thousand civilians made it out of the Soviet Union. While putting the soldiers to work fighting in Italy, the British dispersed the women and children throughout the Commonwealth, leaving many a Polish child to spend the war in Africa or Palestine or such.

Still later, other Poles in the Soviet Union who had not been able to join

General Anders were rounded up to fight under the leadership of General Zygmunt Berling, who, in contrast to General Anders, was a communist. Berling led the so-called Kościuszko Division of the First Army, which was under Soviet control. The army was a first step toward a communist Poland. It fought the Germans on the eastern front, ultimately ending up taking part in the siege of Berlin.

Poles Abroad

In the early days of the war, other Poles were making their way to the west. The government-in-exile was quite properly and legally formed by Poles who happened to be abroad at the time of the outbreak of war. A key figure here was General Władysław Sikorski, who would become head of the military as well as prime minister. Although a general, in the interwar period he had become an opposition politician. In Switzerland, Sikorski had been instrumental in forming a front of opposition known as the Morges Front. A number of Poles who found themselves abroad when war broke out happened to be members of the Morges Front. All the same, there were problems from the outset in getting the Poles abroad to cooperate with each other. Nonetheless, the government worked to create a Polish army, to deal with the Great Powers, and to help the conspiracy that had formed back home.

The Poles' job was made more difficult, as the composition of the government-in-exile was not constant. Prime Minister Sikorski was respected abroad by the Western powers, but he was killed in an airplane crash on July 4, 1943. To this day, the tragic crash is veiled in mystery. Sikorski perished, but the Czech pilot somehow survived. Some Poles persist in believing it was not an accident.

Stanisław Mikołajczyk was forced to try to fill the general's big shoes and assume leadership of the Polish government-in-exile. He became prime minister, while General Kazimierz Sosnkowski took charge of the military. This meant that Mikołajczyk—a member of the Polish People's Party (PSL) and a rather junior politician compared to Sikorski (if also a realist)—did not have as much power as had his predecessor. As it was, Mikołajczyk inherited an unenviable position.

Mikołajczyk's work was made difficult by increasingly fraught relations between the Poles and the Soviets. As of summer 1941 (that is, after the beginning of Operation Barbarossa), Poland and the Soviet Union ostensibly were allies, as both were part of the Allied forces determined to defeat Hitler and the Axis powers. Yet they were uncomfortable bedfellows. Poles were all too aware that Stalin had occupied eastern Polish lands in September 1939 and had subsequently incorporated them into the Soviet Union. What they did not know—or at least, not immediately—was that Stalin had done much more than this.

The Katyń Imbroglio: Massacres and Memories

For the Soviets had taken numerous officers as prisoners of war in the early weeks of the war. These numbered in the vicinity of fifteen thousand. (The regular enlisted men had been let free.) These officers and reserve officers, often the cream of the patriotic Polish intelligentsia, were shipped to a number of Soviet NKVD (that is, secret police) camps at Kozelsk, Ostashkov (both in Soviet Russia), and Starobilsk (in the eastern part of Soviet Ukraine). The officers themselves did not know what their fate would be. Many wrote occasional letters to their families back home. In April 1940, the POWs were transferred to another set of destinations: the forested regions near Katyń, Kalinin, and Kharkiv. At a certain point that spring, all such correspondence ceased.

It turns out that the correspondence ceased because the men ceased to live. It should be added that one woman is known to have perished with the men. This was Janina Lewandowska, a pilot in the reserve. She was executed on April 21 or 22, 1940, at Katyń.

They had been transported, in buses, to one of these destinations, such as Katyń. Each Pole in turn was taken from the van and into a building, where he was handcuffed and led to a soundproof cell. Held on each side by a Soviet guard, a third Soviet shot him from behind in the back of the skull. The dead body was removed, carted off with a host of others, and ultimately thrown into a pit that had been dug in anticipation of the bodies. After the execution, the soundproof cell was quickly rinsed, and the procedure began all over again—until the last of the officers on the bus had been dispatched.

As the fate of the Polish POWs in the Soviet Union demonstrates, it made an enormous difference whether an officer surrendered to the Soviets or to the Germans. Those who ended up in Nazi hands may have spent the rest of the war in view of the Zugspitze, in Bavaria, perhaps not eating well but all the same living to tell the tale. Those officers who ended up in Soviet hands met the fate described above.

That the regular enlisted men were released by the Soviets indicates that Stalin was obsessed—as were the Nazis, if to a lesser extent—with the Polish intelligentsia. Stalin's henchman, Lavrentii Beria, managed to round up another six thousand "undesirables," who met the same fate as the reserve officers—the fate that had been decided by the Politburo. However, while Hitler managed to imprison a number of famous professors, Stalin ordered the systematic elimination of all the reserve officers he could get his hands on. It was Stalin (and his Politburo), and not Hitler, who in one move effected the national decapitation of the best and the brightest of the Poles.

To add insult to injury, many of the families of the Katyń victims were subsequently tracked down and deported to Kazakhstan.

This is how Stalin treated POWs—officers—of a country against which he had not declared war. One can only wonder what he would have done had they been officially at war.

Of course, none of this was immediately known to the families of the reserve officers. Only the cessation of correspondence indicated that, perhaps, not all was well.

The Katyń massacres would become a cause célèbre after Operation Barbarossa had begun. In April 1943, Nazis stumbled across the mass graves at Katyń. When asked about the find, the Soviets claimed the Nazis must have killed the officers. Still, evidence showed that the bodies had lain there for the last two years. Disagreement over this matter, which the Poles asked the Red Cross to investigate, led to a diplomatic break between the Polish government-in-exile and the Soviets later that month. Stalin branded the Poles "reactionary" and did what he could to worsen relations between the Poles and the Great Powers who were their allies. The break with the USSR did not help the Polish cause in the West, for the Allies were more concerned about keeping the Soviet Union in the war than about the fate of Poles.

Polish Contributions in the West

The desire of the Poles who found themselves abroad to fight on the side of the Allies led to their engagement in a number of significant wartime endeavors. Already before World War II, Poles had contributed to solving the mystery of the Enigma machine. Some ended up in England, where they continued to work in counterintelligence.

Poles who had made their way to France proved eager to fight the Germans. They created military formations there, which fought when the Germans invaded France. Some twenty-five thousand made their way to Britain along with the British soldiers. Yet others later traveled from Scotland to fight in Normandy. A large number of Polish pilots flew countless sorties with the British air force, downing over two hundred German planes during the Battle of Britain, some 15 percent of the total.

The Poles who had made their way with General Anders out of the Soviet Union ended up distinguishing themselves at Monte Cassino, Italy, in 1944. Many Poles perished there on the mountain during a week of severe fighting. They were part of the Polish II Corps. Despite—or perhaps because of—the tremendous privation they had already faced, it was the Poles who finally secured the ruins of the monastery. This they did after troops from the United States, Britain, New Zealand, and France had all tried and failed. It was no small accomplishment, if it led later generations of Poles to sing quietly—and sadly—of the red poppies on Monte Cassino.

Poles under German Occupation

Despite the oppressive nature of Nazi occupation, the Poles managed to have a successful underground movement, the largest and most extensive in occupied Europe. They had a long tradition of conspiratorial work, and this tradition stood them in good stead during the war.

The Polish Home Army (for that is what the Polish underground was called) consisted of some four hundred thousand members. Its network of underground couriers, of which Jan Nowak-Jeziorański is an example, supplied the West with information about the war. Home Army members also committed acts of sabotage, punished collaborators, and engaged in partisan warfare.

The Home Army managed to unite members of disparate interwar parties (if not all of them), as all were now fighting for higher stakes. They intended not so much to fight actual battles against the Nazis, given the high cost in reprisals. Rather, they engaged in educational activities, trained cadres, and sought to prepare an armed uprising that would take over once the Nazis were defeated but before the Soviets could come in. Participation in the underground movement came at a cost; by July 1944, some sixty-two thousand conspirators had lost their lives.

The Polish Home Army managed to smuggle a good deal of information out to the West, including pieces of the German-produced V1 and V2 rockets, which were sent to England. Some of this information pertained to a particularly horrible aspect of World War II: the Holocaust.

The Holocaust

Many people associate the Holocaust with Auschwitz. However, to limit one's understanding of the mass murder of European Jews to one location—even one so symbolic—oversimplifies what was a much more layered and complex process. Auschwitz, after all, was both a labor camp, to which Poles and others were sent at the beginning of the war, and an extermination camp. In this way it is unlike Treblinka, Bełżec, Sobibór, and Majdanek. As paradoxical as it may seem, and as shall be seen, most of the Jews of Central and Eastern Europe were murdered before the killing even began at Auschwitz.

We know about Auschwitz so much more precisely because it was a labor camp as well as an extermination camp, with some survivors. There were next to no survivors of the earlier extermination camps, the killing factories, which is where the numerous Jews of Poland met their death.

The process of dealing with the 3.2 million Jews of interwar Poland began even earlier. With the Nazi invasion of Poland, the killing of Jews began, if not in any organized fashion. As early as mid-September 1939, synagogues were being burned.

Jews as well as Poles were expelled from the territories incorporated into the German Reich, the Generalgouvernement serving as a "homeland" or "reservation" for them. Before long, Jews were being herded into ghettos, which quickly became overcrowded. This was also true of the Łódź (German: Litzmannstadt) ghetto, which nonetheless lay on territory incorporated into the Reich. After a visit there on November 2, 1939, Goebbels concluded that the Jews were animals, not human beings: "That's why [killing them] is not a humanitarian [question] but a surgical task. We have to perform radical surgery here. Otherwise Europe will one day be destroyed by this Jewish disease."[*]

Yet the Final Solution did not begin by dealing with the Jewish ghettos in the occupied lands. Rather, it began only after the Nazi invasion of the USSR. This earliest phase of the Final Solution was death by organized shooting. The mobile special operations detachments called Einsatzgruppen, operating behind the advancing front, were responsible for the shooting. At the outset, they were ordered to remove the Bolshevik threat. Soviet commissars and secret police were to be treated like criminals. Still, the Einsatzgruppen killed not only commissars, who were often presumed to be Jews, but also women and children—this from the outset.

Many Jews were killed by the Einsatzgruppen, but not only these units

---

[*]   Cited in Jost Dülffer, *Nazi Germany, 1933–1945: Faith and Annihilation*, trans. Dean Scott McMurry (London: Arnold, 1992), 171.

killed Jews. It turns out that the Wehrmacht—that is, ordinary soldiers—also took part in the killings. This certainly was true for the death pits at Babi Yar, near Kyiv. There 33,771 Jews were shot to death by the SS, the police, and the Wehrmacht. This was a personalized killing, with victim and perpetrator often eerily face-to-face, if only for a moment.

In Vilnius, circa 72,000 Jews were killed with the help of Lithuanians, who not only shot Jews but also organized pogroms. In many instances, it was relatively easy to get help in killing from the local, non-Jewish populations—and this included Poles. In part, this was the consequence of the double occupation—first Soviet, then Nazi—in the eastern borderlands. The locals often blamed their suffering under the Soviets on the Jews. This is where the idea of Judeo-bolshevism was so pervasive.

Such was the face of the Final Solution in its first phase.

The second phase of the Final Solution is what most people associated with the Holocaust. It was initiated by Hitler's deportation of German Jews in October 1941. They were sent to what immediately became—if they were not so already—overpopulated ghettos. Some forty such ghettos had been created for the Jews in the Generalgouvernement in 1940. The Warsaw ghetto alone housed some 425,000 Jews in the space of two square miles. The crowding was tremendous. This in itself was not only humiliating but deleterious for the health of the ghetto inhabitants.

From here, the next step was to defuse the ticking time bombs that were the ghettos. In late 1941, gassing facilities were being experimented with, originally at Chełmno and Bełzec. At the same time, an increasingly desperate Germany began to blame the worldwide Jewish conspiracy for their troubles in fighting the Soviets. They decided to kill the Jews, in part as retribution.

This led to the organization of Operation Reinhardt in 1942—the killing of Polish Jews in the Generalgouvernement (see Map 12.1). The operation began in Chełmno, in a gas van, where some 145,301 from the Wartheland were killed. Subsequently (that is, from March 1942), some 1.3 million Polish Jews were gassed at a series of death factories: at Bełzec, Sobibór, Majdanek, and Treblinka. Not far from Warsaw, the last of these death factories (at Treblinka) operated from July 1942 to November 1943. The extermination of the Jews of the Warsaw ghetto did not go smoothly. There were some escapes, and there was also a rebellion.

All told, in Operation Reinhardt, approximately 1,650,000 Polish Jews were gassed. In Treblinka alone, 700,000 perished. (Compare this to the 200,000 Jews, later, in Auschwitz.) By mid-1942, most of the Jews in Poland and the western parts of the Soviet Union were already dead.

It was only in November 1942 that the young Polish Home Army courier Jan Karski, who had been smuggled into a concentration camp as well as a Jewish ghetto, was able to tell of what he had seen in London. He subsequently was sent to the United States in July 1943, where he talked to President Franklin Delano Roosevelt and Justice Felix Frankfurter, among others. Karski found that few could comprehend—few could or would believe—what he told them.

Karski was not able to tell of the fate of individual Jews, merely to indicate the overall tragedy. While the Polish Home Army officer was on his way to London, Bruno Schulz was still living back in his beloved Drohobych. As odd as it may seem, the writer and artist had been put to work by a local Nazi to paint murals in his Drohobych apartment, including paintings redolent of fairy tales for his children. While this Nazi in a way protected Schulz, the relationship did not save the Polish Jew's life. On November 19, a Gestapo officer who had a quarrel with Schulz's patron shot Schulz in revenge. The Soviet and Nazi occupations are full of similar tragic tales, many of which will never be told.

As for Auschwitz, from 1940 it was a concentration camp. At the concentration camp, some 74,000 non-Jewish Poles died as well as some 15,000 Soviet POWs. In its next iteration, as of 1942, Auschwitz was transformed into a hybrid facility. It was part concentration camp, part extermination camp. Some 200,000 Polish Jews and over 700,000 Jews from elsewhere in Europe were gassed at Auschwitz. Important information about Auschwitz was provided to the outside world by perhaps its most unusual inmate, Captain Witold Pilecki. In 1940 the Home Army officer intentionally walked into a roundup so as to be sent to the camp in order to gain detailed information about it from within. Pilecki would spend nearly three years in the camp before escaping, setting up a clandestine organization while inside and ultimately informing his Home Army superiors in greater and lesser detail about the hell that was Auschwitz.

The geography of the Holocaust is instructive. Jews found in the east (that is, in the lands seized by the Soviets in 1939, then taken by the Nazis in 1941) tended to be executed by organized shooting. Jews in the west made their way to the gas chambers. Auschwitz was located in the Third Reich, in the part of Upper Silesia that had belonged to interwar Poland before the war but which Nazi Germany had claimed for itself at the beginning of the war. Either way, the Holocaust marked the end of a centuries-long history of Jews in the region. The total Jews killed in the Holocaust was about 5.7 million, of which 3 million had been Polish citizens before the war.

Wartime Uprisings

The oppressed populations in the former Polish lands did not simply take this oppression, so to speak, on the chin. They also rebelled, and—with some degree of prior preparation—they rose up. This is as true of the Jewish population as the non-Jewish population. While there were uprisings in the ghettos of Białystok and Będzin, the most famous ghetto uprising took place in Warsaw in 1943.

By that time, the Warsaw ghetto had been reduced to a labor camp. Early in 1943 the Nazis were preparing to liquidate the camp. Realizing the end was drawing near, Jews remaining within the ghetto came together to fight that April. They had established a Jewish Combat Organization and a Jewish Military Union; now about a thousand Jewish fighters constructed well-camouflaged bunkers from which they could shoot at their persecutors. And indeed, some three hundred Germans were injured or killed over the next month in the ghetto. The Jewish fighters' efforts, although heroic, were nonetheless doomed from the outset. Yet they did not fight to win—that would have taken a miracle. Rather, they fought to "rescue human dignity." After routing the Jewish insurgents early in the month, on May 16, 1943, the Nazis finished the job in true symbolic fashion; they dynamited Warsaw's historic Great Synagogue.

A similarly tragic fate was met by many who fought in the Warsaw uprising of 1944. The Polish underground Home Army had seen as one of its main goals the organization of an uprising. It had already been active, in early 1944, in regions the Soviet army was moving into in pursuit of the retreating Germans. Unfortunately for many, they had only two options: they would be interned, or they would be drafted into Berling's army. Still, the Polish partisans helped to liberate certain cities—Vilnius, Lublin, and Lviv—in the east.

An opportunity for a major uprising presented itself in the summer of 1944. In July 1944 a provisional Polish government, under Soviet aegis, was proclaimed in Lublin by a group that styled itself the Polish Committee for National Liberation. Also working together with the Soviets was the communist-sponsored People's Army partisan force, which had been in existence since the end of 1942. The Poles of the non-communist underground desperately wanted to liberate Warsaw themselves, without the help of the approaching Soviet army or any communists, Polish or otherwise.

The Home Army's rising was scheduled to begin on August 1, 1944. Poles attacked the Nazis in Warsaw, in the hopes of seizing control of the city. Unfortunately, the Home Army was left to its own devices, and the rising lasted not days (as had been anticipated) but months.

No help was forthcoming from the Allies. Stalin refused to allow Allied forces to refuel their planes in his country, which would have allowed them to drop supplies for the Polish underground fighters. At the same time, the Red Army, approaching from the east, seemed to encourage the Poles to fight the Nazis over Warsaw. The Red Army, however, did not advance further to help. It inexplicably stopped right on the outside of the city, on the other bank of the Vistula. In this way the Nazis were free to destroy the Polish underground.

The Warsaw Rising of 1944 was another instance when Poland's best and brightest—here, many of the younger generation were involved—perished in defense of their homeland. Massacres took place in the Warsaw district of Wola. Members of the underground tried to escape via the sewers; not all managed to escape.

The uprising proved an utter failure. In the course of the two-month-long rising, some 220,000 Varsovians perished. The rest of the city's inhabitants were subsequently expelled with some ending up being sent to work in Germany or even to concentration camps. Nor was the city itself spared. Himmler ordered the destruction of Warsaw in October 1944, and the city was bombed back to oblivion. Only rubble smoldered where a proud capital had once stood.

Although it ultimately failed, the uprising perhaps had one saving grace. The experience—as for the generations who participated in the Polish uprisings of an earlier century—did bring Poles together from across the political spectrum in order to fight the common enemy. So the uprising strengthened the resolve of yet another generation to persist under pressure. Still, the price paid by the Poles was tremendous.

The heavy losses suffered by both Jewish and Polish populations begs the question Why was there not more cooperation between Poles and Jews during the war? Both were oppressed by the Germans. Here one needs to consider the legacy of interwar anti-Semitism, the fact that the extreme right could make it hard for those Poles who would consider sheltering Jews. That some did was in a way amazing, given the penalty that would meet them if they were caught: they would be executed. Yet some Jews—to be sure, a tiny part of the large prewar population within Poland—were saved and did survive, as is seen through the work of the council for Jewish assistance named Żegota as well as the significant numbers of Poles who since the war have been awarded the distinction Righteous Among the Gentiles by Yad Vashem in Israel.

Nonetheless, some Jews were also betrayed by Poles. This was particularly true of assimilated Jews who, to the Nazis, looked for the most part like the average Pole. Poles might profit in various ways. Gaining Jewish property or money must have motivated many during this hard time. Charges of anti-Semitism notwithstanding, it is true that even some anti-Semites saved Jews, not because they liked them but because their Christian religion dictated they love their neighbor. Yet other Christians forgot that dictum, as seen in the murder of Jews by their Polish neighbors in places such as Jedwabne. Poles today are still coming to grips with this reality. The Jewish shadow lies long on the land where Poles and Jews lived both together and apart for centuries.

More than 90 percent of Poland's Jews perished in the Holocaust. Only in the Baltic states was the percentage of Jewish casualties higher. Since the war, Poles of various generations, particularly since the 1980s, have decried the indifference Poles showed toward the fate of the Jews during the war. That both suffered during World War II is undeniable; yet on the whole they did not suffer together, to pool resources or support each other. Part of the problem was also the demoralization of the war. Human life seemed so expendable, and resistance was costly. Still, not insignificant was the fact that, in the nineteenth and early twentieth centuries (to be sure, when the nation lacked independence), the Poles had not created conditions in which Jews could be more easily integrated into the Polish national community. That some Jews would not have wanted to style themselves Poles is a separate matter. Those who did see themselves as Poles often had a hard time, all the same.

Toward a Postwar Solution

The movement of populations during the war, begun by Hitler and Stalin, continued as the war drew to a close and beyond. Some of this came to be known as ethnic cleansing. Not all of it was the work of the occupying forces, as seen from the clashes between Poles and Ukrainians in Volhynia. Founded in 1942 by some of the Ukrainian policemen who had served under the Nazis, the Ukrainian Insurgent Army (UPA) brutally sought to rid the region of its Polish minority; Poles retaliated in kind. According to one estimate, about 70,000 Poles were murdered, compared to under 20,000 Ukrainians, making this a sore spot for Polish-Ukrainian relations even today.[*]

After the war, population exchanges took place. As the borders shifted westward (Poland lost nearly half of its prewar territory to the Soviet

---

[*] According to Timothy Snyder, *The Reconstruction of Nations: Poland, Ukraine, Lithuania, Belarus, 1569–1999* (New Haven: Yale University Press, 2003), 204–5.

Union), some 780,000 Poles from that region were "repatriated" to their pu-
tative "homeland." The same held true for Ukrainians and Germans on the
territory of the new postwar Polish state. Germans were expelled unceremoniously, even brutally, from the lands now awarded to Poland. These were
territories in the north as well as the west. Poland's Ukrainians faced one of
two fates. Nearly 485,000 Ukrainians living in the territory of Poland were
"repatriated" to the Ukrainian Soviet Socialist Republic. Others managed to
cling to their homesteads until 1947.

The UPA was still fighting the Poles along the southern border of the
new Poland. The assassination of the Polish communist and general Karol
Świerczewski in the region contested by the UPA provided the Polish communist authorities with a ready justification to put an end to its minority
problem in the south. The non-Polish population (whether they considered
themselves Ukrainian or Lemkos, a regional designation) was removed from
its ancestral homeland in the Carpathian piedmont and dispersed within
Poland (primarily in the north and northeast). This forced resettlement was
known as Operation Vistula. In this way, another 140,000 non-Poles were
separated from the land they knew, in the hopes that they would end up assimilating to the Polish majority.

The Poland that was re-created after World War II was a far cry from what
it had been before the war. Both frontiers and populations had shifted. The
expulsion of the Germans as well as the annihilation of the overwhelming
majority of Poland's Jews rendered the country more ethnically homogeneous—more ethnically Polish. The death of so many members of the prewar intelligentsia rendered Poland even more peasant in nature. The moniker of the new entity, the Polish People's Republic (PRL), or simply People's
Poland, was indeed more apt.

CHAPTER 13

People's Poland

From Stalinism to Solidarity

Paradoxically, the postwar permutation of Poland in some ways represented the Poland of which many had long dreamed: a "Poland for the Poles." No longer did Poles have to contend with a sizable ethnic minority. Germans, Belarusians, and Ukrainians either were expelled or found themselves on the other side of the border. Poland's large Jewish population had been annihilated. The postwar settlement, thus, in many ways represented the kind of Poland that Woodrow Wilson may have imagined back in 1918. Even the Poles' access to the sea was now fully guaranteed: much of the Baltic Sea coast formerly controlled by the Germans, including the seaport of Gdańsk/ Danzig, had become part of People's Poland. (The easternmost part of the former Eastern Prussia was annexed by the Soviet Union, to become the region of the Russian Soviet Federative Socialist Republic known as Kaliningrad.)

Yet Roman Dmowski and his nationalists could not have imagined the social makeup of what would come to be known as People's Poland. With the decimation of the Polish intelligentsia (whether through the Katyń massacres, war casualties, the failed Warsaw uprising, or the fact that many Poles who had found themselves out of the country did not return home after the war), the population was much more heavily peasant in origin.

The transformation had been costly. The country had been ravaged by six years of total war. The experience of occupation, sometimes double occupations, had demoralized the population. In a way, having suffered so much, the people had become desensitized to human suffering. They were also still conflicted about the absence of the prewar Jewish population, which had been evident in all of Poland's cities and towns.

Map 13.1: People's Poland

This was seen in the events of summer 1946 in the town of Kielce. The disappearance of a young boy in late July sparked rumors that he had been captured by the Jewish survivors who after the war were living in the building of the Jewish Committee in Kielce. These rumors sparked a pogrom, which spread like wildfire. In the course of the pogrom, some thirty-nine Jews (including women and children) and two Poles were killed. This spawned, in the following months, a mass exodus of Poland's remaining Jews (over sixty thousand) who clearly left the country with bad feelings about the treatment of their Jewish brethren at the hands of Poles.

Communist Beginnings

Yet the first years of communist rule in Poland were nothing like the Poles had imagined. Poles, who had fought so valiantly at the side of the Allies on so many fronts, who had brought news of the Holocaust to the attention of the West, now learned that their erstwhile allies had sold them out. Poles placed the blame squarely on "Yalta," that is, the conference of the Big Three—Winston Churchill, Franklin Delano Roosevelt, and Joseph Stalin—in the Black Sea resort town of Yalta in February 1945. Churchill and Roosevelt had been persuaded to entertain the idea of a division of spheres of influence. Poland would fall within that of the So-viet Union. At Yalta, they reached an agreement with Stalin, according to which the new Polish government would include non-communists; Poles would be compensated in the west for territories lost in the east (at Pots-dam later in 1945 the western border was set at the Oder-Neisse line); and free elections would be held. All this, the leaders of the Western world were assured, would lead to the creation of "a strong, free, independent and democratic Poland."

On paper, the Yalta agreement—while not perfect—did hold out hope. The interwar state had certainly had its flaws. Perhaps this new arrangement would allow Poles to overcome some of the problems they had faced in the first half of the twentieth century? No less a figure than the writer and later Nobel Prize winner Czesław Miłosz later wrote:

> To understand the course of events in Eastern and Central Europe during the first post-war years, it must be realized that the pre-war social conditions called for extensive reforms. It must further be understood that Nazi rule had occasioned a profound disintegration of the existing order of things. In these circumstances, the only hope was to set up a social order which would be new . . . so what was planned in Moscow as a stage on the road to servitude was willingly accepted in the countries concerned as though it were true progress.

Poles could hope that the new arrangement would bring progress, at long last, and would allow the country to move forward from its overwhelm-ing agrarian state toward something more modern. Perhaps it was time for a more progressive social outlook, one that did not overly privilege those born with a silver spoon in their mouths. All Poles needed to get to work, to rebuild their capital, and rethink where they were headed.

If Miłosz is correct, there was some constituency, after the war, for change—at least initially. Of course, when writing *The Captive Mind* in ex-ile, Miłosz already realized that what Moscow had been planning circa 1945 was not true progress for the Poles but rather an early "stage on the road to [Polish] servitude."

Reinterpreting Yalta

Many Poles soon lost their optimism. The Soviets had their own script, and it had little to do with Yalta. First, the Soviets ensured that any identifiable remnants of the Home Army (which ostensibly had been part of the Allied forces) were deported to the Soviet GULag—that is, to the labor camps in Siberia. Some fifty thousand Poles came to experience that hardship. Other Poles were subjected to communist terror within Poland at the hands of the Soviet NKVD, which operated in the country with impunity until the end of 1947, leading to many Poles being imprisoned or ending up in concentration camps. Nor was the principle of personal property respected. The state nationalized all enterprises—that is, factories, businesses, stores. Poland now belonged to the state, and not the state to the people.

Nor did the political realm cheer those who hoped to shape their new state. Disillusion was felt earliest by those whose parties would not be acceptable to the Soviets and their Polish communist allies. The latter labeled the parties of the interwar right fascist—and fascists were unacceptable. This meant there was no room in People's Poland for the party of Roman Dmowski (who died in January 1939) or anything to its right on the political spectrum. Thus, the London Poles were for the most part excluded. By contrast, the Lublin Poles were in charge. The Lublin Poles were communists, many of whom had spent the war in the Soviet Union.

In these early years, the communists were careful to phase themselves in to power; thus at the outset they did countenance some political pluralism. The three main parties that did figure in the Polish political process initially were the PSL (the peasant party), the PPS (socialist party) and PPR (workers' party—read: communist). Stanisław Mikołajczyk, who had served as prime minister of the Polish government-in-exile, returned to Poland. The head of the PSL, he became a deputy prime minister in the new government of national unity established in June 1945. Mikołajczyk hoped that, in this still heavily agrarian country, he could lead his PSL to victory. He was wrong.

The communists first prepared a referendum for June 1946, with three questions on the ballot: 1. Did voters agree that the senate should be abolished? 2. Did they wish for the continuation of the social and economic reforms? 3. And did they wish for the western border of Poland to remain on the Oder-Neisse line? The regime's desired outcome was for Poles to vote three times yes. To determine the strength of the non-communists, Mikołajczyk and his PSL called for voters to say no to the first point. The outcome proved to be grossly falsified: to the first question, it was reported that 68 percent voted yes, whereas in reality nearly three-quarters of the voters voted no.

The referendum took place only weeks before the Kielce pogrom. This may explain why the state reaction to the pogrom was so ineffectual. Perhaps the authorities felt they should allow these Poles to let off some steam. They certainly did not want to be seen coming to the defense of the Jews because of the pervasive association of Jews with communism. This stereotype was far from correct, certainly in the interwar period, where most Jews habitually voted for Piłsudski's first list of candidates. However, after the war, it was clear that certain highly placed communists were of Jewish descent. This helped to strengthen the Jew-Communist (Polish: Żydo-Komuna) connection in people's minds.

The elections to the Seym were scheduled for January 1947. Intimidation and violence characterized the campaign. The general popularity of his party notwithstanding, Mikołajczyk realized he was facing an uphill battle. Stalin was reportedly the final arbiter of the election, determining the percentage of seats that could be had by each party. The populists ended up with not even 15 percent of the total. Learning the results, Mikołajczyk informed foreign correspondents that the results had been falsified. The illusion was over, and Mikołajczyk soon left Poland.

After the election, several of the remaining parties, including the socialists, were co-opted into the communist-run PPR, which then became the PZPR—the Polish United Workers' Party. This was the party to rule Poland for the next decades. By the end of 1948, the PZPR had nearly a million members, which suggests that some Poles had come to accept the new reality.

The new regime was created in an environment that was quickly moving toward the overall view of the world that reigned for nearly half a century—the Cold War. Indeed, Poland hosted the meeting of international communist party representatives at Szklarska Poręba in September 1947. At that time, the Communist Information Bureau (Cominform) was created. This marked the end of supposed coalition politics. The Soviet founder of the Cominform, Andrei Zhdanov, declared that the world was divided into two camps: "the imperialist and anti-democratic camp, on the one hand, and the anti-imperialist and democratic camp, on the other." (Readers should be clear that the first camp he mentioned was the Western world, the second was the Soviet bloc.) The Cold War was on.

The onset of the Cold War ended up favoring the Muscovite faction of the Polish communists, led by Bolesław Bierut, over the "home-grown" communists, led by Władysław Gomułka (who had survived the Stalinist purges of the interwar communist party, because he was in a Polish prison at the time). Gomułka had been the original general secretary of the Polish Workers' Party, the highest post in the land. He lost this position in September 1948, having been accused of "rightist-nationalist deviation."

Stalinism in Poland: Uniformitas Sowjetica Postbellica

One of the few and fortunate German Jews to survive World War II, Victor Klemperer joined the communist party and resumed his career in the new East Germany. In the early years of the Soviet bloc, he made a trip to Poland. Klemperer visited construction sites, department stores, universities, and the like in Warsaw, Gdańsk, and Wrocław. He also attended the three-hour-long May Day parade in Warsaw. As a visiting East German communist, Klemperer had a particularly good vantage point—he was on the podium. Nonetheless, the view elicited this reaction in his famous diary: "This was the dreariest, most uniform, most orchestrated part of our trip to Poland. I survived it. But what did I get out of it? The most complete sense of *uniformitas* imaginable."

Klemperer was remarking upon a hallmark of the post-1948 situation in the Soviet bloc. The countries were to converge in style and substance. It was akin to Napoleon's attempt to imbue his European satellite states, including the Duchy of Warsaw, with his cherished Napoleonic Code—only more so. What was really desired, in Klemperer's words, was a "uniformitas sowjetica postbellica"—a postwar Soviet uniformity. Each country in the East bloc was to become a miniature USSR, with collectivized agriculture, heavy industry, communal housing, even miniature Stalins.

The period of Stalinism (1948–1953) had its own peculiarities and its own raison d'être: to create states in the likeness and image of the USSR. The Stalinist version of the Soviet model was characterized by the primacy of "the Party" (in Poland, the PZPR) over the government. This is why the Party's general secretary carried more weight than any head of state. Organized vertically, the Party hierarchy created a so-called *nomenklatura* or list of party functionaries. Where one stood on the list determined what jobs one might fill and what privileges one might have. Both the Party's leading role and the leading role of the Soviet Union were givens. "Nationalist deviations" from the Soviet model were not permissible.

The PRL was also a police state, complete with surveillance, terror, and occasional purges of party members (the last, for ideological purity and conformity). The Security Service set about destroying what was left of the Polish underground, imprisoning and executing thousands of Poles of varied political views who had fought the Germans. One of these was Witold

Pilecki. Anti-state or anti-Party activities (and there was a long list of these) were harshly punished. An air of mistrust and apprehension prevailed as Poles feared being denounced to the authorities. Arbitrary arrests and detentions were numerous; the Security Service kept personal files on almost a third of adult Poles.

The economy was of the command—not market—ilk. It was run by the central planners, who predetermined production at all levels for a set period in advance, usually five years at a time (Poland's first plan was a Six-Year-Plan, from 1950–1955). These plans budgeted for heavy industry and development—such as the Lenin Steelworks near Kraków, for which a model socialist city, Nowa Huta, was built to house the workers. Prices were arbitrary and usually fixed, as there were no markets to determine the real price of anything. Heavy industry was seen as the country's salvation, as rapid industrialization was desired to bring the Soviet bloc up to Western standards and beyond. To this end, shock workers—that is, those who do more than the specified norm—were held up as national heroes, something that Andrzej Wajda's film *Man of Marble* wonderfully demonstrates.

Under Stalinism, the state essentially was hermetically sealed shut—at least, for its own citizens. Poles traveled only with great difficulty and only with the permission of the authorities. Those fortunate enough to be given a passport for travel abroad were obliged to hand it back upon their return. Travel was generally limited to those who could demonstrate a need to go abroad: officials, representatives of firms involved in foreign trade, academics and artists. In exchange for the privilege, the Security Service sometimes exacted cooperation or reporting from the would-be traveler.

Art and even life were subordinated to politics. Socialist realism—murals of muscled workers and kerchiefed lasses, always smiling—reinforced the excitement with which the new socialist world was being created in People's Poland. Folk song and dance troupes proliferated, these being an approved outlet for expressing national distinctiveness. Such troupes fit the Soviet approach to diversity: "National in form, socialist in content."

Friendship with the Soviet Union was an all-pervasive theme. The most visible symbol of this was Warsaw's Palace of Culture, a gift from Stalin in 1951. The Polish joke was that the best view of Warsaw was found from the top of the Palace of Culture. Why? Because one couldn't see the monstrous building from up there.

Anything—including historical narratives—that might undermine Polish-Soviet friendship was taboo. After the trauma of World War II, Poles were not allowed to mourn fully. They could only mourn those aspects of the war that were sanctioned by the Soviet outlook: thus, no loss of the eastern

Figure 13.1: Poster by Witold Chmielewski and Wiktor Górka advertising the First State Congress of the Collective Farm Movement (1953). An example of socialist realism, this poster depicts smiling workers and a woman in traditional folk costume from the Łowicz region building socialism. The inscription on the Polish flag reads, "To prosperity—to socialism."

borderlands, no paeans to the Home Army, certainly no memories of those murdered at Katyń. (The story is powerfully told in Andrzej Wajda's film *Katyń*.) The communists enthusiastically demonized Germans (for whom no love was lost among the Polish public) as Nazi fascists, modern Teutonic Knights, and the like—linking them to the biggest demon of the Stalinist period, the United States and the capitalist West. The Holocaust that eliminated Poland's prewar large and thriving Jewish population was essentially ignored (to be sure, this was the case everywhere but in Israel at that time) with emphasis on camps like Auschwitz (where Poles also perished), allowing Poles to focus on their own suffering.

Despite the strictures of the Soviet model, there was an important degree of Polish exceptionalism. Compared to the rest of Eastern Europe, staunchly Roman Catholic Poland experienced relatively mild antichurch policies (although that does not make the still very real suffering of the church any less painful) and, less explicably, relatively mild (compared to the rest of Eastern Europe) inter-Party purges. And given the historic predominance of small farms in the Polish lands, collectivization of larger farms proceeded in sluggish fashion; the mainly private agricultural sector even managed to produce foodstuffs for export. Regarding Poland's interwar legacy, although the children of workers and peasants were given precedence over the children of the Polish intelligentsia in higher education, the prewar Polish professoriate was mainly left in place and continued to set the tone there. In sum, the Stalinist model was imposed in order to turn a peasant society into a modern industrial society, as befit what was supposed to be a workers' state. The model fit Poland like the proverbial Procrustean bed ...

Life after Stalin

In 1953 the Poles were in the middle of their first Six-Year-Plan when the unimaginable happened: Stalin died. Yet this did not mean the end of Stalinism. No "thaw" occurred until after the secret speech of the new head of the Communist Party in the USSR, Nikita Khrushchev, at the Twentieth Party Congress in Moscow in February 1956, in which Khrushchev denounced the personality cult and dictatorship of Joseph Stalin, and the excesses of the Stalinist period. Poland's Little Stalin, Bolesław Bierut, happened to be in Moscow for the Party congress, and the revelation may have been too much for him. Still in Moscow, Bierut died two weeks later. Poles, interestingly, were the ones to leak the text of "On the Cult of Personality and Its Consequences" to the West.

In Poland these revelations opened a door that, for all practical purposes, had previously been bolted shut. To be sure, some Poles already had an inkling of some of the inner workings of the system. A highly ranked Polish Security Service officer named Józef Światło escaped to the United States. Through the fall of 1954, Światło broadcast reports via Radio Free Europe; his tales of communist reality within People's Poland proved to be excellent anti-communist propaganda.

Now the door was ajar. Soon it would swing open much wider, bringing some fresh air into the country. Some periodicals, such as the student-run *Po Prostu* (Straight talk) as early as the fall of 1955 managed to gain a broader readership by moving in a reformist—certainly anti-Stalinist—direction.

Nonetheless, Stalinism had shaped a generation of postwar Poles, who had been forced to deal with its peculiar, and peculiarly oppressive, reality. Additionally, the experience of "real socialism" would shape further generations. These new experiences were layered upon Poland's prewar traditions, always simmering under the surface. Still, already in a short period of time, Poland had experienced a sea change. The country physically shifted west, with cities like formerly German Wrocław taking the place of now Soviet Ukrainian Lviv. Intellectually Poles had been forced to shift toward the east (even those who did so kicking and screaming), the country's citizens forced to deal with socialism with a Soviet face.

Facing the Reality of Socialism under Stalinism and Beyond

To be sure, there were some positive sides to the new postwar system. Education became more universal. This allowed some of the formerly disadvantaged—especially the children of workers and peasants—to experience upward mobility, especially if they embraced the regime. And there were plenty of reasons to do so.

One reason had to do with the functioning of the economy. Simply put: "The Plan" had problems. The command economy led to what one economist has termed the "economics of shortage." Indeed, it was hard to anticipate, in advance, what would be needed over a five-year plan. Furthermore, the privileging of Stalinist/communist goals, that is, industrialization and heavy industry, meant that consumer goods were underproduced. Housing was one key area. Poles notoriously waited decades for an apartment—even when they had paid regular increments, for all purchases had to be paid for upfront. The same was true for automobiles. You paid upfront and then waited for delivery, which could take years. Home appliances, such as washing machines, were always hard to obtain.

Because of this, certain groups gained privileged access to certain goods. There were special coupons for newlyweds to help them outfit their apartment—if they could get an apartment of their own. Special coupons allowed expectant mothers to purchase one set of baby clothes, blankets, and cloth diapers for the infant. At a certain point in Polish postwar history (beginning in the late 1970s but experienced more in the 1980s), the most important phrase in the world of socialist shopping was *nie ma* (there isn't any). It was the response to most queries . . .

A real sign of how little the communists cared about supplying even the most basic of goods was that, at this time, there was a perennial shortage of toilet paper. Many had to rely upon the communist party newspaper to serve in its stead.

To obtain these and other undersupplied goods, Poles often stood in line—especially in the early 1980s. They were even known to create line commissions, where names would be written down so someone need not stand all day, or for days on end, to obtain the desired goods.

Standing in lines was not the fate of those at the top of the communist *nomenklatura*. The needs of those favored individuals, who were preoccupied with building communism from above, were somehow taken care of. Other Poles managed to survive socialism by befriending shopkeepers, butchers, and the like—or (better yet) being them. To give a sense of how values were turned upside-down, access to goods gave an individual much more prestige than a college degree.

For the average Pole, a window on the world of Western consumption were the Pewex stores (the acronym stands, rather improbably, for Enterprise of Internal Export). There Poles who had recourse to hard currency could buy goods nowhere else available in Poland. The dollar was king in the Pewex stores; Poles who had relatives in the West were a source of small denominations of these. As Poland's own currency was soft (that is, not exchangeable on the international market), it was worthless there—or anywhere else, frankly, given the ubiquitous shortage of consumer goods.

Polish-Induced Hiccups; or, Toward a Poland for the People

Stalin once quipped that imposing communism on Poland was like saddling a cow. This was doubtless true: saddling the creature was not a pretty sight. Furthermore, one wonders at the sense of it all: what good would a saddled cow be, anyway, and to whom?

Perhaps that the metaphor is best left to Stalin. It may be more fruitful to think of the Polish reaction to communism in terms of mutual indigestion. Poles found the Soviet-style system unpalatable, and this occasioned a case of the hiccups within the Soviet bloc. The hiccups, or belches, caused by People's Poland proved to be more than a few—many more than those caused by other East bloc countries. The resultant indigestion ultimately led to the foreign substance being expelled—much as Rousseau had envisaged nearly two centuries earlier in his *Considerations on the Government of Poland*. Back then the philosophe had advised the Poles: "You may not prevent [your enemies] from gobbling you up; see to it at least that they will not be able to digest you." These serial attacks of hiccups, furthermore, would have ramifications for not only Poles and Poland.

Economic as well as political discomfort could elicit hiccups. Although more nuisance than anything, shortages of basic goods such as those discussed above took their toll on the average Pole. He or she worked long hours and had little to show for it. Actually the Polish saying went, "We pretend to work, and they pretend to pay us." Fits of Polish hiccups—which seemed to be contagious—erupted at discrete moments, even discrete months. The names of certain months immediately bring to the average Pole's mind a certain set of experiences—using our metaphor once again, a certain set of hiccups.

The Polish "June" of 1956

After Bierut's death in March 1956, war at the top ensued within the confines of the Party. The Polish population sensed that something was afoot, internationally as well as domestically. The Cominform, which had paved the way for the spread of the Cold War, was dissolved that same spring. In the wake of Khrushchev's revelations, a nationwide public debate ensued.

In the city of Poznań, workers were the first to react to bad economic news. On June 27, the cash-strapped Polish government reneged on its promise to raise wages. The following day would go down in history as "Black Tuesday." Workers at the former Cegielski factory (now named after Stalin) went on strike, demanding "bread and freedom." The situation on the streets quickly became politicized, as the security services attacked the striking workers. Gaining possession of some of the arms used against them, the workers responded by attacking various buildings, including the PZPR headquarters.

Tanks were sent in. During the unrest, some seventy civilians died along with eight individuals from the side of the government.

The unrest continued beyond this date at various enterprises. Poland in the summer of 1956 was still reeling from the upheaval. The moment was ripe to look for a different kind of inspiration.

On August 26, 1956, many Poles took part in a pilgrimage to Jasna Góra, the site where the icon of Our Lady of Częstochowa, Poland's Black Madonna, hangs. On the day of the pilgrimage, those present in unison swore an oath to the nation. The oath had been penned by Stefan Cardinal Wyszyński, the head of the Roman Catholic Church in Poland. He was under house arrest, but his text reached Jasna Góra nonetheless and had the desired effect on the pilgrims.

The Polish "October" of 1956

It also had an effect on Poland's communists. The Party was shaken by Khrushchev's revelations and by all the turmoil. October proved a political turning point. The leadership of the Party wanted to reinstate Władysław Gomułka as general secretary of the PZPR (he had been under house arrest between 1951 and 1955), that is, restore his position as the most important person in People's Poland.

The Soviets also took an interest in Polish affairs at this moment—a direct interest, as witnessed on October 9. That morning, an airplane carrying Nikita Khrushchev was heading to Warsaw. The leader of the USSR wanted to appear at the Eighth Plenum of the Polish communist party: doubtless he had something he wanted to tell them . . . However, the Polish authorities managed to reroute Khrushchev's plane to a smaller airport. In the course of a full day's discussions with the Soviet leader, Poland's top ranking communists convinced him that they—that is, the PZPR—had not lost control, and that they would still retain control with Gomułka at the head. In this way, Poles were spared the indignity of a Soviet invasion—an indignity visited upon Hungary that same autumn.

Charged with "nationalist deviation" back in 1948, after 1956 Gomułka was able to soften some of the sharp Stalinist edges of communism in Poland, whether concerning religion, the economy, or culture. Hundreds of Soviet officers left the country. Gomułka brought the sluggish process of collectivization—never popular among Poland's numerous farmers—to an end. In the religious and political sphere, after 1956 activists from the lay Catholic organization Znak were able (among other things) to regain control over the respected Catholic weekly *Tygodnik Powszechny*; the lay Catholic movement would grow with the establishment of Clubs for the Catholic Intelligentsia. Note also the establishment and flourishing of the Polish film school. Over the next decades, Poland's best filmmakers—individuals such as Andrzej Wajda, Jerzy Hoffman, Roman Polański, Agnieszka Holland, and Krzysztof Kieślowski—would provide audiences in Poland and around the world with world-class insight into Polish life, past and present.

Nonetheless, Poland remained fully within the East bloc. As Gomułka remarked: "We shall not allow anyone to turn the process of democratization against socialism" ("socialism" being the word of choice in countries that had not yet attained the heights of "communism"). Gomułka simply wanted communism, Polish style. On October 24, the Polish general secretary announced: "An end to meetings and demonstrations. It is time to get on with daily work." As did the general secretary himself. Two days later, Cardinal Wyszyński was released from detention. No less significant, Marshal Konstanty Rokossovsky, the Polish minister of defense, and the rest of the Soviet military officers departed from Poland for the Soviet Union.

Gomułka remained at the helm in the late 1950s and 1960s. As of July 1957, the economics of shortage convinced the general secretary to endorse "meatless Mondays." Yet despite the shortage of meat, Gomułka's Poland was known as "the liveliest barrack in the [Soviet] camp." It also proved quite a musical one: Polish rock-and-roll rocked the East bloc. Annual music festivals at Sopot, Opole, and elsewhere provided singers and bands with a chance to be heard; they in turn provided an inspiring soundtrack to the lives of generations of Poles.

During Gomułka's tenure the system ossified nonetheless. Polish Marxists such as Leszek Kołakowski and many others became disenchanted with the regime. The younger generation also questioned whether the system was developing in the right direction. Among the activists who made a name for themselves at this time were Communist Party members Karol Modzelewski and Jacek Kuroń. The last two penned an open letter dated March 18, 1965, in which they claimed the communist elite was using the system to transform itself into a new ruling class. In sum, "the needs of industrializing an underdeveloped country gave birth to the bureaucracy as a ruling class; it alone could answer these needs, since in the conditions of the country's underdevelopment, it alone adopted industrialization—production for production's sake—as its class interest."* Given this situation, they claimed a workers' revolution was inevitable.

---

*   The Kuroń-Modzelewski Open Letter to the Party, from early 1965, quotation in *From Stalinism to Pluralism*, 2d ed., 110.

A day after publishing the text, Modzelewski and Kuroń were arrested; they soon found themselves in prison and sentenced to jail terms of several years in length.

The Polish Millennium, 1966

Not far on the heels of this persecution of young Marxists who dared to think differently came increased persecution of the Roman Catholic Church. The head of the Polish Roman Catholic church, Stefan Cardinal Wyszyński, had been under house arrest for a number of years (from September 1953 to late October 1956), which as we have seen did not stop him from having an effect on the outcome of 1956. Wyszyński was a very savvy cleric. During his years of imprisonment, he came up with a plan to celebrate Poland's approaching millennium. Even before the cardinal was released from detention on October 26, 1956, he began putting his program into place.

Wyszyński has been called Primate of the Millennium—and for good reason. It was he who prepared the Poles to celebrate Poland's millennium as he understood it. The year of the millennium was 1966—a thousand years after the baptism of Mieszko into the Roman Church, with which one traditionally begins the Polish historical narrative. Yet Wyszyński saw a way to imbue his compatriots with his vision of Poland as a Christian state: Poles would celebrate the Great Novena of the Millennium. Religious novenas usually last nine days. Wyszyński's novena would last nine years—from 1957 to 1966. The Polish nation, furthermore, would renew the religious vows made by King Jan Kazimierz during the Swedish Deluge of the mid-seventeenth century.

In a way, Wyszyński had thrown down the gauntlet. The communists could not let this pass in silence. This religious vision of Poland's millennium stuck in the craw of the communist regime. It preferred to celebrate 1966 as the millennium not of Polish Christianity but of Polish statehood. To this end, the communist authorities proposed to commemorate the Polish millennium by building a thousand schools. They would hold a large final celebration on July 22, 1966—this date being the national holiday after the war, the date of the July Manifesto that created the Polish People's Republic. The communist celebration was replete with military symbolism from Poland's millennial past. And a special emphasis was placed on anti-German themes, as was seen in commemorations of the 550th anniversary of the Battle of Grunwald in 1960.

Nor were the communists above interfering with the Catholic novena. At one point someone rather farcically absconded with the circulating copy of the image of the Black Madonna, so that it might not continue its visitation of parishes. This led to the image's frame itself making the rounds, the message being all too clear to the faithful. Yet more serious steps against the church and the Poles' Roman Catholicism were taken during this period. Religious education in the schools was ended in 1961. A war against crucifixes hanging in schools was begun. And further church construction was impeded.

The situation during the Great Novena of the Millennium was somewhat complicated by the reconciliation of Polish and German bishops in 1965. The Polish episcopate wrote a letter to their German Roman Catholic counterparts in West Germany, in which they acknowledged that wrongs had been committed on both sides during and following World War II, asking for forgiveness as well as granting it. (Incidentally, the bishops' move helped to hasten the recognition by West Germany of Poland's western border, which was not guaranteed by the USSR and West Germany until 1970.)

This rather public, even magnanimous, show of Christian charity on the part of the Polish episcopate enraged the communist regime. The Polish bishops had gone over the heads of the communist officials, in essence engaging in their own foreign diplomacy. And not all Poles understood this forgiveness: after all, since the war German fascists had been the favorite bugbear of the communist regime. How, then, could their bishops approach their German counterparts? The communists tried to profit from this confusion and played the German card for all it was worth.

Still, the culmination of the Great Novena of the Millennium on May 3, 1966 (note that the church used the prewar national holiday of May 3), demonstrated that Poles still valued their Roman Catholic faith. Huge numbers of Poles had made the pilgrimage to Jasna Góra that day—perhaps half a million.

Perhaps a sign that the communists were softening: in the fall of 1967, they granted permission for a church to be constructed in Nowa Huta, their model workers' city outside Kraków.

That same year, the Arab-Israeli War broke out. All of a sudden, Israel became Poland's enemy. This new development was reflected in the events of 1968.

The Polish "March" of 1968

The Polish March was caused by performances of a Romantic play, Adam Mickiewicz's *Forefathers' Eve*, in Warsaw. In this production, the actors played up some of the anti-Russian themes of the famous play. This, naturally, won them larger audiences, who received the play enthusiastically. As a result, although the run of the National Theater's production was to end already on March 30, the production was closed early by the Ministry of Culture and Art, per a decision announced on January 16. The final performance would take place on January 30.

This decision to close down the popular production led to protests, petitions, and demonstrations. Students at the University of Warsaw and other universities spontaneously joined in the protest. Their demonstrations were broken up by ZOMO and ORMO units; these were mobile militarized militias that enthusiastically and brutally clubbed the striking students with metal-tipped rubber truncheons. Students and faculty who participated in the demonstrations were purged.

Yet the events of March were complicated by a fight at the top, within the Party. In his bid for greater power, minister of the interior Mieczysław Moczar sought to play up the "Zionist" menace. As a result, Jews and the "cosmopolitan" intelligentsia were blamed as instigators of the unrest. Here was another example of Jews being turned into scapegoats.

All this led to the expulsion of many of Poland's few remaining Jews from the country, as well as Warsaw University professors such as Leszek Kołakowski (already expelled in 1967), Bronisław Baczko, Zygmunt Bauman, and Włodzimierz Brus. As a result of the anti-Semitic campaign, in the years 1968–1969 some fifteen thousand Jews departed Poland.

These events in Poland overlapped with the Prague Spring in Czechoslovakia. Once again, Poles were spared the invasion that put an end to the Czechoslovak events. (And this time, the Polish army took part in the Soviet bloc invasion of Czechoslovakia in August 1968.) The invasion led to the establishment of the so-called Brezhnev doctrine (after the new general secretary of the USSR), which essentially stated that countries within the Soviet bloc would remain in the Soviet bloc.

The Polish "December" of 1970

By 1970 Gomułka's Poland was in trouble. It simply could not provide the consumer goods—especially foodstuffs—needed by its citizens. The Five-Year-Plans proved ineffectual. Poles had little money, but even the money they had they could not spend with ease. Something had to give.

On December 12, 1970, the authorities announced that prices would rise by 30 percent as of December 14. It is worth noting that the announcement was made on a Saturday evening, thus stores (never open on Sundays) were already closed for the weekend. On Monday morning, the new prices would already be in effect. (It is also worth noting that the price rise had been prepared well in advance—politically as well as otherwise.) Since the average Pole spent three-fifths of his income on food, this change was bound to be costly.

The overall timing of the price hike made it even costlier. The government was raising prices right before the Christmas holiday—the period when most Poles did the most shopping. This could not help but elicit a reaction. It came in the form of strikes along the Baltic Sea coast, in the shipyards of Gdańsk and Gdynia and elsewhere.

If the raising of prices before the Christmas holiday was callous, the response to the strikes was criminal. Gomułka gave permission for the military to shoot at the "counterrevolutionaries." On December 15 alone, seven lives were lost and some five hundred workers were injured. The unrest spread further along the seacoast. On December 17, workers peacefully heading to their shifts at the Lenin Shipyards in Gdynia were shot at. In the course of this and the following days, some forty-five people were killed, and nearly twelve hundred wounded. The situation was becoming critical.

It was time for change at the top. On December 20, Gomułka was replaced as first secretary by Edward Gierek. Well liked by Poland's miners, Gierek had long served as a Party functionary in the city of Katowice in Silesia.

Fortunately for the authorities, Gierek had a populist's touch when addressing his audiences. At one meeting with workers on the seacoast, he asked, "Will you help me?" and the audience fired back, "We will help you!" The Polish original captures the ease of this exchange: "Pomożecie?" to which the reply was "Pomożemy!"

The new communist leader had some ideas about how to shake up People's Poland. Gierek introduced an era of consumption and investment. He emboldened his compatriots to think big. His motto for the nation was "A Pole can do it" (*Polak potrafi*). This propaganda of success as well as the idea that the people's needs would actually be taken into consideration was met with a warm response around the country.

The problem lay in the economics. Gierek's experiment, begun February 1971, focused on foreign trade. Poland's modernization was to be financed and augmented by Western credits, licenses, and imports. Gierek's Poland purchased over three hundred licenses from capitalist countries in 1971–1975. He expected that they would be able to recoup the cost of the licenses (which had to be paid for in hard currency) by exporting goods to the West. They intended to do so in the popular fields of electrical machinery and chemical and electronic industries. At the same time, the regime aimed to increase production of consumer goods. Incomes were also allowed to rise (real wages had risen by 40 percent by 1975), in the hope that the possibility of getting a raise would increase productivity. This was also a period in which Poles had greater freedom to travel, if mainly to countries within the Soviet bloc, and they could do so inexpensively.

In the beginning of the 1970s, Gierek's experiment seemed to be working. Life was looking up. By 1973 Poland had the third fastest national growth rate in the world.

What the Poles could not foresee was the global economic downturn brought on by the international oil crisis, which began in 1973. Having opted to join the world economy, Poland now found itself affected by the world's instability. The price of goods imported from the West rose dramatically at a time when Poland's ability to export meat was declining. With inflation at home and foreign debt skyrocketing, Poland was headed down the path of destruction. It could not make even the interest payments on its debt.

There were other reasons that Poland's centrally planned economy was in trouble. The country was producing expensive machines in grandiose but unproductive new factories, but instead of exporting them to the hard-currency West, it was exporting them to the soft-currency East bloc, leaving Poles lacking the hard currency necessary to service the debt owed to the West. Another example of the planners' general ineptitude was the plan for the production of steel wire, in which all thicknesses of wire were combined into one target tonnage. For the year 1975, the plan was set at 212,536 tons, and this target was exceeded by 6.7 percent. While this sounds promising, the situation was less rosy than it looked on paper, for while 114.1 percent of the demand for 3.0mm wire was satisfied, only 46.2 percent of the planned 0.2mm wire and 54.3 percent of the planned 0.35mm wire was produced. Overproducing the more easily produced thick wire left Poland with a deficit in the no less needed thin wire, which the country was forced to import.

There seemed to be no way for Poland to increase its exports in such a way as to cover the costs of the licenses and the country's growing debt. People's Poland's love-hate relation with the countryside meant that livestock, and thus meat production, was down. And meat was Poland's best export to the hard-currency West. As of 1974, Poland became a net food importer, not exporter. For a country that had long lived by agriculture, this was a shock.

The Polish "June" of 1976

Push came to shove in the summer of 1976. A new set of price hikes was announced, including a 69 percent rise in the price of meat. And the result was predictable. At factories in Radom and Ursus, near Warsaw, large protests broke out. Fighting in the streets ensued between strikers and the ZOMO and the secret police. In the melee, two people perished.

This time, however, the workers were not alone. A group of democratically minded intellectuals that included well-known writers and artists decided to take up their cause. Only a year earlier Poland had agreed to respect human rights, in accordance with the Helsinki Final Act of the Conference on Security and Cooperation in Europe. The intellectuals thus established an organization appropriately named the Committee for the Defense of Workers (KOR), which provided immediate financial assistance to workers who had been repressed and their families. The committee also helped them with their legal defense. The aid was both needed and appreciated.

This development marked a crucial sea change in postwar Polish protest. The intelligentsia had suffered alone in 1968, the workers in 1970. For once, in 1976 both working class and intelligentsia were working together. Perhaps some greater good was yet to come domestically from these hiccups?

The Polish 1978 and 1979

While one series of hiccups was produced by the Polish reaction to the ineptitude of the Soviet-style economy, one can single out a realm in which a different kind of pressure was exerted on the communist regime. This was the religious front. We have already seen how Cardinal Wyszyński managed to create a place for Polish Catholicism in the public sphere. In the late 1970s, the impact of the church was about to skyrocket.

The fateful date was October 16, 1978. On this day, the conclave of cardinals in Rome incredibly elected the fifty-eight-year-old archbishop of Kraków, Karol Wojtyła, as pope. Wojtyła was the first pope in over four centuries who was not Italian.

Although it does not necessarily explain his election by the conclave, Wojtyła's background sheds light on his unique preparation for this honor. Hailing from the town of Wadowice in the south of Poland, the young Wojtyła began his training in an underground seminary during World War II, although he also had exhibited talent as a poet and playwright. Yet his vocation was to serve God.

Ordained a priest in Poland in 1946, shortly thereafter he departed for Rome to complete his doctorate. Father Wojtyła returned to Poland in 1948 and taught for a number of years in Kraków and Lublin. He was elevated to the rank of bishop in 1958 and became archbishop of Kraków in 1964. In the interim, the Polish cleric had participated in the Second Vatican Council in the years 1962–1965. With his command of Italian and other Western languages, he must have made a fine impression there: two years later, he was made a cardinal.

The joy of the average Catholic Pole at hearing the news of Wojtyła's election to the See of Rome in the fall of 1978 knew no bounds. If ever there was a moment of Polish pride, this was it. Naturally, the communists were not nearly as keen; indeed, they were in shock.

The young, articulate, dynamic Wojtyła clearly made an impact on his fellow priests. Yet he made an even greater impact on people in the numerous countries he was to visit over his years as head of the Universal Church. The popularity and influence of this first globetrotting pontiff was unprecedented.

Naturally, one of the countries in which the new pope had enormous influence was Poland. As Pope John Paul II, he made his first visit to Poland in June 1979. The communists were leery. They had prevented him from traveling to Poland earlier in the year for the nine hundredth anniversary of the death of Saint Stanisław, bishop and martyr, fearing that this Polish pope might raise the specter of church-state relations, as they had been in the eleventh century between Bishop Stanisław and King Bolesław the Bold. Once John Paul II was in Poland that summer, the official cameramen in their television broadcasts (for there naturally had to be media coverage) took pains not to pan over the vast crowds that came out to see him.

The pope gave an incredibly powerful sermon in Victory Square in Warsaw, in which he spoke of the Polish nation "giving witness" and famously exhorted his compatriots not to be afraid. Instead of criticizing the communist regime, the Polish pope lent his authority to the unnamed hosts of fellow Poles, past and present, such as the unknown soldier whose tomb lay on the square. Together, he claimed, they all made up Poland. In speaking of the rights of (the little) man, John Paul II empowered each individual to give witness, to act. He also reminded Poles—shades of Wyszyński—that it was impossible to understand Polish history without Christ.

Poles, even those who were not fervent Catholics, seemed to take to heart the pope's message of empowerment and the advancement of the human person. Surely those who wanted their voices to be heard were emboldened these last years. In 1978 a flying university (offering underground lectures) had been established, teaching things that could not be taught in the state schools. And Poles were producing more underground publications.

While Polish society was gaining in confidence, the Polish economy was looking worse and worse. The country's debt continued to spiral out of control. By 1979, Poland's debt to the West had passed the $18 billion mark, to reach $23 billion the next year. By the end of the decade the authorities let it be known that belt-tightening would have to take place on account of the country's huge debts, which needed to be at least serviced, if not paid off.

The Polish "August" of 1980

The communists seemed to have only one trick in their repertoire to deal with budget woes: price increases. It was not a recipe for success in 1980, as it had been neither in 1970 nor in 1976. This time the announcement came in the summer of 1980 that the price of meat would increase. Meat had long been a bellwether of status and prosperity in the country. If Poles could no longer afford it, then Gierek's propaganda of success seemed to ring hollow.

The response of the Polish population was similar to that of 1970: once again, strikes broke out on the Baltic Sea coast. Instigators of the strike in Gdańsk included the crane operator and labor organizer Anna Walentynowicz, who had just lost her job. But the face of the strike in the Gdańsk shipyard came to be an electrician, Lech Wałęsa. The thirty-six-year-old Wałęsa turned out to be a charismatic and dynamic working-class leader.

By 1980 Polish workers had imbued their strike with a degree of creativity. They came up with a new means of protest. This was the round-the-clock sit-down strike on factory grounds. (No more coming and going to work.) Furthermore, they established interfactory strike committees. This last innovation would later allow the workers to create a national structure for the new independent and self-governing trade unions that would be given the name Solidarity.

The strategy of this "Polish August" worked well. On August 31, the government agreed to accept the twenty-one demands formulated by the workers and their advisors from among the intelligentsia (many of whom had been part of KOR). The most important of these demands was the very first: independent, self-governing trade unions. Why was this so crucial? Because, beholden to the Party, the existing government trade unions could not be expected to advocate for the workers' real needs. The decentralized nature of the new independent, self-governing unions meant that it would be harder for the state to gain control over them.

Yet this was not all the workers were seeking. Other demands of the founders of Solidarity included the right to strike; freedom of expression and publication; and the right to have Sunday masses broadcast on television. (Clearly the pope had had an impact.) And indeed, the movement was full of Catholic

Figure 13.2: Here we have the reality of socialism in Poland, circa 1980: masses at a Solidarity trade union rally. One of the banners invokes the Mother of God, Queen of Poland, as well.

symbolism, beginning with the masses that were said during the strikes and including Wałęsa's ubiquitous Our Lady of Częstochowa lapel pin.

The Solidarity trade union movement quickly gained members. By the end of 1980, the new trade unions had some 10 million members—about 75 percent of the employees of state-owned enterprises. This amounted to nearly one-third of the population of Poland. It seemed as though practically every Pole had joined Solidarity.

To add to the euphoria of that year, in December 1980 word came that the Polish émigré writer Czesław Miłosz had been awarded the Nobel Prize for literature.

The Polish Way to the Future . . .

The Solidarity movement was a qualitatively new movement in the East bloc. It was different from the Hungarian reform movement, which had been led by a reform communist. In this it was also different from the Czechoslovaks' search in 1968 for "socialism with a human face."

By 1980 Poles entertained no such delusions of reform communism. Theirs, paradoxically, was a movement of workers against a workers' state. And the movement had the potential to be very dangerous. Witness the Message to the Working People of Eastern Europe, which was sent to Poland's neighbors by the Solidarity congress in the fall of 1981, the first democratically elected body in the Soviet bloc since the 1940s:

> Delegates of the independent self-governing trade union Solidarity, assembled at their first congress in Gdańsk, send the workers of Albania, Bulgaria, Czechoslovakia, the German Democratic Republic, Romania, Hungary, and all the peoples of the Soviet Union words of greeting and support. As the first independent trade union in our postwar history we are deeply aware of the community of our fate. We assure you that, notwithstanding the lies being spread in your countries, we are the authentic representation of 10 million workers which has emerged as the result of workers' strikes. We support all of you who have decided to take the difficult road and fight for free trade unions. We believe that soon our and your representatives will be able to meet to exchange our union experiences.

In this statement, one hears echoes of the old revolutionary slogan, "For our freedom and for yours."

Solidarity had overstepped its original mandate. Although it began as a trade union, it was becoming a political movement. And it was growing. Solidarity even spread to the countryside. Rural Solidarity was finally legalized in May 1981. It was also flexing its new muscle. Throughout 1980 and 1981 periodic strikes continued to plague the country, and a major strike was being planned for December 17.

Such unbridled independent activity could not go unchallenged by the state—especially given the fact that the Soviets were pressuring the Polish communist leadership to restore order in the country. By this point, a series of changes at the top of People's Poland (Stanisław Kania had initially succeeded Gierek) had left General Wojciech Jaruzelski as general secretary of the PZPR, prime minister, and head of the military.

Jaruzelski was a complex character. Born to an impoverished Polish noble family, as a young boy he was deported to the USSR during World War II, where he was orphaned. He habitually wore dark glasses, as his eyes had been seared by the Siberian sun. Yet he came to be a communist, and a military man. Poles generally held their military in high regard. Still, it was Jaruzelski who conducted an anti-Semitic purge of the army in 1967–1968 and sent Polish troops to crush the Czechoslovak Prague Spring in August 1968; and he was minister of national defense in 1970 when the army killed protesting workers on the seacoast. Now all power lay in the hands of the military—more precisely, in Jaruzelski's white-gloved hands.

On December 13, 1981, Jaruzelski announced the imposition of martial law, in the name of the newly established Military Council of National Salvation (WRON) that he headed. This moment had been prepared long in advance. In the wee hours of the night of December 12/13, over five thousand Solidarity activists were preemptively arrested and were soon to be interned in detainment camps. The military were everywhere.

As soon as they learned of the imposition of martial law, other Solidarity activists proceeded to protest. Clashes with the police and ZOMO led to deaths, such as at the Wujek coal mine in Silesia, where nine miners perished.

The rest of the population woke to find they had no recourse to telephone, or to rail or road travel. Denied freedom of association, no public gatherings—even groups congregating on street corners—were allowed. University students were sent home. All individuals were to carry their personal documents on them at all times, as soldiers on patrol checked them.

Society, nonetheless, continued to protest. The thirteenth of every month brought some signs of life. And Solidarity moved into the underground and continued to produce newspapers, pamphlets, and the like. After all, conspiracy was a great Polish tradition that stemmed from the era of partitions through World War II and now into a new age. This time they availed themselves of the mimeograph machine—or, better, the occasional precious photocopy machine, some of which were smuggled in from the United States, the gift of American trade unionists.

The U.S. government under President Ronald Reagan responded, imposing economic sanctions on Poland already in December 1981. Further pressure was placed on the Soviet bloc in ensuing years. The United States upped the nuclear ante while announcing its intention to create the Strategic Defense Initiative, a space-based anti-missile system colloquially referred to as "Star Wars."

Martial law lasted until the summer of 1983. The pope had made his second visit to Poland that spring, only to have an attempt on his life made shortly thereafter back in Rome. By this time, many internees such as Wałęsa had already been released. The electrician turned Solidarity leader was awarded the Nobel Peace Prize in October 1983 yet was not allowed to travel to Stockholm to accept it.

An Uneasy Truce

The return to normality was but a veneer. Beneath the surface, Poland still simmered. The following October a charismatic Warsaw priest, Father Jerzy Popiełuszko, was murdered by officers of the interior ministry. Popiełuszko had a habit—one that clearly annoyed the authorities—of saying masses for the Fatherland . . . The perpetrators were put on trial, but Poles were not satisfied that those at the top who had ordered the murder would ever be held accountable.

The next years represented continued stagnation. Paradoxically, Poland stagnated at the moment when a new and charismatic leader, Mikhail Gorbachev, came to rule the Soviet Union. After 1985 Gorbachev's reform programs of glasnost (more openness) and perestroika (economic restructuring) would open new venues within the Soviet bloc.

Matters came to a head in Poland once again in 1988. A new generation of workers, raised on the myth of Solidarity, went on strike in April and May, only to strike again with even greater force in August. These young workers were getting out of control. They also coined a new and powerful slogan: *Nie ma wolności bez Solidarności!*—There is no freedom without Solidarity!

Times had changed, in Poland and in the region as a whole. That same summer, the authorities approached the old leaders of Solidarity. They proposed to hold round-table talks, in which some members of Solidarity agreed to participate. From February 6 to April 5, 1989, members of the communist camp and moderate members of the Solidarity camp worked to forge an agreement.

The round-table discussions resulted in a portentous compromise. The existing Polish parliament would be revamped. The country would once again have a bicameral legislature: a Senate in addition to a Seym. Yet even more important was the future composition of the legislature. In forthcoming elections, all hundred seats in the Senate would be freely contested. And while 65 percent of the seats in the Seym would be reserved to the ruling party, non-communists could vie for the remaining seats.

This half-free election was set for June 4, 1989. That was Poland's "High Noon." The old Gary Cooper poster from the Hollywood film of the same name was used in the electoral campaign. Solidarity had been relegalized in April and undertook its maiden political campaign—the campaign of its life. Ironically, the Polish election took place the same date as the Tiananmen Square massacre in China.

The election turned out better than anyone in the Solidarity camp could have imagined. The Solidarity camp won 99 of the 100 Senate seats and all

161 freely contested seats of the 460 in the Seym—the maximum it could attain. And the communists accepted the outcome. Thus, instead of a drastic outcome as in China, Poles had decided to cooperate, to work toward a negotiated transition—although what that would entail, exactly, remained to be seen (this was only June 1989).

Regardless, the Solidarity of Lech Wałęsa had been transformed. It served as a parliamentary group and citizens' committees as well as a trade union. Soon it would be further transformed by coming into power.

The compromise nonetheless continued. The communist Jaruzelski assumed the newly created post of president. But who would—could—serve as prime minister? The Poles ultimately ended up having the first non-communist head of government in the entire East bloc. Tadeusz Mazowiecki became prime minister on August 24, 1989.

That summer, this former advisor to Solidarity gave a statesmanlike speech to the assembled parliamentarians. Mazowiecki declared that he wanted to be the prime minister of all Poles, regardless of their views and convictions. He spoke of the new need for the Poles to separate themselves from the past with a thick line. His government—a negotiated, clearly transitional one— would not take responsibility for the past but would move forward.

Mazowiecki could not know what was to come in the Soviet bloc. He could not foresee that Gorbachev would soon allow the countries of the East bloc to embrace a new doctrine, the "Sinatra Doctrine," and do things their own way. How could this first non-communist prime minister know that Poland, with its negotiated breakthrough, would be first in a series of dominoes to fall? Indeed, within the space of half a year, Hungary, Czechoslovakia, East Germany, and Romania had all experienced regime change. Given Poland's lead, they had been able to make even a sharper break with the past than had the trailblazing Poles.

On December 29, 1989, the Third Polish Republic was declared. The crown was restored to Poland's emblem, the white eagle. Soon the communist party building would be transformed into the new stock exchange. Could this, truly, be the end of history?

Epilogue

Poland's "Return" to Europe

Over twenty years have passed since the events of 1989—as much time as the interwar Poles had to shape their polity. It still is not easy to do more than summarize the progress the Poles have made in this relatively short period. Nonetheless, it must be emphasized that Poland has not "returned" to Europe, although that was the buzzword of the early years of transition. Rather, Poland has returned to her rightful place in the community of nations of Europe and, indeed, the world.

Following the partially free elections of June 1989 and their earth-shaking aftermath (the end of Eastern Europe in 1989, of the Soviet bloc, even the Soviet Union, in 1991, and subsequently, of the bipolar world), several things became clear. The Polish Third Republic would be making a series of transitions. It was leaving behind the system imposed on it after World War II. What were the Poles to do now?

There was initial talk in many of the countries of the former Eastern Europe of a "third way," but they ended up opting for the Western way. And so did the Poles. As such, each polity faced what has been called a triple transition.

The first transition concerned the political realm. Poland jettisoned Soviet-style communist dictatorship in favor of a pluralistic democracy. Here there were many growing pains. The Solidarity umbrella may have served well in the partially free election of 1989. Increasingly, though, Poles came to realize that they had disparate views about the way their newly sovereign Polish state should look. And while the "thick line" proposed by Prime Minister Tadeusz Mazowiecki may have kept the peace in a parliament where not all parliamentarians had been freely elected, it soon came to irk those who wanted to rid Poland of its communist baggage. Here Poland paid the price for being the first of the tumbling dominoes of the former East bloc. It was unable to make a clean break with the past and instead had to settle for a negotiated transition. This was a messier situation, but the only one possible in June 1989.

Nonetheless, Poles longed to have fully free elections. None other than Lech Wałęsa came to serve as the first freely elected president in 1990, a job he held until December 1995. Following the presidential election of 1990, the Polish government-in-exile in London, which had continued to exist all these years, passed the baton to the former electrician. Its last president, Ryszard Kaczorowski, and not Jaruzelski, transferred the Polish insignia to the president-elect. The Third Polish Republic had made yet another important transition. It should also be noted that Poland's first female prime minister, Hanna Suchocka, served during Wałęsa's term as president.

While these were positive moves for the country, the transition to fully pluralistic democracy was less than stellar. The Solidarity umbrella blew inside out, as the Solidarity camp broke up into a plethora of parties of varying profiles. Some were run by former intellectuals, such as the successful Democratic Union—later renamed the Freedom Union—of Tadeusz Mazowiecki, Bronisław Geremek, and others. There were parties that might be labeled extremist, such as Roman Giertych's (later) far-right League of Polish Families or Andrzej Lepper's often provocative, populist Self-Defense. Other parties would attract voters in more prosaic or even comical fashion; there was a short-lived party of beer aficionados.

The left of the political spectrum morphed into a more traditional social-democratic party under the leadership of Aleksander Kwaśniewski. This former communist and polished politician surprisingly outperformed the less disciplined Wałęsa during the presidential debates of 1995, when the former electrician turned president bid for yet another term at Poland's helm. Instead, Kwaśniewski won the election and served as president for two terms.

The second transition that Poland had to make in the post-1989 period concerned the economic realm. Here the decision was somewhat simpler. Poland abandoned the centrally planned economy that had created an economics of shortage in favor of a Western-style market economy. Not that the actual transition was made easy. By the end of 1989, Poland's economy was in free fall. The country was experiencing hyperinflation, which at its height amounted to a whopping 640 percent. Poles had to act fast.

The country found its savior in the person of an economic professor named Leszek Balcerowicz. As Poland's finance minister, Balcerowicz worked with

Harvard's Jeffrey Sachs and produced a bold and comprehensive plan that—among other things—took care of the hyperinflation while also renegotiating Poland's vast foreign debts. This "shock therapy" proved extremely effective in jolting Poland out of its old ways. The new regime was also able to profit from the initial euphoria: Poles were willing to suffer at first, if it meant that the overall situation would improve. In this way, Poland made much greater, faster strides than did its neighbors Czechoslovakia and Hungary, where more timid, half-hearted reforms were undertaken. Nonetheless, both the economic restructuring and the question of privatization would continue to prove problematic. Additionally, the economy would have to redirect itself, as exports to the east imploded with the collapse of the Soviet Union in 1991.

The third post-1989 transition was in many ways the easiest. Poland went from being subject to Soviet imperial hegemony to being a fully independent nation-state. It is worth noting that Poland had no territorial designs on lands for which it still had great sympathy—in particular, the cities of Vilnius and Lviv—but which since World War II had become integral parts of Lithuania and Ukraine, respectively. A generation of Poles writing abroad for the respected periodical *Kultura*, published in Paris by Jerzy Giedroyć, had long presented the necessity of accepting Poland's borders. Somehow, this approach was embraced by those engaged in the early years of Poland's now independent foreign policy. Poland rather quickly acknowledged these former Soviet republics' declarations of independence. Indeed, it was the first country formally to recognize Ukrainian independence in December 1991.

At the same time, Poland, although the largest of the former East European states of the Soviet bloc, realized that its interests might best be served by working together with other countries. The most obvious initial group was comprised of its neighbors Hungary and Czechoslovakia (which, after 1992, split amicably into the Czech Republic and Slovakia). It also tried to play the role of elder brother—certainly through the activities of a professor of international law turned Poland's foreign minister, Krzysztof Skubiszewski—to the newly emergent states in the east. In his dealing with Poland's eastern neighbors, Skubiszewski "simply" asked them to adhere to European standards. This standardized and regularized treatment, carrying a certain set of civilizational expectations, may have been one of the reasons why the dissolution of the Soviet Union did not result—certainly not in the countries adjacent to Poland—in territorial disputes. These emerged with a vengeance in the Balkans, where there was no Skubiszewski to set the tone.

Yet from the outset, a number of countries—certainly Poland, Hungary, the Czech Republic, and Slovakia—made it clear: they wanted to "return to Europe." To be sure, they were, and had been, part of Europe from time immemorial. This statement meant that they no longer wanted to be of "Eastern Europe," in its Soviet vintage. Before long they would officially be promoted to the realm of Central Europe.

More than that: Poland and its neighbors wanted to become members of influential Western organizations. The two key organizations, in their view, were NATO and the European Union.

One easily forgets that the countries of the "New Europe" were made to wait, and wait for a long time, for entry into NATO and the European Union. NATO was the first to extend an invitation to Poland and some of its neighbors to join. Accession to NATO nonetheless took a full decade: only as of March 12, 1999, was Poland sure that its borders would be guaranteed by the Western powers.

Securing membership in the European Union took even longer. After 1989, Poland and the other countries of the "new Europe" that wished to apply for EU membership were held to high standards. They had to meet stringent requirements—essentially, they had to be fully ready, legislatively, economically, as well as politically—to become fully functioning parts of the European Union. The west Europeans clearly were concerned that new members would be a drag on the union—something that had not occurred to them when admitting Greece, Spain, or Portugal to the union earlier.

Reaching the threshold for membership in the EU was difficult. Poland had to rise to these new heights at a time when it also had to restructure its economy so as to be able to export to the West. None of this was easy. Still, Poland—together with nine other countries (Cyprus, the Czech Republic, Estonia, Hungary, Latvia, Lithuania, Malta, Slovakia, and Slovenia)—was admitted to the European Union on May 1, 2004. Nearly a decade and a half had passed since Poland began this new journey back into Europe.

Despite the earlier expressed desire to "return to Europe," by 2004 not all Poles were convinced that they wanted membership in the European Union. Might they not be sacrificing their hard-won sovereignty by joining yet another international entity? A referendum was held in the country. It was heartening to see President Aleksander Kwaśniewski, a former communist, work so hard to achieve the goal of Poland joining the European Union—a goal, not incidentally, supported by Pope John Paul II. Ultimately 76.8 percent of Polish voters came out in favor of EU membership.

Despite the positive role played by the now elderly pope, not all was well with the Roman Catholic Church in Poland, which also experienced the pains of transition. Its early interference in politics lost the church much goodwill early on. Poles used to the separation of church and state clearly preferred not being told how to vote.

Nonetheless, the church itself has remained a powerful player within Poland. It has not functioned as a monolith: the establishment by Father Tadeusz Rydzyk of his often controversial Catholic radio station "Radio Maryja" (the most serious charge against it being its anti-Semitism) as well as his developing media empire suggests as much. All this indicates that Polish Catholics are a heterogeneous bunch, running the spectrum from the devout little old ladies pejoratively referred to as "mohair berets" (from their preferred headgear) to Poles who make only infrequent appearances in church, seeing Roman Catholicism as but another traditional attribute of Polishness. The death of John Paul II on April 2, 2005, left the Poles without a truly authoritative Catholic compass.

Adding to the animosity between various groups within Poland was the change in tone of politics after the accession of 2004. This dated from the election to the presidency of Lech Kaczyński in 2005. Kaczyński's Law and Justice Party—run by his identical twin brother, Jarosław—came to power on a platform of fighting corruption and creating a new, purer "Fourth Polish Republic." This ambitious goal was not achieved. While the targets of the Law and Justice Party's ire initially seemed to be the post-communists, the Kaczyńskis spared no kind words for Poland's negotiated transition.

As a consequence, Poles paradoxically proved to be much less enthusiastic about the twentieth anniversary of the revolutions of 1989 than did many other peoples in the region. The latter—particularly the Germans, when celebrating the anniversary of the fall of the Berlin Wall in November 2009—publicly acknowledged the important role played by the Poles who paved the way for them. With the rise of the Law and Justice Party, Polish politics became intensely polarized, with the two main parties, Law and Justice and the relatively new Civic Platform of Donald Tusk, contending for voters' favor not always in a respectful manner (political opponents have often been demonized and/or cast as traitors).

Nor have other Polish achievements been fully appreciated. That Poland weathered the global economic crisis significantly better than much of the continent should be a point of pride for the country's citizens. Yet, in their pursuit of partisan politics, Poles sometimes have lost sight of the larger picture. It remains to be seen whether these two parties will continue to dominate Polish politics, as other, still smaller parties more to the left or right figure as well.

Some of the differences between these two major parties, both lying to the center-right of the political spectrum, have been stylistic. The Law and Justice Party took a much more pugnacious approach to its opponents, while making a point of courting the church. More nationalistic in outlook, it also was more skeptical of the European Union and feared that membership in that organization might curtail Poland's distinctiveness. By contrast, the Civic Platform embraced EU membership, allowing Poles to feel fully citizens of Europe as well as of Poland. Donald Tusk spoke of normalization and mending fences with Poland's neighbors, especially Germany and Russia, powers that still seemed to rub the Kaczyński brothers the wrong way.

The events of April 2010 were a watershed of sorts in Polish politics. Poles wished to commemorate the seventieth anniversary of the Katyń massacres, which Russian president Boris Yeltsin, back in 1991, admitted were the Soviet Union's doing. Prime Minister Donald Tusk first traveled to Smolensk, only to be followed several days later by a presidential plane carrying Lech and Maria Kaczyński as well as a host of Polish dignitaries, military and state officials. The presidential plane crashed right before arrival, killing all ninety-six people onboard.

All of Poland spontaneously burst into mourning. With the loss of so many important, even history-making Poles (for among the dead were also Anna Walentynowicz and Ryszard Kaczorowski) it was as if a second Katyń had taken place. Yet the mourning soon became tempered, once it was learned that the presidential pair would be buried not in Warsaw—the city with which Lech Kaczyński was most identified—but in the crypts of the royal Wawel Cathedral. Poles had debated what might be the appropriate burial place for their president. Since the partitions, the rare honor of a Wawel burial had been granted a mere six outstanding non-royals (generals Prince Józef Poniatowski and Tadeusz Kościuszko, Romantic poets Adam Mickiewicz and Juliusz Słowacki, and generals turned political leaders Józef Piłsudski and Władysław Sikorski). In 2010, not all Poles were sure that President Lech Kaczyński's tragic death was cause enough for him and his wife to be buried in such rarified company. Perceptions that this decision had been made by the bishop of Kraków, Stanisław Cardinal Dziwisz (John Paul II's former secretary), in conjunction with Jarosław Kaczyński, soured many Poles on the whole affair.

While this split in society has continued to have repercussions for the nation (many members of the Law and Justice Party have turned to conspiracy theories in order to explain the crash), the nation nonetheless proved that it could pick up the pieces, fill the offices so tragically vacated, and continue on. The election to the presidency was won by the Civic Platform candidate, Bronisław Komorowski, despite evident electoral goodwill for the counter-candidate, Law and Justice's Jarosław Kaczyński, brother of the deceased president. Under the leadership of Komorowski and Prime Minister Tusk, Poland completed its first ever half-year-long tenure in the rotating presidency of the

Council of the European Union. Poland assumed the presidency in July 2011, barely a year after the plane crash. The overall impression abroad was that the Poles acquitted themselves well. Still, the increasingly vociferous partisanship seen in Polish politics reminds one that Poland is not so different from other countries in the twenty-first century.

Indeed, Poland's reputation has been changing, becoming—perhaps—more "normal." No longer is the country a depressing place haunted by the ghosts of the past and hiding skeletons in its closet. Since 1989 Poles have consistently sought to ferret out the truth about various blank spots in their history. In this they have been assisted by the Institute of National Remembrance, which has jurisdiction over Poland's secret police files, and a new generation of Polish historians. Various revelations have surfaced, not all of them presenting some notable figures in a favorable light.

Yet Poles have persisted in not only adjusting the historical record. They have been making peace with more painful aspects of their past. Such include the often fraught Polish-Jewish relations, with the revelation of the murder of Jews by their Polish neighbors in the town of Jedwabne during World War II serving as an important lightning rod for discussion and reconciliation in the 1990s. Poles have been rediscovering the past, the bad as well as the good.

Despite such revelations, Polish-Jewish relations have also managed to improve. Part of this surely is to be attributed to the example of Pope John Paul II, who did so much to improve relations between the world's Jews and the Roman Catholic Church. He, after all, remembered playing with Jewish neighbors before World War II, and he was witness to the annihilation of the Jews during the war. In the interim, there has been a resurgence of Jewish life in the old Jewish quarter of Kazimierz, in Kraków, and elsewhere in Poland. Jewish memorial sites have been renovated. And a number of Poles have been finding—with some of them embracing—their Jewish roots. Jews are being written back into Polish history, as the recent establishment of the Museum of the History of Polish Jews attests, their lives acknowledged as part of the very fabric of Poland.

There is room for the further improvement of Polish relations with its neighbors, past and present, although much has been done—much more than has been written here. Poles and Germans are on better terms than perhaps they have ever been. As regards Poland's eastern neighbors, Poles took a more favorable view of modern Ukraine during the latter's Orange Revolution. This development spurred both countries to do something creative together: they jointly applied to host the 2012 European soccer championships—and their application proved victorious. Furthermore, the jointly hosted event proved a success. Relationships with other neighbors, such as Lithuania, remain more difficult.

Still, many Poles have come to realize the value of striving for the truth and increasingly understand that the best approach to one's history is an honest acceptance of what actually transpired, whether it puts the nation in a favorable or unfavorable light. In this and other ways, Poland—always creative, never dull—is truly becoming a normal country. What will come next for Poland? Only time will tell.

Suggestions for Further Reading

* signifies a book that transcends the time period in question
\# signifies a primary source—a book that brings to life voices from the past

General Works

Biskupski, M. B. B. *The History of Poland.* Westport, CT: Greenwood Press, 2000.

Davies, Norman. *God's Playground: A History of Poland.* 2 vols. New York: Columbia University Press, 1982.

———. *Heart of Europe: The Past in Poland's Present.* Oxford: Oxford University Press, 1986.

Lukowski, Jerzy, and Hubert Zawadzki, *A Concise History of Poland.* 2d ed. Cambridge: Cambridge University Press, 2006.

Magocsi, Paul Robert. *Historical Atlas of Central Europe.* Revised and expanded edition. Seattle: University of Washington Press, 2002.

Prazmowska, Anita J. *A History of Poland.* New York: Palgrave Macmillan, 2004.

———. *Poland: A Modern History.* New York: I. B. Tauris, 2010.

Zamoyski, Adam. *Poland: A History.* London: Harper Press, 2009.

———. *The Polish Way: A Thousand-Year History of the Poles and Their Culture.* New York: Franklin Watts, 1988.

The Middle Ages and the Renaissance

Długosz, Jan. *The Annals of Jan Długosz. Annales seu cronicae incliti regni Poloniae. An English Abridgement.* Translated by Maurice Michael. Charlton, West Sussex: IM Publications, 1997. #

East-Central Europe in Transition: From the Fourteenth to the Seventeenth Century. Edited by Antoni Mączak, Henryk Samsonowicz, and Peter Burke. Cambridge: Cambridge University Press, 1985. *

Gesta principum Polonorum: The Deeds of the Princes of the Poles. Translated and annotated by Paul W. Knoll and Frank Schaer. Budapest: Central European University Press, 2003. #

Górecki, Piotr. *Economy, Society, and Lordship in Medieval Poland, 1100–1250.* New York: Holmes and Meier, 1992.

———. *Parishes, Tithes, and Society in Earlier Medieval Poland, c. 1000–c. 1250.* Philadelphia: American Philosophical Society, 1993.

Knoll, Paul W. *The Rise of the Polish Monarchy: Piast Poland in East Central Europe, 1320–1370.* Chicago: Chicago University Press, [1972].

Milliman, Paul. *"The Slippery Memory of Men": The Place of Pomerania in the Medieval Kingdom of Poland.* Leiden: Brill, 2013.

Nowakowska, Natalia. *Church, State and Dynasty in Renaissance Poland: The Career of Cardinal Fryderyk Jagiellon (1468–1503).* Aldershot, England: Ashgate, 2007.

The Polish Renaissance in Its European Context. Edited by Samuel Fiszman. Bloomington: Indiana University Press, 1988.

Polonsky, Antony. *The Jews in Poland and Russia.* 3 vols. Oxford: Littman Library of Jewish Civilization, 2010. *

A Republic of Nobles: Studies in Polish History to 1864. Edited by J. K. Fedorowicz, Maria Bogucka, and Henryk Samsonowicz. Cambridge: Cambridge University Press, 1982. *

Sedlar, Jean. *East Central Europe in the Middle Ages, 1000–1500.* Seattle: University of Washington Press, 1994.

Segel, Harold. *Renaissance Culture in Poland: The Rise of Humanism, 1470–1573.* Ithaca: Cornell University Press, 1989.

Stone, Daniel. *The Polish-Lithuanian State, 1386–1795.* Seattle: University of Washington Press, 2001. *

The Early Modern Period (Polish-Lithuanian Commonwealth)

Bogucka, Maria. *The Lost World of the "Sarmatians": Custom as the Regulator of Polish Social Life in Early Modern Times.* Warsaw: Polish Academy of Sciences, Institute of History, 1996.

Citizenship and Identity in a Multinational Commonwealth: Poland-Lithuania in Context, 1550–1772. Edited by Karin Friedrich and Barbara M. Pendzich. Leiden: Brill, 2009.

For Your Freedom and Ours: Polish Progressive Spirit from the 14th Century to the Present. 2d enlarged edition. Edited by Krystyna M. Olszer. New York: F. Unger, 1981. #*

Friedrich, Karin. *The Other Prussia: Royal Prussia, Poland and Liberty, 1569–1772.* Cambridge: Cambridge University Press, 2000.

Frost, Robert I. *After the Deluge: Poland-Lithuania and the Second Northern War, 1655–1660.* Cambridge: Cambridge University Press, 1993.

———. *The Northern Wars: War, State and Society in Northeastern Europe, 1558–1721.* Harlow, England: Longman, 2000.

Hundert, Gershon David. *Jews in Poland-Lithuania in the Eighteenth Century: A Genealogy of Modernity.* Berkeley: University of California Press, 2004.

Kaminski, Andrzej. *Republic versus Autocracy: Poland-Lithuania and Russia, 1686–1697.* Cambridge, MA: Harvard University Press for the Harvard Ukrainian Research Institute, 1993.

Levine, Hillel. *Economic Origins of Antisemitism: Poland and Its Jews in the Early Modern Period.* New Haven: Yale University Press, 1991.

Lukowski, Jerzy. *Liberty's Folly: The Polish-Lithuanian Commonwealth in the Eighteenth Century, 1697–1795.* London: Routledge, 1991.

———. *The Partitions of Poland: 1772, 1793, 1795.* London: Addison Wesley Longman, 1999.

Pasek, Jan Chryzostom. *The Memoirs of Jan Chryzostom z Gosławic Pasek.* Translated by Maria A. J. Swiecicka. New York: Kosciuszko Foundation, 1978. #

Polish Democratic Thought from the Renaissance to the Great Emigration: Essays and Documents. Edited by M. B. Biskupski and James S. Pula. [Boulder, CO]: East European Monographs, distributed by Columbia University Press, 1990. *#

Rosman, Murray J. *The Lords' Jews: Magnate-Jewish Relations in the Polish-Lithuanian Commonwealth during the Eighteenth Century.* Cambridge, MA: Harvard University Press for the Center for Jewish Studies, Harvard University, and the Harvard Ukrainian Research Institute, 1990.

Sinkoff, Nancy. *Out of the Shtetl: Making Jews Modern in the Polish Borderlands.* Providence: Brown Judaic Studies, 2004.

Snyder, Timothy. *The Reconstruction of Nations: Poland, Ukraine, Lithuania, Belarus, 1569–1999.* New Haven: Yale University Press, 2003. *

Social and Cultural Boundaries in Pre-Modern Poland. Edited by Adam Teller, Magda Teter, and Antony Polonsky. Oxford: Littman Library of Jewish Civilization, 2010.

Storozynski, Alex. *The Peasant Prince: Thaddeus Kosciuszko and the Age of Revolution.* New York: Thomas Dunne Books, St. Martin's Press, 2009.

Sysyn, Frank E. *Between Poland and the Ukraine: The Dilemma of Adam Kysil, 1600–1653.* Cambridge, MA: Harvard University Press for the Harvard Ukrainian Research Institute, 1985.

Tazbir, Janusz. *A State without Stakes: Polish Religious Toleration in the Sixteenth and Seventeenth Centuries.* Translated by A. T. Jordan. [New York]: Kosciuszko Foundation, 1972.

Teter, Magda. *Jews and Heretics in Catholic Poland: A Beleaguered Church in the Post-Reformation Era.* Cambridge: Cambridge University Press, 2006.

Walicki, Andrzej. *The Enlightenment and the Birth of Modern Nationhood: Polish Political Thought from Noble Republicanism to Tadeusz Kościuszko.* Notre Dame, IN: University of Notre Dame Press, 1989.

Wolff, Larry. *Inventing Eastern Europe: The Map of Civilization on the Mind of the Enlightenment.* Stanford: Stanford University Press, 1994.

Zamoyski, Adam. *The Last King of Poland.* London: J. Cape, 1992.

Zolkiewski, Stanislaw. *Expedition to Moscow: A Memoir.* London 1959. #

The Long Nineteenth Century (Era of Partitions)

Antisemitism and Its Opponents in Modern Poland. Edited by Robert Blobaum. Ithaca: Cornell University Press, 2005. *

Bilenky, Serhiy. *Romantic Nationalism in Eastern Europe: Russian, Polish, and Ukrainian Political Imaginations.* Stanford Studies on Central and Eastern Europe, ed. Norman Naimark and Larry Wolff. Stanford: Stanford University Press, 2012.

Blejwas, Stanislaus A. *Realism in Polish Politics: Warsaw Positivism and National Survival in Nineteenth Century Poland.* New Haven: Yale Concilium on International and Area Studies; Columbus, Oh.: Distributed by Slavica Publishers, 1984.

Blobaum, Robert. *Feliks Dzierżynski and the SDKPiL: A Study of the Origins of Polish Communism.* Boulder, CO: East European Monographs; distributed by Columbia University Press, 1984.

———. *Rewolucja: Russian Poland, 1904–1907.* Ithaca: Cornell University Press, 1995.

Brock, Peter. "Polish Nationalism." In *Nationalism in Eastern Europe.* Edited by Peter F. Sugar and Ivo J. Lederer. Seattle: University of Washington Press, 1969.

———. *Polish Revolutionary Populism: A Study in Agrarian Socialist Thought from the 1830s to the 1850s.* Toronto: University of Toronto Press, 1977.

Dabrowski, Patrice M. *Commemorations and the Shaping of Modern Poland.* Bloomington: Indiana University Press, 2004.

Fountain, Alvin Marcus, II. *Roman Dmowski: Party, Tactics, Ideology, 1895–1907.* Boulder, CO: East European Monographs, distributed by Columbia University Press, 1980.

Frank, Alison Fleig. *Oil Empire: Visions of Prosperity in Austrian Galicia.* Cambridge, MA: Harvard University Press, 2005. *

Hagen, William W. *Germans, Poles, and Jews: The Nationality Conflict in the Prussian East, 1772–1914.* Chicago: Chicago University Press, 1980.

Hetherington, Peter. *Unvanquished: Joseph Pilsudski, Resurrected Poland and the Struggle for Eastern Europe.* 2d ed. Houston: Pingora Press, 2012. *

Himka, John-Paul. *Galician Villagers and the Ukrainian National Movement in the Nineteenth Century.* New York: St. Martin's Press, 1988.

———. *Socialism in Galicia: The Emergence of Polish Social Democracy and Ukrainian Radicalism (1860–1890).* Cambridge, MA: Harvard University Press for the Harvard Ukrainian Research Institute, 1983.

Jedlicki, Jerzy. *A Suburb of Europe: Nineteenth-Century Polish Approaches to Western Civilization.* Budapest: Central Europe University Press, 1999.

Kieniewicz, Stefan. *The Emancipation of the Polish Peasantry.* Chicago: Chicago University Press, 1969.

Kulczycki, John J. *School Strikes in Prussian Poland, 1901–1907: The Struggle over Bilingual Education.* Boulder, CO: East European Monographs, distributed by Columbia University Press, 1981.

Ludwikowski, Rett. *Continuity and Change: Conservatism in Polish Political Thought.* Washington, DC: Catholic University of America Press, 1991. *

Michlic, Joanna Beata. *Poland's Threatening Other: The Image of the Jew from 1880 to the Present.* Lincoln: University of Nebraska Press, 2006. *

Naimark, Norman M. *The History of the "Proletariat." The Emergence of Marxism in the Kingdom of Poland, 1870–1887.* Boulder, CO: East European Monographs, distributed by Columbia University Press, 1979.

The Origins of Modern Polish Democracy. Edited by M. B. B. Biskupski, James S. Pula, and Piotr J. Wrobel. Athens: Ohio University Press, 2010. *

Pekacz, Jolanta T. *Music in the Culture of Polish Galicia, 1772–1914.* Rochester, NY: University of Rochester Press, 2002.

Porter, Brian A. *When Nationalism Learned to Hate: Imagining Modern Politics in Nineteenth Century Poland.* Oxford: Oxford University Press, 2000.

Remy, Johannes. *Higher Education and National Identity: Polish Student Activism in Russia, 1832–1863.* Helsinki: Suomalaisen Kirjallisuuden Seura, 2000.

Słomka, Jan. *From Serfdom to Self-Government: Memoirs of a Polish Village Mayor, 1842–1927.* London: Minerva, [1941]. *#

Snyder, Timothy. *Nationalism, Marxism, and Modern Central Europe: A Biography of Kazimierz Kelles-Krauz, 1872–1905.* Cambridge, MA: Harvard University Press for the Harvard Ukrainian Research Institute, 1997.

Stauter-Halsted, Keely. *The Nation in the Village: The Genesis of Peasant National Identity in Austrian Poland, 1848–1914.* Ithaca: Cornell University Press, 2001.

Trzeciakowski, Lech. *The Kulturkampf in Prussian Poland.* Translated by Katarzyna Kretkowska. New York: East European Monographs, 1990.

Walicki, Andrzej. *Philosophy and Romantic Nationalism: The Case of Poland.* Oxford: Clarendon Press; New York: Oxford University Press, 1982.

———. *Poland between East and West: The Controversies over Self-Definition and Modernization in Partitioned Poland.* Cambridge, MA: Ukrainian Research Institute, Harvard University, 1994.

———. *Russia, Poland, and Universal Regeneration: Studies on Russian and Polish Thought of the Romantic Period.* Notre Dame, IN: University of Notre Dame Press, 1991.

———. *The Three Traditions in Polish Patriotism and Their Contemporary Relevance.* Bloomington, IN: Polish Studies Center, 1988. *

Wandycz, Piotr S. *The Lands of Partitioned Poland, 1795–1918*. Seattle: University of Washington Press, 1974.

Weeks, Theodore R. *From Assimilation to Antisemitism: The "Jewish Question" in Poland, 1850–1914*. DeKalb: Northern Illinois University Press, 2006.

———. *Nation and State in Late Imperial Russia: Nationalism and Russification on the Western Frontier*. DeKalb: Northern Illinois University Press, 1996.

Wolff, Larry. *The Idea of Galicia: History and Fantasy in Habsburg Political Culture*. Stanford: Stanford University Press, 2010. *

Zamoyski, Adam. *Holy Madness: Romantics, Patriots, and Revolutionaries, 1776–1871*. London: Weidenfeld and Nicolson, 1999.

Zawadzki, Hubert. *A Man of Honour: Adam Czartoryski as a Statesman of Russia and Poland, 1795–1831*. Oxford: Clarendon and Oxford University Press, 1993.

Zimmerman, Joshua D. *Poles, Jews, and the Politics of Nationality: The Bund and the Polish Socialist Party in Late Tsarist Russia, 1892–1914*. Madison: University of Wisconsin Press, 2004.

The Short Twentieth Century (1918–1989)

Ash, Timothy Garton. *The Magic Lantern: The Revolution of '89 Witnessed in Warsaw, Budapest, Berlin, and Prague*. New York: Random House, 1990. #

———. *The Polish Revolution: Solidarity*. Revised and updated edition. London: Penguin, 1999.

Bjork, James E. *Neither German nor Pole: Catholicism and National Indifference in a Central European Borderland*. Ann Arbor: University of Michigan Press, 2008.

Bór-Komorowski, T[adeusz]. *The Secret Army*. Nashville: Battery Press, 1984. #

Cole, Daniel H. *Instituting Environmental Protection: From Red to Green in Poland*. New York: Macmillan Press and St. Martin's Press, 1998.

Connelly, John. *Captive University: The Sovietization of East German, Czech, and Polish Higher Education, 1945–1956*. Chapel Hill: University of North Carolina Press, 2000.

Coutouvidis, John, and Jaime Reynolds. *Poland, 1939–1947*. New York: Holmes and Meier, 1986.

Curp, T. David. *A Clean Sweep? The Politics of Ethnic Cleansing in Western Poland, 1945–1960*. Rochester, NY: University of Rochester Press, 2006.

Davies, Norman. *White Eagle, Red Star: The Polish-Soviet War, 1919–1920*. London: Macdonald, 1972.

Fidelis, Malgorzata. *Women, Communism and Industrialization in Postwar Poland*. Cambridge: Cambridge University Press, 2010.

Fleming, Michael. *Communism, Nationalism and Ethnicity in Poland, 1944–50*. London: Routledge, 2010.

From Stalinism to Pluralism: A Documentary History of Eastern Europe since 1945. Edited by Gale Stokes. 2d ed. Oxford: Oxford University Press, 1996. *#

Gross, Jan Tomasz. *Neighbors: The Destruction of the Jewish Community in Jedwabne, Poland*. Princeton, NJ: Princeton University Press, 2001.

———. *Polish Society under German Occupation: The Generalgouvernement, 1939–1944*. Princeton, NJ: Princeton University Press, 1979.

———. *Revolution from Abroad: The Soviet Conquest of Poland's Western Ukraine and Western Belorussia*. Expanded edition. Princeton, NJ: Princeton University Press, 2002.

Hicks, Barbara. *Environmental Politics in Poland: A Social Movement between Regime and Opposition*. New York: Columbia University Press, 1996.

Huener, Jonathan. *Auschwitz, Poland, and the Politics of Commemoration, 1945–1979*. Athens: Ohio University Press, 2003.

Jolluck, Katherine R. *Exile and Identity: Polish Women in the Soviet Union during World War II*. Pittsburg: Pittsburg University Press, 2002.

Karski, Jan. *The Story of a Secret State*. Boston: Houghton Mifflin, 1944. #

Kassow, Samuel. *Who Will Write Our History? Emanuel Ringelblum, the Warsaw Ghetto, and the Oyneg Shabes Archive*. Bloomington: Indiana University Press, 2007.

Kenney, Padraic. *A Carnival of Revolution: Central Europe, 1989*. Princeton, NJ: Princeton University Press, 2002.

———. *Rebuilding Poland: Workers and Communists, 1945–1950*. Ithaca: Cornell University Press, 1997.

Kersten, Krystyna. *The Establishment of Communist Rule in Poland*. Translated by John Micgiel and Michael H. Bernhard. Berkeley: University of California Press, 1991.

Kubik, Jan. *The Power of Symbols against the Symbols of Power: The Rise of Solidarity and the Fall of State Socialism*. University Park: Pennsylvania State University Press, 1994.

Kunicki, Mikolaj Stanislaw. *Between the Brown and the Red: Nationalism, Catholicism, and Communism in Twentieth-Century Poland. The Politics of Boleslaw Piasecki*. Athens: Ohio University Press, 2012.

Laba, Roman. *The Roots of Solidarity: A Political Sociology of Poland's Working-Class Democratization*. Princeton, NJ: Princeton University Press, 1991.

Lebow, Katherine. *Unfinished Utopia: Nowa Huta, Stalinism, and Polish Society, 1949–56*. Ithaca: Cornell University Press, 2013.

Lipski, Jan Józef. *KOR: A History of the Workers' Defense Committee in Poland, 1976–1981*. Translated by Olga Amsterdamska and Gene M. Moore. Berkeley: University of California Press, 1985.

Martin, Sean. *Jewish Life in Cracow, 1918–1939*. London: Vallentine Mitchell, 2004.

McDonald, Bernadette. *Freedom Climbers*. Vancouver: Rocky Mountain Books, 2011.

Monticone, Ronald C. *The Catholic Church in Communist Poland, 1945–1985: Forty Years of Church-State Relations*. Boulder, CO: East European Monographs, distributed by Columbia University Press, 1986.

Nowak, Jan. *Courier from Warsaw*. Detroit: Wayne State University Press, 1982. #

Paczkowski, Andrzej. *The Spring Will Be Ours: Poland and the Poles from Occupation to Freedom*. University Park: Pennsylvania State University Press, 2003.

Paderewski, Ignace Jan. *The Paderewski Memoirs*. With Mary Lawton. New York: Da Capo Press, 1980. *#

Paul, Allen. *Katyn: Stalin's Massacre and the Triumph of Truth*. DeKalb: Northern Illinois University Press, 2010.

Pease, Neal. *Rome's Most Faithful Daughter: The Catholic Church and Independent Poland, 1914–1939*. Athens: Ohio University Press, 2009.

Pilecki, Witold. *The Auschwitz Volunteer: Beyond Bravery*. Translated by Jarek Garliński. Los Angeles: Aquila Polonica, 2012. #

Piłsudski, Józef. *The Year 1920 and Its Climax: Battle of Warsaw during the Polish-Soviet War, 1919–1920*. New York: Pilsudski Institute of America, 1972. #

Plach, Eva. *The Clash of Moral Nations: Cultural Politics in Pilsudski's Poland, 1926–1935*. Athens: Ohio University Press, 2006.

Polish Paradoxes. Edited by Stanislaw Gomulka and Antony Polonsky. London: Routledge, 1990.

Polonsky, Antony. *Politics in Independent Poland, 1921–1939: The Crisis of Constitutional Government.* Oxford: Clarendon Press, 1972.

Polonsky, Antony, and Joanna B. Michlic. *The Neighbors Respond: The Controversy over the Jedwabne Massacre in Poland.* Princeton, NJ: Princeton University Press, 2004.

Pomian-Szrednicki, Maciej. *Religious Change in Contemporary Poland: Secularization and Politics.* London: Routledge and Kegan Paul, 1982.

Porter, Brian A. *Faith and Fatherland: Catholicism, Modernity, and Poland.* New York: Oxford University Press, 2011. *

Redlich, Shimon. *Together and Apart in Brzezany: Poles, Jews, and Ukrainians, 1919–1945.* Bloomington: Indiana University Press, 2002.

Shore, Marci. *Caviar and Ashes: A Warsaw Generation's Life and Death in Marxism, 1918–1969.* New Haven: Yale University Press, 2006.

Skaff, Sheila. *The Law of the Looking Glass: Cinema in Poland, 1896–1939.* Athens: Ohio University Press, 2008. *

Snyder, Timothy. *Bloodlands: Europe between Hitler and Stalin.* New York: Basic Books, 2010.

———. *Sketches from a Secret War: A Polish Artist's Mission to Liberate Soviet Ukraine.* New Haven: Yale University Press, 2005.

Terry, Sarah Meiklejohn. *Poland's Place in Europe: General Sikorski and the Origins of the Oder-Neisse Line, 1939–1943.* Princeton, NJ: Princeton University Press, 1983.

Toranska, Teresa. *"Them": Stalin's Polish Puppets.* New York: Harper and Row, 1987. #

Wandycz, Piotr S. *Soviet-Polish Relations, 1917–1921.* Cambridge, MA: Harvard University Press, 1969.

Watt, Richard M. *Bitter Glory: Poland and Its Fate, 1918 to 1939.* New York: Simon and Schuster, 1982.

Zamoyski, Adam. *Warsaw 1920: Lenin's Failed Conquest of Europe.* London: HarperPress, 2008.

Zawodny, J. K. *Death in the Forest: The Story of the Katyn Forest Massacre.* Notre Dame, IN: University of Notre Dame Press, 1962.

After 1989

Cooley, Timothy J. *Making Music in the Polish Tatras: Tourists, Ethnographers, and Mountain Musicians.* Bloomington: Indiana University Press, 2005.*

Dunn, Elizabeth C. *Privatizing Poland: Baby Food, Big Business, and the Remaking of Labor.* Ithaca: Cornell University Press, 2004.

Hoffman, Eva. *Exit into History: A Journey through the New Eastern Europe.* New York: Viking, 1993.

Kenney, Padraic. *The Burdens of Freedom: Eastern Europe since 1989.* New York: Fernwood Publications and Zed Books, distributed in the United States by Palgrave Macmillan, 2006.

Shore, Marci. *The Taste of Ashes: The Afterlife of Totalitarianism in Eastern Europe.* New York: Crown, 2013.

Zubrzycki, Geneviève. *The Crosses of Auschwitz: Nationalism and Religion in Post-Communist Poland.* Chicago: University of Chicago Press, 2006.

Index